THE SYSTEMATICS ASSOCIATION
SPECIAL VOLUME No. 17(a)

THE SHORE ENVIRONMENT

VOLUME 2: ECOSYSTEMS

Edited by

J. H. PRICE

Department of Botany, British Museum (Natural History)

D. E. G. IRVINE

Department of Food and Biological Sciences, Polytechnic of North London

and

W. F. FARNHAM

Department of Biological Sciences, Portsmouth Polytechnic

1980

Published for the

SYSTEMATICS ASSOCIATION

by

ACADEMIC PRESS

LONDON NEW YORK TORONTO SYDNEY SAN FRANCISCO

ACADEMIC PRESS INC. (LONDON) LTD.
24-28 Oval Road
London NW1 7DX

U.S. Edition published by
ACADEMIC PRESS INC.
111 Fifth Avenue
New York, New York 10003

British Library Cataloguing in Publication Data

The shore environment.
Vol. 2: Ecosystems. – (Systematics Association. Special volumes; 17B ISSN 0309-2593).
1. Seashore ecology – Congresses
2. Benthos – Congresses
I. Price, J. H. II. Irvine, David Edward Guthrie III. Farnham, W.F. IV. Series
574.5′2636 QH541.5.S35 80-40927

ISBN 0-12-564702-6

PRINTED IN GREAT BRITAIN BY THE ALDEN PRESS, OXFORD

Contributors and Participants

Contributors are indicated by an asterisk

Alvarez, Dr R. A., *Departmento de Zoologia, Universidad de Oviedo, Spain.*

Angus, S., *Nature Conservancy Council, Old Bank Road, Goldspie, Sutherland, Scotland.*

Astthorsson, O., *Department of Zoology, The University, Tillydrome Avenue, Aberdeen, Scotland.*

Baker, Dr J. M., *Oil Pollution Research Unit, Orielton Field Centre, Pembroke, Dyfed SA71 5EZ, Wales.*

Bartrop, Miss J., *Scottish Marine Biological Association, Dunstaffnage Marine Research Laboratory, P.O. Box 3, Oban, Argyll PA34 4AD, Scotland.*

Batty, L., *Medina Valley Field Centre, Dodnor Lane, Newport, Isle of Wight PO30 5TE, England.*

Beale, M., *Cobnor House, Chidham, Chichester, Sussex, England.*

*Bennell, Miss S. J., *Marine Science Laboratories, Menai Bridge, Anglesey, Gwynedd LL59 5EH, Wales.*

*Beveridge, Miss C. M., *Marine Science Laboratories, Menai Bridge, Anglesey, Gwynedd LL59 5EH, Wales.*

Bird, Miss C. J., *Atlantic Regional Laboratory, 1411 Oxford St., Halifax, Nova Scotia, Canada.*

Bishop, Miss G. M., *The Laboratory, Citadel Hill, Plymouth, Devon PL1 2PB England.*

Boalch, Dr G. T., *The Laboratory, Citadel Hill, Plymouth, Devon PL1 2PB, England.*

Bolton, Dr J. J., *Department of Biology, Memorial University of Newfoundland, St. John's, Newfoundland, A1C 5S7, Canada.*

*Boney, Professor A. D., *Department of Botany, The University, Glasgow G12 8QQ, Scotland.*

*Budd, J. T. C., *Department of Geography, Portsmouth Polytechnic, Lion Terrace, Portsmouth PO1 3HE, England.*

Butler, Mrs Y. M., *Portsmouth Polytechnic Marine Laboratory, Ferry Road, Hayling Island, Hants. PO11 0DG, England.*

Chater, K. W. A., *B.P. Chemicals Ltd., Devonshire House, Mayfair Place, Piccadilly, London W1X 6AY, England.*

*Clokie, J. J. P., *University Marine Station, Millport, Isle of Cumbrae, Scotland.*

Cooke, Mrs F. P., *8 Menai View Terrace, Bangor, Gwynedd, Wales.*

*Coppejans, Dr E., *Laboratorium voor Morfologie, Systematiek en Ecologie van de Planten, Rijksuniversiteit – Gent, K.L. Ledeganckstraat 35, B.9000, Gent, Belgium.*

*Coulson, M. G., *Department of Geography, Portsmouth Polytechnic, Lion Terrace, Portsmouth, PO1 3HE, England.*

Critchley, A., *Portsmouth Polytechnic Marine Laboratory, Ferry Road, Hayling Island, Hants. PO11 0DG, England.*

Crothers, J. H., *Leonard Wills Field Centre, Nettlecombe Court, Williton, Taunton, Somerset, England.*

Culley, Dr M., *Portsmouth Polytechnic Marine Laboratory, Ferry Road, Hayling Island, Hants. PO11 0DG, England.*

*Dalby, Dr D. H., *Department of Botany, Imperial College of Science and Technology, London SW7 2AZ, England.*

De Groot, Dr S. J., *Rijksinstituut voor Visserijonderzoek, Haringkade 1-POB 68, Ymuiden, The Netherlands.*

De Vos, Miss, D., *Laboratorium voor Morfologie van de Planten, Rijksuniversiteit – Gent, K.L. Ledeganckstraat 35, B.9000 Gent, Belgium.*

Dipper, Dr F. A., *Nature Conservancy Council, Godwin House, George Street, Huntingdon, Cambs. PE18 6BU, England.*

*Earll, Dr R. C., *Zoology Department, University of Manchester, Oxford Road, Manchester M13 9PL, England.*

*Farnham, Dr W. F., *Department of Biological Sciences, Portsmouth Polytechnic Marine Laboratory, Ferry Road, Hayling Island, Hants. PO11 0DG, England.*

*Fletcher, Dr A., *Documentation and Information Retrieval Section, Leicestershire Museums Service, 96 New Walk, Leicester LE1 6TD, England.*

*Fletcher, Dr R. L., *Department of Biological Sciences, Portsmouth Polytechnic Marine Laboratory, Ferry Road, Hayling Island, Hants. PO11 0DG, England.*

Freytag, Dr J., *14 Ashley Gardens, Petersham, Richmond-on-Thames, Surrey, England.*

*George, Dr J. D., *Department of Zoology, British Museum (Natural History), Cromwell Road, London SW7 5BD, England.*

Goodman, K., *Department of Zoology, The University, Tillydrome Avenue, Aberdeen, Scotland.*

Guiry, Dr M. D., *Department of Botany, University College, Galway, Ireland.*

Guiry, Mrs W., *Department of Botany, University College, Galway, Ireland.*

Harvey, R., *Scottish Marine Biological Association, Dunstaffnage Marine Research Laboratory, P.O. Box 3, Oban, Argyll PA34 4AD, Scotland.*

Hawkins, S. J., *Marine Biology Station, Port Erin, Isle of Man, England.*

*Hayward, Dr P. J., *Department of Zoology, University College, Singleton Park, Swansea SAZ 8PP, Wales.*

Hesthagen, I. H., *Institutt for Marinbiologi, University of Oslo, P.O. Box 1064, Blindern, Oslo 3, Norway.*

Hibbert, Dr F. A., *Department of Biological Sciences, Portsmouth Polytechnic, King Henry I Street, Portsmouth PO1 2DY, England.*

*Hiscock, Dr K., *Oil Pollution Research Unit, Orielton Field Centre, Pembroke, Dyfed SA71 5EZ, Wales.*

Hoek, Professor C. Van Den, *Department of Systematic Botany, Biological Centre, University of Groningen, Kerklaan 30, P.O. Box 14, 1750 AA Haren, The Netherlands.*

Holmsgaard, J. E., *Litex Industry, P.O. Box 7, 2600 Glostrup, Denmark.*

*Hooper, R. G., *Department of Biology, Memorial University of Newfoundland, St. John's, Newfoundland A1C 5S7, Canada.*

Housden, Miss P. R., *Portsmouth Polytechnic, Marine Laboratory, Ferry Road, Hayling Island, Hants. PO11 0DG, England.*

Houston, M. C. M., *Southern Water Authority, Eastleigh House, 2 Market Street, Eastleigh, Hants., England.*

Houvenaghel, Dr G. T., *Laboratoire de Zoologie, C.P. 160, Université Libre de Bruxelles, 50 Av. F.D. Roosevelt, B-1050 Bruxelles, Belgium.*

Howson, Miss C., *Department of Botany, The University, Glasgow G12 8QQ, Scotland.*

*Hughes, Dr R. N., *Department of Zoology, University College of North Wales, Bangor, Gwynedd LL57 2UW, Wales.*

Hunnam, Dr P. J., *Aquatic Biological Consultancy Services Ltd., 135 New London Road, Chelmsford, Essex CM2 0QT, England.*

Irvine, Dr D. E. G., *Department of Food and Biological Sciences, Polytechnic of North London, Holloway Road, London N7 8DB, England.*

Jackson, D., *Department of Biology, University of Essex, Wivenhoe Park, Colchester, Essex CO4 3SQ, England.*

*John, Dr D. M., *Department of Botany, British Museum (Natural History), Cromwell Road, London SW7 5BD, England.*

Jones, Dr E. B. G., *Department of Biological Sciences, Portsmouth Polytechnic, King Henry I Street, Portsmouth PO1 2DY, England.*

*Jones, Dr W. E., *Marine Science Laboratories, Menai Bridge, Anglesey, Gwynedd LL59 5EH, Wales.*

*Knight, S. J. T., *Scottish Marine Biological Association, Dunstaffnage Marine Research Laboratory, P.O. Box 3, Oban, Argyll PA34 4AD, Scotland.*

Lambe, Dr E., *Department of Botany, University College, Galway, Ireland.*

*Lewis, Dr J. R., *Wellcome Marine Laboratory, University of Leeds, Robin Hood's Bay, Yorkshire YO22 4SL, England.*

*Lieberman, Mrs D., *Department of Botany, University of Ghana, P.O. Box 55, Legon, Ghana.*

*Lieberman, Dr M., *Department of Zoology, University of Ghana, P.O. Box 55, Legon, Ghana.*

Lindsey, Dr B. I., *Applied Science Department, Brighton Technical College, Pelham Street, Brighton, Sussex BN1 4FA, England.*

Littler, Mrs D., *Department of Ecology and Evolutionary Biology, University of California, Irvine, California 92717, U.S.A.*

*Littler, Dr M. M., *Department of Ecology and Evolutionary Biology, University of California, Irvine, California 92717, U.S.A.*

Lowthion, D., *Southern Water Authority, Eastleigh House, 2 Market Street, Eastleigh, Hants., England.*

*Lüning, Dr K., *Biologisch Anstalt Helgoland, 2192 Helgoland, West Germany.*

Lyes, Dr M. C., *National Board for Science and Technology, Shelbourne Road, Dublin 4, Ireland.*

*Mack-Smith, S., *Marine Science Laboratories, Menai Bridge, Anglesey, Gwynedd LL59 5EH, Wales.*

*McConnell, B., *Marine Science Laboratories, Menai Bridge, Anglesey, Gwynedd LL59 5EH, Wales.*

*Mitchell, J. S., *Marine Science Laboratories, Menai Bridge, Anglesey, Gwynedd LL59 5EH, Wales.*

*Mitchell, Dr R., *Nature Conservancy Council, P.O. Box 6, Godwin House, George Street, Huntingdon, Cambs. PE18 6BU, England.*

*Nicholls, D. J., *Department of Biological Services, Portsmouth Polytechnic, King Henry I Street, Portsmouth PO1 2DY, England.*

Niell, Dr F. X., *Instituto de Investigaciones Pesqueras, Muelle de Bouzas, Vigo, Spain.*

O'Sullivan, G., *Department of Zoology, University College, Belfield, Dublin, Ireland.*

Palmer, C., *Portsmouth Polytechnic Marine Laboratory, Ferry Road, Hayling Island, Hants. PO11 0DG, England.*

Peattie, Mrs M., *Ministry of Agriculture, Fisheries and Food, Westminster House, Horseferry Road, London SW1, England.*

*Platt, Dr H. M., *Department of Zoology, British Museum (Natural History), Cromwell Road, London SW7 5BD, England.*

*Polderman, Drs P. J. G., *Polarisstraat 12, 3235 Th Rockanje, The Netherlands.*

*Powell, H. T., *Scottish Marine Biological Association, Dunstaffnage Marine Research Laboratory, P.O. Box 3, Oban, Argyll PA34 4AD, Scotland.*

Powell, Miss P. E., *Institute of Naval Medicine, Crescent Road, Alverstoke, Hants., England.*

*Price, J. H., *Department of Botany, British Museum (Natural History), Cromwell Road, London SW7 5BD, England.*

Pringle, Dr J. D., *Resource Branch, Department of Fisheries and Oceans, P.O. Box 550, Halifax, Nova Scotia, Canada.*

Raffaelli, Dr D. G., *Department of Biology, University of Essex, Wivenhoe Park, Colchester, Essex CO4 3SQ, England.*

*Russell, Dr G., *Department of Botany, University of Liverpool, P.O. Box 147, Liverpool L69 3BX, England.*

*Shaw, Miss K. M., *Biometrics and Computing Section, British Museum (Natural History), Cromwell Road, London SW7 5BD, England.*

*South, Professor G. R., *Department of Biology, Memorial University of Newfoundland, St. John's, Newfoundland, A1C 5S7, Canada.*

Streeter, Miss J., *Gilbert White Museum, Selbourne, Hants., England.*

*Swaine, Dr M. D., *Department of Botany, University of Aberdeen, Tillydrome Avenue, Aberdeen, Scotland.*

*Tittley, I., *Department of Botany, British Museum (Natural History), Cromwell Road, London SW7 5BD, England.*

Thomas, N., *Portsmouth Polytechnic Marine Laboratory, Ferry Road, Hayling Island, Hants. PO11 0DG, England.*

Thorpe, Dr C., *Portsmouth Polytechnic Marine Laboratory, Ferry Road, Hayling Island, Hants. PO11 0DG, England.*

Van Vlymen, C., *Slapton Ley Field Centre, Slapton, Kingsbridge, Devon TQ7 2QP, England.*

*Warwick, Dr R. M., *Institute for Marine Environmental Research, Prospect Place, The Hoe, Plymouth, Devon, England.*

*Wheeler, A., *Department of Zoology, British Museum (Natural History), Cromwell Road, London SW7 5BD, England.*

*Whittick, Dr A., *Department of Biology, Memorial University of Newfoundland, St. John's, Newfoundland A1C 5S7, Canada.*

*Wilkinson, Dr M., *Department of Brewing and Biological Sciences, Heriot-Watt University, Chambers Street, Edinburgh EH1 1HX, Scotland.*

*Withers, Dr R. G., *Portsmouth Polytechnic Marine Laboratory, Ferry Road, Hayling Island, Hants. PO11 0DG, England.*

Preface

There has recently been considerable activity in those fields relevant to benthic marine inshore ecology. Some of this activity has been aimed principally at the study of plants, but the much greater proportion has still been carried out by zoologists. In addition to that bias, locational rather than organismic studies in the benthic field have swung more towards the subtidal than the intertidal, despite the very considerable logistic problems and therefore much greater consumption of time involved.

By no means has all this been field activity, nor even the testing of practical issues in the controlled environment of the laboratory. Conceptual, theoretical, statistical and mathematical aspects of benthic ecology have been avidly pursued by some schools and individuals, the results of which activity have not always avoided the categorization "ad nauseam" in the eyes of some of the more directly practical amongst ecologists. Organization, exploitation, population studies, conservation, and other more specialized aspects of benthic ecology have similarly been explored, but in many parts of the world all those aspects mentioned have tended to be pursued as though they were isolable from the many other aspects without adversely affecting results or biasing approaches adopted. This is clearly not the truth, as particularly benthic ecologists working in the intertidals of the U.S.A. have recently ably demonstrated in both theory and practice. Neither benthic ecology as a whole nor its various contributory aspects can ever be divorced from affecting and being affected by all other such disciplines as taxonomy and applied (commercial and industrial) studies. Coastal land-use planning, for whatever purpose, and the extent to which plans have been effectively followed or disregarded have obvious local and often much more widespread importance. The extent of interrelated effects has been well summarized as regards the structure of communities by Lubchenco and Menge (1978; *Ecol. Monogr.* 48, 68), in their comment that such structure has "... several important characteristics ... which are usually treated as separate phenomena, but are in fact intimately related and can best be understood if investigated together. In particular, patterns of species diversity, succession, and stability and life histories need to be better integrated. Further, the regulating mechanisms must be separated from the patterns". The spirit behind this comment could be equally well applied in the interdisciplinary relations of ecology with, for example, taxonomy.

Many of the chapters included in these volumes emphasize the need for integration of approaches and the requirement for long-term consistency of study area and approach to produce optimal results. Others explore further into concept, theory, method and application, often cutting across hitherto rarely-breached boundaries of compartmentalization. Mathematical presentation has been kept to a minimum commensurate with understanding and clarity. Any further development of the mathematical approach is presented in the form of appendices to individual chapters. A bone of contention is the use of "substrate" cf. "substratum"; the decision has been left to the discretion of the original authors. In this and any other cases where meanings were unlikely to be obscure, we saw little point in making immense issues out of standardization of rendering. The situation is the same where North American authors have employed essentially American terminology such as, for example, "fall" instead of "autumn"; unless obscurity resulted, the original rendering remains unchanged. The term "shore environment", incidentally, important since utilized in the title, is here taken as covering the supratidal within the sphere of marine influence, the intertidal, and the adjacent subtidal levels.

Despite recent publications exploring similar fields, we feel that the present volumes are balanced in such a way that intergroup treatments and other relatively neglected fields are given more of the emphasis now required. Similarly, generally unexplored aspects of methodology or available equipment are treated more widely. In each case, we would have expanded the coverage further to include other intergroup relations or other aspects of method had an appropriate expert existed or been free to undertake the task. For those imbalances created by remaining lacunae we apologize, but express the hope that their recognizable presence will stimulate further studies and appropriate publications. Since the overall bulk of the final collated scripts required production as two volumes

(Vol. 1: Methods; Vol. 2: Ecosystems) rather than as the initially projected single work, maintenance of the original symposium sections and order of chapters has not been feasible. Division into the two volumes has been carried out on as logical a basis as possible, but inevitably some papers would have been equally appropriate in either volume. We believe that contributors will not find difficulties with the decision finally reached on chapter order.

For our part, we feel as organizers that this international meeting achieved to a high degree the stimulating interchange of ideas originally sought. Certainly, we were surprised and gratified by the extent of interest, response, and subsequently participation. In large part, the contributors kept to limits of time and space as laid down for both presentation and final production of manuscript, for which we should like to express our thanks, as appropriate. Thanks also go to all those who assisted in making the organization of the meeting such a success, particularly the various staff of Portsmouth Polytechnic. We should especially like to record our gratitude to the President, Dr W. Davey, C.B.E., for the hospitality shown during our visit.

The success of the meeting would not have been reflected in the standard of the resultant volumes had it not been for the high degree of concern and cooperation shown by Academic Press and by our major Sponsoring Body, the Systematics Association. The volumes most appropriately appear in the latter's Special Volume Series. Thanks are also due to our other Sponsors for the financial assistance that helped to create and sustain international participation; these were the Natural Environment Research Council, Portsmouth Polytechnic, the British Council, British Petroleum, and the British Phycological Society.

July 1980
London

J. H. Price
D. E. G. Irvine
W. F. Farnham

Contents

Volume 2

LIST OF CONTRIBUTORS AND PARTICIPANTS . . v

PREFACE xi

SYSTEMATICS ASSOCIATION PUBLICATIONS . . xix

1 The Description and Classification of Sublittoral Epibenthic Ecosystems

KEITH HISCOCK and ROGER MITCHELL 323

2 Phytosociological Studies on Mediterranean Algal Vegetation. Rocky Surfaces of the Photophilic Infralittoral Zone

E. COPPEJANS 371

3 Ecological and Phenological Aspects of the Marine Phytobenthos of the Island of Newfoundland

ROBERT G. HOOPER, G. ROBIN SOUTH and ALAN WHITTICK 395

4 Estuarine Benthic Algae and their Environment: A Review

MARTIN WILKINSON 425

5 Niche and Community in the Inshore Benthos, with Emphasis on the Macroalgae

J. H. PRICE 487

6 Southern California Rocky Intertidal Ecosystems: Methods, Community Structure and Variability

MARK M. LITTLER 565

7 The Assessment of Changes in Intertidal Ecosystems Following Major Reclamation Work: Framework for Interpretation of Algal-dominated Biota and the Use and Misuse of Data

J. J. P. CLOKIE and A. D. BONEY 609

8 Fish-Algal Relations in Temperate Waters

ALWYNE WHEELER 677

9 Predation and Community Structure

ROGER N. HUGHES 699

10 The Significance of Freeliving Nematodes to the Littoral Ecosystem

H. M. PLATT and R. M. WARWICK 729

11 Invertebrate Epiphytes of Coastal Marine Algae

P. J. HAYWARD 761

12 Marine and Maritime Lichens of Rocky Shores: Their Ecology, Physiology and Biological Interactions

A. FLETCHER 789

13 The Algal Communities on Floating Structures in Portsmouth and Langstone Harbours (South Coast of England)

R. L. FLETCHER 843

14 Studies on Aliens in the Marine Flora of Southern England

W. F. FARNHAM 875

15 Control of Algal Life-history by Daylength and Temperature

K. LÜNING 915

TAXONOMIC INDEX II1

SUBJECT INDEX IIxxi

Contents of Volume 1

LIST OF CONTRIBUTORS AND PARTICIPANTS . . v

PREFACE xi

SYSTEMATICS ASSOCIATION PUBLICATIONS . . xix

1 Objectives in Littoral Ecology – A Personal Viewpoint

J. R. LEWIS 1

2 Field Teaching Methods in Shore Ecology

W. EIFION JONES 19

3 Photography as a Marine Biological Research Tool

J. DAVID GEORGE 45

4 Monitoring and Exposure Scales

D. H. DALBY 117

5 Methods of Data Collection and Processing in Rocky Intertidal Monitoring

W. E. JONES, S. BENNELL, C. BEVERIDGE, B. McCONNELL, S. MACK-SMITH, J. MITCHELL and A. FLETCHER 137

6 Applications of Simple Numerical Methods to the Analysis of Intertidal Vegetation

G. RUSSELL 171

7 The Permanent Quadrat Method, a Means of Investigating the Dynamics of Saltmarsh Algal Vegetation

P. J. G. POLDERMAN 193

8 Numerical and Field Methods in the Study of the Marine Flora of Chalk Cliffs

IAN TITTLEY and KATHLEEN M. SHAW 213

9 Remote Sensing and Field Sampling of Mudflat Organisms in Langstone and Chichester Harbours, Southern England

M. G. COULSON, J. T. C. BUDD, R. G. WITHERS and D. J. NICHOLLS 241

10 Strategies of Data Collection and Analysis of Subtidal Vegetation

DAVID M. JOHN, DIANA LIEBERMAN, MILTON LIEBERMAN and M. D. SWAINE 265

11 The Development and Use of a Computer-based System for Handling Habitat and Species Information from the Sublittoral Environment

R. C. EARLL 285

12 The Survey and Nature Conservation Assessment of Littoral Areas

S. J. T. KNIGHT and R. MITCHELL 303

TAXONOMIC INDEX Ii

SUBJECT INDEX Ivii

Systematics Association Publications

1. BIBLIOGRAPHY OF KEY WORKS FOR THE IDENTIFICATION OF THE BRITISH FAUNA AND FLORA
   3rd edition (1967)
   Edited by G. J. Kerrich, R. D. Meikle and N. Tebble
2. FUNCTION AND TAXONOMIC IMPORTANCE (1959)
   Edited by A. J. Cain
3. THE SPECIES CONCEPT IN PALAEONTOLOGY (1956)
   Edited by P. S. Sylvester-Bradley
4. TAXONOMY AND GEOGRAPHY (1962)
   Edited by D. Nichols
5. SPECIATION IN THE SEA (1963)
   Edited by J. P. Harding and N. Tebble
6. PHENETIC AND PHYLOGENETIC CLASSIFICATION (1964)
   Edited by V. H. Heywood and J. McNeill
7. ASPECTS OF TETHYAN BIOGEOGRAPHY (1967)
   Edited by C. G. Adams and D. V. Ager
8. THE SOIL ECOSYSTEM (1969)
   Edited by J. Sheals
9. ORGANISMS AND CONTINENTS THROUGH TIME (1973)†
   Edited by N. F. Hughes

LONDON. Published by the Association

Systematics Association Special Volumes

1. THE NEW SYSTEMATICS (1940)
   Edited by Julian Huxley (Reprinted 1971)
2. CHEMOTAXONOMY AND SEROTAXONOMY (1968)*
   Edited by J. G. Hawkes
3. DATA PROCESSING IN BIOLOGY AND GEOLOGY (1971)*
   Edited by J. L. Cutbill
4. SCANNING ELECTRON MICROSCOPY (1971)*
   Edited by V. H. Heywood
5. TAXONOMY AND ECOLOGY (1973)*
   Edited by V. H. Heywood
6. THE CHANGING FLORA AND FAUNA OF BRITAIN (1974)*
   Edited by D. L. Hawksworth
7. BIOLOGICAL IDENTIFICATION WITH COMPUTERS (1975)*
   Edited by R. J. Pankhurst

*Published by Academic Press for the Systematics Association
†Published by the Palaeontological Association in conjection with the Systematics Association

8. LICHENOLOGY: PROGRESS AND PROBLEMS (1977)*
   Edited by D. H. Brown, D. L. Hawksworth and R. H. Bailey
9. KEY WORKS (1978)*
   Edited by G. J. Kerrich, D. L. Hawksworth and R. W. Sims
10. MODERN APPROACHES TO THE TAXONOMY OF RED AND BROWN ALGAE (1978)*
    Edited by D. E. G. Irvine and J. H. Price
11. BIOLOGY AND SYSTEMATICS OF COLONIAL ORGANISMS (1979)*
    Edited by G. P. Larwood and B. R. Rosen
12. THE ORIGIN OF MAJOR INVERTEBRATE GROUPS (1979)*
    Edited by M. R. House
13. ADVANCES IN BRYOZOOLOGY (1979)*
    Edited by G. P. Larwood and M. B. Abbott
14. BRYOPHYTE SYSTEMATICS (1979)*
    Edited by G. C. S. Clarke and J. G. Duckett
15. THE TERRESTRIAL ENVIRONMENT AND THE ORIGIN OF LAND VERTEBRATES (1980)*
    Edited by A. L. Panchen
16. CHEMOSYSTEMATICS: PRINCIPLES AND PRACTICE (1980)*
    Edited by F. A. Bisby, J. G. Vaughan and C. A. Wright
17. THE SHORE ENVIRONMENT: METHODS AND ECOSYSTEMS (2 VOLUMES) (1980)*
    Edited by J. H. Price, D. E. G. Irvine and W. F. Farnham

*Published by Academic Press for the Systematics Association

1 | The Description and Classification of Sublittoral Epibenthic Ecosystems

KEITH HISCOCK

Oil Pollution Research Unit, Field Studies Council, Orielton Field Centre, Pembroke, Dyfed, Wales

and

ROGER MITCHELL

Chief Scientist Team, Nature Conservancy Council, Godwin House, Huntingdon, England

Abstract: The basis of a strategy for safeguarding marine ecosystems in Britain's shallow seas is the selection of sites of nature conservation importance. Central to this process is the classification of marine ecosystems to provide a framework for the selection and assessment of key marine conservation areas. Despite many attempts to classify marine benthic communities and their physical habitat, no comprehensive system has been developed. Nevertheless, a means of describing and classifying sublittoral habitats and communities, outlined in this chapter, has been devised and found adequate in use. The description and classification of recurrent sublittoral epibenthic communities has proved more difficult; an analysis of examples of community types is undertaken in relation to the similarity of species composition and stability. Although some communities are intrinsically unstable, the majority of epibenthic communities show little overall variation once established. It is concluded that the suggested framework for classification will assist in descriptive survey and in the understanding of the structure, recurrence and stability of sublittoral epibenthic communities.

Systematics Association Special Volume No. 17(b), "The Shore Environment, Vol. 2: Ecosystems", edited by J. H. Price, D. E. G. Irvine and W. F. Farnham, 1980, pp. 323–370, Academic Press, London and New York.

INTRODUCTION

In developing a strategy for the nature conservation of Britain's shallow seas, the safeguarding of habitats is considered to be the best approach (Mitchell, 1977). This strategy depends on the selection of sites of nature conservation importance which will eventually become statutory nature reserves or will be notified to the relevant executive authorities as sites of conservation interest. Mitchell (1979) described a site selection process, adapted from that developed for terrestrial ecosystems, designed to identify a series of sites which give acceptable representation of all the more important features within the range of variation of British marine ecosystems. The first of the two steps involved in this process is the identification and recording of primary scientific data for the site in terms of the physical habitat and biota. On the basis of the intrinsic features described, and within the framework of the classification of ecosystem types, the second step is to select those sites which should constitute the national series of key marine conservation areas. This chapter is concerned with the classification of ecosystems which is central to the site selection process. It is essential that, in this very practical application, a workable framework for the description of marine ecosystems is adopted, in particular for comparing different sites of similar quality. Many terrestrial, but relatively few marine, ecosystems are already classified by habitat, biotope, biocoenosis, community or association. However, the style in which sublittoral epibenthic plant and animal assemblages are described varies widely from worker to worker and survey to survey. It seems important to work towards the application of similar criteria and methods which (i) can be more objectively applied for the description of epibenthic groups of organisms in a meaningful way and (ii) are, if possible, productive of results suitable for computer storage and analysis. Only then can we compare the descriptions of different areas to discover whether recurrent communities are present. This chapter therefore considers how previous methods of classification have been applied and suggests a framework for the description and classification of sublittoral habitats and epibenthic groups of organisms in the context of the British Isles.

BASIC DEFINITIONS AND THE CLASSIFICATION OF COMMUNITIES

The need to describe succinctly the mixture of different organisms collected from the seabed at any one location has over the past 100 years led to the use of a variety of terms and methods of description. Some terms were taken from terrestrial ecology and others have been introduced by benthic ecologists in an attempt to define their findings exactly. While many terms have identical or very similar meanings, some have been misused or broadened beyond their original meaning and ecologists have sometimes unwittingly used words which have very specific meanings other than those which were intended. It is therefore appropriate to discuss the terminology which we propose should be used in describing the groups of plants and animals which constitute the epibenthos.

In 1913, Petersen described the animal "communities" of the seabed off Denmark. The communities of Petersen (1913, 1918) have provided the basis for the description of sublittoral benthos by many workers and continue to be used today. The term "community" was, according to Jones (1950), used by Petersen in the sense of Molander (1928) such that "an animal community or association is a regularly recurring combination of certain type animals, as a rule also strongly represented numerically". The number of species listed in the definition of a community in the sense of Petersen is small and restricted to dominant or characteristic organisms which are, in general, faithful to the community. A term which expresses a very similar concept to that of the Petersen community and also includes the definition of characteristic species is the "biocoenosis" (first used by Möbius, 1877). However, the two terms are not identical in meaning and, according to Glémarec (1973), the description of a biocoenosis embraces *all* of the organisms living in a particular habitat, as well as the characterizing species.

The term "community" used both in the sense of Petersen and as by many benthic ecologists is not widely accepted. Terrestrial ecologists use "community" in a very general sense to include any group of organisms present in a particular habitat. "Association", which is considered synonymous with "community" by Molander (1928) and Jones (1950), is used by botanists to refer to an assemblage of plants with a definite floristic composition. "Association" is also used to describe a relationship in which the presence of one organism depends on the presence of another. For instance, the commensal association of the anemone *Adamsia palliata*[*] with the hermit crab *Pagurus* (*Eupagurus*) *prideuxi* Leach.

A further consideration in defining a community is given by Allee *et al.* (1949) who require that "given radiant energy, it is self-sustaining". This aspect of a community definition is further supported by Macfadyen (1963) who argues that benthic animal communities lacking any primary photosynthetic source of food cannot be regarded as a biotic community but should be considered part of a wider community which includes the plankton. This conclusion is not subscribed to here partly because many epibenthic organims rely on suspended particulate matter as a primary source of food, rather than on the plankton. Furthermore, such considerations make the definition of particular communities extremely difficult.

The most important difference between the definition of community given by Molander (1928) and that used by most ecologists involves recurrence. During fieldwork, it may be required simply to describe the group of organisms found at a particular site and to consider only at a much later date whether that group is representative of a certain recurrent community, or even whether communities in the sense of Petersen (1918) exist in the habitat being studied. It is not appropriate to use the term "population" (as in Lewis, 1964, and Pérès, 1967b) when referring to the assemblage of organisms present on the seabed. The generally-accepted definition of a population is that used by Odum (1971): "groups of individuals of any one kind of organism". The term is often qualified as "single-species" population. The French word "peuplements", which is widely used in describing assemblages of organisms, is polyspecific and, as pointed out by Glémarec (1973), cannot be translated directly as the French or English word "population". We therefore follow terrestrial ecologists and adopt the loose use of the term "community", to include any group of organisms present in a particular habitat. The term "community" is used here in the sense of Petersen (as defined by Molander, 1928) only when reference is to a named community as, for instance, "the *Modiolus modiolus* community".

---

[*]Nomenclature and authorities for animals follow data in "Plymouth Marine Fauna" (Mar. biol. Ass., 1957) where applicable.

Most authors now describe plant and animal communities according to both the environmental conditions (referred to as habitat or biotope) and the characteristic or dominant species. We consider that the physical habitat together with the biota represents the ecosystem. Jones (1950) notes that "every community is the product of a given range of environmental conditions" and suggests that "the only consistent way to divide the fauna into communities is to survey it in relation to the environment and to erect communities based on more or less definite limits to the physical conditions". This approach is subscribed to in this chapter and expanded later.

Several authors, in describing benthic communities, refer to facies or sub-communities. Such facies retain the main features of the communities but include their own characteristic species. An example of this approach can be seen in Cabioch (1968). L'Hardy-Halos *et al.* (1973) and Castric-Fey (1974) describe rocky sublittoral biota by reference to the different biological strata present. The use of a system of stratification follows the work of terrestrial botanists (see, for instance, Whittaker, 1970). However, its usefulness in describing marine biota is here considered limited.

The success of attempts to classify benthic communities has been varied. For instance, the classification of vertical zones on rocky shores has been very successful and the zones described by Lewis (1964), Stephenson and Stephenson (1972) and Pérès and Molinier (1957) can be easily observed. Furthermore, particular rocky shore plant and animal communities occur in the same conditions of wave exposure at widely different locations, as exemplified by the success of the biologically defined exposure scale (Ballantine, 1961). However, the classification of all sedimentary benthic assemblages of organisms into a small number of recurrent communities or associations such as those described by Petersen (1913), Jones (1950), Thorson (1957) and Glémarec (1973) has had only limited success. Many intermediate communities occur, and in some areas of seabed the assemblages of organisms present defy classification into communities characterized by dominant species. In view of the difficulty experienced in classifying *sedimentary* benthos into a few communities, the possibility of any comprehensive classification of *rocky* sublittoral communities, where a greater number of species occurs and where the potential range of habitat heterogeneity and environmental variability is much higher, seems remote. Nevertheless, as described below, a classification which is suitable for many situations is being developed.

DESCRIPTION AND CLASSIFICATION OF HABITATS AND COMMUNITIES

1. Introduction

Hiscock (1979) summarizes the very wide range of environmental conditions important in determining the plant and animal communities present on the seabed and shows a record card used to describe habitat features of a site. This method of classifying habitats is used here as a framework for the description of those habitats and of the assemblages of plants and animals present in particular habitats. It is not practicable to include all possible habitat categories and the framework has to be an open one so that, for example, a worker can if he so wishes include artificial substrata as a separate category. The classification also indicates the range of environmental conditions present in the sublittoral and should enable the definition of similar habitats for studies aimed at investigating variability due to particular environmental conditions. The classification is summarized in Fig. 1 and explained below.

2. Geographical Location

The composition of sublittoral benthos in terms of the main orders, families and often genera represented in a particular habitat is similar all around the British Isles. However, the species present in and often characteristic of particular communities are frequently different in the north and east compared to the south and west. These differences, which result primarily from different temperature regimes, are reflected in the meeting of two major biogeographical provinces in the British Isles: the Mediterranean-Atlantic and the Arctic-Boreal. These and other biogeographical regions have been most clearly classified by Ekman (1953) for animals and in a similar way by Børgesen and Jónsson (1905) for algae. Table I defines the limits of these biogeographical areas; the classification of Ekman (1953) is preferred. Further biogeographical provinces can be defined for smaller areas, such as the seven suggested by Holme (1966) for the English Channel.

Table I. The main biogeographical areas described by Ekman (1953) and Bøgesen and Jónsson (1905)

Name of area: Ekman (1953)	Name of area: Bøgesen and Jónsson (1905)	Extent
Arctic	Arctic	Extends south to the north of Norway.
Arctic-Boreal	Sub-Arctic	Extends to near the south of the British Isles.
	Boreal-Arctic	Extends from the Arctic as far south as the Atlantic coast of North Africa.
Boreal		Centred in the North Sea. Includes all of British Isles.
	Cold-Boreal	Extends northwards to Iceland, the Faroes and northern Norway and south to the Mediterranean and North Africa.
Mediterranean-Boreal	Warm-Boreal	Extends to near the north of the British Isles.
Mediterranean-Atlantic	—	Extends northwards to the English Channel and western approaches.

No exact limit can be placed on the major biogeographical areas. Each species has slightly different tolerances to the many environmental factors that vary and may cause extinction from one province to the next. Therefore, each species may finally disappear at a location along the coast different to the extinction points of other species that occur within the same biogeographical category. Some abrupt common boundaries do occur, for instance at headlands where residual currents sweep offshore or where large areas of unsuitable substratum are present near the limits of distribution for particular species (see, for instance, Holme, 1966, and Cabioch *et al.*, 1977). Enclosed areas such as the Irish Sea, Bristol Channel and English Channel often show localized biogeographical changes, with oceanic or Mediterranean-Atlantic species becoming progressively less abundant and eventually disappearing along the coast away from the open ocean.

Fig. 1. A framework for the description of sublittoral habitats and communities in coastal waters of the north-east Atlantic. * = Features noted only if a part of the habitat is being described.

Category		Features included in classification									
Geographical location		Area of survey									
Divisions of the sublittoral zone		Sublittoral fringe	Infralittoral			Circalittoral					
			Upper Infralittoral	Lower Infralittoral		Upper Circalittoral	Lower Circalittoral				
Substratum & topographical features	Sediments	Clean gravel	Muddy gravel	Maerl	Coarse sand	Fine clean sand	Muddy sand	Sandy mud	Mud	Mixed sediments	
	Rock	Bedrock	Boulders 50 cm +	Boulders 15 to 50 cm	Pebbles 2.5 to 15 cm						
	Topographical features	Upward facing surfaces	Steeply inclined surfaces and cliffs (75 to 100°)	Overhangs (100 to 135°)	Steep overhangs and cave roofs (135° +)	Walls of caves	Sides of Crevices	Potholes	Undersides of rocks	Open gullies (< 75°)	Steep-sided gullies (75° +)
	Other* substrata (examples)	Kelp holdfasts	Kelp stipes	Kelp fronds	Pier piles	Pontoons and buoys	Wreck				
Substratum mobility* & scour		Substratum mobile	Scour present								

Fig. 1. (continued)

<table>
<tr><th>Category</th><th colspan="13">Features included in classification</th></tr>
<tr><td>Exposure to wave action</td><td>Very exposed</td><td colspan="2">Exposed</td><td colspan="3">Semi-exposed</td><td colspan="4">Sheltered</td><td colspan="2">Very sheltered</td><td>Extremely sheltered</td></tr>
<tr><td>Exposure to tidal streams</td><td colspan="2">Very exposed</td><td colspan="3">Exposed</td><td colspan="3">Semi-exposed</td><td colspan="3">Sheltered</td><td colspan="2">Very sheltered</td></tr>
<tr><td>Presence of* sand and silt</td><td colspan="3">Sand on rocks and organisms</td><td colspan="4">Thin/flocculent cover of silt on rocks and organisms</td><td colspan="6">Thick cover of silt on rocks and organisms</td></tr>
<tr><td>Rock type*</td><td colspan="3">Calcareous</td><td colspan="4">Highly fissured</td><td colspan="6">Friable</td></tr>
<tr><td>Salinity*</td><td colspan="5">Low</td><td colspan="8">Variable</td></tr>
<tr><td>Other environ-* mental features present and notes</td><td colspan="13"></td></tr>
<tr><td>Community present</td><td colspan="4">Dominant or abundant species or species group</td><td colspan="5">Other species of frequent or higher abundance</td><td colspan="4">Other species</td></tr>
</table>

In discussion of the location of conservation areas, it is important to recognize the presence of biogeographical provinces and to select similar habitats for conservation in the major provinces. For purposes of survey and description of the communities present at each site visited, it is necessary to record only the location of the site along the coast. Following the completion of the survey of a large area, comparison of sites to establish whether biogeographical provinces are present can be considered. In comparison of the communities present at a particular geographical location with those of another area, the main biogeographical province should be noted.

3. Depth Zones

The underwater observer studying hard surfaces from shallow to deep water will find marked changes in the communities present at different depths. In view of the different characteristics of these zones and the different habitats which they offer, it seems important to both characterize and name them. Figure 2 shows a typical example of the zonation of conspicuous sublittoral species with depth on an open Atlantic coast; it can be seen that the majority of algae, including *Laminaria hyperborea,** extend to a similar depth. *Laminaria hyperborea* has been shown to extend to a depth, measured from mid-tide level on the French coast, at which about 1% of surface illumination is present (Boulter *et al.*, 1974; Castric-Fey, 1974). According to Pérès (1967a) this 1% level is reflected in the maximum extent of photophilic algae which, in turn, provides a basis for the division of the sublittoral zone into "infralittoral" and "circalittoral" sub-zones,† in the terminology of Pérès and Molinier (1957). However, particularly in British waters, it is important that the zones are indicated by the plants and animals which characterize them and not by such a highly variable factor as the percentage of surface illumination which is present. In such British waters, the levels *dominated* by erect algae, including the *Laminaria hyperborea* forest, provide the most suitable characterization of the infralittoral sub-zone, and the animal-dominated area characterizes the circalittoral sub-zone.

---

*Nomenclature and authorities for benthic macroalgae follow data in Parke and Dixon (1976).

†Zones are defined in full later (pp. 337–338).

It is important to note here that, although the light regime (1% of surface illumination level) which separates the two sub-zones at most locations in both the Mediterranean and north-east Atlantic appears similar, the circalittoral zone in the Mediterranean is often dominated or characterized by algae.

The maximum downward extent of the whole sublittoral zone is defined as the greatest depth to which photosynthetic plants can grow. Underwater, this limit is very difficult to distinguish on the basis of the organisms which can be seen. However, work carried out by J. Clokie (personal communication) on the west coast of Scotland shows that the algae "*Conchocelis*" and *Lithothamnion sonderi* are present in greater depths than any other algae, reaching about twice the depth to which most species of erect foliose algae occur.

The real downward extent of the sublittoral, and therefore the circalittoral (*sensu* Pérès and Molinier, 1957), is often ignored by field-workers and the latter term is used to refer to depths greater than that to which algae can survive. Pérès (1967b) described a similar problem in the Mediterranean and suggested that, if rocks are absolutely devoid of algae, a further category is required to describe them: the bathylittoral. The "offshore rocky bottom biocoenosis" occurs at about 250 m in the Mediterranean and, according to Pérès (1967b), corresponds to a bathylittoral zone; it exhibits similarities to the animal assemblages which we include in the circalittoral for the British Isles. However, in view of the difficulty of establishing during fieldwork whether one is in the sublittoral, bathylittoral or bathyal zone we propose, for the moment, to retain the classification of depth zones as extending, in nearshore areas, to the circalittoral zone only. Further systematic surveys of the distribution of species with depth may reveal a distinctive change in the assemblage of animals present in different depths, corresponding to the disappearance of microscopic or indistinct algae. A change which could be defined and recognized by field-workers would provide the basis for separation of sublittoral and bathylittoral zones.

The strength of wave action also influences the depth distribution of some species and appears to be particularly important in determining the presence of some animal species in shallow water. Increasing siltation with depth, resulting from attenuation of wave

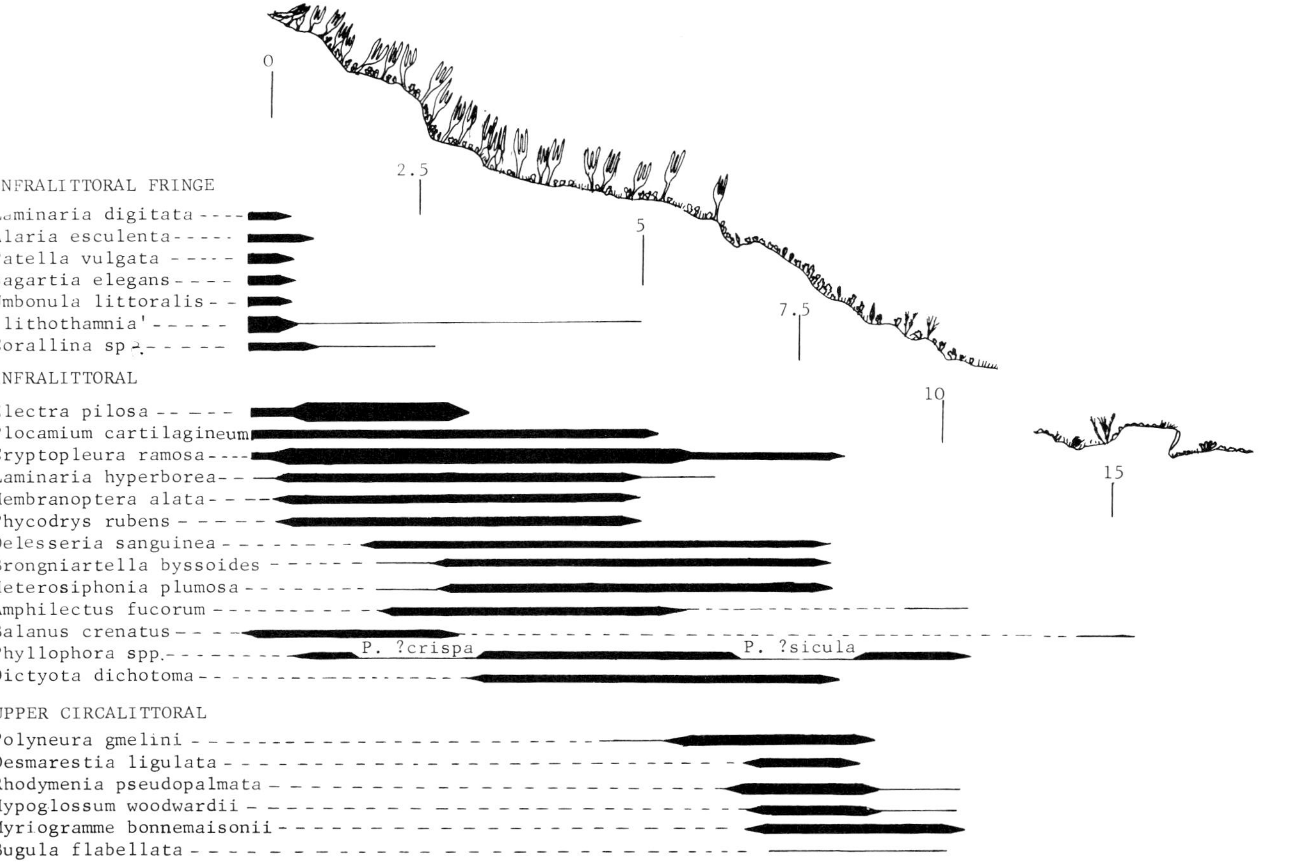
0
2.5
5
7.5
10
15
INFRALITTORAL FRINGE
Laminaria digitata
Alaria esculenta
Patella vulgata
Sagartia elegans
Umbonula littoralis
'lithothamnia'
Corallina spp.
INFRALITTORAL
Electra pilosa
Plocamium cartilagineum
Cryptopleura ramosa
Laminaria hyperborea
Membranoptera alata
Phycodrys rubens
Delesseria sanguinea
Brongniartella byssoides
Heterosiphonia plumosa
Amphilectus fucorum
Balanus crenatus
Phyllophora spp.
P. ?crispa
P. ?sicula
Dictyota dichotoma
UPPER CIRCALITTORAL
Polyneura gmelini
Desmarestia ligulata
Rhodymenia pseudopalmata
Hypoglossum woodwardii
Myriogramme bonnemaisonii
Bugula flabellata

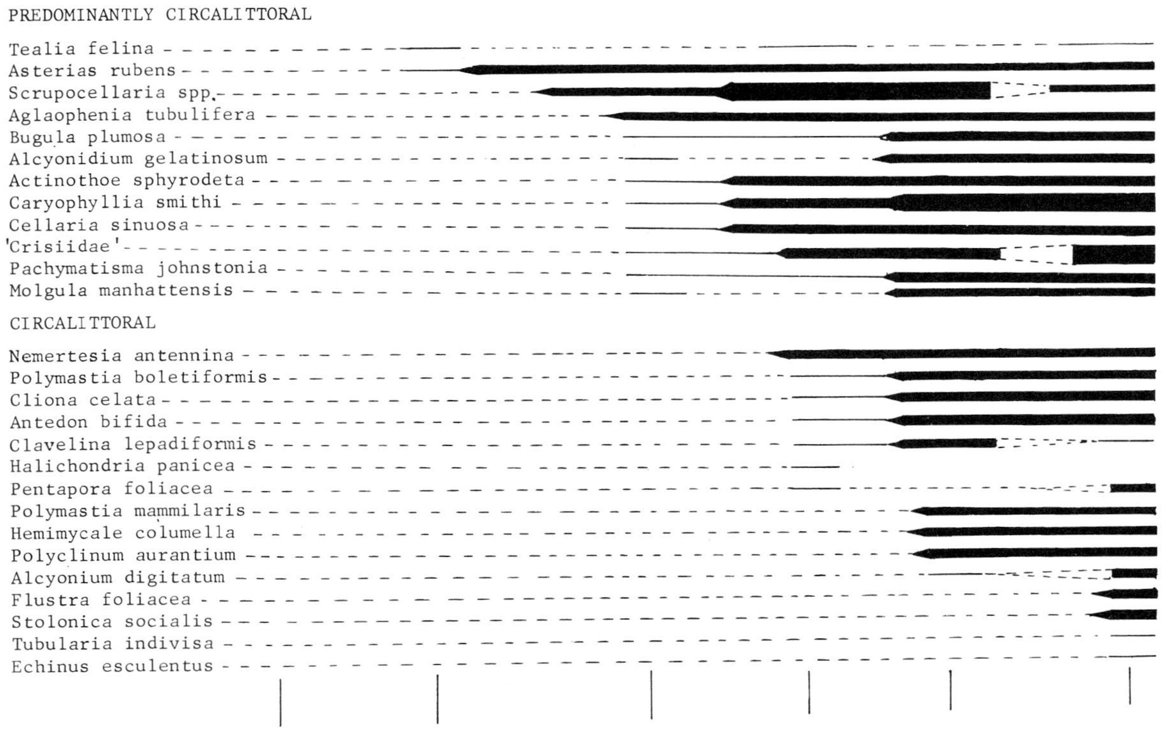

Fig. 2. The distribution of sublittoral species with depth and the main zones present on the west coast of Ramsey Island, West Wales. From Hiscock (1978).

action, similarly affects zonation. Riedl (1964) has suggested the presence of different zones resulting from multi-directional or two-directional water movement. However, any attempt to incorporate such a consideration into a classification scheme would be beset with problems similar to those of describing the light regime present and cannot be considered practical.

Only in a few areas will algal growth on rocks be prevented by factors other than light. For instance, at some extremely exposed sites, wave action may be so severe that kelps and foliose algae cannot survive and surge-tolerant animals such as barnacles and encrusting sponges will dominate the rock in shallow water (as in the case of rocks off the west coast of Ramsey Island). In areas exposed to strong tidal streams, suspension-feeding animals often thrive and compete successfully for living space with the algae which would, in shelter, dominate the rock (for instance, in the Swellies, Menai Strait).

The recognition by Glémarec (1973) of an "infralittoral zone", for sedimentary benthos, according to temperature is less useful for epibiota, particularly on sublittoral rocks, and is not in accord with the classification of Pérès and Molinier (1957). However, for animal assemblages living in or on sediments, the division of communities into infralittoral and circalittoral sub-zones according to algal domination cannot be applied and the term sublittoral is preferred.

A further separation of distinctly different communities at different depths occurs as a result of the temperature regime above and below the thermocline. Above the thermocline, waters are subject to large temperature-changes throughout the year, whilst below it such changes are slight. The two zones are described by Glémarec (1973) as "open sea" and "coastal" circalittoral "étages". The depth of the thermocline which separates the two zones is determined by both hydrodynamic conditions and the local topography. In calm waters the thermocline might rise to 40 m, but generally the cold waters are limited to depths below 70–80 m. Castric-Fey (1974) places the separation of the open sea and coastal "étages" at 40–47 m according to animal communities present off the Îles de Glénan (north France), while Könnecker (1977) describes stenohaline, stenothermal offshore communities below 40 m off Galway Bay (west Ireland). The "prelittoral" and "frontolittoral zones" of Cabioch (1968), which are separated at about the 80 m isobath, are probably equivalent to the open sea and coastal zones (Glémarec, 1973). In view of Glémarec's definition of the circalittoral, which does not accord with that of Pérès and Molinier (1957), the term "sublittoral" is here preferred for use when referring to the open sea and coastal zones. The framework for classification (Fig. 1) is for the coastal sublittoral zone.

A single term is necessary to describe each of the main zones so as to avoid long descriptions such as "the animal-dominated zone with sparse algae present". Further, the description of depth zones according to the characteristic species present (see, for instance, Castric-Fey *et al.*, 1973) does not provide a system which permits comparison between areas, although it is useful within a limited geographical location. Hedgepeth (1957) reviewed the terminology applied to depth zones and, in an addendum, noted the system proposed in the same year by Pérès and Molinier. The Pérès and Molinier nomenclature is preferred here as a basis for the division of the main zones and has been found easy to apply in the field. The system has been applied to the north-east Atlantic in approximately the same sense as that used in Castric-Fey *et al.* (1973) for the Brittany coast. Castric-Fey *et al.* use the term "horizon" in preference to "zone" because the former is stated more clearly to represent the concept of a series of horizontal bands (Castric-Fey, 1974). However, "depth zone" and "zonation" are retained here because of the widespread use of the terms.

The following terminology is therefore defined, as a basis for separating the main habitat zones related to the domination of rock surfaces by algae or animals at different depths.

The SUBLITTORAL zone extends from the upper limit of the large kelps (*Alaria, Laminaria* and *Saccorhiza* in the north-east Atlantic) to, by strict definition, the greatest depth at which photosynthetic plants can grow. However, for practical purposes the sublittoral is considered to include all depths below the littoral;

The SUBLITTORAL FRINGE is the transition zone between littoral zone and sub-littoral zone and, on the open coast, lies above the main *Laminaria hyperborea* population;

The INFRALITTORAL sub-zone is that part of the sublittoral zone dominated by photophilous algae (large kelp plants according to Pérès and Molinier, 1957). It is most convenient to consider the infralittoral to apply to any levels that are dominated by subtidal erect algae, as kelp plants are sometimes absent;

The CIRCALITTORAL sub-zone is that part of the sublittoral zone that extends below the levels dominated by photophilous algae. This is taken here as the sub-zone below the domination of all erect algae.

We have divided the infralittoral and circalittoral sub-zones further into:

An UPPER INFRALITTORAL where a forest of Laminariales is present;

A LOWER INFRALITTORAL where Laminariales are absent or sparse but dense algae dominate the rock;

An UPPER CIRCALITTORAL where animals predominate but scattered erect algae are present;

A LOWER CIRCALITTORAL where erect algae are absent.

4. *Substratum and Topographical Features*

The presence of particular species depends primarily on the presence of suitable substrata within particular depth zones. Many species burrowing in sediments are particularly sensitive to the sediment grade and mixture. Truly epifaunal species are much less affected by sediment type, or are dependent mainly on the presence and type of hard substrata and mobility of the latter. Since many studies of epifaunal species also include visible infauna, a wide range of sediment mixtures is included in Fig. 1. However, an observer working on the seabed should note the exact nature of the sediments. For instance, mud will sometimes be found to be a veneer of mud over muddy gravel, and such features can greatly affect the species present. The notations used to describe sediments are taken mainly from Glémarec (1973), with additions. For the purposes of the present classification, rock substrata are described as: bedrock; boulders 50 cm +; boulders 15–50 cm; pebbles 2.5–15 cm.

Many topographical features such as overhangs and cliffs have species present which are distinctly different from those of the surrounding rock surfaces. The importance of inclination of rock surfaces in determining the species present was recognized by Drach (1959), who listed eight categories of rock surfaces. Castric-Fey (1974) redefined and added to the categories listed by Drach, and her list is used here in arriving at a suitable classification. However, the biologist-diver cannot be expected to utilize too detailed a categorization and we have aimed to keep the list of features as simple as possible. We have therefore identified topographical features which are likely to present easily distinguished communities that are reasonably practical for the field worker to identify and record *in situ*. In a study aimed at describing the effects of topography on the communities present, a more carefully defined list of categories might be required.

Many organisms provide a substratum or shelter for a distinctive community of species. Only a few widespread biotic habitats are listed in Fig. 1. Distinctive communities are also often associated with the structures placed on and above the seabed by man. The most common ones to be encountered are pier piles, pontoons/buoys, or wrecks, and all these are included in Fig. 1.

5. Substratum Mobility and Scour

The epibiota which is present on rocks depends partly on the stability of the substratum. For instance, small boulders in a wave-sheltered area will support a similar flora and fauna to that of adjacent bedrock but, in a wave-exposed situation, a community of fast-growing species which have colonized since the boulder was last disturbed by wave action will be present. Similarly, scour resulting from the movement of sand, gravel, pebbles and boulders adjacent to bedrock will largely determine the species present. Whether or not rocks are mobile or whether scour occurs can only be surmised, but such surfaces should be considered a separate habitat.

6. Exposure to Wave Action and Tidal Streams

The strength of wave action and tidal streams is of great importance in determining the epifauna and flora present, particularly on rock substrata. Little account has been taken of the effect of water movements in classifications of infaunal benthic associations, partly because the grade of sediment reflects to some extent the strength of water movements and partly because infaunal species are little affected by the direct action of tidal streams and wave oscillations. Exposure grades are difficult to assess for sublittoral areas, but it is considered that the scales developed by Hiscock (1976, and summarized in Hiscock, 1979), provide a practical method of classifying exposure.

7. The Presence of Silt and Sand on Rocks

The presence of silt falling on to or smothering epibenthic organisms is important and the classification therefore includes this feature. The worker interpreting field records must bear in mind that silt may only be deposited in calm weather but, for surveys carried out in summer, the maximum amount of silt likely to accrete will probably be observed. Sand overlying rocks or mixed in with organisms probably also tends to smother, but scour is a more important factor here. Sand overlying rocks or mixed in with undergrowth is recorded as a separate category.

8. Rock Type

It seems likely that rock type will be of greatest importance to epibenthic species in the case of friable, easily penetrated (usually calcareous) or highly fissured rocks; these rock types should therefore be mentioned in describing habitats.

9. Salinity

Where salinity is variable or reduced, plant and animal communities will be affected and any classification of sublittoral communites in such a situation should include a note of the salinity regime.

10. Other Features and Notes

Important widely occurring features have been mentioned above. Other factors may affect sublittoral communities and their description will therefore be important in classification. Such features include, for example, de-oxygenation, warming by effluents and local pollution effects.

In providing a strictly defined framework for categorizing a very variable environment, and for including all species within one community defined by a few habitat criteria, the field-worker is prevented from qualifying particular observations which do not fit into the framework. It is therefore important to note such observations.

11. Community Present

The community(-ies) present in any one habitat must be described in a manner precise enough to ensure that the dominant or most abundant species recorded will enable the later recognition of characteristic species in recurrent communities. Quantitative or semi-quantitative data are considered necessary if the species most important in characterizing the community are to be identified. However, the methods normally used to sample or observe epibenthic communities and the nature of the organisms allow only the use of semi-quantitative recording. Remote methods of sampling employ dredges to collect from an ill-defined area of seabed, whilst divers often make only estimates of density or percentage cover to maximize the information which they obtain in one brief excursion to the seabed. Furthermore, the necessity of recording percentage cover for some species and density for others prevents the direct comparison of even quantitative data, because the units of measurements are different. The use of an abundance scale such as that described by Hiscock (1979) provides the same range of comparable notations for different species recorded in different units and gives an indication of their real abundance by taking account of the maximum amount in which they are known to occur.

In Fig. 1, we have suggested the recording of dominant or abundant species, species of frequent or higher occurrence and other species present, in each habitat investigated. Often, this will be a summary of more detailed records, including quantitative data.* An example of this approach is shown in Table II. It is particularly important to note species which are frequent as a separate category since, in some locations, no single species is present in quantities large enough to be described as abundant.

12. Conclusion

Most of the criteria listed for the definition of the habitat have been incorporated in check-lists used to describe a wide variety of sites

*Subsequent to the preparation of this chapter, all community descriptions drawn up by us have employed Abundant, Common, Frequent, Occasional and Rare assessments for constituent species.

Table II. Results of a brief descriptive survey of one site (Graves End, Pwll-du Head, Gower) by two divers organized according to the framework in Fig. 1

General description of habitat: Broken rock slope of limestone bedrock with some small boulders, pebbles and clean sand present. Very exposed to wave action above 2 m, exposed to wave action below 2 m, semi-exposed to tidal streams.

Species present in different habitats in the main zones:

SUBLITTORAL FRINGE/UPPER INFRALITTORAL (+ 0.6 to 0 m)

Upward Facing Surfaces. Bedrock.

Dominant species: *Laminaria hyperborea.*

Abundant species: *Plocamium cartilagineum, Cryptopleura ramosa, Polycarpa pomaria.*

Frequent + species: *Phyllophora pseudoceranoides, Corallina* sp., *Hypoglossum woodwardii, Cladophora* sp., *Chaetomorpha* sp., *Halichondria panicea, Sabellaria spinulosa, Sidnyum turbinatum, Ophlitaspongia seriata.*

Other species: ?*Phyllophora sicula, Polyneura gmelinii, Hymeniacidon perleve, Dysidea fragilis, Amphilectus fucorum, Aglaophenia* sp., *Tealia felina, Botryllus schlosseri, Polyclinum aurantium,* ?*Dasychone bombyx, Jasminiera elegans, Grantia compressa.*

Kelp stipes

Frequent + species: *Membranoptera alata, Palmaria palmata.*

Other species: *Cryptopleura ramosa.*

LOWER INFRALITTORAL

Upward Facing Surfaces. Bedrock (0 to 1 m).

Abundant species: *Calliblepharis ciliata.*

Frequent + species: *Plocamium cartilagineum, Phyllophora pseudoceranoides, Rhodymenia delicatula, Hypoglossum woodwardii, Polyneura gmelinii, Dictyota dichotoma, Hymeniacidon perleve, Aglaophenia* sp., *Sabellaria spinulosa, Sidnyum turbinatum, Distaplia rosea,* ?*Dasychone bombyx/Jasminiera elegans, Polycarpa pomaria.*

Other species: *Schottera nicaeensis,* "lithothamnia", *Rhodymenia delicatula, Rhodymenia pseudopalmata* var. *ellisiae, R. pseudopalmata* var. *pseudopalmata, Radicilingua thysanorhizans, Heterosiphonia plumosa, Rhodomela confervoides, Laminaria hyperborea, Taonia atomaria, Ulva* sp., *Bryopsis plumosa, Cliona* sp. (boring), *Tethya aurantia, Haliclona oculata, Tubularia indivisa, Halecium halecinum, Nemertesia ramosa, Nemertesia antennina, Alcyonium digitatum, Pomatoceros triqueter, Balanus crenatus,* Caprellidae, *Macropipus puber, Hiatella arctica, Crisia denticulata, Bugula plumosa, Bugula turbinata, Scrupocellaria scruposa, Asterias rubens, Clavelina lepadiformis, Hemimycale columella, Bowerbankia* sp.

Table II. (Continued)

Kelp Stipes

Abundant species: *Phycodrys rubens.*

Other species: *Membranoptera alata, Cryptopleura ramosa.*

(*Callithamnion* sp. was noted as present in potholes at 1.1 m. *Bugula plumosa* and *Bugula turbinata* were noted as frequent on vertical surfaces at 1.1 m.)

CIRCALITTORAL (1 to 3.6 m)

Upward Facing Surfaces. Bedrock.

Frequent + species: *Rhodymenia pseudopalmata* var. *ellisiae, Hypoglossum woodwardii, Polyneura gmelinii, Ciocalypta penicillus,*[a] *Tubularia indivisa, Halecium halecinum, Hydrallmania falcata, Aglaophenia* sp., *Nemertesia antennina, Alcyonium digitatum, Sabellaria spinulosa, Phoronis hippocrepia,*[a] Caprellidae, Jasiidae, *Mytilus edulis* (juveniles), *Sidnyum turbinatum, Distaplia rosea, Polycarpa pomaria, Sertularia cupressina.*

Other species: *Rhodymenia pseudopalmata* var. *pseudopalmata, Polymastia mammilaris, Cliona* sp. (boring), *Suberites domuncula, Haliclona oculata, Plumularia setacea, Tealia felina, Sagartia elegans, Balanus crenatus,*[a] *Pagurus* sp., *Bugula plumosa, Bugula turbinata, Alcyonidium gelatinosum, Asterias rubens.*

---

[a]Present adjacent to sand.

(Algae were frequent only in shallow water. At 3.6 m, only a few individual plants of *R. pseudopalmata* var. *ellisiae* and *P. gmelinii* were observed.)

in south-west Britain during the past three years. The criteria have been found to be adequate and relevant to the interpretation of species data. The listing of species present in separate habitats to describe a separate community within each habitat has been used during 1979 and found to provide an excellent method for the detailed description of communities and the presentation of results by biologists using diving techniques to survey large areas of seabed. Table III summarizes the results of an extensive survey in which the range of major habitats and species characteristic of the different communities are identified.

The use of the framework for classification described here requires a great deal of discipline on the part of the diver trying to survey large areas of seabed in (a) making complete and separate lists for different habitats, and (b) noting abundance for all conspicuous species. However, where observations over small areas of seabed and quantitative samples are the basis for description, the definition of a single habitat and the listing of species is easily carried out (see, for instance, Table IV).

Comparison of species lists from the same habitat type in different locations will provide sufficient information for a decision on whether recurrent communities with a similar species composition and the same dominant, abundant or frequent species can be identified. The latter type of survey (Table IV) inevitably provides the best basis for description and comparison, but the time spent in fieldwork and in sample analysis is very much greater than for surveys of large areas listing conspicuous species.

DESCRIPTIONS OF RECURRENT SUBLITTORAL COMMUNITIES

1. *Introduction*

Several descriptions of sublittoral epibenthic plant and animal assemblages have now been published or are available to the authors as limited circulation reports or unpublished data. Reports which describe and compare the fauna and flora found at different sites in terms of associations or communities and their dominant or characteristic species are particularly valuable in considering the most effective means of describing communities. Also, the work now being completed is enabling the description of communities which do recur under similar environmental conditions in different locations. Sublittoral algal assemblages were described by Kain (1960) for the Isle of Man, Smith (1967) for Anglesey, Norton and Milburn (1972) for Argyll, Tittley *et al.* (1976) for Sullom Voe in Shetland, and Price and Tittley (1978) for Mull. Epibenthic animal assemblages were described by Jones (1951) for the Isle of Man, Warwick and Davies (1977) for the Bristol Channel, Könnecker (1977) for Galway Bay, and Erwin (1977) for Strangford Lough. Hiscock (1976) described sublittoral fauna present around Lundy, Anglesey and Lough Ine. The distribution of algae and animals was described by Hunnam (1976) for Skomer, by Earll (in Institute of Terrestrial Ecology, 1975) for Shetland, by Dixon *et al.* (1978) for part of the Dorset coast, and by Hiscock and Hiscock (1980, in press) for Roaringwater Bay, south-west Ireland. Work has also been carried out by the authors in various parts of south-west Britain and in the Outer Hebrides; this is being reported to the Nature Conservancy Council in a series of limited-circulation reports. Several descriptions of single locations are also useful, including the work of Knight-Jones and Nelson-Smith (1977), Hiscock and Hoare (1975), and Norton *et al.* (1977). Descriptions of particular communities were given by Warner (1971) for *Ophiothrix fragilis* and Roberts (1975) for *Modiolus modiolus*. Work carried out on the Atlantic coast of France is also relevant to the description of ecosystems present around the British Isles and the studies of Cabioch (1968) and Castric-Fey *et al.* (1973) are particularly notable.

In comparing descriptions of separate communities to discover whether similar assemblages of organisms occur in different locations, it is important initially to consider how similar the different assemblages have to be if they are to be considered as a recurrent community, and also to define the importance of characterizing species.

Thorson (1957) requires, amongst other things, that a characterizing species is conspicuous, occurs in at least 50% of the standard sampling units (0.1 m^2 in depths shallower than 200 m) and contributes at least 5% of the total living weight per standard unit. However, he also notes that "common sense combined with experience and intuition play an important part in selecting such species". Other authors (for instance, Davis, 1925) designate characteristic species for a particular single location by an arbitrary cut-off point in the numerical dominance of species (for instance by ranking the percentages each species contributes to the total number of individuals at each station, followed by summing in descending order of abundance until 50% is reached). The second method is unlikely to

Table III. Sublittoral communities present around Ramsey Island. Adapted from Hiscock (1978).

Zonation with depth (all coasts) on stable rock

SUBLITTORAL FRINGE. Dominated by encrusting calcareous algae ("lithothamnia") with *Laminaria digitata, Corallina* sp. and *Umbonula littoralis* present. *Sagartia elegans, Alaria esculenta* and *Patella* sp. present on wave-exposed coasts.

INFRALITTORAL. Dense algal growth of a wide vareity of species including, in particular, *Laminaria hyperborea, Cryptopleura ramosa, Plocamium cartilagineum, Delesseria sanguinea, Heterosiphonia plumosa, Dictyopteris membranacea* and *Dictyota dichotoma*. Wave-sheltered communities include, in addition, *Saccorhiza polyschides, Calliblepharis ciliata, Kallymenia reniformis, Rhodomela* sp. and, on small stones, *Stenogramme interrupta.*

UPPER INFRALITTORAL. Characterized by a forest of *Laminaria hyperborea* and associated species including *Membranipora membranacea, Obelia geniculata, Palmaria palmata, Phycodrys rubens* and *Membranoptera alata. Laminaria saccharina* and *Halidrys siliquosa* often present at the lower limit of dense *L. hyperborea* or where semi-stable substrata present.

LOWER INFRALITTORAL. Kelp sparse or absent. Characterized by a wide variety of foliose algae.

UPPER CIRCALITTORAL. Predominately animals. Characterized by the algae *Rhodymenia pseudopalmata, Myriogramme bonnemaisonii, Hypoglossum woodwardii* and *Phyllophora sicula.*

CIRCALITTORAL COMMUNITIES. Separated into several communities described below. Widespread species include *Sertularia argentea, Nemertesia antennina, N. ramosa, Alcyonium digitatum, Actinothoe sphyrodeta, Caryophyllia smithi, Crisia eburnea, Bugula plumosa, Cellaria sinuosa, Flustra foliacea, Pentapora foliacea, Alcyonidium gelatinosum, Asterias rubens* and *Pachymatisma johnstonia.*

Circalittoral communities

Stable rocks exposed or very exposed to tidal streams and, off the west coast, very exposed to wave action. Characterized by a *Halichondria panicea-Tubularia indivisa* community with extensive patches of *Balanus crenatus,* encrusting sponges, *Amphisbetia operculata* and *Sagartia elegans.* Many widely distributed species absent.

Stable rocks very exposed to wave action and exposed or semi-exposed to tidal streams. Characterized by dense Bryozoa + Hydrozoa, *Polyclinum aurantium* and, at some sites, *Molgula manhattensis.*

Semi-stable rocks exposed or very exposed to wave action and semi-exposed to tidal streams. Characterized by encrusting Bryozoa, particularly *Escharoides coccineus* and *Pomatoceros triqueter.*

Table III. (Continued)

Stable small boulders and stones semi-exposed to tidal streams and semi-exposed to or sheltered from wave action. Characterized by dense Bryozoa + Hydrozoa with *Ophiocomina nigra* at some depths. *Cellepora pumicosa* and *Halecium halecinum* probably characteristic on the east coast.
Mobile or semi-mobile gravel and small stones very exposed to tidal streams, sheltered from wave action. Similar but reduced fauna to stable stones. Encrusting Bryozoa and *Pomatoceros triqueter* probably characteristic.
Silty bedrock semi-exposed to wave action, sheltered from tidal streams. Characterized by the absence of dense Bryozoa/Hydrozoa and by the presence of large numbers of *Molgula manhattensis* and *Suberites carnosus.*
Stable sand, gravel and gravel covered by mud sheltered from vigorous water movement. Characterized by visible infauna species including *Sabella penicillus, Cerianthus lloydi, Peachia hastata, Myxicola infundibulum* and by a mobile epifauna including *Ophiura* sp(p). and gobies.
Mobile sand very exposed to wave action, sheltered from or semi-exposed to tidal streams. Characterized by absence of epifauna except *Pagurus bernhardus.*

select large conspicuous species as characteristic because they occur in low densities and, particularly from the point of view of *in situ* surveys of epibenthos, the use of conspicuous species to characterize communities is important.

The recognition of characteristic species, or species most abundant in particular habitats or recurrent communities, and the separation of different recurrent communities can be carried out by numerical analysis using techniques such as those described by Moore (1973); these are very valuable in sorting results objectively and with the same degree of thoroughness, using the same criteria for all samples.

Studies of epibenthic assemblages have been carried out using a wide variety of methods, ranging from the collection of quantitative samples and identification of all species collected to the listing of only conspicuous species which could be recognized *in situ*. Comparison of the results of different workers is therefore sometimes difficult and at present it is not usually possible to apply particular criteria in assessing whether the community in one location can be considered the same as that in a different area. However, most authors give some indication of the abundance of each species, which enables the comparison of characterizing species from each area. The application of the method described here for recording the abundance of

Table IV. Circalittoral animal communities on cliffs in the region of Lough Ine. Excluding species recorded as Rare and only present at one location. Species recorded as Abundant are listed in heavy type. Species recorded as Frequent or Common are listed in italics. Adapted from Hiscock (1976), Table 4.

Carrigathorna	Whirlpool Cliff	Island Cliff
Circalittoral communites on cliff surface very sheltered from tidal streams and very exposed to wave action with little silt present.	Circalittoral communities on cliff surface semi-exposed to tidal streams and extremely sheltered from wave action. No silt present.	Circalittoral communities on cliff surface very sheltered from tidal streams and extremely sheltered from wave action. Thin/ flocculent cover of silt.
Suberites carnosus	Suberites carnosus	Suberites carnosus
Cliona celata	Cliona celata	Polymastia boletiformis
Polymastia boletiformis	Polymastia boletiformis	*Tethya autantia*
Tethya aurantia	Tethya aurantia	**Stelligera stuposa**
Dysidea fragilis	Stelligera stuposa	*Dysidea fragilis*
Haliclona sp.	Dysidea fragilis	*Jophon hyndmani*
Amphilectus fucorum	Haliclona sp.	*Eudendrium ramosum*
Halecium halecinum	Amphilectus fucorum	Kirchenpaueria pinnata
Sertularella polyzonias	*Eudendrium ramosum*	*Aurelia aurita (scyphistomae)*
Amphisbetia operculata	Halecium halecinum	*Parerythropodium hibernicum*
Kirchenpaueria pinnata	Sertularella polyzonias	*Caryophyllia smithi*
Nemertesia antennina	Amphisbetia operculata	Corynactis viridis
Aglaophenia sp.	Aurelia aurita (scyphistomae)	Harmothoe sp.
Alcyonium digitatum	Alcyonium digitatum	Eulalia viridis
Anemonia sulcata	Parerythropodium hibernicum	Castalia punctata
Tealia felina	Caryophyllia smithi	Lysidice ninetta
Caryophyllia smithi	**Corynactis viridis**	Potamilla reniformis
Corynactis viridis	*Harmothoe* sp.	*Hydroides norvegicus*
Eulalia viridis	*Phyllodoce lamelligera*	*Pomatoceros triqueter*
Harmothoe sp.	*Eulalia viridis*	Verruca stroemia
Phyllodoce lamelligera	Castalia punctata	Balanus balanus
Lysidice ninetta	Syllis prolifera/variegata	*Janira maculosa*
Castalia punctata	*Lysidice ninetta*	Lysianassa ceratina
Pomatoceros triqueter	*Potamilla reniformis*	Gitana sp.
Verruca stroemia	*Hydroides norvegicus*	*Lembos websteri*
Balanus balanus	*Pomatoceros triqueter*	**Corophium bonelli**
Pyrogoma anglicum	Verruca stroemia	Cingula semicostata
Stenothoe minuta	Balanus balanus	*Alvania* punctura
Lembos websteri	Pyrgoma anglicum	Rissoa parva
?*Hippolyte sp.*	*Lysianassa ceratina*	Bittium reticulatum
Calliostoma zizyphinum	*Lembos websteri*	Heteranomia squamula
Tricolia pullus	**Corophium bonelli**	Chlamys varia (juv.)
Cingula semicostata	Calliostoma zizyphinum	Kellia suborbicularis
Alvania punctura	Tricolia pullus	Cerastoderma sp. (juv.)
Rissoa parva	Rissoa parva	*Hiatella arctica*
Bittium reticulatum	Bittium reticulatum	*Scrupocellaria scruposa*
Nassarius incrassatus	Nassarius incrassatus	Scrupocellaria scrupea

Table IV. (Continued)

Carrigathorna	Whirlpool Cliff	Island Cliff
Onchidella celtica	Modiolus phaseolinus	Scrupocellaria reptans
Modiolus phaseolinus	Mytilus edulis (juv.)	Crisidia cornuta
Musculus marmoratus	*Musculus marmoratus*	Crisia denticulata
Heteranomia squamula	*Heteranomia squamula*	Crania anomala
Chlamys varia (juv.)	Chlamys varia (juv.)	Henricia sp.
Cerastoderma sp. (juv.)	*Kellia suborbicularis*	Asterias rubens
Hiatella arctica	*Hiatella arctica*	Marthasterias glacialis
Scrupocellaria scruposa	Scrupocellaria scruposa	Ophiothrix fragilis (juv.)
Scrupocellaria scrupea	Scrupocellaria scrupea	*Amphipholis squamata*
Scrupocellaria reptans	Scrupocellaria reptans	*Distaplia rosea*
Crisidia cornuta	Crisidia cornuta	*Diplosoma listerianum*
Crisia denticulata	Crisia denticulata	*Ascidiella aspersa*
Crania anomala	Henricia sp.	*Pyura tesselata/Polycarpa* sp.
Antedon bifida	Marthasterias glacialis	
Henricia sp.	Ophiothrix fragilis (juv.)	
Asterias rubens	Amphipholis squamata	
Marthasterias glacialis	Echinus esculentus	
Ophiothrix fragilis (juv.)	*Ascidiella aspersa*	
Amphipholis squamata		
Echinus esculentus		
Cucumaria normanni		

species should enable objective criteria to be applied to identify similar communities. For instance, two separate communities might be considered similar if both include more than 50% of "frequent" species. In addition, the amount of work which has been carried out since sublittoral rocky areas could be effectively studied by diving is small, and it is not at present possible to give a reasonably comprehensive overview of the epibenthic communities which occur in British waters. Therefore, examples are chosen of a few epibenthic communities with which the authors are familiar and which represent a small fraction of the habitats and communities occurring around the coast. These examples provide an indication of how well the concept of recurrent communities can be applied to sublittoral epibenthos. Three main points should, however, be made regarding epibenthic communities. It is often appropriate to name communities by the habitat conditions in/on which they occur, for instance, kelp stipes. Some communities are characterized, and can therefore be named, by groups of organisms which dominate the seabed, for instance, erect Hydrozoa and Bryozoa. Where a community is named for particular characteristic organisms, it seems essential that those organisms should be present in every example of the community.

2. *The* Modiolus modiolus *Community of Tide-exposed Seabed*

Beds of the horse mussel *Modiolus modiolus* cover extensive areas of seabed in several parts of the British Isles, but particularly off the northern coasts. Epifaunal populations of *Modiolus* occur on stable rock or wherever shells and stones are present on sediments for initial colonization. The *Modiolus* community appears to be a good example of an epifaunal assemblage which recurs under similar conditions in different locations. Descriptions of *Modiolus* communities in British coastal waters have been published by Jones (1951) for the south coast of the Isle of Man, Roberts (1975) for Strangford Lough and by Warwick and Davies (1977) for the Bristol Channel. Further records are available in limited circulation reports for Shetland by Earll (in ITE, 1975 and personal communication), Addy and Griffiths (1977), Addy (1977), Hiscock and Hainsworth (1976), and from unpublished observations made by K. Hiscock. Table V compares the species found at a location in Shetland and in Strangford Lough. Despite the different methods of sampling and recording used by the different authors at two widely different locations, 38% of all the species and 73% of the most abundant species present in Shetland were also recorded in Strangford Lough. A comparison with the work of Jones (1951) reveals further similarity between the three sets of data. The close similarity allows the description "*Modiolus modiolus* community" to be used in a meaningful way. However, of the two areas compared in detail, many of the dominant or most abundant species were different and only *Modiolus modiolus, Ophiothrix fragilis* and *Echinus esculentus* were present in both. Furthermore, Petersen (1918) distinguishes the most important characterizing species as *M. modiolus, Ophiopholis aculeata, Trophonia* (= *Pherusa*) *plumosa* (O.F. Müll.) and *Balanus* spp., thus leaving only *Modiolus* as the consistently abundant or dominant species. It is particularly notable that *O. aculeata* was not recorded in the Strangford *Modiolus* community but is recorded by Erwin (1977) from Strangford. The observations of Earll (in ITE, 1975) are useful in noting that the components of the *Modiolus* community in Shetland vary from site to site and tend towards an increasing number of epifaunal ascidians at sheltered sites and of *Ophiothrix fragilis, Ophiocomina nigra* and *Psammechinus miliaris* at more exposed locations. Many of the large epifaunal species which occur with *Modiolus* are widespread in Shetland and the association is therefore largely one of species with similar environmental requirements which occur together. In view of the variability likely to occur in associated species depending on environment, it seems important to add a description of the major environmental factors affecting differences in the description.

The concept that *Modiolus* must, as a characteristic species, always be present in a "*Modiolus* community" has to be considered. Spärk (1929) does not consider that a species used to name a particular community needs to be present in order to identify that community. Given such an attitude, the field-worker is given the opportunity to be highly subjective in the description and classification of the community being recorded. For instance, Warwick and Davis (1977) working in the Bristol Channel, have tried to adhere to the original communities defined by Petersen (1913) and have adopted a very broad interpretation of the *Modiolus* community. Although including many of the species found in other *Modiolus* communities, only nine out of 45 sites sampled included *Modiolus*. Furthermore, the density of *Modiolus* at the sites where it was present does not satisfy the criteria established by Thorson (1957) for the definition of a characteristic species. If authors set themselves the task of fitting their findings into the descriptions of other workers then a very broad definition of a recurrent community is required. Indeed, it seems neither realistic nor useful to assume that previous classifications can always be applied.

3. *The* Ophiothrix fragilis *Community*

Dense beds (over 1000 individuals per square metre) of the brittle star *Ophiothrix fragilis* occur on unbroken, usually horizontal seabed in wave-sheltered areas all around the British Isles. The beds often extend over many hectares or even square kilometres of seabed (see, for instance, Brun, 1969), and appear to be a stable feature of many areas. Warner (1971) notes that the populations

Table V. Invertebrate species present in a *Modiolus modiolus* community present between Calback Ness and Little Roe Island in Shetland and in Strangford Lough, Northern Ireland

Shetland		Strangford Lough	
Prominent species present in large numbers (> 1/10 m²) recorded by Hiscock and Hainsworth, 1976, and unpublished records by Hiscock, 1978.	"Syllidae"	*Abundant species*	Cancer pagurus
	Nephthys hombergi		Goneplax rhomboides
	Audouinia tentaculata	Sertularella polyzonias	Pinnotheres pissum
	Lanice conchilega	Plumularia setacea	Hyas araneus
	Balanus balanus[a]	Porcellana longicornis[a]	Macropodia rostrata
	Janira maculosa	Pagurus bernhardus[a]	Tonicella rubra
Halecium halecinum	Podoceropsis excavata	Macropipus depurator	Diodora apertura
Kirchenpaueria pinnata	Galathea intermedia	Inachus dorsettensis[a]	Calliostoma zizyphinum
Pomatoceros triqueter[a]	Porcellana longicornis[a]	Buccinum undatum[a]	Gibbula cineraria[a]
Terebellidae (?Polymnia nebulosa[a])	Pagurus bernhardus[a]	Chlamys varia	Capulus ungaricus
Gibbula cineraria[a]	Pagurus pubescens	Chlamys opercularis[a]	Trivia monacha
Modiolus modiolus[a]	Macropipus depurator	Modiolus modiolus[a]	Ocenebra erinacea
Chlamys opercularis[a]	Inachus sp.[a]	Hiatella arctica[a]	Neptunea antiqua
Ophiothrix fragilis	Hyas araneus	Crisia denticulata	Pleurobranchus membranaceus
Ophiopholis aculeata	'Chiton'	Asterias rubens[a]	Nucula tenuis[a]
Antedon bifida[a]	Acmaea virginea	Ophiothrix fragilis[a]	Musculus marmoratus
Echinus esculentus[a]	Margarites groenlandicus	Ophiocomina nigra[a]	Mytilus edulis
	Gibbula tumida	Echinus esculentus[a]	Anomia ephippium
Qualitative records of species not included in the previous column from Addy and Griffiths, 1977, and Addy, 1977, and species present in small numbers (< 1/10 m²) recorded by Hiscock and Hainsworth, 1976, and Hiscock, 1978.	Buccinum undatum[a]		Pecten maximus
	Nassarius incrassatus	*Other species*	Chlamys distorta[a]
	Nucula spp. (juv.)[a]		Chlamys tigerina
	Monia patelliformis	Alcyonium digitatum[a]	Arctica islandica
	Chlamys distorta[a]	Tealia felina[a]	Cerastoderma edule
	Cultellus pellucidus	Adamsia palliata	Dosinia exoleta
	Ensis arcuatus	Tubulanus annulatus	Venus fasciata
	Hiatella arctica[a]	Lineus longissimus	Venerupis rhomboides

Table V. (Continued)

Shetland		Strangford Lough	
Virgularia mirabilis	Asterias rubens[a]	Lepidonotus squamatus[a]	Venerupis saxatilis
Alcyonium digitatum[a]	Crossaster papposus[a]	Nereis diversicolor	Tellina fabula
?Peachia hastata	Solaster endeca	Stylarioides plumosa	Umbonula littoralis
Tealia felina[a]	Ophiopholis sp. (juv.)	Polymnia nebulosa[a]	Antedon bifida[a]
Metridium senile	Ophiocomina nigra[a]	Sabella pavonina	Crossaster papposus[a]
Lucernaria quadricornis	Amphiura filiformis	Serpula vermicularis	Henricia sanguinolenta
Halosydna gelatinosa	Psammechinus miliaris	Hydroides norvegica	Marthasterias glacialis
Harmothoe spinifera	Echinocyamus pusillus	Pomatoceros triqueter[a]	Cucumaria saxicola
Lepidonotus squamatus	Strongylocentrotus droebachiensis	Spirorbis spirillum	Cucumaria lactea
		Golfingia vulgaris	Clavelina lepadiformis
		Balanus balanus[a]	Ciona intestinalis
		Nepthrops norvegicus	Corella parallelogramma
		Galathea dispersa	Ascidia mentula
		Macropipus puber	Dendrodoa grossularia
		Carcinus maenas	Molgula sp.

[a] Species present in both locations.

sampled by Allen (1899) were still present to be photographed by Vevers (1952). Also, dense *Ophiothrix fragilis* beds occur on a wide variety of substrata, from sand to rock. This brittle star is a truly dominant species and must smother most areas of seabed over which it is present, thus preventing establishment of many other species. However, several species do occur in the beds and some are listed in Table VI. Of the 22 species listed, it is considered here that only five might benefit by feeding on *Ophiothrix: Sagartia elegans* var. *miniata, Tealia felina, Luidea ciliaris, Asterias rubens* and *Crossaster papposus*. All the other species are most likely present because environmental conditions are suitable or because another food supply (for instance, infaunal bivalves in the case of *Buccinum undatum*) is present. Of the species likely to feed on *Ophiothrix*, the anemone *Tealia felina* is the only species consistently present in *Ophiothrix* beds. *Alcyonium digitatum*, also recorded in the same location as the brittle star populations studied, is a passive suspension feeder widely distributed throughout the British Isles and thriving in areas exposed to current flow; it is likely to be characteristic of the habitat in the absence of *Ophiothrix*.

In a dense bed of *Ophiothrix fragilis*, the brittle star clearly excludes many species and attracts a few others, while some species, independent of the *Ophiothrix* and thriving in the conditions present, survive smothering.

4. *Algae and Animals Associated with* Laminaria hyperborea

The large kelps, of which *Laminaria hyperborea* is the most common, provide a well-defined habitat on which distinctive communities of associated plants and animals develop. These communities are different on the fronds, on the stipes, and in the holdfasts. Thus, the three parts of the kelp plant provide three different habitats. The frond usually supports a limited attached fauna, with *Obelia dichotoma, Patina pellucida* and *Membranipora membranacea* commonly present, while the holdfast includes a very large number of species (389 in holdfasts collected from the north-east coast of Britain by Moore, 1973). Descriptions of holdfast faunas have been made by several workers, but particularly detailed studies have been carried out by Jones (1971) and Moore (1973). The latter

Table VI. Species often recorded from dense beds of *Ophiothrix fragilis* at nine locations in the British Isles. Only species which can be observed *in situ* have been included and species present in small amounts at only one or two sites or present at only one site (57 out of the total of 79 species) have been excluded from this table.

Substrate	muddy or sandy gravel, some rock, Torbay[a]	slate pebbles, Lundy[b]	bedrock, North Devon[b]	limestone bedrock, South Pembrokeshire[b]	bedrock, South-west Ireland[b]	gravel, pebbles, some rock, Anglesey, Menai Strait[b]	rock, pebbles, Anglesey, North coast[c]	gravel and pebbles, Isle of Man[d]	rock, Shetland[b]
Cliona celata	—	—	—	+	+	+	—	—	—
Haliclona oculata	—	—	—	++	—	+	—	—	—
Halecium halecinum	+	—	—	+	+	+	—	—	+
Nemertesia antennina	+	++	++	+	+	—	—	+	—
Hydrallmania falcata	—	—	—	—	+	+	—	+	—
Aglaophenia sp(p).	+	—	—	++	+	—	—	—	—
Cerianthus lloydi	++	—	—	—	—	+	—	—	—
Sagartia elegans var. *miniata*	—	—	+	—	++	+	—	—	—
Tealia felina	+	++	++	++	++	+	+	+	+
Alcyonium digitatum	+	+	+	++	+	++	+	+	+
Modiolus modiolus	—	—	—	—	—	—	—	+	++
Calliostoma zizyphinum	—	—	—	—	+	—	—	+	+
Buccinum undatum	+	—	—	—	—	+	—	—	+
Pagurus bernhardus	++	—	—	+	—	+	—	—	+
Alcyonidium gelatinosum	—	++	++	—	+	—	—	—	—
Ophiocomina nigra	—	+	+	—	+	—	—	—	+
Luidea ciliaris	—	++	—	—	+	—	—	+	+
Asterias rubens	+	—	—	+	+	+	+	+	+
Crassoster papposus	—	—	—	—	—	+	+	+	+
Echinus esculentus	—	—	—	—	+	—	—	+	++
Metridium senile	+	—	—	—	++	—	—	—	—
Antedon bifida	+	—	—	++	+	—	+	—	+

+ = present in small amounts, ++ = present in large amounts.
[a]Warner (1979).
[b]Hiscock (unpublished).
[c]Hiscock (1976).
[d]Brun (1969).

author establishes five separate communites for the area sampled in north-east Britain.

Several reports are now available of the stipe epiflora present on *L. hyperborea* from a wide variety of locations. Table VII compares the species listed (in publications or in limited-circulation and unpublished reports) as present on kelp stipes. It can be seen that several species are almost always present. Furthermore, many of the species do not generally occur on surrounding rocks but are found specifically on stipes in the sublittoral zone and these are noted as characteristic of the community. In the fairly simple summary which we have presented, we have not considered the changes which take place as the kelp plant gets older. It should be borne in mind that algal growth on stipes increases with the age of the "host" plant but that, in sheltered areas where plants grow to a considerable age, animal communities often form a significant part of the kelp stipe community. Further, the species found on stipes are affected by depth, shading and grazing. For instance, Norton *et al.* (1977) note that at 3 m depth *Membranoptera alata, Polysiphonia* spp., and *Palmaria palmata* were the most abundant stipe epiphytes, but were almost completely supplanted by *Cryptopleura ramosa* and *Phycodrys rubens* at 6 m.

5. *The* Dendrodoa grossularia–Clathrina (= Leucosolenia) coriacea *(Montagu) Community Present under Overhangs in Wave-exposed Locations*

The two species named as characteristic of this community have been observed together by one author (K. H) only under overhangs or on vertical surfaces at wave-exposed sites. Table VIII lists the main species which are present in the community at four locations where it has been observed. It can be seen that there is a high degree of constancy in the composition of the separate assemblages of organisms. Other conspicuous species which are present in large amounts in all four communities are also often present in the absence of *Clathrina* and *Dendrodoa* and, in the case of *Pachymatisma johnstonia* and *Corynactis viridis*, occur most commonly on vertical surfaces or overhangs. *Steletta grubii* has only been recorded by the authors from the three locations listed in Table VIII and may be restricted to the habitat described here. (*S. grubii* has also been

Table VII. Algae associated with kelp stipes. Species present in small amounts at only one or two sites or present at only one site (48 out of the total of 65 species) have been excluded from this table. Species found solely or mainly on stipes in the sublittoral are indicated by an asterisk (*). All records of separate *Polysiphonia* species are listed in one line.

	Shetland[a,b]	Mull[c]	South-west Ireland[d]	Skokholm[e]	South Pembrokeshire[f]	Gower[e]	North Devon[e]	Lundy[e]	West Cornwall[e]
Plocamium cartilagineum	++	++	—	—	+	—	—	+	+
Phyllophora sicula	—	—	—	—	—	—	+	++	++
Callophyllis laciniata	++	++	+	+	+	—	—	+	++
*Palmaria palmata**	—	++	++	++	++	++	++	++	++
Lomentaria articulata	—	++	—	—	—	—	—	—	+
Ptilota plumosa	++	++	—	+	—	—	—	—	—
Cryptopleura ramosa	+	++	++	++	++	+	++	++	++
Delesseria sanguinea	+	+	—	—	—	—	—	—	+
*Membranoptera alata**	+	++	++	+	++	++	++	++	++
*Phycodrys rubens**	++	++	++	++	++	++	++	++	++
Brongniartella byssoides	+	—	—	—	—	—	—	+	+
Polysiphonia spp.	++	++	++	+	++	+	+	++	+
"Ectocarpoids"	++	++	—	—	—	—	++	++	—
Desmarestia aculeata	+	—	—	—	—	—	—	+	+
Desmarestia viridis	+	+	—	—	—	—	—	+	—
Dictyota dichotoma	—	+	—	+	—	—	—	+	—
Ulva lactuca	+	+	—	—	+	—	—	—	—

+ = present in small amounts, ++ = present in large amounts at any single location within the area studied.
[a]Tittley *et al.* (1976).
[b]Hiscock and Hainsworth (1976).
[c]Price and Tittley (1978).
[d]Norton *et al.* (1977).
[e]Hiscock (unpublished).
[f]Cartlidge and Hiscock (1979).

Table VIII. Main components of the *Dendrodoa–Clathrina* community present under overhangs or on vertical rock at wave-exposed locations in South Pembrokeshire. Species recorded at only one site (10 out of 25) not included.

	The Wick Skomer	Twinlet Bay, Skokholm	Crow Rock, Linney Head	Blucks Pool, Freshwater West
Clathrina coriacea	+++	++	+	++
?*Myxilla rosacea*/?*Amphilectus fucorum*	++	+	++	++
Pachymatisma johnstonia	++	++	++	++
Halichondria panicea	+	++	–	–
Steletta grubii	–	++	+	++
Tubularia indivisa	+	++	+	+
Aglaophenia sp.	++	++	++	++
Actinothoe sphyrodeta	++	–	–	+
Corynactis viridis	++	++	+	–
Alcyonium digatatum	–	++	++	++
Filograna implexa	++	++	+	+
Scrupocellaria sp(p).	++	++	++	+
Crisiidae	++	++	+	+
Bugula plumosa	+	+	–	+
Dendrodoa grossularia	+++	+++	++	++

+ Occasional or rare; ++ Frequent or common; +++ Abundant or dominant.

recorded by Dixon *et al.* (1978) as present at the top of a ledge on sublittoral rocks off Dorset.)

It may be that the recurrent community described here is merely a variation of a community of overhanging or vertical rocks in wave-exposed areas. At present, we have named the assemblage of species present as a community, although observed at only four different locations; a future decision that the *Dendrodoa–Clathrina* community is merely a part of the community of overhanging or vertical rocks in wave-exposed areas will require a great deal more information.

THE DEVELOPMENT OF COMMUNITIES AND THEIR STABILITY

1. Introduction

In describing sublittoral epibenthic communities, it is important to consider the time taken in their development, the presence or absence of a climax, and their stability (resilience) over time. Such data are important in the selection of representative ecosystems for conservation areas, and in the manner in which they are managed. In addition, in assessing the effects of potential deleterious change in marine ecosystems as a consequence of pollution, disturbance or exploitation, it is important to be able to predict reliably whether the same communities as were previously present will recur.

2. Development

The broad pattern of ecosystem development, reviewed most recently by Fishelson (1977) for marine areas, suggests a period of succession starting with colonization by a large number of species, followed by competition and dominance by fewer species, and terminating in an "ecologically stable climax". This climax is followed by an "enrichment period", during which new species are added to the basic community. Highly diverse communities take a long period of time to develop and environmental stability is important to the recruitment and survival of a large number of species. This theory is expounded in the stability–time hypothesis of Sanders (1968), where it is also suggested that in unstable, and therefore stressful, environments a low diversity of eurytopic (physiologically tolerant) species is present, whilst in stable or predictable environments a high diversity of stenotopic (low physiological tolerance) species is present.

The development of sublittoral epibenthic communities has been studied, usually for short periods of time, using settlement panels or cleared surfaces. One of the most detailed studies is that described by Sutherland and Karlson (1977) in Beaufort, North Carolina. They noted that five different patterns of initial community development occurred on 21 plates submerged from May to November in 1971, whilst only two types of initial development were recorded from 20 plates submerged over the same months in 1972. They concluded that the differences occurred because of variable local recruitment. Sutherland and Karlson (1977) also found little evidence for convergence of the different community types with time and noted that no stable climax was developed during the $2\frac{1}{2}$ to $3\frac{1}{2}$ years of study. Furthermore, they concluded that changes in community structure were likely to continue and that a stable climax was not present in the community. Similar results for the initial development of algal communities were obtained by Kain (1975). Here, the dominant colonizing species initially present on cleared areas were different both in relation to the time of year at which the areas were cleared and on areas cleared in the same month in different years. For instance, on concrete blocks cleared in November, the main colonizers were *Saccorhiza polyschides* in 1968, *Desmarestia viridis* in 1969, and a mixture of *D. viridis* and *Alaria esculenta* in 1970. However, it is particularly notable that, in most cases, *Laminaria hyperborea* had regained dominance after two years and species composition and biomass similar to virgin forest were obtained after about three years (probably the "ecologically stable climax" of Fishelson, 1977). Kain (1975) recorded return to virgin-forest populations after three years and our own observations indicate further probable changes, as the *L. hyperborea* continues to grow (to an age of about eight years in sheltered areas), with increasing shading as the plants get larger and the development of an animal-dominated rather than algal-dominated stipe cover. The time taken for cleared areas described by Kain (1975) to return to a near virgin-forest situation is similar to that recorded by Foreman (1977) for communities of algae recovering from urchin grazing in the Strait of Georgia. Here, four to six years elapsed before return to an "ecological climax". Furthermore, it is interesting that both Kain (1975) and Foreman (1977) noted that recovery was slower in deeper water than in shallow water.

All the studies of development of epifaunal communities known to the authors are for short periods of time or, where it is concluded that a climax has been reached, for short-lived species. Many sublittoral epibenthic species live for several decades; recruitment and growth to full size are therefore doubtless slow. It is thus clear that inadequate information is yet available to describe fully the time taken for a climax to develop.

3. Stability

It seems likely that most communities will include: (a) long-lived species, with a steady low level of recruitment, which show little change in abundance with time; (b) species very susceptible to slight changes in environmental conditions which may suffer sudden large changes in abundance; (c) seasonal species which vary greatly in abundance through the year; (d) opportunistic species, which have a high reproductive potential and rapidly colonize following the elimination of another species. The degree to which change occurs in any particular community will depend on the proportions of the various types of species present and the stability of the environment surrounding them.

Sutherland (1974) and Gray (1977) have described, based on the work of Lewontin (1969), different forms of stability in marine ecosystems. A community which includes the same dominant or characteristic species over a period of time is described as being in "global stability", whilst where several community types with different dominant species have developed in the same habitat, "multiple stable points" are present. Communities with multiple stable points are described as being in "neighbourhood stability" and environmental perturbations can lead to switching from one community with a particular dominant or characteristic species to a different community. It is therefore important to establish whether multiple stable points exist throughout the life of the assemblage of organisms present at a particular location, or whether the presence of several alternative stable points is merely a part of the development of a single community which in the end is stable or in which variability is minor. Gray (1977), who described studies of the infauna of sediments, and Sutherland and Karlson (1977), who based their discussion mainly on studies of settling panels, have concluded that global stability does not generally occur and that multiple stable points exist in sublittoral communities. Furthermore, Sutherland (1974) demonstrated that such multiple stable points exist on rocky shores and on coral reefs. If more than one climax can develop following succession and if multiple stable points exist under similar conditions, then, as Gray (1977) stated, it will be difficult to classify distinctive communities which can be expected to recur under particular environmental conditions.

However, the situations which Sutherland (1974), Gray (1977), and Sutherland and Karlson (1977) described are not necessarily representative of the majority of natural communities. It is particularly notable that Sutherland (1974) chose examples where important grazing species had been experimentally excluded in order to demonstrate the presence of alternative stable points. Both on settlement panels and in sediments, many species are short-lived. In such a situation, where death of a population of a particular species results in space being made available, recruitment will depend on the time of year and the larvae available for settlement. In circalittoral epibenthic animal communities, many or most of the sessile species are long-lived and there are few important grazing species, predators or species capable of massive settlement and smothering. Thus, we must consider natural sublittoral epibenthic communities as a different case and search for examples which might provide clues regarding their stability and variability.

Our first conclusion is that there is little evidence available on which to base any consideration of the stability of sublittoral epibenthic communities. The impression of many biologists familiar with particular areas is that the conspicuous epibiota is very similar from year to year. One of the authors (R. M.) found this to be so in observations in Southampton Water and the Solent from 1968 to 1971, as did K. H. around Lundy and North Devon from 1970 to 1978 and Anglesey from 1971 to 1975. However, such observations have not often been tested. The sublittoral sampling carried out in 1956 by Knight-Jones (Knight-Jones and Nelson-Smith, 1977) across the Menai Strait provided a basis for the assessment of change over several years, and in 1976 the same transect was sampled again by Hoare and Peattie (1979). They found that there was little change in the main species present in 1976 when compared with 1956. Similarly, Gulliksen (1977), who studied sublittoral communities in the western Baltic, concluded that no overall profound changes in the species composition seemed to have occured, on the basis of samples collected in 1974 and 1975, although mortality during the winter appeared to have reduced population densities. T. Lundälv (personal communication), working on the coast of Sweden, has found that variability in rocky sublittoral communities varied widely between different environments, being both much greater on exposed coasts than on sheltered ones and also correlated with depth. P. Dyrynda (personal communication), working in several sublittoral locations around Britain, has found considerable variability in populations of some sponges, bryozoans and ascidians throughout the year. Large seasonal changes and annual fluctuations in the abundance of nudibranchs are known to occur (Miller, 1962; G. Brown, personal communication). It is similarly well-known that populations of mussels, *Mytilus edulis*, vary greatly in different years (see, for instance, Lewis, 1977). On the Gower coast, a great increase in the abundance of mussels on sublittoral rocks has been noted since about 1974, with only very localized occurrences in the previous 15 years (A. Osborne, personal communication). In a survey carried out by one author (K. H.) in 1978, populations of *Asterias rubens* were very high and large areas of dead mussels were present, together with bared rock on which the remains of byssus threads were still attached but over which opportunistic species such as the hydroid *Obelia dichotoma* had settled. Similar smothering of sessile organisms on rocks by the development of, for instance, dense beds of *Ophiothrix fragilis* might occur. However, the presence of such dominant species on the rocky seabed is unusual.

Patchiness of dominant, abundant or characterizing species in apparently the same environmental conditions at the same location also indicates some degree of instability. However, it may be that the same communities are always present but develop in different areas in different years, thus giving the casual observer the impression of stability. Such patchiness in dominant or abundant species has been observed along a few hundred metres of sublittoral horizontal limestone bedrock off Stackpole Head in Pembrokeshire where, at between 13 and 14 m, *Molgula manhattensis, Ophiothrix fragilis, Cellepora pumicosa, Distomus variolosus* and *Alcyonium digitatum* characterized different areas of seabed, but were absent or present in only small amounts on adjacent areas.

4. Conclusion

It seems likely that, for instance, when a plant of a dominant species such as a large kelp dies, or where an *Ophiothrix* bed is swept away, a succession will occur that is marked by several different stages of domination by different species for a few months or even years. Settlement and recruitment is opportunistic and depends on the time of year and the presence in the plankton of larvae or spores ready to settle. Any patchy loss of dominant species will lead to patchy colonization and the discontinuous distribution of abundant or dominant species in similar habitats. Some epibenthic communities will be in a continuous state of development and destruction where the substratum is unstable and mobilized during severe storms. Instability will most likely be a feature of wave-exposed locations because of the infrequent but violent disturbances which occur. Thus, species characteristic of sheltered areas may settle on an exposed coast during summer and even grow to dominate rock but will be destroyed during autumn storms. Also, some species populations may develop on bare rock and be stable for several years until an unusually severe storm occurs. In consequence, it is expected that shallow-water communities, where wave action is strongest, will be more variable than those in deep water, where wave action is attenuated and the range of water movement less variable. However, in deep water where tidal streams are weak, variable wave action has an effect different to that of direct destruction in that it allows, during calm weather, the deposition of silt; this may be important in causing smothering and therefore variable abundance of short-lived species intolerant of siltation. The more stable or predictable the environmental conditions, the more stable and/or diverse will be the communities present, according to the stability–time hypothesis.

Although, from mainly subjective observations, the likely instability of some sublittoral epibenthic communities has been emphasized in the above discussion, it is suggested that little overall variability occurs in the majority of such communities. In particular, animal communities on stable rock in depths below the zone where severe multi-directional wave action is often present are expected to show little variability in sessile species present. Small changes will occur in species composition due to seasonal transients. Major changes might be observed consequent on invasion by smothering species such as *Mytilus edulis* or *Ophiothrix fragilis*, through predation, by such species as *Asterias rubens*, of an established mussel bed, or from grazing by large populations of *Echinus esculentus*; in the majority of areas, however, the picture will be one of stability.

GENERAL CONCLUSIONS

It is intended that this chapter should provide field-workers with a practical framework for the description of sublittoral habitats and of the assemblages of organisms present in those habitats. The classification suggested can be neither comprehensive nor capable of application in every situation likely to be encountered underwater. Nevertheless, it is considered useful to suggest a structured framework for the descriptive survey of the majority of situations, so that comparisons can be carried out between sites and between the results of different teams. Species data from strictly quantitative information, particularly where all of the macrobenthic species in a given area are sampled, can be subjected to a wide range of analytical techniques producing much greater amounts of information than is usual for the results of descriptive survey, involved mainly here.

Although it is intended that the information given might assist in understanding the structure, recurrence and stability of sublittoral epibenthic communities, it is acknowledged that this is very much a preliminary appraisal. A great deal more work is required to consolidate information and impressions on the similarity of communities in similar habitats, on the development of communities, and on the stability of established populations and communities. In the poorly-studied nearshore rocky sublittoral with its wide range of habitats and species, the process of survey and assessment will necessarily be a long one.

ACKNOWLEDGEMENTS

This paper is in part based on the work commissioned by the Nature Conservancy Council to describe sublittoral ecosystems in south-west Britain as part of its nature conservation research programme. We are grateful to Dr Brian Dicks, John Addy, John Hartley and Catherine Mitchell for useful discussion and comments on the manuscript.

REFERENCES

Addy, J. M. (1977). "Sublittoral Macrobenthic Survey in Sullom Voe, Shetland. May 1977". Shetland Oil Terminal Environmental Advisory Group/Field Studies Council Oil Pollution Research Unit (unpublished report).

Addy, J. M. and Griffiths, P. W. (1977). "Sublittoral Macrobenthic Survey in Sullom Voe, Shetland. May 1976". Sullom Voe Environmental Advisory Group/Field Studies Council Oil Pollution Research Unit (unpublished report).

Allee, W. C., Emerson, A. E., Park, O., Park, T. and Schmidt, K. P. (1949). "Principles of Animal Ecology". W. B. Saunders Co., Philadelphia.

Allen, E. J. (1899). On the fauna and bottom deposits near the thirty fathom line from the Eddystone Grounds to Start Point. *J. mar. biol. Ass. U.K.* 5, 365–542.

Ballantine, W. J. (1961). A biologically defined exposure scale for the comparative description of rocky shores. *Fld Stud.* **1**(3), 1–19.

Børgesen, F. and Jónsson, H. (1905). The distribution of the marine algae of the Arctic Sea and the northernmost part of the Atlantic. *In* "Botany of the Faeröes based upon Danish Investigations" (E. Warming, ed.), Appendix I–XXVIII. John Weldon and Co., London.

Boulter, J., Cabioch, L. and Grall, J. -R. (1974). Quelques observations sur la pénétration de la lumière dans les eaux marines au voisinage de Roscoff et ses conséquences écologiques. *Bull. Soc. phycol. Fr.* **19**, 129–140.

Brun, E. (1969). Aggregation of *Ophiothrix fragilis* (Abildgaard) (Echinodermata: Ophiuroidea). *Nytt Mag. Zool.* **17**, 153–160.

Cabioch, L. (1968). Contribution à la connaissance des peuplements benthiques de la manche occidentale. *Cah. Biol. mar.* **9** (suppl.), 493–720.

Cabioch, L., Gentil, F., Glaçon, R. and Retiere, C. (1977). Le macrobenthos des fonds meubles de la Manche: distribution générale et ecologie. *In* "Biology of Benthic Organisms" (B. F. Keegan, P. Ó. Céidigh and P. J. S. Boaden, eds), pp. 115–128. Pergamon Press, Oxford.

Cartlidge, D. and Hiscock, K. (1979). "Field Survey of Sublittoral Habitats and Species in South Pembrokeshire". Nature Conservancy Council, Huntingdon/Field Studies Council Oil Pollution Research Unit, Orielton Field Centre, Pembroke (unpublished report).

Castric-Fey, A. (1974). "Les peuplements sessiles du benthos rocheux de l'Archipel de Glénan (Sud Bretagne). Ecologie descriptive et expérimentale". Thèse de Doctorat, Université de Paris VI.

Castric-Fey, A., Girard-Descatoire, A., Lafargue, F. and L'Hardy Halos, M. T. (1973). Etagement des algues et des Invertébrés sessiles dans l'Archipel de Glénan. Définition biologique des horizons bathymétriques. *Helgoländer wiss. Meeresunters.* **24**, 490–509.

Davis, F. M. (1925). Quantitative studies of the fauna of the sea bottom. No. 2. Results of the investigations in the southern North Sea. *Fish. Invest.* ser. II 8(4), 1–50.

Dixon, I., Harrison, K., Hodder, J. and Roberts, C. (1978). "Report of the Second Dorset Underwater Survey. July 1977 to March 1978". Dorset County Council/Nature Conservancy Council/Dorset Naturalists Trust.

Drach, P. (1959). Méthodes et plan de travail pour l'exploration biologique en scaphandre autonome. *Proc. int. Congr. Zool., Lond.* **15**, 254–257.

Ekman, S. (1953). "Zoogeography of the Sea". Sidgwick and Jackson, London.

Erwin, D. G. (1977). A diving survey of Strangford Lough: the benthic communities and their relation to substrate – a preliminary account. *In* "Biology of Benthic Organsims" (B. F. Keegan, P. Ó Céidigh and P. J. S. Boaden, eds), pp. 215–224. Pergamon Press, Oxford.

Fishelson, L. (1977). Stability and instability of marine ecosystems, illustrated by examples from the Red Sea. *Helgoländer wiss. Meeresunters.* **30**, 18–29.

Foreman, R. E. (1977). Benthic community modification and recovery following intensive grazing by *Strongylocentrotus droebachiensis. Helgoländer wiss. Meeresunters.* **30**, 468–484.

Glémarec, M. (1973). The benthic communities of the European North Atlantic continental shelf. *Oceanogr. mar. Biol. ann. Rev.* **11**, 263–289.

Gray, J. S. (1977). The stability of benthic ecosystems. *Helgoländer wiss. Meeresunters.* **30**, 427–444.

Gulliksen, B. (1977). Studies from the "UWL Helgoland" on the macrobenthic fauna of rocks and boulders in Lübeck Bay (Western Baltic Sea). *Helgoländer wiss. Meeresunters.* **30**, 519–526.

Hedgepeth, J. W. (1957). Classification of marine environments. *Mem. geol. Soc. Am.* **67**(2), 17–28.

Hiscock, K. (1976). "The influence of water movement on the ecology of sublittoral rocky areas". Ph. D. thesis, University of Wales.

Hiscock, K. (1978). "Field survey of sublittoral habitats and species around Ramsey". Nature Conservancy Council, Huntingdon/Field Studies Council Oil Pollution Research Unit, Orielton, Pembroke (unpublished report).

Hiscock, K. (1979). Systematic surveys and monitoring in nearshore sublittoral areas using diving. *In* "Monitoring the Marine Environment" (D. Nichols, ed.), pp. 55–74. Symposia of the Inst. of Biol., No. 24. Institute of Biology, London.

Hiscock, K. and Hainsworth, S. (1976). "Biological surveys of sublittoral rocky areas at the northern end of Calback Ness, Shetland". Sullom Voe Environmental Advisory Group/Field Studies Council Oil Pollution Research Unit (unpublished report).

Hiscock, K. and Hiscock, S. (in press). Sublittoral plant and animal communities in the area of Roaringwater Bay, south-west Ireland. *J. Sherkin Is.* **1**.

Hiscock, K. and Hoare, R. (1975). The ecology of sublittoral communities at Abereiddy Quarry, Pembrokeshire. *J. mar. biol. Ass. U.K.* **55**, 833–864.

Hoare, R. and Peattie, M. E. (1979). The sublittoral ecology of the Menai Strait. I. Temporal and spatial variation in the fauna and flora along a transect. *Estuar. cst. mar. Sci.* 9, 663–675.

Holme, N. A. (1966). The bottom fauna of the English Channel. Part II. *J. mar. biol. Ass. U.K.* **46**, 401–493.

Hunnam, P. J. (1976). "A Preliminary Description of the Sublittoral Habitats and Associated Biota within the Skomer Marine Reserve, Dyfed, Wales". West Wales Naturalist Trust, Haverfordwest (unpublished report).

Institute of Terrestrial Ecology (1975). "Report to the NCC of Some Aspects of the Ecology of Shetland. VI. The Coast of Shetland. 6.4. Sub-littoral Biota". Institute of Terrestrial Ecology, Merlewood (unpublished report).

Jones, D. J. (1971). Ecological studies on macro-invertebrate populations associated with polluted kelp forests in the North Sea. *Helgoländer wiss. Meeresunters* **22**, 417–441.

Jones, N. S. (1950). Marine bottom communities. *Ext. Biol. Rev.* **25**, 283–313.

Jones, N. S. (1951). The bottom fauna of the south coast of the Isle of Man. *J. Anim. Ecol.* **20**, 132–144.

Kain, J. M. (1960). Direct observations on some Manx sublittoral algae. *J. mar. biol. Ass. U.K.* **39**, 609–630.

Kain, J. M. (1975). Algal recolonisation of some cleared subtidal areas. *J. Ecol.* **63**, 739–765.

Knight-Jones, E. W. and Nelson-Smith, A. (1977). Sublittoral transects in the Menai Straits and Milford Haven. *In* "Biology of Benthic Organisms" (B. F. Keegan, P. Ó Céidigh and P. J. S. Boaden, eds), pp. 379–390. Pergamon Press, Oxford.

Könnecker, G. (1977). Epibenthic assemblages as indicators of environmental conditions. *In* "Biology of Benthic Organisms" (B. F. Keegan, P. Ó Céidigh and P. J. S. Boaden, eds), pp. 391–396. Pergamon Press, Oxford.

Lewis, J. R. (1964). "The Ecology of Rocky Shores". English Universities Press, London.

Lewis, J. R. (1977). The role of physical and biological factors in the distribution and stability of rocky shore communities. *In* "Biology of Benthic Organisms" (B. F. Keegan, P. Ó Céidigh and P. J. S. Boaden, eds), pp. 417–424. Pergamon Press, Oxford.

Lewontin, R. C. (1969). The meaning of stability. *Brookhaven Symp. Biol.* **22**, 13–24.

L'Hardy-Halos, M. -Th., Castric-Fey, A., Girard-Descatoire, A. and Lafargue, F. (1973). Recherches en scaphandre autonome sur le peuplement végétal du substrat rocheux: l'Archipel de Glénan. *Bull. soc. Scient. Bretagne* **48**, 103–128.

Macfadyen, A. (1963). "Animal Ecology". Pitman, London.

Marine Biological Association (1957). "Plymouth Marine Fauna" (3rd edn). Mar. Biol. Ass., U.K., Plymouth.

Miller, M. C. (1962). Annual cycles of some Manx nudibranchs, with a discussion on the problem of migration. *J. Anim. Ecol.* **31**, 545–569.

Mitchell, R. (1977). Marine wildlife conservation. *In* "Progress in Underwater Science" (K. Hiscock and A. D. Baume, eds), pp. 65–81. Pentech Press, London.

Mitchell, R. (1979). Marine wildlife conservation in the coastal zone. *In* "Monitoring the Marine Environment" (D. Nichols, ed.), pp. 181–193. Institute of Biology, Symposium No. 24, London.

Möbius, K. (1877). "Die Auster und die Austernwirtschaft". Hempel and Parry, Berlin.

Molander, A. R. (1928). Animal communities of soft bottom areas in the Gullmar Fjord. *Kristinebergs Zoologiska Stat.* 1877–1927, No. 2, 1–90.

Moore, P. G. (1973). The kelp fauna of north-east Britain. II. Multivariate classification: turbidity as an ecological factor. *J. exp. mar. Biol. Ecol.* **13**, 127–163.

Norton, T. A. and Milburn, J. A. (1972). Direct observations on the sublittoral marine algae of Argyll, Scotland. *Hydrobiologia* **40**, 55–68.

Norton, T. A., Hiscock, K. and Kitching, J. A. (1977). The ecology of Lough Ine. XX. The *Laminaria* forest at Carrigathorna. *J. Ecol.* **65**, 919–941.

Odum, E. P. (1971). "Fundamentals of Ecology" (3rd edn). W. B. Saunders Co., Philadelphia.

Parke, M. W. and Dixon, P. S. (1976). Check-list of British marine algae – third revision. *J. mar. biol. Ass. U.K.* **56**, 527–594.

Pérès, J. M. (1967a). Les biocoenoses benthiques dans la système phytal. *Recl Trav. Stn mar. Endoume* **58**, 3–113.

Pérès, J. M. (1967b). The Mediterranean benthos. *Oceanogr. mar. Biol. ann. Rev.* **5**, 449–533.

Pérès, J. M. and Molinier, R. (1957). Compte/rendu du colloque tenue à Gênes par la comité du benthos de la Commission Internationale pour l'Exploration Scientifique de la Mer Mediterranée. *Recl Trav. Stn. mar. Endoume* **22**, 5–15.

Petersen, C. G. J. (1913). Valuation of the sea. II. The animal communities of the sea-bottom and their importance for marine zoogeography. *Rep. Dan. biol. Stn* **21**, 1–44.

Petersen, C. G. J. (1918). The sea bottom and its production of fish food. *Rep. Dan. biol. Stn* **25**, 1–62.

Price, J. H. and Tittley, I. (1978). Marine ecosystems. *In* "The Island of Mull. A Survey of its Flora and Environment" (A. C. Jermy and J. A. Crabbe, eds), pp. 8.1–8.31. British Museum (Natural History), London.

Riedl, R. (1964). Die Erscheinungen der Wasserbewegung und ihre Wirkung auf Sedentarien im mediterranen Felslitoral. *Helgoländer wiss. Meeresunters.* **10**, 155–186.

Roberts, C. D. (1975). Investigations into a *Modiolus modiolus* (L.) (Mollusca: Bivalvia) community in Strangford Lough, N. Ireland. *Rep. Underwater Ass.* **1**(NS), 27–49.

Sanders, H. L. (1968). Marine benthic diversity: a comparative study. *Am. Nat.* **102**, 243–282.

Smith, R. M. (1967). Sublittoral ecology of marine algae on the North Wales coast. *Helgoländer wiss. Meeresunters* **15**, 467–479.

Spärk, R. (1929). Preliminary survey of the results of quantitative bottom investigations in Iceland and Faroe waters, 1926–27. *Rapp. P. -v. Réun. Cons. perm. int. Explor. Mer* **57**, 1.

Stephenson, T. A. and Stephenson, A. (1972). "Life between Tidemarks on Rocky Shores". Freeman, San Francisco.

Sutherland, J. P. (1974). Multiple stable points in natural communites. *Am. Nat.* **108**, 859–873.

Sutherland, J. P. and Karlson, R. H. (1977). Development and stability of the fouling community at Beaufort, North Carolina. *Ecol. Monogr.* **47**, 425–446.

Thorson, G. (1957). Bottom communities (sublittoral or shallow shelf). *Mem. geol. Soc. Am.* **67**, 461–534.

Tittley, I., Irvine, D. E. G. and Jephson, N. A. (1976). The infralittoral marine algae of Sullom Voe, Shetland. *Trans. bot. Soc. Edinb.* **42**, 397–419.

Vevers, H. G. (1952). A photographic survey of certain areas of the sea floor near Plymouth. *J. mar. biol. Ass. U.K.* **31**, 215–222.

Warner, G. F. (1971). On the ecology of a dense bed of the brittle star *Ophiothrix fragilis*. *J. mar. biol. Ass. U.K.* **51**, 267–282.

Warwick, R. M. and Davies, J. R. (1977). The distribution of sublittoral macrofauna communities in the Bristol Channel in relation to substrate. *Estuar. cst. mar. Sci.* **5**, 111–222.

Whittaker, R. H. (1970). "Communities and Ecosystems". Macmillan, London.

2 Phytosociological Studies on Mediterranean Algal Vegetation: Rocky Surfaces of the Photophilic Infralittoral Zone

E. COPPEJANS

Laboratorium voor Morfologie, Systematiek en Ekologie van de Planten, Rijksuniversiteit Gent, K. L. Ledeganckstraat, 35, B.9000, Gent, Belgium

Abstract: No thorough bionomic study of the photophilic infralittoral algal vegetation of western Mediterranean rocky surfaces exists, despite the fact that this vegetation-type covers large areas along the coasts.

A description of the biotope to be studied is first presented; thereafter, different features and problems arising with the Mediterranean algal vegetation are discussed. Particularly in this biotope, the overall size and height of the constituents are small, so that we had to develop sampling procedures and methods of detailed laboratory study. Quadrats of 20 × 20 cm were the samples;* rock surface of the whole sample area was removed with hammer and chisel so that the smaller algae and crustose forms in the underlying flora were not missed. Following a minimum area study, the homogeneity of the vegetation from which the samples were taken was checked.

Species diversity appears to be very high in this biotope and a list of rarer taxa has been compiled. As yet, phytosociological interpretation has not been attempted since we lack data from some seasons. A survey of previously

*The French term "relevé" has generally been translated here as "sample" (Editors). A more precise and detailed equivalent is required elsewhere; see footnote to p. 51.

Systematics Association Special Volume No. 17(b), "The Shore Environment, Vol. 2: Ecosystems", edited by J. H. Price, D. E. G. Irvine and W. F. Farnham, 1980, pp. 371–393, Academic Press, London and New York.

recognized bionomic categories is presented for the photophilic infralittoral algal vegetation.

Résumé: Les végétations algales de l'infralittoral photophile sur substrat rocheux du bassin méditerranéen occidental n'ont pas encore été le sujet d'études phytosociologiques approfondies malgré le fait qu'elles couvrent d'énormes surfaces le long des côtes.

Après un essai de délimitation du biotope à étudier, divers problèmes, propres aux végétations algales méditerranéennes sont discutés. A cause de la miniaturisation de ces populations, surtout dans le biotope étudié, nous devions effectuer une procédure d'échantillonage et l'étude détaillée des relevés au laboratoire. Ces relevés de 20 × 20 cm fûrent effectués en cassant le substrat à l'aide de marteau et burin; ainsi les petites algues et les algues encroûtantes de la sous-strate sont également récoltées. Après une étude d'aire minima, l'homogénéité de la végétation étudiée a été vérifiée.

La richesse floristique semble être trés élevée dans ce biotope, et un grand nombre, d'espèces extrêmement rares a été identifié. Une interprétation phytosociologique de nos données n'a pas encore été effectuée à cause du manque de données de certaines saisons. Un aperçu des classifications bionomiques antérieures des végétations algales de l'infralittoral photophile est donné.

INTRODUCTION

Whereas ecological data on terrestrial plants have been sought since the beginning of the last century, and terrestrial vegetation has been studied by rigorous phytosociological methods for over 50 years, this is not at all the case for marine vegetation. Some of the phycologists who worked along the coasts of the Atlantic Ocean during the last century added only, as ecological data to their herbarium specimens, the tidal level at which they had been collected.

The Mediterranean Sea has small tides, roughly 30 cm in amplitude; this is mainly due to the effects of wind and pressure-systems. Sampling below the water surface remained extremely fragmentary until recently, especially on rocky surfaces where dredging is excluded. It was not until the studies of Funk (1927) at Naples and of J. Feldmann (1937) at Banyuls that important ecological information on Mediterranean infralittoral seaweeds was recorded. Even then, it was difficult to describe the exact biotope (horizontal rock, vertical rock, overhanging rocky surfaces, precise depth) of the algae collected, since they were dredged.

Molinier (1960) carried out pioneering phytosociological studies of the algal communities near the water surface at Cap Corse; for this purpose, he used a simple Braun–Blanquet method.

The development and popularization of SCUBA diving made possible *in situ* studies of the marine infralittoral biotope. This diving technique is not without its problems, as it still remains difficult to carry out a relevé* near the surface because of water movement. At greater depths, only one or two relevés per dive are possible as availability of air and physical activities are limited.

Boudouresque, himself a diver, was the first to carry out (in the 1960s) quantitative ecological recording in the infralittoral by developing a bionomic technique adapted for immersed marine benthic vegetation.

The method was derived from the Braun–Blanquet school (Boudouresque, 1971a) and was used for the study of sciaphilic (shade-requiring) vegetation. He defined distinct sociological categories (Boudouresque, 1970, 1971b, 1972, 1974a, b).

We used this same method to study the so-called "photophilic (light-requiring) infralittoral algal vegetation" of the western Mediterranean basin. This had never previously been thoroughly studied, although widespread along the shores.

PHYSICAL CHARACTERISTICS OF THE PHOTOPHILIC INFRALITTORAL BIOTOPE

The existing literature does not give a well-defined description of the photophilic infralittoral biotope. According to Pérès and Picard (1956, 1958, 1964) and Pérès (1967), the infralittoral zone starts at low-water level and extends down to the deepest levels of marine phanerogams. The lower limit depends on the turbidity of the water and lies at an average depth of 35 m. The infralittoral zone is bionomically characterized by the luxuriance of the flora, both of seaweeds and marine phanerogams. Pérès and Picard did not separate the photophilic and sciaphilic biotopes within the infralittoral zone, as faunistically they did not find any differences.

Feldmann (1937, 1962) assumed that the boundary between photophilic and sciaphilic algae is at a depth of 5–10 m where, as he

---

*"A relevé refers to a site analyzed with detailed records of total species present, their relative importance, and other analytic characters of the flora and habit" (A. R. O. Chapman, 1979).

Table I. Monthly values of the sun energy in cal/cm^2/day at different depths, in the region of Banyuls-sur-Mer (Weinberg, personal communication)

Month	E_{tot}	E_{480}	E_{0^-}	E_{10^-}	E_{20^-}	E_{30^-}	E_{40^-}
January	163.52	17.99	14.24	1.047	0.123	0.014	0.002
February	223.17	24.55	20.80	1.545	0.184	0.022	0.003
March	337.38	37.11	32.74	2.741	0.367	0.049	0.007
April	415.58	45.72	40.95	4.770	0.889	0.166	0.031
May	521.26	57.34	51.91	9.388	2.717	0.786	0.228
June	564.96	62.15	56.27	13.876	5.475	2.160	0.852
July	560.11	61.61	55.84	16.158	7.481	3.464	1.604
August	488.86	53.78	48.73	14.532	6.933	3.308	1.578
September	367.13	40.38	36.01	9.429	3.950	1.655	0.693
October	254.00	27.74	24.18	4.691	1.456	0.542	0.140
November	169.46	18.64	15.26	2.045	0.438	0.094	0.020
December	133.99	14.74	11.48	1.073	0.161	0.024	0.004

E_{tot} = total light energy, just above the surface of the sea.
E_{480} = light energy of wavelength of 480 nm.
E_{0^-} = light energy just below the surface of the sea.
$E_{10^-,etc.}$ = light energy at a depth of 10 m, etc.

says, "light-liking algae are replaced by shade-liking ones". This only shifts the problem as there existed no list of shade-liking algae.

Therefore, we investigated the possibility of defining the photophilic infralittoral biotope by physical factors. Results were as follows:

(a) The light quantity does not show a clear-cut threshold value (Table I). At Banyuls, the 10% value for the light penetration lies at less than 10 m depth in winter and at more than 20 m in summer (Weinberg, 1975). This is due to the higher turbidity of the water in winter (Fig. 1); as a consequence, the winter season represents more pronounced difference in greater depths than it does closer to the surface.

(b) A thermocline is only present in summer, as turbulence of the water is too great during the winter (Fig. 2). Thermocline depth fluctuates daily; at Banyuls, it is between 15 and 30 m (Weinberg, 1975).

(c) On the basis of turbulence, Riedl (1964) divided the infralittoral zone into three sub-zones (Fig. 3): an upper one, 0–2 m in depth, with multi-directional movements of the water; a second one, from 2 m to 10–12 m depth, with bi-

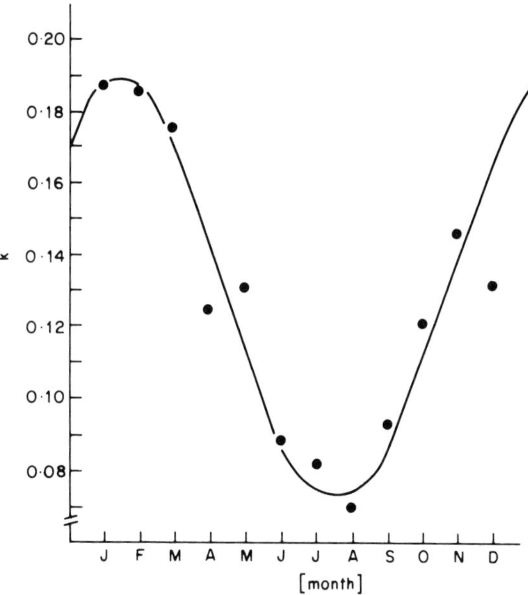

Fig. 1. Annual variations of the extinction coefficient *k* in the region of Banyuls-sur-Mer (after Weinberg, 1975).

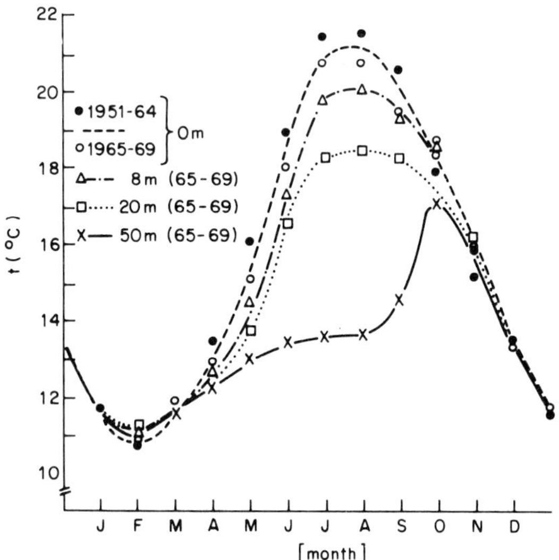

Fig. 2. Annual variations of the temperature at different depths, in the region of Banyuls-sur-Mer (after Weinberg, 1975).

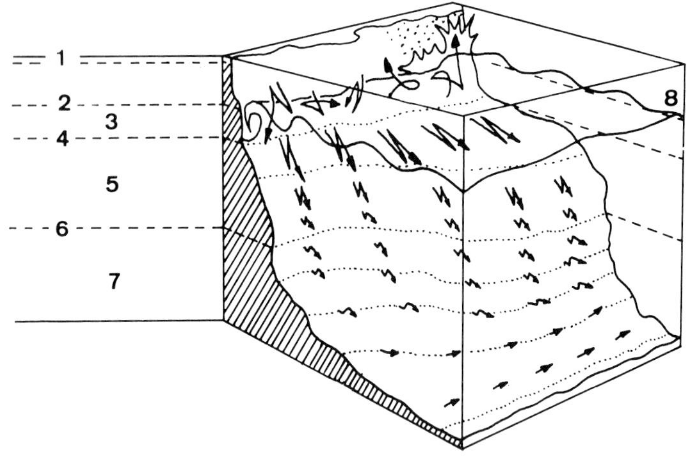

Fig. 3. Hydrodynamic zones (after Riedl, 1964). 1, Upper limit of the spray of the waves. 2, Water level with calm sea. 3, Zone of multi-directional water movements. 4, First critical level. 5, Zone of bi-directional water movements. 6, Second critical level. 7, Zone of uni-directional water movements. 8, Water surface.

directional movements; the lowest one, with a uni-directional movement of the water (the general coastal current).

It is still not known if the lower boundary coincides with a biological boundary. The physical factors (light, temperature, water movement) do not give a clear-cut boundary between the photophilic and sciaphilic infralittoral zones, but some features indicate that this must be around 15 m depth. Quadrat samples were taken down to 20 m, and even some at 30 m, always on horizontal substrata without any shade.

FEATURES AND PROBLEMS PERTINENT TO THE MEDITERRANEAN ALGAL VEGETATION

Because of the small size of Mediterranean algae generally, particularly in the biotope studied here (the largest algae in our relevés were only 10 cm high), and of the difficulty in distinguishing differentiating characters under water, it was impossible definitely to identify algal species *in situ*. In the relevé REC 5, containing (after laboratory study) 109 spp., only *Padina pavonica* (L.) Lamour. could be identified *in situ*. Therefore, it was necessary to utilize a sampling procedure and to undertake detailed study of the samples in the laboratory. The rocky substratum was removed by hammer and chisel, so that the smaller and crustose algae of the underlying flora were sampled as well. All the fragments of the relevé have to be studied microscopically, which results in a long sorting time, even when Cyanophyceae and Bacillariophyceae are excluded.

The fact that species cannot be identified *in situ* has important consequences; according to the Braun–Blanquet method, a relevé has to be taken in homogeneous vegetation. Therefore, we had to determine whether "homogeneous" vegetation, as seen with the naked eye, really is homogeneous (see section on Homogeneity, p. 382).

Another consequence of the miniaturization of the algal vegetation is the fact that the minimum area is very small. An important part of our research was to determine the minimum area for the biotope studied.

THE QUALITATIVE MINIMUM AREA

Whereas it seems easy to give an approximate definition of the "qualitative minimum area" (the smallest surface where almost all the species of the community studied are present), it is much more difficult to give a rigorous definition (avoiding the qualification "almost all the species"). This problem has been studied by a large number of terrestrial phytosociologists. Tüxen (1970) gives 170 references on that subject; Gleason (1922, 1925), Moravec (1973) and van der Maarel (1970) present extra ones. Marine phytosociologists, on the contrary, have only recently considered this concept. Boudouresque (1974b) made a minimum area study of the sciaphilic algal vegetation of the Mediterranean Sea, and we have determined it for the photophilic infralittoral biotope (Dhondt, 1976; Dhondt and Coppejans, 1977). Some other minimum area studies for algal vegetation have been carried out more recently (Cinelli *et al.*, 1977a, b).

Different authors have proposed a range of methods for calculating the minimum area; they mainly need the species numbers of a series of quadrats of increasing area to draw a species/area curve. For that purpose two series of 11 relevés were made, using the "multiple plot procedure" (quadrats not overlapping); one series was at Banyuls and the other at Port-Cros (France), at 4 m depth, in "homogeneous"

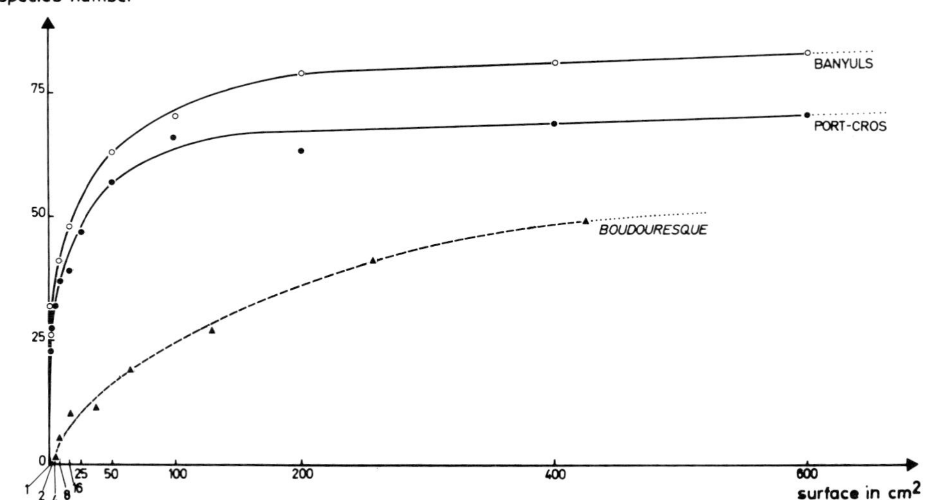

Fig. 4. Species/area curves of the algae of the photophilic biotope from Banyuls and Port-Cros (own observations) and of the sciaphilic biotope (Boudouresque, 1974b).

vegetation. Quadrat areas were 1 x 1 cm, 1 x 2 cm, 2 x 2 cm, 2 x 4 cm, 4 x 4 cm, 5 x 5 cm, 5 x 10 cm, 10 x 10 cm, 10 x 20 cm, 20 x 20 cm and 20 x 30 cm. After sorting the relevés and carrying out a Bravet–Pearson correlation analysis on the species numbers/relevé, a species/area curve was drawn. This is a parabolic curve (Fig. 4). According to the definition of Braun–Blanquet, the minimum area is reached where the curve becomes more or less horizontal; we can conclude that, for the vegetation studied, this area is reached between 100 and 200 cm^2. There are more accurate methods to determine objectively the minimum area on these curves. In the tangent-method of Cain and Castro (1959), the minimum area is reached when an increase of 10% of the surface results in an increase of 10% of the species number (method 1); for more precision, that area can be considered to be reached when an increase of 10% of the surface results in an increase of 5% of the species number (method 2). The following results were obtained:

	Banyuls	Port-Cros
method 1	115 cm^2	135 cm^2
method 2	250 cm^2	250 cm^2

Vestal (1949) developed another procedure, in which a semi-logarithmic plotting of the species/area curve (species-log area) is involved. On this curve, two points are determined such that the area at point 2 is 50 times larger than at point 1 and that the species number of point 2 is double that of point 1. Point 2 is then "the area definitive for composition" (Vestal, 1949). This was found to be 200 cm^2 at both Banyuls and Port-Cros.

Du Rietz *et al.* (1920) determined the minimum area by means of frequency/area or constant species/area curves (a constant species being a species present in 91–100% of the quadrats). According to these authors, the minimum area is obtained when the total number of constant species of the vegetation studied is achieved (Fig. 5). Values for this minimum area at Port-Cros and Banyuls were 100 cm^2 and 200 cm^2, respectively.

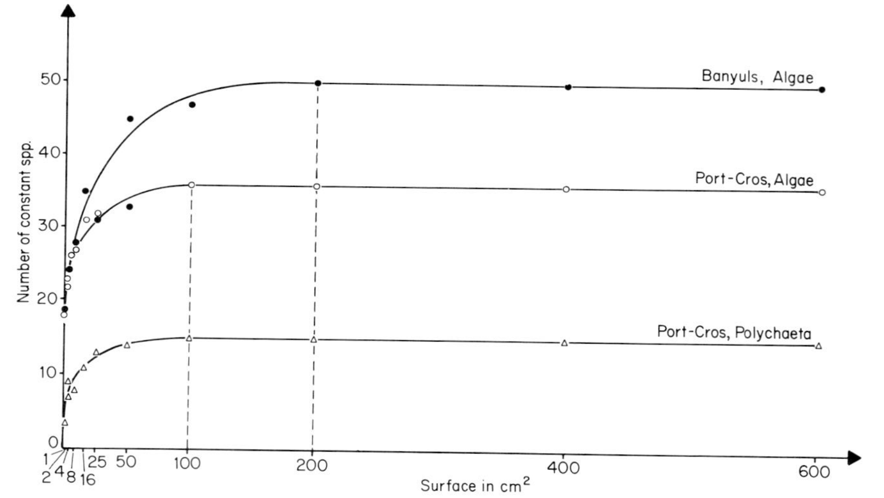

Fig. 5. Constant species/area curves of the algae (and Polychaeta) of the photophilic biotope from Banyuls and Port-Cros.

In conclusion, it is clear that the values of minimum area ((100)–200–(250) cm^2) depend on the method used, and that it undoubtedly is much smaller than the relevé area used (400 cm^2). This is the case for both sites, Banyuls and Port-Cros. Boudouresque (1974b) calculated the minimum area for circalittoral (sciaphilic) vegetation at 200 cm^2; Cinelli *et al.* (1977a) for vegetation dominated by *Cystoseira mediterranea* Sauv., at 150–200 cm^2; Cinelli *et al.* (1977b) for harbour vegetation, at 100–150 cm^2.

SPECIES DIVERSITY; EPIPHYTISM

Although the area of the relevé is so small (20 x 20 cm), the species diversity is very high within the taxonomic groups considered (Chlorophyceae, Bryopsidophyceae, Phaeophyceae, and Rhodophyceae); the average was 70 spp./relevé, with up to 109 spp. in some cases (Coppejans and Boudouresque, 1975). This is very high when compared with other biotopes studied using the same method. Superficial sciaphilic vegetation on exposed rocky coasts averaged 30–50 spp.; on sheltered coasts, 30–75 spp.; in harbours, 30–40 spp. (Boudouresque, 1971c). This high species diversity is partly due to the smaller algae of the underlying vegetation, partly to the epiphytes on the larger algae. The number of epiphytes can sometimes be quite impressive. Whilst Nasr and Aleem (1949) found 12 epiphytic spp. on one specimen of *Halopteris filicina* (Grat.) Kütz. in August along the Egyptian coast, 30 epiphytic taxa were once found on one specimen of *Stypocaulon scoparium* (L.) Kütz. (10 cm high), collected at Port-Cros in September at 20 m depth. The species included *Corallina granifera* Ellis et Sol.; *Jania rubens* (L.) Lamour.; *Jania corniculata* (L.) Lamour.; "*Falkenbergia rufolanosa*" (Harv.) Schmitz; *Spyridia filamentosa* (Wulf.) Harv.; *Plocamium cartilagineum* (L.) Dixon "var. *uncinatum*" J. Ag.; *Laurencia obtusa* (Huds.) Lamour.; *Dasya rigidula* (Kütz.) Ardiss.; *Wrangelia penicillata* C. Ag.; *Dictyota linearis* (C. Ag.) Grev.; *Ceramium byssoideum* Harv.; *Myriactula stellulata* (Harv.) Levr.; *Stilophora rhizodes* (Turn.) J. Ag.; *Giraudya sphacelarioides* Derb. et Sol.; *Antithamnion plumula* (Ellis) Thur. var. *bebbii* (Reinsch) J. Feldm.; *Lejolisia mediterranea* Born.; *Crouania attenuata* (Bonnem.) J. Ag. f. *bispora* (Crouan frat.) Hauck; *Discosporangium mesarthrocarpum* (Menegh.) Hauck; *Nitophyllum punctatum* (Stackh.) Grev.; *Rhodophyllis divaricata* (Stackh.) Papenf.; *Griffithsia barbata* (Sm.)

C. Ag.; *Ceramium diaphanum* (Lightf.) Roth; *Ceramium cingulatum* Web. v. Bosse: *Elachista intermedia* Crouan frat.; *Kuckuckia spinosa* (Kütz.) Kornm.; *Corynospora pedicellata* (Sm.) J. Ag. var. *tenuis* G. Feldm.; *Castagnea cylindrica* Sauv.; *Chondria mairei* G. Feldm.; *Bonnemaisonia* sp.; *Polysiphonia* sp.

Frequent epiphytes on other algae are: *Fosliella* spp.; representatives of the Chaetophorales (*Ulvella, Pringsheimiella, Phaeophila, Entocladia*); representatives of the Acrochaetiales; diverse Bangiophyceae (*Erythrocladia, Erythrotrichia, Chroodactylon, Goniotrichum*).

HOMOGENEITY; SIMILARITY

As mentioned in an earlier section, the relevés have to be taken from "homogeneous" vegetation; therefore, we checked if the impression of homogeneity agreed with the reality. Four contiguous relevés (of 20 × 20 cm) were made at Port-Cros and three relevés (of 10 × 20 cm) at Banyuls. After sorting them, the similarity coefficients were calculated by a series of formulae (Coppejans, 1977a, b). For mathematical background, the following references were used: Augarde (1957), Ceska (1966, 1968), Godron (1966), Goodall (1973), Gounot and Calleja (1962). The similarity tests fall into two groups; those that are based on the number of species present in the relevés and those based on the coverage of these species.

The similarity tests based on presence–absence of species (*vide*, for details, Coppejans, 1977a, c; those used were of Ceska, Kulczynski, Sørensen, Ochiai and Barkman, Jaccard and Sneath, Sokal and Sneath) all gave similar results. Those of Jaccard and of Sokal gave rather lower values, but when these were multiplied by a constant factor (Jaccard × 1.24; Sokal × 1.70) they became comparable with the other values. The average similarity value lies around 75%. This proves that the quadrat area used, 20 × 20 cm (and even 10 × 20 cm), is representative for the species-composition. These results are very high, compared with those of Boudouresque (1974b); for two relevés of 200 cm^2 made in a sciaphilic vegetation, he found the similarity coefficient of Sørensen to be 64.6%, whereas we found 77% for relevés of the same surface at Banyuls. This conflicts with the cautious conclusion of Boudouresque (1974b, p. 154): "L'aire minima varie d'un peuplement à l'autre. Son étude dans chaque type de peuplement et dans chaque région, est donc nécessaire, et il serait intéressant de rechercher si le seuil de similitude de 65% peut être considéré comme très général en milieu marin." According to our results this last supposition is not true, as the threshold value of similarity in photophilic vegetation is higher (75–80%, as in terrestrial vegetation).

The different similarity tests based on the coverage of the species (*vide*, for details, Coppejans, 1977a, b; those used were of Czekanowski, Kulczynski, Monthoux, Ruzicka, Spearman in Weber, 1972: 538) give rather divergent results.

As a general conclusion on this homogeneity study, we can say that the similarity-coefficients obtained by divergent formulae and based on different data (species number, percentage cover) are very high, much higher than those in marine sciaphilic vegetation, equalling those in terrestrial vegetation.

SAMPLING; STUDY OF THE SAMPLES

After the preliminary investigation of the photophilic infralittoral biotope, of the minimum area and of the homogeneity of the vegetation to be studied, the phytosociological investigation itself was commenced. So as to study photophilic algae at different depths and from different seasons and regions, sampling was done in homogeneous vegetation (see previous section) on horizontal or slightly inclined rocky surfaces, at depths of 2–25 m below C.D. The location of the relevés was taken at random by throwing away the chisel and taking the sample where it finally lay. This is important to provide the objective data needed for certain statistical methods. Date, depth, declivity and direction of the slope, coverage and maximum height of the vegetation were noted over a surface of 20 x 20 cm (see section on Qualitative Minimum Area).

The substratum was removed with hammer and chisel, to sample smaller and crustose algae of the underlying flora. All fragments were placed in plastic-bags, formalinized (4%) on arrival at the laboratory, and stored in the dark to reduce bleaching of the specimens. Over 100 relevés were recorded from March 1973 to July 1978; they were spread over winter and summer seasons at Banyuls (near the French–Spanish border); Marseille; the nature-reserve of Port-Cros, an island in front of Le Lavandou; and the bay of Calvi (Corsica).

Sorting through the relevés is extremely time-consuming, as each fragment in the samples is studied under a binocular microscope; the smaller algae and their epiphytes were also identified under the microscope (Cyanophyceae and Bacillariophyceae were excluded). Species diversity being very important (see that section), in total we identified 280 algal taxa, of which 40 were Chlorophyceae, 65 Phaeophyceae and 175 Rhodophyceae. These comprehensive species-lists are of great importance for later phytosociological analysis of the data. The presence, nature and frequency of the reproductive structures have also been noted and quantified. A reproductive coefficient and the reproductive density can be calculated from these data (Boudouresque, 1971a); these are, of course, time-linked. After the species list was completed, a percentage-cover was given to each species. We did not use the scale of Braun–Blanquet as it seemed too imprecise, especially for comparing the coverages of the epiphytes and of the smaller algae.

A sociability-factor could not be deduced as the samples consisted only of fragments of the original vegetation.

On the basis of the species lists, the ratios of different algal groups can be calculated; R/P (ratio of numbers of species of Rhodophyceae to Phaeophyceae) can be used to characterize the flora of a region. The ratios of the different orders within the Rhodophyceae can be used to characterize a biotope within a floristic province.

The distribution of the species present in the relevés over the different ecological algal groups ("groupes écologiques"; Boudouresque, 1970, 1971a) can also give important information about the population studied. All the above-mentioned data can be subjected to different ordination methods for identifying sociological units. For the photophilic vegetation, we still need more data so as to take the seasonal variation into account. From the species lists of the different quadrat-samples, it already seems that the depth where *Stypocaulon scoparium* is replaced by *Halopteris filicina* indicates the lower limit of photophilic algal vegetation in the western Mediterranean basin.

SYSTEMATICS

In sorting thoroughly the relevés, one is regularly confronted by identification and taxonomic problems. Boudouresque (1971c, p. 82) stated that:

> Contrairement à ce qui se passe dans le domaine terrestre (au moins dans nos régions) la systématique des végétaux marins reste extrêmement complexe. Est-il besoin de préciser qu'aucun ordinateur, qu'aucune méthodologie, si valable soit-elle, ne saurait remplacer une détermination exacte? Un travail de bionomie effectué sur des bases systématiques incertaines est une architecture compliquée bâtie sur des sables mouvants.

In the 100 relevés studied we identified, as stated above, 280 algal taxa (40 Chlorophyceae; 65 Phaeophyceae; 175 Rhodophyceae). Some of the specimens did not agree with any described taxon. *Polysiphonia banyulensis* Copp. has been described as a new species (Coppejans, 1976a, 1978a) and recorded since at Calvi (Corsica) and at Naples. For some other taxa, we either did not have enough specimens or did not find all the reproductive structures necessary for a complete description. We called them "species novae ineditae" and illustrated them (Coppejans, 1977a: *Sphacelaria papilioniformis, Lomentaria pennata, Myriogramme unistromatica, Peyssonnelia* sp. and a Ceramiacean belonging to the tribe Wrangelieae).

We also recorded taxa new to the Mediterranean Sea: *Ceramium cingulatum* Web. v. Bosse, described from the Indian Ocean and only found twice since the type collection, was present in our relevés at Banyuls, Marseille and Port-Cros (Coppejans, 1977b). *Ceramium taylori* Dawson, described from the North American Pacific coast and recently found by Verlaque at Marseille, was present in our relevés from the three areas studied. *Ceramium fastigiatum* (Roth) Harv. var. *flaccidum* (Børg.) Petersen has been described as an epiphyte on roots of mangrove-plants in the Caribbean Sea. We noticed it in relevés from Banyuls and Port-Cros. *Fosliella farinosa* (Lamour.) Howe var. *chalicodictya* Taylor had not been found since its type collection in the Caribbean Sea. We found it at Banyuls and Port-Cros (Coppejans, 1976b). It has also recently been collected by Boudouresque in Corsica. The record of *Lophosiphonia scopulorum* (Harv.) Womersley at Banyuls added this species to the Mediterranean flora (Coppejans, 1976b). Apart from these taxa new to the Mediterranean Sea, we also recorded species new to the French flora. *Myrionema liechtensternii* Hauck, described last century from the Adriatic Sea and never collected since, was found at Banyuls and, more frequently, at Port-Cros (Coppejans and Dhondt, 1976). *Dilophus mediterraneus* Ercegović, described from the Adriatic Sea, was frequently recorded at Port-Cros. Hitherto, *Griffithsia tenuis* C. Ag. was only known to occur in the Adriatic Sea and along the coasts of north Africa. It was a rare species in our relevés from Port-Cros. *Lophosiphonia cristata* Falkenb. has only been mentioned from Tobruk (Libya) since its original discovery at Naples, where it has not been found again. We recorded it at Port-Cros (Coppejans and Boudouresque, 1976a). *Sphacelaria fusca* (Huds.) C. Ag., already known from the Atlantic coasts of France, has been found along the Mediterranean French coast for the first time, at Banyuls, Marseille and Port-Cros. In total, we have added 15 taxa to the known French marine algal flora. A list of species rarely recorded for the Mediterranean has also been compiled; these included *Cladophoropsis modonensis* (Kütz.) Børg., *Siphonocladus pusillus* (Kütz.) Hauck, *Choristocarpus tenellus* (Kütz). Zanard. (Coppejans and Boudouresque, 1976b), *Colpomenia peregrina* Sauv., *Discosporangium mesarthrocarpum* (Menegh.) Hauck (Augier *et al.*, 1975), *Lobophora variegata* (Lamour.) Womersley, *Aphanocladia stichidiosa* (Funk) Ardré, *Chondria mairei* G. Feldm., *Lomentaria chylocladiella* Funk, *L. verticillata* Funk, and *Myriogramme distromatica* (Rodr.) Boud.

Some rare reproductive structures have also been observed. The gonimoblasts of *Antithamnion spirographidis* Schiffner were never seen in nature before. The propagules of *Fosliella farinosa* (Lamour.) Howe var. *farinosa*, figured in 1881 for *F. farinosa* var. *solmsiana* (Falkenb.) Foslie by Solms-Laubach, have never been observed since. We have recorded them in Corsica (Coppejans, 1978b).

On the basis of the species lists from the different relevés, we drew up an autecological and phenological "card" for each species. This information, combined with data from the literature, permitted the construction of an autecological, synecological and phenological image for each sampled species.

PHYTOSOCIOLOGY

Thus far, we have been unable to make winter observations at Banyuls or summer observations at Marseille. This makes it somewhat premature to give a phytosociological interpretation of our data. Nevertheless, we present a brief survey of previous bionomical groupings of the photophilic infralittoral algal vegetation. The zoologists, who give less importance to the algae, as well as those phycologists who adopt a simple solution, accept that the photophilic infralittoral vegetation is characterized by only one biocoenosis, the "Biocoenosis of the Photophilic Algae", ranging in depth from 2 to 25 (45) m. This oversimplifies the situation even when one distinguishes different facies, zones or populations within this biocoenosis. Other authors are over-influenced by the physiognomical diversity of the biotope. Using an imprecise bionomical method, they divide this zone into as many associations or communities as there are dominant algae. In this way, the infralittoral has been divided into:

different Associations: Feldmann, J. (1937); Zalokar (1942); Giaccone and Pignatti (1967); Giaccone *et al.* (1973); Nasr and Aleem (1949);
different Phytocoenoses: Giaccone (1965);
different Populations: Bellan-Santini (1962);
different Populations + facies: Pérès (1967);
different Communities: Ernst (1959);
different Biocoenoses: Molinier (1960); Boudouresque (1971a).

These latter authors divided the biocoenosis of the photophilic algae (*sensu lato*) into three: the Schotterion, as the underlying vegetation of the larger *Cystoseira* spp.; the Cystoseiretum strictae, at places with strong turbulence from just below the water-surface down to 50 cm depth; the Cystoseiretum crinitae, below that. We restricted our research to the study of the Cystoseiretum crinitae.

A third supposition is that the infralittoral vegetation forms a climax-cycle in which, starting from an initial association dominated by *Jania rubens* (L.) Lamour., eventually results a climax-association with *Posidonia oceanica* (L.) Delile (Potamogetonaceae, a marine phanerogam), with transitional associations (Molinier, 1954, 1955; Molinier and Picard, 1953, 1954; Pérès and Picard, 1955). All the latter authors based their interpretation on the data from a restricted area or from one season; they took only the "larger" algae into account to describe the above-mentioned groupings. Owing to this, they only mention a small number of "larger" species, not taking the smaller and (according to Boudouresque's results) often more characteristic ones into account, e.g. Giaccone (1965), 10 m depth, 1 m^2 quadrat, 7 spp; 4 m^2, 12 spp; Giaccone and de Leo (1966), 0.5 m depth, 8 m^2, 23 spp; 4 m, 1 m^2, 12 spp; 35 m, 6 m^2, 16 spp; Giaconne (1968), 60 m, 100 m^2, 23 spp.

The "transect-method" is rather physiognomical; by making such transects, one can distinguish different vegetation zones (as in Coppejans, 1970, 1972, 1974; Gamulin-Brida, 1965; Giaccone and

Pignatti, 1967; Huvé *et al.*, 1963; Larkum *et al.*, 1967). These authors again characterize the different zones by only a restricted number of larger algae. The results of such transect methods become absolutely useless (for bionomical interpretation) when all the noted algae are listed without recording the depth or the microbiotope (horizontal, vertical, overhanging rock-surface). Such lists are presented in Giaccone *et al.* (1972) for 0–38 m; in Giaccone *et al.* (1973) for 0–60 m; in Giaccone and Sortino (1974) for 0–50 m. Nevertheless these works have a positive value for the construction of species inventories for the area studied. The method of phytosociological relevés has been used only occasionally for studying photophilic marine algal vegetation, e.g., as in Cinelli (1969); Giaccone (1965, 1971, 1977); Giaccone *et al.* (1973); Molinier (1960); Pignatti (1962).

CONCLUSIONS

Our research aimed to contribute a better understanding of the phytosociological units within the photophilic vegetation in the Mediterranean sea. This was achieved by means of a rigorous bionomical method requiring the preliminary study of such factors as minimum area, homogeneity and species-composition. The fauna has been completely excluded from this study, as it had already been the subject of thorough studies by Bellan-Santini (1962, 1968, 1969); Gamulin-Brida (1965, 1974); Ledoyer (1968); Tortonese (1958). More winter observations are required fully to take into account the seasonal variation of the photophilic algal vegetation before our data are submitted to different ordination methods for identifying sociological units within the Cystoseiretum crinitae. It appears that the depth at which *Stypocaulon scoparium* is replaced by *Halopteris filicina* indicates the lower limit of photophilic algal vegetation in the western Mediterranean basin.

ACKNOWLEDGEMENTS

I should like to thank Dr C. -F. Boudouresque for his help and encouragement during this study, which formed part of my doctoral thesis. I should also like to acknowledge the facilities provided by the directors of the marine stations at Banyuls, Marseille, Port-Cros and Calvi. Dr W. F. Farnham criticized a draft of this manuscript.

REFERENCES

Augarde, J. (1957). Contribution à l'étude des problèmes de l'homogénéité en phytosociologie. *Bull. Serv. Carte phytogéogr.* sér B **2**, 11–24.

Augier, H., Boudouresque, C. -F. and Coppejans, E. (1975). Présence de *Discosporangium mesarthrocarpum* (Men.) Hauck à Port-Cros. *Trav. scient. Parc natn. Port-Cros* **1**, 77–78.

Bellan-Santini, D. (1962). Étude floristique et faunistique de quelques peuplements infralittoraux de substrat rocheux. *Recl Trav. Stn mar. Endoume* **26**, 237–298.

Bellan-Santini, D. (1968). Conclusions d'une étude quantitative dans la biocénose des algues photophiles en Méditerranée sur les côtes de Provence (France). *Mar. Biol., Berl.* **1**, 250–256.

Bellan-Santini, D. (1969). Contribution à l'étude des peuplements infralittoraux sur substrat rocheux (Étude qualitative et quantitative de la frange supérieure). *Recl Trav. Stn mar. Endoume* **47**, 5–294.

Boudouresque, C. -F. (1970). "Recherches de bionomie analytique, structurale et expérimentale sur les peuplements benthiques sciaphiles de Méditerranée occidentale (fraction algale)". Thèse au centre Universitaire de Marseille-Luminy.

Boudouresque, C. -F. (1971a). Contribution à l'étude phytosociologique des peuplements algaux des côtes varoises. *Vegetatio* **22**, 83–184.

Boudouresque, C. -F. (1971b). Sur les phytocoenoses sciaphiles superficielles en Méditerranée occidentale. *Rapp. P. -v. Réun. Commn int. Explor. scient. Mer méditerr.* **20**, 193–196.

Boudouresque, C. -F. (1971c). Méthodes d'étude qualitative et quantitative du benthos (en particulier du phytobenthos). *Téthys* **3**, 79–104.

Boudouresque, C. -F. (1972). Recherches de bionomie analytique structurale et expérimentale sur les peuplements benthiques sciaphiles de Méditerranée occidentale (fraction algale). La sous-strate sciaphile d'un peuplement photophile de mode calme, le peuplement à *Cystoseira crinita. Bull. Mus. Hist. nat. Marseille* **32**, 253–263.

Boudouresque, C. -F. (1974a). Recherches de bionomie analytique structurale et expérimentale sur les peuplements benthiques sciaphiles de Méditerranée occidentale (fraction algale): le peuplement épiphyte des rhizomes de Posidonies (*Posidonia oceanica* Delile). *Bull. Mus. Hist. nat. Marseille* **34**, 269–283.

Boudouresque, C. -F. (1974b). Aire minima et peuplements algaux marins. *Bull. Soc. phycol. Fr.* **19**, 141–157.

Cain, S. and Castro, O. (1959). Manual of vegetation in Wyoming. *Am. J. Bot.* **30**, 240–247.

Ceska, A. (1966). Estimation of the mean floristic similarity between and within sets of vegetational relevés. *Folia geobot. phytotax. bohemoslovaca* **1**, 93–100.

Ceska, A. (1968). Application of association coefficients for estimating the mean similarity between sets of vegetational relevés. *Folia geobot. phytotax. bohemoslovaca* **3**, 57–64.

Chapman, A. R. O. (1979). "Biology of Seaweeds Levels of Organisation", University Park Press, Baltimore.

Cinelli, F. (1969). Primo contributo alla conoscenza della vegetazione algale bentonica del litorale di Livorno. *Pubbl. Staz. zool. Napoli* **37**, 545–566.

Cinelli, F., Boudouresque, C. -F., Fresi, E., Marcot, J. and Mazzella, L. (1977a). L'aire minima du phytobenthos dans le port de Sant d'Angelo (Ischia, Italie). *Rapp. P. -v. Réun. Commn int. Explor. scient. Mer méditerr.* **24**, 149–152.

Cinelli, F., Fresi, E., Idato, E. and Mazzella, L. (1977b). L'aire minima du phytobenthos dans un peuplement à *Cystoseira mediterranea* de l'île d'Ischia (Golfe de Naples). *Rapp. P. -v. Réun. Commn int. Explor. scient. Mer méditerr.* **24**, 113–115.

Coppejans, E. (1970). "Systematisch-ekologische studie van de wierpopulatie op de rotskusten van Le Dramont, St. Raphaël (Var, Frankrijk)". Licenciaats-thesis Rijksuniversiteit Gent.

Coppejans, E. (1972). Résultats d'une étude systématique et écologique de la population algale des côtes rocheuses du Dramont, St. Raphaël (Var, France). *Biol. Jaarb. Dodonaea* **40**, 152–180.

Coppejans, E. (1974). A preliminary study of the marine algal communities on the islands of Milos and Sikinos (Cyclades-Greece). *Bull. Soc. r. Bot. Belg.* **107**, 387–406.

Coppejans, E. (1976a). Sur *Polysiphonia banyulensis* nov. sp. (Ceramiales – Rhodophyceae). *Vie Milieu* **25**, 179–187.

Coppejans, E. (1976b). *Fosliella farinosa* (Lamouroux) Howe var. *chalicodictya* Taylor (Rhodophyceae – Cryptonemiales) et *Lophosiphonia scopulorum* (Harvey) Womersley (Rhodophyceae – Ceramiales) récoltées en Méditerranée nord-occidentale. *Biol. Jaarb. Dodonaea* **44**, 101–111.

Coppejans, E. (1977a). "Bijdrage tot de studie van de wierpopulaties (Chlorophyceae, Phaeophyceae, Rhodophyceae) van het fotofiel infralittoraal in het noordwestelijk mediteraan bekken". Doktoraatsthesis Rijksuniversiteit Gent.

Coppejans, E. (1977b). Végétation marine de l'île de Port-Cros (Parc National). XV. *Ceramium cingulatum* Weber von Bosse nouvelle pour la Méditerannée et quelques populations d'une *Ceramium* sp. à parasporocystes. *Biol. Jaarb. Dodonaea* **45**, 51–61.

Coppejans, E. (1977c). Résultats d'une étude d'homogénéité de peuplements algaux photophiles sur substrat rocheux à Banyuls et à Port-Cros. *Rapp. P. -v. Réun. Commn int. Explor. scient. Mer méditerr.* **24**, 143–144.

Coppejans, E. (1978a). Données supplémentaires sur *Polysiphonia banyulensis* Coppejans (Ceramiales, Rhodophyceae). *Vie Milieu*, in press.

Coppejans, E. (1978b). Sur les propagules de *Fosliella farinosa* (Lamouroux) Howe var. *farinosa* (Rhodophyceae – Cryptonemiales). *Bull. Soc. r. Bot. Belg.* **111**, 55–61.

Coppejans, E. and Boudouresque, C. -F. (1975). Sur la richesse floristique de certains peuplements photophiles infralittoraux de Port-Cros (Var, France). *Rapp. P. -v. Réun. Commn int. Explor. scient. Mer méditerr.* **23**, 79–80.

Coppejans, E. and Boudouresque, C. -F. (1976a). Végétation marine de l'île de Port-Cros (Parc National). XII. Sur *Acrochaetium molinieri* sp. nov. et *Lophosiphonia cristata* Falkenberg. *G. Bot. ital.* **110**, 219–229.

Coppejans, E. and Boudouresque, C. -F. (1976b). Présence de *Choristocarpus tenellus* (Kütz.) Zan. à Port-Cros. *Trav. scient. Parc. natn. Port-Cros* 2, 195–197.

Coppejans, E. and Dhondt, F. (1976). Végétation marine de l'île de Port-Cros (Parc National). XIII. *Myrionema liechtensternii* Hauck (Phaeophyta-Chordariales), nouvelle pour la flore algologique de France. *Biol. Jaarb. Dodonaea* **44**, 112–117.

Dhondt, F. (1976). "Minimumareaalstudie van wiervegetaties op rotskusten te Port-Cros en Banyuls (Frankrijk, Middellandse zee)". Licenciaatsthesis Rijksuniversiteit Gent.

Dhondt, F. and Coppejans, E. (1977). Résultats d'une étude d'aire minima de peuplements algaux photophiles sur substrat rocheux à Banyuls et à Port-Cros. *Rapp. P. -v. Réun. Commn int. Explor. scient. Mer méditerr.* **24**, 141–142.

Du Rietz, G., Fries, T. and Osvald, H. (1920). Gesetze der Konstitution natürlicher Pflanzengesellschaften. *Flora och Fauna* 7, 1–47.

Ernst, J. (1959). Studiën über die Seichtwasser-Vegetation der Sorrentiner Küste. *Pubbl. Staz. zool. Napoli* **30** (Suppl.), 470–518.

Feldmann, J. (1937). Recherches sur la végétation marine de la Méditerranée: La Côte des Albères. *Revue algol.* **10**, 1–336.

Feldmann, J. (1962). La végétation benthique de la Méditerranée, ses particularités et ses problèmes. *Pubbl. Staz. zool. Napoli* 32 (Suppl.), 170–180.

Funk, G. (1927). Die Algenvegetation des Golfs von Neapel nach neueren ökologischen Untersuchungen. *Pubbl. Staz. zool. Napoli* 7 (Suppl.), 1–507.

Gamulin-Brida, H. (1965). Contributions aux recherches sur la bionomie benthique de la baie de Porto Paone (Naples, Italie). Répartition des biocoenoses benthiques. *Pubbl. Staz. zool. Napoli* **34**, 476–500.

Gamulin-Brida, H. (1974). Biocoenoses benthiques de la mer Adriatique. *Acta adriat.* **15**, 1–102.

Giaccone, G. (1965). Le fitocenosi marine nel settore rosso de Capo Zafferano (Palermo). *Lav. Ist. bot. Giard. Col. Palermo* **22**, 1–69.

Giaccone, G. (1968). Aspetti della biocenosi coralligena in due stazioni dei bacini occidentale ed orientale del Mediterraneo. *G. Bot. ital.* **102**, 537–541.

Giaccone, G. (1971). Contributo allo studio dei popolamenti algali del basso Tirreno. *Annali Univ. Ferrara,* Sez. IV, **4**, 17–43.

Giaccone, G. (1977). Classification des peuplements phytobenthoniques de Méditerranée. *Rapp. P. -v. Réun. Commn int. Mer méditerr.* 24, 103–104.

Giaccone, G. and De Leo, A. (1966). Flora e vegetazione algale del Golfo di Palermo (II Contributo). *Lav. Ist. bot. Giard. Col. Palermo* 22, 1–69.

Giaccone, G. and Pignatti, S. (1967). Studi sulla produttività primaria del fitobentos nel Golfo di Trieste II. La Vegetazione del Golfo di Trieste. *Nova Thalassia* 3, 1–28.

Giaccone, G. and Sortino, M. (1974). Zonazione della vegetazione marina delle Isole Egadi (Canale di Sicilia). *Lav. Ist. bot. Giard. Col. Palermo* **25**, 164–183.

Giaccone, G. Scamacca, B., Cinelli, F., Sartoni, G. and Furnari, G. (1972).

Studio preliminare sulla tipologia della vegetazione sommersa del Canale di Sicilia e isole vicine. *G. Bot. ital.* **106**, 211–229.

Giaccone, G., Sortino, M., Solazzi, A. and Tolomio, C. (1973). Tipologia e distribuzione estiva della vegetazione sommersa del'Isola di Pantelleria. *Lav. Ist. bot. Giard. Col. Palermo* **25**, 103–119.

Gleason, H. (1922). On the relation between species and area. *Ecology* **3**, 158–162.

Gleason, H. (1925). Species and area. *Ecology* **6**, 66–74.

Godron, M. (1966). Application de la théorie de l'information à l'étude de l'homogénéité et de la structure de la végétation *Oecol. Pl.* **1**, 187–197.

Goodall, D. (1973). Sample similarity and species correlation. *In* "Ordination and Classification of Communities" (R. H. Whittaker, ed.), pp. 105–156. W. Junk, The Hague.

Gounot, M. (1969). "Méthodes d'Étude Quantitative de la Végétation". Masson, Paris.

Gounot, M. and Calleja, M. (1962). Coëfficient de communeauté, homogénéité et aire minimale. *Bull. Serv. Carte phytogéogr. Sér.* B 7, 181–200.

Huvé, H., Huvé, P. and Picard, J. (1963). Aperçu préliminaire sur le benthos littoral de la côte rocheuse adriatique italienne. *Rapp. P. -v. Réun. Commn int. Mer méditerr.* **17**, 93–102.

Larkum, A., Drew, E. and Crossett, R. (1967). The vertical distribution of attached marine algae in Malta. *J. Ecol.* **55**, 361–371.

Ledoyer, M. (1968). Ecologie de la faune vagile des biotopes méditerranéens accessibles en scaphandre autonome. *Recl Trav. Stn mar. Endoume* **44**, 1–60.

Molinier, R. (1954). Première constribution à l'étude des peuplements marins superficiels des îles Pithyuses (Baléares). *Vie Milieu* 5, 226–242.

Molinier, R. (1955). Aperçu de bionomie marine sur les côtes septentrionales de la Sardaigne. *Bull. Stn Aquic. Pêche Castiglione* N.S., 7, 373–400.

Molinier, R. (1960). Etude des biocoenoses marines du Cap Corse. *Vegetatio* 9, 121–312.

Molinier, R. and Picard, J. (1953). Recherches analytiques sur les peuplements littoraux méditerranéens se développant sur substrat solide. *Recl Trav. Stn mar. Endoume* **4**, 1–18.

Molinier, R. and Picard, J. (1954). Nouvelles recherches bionomiques sur les Côtes Méditerranéennes françaises. *Recl Trav. Stn mar. Endoume* **13**, 9–19.

Moravec, J. (1973). The determination of the minimal area of phytocoenoses. *Folia geobot. phytotax. bohemoslovaca* 8, 23–47.

Nasr, A. and Aleem, A. (1949). Ecological studies of some marine algae from Alexandria. *Hydrobiologia* **1**, 251–289.

Pérès, J. -M. (1967). Les biocoenoses benthiques dans le système phytal. *Recl Trav. Stn mar. Endoume* **42**, 1–113.

Pérès, J. -M. and Picard, J. (1955). Biotopes et biocoenoses de la Méditerranée occidentale comparés à ceux de la Manche et de l'Atlantique nord-orientale. *Archs Zool. exp. gén.* **92**, 1–72.

Pérès, J. -M. and Picard, J. (1956). Considérations sur l'étagement des formations benthiques. *Recl Trav. Stn mar. Endoume* **16**, 1–22.

Pérès, J. -M. and Picard, J. (1958). Manuel de bionomie benthique de la mer Méditerranée. *Recl Trav. Stn mar. Endoume* **23**, 5–122.

Pérès, J. -M. and Picard, J. (1964). Nouveau manuel de bionomie benthique de la mer Méditerranée. *Recl Trav. Stn mar. Endoume* **31**, 5–137.

Pignatti, S. (1962). Associazioni di alghe marine sulla costa veneziana. *Memorie Ist. veneto Sci.* **32**, 1–134.

Riedl, R. (1964). Lo studio del litorale marino in rapporto alla moderna biologia. *Atti seminar. Stud. Biol.* **1**, 1–30.

Tortonese, E. (1958). Bionomia marina della regione costiera fra punta della chiappa e Portofino (Riviera ligure di levante). *Archo Oceanogr. Limnol.* **11**, 167–210.

Tüxen, R. (1970). Bibliographie zum Problem des Minimum-Areals und der Art-Areal Kurve, *Exerpta bot.* Sect. B, **10**, 291–314.

van der Maarel, E. (1970). Vegetationsstruktur und Minimum-Areal in einem Dünen-Trockenrasen. *In* "Gesellschaftsmorphologie" (R. Tüxen, ed.), pp. 218–239. W. Junk, The Hague.

Vestal, A. (1949). Minimum areas for different vegetations. Their determination from species-area curves. *Illinois biol. Monogr.* **20**, 1–129.

Weber, E. (1972). "Grundriss der Biologischen Statistik". Gustav Fischer Verlag, Stuttgart.

Weinberg, S. (1975). Ecologie des Octocoralliaires communs du substrat dur dans la région de Banyuls-sur-Mer. *Bijdr. Dierk.* **45**, 50–70.

Zalokar, M. (1942). Les associations sous-marines de la côte adriatique au dessous de Velebit. *Bull. Soc. bot. Genève* **33**, 1–24.

3 | Ecological and Phenological Aspects of the Marine Phytobenthos of the Island of Newfoundland*

ROBERT G. HOOPER, G. ROBIN SOUTH AND

ALAN WHITTICK‡

Department of Biology, Memorial University of Newfoundland, St. John's, Newfoundland, Canada

Abstract: Detailed floristic studies of the marine algae of insular Newfoundland have been carried out over the last 12 years. These studies indicate that the benthic marine algal communities fall into two broad phytogeographic categories; the west and south coast, and the northern and eastern coasts, which face the open Atlantic. Three representative localities were studied and the vertical distribution of a subsample of the component species examined, using simple hierarchical agglomerative clustering techniques in a manner designed to reveal broad ecological groupings. The detailed distribution of the community types at one of these locations, Bonne Bay, a deep fiord on the west coast of the Island, is described. The phenology of selected algal species characteristic of these communities is reported in terms of growth and reproduction.

The open Atlantic association is characteristic of much of the flora of the western North Atlantic, north of Cape Cod, but is modified in the intertidal

---

*A contribution to the Canada/MAB project No. 8: *Inventory of Canadian Biological Resources*.

‡Much of the fieldwork, field interpretation and analysis was conducted by R. G. H. G. R. S. initiated the program and gave overall support, continuity and direction throughout. A. W. was involved in portions of the fieldwork and was largely responsible for the numerical analysis and compilation.

Systematics Association Special Volume No. 17(b), "The Shore Environment, Vol. 2: Ecosystems", edited by J. H. Price, D. E. G. Irvine and W. F. Farnham, 1980, pp. 395–423, Academic Press, London and New York.

and shallow subtidal by ice scour damage. In sheltered localities on the south and west coasts, the flora is enriched by the addition of northern species at their southern limits and southern species at their northern limits. The southern elements are confined to the immediate subtidal, while the northern species occur mainly in deep water, reaching maximum development below 25 m. The enriched south and west coast floras are maintained in sheltered localities by the development of a stable summer thermocline, which allows the deep-water masses to remain colder than the ambient Atlantic temperatures. Conversely, the surface temperatures exceed those of the open coast in summer, and permit development of warmer-water species.

Seasonal aspects of the flora are marked and were studied in detail at Bonne Bay. On the basis of vegetative growth, two main groups occur, with a summer–fall and a winter–spring flora. In terms of reproductive periodicity, three groups occur: winter (December–April); spring (March–July) and summer–fall (June–November). While temperature is indicated as a major factor controlling the initiation and cessation of growth and reproduction, photoperiodic and other responses must be considered for some of the species.

INTRODUCTION

A long-term floristic and ecological study of the benthic marine algae of Newfoundland has been in progress since 1967. The limited previous marine phycological work in the area is described in South and Cardinal (1973). Other than the collections (a few species, some doubtfully from Newfoundland) made by Sir Joseph Banks in 1766 (Lysaght, 1971), the only significant references to Newfoundland marine algae prior to this investigation are those of De la Pylaie (1824, 1829), Taylor (1957), Wilce (1959), Lee (1968, 1969) and Mathieson *et al.* (1969). The French Islands of St Pierre and Miquelon, usually included in the region in general accounts (South 1970, 1976a), received more attention and the algae were reported by Hariot (1889) and Le Gallo (1947, 1949). The Newfoundland study forms part of a more general investigation of the flora of marine algae of eastern Canada (South and Cardinal, 1970, 1973; South 1976b).

From a marine phytogeographic standpoint, the island of Newfoundland is generally regarded as transitional between the New England flora to the south, and the arctic flora to the north. In the absence of an adequate data base, however, little more can be said. The major, long-term objective of this study has been, therefore, to acquire sufficient information to permit a clear understanding of the composition, distribution, affinities and ecology of the marine algal flora. In order to meet these requirements, several approaches have been adopted: a cataloguing of the component species; description of their horizontal and vertical distributions; description of their phenology; determination of factors responsible for the observed spatial and temporal patterns. Development of a comprehensive herbarium and expanding field data files have been the backbone of the study, and now provide the data base which can be drawn on.

Cataloguing of the species has been completed, with original and revised check-lists now available for eastern Canada (South and Cardinal, 1970; South 1976b), and Newfoundland, Labrador and the French Islands of St Pierre and Miquelon (South, 1970, 1976a).

The description of the horizontal and vertical distribution of the species in Newfoundland presented a formidable logistic challenge. The island occupies 106 000 km^2, and is the world's sixteenth largest island, comparable in size with Cuba or Iceland. There are more than 8000 km of highly indented coastline, spanning latitudes 46 to 52°N. Most of the coast is rocky and favourable for attachment of algae. The small tidal range, from 1.5 to 2.5 m, requires most of the fieldwork to be dependent on divers. Nevertheless, much of the work is now completed.

To date, more than 700 collecting localities have been visited (Fig. 1), many of them repeatedly, over all seasons, and using SCUBA. More than 16 000 collections have been made, and the accessions to the Phycological Herbarium, Memorial University of Newfoundland (NFLD) now total *c.* 30 000. An exsiccata, *Algae Terrae Novae*, has been completed, with 200 numbers issued in nine sets over a ten-year period (South 1973; South and Hooper, 1980) and more than 12 000 specimens distributed to over 60 institutions. A reference base to the Newfoundland algae is therefore widely available.

Records of locality, depth, phenology and the general ecological conditions are included with all voucher specimens. For more than 75% of the flora, which comprises 264 species of benthic Rhodophyta, Phaeophyta and Chlorophyta (South, 1976a), year-round observations on horizontal and vertical distribution, phenology and ecology are now available, either from a few selected sites or from many sites. Other than the coast of the Great Northern Peninsula and the south coast from Fortune Bay to Rose Blanche, both regions inaccessible by road, much of the island has been covered. Particularly detailed data are available from Bonne Bay, Placentia Bay, and the North Avalon Peninsula. Using this large data base, an attempt can now be made on the synthetic phase of the project – an analysis of the observed spatial and temporal distributions of the species.

The large volume of this data base predicates that the synthetic approach must be numerical and therefore must involve the use of modern high-speed computers. The numerical description of vegetation has given great stimulus to the development of various efficient multivariate sorting and grouping techniques, which are now routinely applied in terrestrial ecology. The use of these techniques in the description of benthic marine algal distribution has been more limited and Boudouresque (1971) has reviewed some of these as they have been applied to marine plant communities. In the main there have been two approaches, differing vastly in scale. At the phytogeographic level whole floras have been compared (van den Hoek, 1975; Lawson, 1978), while at the opposite extreme detailed studies based on small quadrat samples have been used to elucidate distributions in restricted areas, such as intertidal communities (Russell, 1972). Our approach falls between these two extremes in that it is of necessity phytogeographic in scope, but in addition reveals broad ecological distributions. Year-round observations have allowed an assessment of temporal patterns of both reproductive and vegetative phases of the component species.

MATERIALS AND METHODS

Figure 1 shows the total number of locations in insular Newfoundland from which we have collection data. The data have been obtained over a 12-year period. However, we have chosen three sites for discussion in this paper (Fig. 1): area A is the northern part of the Avalon Peninsula; area P is the head of Placentia Bay; area B is Bonne Bay. Of all the areas we have examined in insular Newfoundland, we have the most extensive and systematic collections from these locations.

Study area A has a flora typical of the open Atlantic coast of eastern Canada; it is subject to high exposure and to the open north Atlantic temperature regimes, and in addition its intertidal receives periodic scouring by drifting pack ice. It is under the direct influence

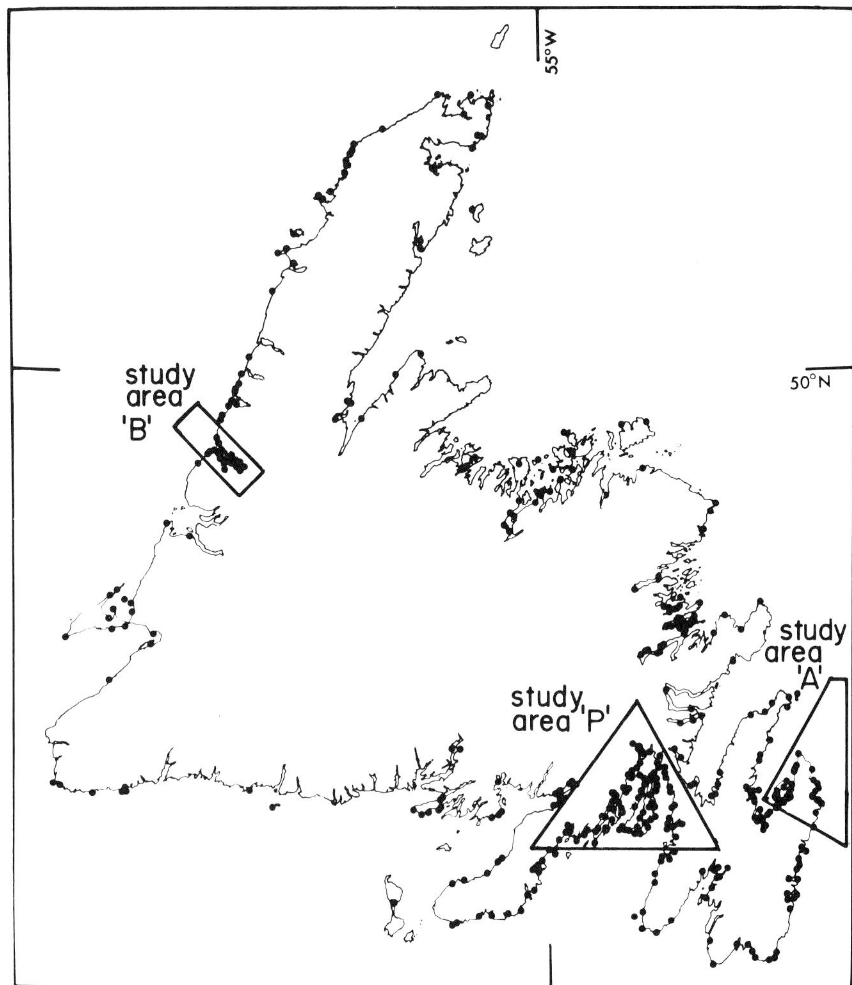

Fig. 1. Insular Newfoundland, with sampling stations (●) visited (1967–spring 1978). The main concentration of sampling is in the three study areas, Bonne Bay (B), Placentia Bay (P) and North Avalon (A).

of the arctic waters of the Labrador Current. Study area P is more sheltered, with less overall exposure, more stable water masses and little or no intertidal ice scour. It is only slightly influenced by the Labrador Current. Study area B has been chosen for detailed analysis and presentation in this paper, with the coastline (Fig. 2) divided into 60 stations separated by 1–2 km sections of shore.

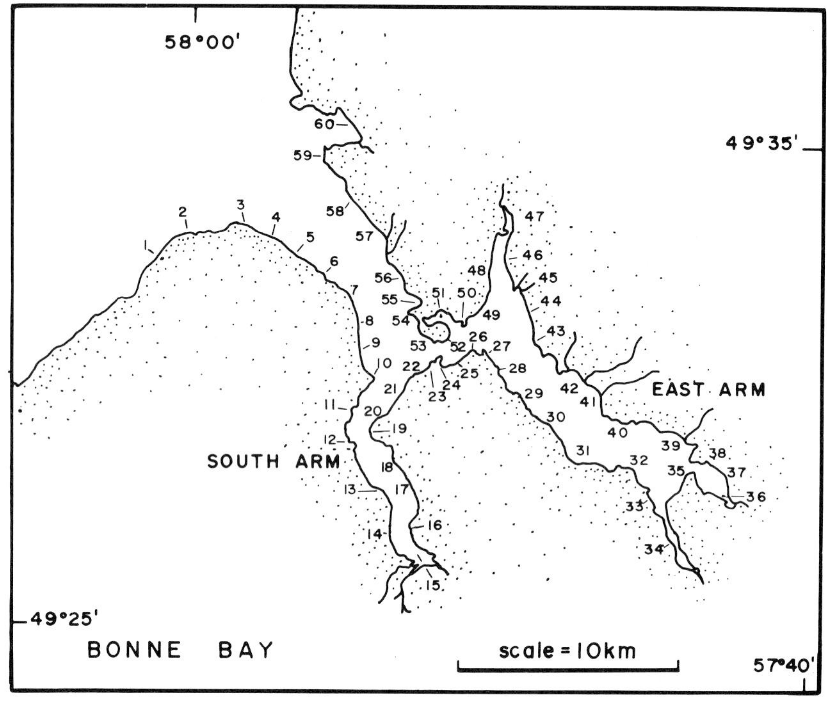

Fig. 2. Bonne Bay (Area B) showing the location of the 60 study sites.

Bonne Bay is a small fiordic embayment. The physiography is primarily the result of glaciation followed by some post-glacial rebound emergence and a relatively small degree of erosion. It is divided into two deep glacial troughs. The outer trough starts in the South Arm and extends more than 10 km west of the bay proper, into the Gulf of St Lawrence. The East Arm is a distinctly separate trough joined to the rest of Bonne Bay by a shallow (less than 15 m) sill across the Narrows, which is less than 500 m wide. Both troughs are roughly "U"-shaped and both are very deep (about 250 m in the case of the East Arm).

The shore line is quite regular, with no islands. Minor differences in topography are usually due to estuarine sedimentation, glacial boulders and moraines, or rock falls. Basement geology is mainly sedimentary (shales, limestone, and so on) often secondarily covered with unsorted glacial and biogenous sediments. The major estuary is

Lomond River (Stn 34). Smaller estuaries occur at Glenburnie (Stn 15), Deer Arm (Stn 47) and several minor locations.

During most winters, the East Arm and the southern portions of the South Arm freeze. The outer parts of the bay are often covered with sea-ice, originating in the Gulf of St Lawrence and carried into the bay by the prevailing westerly winds. This sea-ice tends to scour the intertidal of the outer north-west shores (Stns 55–58; Stn 1–3 and 59). Those stations with the local land-fast ice are protected from sea-ice intertidal scouring because the local ice remains until after the sea-ice has disappeared. An ice foot partially protects the rich south-west (Stns 4–9) and south narrows (Stns 19–22) intertidal floras.

Station 24, Gadd's Point, marks the narrowest point separating the East Arm from the outside of the bay. Strong tidal currents past this station are responsible for the richest floral associations in Bonne Bay.

Areas A and P are represented by a large number of collections, but these are not as regularly spaced as those from area B. The data at the three areas have been obtained over eight years, and at all sites collections of algae have been made from the high intertidal to depths in excess of 40 m, using SCUBA. For each species, additional data collected included depth, substrate type, water temperature, exposure and reproductive status of the species. Temperature depth profiles for each site have been obtained. Specimens have been preserved (*in Herb.* NFLD) using normal herbarium procedures, and it is these collections plus direct observations that have provided the data base for the results presented here.

Only 120 of the 264 recorded species were considered in this study (Table 1). The excluded species fall into two categories. The first category includes species of doubtful taxonomic status, in groups which require urgent and critical revision, and hence cannot be identified with certainty (e.g. species of *Streblonema*). The second excluded group consists of rare species, defined as those which have only been found at one locality within the study areas and which thus contribute little to the overall ecology (e.g. *Callithamnion tetragonum* (With.) C. Ag.). To qualify for inclusion within one of the three study sites, species must occur at more than one locality and have been collected on more than one occasion.

In analysis of the overall relationships between the three study

Table I. Benthic Chlorophyta, Phaeophyta and Rhodophyta occuring within five depth ranges at three Newfoundland localities

Location	Bonne Bay (B)					Placentia Bay (P)					N. Avalon Peninsula (A)				
Depth range	1	2	3	4	5	1	2	3	4	5	1	2	3	4	5
CHLOROPHYTA															
Blidingia minima	*					*					*				
Bryopsis hypnoides		*	*				*	*							
Capsosiphon fulvescens	*					*									
Chaetomorpha linum			*				*	*							
Chaetomorpha melagonium		*	*				*	*				*			
Cladophora pygmaea				*	*			*	*						
Cladophora rupestris	*	*				*	*					*			
Cladophora sericea		*	*				*	*				*			
Codiolum pusillum	*					*					*				
Derbesia marina			*					*				*	*		
Enteromorpha sp.	*	*				*	*					*			
Monostroma grevillei		*					*					*	*		
Monostroma undulatum		*	*				*	*				*	*		
Percursaria percursa	*					*									
Prasiola stipitata	*					*					*				
Rhizoclonium riparium	*	*				*	*				*	*			
Spongomorpha aeruginosa		*				*	*				*	*			
Spongomorpha arcta		*	*				*	*				*			
Ulothrix flacca	*	*				*	*				*	*			
Ulva lactuca		*	*				*	*				*	*		
Ulvaria obscura		*					*					*			
Urospora penicilliformis	*	*				*					*	*			
Urospora wormskioldii		*	*					*				*	*		
PHAEOPHYTA															
Acrothrix novae-angliae		*	*					*							
Agarum cribrosum			*	*	*		*	*	*	*			*	*	*
Alaria esculenta		*					*	*				*	*		
Ascophyllum nodosum	*	*				*	*								
Asperococcus fistulosus	*	*				*	*								
Chorda filum		*	*				*	*				*	*		
Chorda tomentosa		*	*				*	*				*	*		
Chordaria flagelliformis	*	*				*	*	*			*	*	*		
Delamarea attenuata		*					*	*			*				
Desmarestia aculeata		*	*	*	*			*	*	*			*	*	*
Desmarestia viridis		*	*	*	*		*		*	*		*	*	*	
Dictyosiphon foeniculaceus		*	*				*	*				*	*		
Ectocarpus fasciculatus		*					*					*			
Ectocarpus siliculosus		*	*				*	*				*	*		
Eudesme virescens		*	*				*	*				*	*		
Fucus distichus	*					*					*				
Fucus edentatus		*					*					*			

Table I. (Continued)

Location	Bonne Bay (B)					Placentia Bay (P)					N. Avalon Peninsula (A)				
Depth range	1	2	3	4	5	1	2	3	4	5	1	2	3	4	5
Fucus evanescens							*								
Fucus spiralis	*					*					*				
Fucus vesiculosus	*	*				*	*				*				
Giffordia granulosa		*	*					*							
Halopteris scoparia		*	*				*	*							
Haplospora globosa		*	*				*	*					*		
Isthmoplea sphaerophora		*				*									
Laminaria digitata		*					*					*	*		
Laminaria longicruris		*	*	*	*		*	*	*	*					
Laminaria solidungula				*	*				*	*					
Melanosiphon intestinalis	*					*					*				
Myriocladia lovenii		*	*					*	*						
Papenfussiella callitricha							*	*				*	*		
Petalonia fascia	*	*				*	*				*	*			
Petalonia zosterifolia		*					*				*	*	*		
Pilayella littoralis	*	*	*			*	*	*			*	*	*		
Punctaria latifolia		*					*	*				*			
Punctaria plantaginea		*	*				*	*				*			
Saccorhiza dermatodea		*	*				*	*				*	*		
Scytosiphon lomentaria	*	*	*			*	*	*			*	*			
Sphacelaria cirrosa							*								
Sphacelaria plumosa		*	*	*	*		*	*	*	*					
Sphaerotrichia divaricata		*					*								
Stictyosiphon soriferus		*	*	*	*			*	*						
Tilopteris mertensii		*					*	*					*		
RHODOPHYTA															
Ahnfeltia plicata		*	*				*	*							
Antithamnion cruciatum							*	*							
Antithamnion floccosum		*	*				*	*				*	*	*	
Antithamnion pylaisaei		*	*	*	*		*	*	*	*		*	*	*	*
Audouinella alariae		*					*					*			
Audouinella membranacea		*	*	*	*		*	*	*	*			*	*	*
Audouinella purpurea	*	*				*	*	*				*	*		
Bangia atropurpurea	*	*				*	*				*				
Bonnemaisonia hamifera		*	*	*			*	*	*						
Callithamnion corymbosum		*	*				*	*							
Callophyllis cristata			*	*	*		*	*	*	*			*	*	*
Ceramium rubrum		*	*	*			*	*	*			*			
Ceratocolax hartzii					*			*	*	*					
Chondrus crispus	*	*				*	*	*							
Choreocolax polysiphoniae	*					*	*	*							
Clathromorphum circumscriptum		*	*	*			*	*	*			*		*	

Table I. (Continued)

Location	Bonne Bay (B)					Placentia Bay (P)					N. Avalon Peninsula (A)				
Depth range	1	2	3	4	5	1	2	3	4	5	1	2	3	4	5
Clathromorphum compactum							*	*	*					*	*
Corallina officinalis		*	*				*	*				*		*	
Cystoclonium purpureum		*	*				*	*							
Dumontia incrassata		*					*								
Gigartina stellata	*					*	*								
Halosaccion ramentaceum		*					*	*				*	*		
Hildenbrandia rubra	*	*	*	*	*	*	*	*	*	*	*	*	*	*	*
Leptophytum laeve			*	*	*			*	*	*				*	*
Lithothamnium glaciale			*	*	*		*	*	*	*		*	*	*	*
Lithothamnium lemoineae			*	*				*	*				*	*	*
Lithothamnium tophiforme					*					*					
Membranoptera alata				*	*			*	*	*			*	*	*
Neodilsea integra				*	*				*	*					
Odonthalia dentata					*					*					
Palmaria palmata	*	*				*	*	*				*	*		
Pantoneura baerii		*	*	*	*		*	*	*	*					*
Petrocelis middendorfii						*	*								
Peyssonnelia rosenvingii				*	*				*	*			*	*	*
Phycodrys rubens		*	*	*	*		*	*	*	*			*	*	*
Phyllophora pseudoceranoides		*	*				*	*							
Phyllophora truncata			*	*	*		*	*	*	*					
Phymatolithon laevigatum		*	*	*			*	*				*	*		
Phymatolithon lenormandii		*					*								
Phymatolithon rugulosum							*	*					*	*	
Plumaria elegans	*	*	*			*	*	*							
Polyides rotundus		*	*				*	*							
Polysiphonia arctica					*				*	*					
Polysiphonia flexicaulis		*	*	*			*	*				*	*		
Polysiphonia lanosa	*	*				*	*								
Polysiphonia nigrescens		*	*				*	*							
Polysiphonia urceolata		*	*	*			*	*				*	*	*	
Porphyra linearis	*	*				*	*				*	*			
Porphyra miniata		*	*				*	*				*	*		
Porphyra umbilicalis	*	*				*	*				*	*			
Ptilota serrata			*	*	*		*	*	*	*			*	*	*
Rhodomela confervoides		*	*	*	*	*	*	*	*	*		*	*	*	
Rhodophyllis dichotoma				*	*				*	*					
Rhodophysema elegans		*	*				*	*							
Turnerella pennyi					*					*				*	*

areas, the benthos was arbitrarily divided into five depth ranges. These are: *Zone 1*: high water to 1 m above extreme low water; *Zone 2*: 1 m above extreme low water to 2 m below; *Zone 3*: 2–10 m depth subtidal; *Zone 4*: 10–25 m depth subtidal; *Zone 5*: Below 25 m depth subtidal (Table I). In area B, however, species distributions at the 60 sites were considered in terms of three depth ranges: *Zone 1*: intertidal; *Zone 2*: extreme low water to 10 m depth; *Zone 3*: below 25 m.

The data in Table I were subjected to cluster analysis. The presence and absence data for the 15 samples (3 sites, 5 depths) generated a similarity matrix using the Jaccard (1908) coefficient, which only takes into account positive matches of data. Arguments for the choice of coefficients which excluded negative matches when working in marine communities distributed over a depth range are given by Field (1968). Clustering was by group average sorting (Sokal and Michener, 1958), which of the simpler hierarchical agglomerative techniques produces the best ecologically interpretable clusters. Jardine and Sibson (1971) have criticized the use of this sorting technique with binary data, but the use of their recommended single linkage clustering techniques produced extreme chaining and few clear clusters emerged. In addition to clustering of both sites and depths on species occurrence, the generation of a similarity matrix based on the transpose of the initial data matrix and its subsequent clustering yields groups of species based on the distribution of the samples.

For study area B, Bonne Bay, similar analyses were performed, but there the 60 sites and their species provided the data, and the three chosen depth ranges were dealt with separately. Species and site clustering were performed, with a total of six analyses.

In an attempt to assess the temporal distribution and seasonal reproductive status of selected Bonne Bay species, cluster analyses were performed. The clustering strategy was essentially the same as above, with the addition of a simple matching coefficient (Sneath and Sokal, 1973) which gives equal weighting to both positive and negative matches, the justification being that the absence of a reproductive structure has importance equal to that of its presence in year-round phenological studies. Two cluster analyses of phenological data were made, one on vegetative presence, involving those species which possess alternate or otherwise cryptic phases in their seasonal pattern, the second on species which show a marked reproductive (fertile) seasonal periodicity. Fertility is defined as the production and release of spores or gametes. A limited number of species was examined and scored on a monthly basis for presence or absence in the first instance, and for the possession of functional reproductive structures in the second.

RESULTS AND DISCUSSION

Figure 3 shows the result of cluster analysis of the five depths at three sites, based on the presence and absence of species. The three major clusters which emerge are not the three areas A, B and P, but represent three depth ranges: Zone 1, the high intertidal community; Zones 2 and 3, the low intertidal to 10 m depth; Zones 4 and 5, the deep subtidal. It is also apparent that Bonne Bay (B) and Placentia Bay (P) are more closely related to each other than to the North Avalon area (A). Figure 4 shows the cluster analysis of the 120 species from the above samples. Three major groups again emerge; the first (*Fucus evanescens** to *Porphyra umbilicalis**) consists mainly of intertidal species, but with some extension into the immediate subtidal. The second group (*Monostroma grevillei* to *Rhodophysema elegans*) is principally composed of species found in the immediate subtidal, but extending into the low intertidal. The third group (*Bonnemaisonia hamifera* to *Turnerella pennyi*) is exclusively subtidal and includes the species found at the greatest depths.

Each of the above groups can be further subdivided. The first major group contains a subgroup (*Blidingia minima* to *Melanosiphon intestinalis*) which is characteristic of the uppermost limits of the intertidal at all sites.

The second major group shows a number of subgroups; species from *Monostroma grevillei* to *Audouinella alariae* are found in Zone 2 at all sites, but in this zone *Sphaerotrichia divaricata* and *Phymatolithon lenormandii* are restricted to areas B and P. Of the other species in this general depth range, *Acrothrix novae-angliae* to *Rhodophysema elegans* are restricted to Bonne Bay and Placentia Bay, while the remnants of this group from *Alaria esculenta* to *Porphyra miniata* are found at all sites.

---

*Nomenclature, including authorities, follows that in South (1976b).

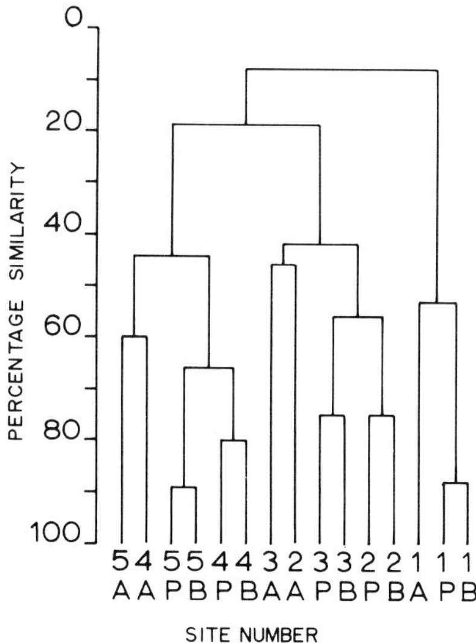

Fig. 3. Cluster analysis for five depth ranges (1 = upper intertidal to 1 m above low water, 2 = 1 m above low water to 2 m below, 3 = 2 m to 10 m below low water, 4 = 10 m to 25 m below low water, 5 = below 25 m below low water) in the three study areas, North Avalon (A), Placentia Bay (P) and Bonne Bay (B), based on 120 species of benthic algae.

The third major group divides into two distinct subgroups. One subgroup (*Cladophora pygmaea* to *Turnerella pennyi*) occurs in the deepest zones, and with the exception of *T. pennyi* the species are restricted to areas B and P. The other subgroup contains species (*Lithothamnium lemoineae* to *Rhodomela confervoides*) which are ubiquitous, with extended depth ranges, and a few species (*Stictyosiphon soriferus* to *Phyllophora truncata*) which are restricted to B and P, but do not extend into the deepest zones. Other species groups not mentioned above occupy different depth zones at the three study areas and hence are not associated with the above clusters. Two major conclusions can be drawn from a synthesis of these data:

(1) Bonne Bay and Placentia Bay are floristically similar and possess a richer flora than the North Avalon area.

(2) There are two depth zones where this floristic difference is most marked, the immediate subtidal and the deep subtidal (Zone 5, below 25 m).

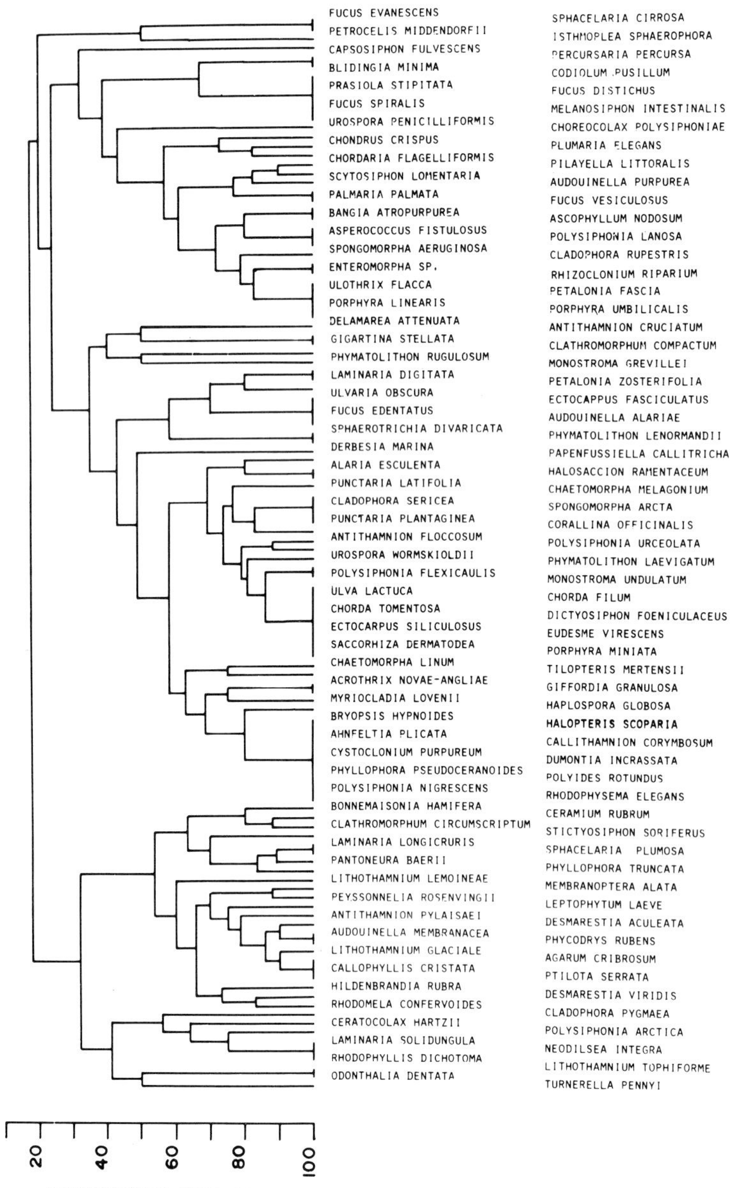

Fig. 4. Cluster analysis of 120 species of benthic algae based on their occurrence in five depth ranges at the three study sites.

The species which characterize and enrich the deep flora of both Bonne Bay and Placentia Bay, but which are absent from the Avalon, are *Odonthalia dentata, Lithothamnium tophiforme, Rhodophyllis dichotoma, Neodilsea integra, Laminaria solidungula* and *Polysiphonia arctica.* All are considered northern species and approach the southern limits of their western Atlantic distribution in Newfoundland.

Species characterizing the immediate subtidal in these two areas are scattered between the major clusters, but include such species as *Callithamnion corymbosum, Plumaria elegans*, and others mentioned above. They do not form a discrete group in the dendrogram (Fig. 4) because of their relatively extended depth ranges, in many instances from the low intertidal to all but the deepest subtidal. They are also absent from the high intertidal zones. These species are usually considered southern, with insular Newfoundland marking the northern limits of their ranges in the western Atlantic.

We believe that these two groups of species are found at the two areas B and P because of the relatively sheltered nature of those areas; this allows the development of a stable water column and the establishment of a discrete and stable thermocline during the summer months. Figure 5 shows the month-by-month mean surface temperature and mean temperature at 30 m depth for the North Avalon (A) and Bonne Bay (B); four temperature/depth profiles, two at each area for February and August, the coldest and warmest months of the year, are also given. There is little difference between sites or depths during the winter and spring months, but in summer and fall dramatic differences are seen. The surface temperatures at Bonne Bay are higher than those occurring at the Avalon site; conversely, the deep water in Bonne Bay is considerably colder. The depth temperature profiles reveal a marked temperature stratification in Bonne Bay in August, but no such discrete thermocline in the shallow water of the North Avalon area. In the Avalon area thermoclines do occur, but for the most part are transitory or situated at greater depths. Bathythermograph profiles in Placentia Bay (not given) are similar to Bonne Bay, but lack the extreme stability which characterizes the inner part of this fiordic system. It is likely that the southern species are maintained by the higher summer temperatures which occur in the immediate subtidal, while the northern, deep-water species owe their persistence to the maintenance of deep cold water masses within the photic zone.

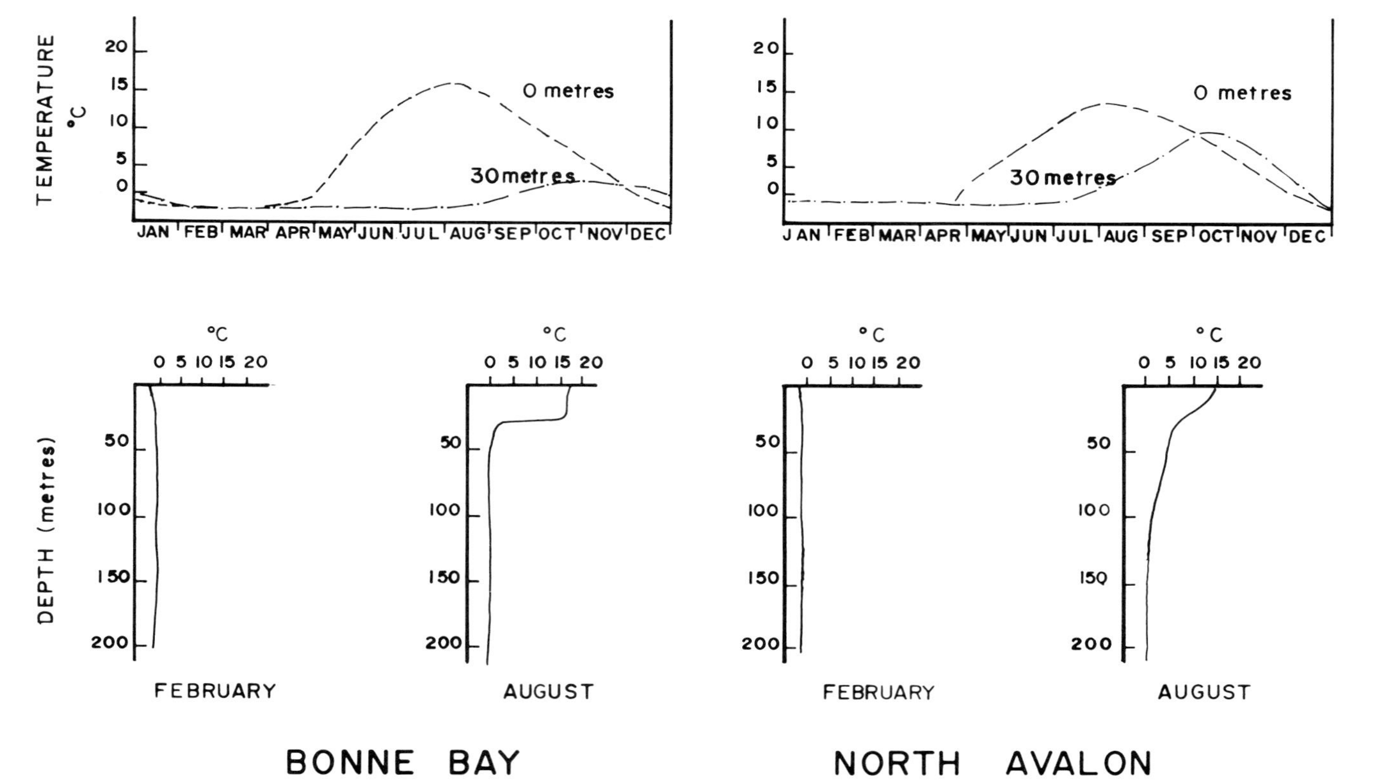

Fig. 5. Annual temperature cycles at Bonne Bay and from North Avalon at the surface (0 m) and at 30 m depth. Bathythermograph profiles for the two sites in February and August.

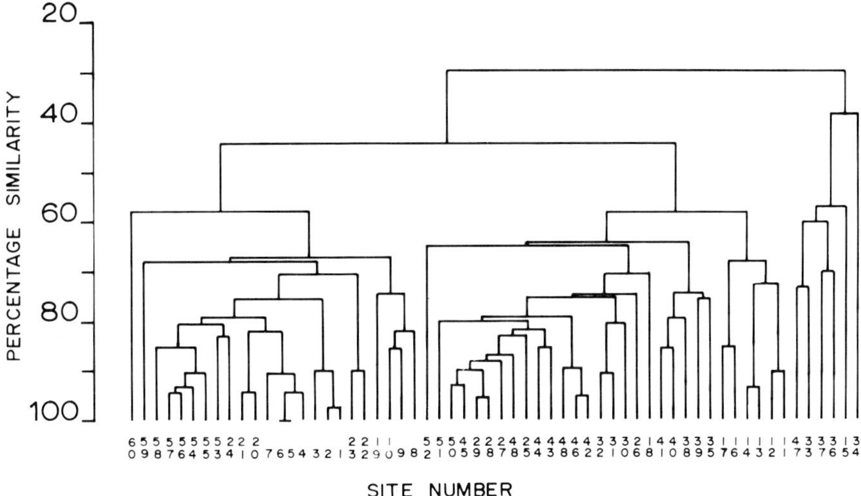

Fig. 6. Cluster analysis of 60 intertidal sites from Bonne Bay (Fig. 2) based on the intertidal algal flora.

The study has revealed three major groups of species which, for the most part, are characteristic of the intertidal, the immediate subtidal and the deep subtidal. It does not, however, permit an ecological comparison between species occurring over a wide range of habitats within the three areas. The detailed analysis of the distribution of the species at Bonne Bay allowed a more detailed ecological study from 60 sites.

Figure 6 shows the relationships of the 60 intertidal sites at Bonne Bay. The numbers correspond to the numbers on the map (Fig. 2). Three major divisions emerge. The first, from sites 60–8, includes the outermost portions of the bay subject to high exposure, including ice scour. Excluded from this group are sites at the head of the South Arm and all the sites of the East Arm. Site 60 is unique in the paucity of its flora, brought about by the shallow, shelving nature of the intertidal substrate. Sites 52–11 include those in the East Arm and in the inner part of the South Arm. A major subgroup in this division are sites 17–11, which have a steep, relatively unstable substrate. The third major divison, sites 47–34, is estuarine; in addition to reduced salinity, the substrate is mostly silty or muddy.

Figure 7 shows the species relationships between the 60 sites. One

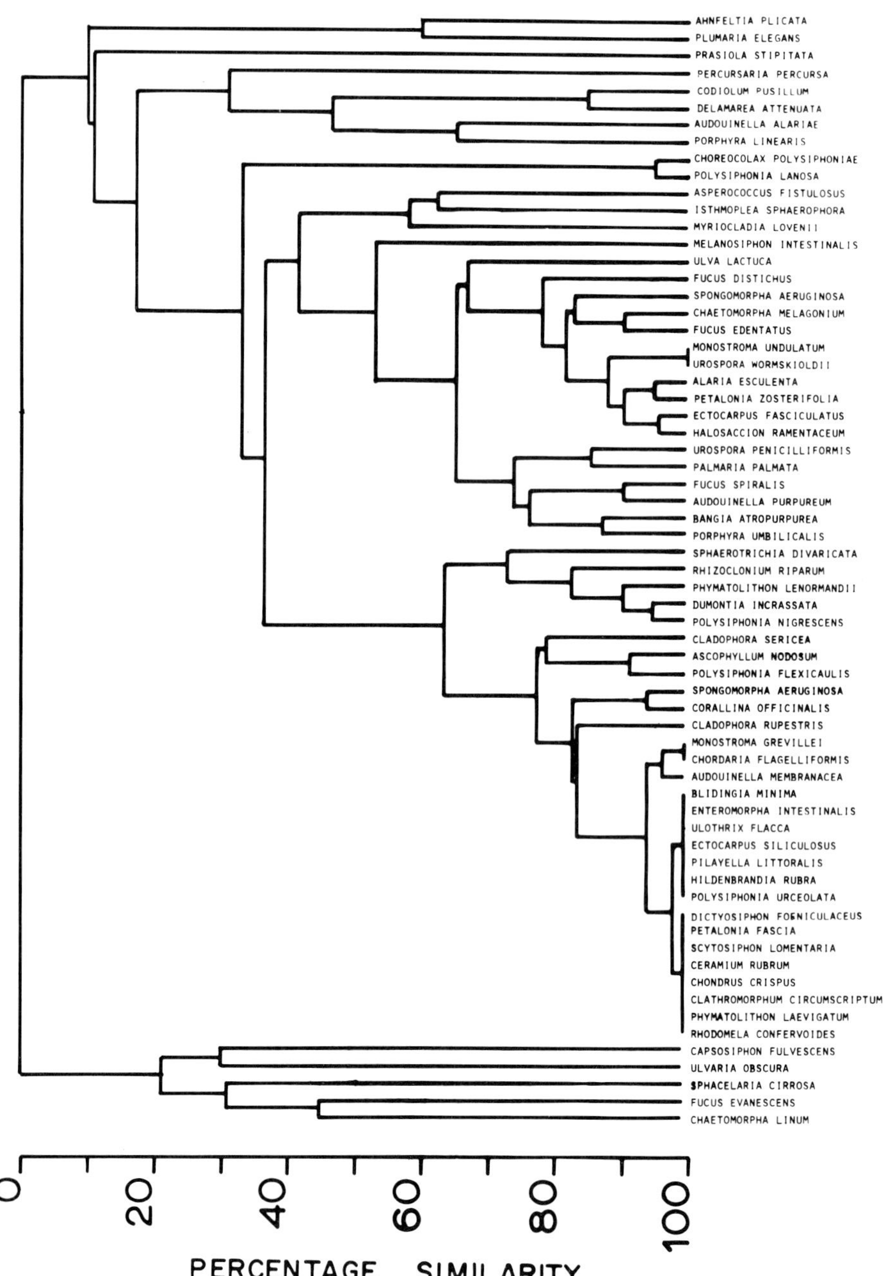

Fig. 7. Cluster analysis of the intertidal algal species of Bonne Bay based on their 60 sampling sites.

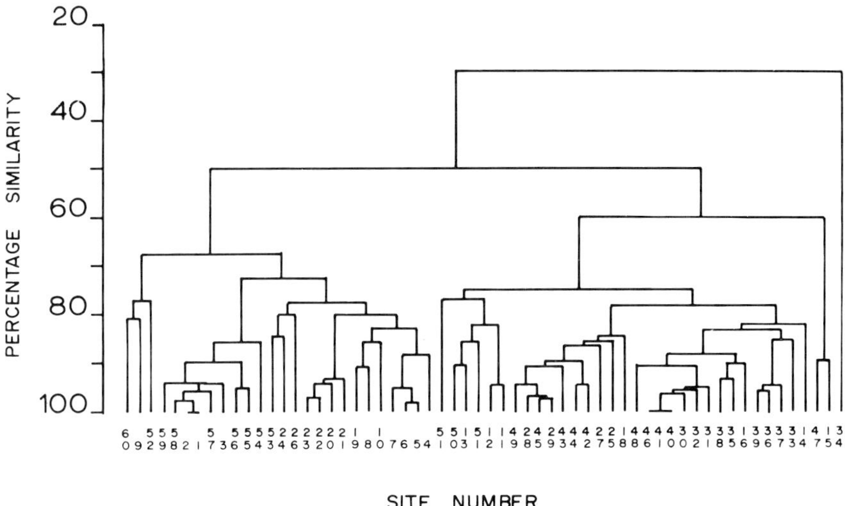

Fig. 8. Cluster analysis of 60 subtidal sites from Bonne Bay (0 to 10 m depth) based on the algal flora.

group (*Chaetomorpha linum* to *Capsosiphon fulvescens*) includes the species which are mainly limited to the estuarine sites. A second group (*Rhodomela confervoides* to *Cladophora sericea*) is of ubiquitous species, found in all but the estuarine sites; a third group (*Polysiphonia nigrescens* to *Sphaerotrichia divaricata*) is confined to the more sheltered parts of the bay, in the South and East Arms. The fourth group (*Porphyra umbilicalis* to *Ulva lactuca*) contains species largely confined to the outer, more exposed portions of Bonne Bay. The remnants are species of more scattered distribution, usually with more narrow ecological amplitudes (e.g. *Ahnfeltia plicata* is found in sandy situations, *Melanosiphon intestinalis* is confined to those sites which have high intertidal pools, and *Prasiola stipitata* to nitrogen-rich areas).

Figure 8 is the dendrogram of the same 60 sites, but for the subtidal over a depth range of 0–10 m. Sites 59–4 are the most exposed sites of the bay, 51–34 the more sheltered inner parts. Sites 47–34 of this group are estuarine, the extreme example being site 34, which in addition to possessing reduced salinity lacks a solid substrate. Within the sheltered group, sites 51–11 have an impoverished flora due to lack of suitable substrate for all but the smallest and most ephemeral of species. The first three sites on the dendrogram, 60–52, are unique in that they are harbours with a characteristic flora found on wooden pilings, but where the natural substrate supports only a sparse flora. The equivalent species dendrogram for the subtidal groups is given in Fig. 9. The group from *Polysiphonia urceolata* to *Halopteris scoparia* is found in all but the most estuarine of sites. The group *Palmaria palmata* to *Haplospora globosa* tends to have a distribution restricted to the outer parts of the Bay, while the remaining species have more scattered and restricted distributions.

Figure 10 is a dendrogram of the sites below 25 m depth. These depths are represented at only 50 of the sites. Sites 59–1 are found on the outer coast, an area of exposure and water mixing with a deeper and less stable thermocline. Absent from these sites are the northern species characteristic of the deep water of Bonne Bay. These include *Rhodophyllis dichotoma, Neodilsea integra, Polysiphonia arctica, Pantoneura baerii, Lithothamnium tophiforme, Odonthalia dentata* and *Laminaria solidungula.* Sites 58–30 contain the normal deep-water species complement typical of most of the bay at this depth. Sites 58–25 are floristically the richest. Sites 17–11 have unstable substrates, and are species-poor, lacking the larger deep-water algae (e.g. *Laminaria* spp., *Agarum cribrosum*). The deep-water species distributions (Fig. 11) are almost impossible to interpret. The group of species from *Polysiphonia arctica* to *Antithamnion pylaisaei* is present at nearly all sites, except the above mentioned, while the remainder have a more scattered distribution determined by micro-habitat conditions; they are not examined here.

Of the environmental factors considered, exposure, substrate type and stability, and estuarine conditions are the most pronounced. There are, however, many species for which no obvious distribution patterns have emerged. These are most likely influenced by micro-habitat and microenvironmental factors which cannot be accommodated in the relatively coarse sampling undertaken in this study.

A further major dimension is that of vegetative and reproductive periodicity. Using the same sampling techniques on selected species in Bonne Bay, but on a year-round basis, it is possible to add a temporal dimension.

Figure 12 is a dendrogram of the monthly occurrence of 29 algal species which show marked seasonal periodicity in Bonne Bay. All

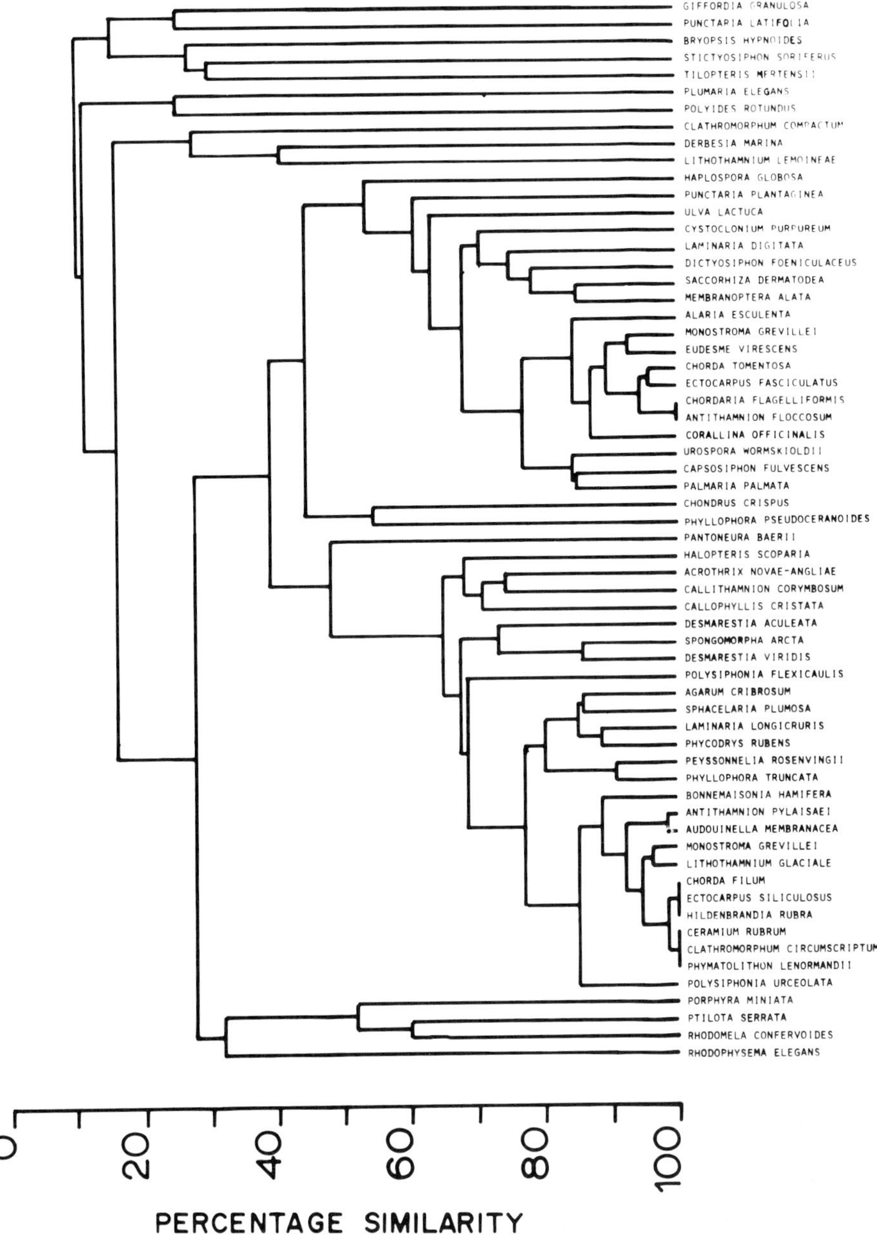

Fig. 9. Cluster analysis of the subtidal algal species of Bonne Bay (0 to 10 m depth) based on their occurrence at 60 sampling sites.

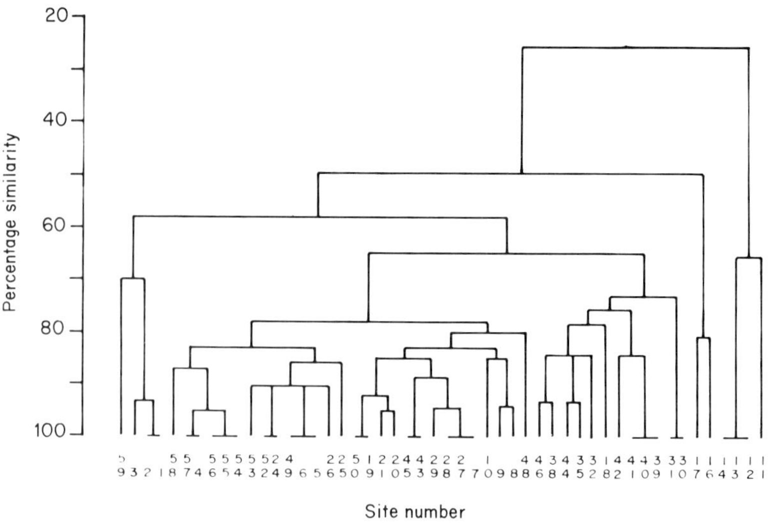

Fig. 10. Cluster analysis of 50 deep subtidal sites (below 25 m) from Bonne Bay based on the algal flora.

are restricted to the intertidal or to the shallow subtidal. Many (e.g. *Monostroma* spp., *Chorda* spp., *Porphyra* spp.) possess heteromorphic life histories, while others (e.g. *Callithamnion corymbosum*; Whittick, 1978) are known to persist in this region in a reduced vegetative state. Two major groups are evident (Fig. 12). Those from *Porphyra miniata* to *Cladophora sericea*, with a summer–fall distribution, and those from *Porphyra linearis* to *Monostroma undulatum*, which are predominantly winter–spring species. Within the first major division two clear subgroups can be seen; those from *Porphyra miniata* to *Dictyosiphon foeniculaceus*, which appear in the spring and persist through the summer, often into the fall and winter, and those from *Callithamnion corymbosum* to *Cladophora sericea*, which appear in the summer months and may persist through into early winter. The second major subdivision can be further subdivided into two elements, showing the converse of the two subgroups of the first division. The species within the group from *Porphyra linearis* to *Audouinella alariae* commence growth in the fall or early winter and persist through the spring. The other group, *Dumontia incrassata* to *Monostroma undulatum*, is essentially confined to the winter and

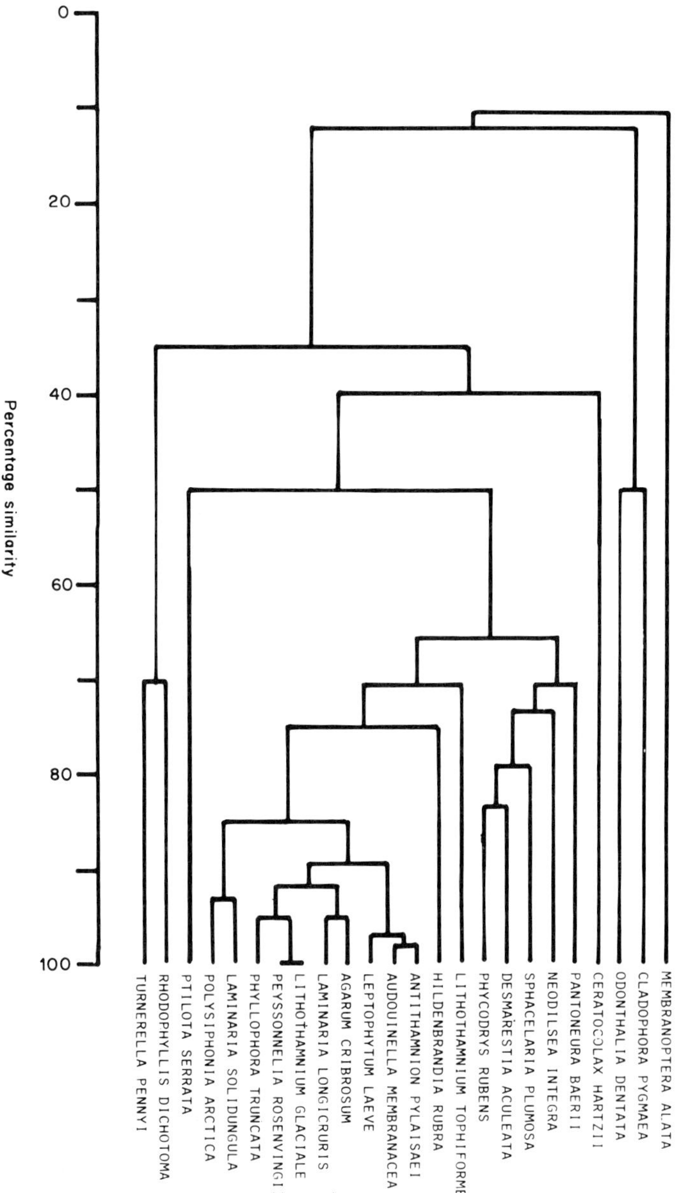

Fig. 11. Cluster analysis of the deep subtidal algal species of Bonne Bay (below 25 m depth) based on their occurrence at 50 sampling sites.

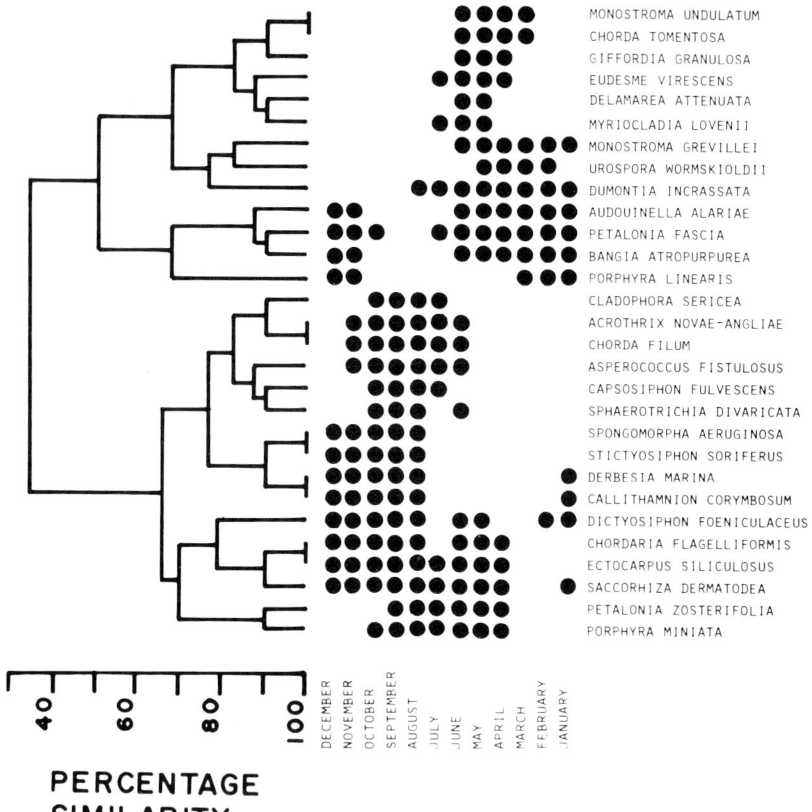

Fig. 12. Cluster analysis, showing vegetative phenology, based on monthly presence (●), of Bonne Bay benthic algal species with marked seasonal occurrences.

spring months, not appearing until the water temperature reaches a required minimum and including some (e.g. *Urospora wormskioldii* to *Monostroma undulatum*) that disappear abruptly when temperatures increase in the early summer.

Similar trends are seen in Fig. 13, which is the dendrogram of the reproductive state of 56 species of algae from Bonne Bay. Three major divisions emerge. Species in the division from *Turnerella pennyi* to *Antithamnion floccosum* become fertile in fall or early winter and persist in this state into the spring. The second major division includes species from *Porphyra miniata* to *Dictyosiphon*

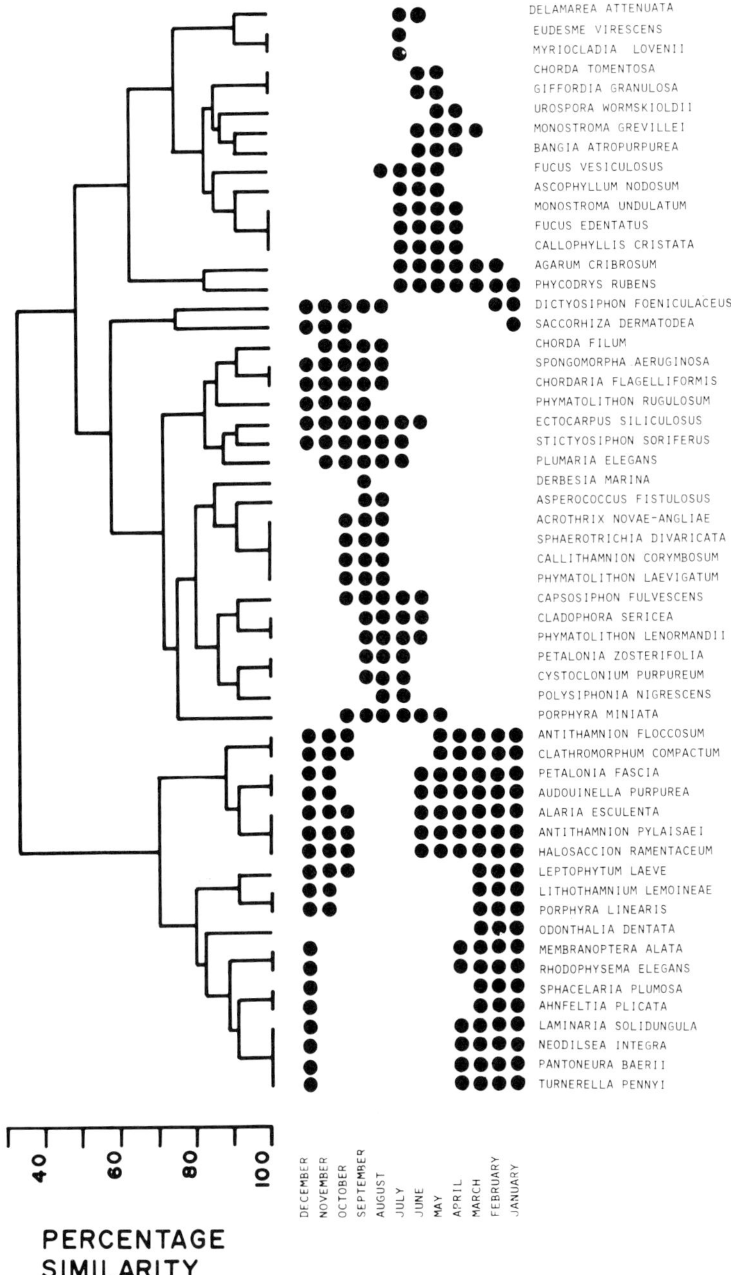

Fig. 13. Cluster analysis showing the reproduction phenology of selected Bonne Bay benthic algae, based on monthly occurrence (●) of functional reproductive structures.

foeniculaceus, with reproductive periods essentially confined to the summer and fall, but with two species (*Saccorhiza dermatodea* and *Dictyosiphon foeniculaceus*) remaining fertile in the early winter. The third division, *Phycodrys rubens* to *Delamarea attenuata*, is principally of plants which become fertile in the first half of the year. *Phycodrys rubens* and *Agarum cribrosum* form one subgroup of species which become fertile in January, while the species in the group bounded by *Callophyllis cristata* and *Chorda tomentosa* do not become fertile until late spring. The three remaining species, *Myriocladia lovenii, Eudesme virescens* and *Delamarea attenuata*, have a reproductive period restricted to the middle of the year.

A comparison of Figs 12 and 13 with Fig. 5, showing the annual cycle of temperature in Bonne Bay, indicates temperature as a major factor controlling both the initiation and cessation of growth and reproduction. However, the behaviour of many groups of species cannot be explained on the basis of temperature alone and these groups, which abruptly initiate growth and reproduction in the spring and fall, are probably under some form of photoperiodic or photosynthetic control. Of special interest in this regard are the species found in Bonne Bay and Placentia Bay but absent from the North Avalon area. The species at their northern limits, confined to the shallow water, grow and reproduce in the second half of the year when water temperatures are at a maximum. The deep-water, northern species, have their reproductive periods in the first half of the year when temperatures are at a minimum. This is further evidence in support of our conclusion that populations of these species are temperature-sensitive and are maintained by water stratification during the summer months.

CONCLUSIONS

This study has shown that it is possible, based on large resources of systematically gathered herbarium and field data, to delimit species distributions, large-scale ecological groupings, and seasonal patterns of growth and reproduction, using simple numerical techniques. The method, however, has many limitations; broad ecological categories can be determined, but the sample size precludes detailed analysis. The problem of the scale factor can be seen on all the species dendrograms, where there occur groupings of species that seem to have little in common beyond their mutual exclusion from other groups. A second problem is that the method does not take into account any estimation of measurements of abundance of species. As presented in this paper, the floras of Bonne Bay and Placentia Bay appear very similar; an examination of the largely unscoured intertidal of Placentia Bay would, however, show higher densities of plants.

Work is continuing on these problems and detailed small-scale quadrat studies, together with the collection of multivariate environmental data, are planned to investigate the distribution and ecological relationships of selected species. Detailed autecological studies, using year-round field sampling coupled with culture studies in the laboratory under defined environmental conditions, are also being actively pursued. They have already been successful in elucidating some of the factors controlling the growth and reproduction of several of the southern species at their northern limits (Whittick and Hooper, 1977; Whittick 1977, 1978; Whittick and West, 1979; South and Hooper, 1976) and northern species at their southern limits (South *et al.*, 1972; Hooper and South, 1977).

The preliminary nature of this study should be emphasized; the limitations imposed by the size of the region and the large resources necessary to carry out such an extensive programme should not be overlooked. Despite these limitations, however, the data now available on the benthic macrophytes of this large region at such (oceanographically) northerly locations are more extensive than for any comparable region in the world. In providing this first major overview of the phytobenthos of insular Newfoundland, even with the obvious limitations, a meaningful basis for future investigation becomes available. In addition, the conclusions will hopefully allow the interpretation of events in comparable cold-water environments in the northern hemisphere.

ACKNOWLEDGEMENTS

The support of NRC (NSERC) Grant A-4648 (G. R. S.) has continued throughout this project and is gratefully acknowledged. Additional substantial support was obtained from Memorial University of Newfoundland (especially through the Placentia Bay Environmental Studies Project, directed by Dr W. D. Machin); Newfoundland and Labrador Hydro Ltd (Conception Bay); Parks Canada (Bonne Bay); the International Biological Programme (Bonne Bay); Gary Hunter; and NRC (NSERC) Grant A-9900 (A. W.). Of the many who assisted in the extensive field work, we are especially indebted to Marlene Roberge, Sheila Gibbons, D. Reddin, G. Fenwick, B. Bennett and D. W. Keats. We are indebted to Roy Ficken for expert photographic assistance.

REFERENCES

Boudouresque, C. F. (1971). Méthodes d'études qualitative et quantitative du benthos (en particulier du phytobenthos). *Tethys* 3, 79–104.

De La Pylaie, A. J. M. B. (1824). Quelques observations sur les productions de l'Ile de Terre-Neuve, et sur quelques algues de la côte de France appartenant au genre Laminaire. *Annls. Sci. nat.* 4, 174–184.

De La Pylaie, A. J. M. B. (1829) "Flore de l'Ile de Terre Neuve et des Isles Saint Pierre et Miclon". Paris, 128 pp.

Field, J. E. (1968). The use of the information statistic in the numerical classification of heterogenous systems. *J. Ecol.* 57, 505–509.

Hariot, P. (1889). Liste des algues reçueillies à l'île Miquelon par le docteur Delamare. *J. Bot., Paris* 3, 154–157; 181–183; 194–196.

Hoek, C. van den (1975). Phytogeographic provinces along the coasts of the northern Atlantic Ocean. *Phycologia* 14, 317–330.

Hooper, R. G. and South, G. R. (1977). Distribution and ecology of *Papenfussiella callitricha* (Rosenv.) Kylin (Phaeophyceae, Chordariaceae). *Phycologia* **16**, 153–157.

Jaccard, P. (1908). Nouvelles recherches sur la distribution florale. *Bull. Soc. Vaud. Sci. Nat.* 44, 223–270.

Jardine, N. and Sibson, R. (1971). "Mathematical Taxonomy". Wiley, London.

Lawson, G. W. (1978). The distribution of seaweed floras in the tropical and subtropical Atlantic Ocean: a quantitative approach. *Bot. J. Linn. Soc.* **76**, 177–193.

Lee, R. K. S. (1968). A collection of marine algae from Newfoundland. I. Introduction and Phaeophyta. *Naturaliste can.* **95**, 957–978.

Lee, R. K. S. (1969). A collection of marine algae from Newfoundland. II. Chlorophyta and Rhodophyta. *Naturaliste can.* **96**, 123–145.

Le Gallo, C. (1947). Algues marines des Iles Saint Pierre et Miquelon. *Naturaliste can.* 74, 293–318.

Le Gallo, C. (1949). Esquisse générale de la flore vasculaire des Iles Saint Pierre et Miquelon, suivie d'un supplement sur les algues marines. *Contr. Inst. bot. Univ. Montréal* 65 (Suppl.), 60–81.

Lysaght, A. M. (1971). "Joseph Banks in Newfoundland and Labrador, 1766. His Diary, Manuscripts and Collections". University of California Press, Berkeley.

Mathieson, A. C., Dawes, C. J. and Humm, H. J. (1969). Contributions to the marine algae of Newfoundland. *Rhodora* **71**, 110–159.

Russell, G. (1972). Phytosociological studies on a two zone shore I: Basic pattern. *J. Ecol.* **60**, 539–545.

Sneath, P. H. A. and Sokal, R. R. (1973). "Numerical Taxonomy". W. H. Freeman and Co., San Francisco.

Sokal, R. R. and Michener, C. D. (1958). A statistical method for evaluating systematic relationships. *Univ. Kansas Sci. Bull.* **38**, 1409–1438.

South, G. R. (1970). Checklist of marine algae from Newfoundland, Labrador and the French Islands of St. Pierre and Miquelon. *Mem. Univ. Nfld Mar. Sci. Res. Lab. tech. Rep.* **2**, 1–20.

South, G. R. (1973). Algae Terrae Novae, a new exsiccata of Newfoundland benthic marine algae. *Taxon* **22**, 451–454.

South, G. R. (1976a). Checklist of marine algae from Newfoundland, Labrador and the French Islands of St. Pierre and Miquelon – first revision. *Mem. Univ. Nfld Mar. Sci. Res. Lab. tech. Rep.* **19**, 1–34.

South, G. R. (1976b). Checklist of marine algae of eastern Canada – first revision. *J. mar. biol. Ass. U.K.* **56**, 817–43.

South, G. R. and Cardinal, A. (1970). A checklist of marine algae of eastern Canada. *Can. J. Bot.* **48**, 2077–2095.

South, G. R. and Cardinal, A. (1973). Contributions to the flora of marine algae of eastern Canada, 1. Introduction, historical review and key to the genera. *Naturaliste can.* **100**, 605–630.

South, G. R. and Hooper, R. G. (1976). *Stictyosiphon soriferus* (Phaeophyta, Dictyosiphonales) from Eastern North America. *J. Phycol.* **12**, 24–29.

South, G. R. and Hooper, R. G. (1980). Algae Terrae Novae: exsiccata of Newfoundland benthic marine algae. II. Deposition of Sets. *Taxon* **29**, 97–99.

South, G. R., Hooper, R. G. and Irvine, L. M. (1972). The life history of *Turnerella pennyi* (Harv.) Schmitz. *Br. phycol. J.* **7**, 221–233.

Taylor, W. R. (1957). "Marine Algae of the Northeastern coast of North America". Ann Arbor, University of Michigan.

Whittick, A. (1977). The reproductive ecology of *Plumaria elegans* (Bonnem.) Schmitz (Ceramiaceae: Rhodophyta) at its northern limits in the western Atlantic. *J. exp. mar. Biol. Ecol.* **29**, 223–230.

Whittick, A. (1978). The life history and phenology of *Callithamnion corymbosum* (Rhodophyta: Ceramiaceae) in Newfoundland. *Can. J. Bot.* **56**, 2497–2499.

Whittick, A. and Hooper, R. G. (1977). The reproduction and phenology of *Antithamnion cruciatum* (Rhodophyta: Ceramiaceae) in insular Newfoundland. *Can. J. Bot.* **55**, 520–524.

Whittick, A. and West, J. A. (1979). The life history of a monoecious species of *Callithamnion* (Rhodophyceae, Ceramiaceae) in culture. *Phycologia* **18**, 30–37.

Wilce, R. T. (1959). The marine algae of the Labrador Peninsula and Northwest Newfoundland. (Ecology and Distribution). *Natl Mus. Can. Bull.* **158**, 1–103.

4 | Estuarine Benthic Algae and their Environment: A Review

MARTIN WILKINSON

Department of Brewing and Biological Sciences,
Heriot-Watt University, Edinburgh, Scotland

Abstract: The current state of knowledge concerning the distribution between estuaries, and horizontal and vertical distribution within estuaries, of macrobenthic and microbenthic algae, other than salt-marsh algae, is reviewed. Also reviewed is current information on the effects on the estuarine algae of those environmental factors most likely to influence these distributions. The factor effects are considered from the points of view of both field observations and laboratory tolerance experiments. The literature on the physiological basis of the results of tolerance experiments is also considered. Particular attention is paid to pollution as a factor and to the role of subspecific variation in conditioning estuarine algal distributions; factor effects on the life processes of algae within their distribution ranges are similarly examined.

INTRODUCTION

For this review a narrow definition of an estuary is accepted, namely the lower reaches of a river subject to either or both of the factors of tidal influence and of lowered salinity due to mixing of sea water and fresh water. Comparisons are made with other brackish environments such as fjords and lagoons, which are encompassed within wider definitions of an estuary. Differences in algal vegetation

Systematics Association Special Volume, No. 17(b), "The Shore Environment, Vol. 2: Ecosystems", edited by J. H. Price, D. E. G. Irvine and W. F. Farnham, 1980, pp. 425–486, Academic Press, London and New York.

between these environments might reflect differences in hydrographic conditions and thereby give field evidence as to the effect of particular factors. Within these environments both multicellular benthic algae and benthic microalgae are considered because in some situations they go together inseparably to make up the visible estuarine vegetation. None the less the difference in approach to these groups requires that they should largely be considered separately. Most of the review is devoted to multicellular algae, with occasional comments on microalgae where appropriate. The microalgae are described in a highly selective summary at the end. Salt-marsh algae have been excluded. Most of the published work relates to descriptions of distributions, but causal factors in distribution are here considered as are affects of general estuarine conditions on the algae. Because of the particular pollution problems in estuaries, pollution effects on estuarine algae are described and subspecific variation in this highly variable environment is reviewed. This review is selective, and more detail on salinity as a factor can be found in Gessner and Schramm (1971) and on benthic diatoms in Round (1971).

DISTRIBUTION

1. *Introduction*

A very strong transition exists in estuaries between the two classic environments, the sea and the fresh water. An attempt is made in this section to describe the reaction of fresh water and marine algae to this in terms of the distribution of different species within the transition zone. Because of the pattern of salinity distribution in many estuaries both vertical and horizontal gradients occur on the shore. The differences in distributions between one estuary and another are compared and a brief study of other brackish habitats with different hydrographic regimes is included. Attempts to classify the variation in distribution patterns found have included classification of zones within estuaries, of types of estuary on the basis of algae present and of types of algae on the basis of their distribution patterns in many estuaries. These classifications are presented but found to be insufficiently developed in the present state of knowledge of the algae.

2. Sampling

Sampling of estuarine algae to record distribution can be carried out qualitatively or quantitatively. Qualitative sampling may not reveal all the microscopic or less abundant species. Consequently the technique of culturing salt-marsh mud to isolate microscopic species (Stewart and Pugh, 1963) has been extended to estuarine muds by Gayral and de Mazancourt (1958) and by Lepailleur (1971). A field culture technique for microscopic species is the use of artificial substrata. This technique has, for example, been employed by Moore and McIntire (1977), using PVC plates, to study the distribution of littoral diatoms. Qualitative sampling may indicate horizontal distribution along an estuary in relation to water quality parameters, such as salinity, with the complicating factor of tidal emersion removed by investigating the permanently submerged flora on buoys, as has been done by Grieve and Robertson (1864) and by Milne (1940). Quantitative sampling presents more of a problem for the worker concerned with the multicellular rather than the unicellular algae. The latter have conventionally been sampled quantitatively in a wide range of environments. The techniques of quantification applied to multicellular algae on the open coast, such as direct counting and biomass measurements of individual species, are less applicable in estuaries, where the flora is dominated by mats of green and blue-green algae. Identification requires microscopic examination in the laboratory and individuals of a single species cannot be distinguished from each other. The only practicable approach so far found is to record the percentage frequency of occurrence of each species in point samples of the algal mat taken from 25 different sub-quadrats within a larger quadrat. This technique has been applied to the more marine vegetation at the mouth of the Dee estuary, Cheshire, by Russell (1972) and is currently being applied to upstream mats of algae by Wilkinson (unpublished) and Tittley (personal communication).

3. Identification

After sampling, identification presents a problem with estuarine algae since the variability of estuarine conditions induces plastic responses in morphology. The extent of these responses may vary between estuaries with variation in the hydrographic regime and identification problems are further complicated by the dominance in estuaries of marine taxa which are noted for their taxonomic difficulty, e.g. the genus *Enteromorpha*. Variation is considered in a later section of this review.

One major component of estuarine floras, the genus *Vaucheria*, presents a particular problem in identification to species level. Such identification is necessary since distinct distribution patterns in relation to salinity and other estuarine factors have been shown for *Vaucheria* species by Knutzen (1973) and by Simons (1975). Specific identification depends on observation of reproductive structures, which are rare in field material, and the laboratory treatment of *Vaucheria* after collection to induce formation of reproductive organs has been described by Simons and Vroman (1973).

4. *Horizontal Distribution and Species Composition*

The general pattern of distribution of multicellular algae along estuaries has been described by a number of authors, principally Doty and Newhouse (1954), den Hartog (1971), Tittley and Price (1977), Wilkinson (1973a) and Wilkinson *et al.* (1976), and can be summarized as follows:

(i) Colonization of most of the length of the estuary is by marine species with freshwater species predominating only near the head of the estuary.

(ii) There is a progressive reduction in species number going upstream which is brought about by a selective attenuation, firstly of red and then secondly of brown algae. Green algae, although not necessarily becoming more numerous in terms of species, become relatively more important going upstream.

(iii) In the mid-reaches of the estuary there are a few species confined to brackish-water, such as *Fucus ceranoides** and certain *Vaucheria* spp.

This pattern is repeated through most of the estuaries listed in Table I.

---

*For all species present within the area which it covers, the current British check-list (Parke and Dixon, 1976) has been used as the basis for nomenclature and authorities.

Table I. Some descriptions of multicellular algal distribution in estuaries

Reference	River	Location
Alexander *et al.* (1935)	Tees	N.E. England
Alexander (1932)	Tay	Scotland
Behre (1961)	Weser	W. Germany
Cardinal and Villalard (1971)	St Lawrence	Canada
Conover (1958)	Coonamessatt	N.E. coast, U.S.A.
Cotton (1912)	Newport	Eire
	Bunowen	Eire
	Westport	Eire
Donze (1968)	Umia	Spain
	Ulla	Spain
Doty and Newhouse (1954)	Oyster	N.E. coast, U.S.A.
Edwards (1972)	Tyne	N.E. England
	Tees	N.E. England
	Wear	N.E. England
Gillham (1957)	Exe	S.W. England
den Hartog (1959)	Dutch Delta area[a]	Holland
Holmes (1888)	Blackwater	S.E. England
Lepailleur (1971)	Orne	France
Lindgren (1965)	Two estuaries near Gøtebørg	Sweden
Mathieson and Fralick (1973)	Merrimack	N.E. coast, U.S.A.
	Great Bay	N E. coast, U.S.A.
Mathieson and Fralick (1972)	Hampton-Seabrook	N.E. coast, U.S.A.
Mathieson and Fuller (1969)	Chesapeake Bay	Eastern U.S.A.
	Patuxent	Eastern U.S.A.
Milligan (1965)	Blackwater	S.E. England
Milne (1940)	Tamar	S.W. England
Munda (1972b)	various small estuaries	Iceland
Munda (1978a)	various small estuaries	Iceland
Nelson-Smith (1965, 1967)	Milford Haven	Wales
Nienhuis (1975)	Dutch Delta area[a]	Holland
Price *et al.* (1977)	Boston Haven	E. England
	Nene	E. England
Priou and Serpette (1954)	various	Brittany, France
Wallentinus (1976)	Trosa	Sweden
Tittley and Price (1977)	Thames	E. England
Wildish (1971)	Medway	E. England
Wilkinson (1973a)	Wear	N.E. England
Wilkinson (1973b)	Clyde	Scotland
Wilkinson (1975)	Tarff, Dee	Scotland
	Urr, Fleet	Scotland
Wilkinson and Roberts (1974)	Add	Scotland
Zimmerman and Livingston (1976)	Appalachee	S.E. coast, U.S.A.

[a]This includes the estuaries of the Rivers Rhine, Meuse and Scheldt.

Few authors have detailed distribution of epilithic blue-green algae along estuarine gradients, even though these may be a conspicuous component of estuarine floras. One account where this has been done is that of Priou and Serpette (1954). This general pattern applies to estuaries with both large and small numbers of species. Mathieson and Fralick (1972) have suggested that species number may be greater in larger estuaries, but the author's unpublished observations suggest that in smaller estuaries species total is very variable, probably depending on factors such as sediment loading and degree of pollution.

Attempts to classify estuarine algal distributions have involved recognition of distributions along estuaries, and distributions between estuaries. Some authors have attempted to correlate the distribution of algae along estuaries with the different salinity zones distinguished in large estuaries under the Venice system for the classification of brackish-water (den Hartog, 1959, 1960, 1971; Tittley and Price, 1977). That such a classification is not universally applicable is shown by the slight modifications which Tittley and Price had to make to accommodate data from the Thames estuary. Doty and Newhouse (1954) could not divide the algae of the Oyster River into any zones and, using long-term salinity data supplied by the Clyde River Purification Board, Wilkinson (unpublished) has not been able to subdivide the flora of the Clyde estuary, as given by Wilkinson (1973b), into Venice zones. The major problem in doing this is that each estuary is hydrographically individual and so precisely similar algal distributions in relation to hydrographically correlated factors would not be expected in every estuary. It is also difficult to decide which value of salinity is most meaningful when algae of both long and short life-span are involved. One could consider salinity ranges or means and these could be on a short-term or long-term basis; different approaches would be relevant for different species. Despite the inability of the Venice system to be rigidly applied numerous authors have referred to particular species using Venice terminology, such as "oligohaline" or "mesohaline", clearly indicating that estuarine species must have broadly predictable salinity ranges even though details may differ between different estuaries.

Wilkinson *et al.* (1976) have suggested on the basis of a survey of 15 British estuaries that superimposed on the general pattern described above is a further pattern, on the basis of which the estuaries can be divided into three categories using algae present in the mid and upper reaches as follows:

(i) Mainly Chlorophyta and *Vaucheria* spp.

(ii) Upper part of eulittoral zone occupied mainly by Chlorophyta and *Vaucheria* spp. but lower dominated by *Melosira nummuloides* (Dillw.) C. Ag., a centric diatom forming filaments aggregated together in dense brown mats.

(iii) Chlorophyta, *Vaucheria* spp. and very conspicuous blue-green algae forming gelatinous masses, e.g. *Rivularia* and *Nostoc*.

A survey by Wilkinson (as yet unpublished) of a further 45 estuaries, both large and small, has indicated that most estuaries appear Chlorophyta-dominated, i.e. of category (i). None the less, further examples of category (iii) appear in the literature, e.g. Cotton (1912). Category (ii) has not been reported by any other authors but it is noteworthy that Wilkinson *et al.* correlated the dominance of *M. nummuloides* with organic pollution and other authors, e.g. Munda (1967), have also reported that it is more abundant in such conditions. Abundance would appear to be important in characterizing the flora of an estuary. In Wilkinson's unpublished further survey (see above), he found that species lists for particular estuaries all appeared to be drawn from a common pool of relatively few species while differences between estuaries existed in terms of which species were abundant. This may explain the apparent contradiction between Cotton (1912), who reported that flora of the inner reaches of different estuaries was different, and Munda (1969, 1972b) who has commented on the similarity of the inner flora compared with the difference in the outer flora. The inner flora is likely to be a group of species of wide ecological amplitude while, in the less harsh conditions of the outer estuary, species of lesser amplitude may be at an advantage. Differences in ecological requirements of the inner and outer flora are well illustrated by Mathieson (1978) in the Great Bay estuary system, New Hampshire, where the inner flora consists of seasonally dynamic warm-water species and the outer flora consists of a separate floristic unit, the cold-water perennial species.

Individual species of algae found in estuaries have been classified in a variety of ways according to their distribution. The most basic classification is into marine, freshwater and brackish-water species. Marine species have, in turn, been classified into stenohaline with little tolerance of salinity variation, and euryhaline, with wide salinity tolerance. den Hartog (1971) has described the relative distributions of these categories of species between nine different zones occurring between the freshwater river and the sea in the Dutch Delta Area. The zones were distinguished on the basis of the presence of tidal rise and fall of water level, reversal of current flow with tidal rise and fall, influence of marine salt and influence of fresh water. In the marine environment he recognized a true marine euhalinicum characterized by stenohaline forms, while at the mouth of the estuary was an estuarine euhalinicum, subject to an annual short drop in salinity resulting in colonization by stenohaline annuals rather than stenohaline perennials. In the brackish part of the estuary he recognized three zones, characterized by different salinity or chlorinity ($^0/_{00}$ Cl) limits. These were (i) the polyhalinicum (10–16.5 $^0/_{00}$ Cl) where marine species number was reduced and brackish water species were rare, (ii) the mesohalinicum (1.8–10 $^0/_{00}$ Cl) characterized by large daily salinity fluctuations with a corresponding abundance of brackish-water species and restriction of marine species to very euryhaline ones, and (iii) the oligohalinicum (0.3–1.8 $^0/_{00}$ Cl) with a reduction in brackish species, a further reduction in marine species and the appearance of salt tolerant freshwater species. The freshwater part was subdivided into three estuarine zones in addition to a fourth zone in the true freshwater river. The lowest zone was the marginal freshwater zone in which freshwater moves up and down and current changes direction with the tide. This zone was unstable because of an annual short influx of salt water so that only a few species of each category occur here. The estuarine freshwater zone was similar except for lack of salt penetration. This had a rich freshwater flora and a very small marine element. Upstream of this was the "stuw" zone which still had tidal rise and fall but the current always flowed towards the sea. This was poor in species, which were all freshwater.

Lists of marine species penetrating into each of the brackish-water zones have been presented by various authors. For example, den Hartog (1967) has given lists of indicator species for each zone. These lists are not reproduced here for the meso- and polyhaline zones, since there are differences between authors. Reasons for differences in salinity zone penetration of particular algae in different localities can be found in other environmental factors such as substratum, temperature and the particular pattern of salinity variation. More information is obtained on this by comparing estuarine distributions with those in other brackish habitats, as is done later in this review. Most agreement between authors is found in the species of the oligohaline zone. Nienhuis (1975) lists the following oligohaline zone species from the Dutch Delta area:

(i) Marine species; *Rhodochorton purpureum* (= *Audouinella purpurea*), *Hildenbrandia prototypus* (= *rubra*), *Fucus vesiculosus*, *Urospora penicilliformis*, *Ulothrix flacca*, *U. pseudoflacca*, *U. subflaccida*, *Blidingia marginata*, *Monostroma oxyspermum*.

(ii) Species occurring throughout from fresh to sea water; *Rhizoclonium riparium*, *Blidingia minima*.

(iii) Freshwater species with a slight brackish-water tolerance; *Ulothrix tenerrima* (Kütz.) Kütz., *U. variabilis* (Kütz.) Kütz., *U. oscillarina* Kütz., *Cladophora okamurai* (Ueda) Hoek.

Penetration of freshwater species into estuaries has also been described by Doty (1947), Gillham (1957) and Priou and Serpette (1954), among others.

From the literature it is difficult to define what is meant by a brackish-water species. Most of the algae present, and even dominant, in the brackish reaches of estuaries are present somewhere on the open coast although they may be restricted to more extreme habitats in the intertidal zone, e.g. *Blidingia minima* at the top of the eulittoral zone (den Hartog, 1967). These are therefore euryhaline marine species and may simply be most abundant, in some cases, in estuaries because the estuarine advantage of their wide ecological amplitude puts them at a disadvantage on the open coast when competing with more precisely adapted species. An extreme example of this is *Fucus ceranoides*, which seems to be the most characteristic brackish-water alga in Britain. Its experimentally-determined salinity tolerance suggests that it could survive on the open coast (Burrows, 1964), but in practice it is restricted to the most extreme habitats on the coast where fresh water runs over the rocks during low tide. Simons (1975) has suggested that truly brackish species can be recognized by their ability to reproduce in brackish habitats. Presumably this should indicate that they are growing in near-optimum conditions compared with many euryhaline marine species whose reproduction is impaired at low salinity as described later. Relatively few species appear to be truly brackish-water species. Simons (1975) has given distributional ranges for brackish *Vaucheria* species in Dutch estuaries and Knutzen (1973) has also described the separation of *Vaucheria* into marine and brackish species in Norway. Waern (1952) commented on the paucity of brackish species in river mouths leading into the Baltic as being similar to the case with animals in the Baltic. He gave *Ceramium tenuicorne* (Kütz.) Waern, *Porterinema fluviatile* (Porter) Waern and possibly *Monostroma balticum* (Aresch.) Wittr. as true brackish algae. Since then, Rhodes (1972) has reported *Porterinema* from more saline habitats in the U.S.A. and has concluded that it is euryhaline marine. Another genus which, like *Vaucheria*, has a number of important representatives in brackish water is *Cladophora* but the salinity limits given for various *Cladophora* species by Söderström (1963) show that they are all freshwater and marine forms which extend into brackish environments. It seems therefore that there are relatively few truly brackish-water algae. Species whose optimum growth occurs at reduced salinity in culture might be regarded as brackish (van den Hoek, personal communication). As yet there is insufficient published culture evidence to investigate this idea further.

Two other attempts to classify estuarine algal species are those of Wilkinson (1977b) and of von Wachenfeldt (1969).

Wilkinson recognized three categories:

(i) Species restricted as obvious forms to one particular type of estuary, e.g. *Melosira nummuloides*, and characteristic of that type.

(ii) Species occurring widely throughout most or all of the lengths of most estuaries, e.g. *Enteromorpha intestinalis*.

(iii) Species occurring in most estuaries but restricted to a narrow range or ecological situation within them, e.g. *Monostroma oxyspermum*.

Von Wachenfeldt distinguished the following four groups of species:

(i) Species with a definite inner limit and no effect on morphology, life history or vertical distribution with distance along the salinity gradient, e.g. *Ascophyllum nodosum*.

(ii) Species with a relatively marked inner limit and no effect on morphology, life history or vertical distribution but with decreasing abundance with distance along the salinity gradient, e.g. *Fucus serratus*.

(iii) Species with a diffuse inner limit and with decreasing abundance and with changes in vertical distribution and morphology along the gradient, e.g. *Dilsea edulis* (= *carnosa*).

(iv) Species, with an oscillating inner limit, which are sterile and which decrease in abundance, change in morphology and in vertical distribution, e.g. *Antithamnion plumula*.

The existence of these various species classifications seems confusing, since there does not appear to be any great degree of correlation between one classification and another. den Hartog's and Nienhuis's classification is based on the application of the Venice system and other criteria to one large estuarine complex, while Wilkinson's classification is based on a comparison of distributions between a large number of estuaries, all of which are smaller than those of den Hartog and Nienhuis. von Wachenfeldt's classification is based on the more stable situation of a salinity gradient in the Baltic Sea and in these stable conditions is characterized by the intervention of large numbers of marine species. As synoptic studies are undertaken on estuarine algae and more work is done on physiological ecology of the algae, it should become possible to present a more universally applicable classification of estuarine species.

The classifications of estuarine species described above have assumed that each estuarine species is abundant under one particular set of conditions. However, some estuarine algae have a bimodal distribution with abundance under contrasting sets of conditions and absence or relative rarity in intermediate situations, e.g. *Phormidium corium* (= *Schizothrix rubella*) in the cleanest and most polluted parts of a sewage polluted fjord (Munda, 1967). As detailed later, *Capsosiphon fulvescens* has been described from very unpolluted situations and also as characteristic of sewage pollution.

Species distribution patterns in estuaries may change with season as a result of rainfall (altering salinity or hydrographic regimes) or of temperature changes affecting salinity tolerance. Seasonal migration of *Stilophora rhizodes* in the Coonamessatt River (Conover, 1958) is an example of this. Not all algae respond to such changes. *Petalonia fascia* did not migrate seasonally in the Coonamessatt River, while den Hartog (1970) has described another less regular situation; an abnormally dry summer in 1959 when there was a 20 km displacement of the 0.3 ‰ Cl isohaline in the Dutch Delta estuaries. This was accompanied by an upstream movement of *Porphyra umbilicalis* but the other fast-growing pioneer species (including *Petalonia fascia*) did not migrate upstream. It has even been suggested by Doty (1947) that fast-growing species might utilize the interval between successive spring tides, this in order to explain the occurrence of the freshwater species *Ulothrix zonata* (Web. et Mohr) Kütz. in mouths of creeks reached by the highest spring tides in Oregon.

Finally, species distribution may be modified by factors in estuaries other than the salinity gradient. For example, Niemeck and Mathieson (1976) have reported a patchy distribution for *Fucus spiralis* in the Great Bay System, New Hampshire, within a wide salinity tolerance range (3–32‰), as a result of its being confined to certain types of rock, and den Hartog (1967) has reported that *Bangia* and *Rhizoclonium* in the Dutch Delta estuaries only extend through to fresh water under polluted conditions.

5. Vertical Distribution

Since estuaries are tidal they show a vertical zonation pattern of intertidal algae. This is modified from the particular pattern of the open coast by the reduction in species present. A further difference from the open coast is that the water which covers the intertidal zone at high tide may be stratified with respect to salinity. This may reinforce and intensify the gradient of increasing euryhalinity with increasing height on the shore suggested for open coast plants by den Hartog (1968). This intensification might lead one to expect a particularly well-marked vertical zonation pattern, while the variation in hydrographic conditions and hence in salinity distribution with depth from one estuary to another might give rise to variation in the zonation pattern between estuaries. Chapman (1973) has suggested that the primary determinant in open coast vertical algal zonation is interspecific competition. With the reduced number of species going upstream interspecific competition could be reduced, resulting in less well-defined zonation. Also a reduction in competition going upstream is likely to be accompanied by increasing variability in the physical and chemical environment. This may result in a change from biotic to abiotic causes as primary determinants of vertical zonation in estuaries.

In the absence of experiments specifically designed to test the points above it is not possible to reach definite conclusions. However, a comparison of vertical distributions reported in the literature provides circumstantial evidence in support.

The accounts of vertical distribution are given by Behre (1961), Cotton (1912), Donze (1968), den Hartog (1959), Hopkins (1964b), Munda (1972b), Nienhuis (1975), Price *et al.* (1977), Priou and Serpette (1954), Tittley and Price (1977), Russell (1972) and Cox (1977a). Combining these results with unpublished observations of the present author the following generalizations can be made:

(i) A well-marked pattern of vertical zonation does exist in many estuaries.

(ii) Bands of fucoids may be present in the outer parts of an estuary but the vertical salinity gradient at high tide is reflected in the replacement of uppermost bands of fucoids, e.g. of *Pelvetia*, with more euryhaline green algae such as *Blidingia* and *Rhizoclonium*.

(iii) In estuaries which are completely flushed by fresh water at low tide, fucoids may be replaced below low water mark by other euryhaline algae such as *Enteromorpha*.

(iv) In upper parts of estuaries, fucoid bands are replaced by bands of smaller species, particularly important band-forming species in British estuaries being *Rhizoclonium riparium*, *Blidingia minima*, *Phormidium* spp., *Vaucheria* spp., *Audouinella purpurea*, *Enteromorpha intestinalis*, *E. prolifera* and *Monostroma oxyspermum*.

In the most upstream parts the top band may be dominated by bryophytes and in completely flushed estuaries the *Enteromorpha* band at the bottom may be replaced by or mixed with aquatic mosses such as *Fontinalis*. Some vertical zonation patterns are shown in Fig. 1.

Russell (1972) worked on a shore at the mouth of the Dee estuary in Cheshire which showed a relatively marine flora. None the less, the zonation pattern differed from that of the open coast in being a two-zone shore with a sharp distinction between the littoral fringe and the eulittoral zone; the third zone of the open coast, the sub-littoral fringe, was missing and this was attributed to the presence of sand and mud. Cox (1977a) suggested that such two-zone shores might be the normal situation in the lower reaches of estuaries since these are normally more turbid than open coastal areas. She illustrated her suggestion using the vertical distribution of tube-dwelling diatoms

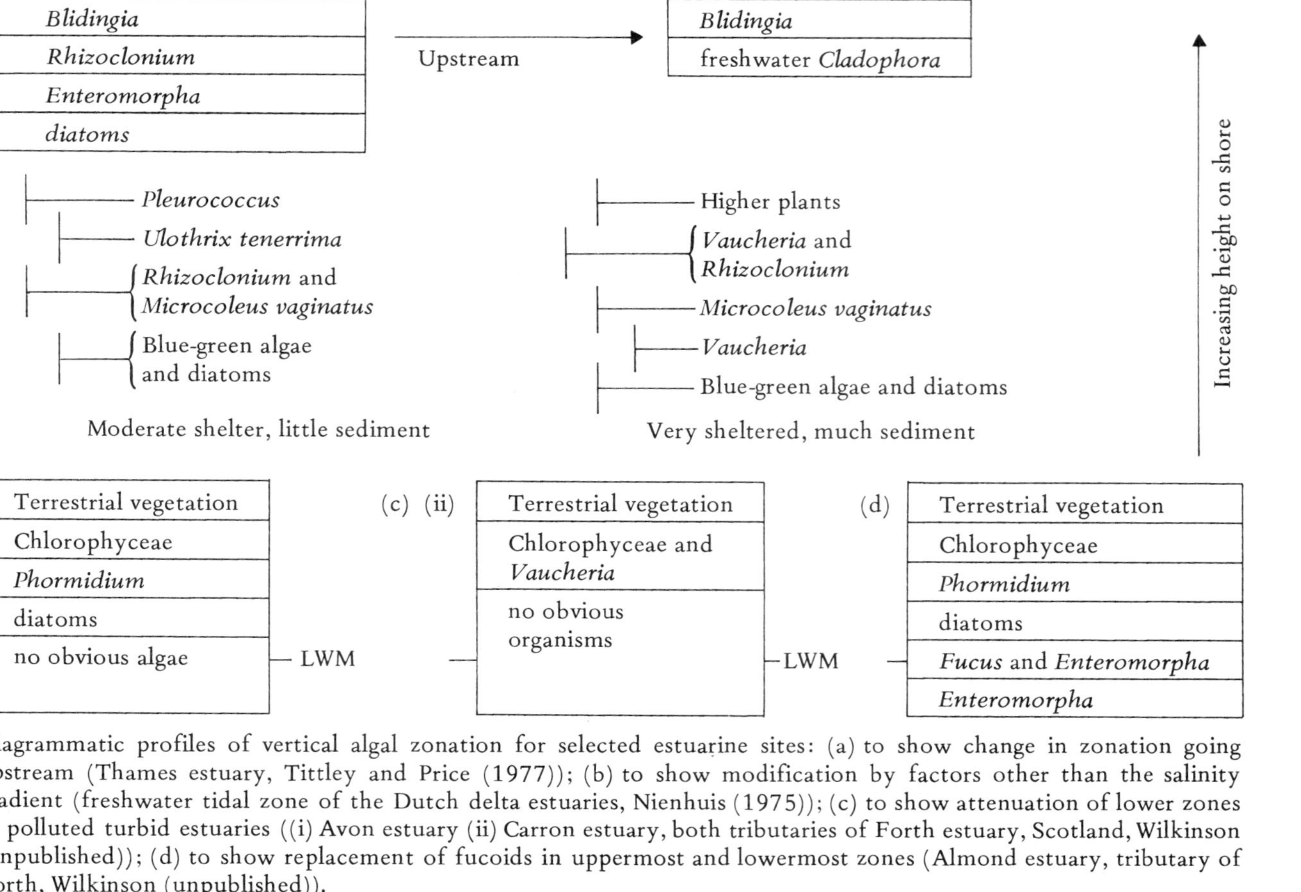

Fig. 1. Diagrammatic profiles of vertical algal zonation for selected estuarine sites: (a) to show change in zonation going upstream (Thames estuary, Tittley and Price (1977)); (b) to show modification by factors other than the salinity gradient (freshwater tidal zone of the Dutch delta estuaries, Nienhuis (1975)); (c) to show attenuation of lower zones in polluted turbid estuaries ((i) Avon estuary (ii) Carron estuary, both tributaries of Forth estuary, Scotland, Wilkinson (unpublished)); (d) to show replacement of fucoids in uppermost and lowermost zones (Almond estuary, tributary of Forth, Wilkinson (unpublished)).

in the lower Severn estuary and showed (Cox, 1977a, b) that there was a correspondence between the vertical heights reached on the shore by each species and its horizontal penetration along the salinity gradient. She noted that the tube-dwelling diatoms exhibited brackish-water submergence, i.e. a tendency for species which are intertidal at high salinities to descend in vertical level eventually becoming sublittoral in brackish-water. den Hartog (1968) has distinguished three types of brackish-water submergence in algae:

(i) Upper limit submergence where only the upper limit becomes reduced in level, due possibly to salinity stratification or to reduction of tides so that sublittoral species cannot penetrate the eulittoral zone.

(ii) Basal submergence where the lower limit goes down with decreasing salinity, presumably because this removes competition by stenohaline species. Many of the euryhaline green algae such as *Enteromorpha*, *Rhizoclonium*, and *Ulothrix* fall into this category.

(iii) Total submergence where both upper and lower limits go down with decreasing salinity. This is more characteristic of areas such as the Baltic than of true estuaries. Intertidal species follow a particular isohaline downwards until light penetration becomes limiting.

Two examples of brackish-water submergence from British estuaries are (i) Chater's (1927) description of *Fucus ceranoides* in the Aberdeenshire Dee appearing in the *Fucus spiralis* zone at the seaward end and gradually broadening its limits going upstream, and (ii) Edwards's (1975) statement that *Prasiola stipitata* and *Rosenvingiella polyrhiza* in the Rivers Tyne, Tees and Wear occur at a lower level in the estuary than on the surrounding open coast.

Factors other than the salinity gradient may bring about changes in the vertical zonation. Nienhuis (1975) has presented, for the Dutch Delta estuaries, three possible vertical zonation patterns which occur under different combinations of shelter and sediment loading in the freshwater tidal area. Tittley and Price (1977) have shown that the physical nature of the substratum, e.g. brick or concrete, can have a profound influence on zonation pattern in the mid-reaches of the Thames estuary.

6. Comparison with some other Brackish Habitats

The distribution patterns described above are at present so poorly known that a number of unresolved problems are seen. One approach to determining the factors affecting distributions of particular estuarine species might be to compare distributions between environments of known but differing salinity patterns. This is suggested as a deliberate exercise in comparing unlike situations. The concept of using a control estuary against which to judge distributions in another as suggested by Alexander (1932), Alexander *et al.* (1935) and Edwards (1972) is a different type of exercise in which it is erroneously assumed that two estuaries can be assumed to be hydrographically similar. Such a practice has been condemned by Gray (1976). Other habitats which can validly be compared with estuaries, provided hydrographic differences are understood, include fjords, saline lagoons and the Baltic Sea.

Fjordic estuaries usually differ from typical coastal plain estuaries in the relatively large volume of sea water compared with fresh water, giving rise to a marked stratification. Combined with low turbidity, this seems to result in a well-developed sublittoral vegetation of marine-derived species exhibiting brackish-water submergence. The salinity fluctuations occur mainly in the surface layers and are on a seasonal basis (connected with melting snow) rather than on a daily basis. This offers relatively stable reduced salinity conditions at the surface. The result is greater penetration upstream of red and brown euryhaline marine algae. An example is *Dictyosiphon*, which has been found at salinities in fjords lower than those at which it occurs in estuaries. This has been reported from Icelandic fjords (Munda, 1969, 1972b, 1978a, b), the Hardangerfjord, Norway (Jorde and Klavestad, 1963), and the Oslofjord (Sundene, 1953). Breivik (1958) has correlated the absence of red and brown algae from the surface waters of the innermost part of a small Norwegian fjord with the fact that the species concerned are summer forms and the surface salinity is reduced in summer. It seems possible, therefore, to speculate that turbidity restricts the sublittoral vegetation in estuaries and the extent of fluctuation in salinity inhibits intertidal penetration of red and brown algae. There could, however, be other reasons restricting red and brown algae. For example, Lein *et al.* (1974) have suggested that pollution from a paper mill restricts red and brown algal penetration of the Iddefjord. None the less, comparison with further environments will show the importance of salinity stability.

Reports of algal distribution in the brackish lagoons on the Texas coast (Conover, 1958, 1964; Edwards and Kapraun, 1973) show red and brown algae existing in quantity at lower salinities than in estuaries. This may be correlated with the fact that, as in fjords, the salinity varies on a seasonal rather than on a daily basis. A problem in comparing the Texas lagoons with the estuaries of north-west Europe lies in the temperature difference since, as discussed elsewhere in this review, salinity tolerance varies with temperature.

No such problems exist in comparison with the Baltic Sea, which offers the best evidence for the role of salinity stability. The Baltic is a virtually tideless sea with a gentle salinity gradient from full sea water in the North Sea to almost fresh water at its innermost end around Finland. Salinity variations are relatively small at any particular site in the Baltic. Under these conditions, many marine species can penetrate to much lower salinities than in estuaries, as shown by the salinity limits for a variety of species in the two environments given by den Hartog (1967). The same argument applies to the ability of freshwater species to penetrate downstream. This reaches its climax in the Baltic, where the two most important belt-forming organisms in parts of the inner Baltic can be the freshwater species *Cladophora glomerata* and the marine species *Fucus vesiculosus* in the one vertical profile. As in fjords, the clear waters of the Baltic are able to support rich sublittoral vegetation even at low salinity. All the above points are illustrated by many papers on Baltic algae. A few noteworthy examples are Kristiansen (1972), Ravanko (1968), Waern (1952, 1965) and Wallentinus (1976).

The conclusions to be drawn from these comparative studies are that fluctuating salinity and heavy silt load are probably important factors influencing algal distributions in an estuary. Proof of this can only come from laboratory and field experimentation on particular factors or combinations of factors.

EFFECTS OF ENVIRONMENTAL FACTORS

1. Introduction

Although most of the algae colonizing estuaries are marine in origin this review has been specifically restricted to effects which have been reported from observations in estuaries and to consideration, in particular, of salinity as an environmental factor, because of its importance in estuaries and its lack of consideration in many marine investigations. Comparing the marine and estuarine environments, Wilkinson (1977a) has selected six factors which are thought most likely to influence algal distribution within and between estuaries. These are:

(i) salinity distribution;
(ii) chemical composition of the fresh-water inflow;
(iii) altered biotic relationships resulting from reduced species diversity in estuaries;
(iv) heterotrophic potential of the algae in relation to loading with organic materials and reduction of light penetration;
(v) turbidity and sediment loading;
(vi) nature of the substratum.

The effect of each of these factors in regulating estuarine algal distribution will be reviewed. Other changes in algae which occur within their distribution range, e.g. limitation of size or of reproductive potential, will be considered in a later section of this review since these effects cannot, in the main, be ascribed as yet to any particular environmental factor.

The literature on the effects of all these factors, except for salinity, in estuaries is very sparse. This is probably a reflection of a widely held belief that salinity is the overriding factor in estuaries. However, the review will show that within a plant's salinity range its distribution may be determined by other factors such as substratum availability (e.g. the example, already quoted, of *Fucus spiralis* distribution reported by Niemeck and Mathieson, 1976). Two further complicating factors in estuaries are:

(i) The hydrographic pattern of the estuary may modify several factors simultaneously, so that these factors are correlated and their effects cannot easily be unravelled from field investigations. Two examples are the correlation of salinity and exposure reported by Donze (1968) and the correlation of salinity and temperature reported by Hanisak (1979).
(ii) Not only the range of variation but also the duration of extreme values of factors need to be considered. This approach was used to explain the penetration of an estuary by the freshwater red alga *Lemanea fucina* [= *Sacheria*

fucina (Borg) Sirodot] on the basis of its time-intensity tolerance to salinity (Wood and Straughan, 1953).

The methods available for study of factor effects fall broadly into two fields:

(i) correlation of observed field distributions with measurements of environmental factors;

(ii) tolerance experiments.

The correlation of distributions with factor measurements is a difficult approach because of the problem of obtaining representative measurements of highly variable environmental factors. Even if a large measurement programme can be mounted, there remains the problem of which particular values of any factor to use. Short-term averages might be more meaningful when considering algae of short life-span, but long-term averages are likely to be more accurate. Extremes have to be tolerated by the algae, yet den Hartog (1970) has advocated the use of long-term averages. In den Hartog's situation, dealing with large estuaries such as that of the River Rhine, the extremes will not regularly vary by large amounts from average values and such small variations can probably be tolerated by euryhaline algae. However, when present in small completely flushed estuaries a plant may have to withstand salinity fluctuations on most tides of most of the range between fresh water and sea water. Despite the difficulties there have been such attempts to correlate algal distribution and factor intensity as that of Conover (1958). Some workers, as explained below, have attempted to test field correlations by a further stage of experimental tolerance testing, but this approach has been partially refuted by McIntire (1978) who has suggested that a more precise approach to field correlation using multivariate mathematical techniques such as ordination, principal components analysis, canonical correlation and so on, is more meaningful. McIntire obtained interesting and good factor correlations working on diatoms. As yet, no-one has applied these techniques to multicellular algae in estuaries so their full value in this field cannot be assessed.

It is probably true that tolerance experiments on single factors yield a limited amount of useful information. This approach can be improved in a number of ways:

(i) Performance of experiments in which combined effects of several factors can be investigated simultaneously, e.g. the work of Prange (1978) on *Blidingia minima*. Most workers have simply varied parameters of water chemistry simultaneously. This only requires a simple set-up with a single culture vessel for each combination of conditions. A more complex approach is to simulate physical factors such as desiccation and tidal movement simultaneously with chemical factors, as has been done for benthic diatoms in a special apparatus by Wulff and McIntire (1972) and by McIntire and Wulff (1969).

(ii) Russell and Fielding (1974) have introduced a further dimension into tolerance-testing by investigating, using a modification of the de Wit replacement series technique, the effects of various combined levels of factors on competition between species in mixed culture. They pointed out that this technique could not so easily be applied to algae as to higher plants because of complications arising from the non-linear nature of the sigmoid algal growth curve. They were able to circumvent this problem by using a modified method in which three species were tested in all possible combinations of any two species.

(iii) Tolerance experiments can also be extended by transplanting organisms in the field from one set of conditions to another and observing survival and growth. Pollution effects in brackish water on *Ascophyllum* have, for example, been studied in this way by Rueness (1973).

2. Salinity

Although there have been numbers of studies of horizontal distributions of algae along estuaries (Table I) only a few of these have given specific salinity values for the extent of penetration of various species. In order to find a reasonable number of papers quoting salinity limits it is necessary to include environments with seasonal rather than daily salinity fluctuations, e.g. the Texas lagoons. Salinity limits for particular species have been quoted, among others, by Chater (1927), Druehl (1978), Conover (1964), Edwards and Krapraun (1973), Jorde and Klavestad (1963), Mathieson and Fuller (1969), Nienhuis (1975), and Söderström (1963). Comparison of these lists shows that, even allowing for differences in salinity variability between different types of environments, some species appear to have the same tolerance in different localities while others appear to have different tolerances. For example, *Petalonia fascia* was regarded by Edwards and Kapraun as stenohaline, being restricted to 26–30 ‰ salinity, but Munda (1978b) reported it as a component of the mesohalinicum in Icelandic fjords and Kristiansen (1972) has reported it from salinities as low as 9 ‰ in the Baltic Sea. Similarly, *Cladophora albida* is also reported as stenohaline (26–30 ‰) by Edwards and Kapraun but has been found at salinities as low as 15‰ in the Baltic Sea by Söderström (1963). den Hartog (1959) has reported *Porphyra leucosticta* from the polyhalinicum, with variable salinity, of Dutch estuaries and also from an environment with stable polyhaline salinity in a canal. These three species are merely given as examples and further instances could be quoted. They illustrate how dangerous it is to believe that a salinity limit determined for a species by field observation in one locality will necessarily apply in other localities. This probably results from the following three points:

(i) The degree of stability of the salinity may vary from habitat to habitat.
(ii) Other environmental factors may override or interact with salinity in setting distributional limits.
(iii) Separate races for salinity tolerance may exist within a single species.

Considering first the stability of salinity, den Hartog (1967) has demonstrated that marine species penetrate to much lower salinities in the stable salinities of the Baltic Sea than in the variable environment of Dutch estuaries. In the examples quoted above, a possible exception to this general rule is seen in *Porphyra leucosticta*, which shows broadly the same tolerance to lowered salinity in both stable and unstable environments. As a polyhaline species, it has only a slight tolerance to lowered salinity and perhaps indicates that a marked effect of the degree of variability of salinity is most likely to be seen in those species with the widest overall salinity tolerance. It would seem that the reaction to variable salinity may be as important a factor as the level of salinity itself. An example which might support this is a consideration of two species with contrasting distribution patterns. Nienhuis (1975) has reported that *Rhizoclonium riparium*, which can grow in a full range of salinities from fresh to sea water, is most abundant in parts of the Dutch Delta estuaries where the salinity fluctuations are greatest. den Hartog (1972) has pointed out that *Bangia atropurpurea*, a species which can also withstand all salinities within the range from full sea water to fresh water, is absent in the Dutch Delta from intermediate habitats with a fluctuating salinity. Two attempts to classify species on salinity tolerance have not fully taken account of this:

(i) Edwards and Kapraun (1973) recognized three groups of species on the basis of the range of salinity fluctuation tolerated in a Texas lagoon:

very euryhaline	salinity range	21–40 ‰
euryhaline		11–20 ‰
stenohaline		10 ‰ or less

This classification is based solely on range and takes no account of absolute values tolerated.

(ii) Jorde and Klavestad (1963) distinguished two types of species in the Hardangerfjord:
  (a) those species which tolerate great changes in salinity and are tolerant especially to very low salinities;
  (b) those species with a narrower tolerance range which only penetrate upstream to higher average salinities and colonize relatively stable situations.

While Jorde and Klavestad's classification does take account of both range and actual limits, it can still only be applied to the environment in which it was determined since it does not account for apparently different limits quoted for the same species by different authors. The explanations of this phenomenon may lie in the modifying or interacting effects of other factors with salinity.

There are reports in the literature of salinity limits for distribution being modified by temperature, substratum, sediments, pollution and nutrients.

Temperature may affect distributions by regulating salinity tolerance. The experimental demonstration of this will be considered later. At this stage field evidence only is presented. Druehl (1978), in a study of the distribution of *Macrocystis integrifolia* Bory in lowered salinity waters off the coast of British Columbia, noted that the species was present in localities where low salinities occurred during winter (i.e. the colder season) or where there was little seasonal variation of salinity and temperature. This suggests that salinity reduction is better tolerated at low temperature and this is in accord with the differences in salinity range for *Petalonia* in the Baltic and in the Texas lagoons already quoted. The higher salinity tolerance was seen in the Baltic, which was the colder environment. Conover (1964), working in Texas lagoons, recognized two types of species distribution: from normal to hyposaline conditions and from normal to hypersaline conditions. He found that lowered temperature in the water increased the tolerance of the former to lower salinities and the latter to higher salinities. However, other examples present exactly the opposite situation. Jorde and Klavestad (1959) have shown that *Stictyosiphon* is present in high salinities on the open coast only when temperature is low; when the temperature rises, it only survives in the lower salinities within a fjord where it is dominant. In this case tolerance of low salinities is increased with increasing temperature. This is the situation which has been reported as explaining the greater species diversity of tropical estuaries compared with temperate ones (Doty and Newhouse, 1954). The solution to this apparent contradiction may lie in considering a third factor which is directly related to salinity and temperature. Conover (1958) noted that species distributions were more precisely correlated with density of the water than with its salinity. Salinity is the major property of the water which gives rise to its density. Salinity does not vary with temperature but density does. Hence density is a single factor which is the combined result of salinity and temperature. Although Conover found a correlation with density, he suggested it was only apparent and perhaps not meaningful. The most likely way in which density could be implicated is that it, and not salinity, determines the movement of a parcel of water relative to other parcels of water and hence sets up the stratification pattern. By favouring particular densities, a species may be adhering to a specific parcel of water with a particular chemical composition and concomitant effects. This does seem unlikely, since the same parcel of water would have a different density at a different temperature and then the correlation would break down. However, no firm conclusion can be reached.

Since the sea water and fresh water which mix to produce brackish water in an estuary are not only of a different salinity but sometimes also at different temperatures, a temperature gradient which parallels the salinity gradient can be formed along an estuary. Malinowski and Ramus (1973) concluded from a field study that *Codium fragile* ssp.

tomentosoides was limited by a certain combination of salinity and temperature, but Hanisak (1979) has pointed out that the correlation in the field between salinity and temperature masks the effects of either factor taken singly; he has shown experimentally that the salinity tolerance of this plant is wider than Malinowski and Ramus had deduced. This example illustrates the difficulty in inferring environmental factor effects from field studies without the use of sophisticated mathematical techniques or of tolerance experiments.

An example of the effect of substratum is given by Gillham (1957) who concluded that the nature of the substratum was more important than salinity in fixing the upstream limit of *Fucus ceranoides* in the Exe estuary in Devon. Regarding the effect of exposure, Jorde and Klavestad (1960) have suggested that *Sphacelaria plumosa* has a wide salinity tolerance but its occurrence in many low salinity environments in the Norwegian fjords is prevented by a requirement for a high degree of shelter from wave action, so that a field study of its distribution would show a greater correlation with exposure than with salinity. Pekkari (1973) has described the occurrence of *Fucus vesiculosus* beyond its normal inner salinity limit in the Baltic when the water is enriched with nutrients from sewage. In one particular locality in the inner Baltic (Brahestad), this results in *F. vesiculosus* living in an otherwise freshwater-type environment. Similarly, den Hartog (1967) has observed in Holland that *Rhizoclonium riparium* and *Bangia atropurpurea* only penetrate right through estuaries to the freshwater zone under polluted conditions. Lein *et al.* (1974) have reported that fucoids penetrate further into the Iddefjord in polluted localities and they suggested that pollution rather than salinity limits the distributions. An opposite phenomenon has been described by Lindgren (1965), who found *Cladophora rupestris*, *Fucus spiralis* and "*Trailliella intricata*" to have a higher salinity limit under polluted conditions. Since he was comparing a polluted and an unpolluted estuary which could have varied in many other features, it is possible that salinity was not the important factor.

Two processes seem to be involved in the examples cited above. In the case of substratum and exposure effects a plant is not able to occupy its full salinity tolerance range because it has a narrower range for another environmental factor. In the case of temperature effects, the plant's, and possibly the nutrients', physiological tolerance to salinity may itself be modified through the action of another environmental factor. Which of these processes is at work in a particular situation can only be determined by carrying out experimental work on tolerances.

Experimental studies on the effects of salinity on algae fall into three classes which will be considered separately. These are:

(i) experiments on survival and growth rates;

(ii) experiments on a wide variety of cytological and developmental phenomena;

(iii) experiments on the rates of photosynthesis and respiration.

Experiments on survival and growth at different salinities have been carried out as shown in Table II. Studies have been carried out therefore on a wide range of species characteristic of different situations. In general there is a correspondence shown in these experiments between salinity tolerance and distribution in nature; the wider the salinity tolerance, the greater the upstream penetration of the species. This is in accord with the early work of Biebl (1952) who divided open coast algae into three categories on the basis of, among other factors, their tolerance to salinity. He distinguished sublittoral, low-water and tide pool, and intertidal species, and showed that the salinity tolerance of each category was related to the extent of salinity fluctuations in each of the three environments in the field.

It seems likely that some of the salinity tolerance ranges reported in these experiments are wider than those apparently tolerated in nature by the species concerned. An extreme example of this is the survival of freshwater algae in about 60% sea water (Munda, 1972a). This is well exemplified by a comparison of *Fucus ceranoides* and *F. serratus* (Burrows, 1964). These species are restricted in nature, *F. serratus* to the lower littoral and upper sublittoral of the open coast, *F. ceranoides* to the brackish reaches of estuaries. Yet in culture they both tolerated a similarly wide range of salinities. The difference appeared when Burrows modified the experiments by providing a daily alternation of salinities. *F. ceranoides* then fared much better than *F. serratus*. This higher tolerance to fluctuating salinity in *F. ceranoides* is in accord with its occurrence in brackish parts of estuaries. The importance of variation of salinity tolerance with age of plant was also illustrated by Burrows. *F. ceranoides* eggs developed resistance to fresh water much more quickly than those of *F. serratus*, making successful reproduction of *F. ceranoides* more likely under estuarine conditions.

Table II. Some experiments in which survival and growth have been measured at different salinities for marine, estuarine and freshwater algae

Species	Author
Cladophora fracta	Munda (1972a)
Blidingia minima	Prange (1978)
Enteromorpha intestinalis	Reed and Russell (1978a, b); Black (1971)
E. flexuosa	Townsend and Lawson (1972)
Eugomontia sacculata	Wilkinson (1974)
Rhizocolonium riparium	Nienhuis (1975)
Ulothrix flacca	Russell and Fielding (1974)
Fucus vesiculosus	Munda (1977a); Boyle and Doty (1949)
F. ceranoides	Burrows (1964)
F. serratus	Burrows (1964)
Chorda filum	Norton and South (1969)
Saccorhiza polyschides	Norton and South (1969)
Ectocarpus siliculosus	Russell and Fielding (1974)
Sphaerotrichia divaricata	Boyle and Doty (1949)
Polysiphonia lanosa	Boney (1964)
Bangia atropurpurea	den Hartog (1972); Sheath and Cole (1978)
Erythrotrichia carnea	Russell and Fielding (1974)
Delesseria sanguinea	Hoffman (1959)
Caloglossa leprieurii (Mont.) J. Ag.	Yarish *et al.* (1977)
Bostrychia radicans Mont.	Yarish *et al.* (1977)
Benthic diatoms	Admiraal (1977b); Wulff and McIntire (1972)
Melosira nummuloides	Wilkinson *et al.* (1976)
Phormidium spp.	Stam and Holleman (1975)
Tribonema vulgare Pascher	Munda (1972a)
Vaucheria geminata Heering	Munda (1972a)

The interaction of factors other than salinity variation with straight salinity tolerance has been shown in some of the experiments. The factors concerned are temperature, desiccation, light intensity, calcium levels and competition from other species.

Ohno (1969) found that the optimum salinity for growth of various intertidal algae decreased when temperature was decreased in culture. Decreased temperature also increased tolerance to lower salinity in *Sphaerotrichia divaricata* according to Boyle and Doty (1949), who found that 80% of sea water did not cause low salinity injury at 6°C but did so at higher temperatures. Wilkinson *et al.* (1976) found that the centric diatom *Melosira nummuloides* was tolerant of lower salinities at lower temperatures. All three examples suggest wider salinity tolerance at lower temperature, but Hanisak (1979) has given a slightly wider tolerance range in culture at *higher* temperature for *Codium fragile* ssp. *tomentosoides* which grew from 18–42‰ at 12°C but 18–48‰ at 18° and 24°C. Therefore it would appear that the varying effect of temperature on salinity tolerance, already described from field results, may also be found in survival and growth experiments.

The interaction of salinity and desiccation has been studied in *Enteromorpha flexuosa* in Ghana by Townsend and Lawson (1972) who found, using a tide-simulating machine, that desiccation resistance was linearly related to the salinity at which the plants had been cultured. In contrast to this is the result of Schramm and Ohno (1973), who found that salinities in the range 5–40‰ did not affect the rate of water-loss on drying of *Fucus vesiculosus*. It is not safe to conclude on such limited evidence that different algae respond in different ways. Schramm and Ohno used an artificial seawater medium, while Townsend and Lawson used natural sea water diluted with distilled water. Ionic ratios would therefore be different in the two media at the same salinities and this could have some, as yet undetected, effect on the ability of the plant to control water loss. It is particularly interesting in this context that den Hartog (1968) has suggested that the higher a plant grows in the intertidal zone of the open coast the greater its salinity tolerance as well as its desiccation tolerance will need to be. It is therefore not unreasonable to expect a relation between tolerance to salinity and to desiccation.

One particular ion has been linked with salinity tolerance but not with desiccation tolerance of plants. Hoffman (1959) found that an increased level of calcium in the culture medium allows *Delesseria sanguinea* to survive at otherwise fatal salinities of 10, 5 and 1‰. There are a number of other records, described later, of calcium and of other ions affecting the response to salinity of photosynthesis and respiration but no further results have been found relating to overall growth.

Unexpectedly, light intensity has been linked by experiments to the physiological tolerance of plants to salinity rather than just found to be a modifying factor limiting distribution within a salinity tolerance range. Wulff and McIntire (1972) cultured assemblages of benthic diatoms in a laboratory model ecosystem under various conditions of light intensity, salinity, temperature and dessication; they found that a sudden change in salinity had a much greater effect on the diatom assemblages at higher light than at lower light intensity. The effect was mainly in the form of a reduction in diversity index.

Another of the more complex type of tolerance experiment in which light intensity has been studied is the competition experiment, based on the de Wit replacement series, of Russell and Fielding (1974). Competition between *Ulothrix flacca*, *Erythrotrichia carnea*, and *Ectocarpus siliculosus* was investigated under various combinations of salinity, light intensity and temperature. They found that all three species appeared to lose competitive ability at low salinity and suggested that this was in accord with the less sharp zonation patterns in estuaries.

Besides competition, another important biotic factor is grazing. Wilkinson *et al.* (1976) observed that the centric diatom *Melosira nummuloides* was present as a littoral form in the Clyde estuary, Scotland, over a much narrower salinity range than its experimentally determined one. Field culture experiments in cages which excluded periwinkles suggested that it could survive well outside its normal range in the estuary if grazing was controlled.

So far the results of experiments above have been described on the intuitive assumption that results for a particular species will apply to all members of that species. However, it was suggested earlier that geographical differences in field observations of salinity limits might be explained by the existence of different races within a species. There is evidence that salinity tolerance determined experimentally is different for different populations of a species. For example, Munda (1977a) found that *Fucus vesiculosus* from Helgoland was less tolerant than material from Iceland and the Baltic. This and other examples are discussed further in the section of this review on intraspecific variation.

The cytological and developmental phenomena experimentally studied in relation to salinity are chloride loss, cell division, regeneration and various parts of the reproductive process.

Ohno (1976) found that chloride loss after transfer to distilled water increased linearly with the salinity at which plants had been cultured. More interestingly, the loss was greater at all salinities for sublittoral than for intertidal species. It is conceivable that at low salinities, where external chloride is very low, the sublittoral plants' intracellular chloride level is much more likely to drop to a very low level than that of the intertidal plants. Since intracellular chloride has been shown to be necessary for photosynthesis (Bové *et al.*, 1963), this could explain the difference in survival at reduced salinity for sublittoral and intertidal species as reported by Biebl (1952). If similar differences in ability to retain chloride were found between open coast and estuarine species this might provide a partial physiological explanation of salinity tolerance of estuarine algae. This has not so far been demonstrated.

Brown (1977) has observed salinity effects on cell division. He found that *Stichococcus bacillaris* grew in culture from freshwater salinities right through to 40 ‰ artificial sea water. Cell division was maximum at low salinity, 2 ‰, but adherence of cells was greater at high salinity so that chain length increased with increasing salinity. Eaton *et al.* (1966) found that a wide range of salinities had no effect on regenerative capacity of cut fragments of *Enteromorpha intestinalis*. The importance of this conclusion may lie in allowing reproduction by fragmentation at low salinity when other reproductive processes may be impaired. There is evidence that reproduction of *E. intestinalis* by zoospores is affected by salinity. This process can be considered in four stages, each of which is affected. Kapraun (1970) suggested that some *Enteromorpha* species produced spores best in a salinity below that which was best for growth. Lersten and Voth (1960) found that swarmers of *E. intestinalis* were discharged most readily in full sea water and this was inhibited at low salinity. Black (1971) found that zoospores did not survive after release in fresh water and Christie and Shaw (1968) found that settlement of zoospores was poor at low salinity. On balance these results suggest that reproduction by spores would be considerably inhibited at low salinity in *E. intestinalis* and ability of detached fragments drifting upstream to regenerate rhizoids and re-attach might become important in population maintenance. The importance of this point is further discussed in the later section on intraspecific variation. *E. intestinalis* is a very euryhaline alga. If salinity were found to inhibit rhizoid production in more stenohaline algae this could provide a further partial explanation of distribution of estuarine populations in response to salinity. Experimental evidence for this is currently lacking.

Experiments to determine rates of photosynthesis and/or respiration in relation to salinity have been carried out by the authors listed in Table III.

Table III. Some published work on measurement of algal photosynthesis and/or respiration in relation to salinity

Author	Species used
Admiraal (1977b, d)	Benthic diatoms
Dawes *et al.* (1978)	Six species from Florida mangroves and saltmarshes
Fromageot (1923)	*Ulva lactuca*
Kjeldsen and Phinney (1972)	Seven species of marine algae
Hammer (1968)	Marine algae
Gessner (1969)	*Dictyopteris membranacea*
Legendre (1921)	*Fucus serratus, Ulva lactuca*
McIntosh and Dawes (1978)	*Bostrychia binderi* Harv.
Mathieson and Dawes (1974)	Five species of *Eucheuma*
Munda and Kremer (1977)	*Fucus spiralis, F. vesiculosus*
Nellen (1966)	*Fucus serratus, Delesseria sanguinea*
Ogata and Matsui (1965)	*Ulva pertusa* Kjellm., *Porphyra tenera* Kjellm., *Gelidium amansii* Lamour.
Ogata and Schramm (1971)	*Porphyra umbilicalis*
Ogata and Takada (1968)	Various marine algae
Ohno (1976)	*Fucus vesiculosus, Laminaria saccharina, Porphyra umbilicalis*
Prange (1978)	*Blidingia minima*
Yarish *et al.* (1978)	*Caloglossa leprieurii, Bostrychia radicans, Polysiphonia subtilissima* Mont.

In general the results from most of these authors show that the rate of photosynthesis decreases and the rate of respiration increases with reduced salinity, at least at low salinities, giving a reduction in net photosynthesis. The exact pattern of change with salinity and the position of the salinity minimum and optimum has been found to correlate with estuarine penetration of the various species in some cases. For example, in the seven species investigated by Kjeldsen and Phinney (1972) two groups could be recognized: those in which the estuarine distribution was in accord with combined effects of salinity and temperature on photosynthesis, and those in which the field distribution was narrower than the laboratory studies on photosynthesis indicated. In the latter case further factors were suggested as limiting the distribution. Mathieson and Dawes (1974) also investigated the effect of temperature on the salinity response. They found that tolerance to reduced salinity for photosynthesis was greater at lower temperature and that the temperature optimum was increased with increasing salinity, This accords with most but not all of the salinity–temperature interactions on survival and growth rate described earlier. There is a problem in determining the validity of results on rates of photosynthesis and respiration from laboratory culture. Acclimation of the plants before the experiment in the conditions under which they were to be tested was considered desirable by some authors. Nellen (1966) pointed out that a short-term exposure of 30 min stimulated rates of photosynthesis and respiration. To attempt to reduce this effect by acclimation may not be valid ecologically if the acclimation period exposes the plants to constant conditions for longer than they would be under constant conditions in the field. This is likely to be a particularly short length of time for the highly variable estuarine environment and yet relatively long acclimation times of 24 h were used by Ohno (1976) and 48 h by Dawes *et al.* (1978). Yarish *et al.* (1978) experimented with acclimation times from 0–16 days in 0–35 $^0/_{00}$ salinity and found optimum times up to 4 days. Ohno found that photosynthesis was faster after 24 h acclimation in *Enteromorpha intestinalis*, *Laminaria saccharina* and *Fucus vesiculosus*, while Admiraal (1977b) found that preconditioning had no effect on salinity response for photosynthesis in benthic diatoms. Ogata and Takada (1968) found a more drastic response, in that some species responded well to acclimation while others were killed. Again, it does not follow that the killed species would have failed to survive or photosynthesize in the field if the conditions of acclimation were only of short duration. It is probably safe to conclude that these experiments indicate the shape of the salinity response curves but do not necessarily give valid absolute measurements of the processes. For species living in a variable environment, recovery from inhibition of a process induced by extreme conditions is necessary. An interesting contrast is provided by Gessner (1969) and Nellen (1966). Gessner was working with *Dictyopteris membranacea*, which shows less salinity tolerance in its field distribution than *Fucus serratus* and *Delesseria sanguinea*, with which Nellen was working. Fresh water gave a total breakdown of photosynthesis and respiration in *Dictyopteris* within an exposure of one minute, whilst after exposure below 20‰ only partial recovery occurred after return to full sea water; in *Fucus* and *Delesseria*, inhibition by very low salinity was completely reversed on return to sea water. This ability to recover may be an important physiological attribute, insufficiently investigated, in euryhaline algae. Gessner attributed the rapid destruction of the processes in *Dictyopteris* to a rapid efflux of ions. He used chloride only as a marker ion and assumed that other ions left the plant at a similar rate, but it might be appropriate to lay particular stress on the efflux of chloride because of its involvement, mentioned earlier, in photosynthesis.

Besides chloride some other ions, namely bicarbonate and calcium, have been more definitely implicated in modification of the salinity response of photosynthesis. Ogata and Matsui (1965) pointed out that salinity, pH, osmotic pressure and carbon dioxide are all inter-related in the marine environment. By use of buffers, they were able to isolate each of these factors in separate experiments, finding that while salinity and pH affected the performance of the plants through direct effects on the protoplasm, maintenance of the carbon dioxide supply in the external medium reduced the inhibition of photosynthesis at low salinity. Ohno (1976), Hammer (1968) and Legendre (1921) also found that marine algae gave high photosynthetic rates at low salinity with added bicarbonate. McIntosh and Dawes (1978) compared the effect of diluting sea water with distilled water and with spring water and found that the photosynthetic rate was higher and the salinity peak was lower if spring water was used. They attributed this to the levels of bicarbonate and of nutrients. These experiments clearly indicate that bicarbonate levels influence the salinity response; there is no direct experimental evidence for the effect of nutrients on macroalgae, although Admiraal (1977d) found that levels of ammonium nitrogen in polluted estuaries in Holland could inhibit photosynthesis in benthic diatoms. McIntosh and Dawes also found that added calcium in the culture medium allowed maintenance of a higher photosynthetic rate for a longer time at low salinity. This accords with Hoffman's (1959) finding that calcium allowed *Delesseria* to survive at low salinity.

Finally, the growth habit of plants may enable them to avoid exposure to ambient salinities. After experimental work, Dawes *et al.*

(1978) concluded that *Cladophora repens* (J. Ag.) Harv. [= *C. coelothrix* Kütz.] was protected from salinity fluctuations and desiccation in mangrove swamps by its turf-forming habit.

3. Chemical Composition of the Water

This is the second of the factors stressed by Wilkinson (1977a). The ionic composition of rivers is highly variable relative to that of sea water (Phillips, 1972) and therefore with decreasing salinity there will be increasing differences in water chemistry between estuaries. Gessner and Schramm (1971) considered that the differences between four species of red algae in ability to tolerate lack of calcium at low salinity (Schwenke, 1958) was important since sea water was of constant composition. In estuaries, this difference between species may become very important. Furthermore, nutrient and trace metal levels are profoundly altered in industrialized estuaries by domestic and industrial discharges. Evidence has already been presented in this review that calcium, chloride and bicarbonate levels, which vary at low salinity, affect growth and photosynthesis. Further literature surveyed below suggests that relative variations of potassium, sodium, calcium and chloride affect distribution. As insufficient data are available for estuarine algae, marine and other brackish work is included.

Black (1971) and Black and Weeks (1972) on *Enteromorpha intestinalis* and Eppley (1958) on *Porphyra perforata* J. Ag. have suggested that the internal ionic composition of the algae is maintained by active extrusion of sodium and uptake of potassium and chloride at all salinities, with calcium being necessary to maintain membrane selectivity to sodium and potassium (Eppley and Cyrus, 1960). Droop (1958), working on euryhaline phytoplankton, showed that sodium supply at low salinity was more critical than that of calcium because of the relative magnitudes of the plant requirements and average freshwater levels of the two ions. Despite active uptake, internal chloride levels remain in direct proportion to external levels in *Porphyra umbilicalis* and in three *Fucus* species (Ohno, 1976; Munda, 1964; Munda and Kremer, 1977). On sudden transfer to distilled water there is a rapid loss of chloride (Gessner, 1969), but this is thought to occur mainly from the free space (Gessner and Hammer, 1968), so it may not have a serious effect. Therefore, variations in the external environment can affect the maintenance of the internal levels of major inorganic ions, although the evidence is as yet insufficient to present a clear picture.

Less clear still are the effects of this internal variation. The possible rôle of changing chloride levels on photosynthetic rate has already been mentioned. Munda (1964) has repeated an earlier suggestion of Overbeck that the Ca^{2+} Mg^{2+}/Cl^{-} ratio may be important in setting distribution limits for *Fucus*. With decreasing salinity, this ratio will change internally in some species, since *Porphyra perforata* actively accumulates calcium (Eppley, 1958) and some fucoids show increasing internal calcium and magnesium and decreasing chloride with decreased salinity (Munda, 1964).

The effect of ion imbalance should be sought on a variety of physiological processes rather than just in maintenance of osmotic equilibrium, since the latter has been shown in *Stichococcus bacillaris* (Brown, 1977) and in fucoids (Munda, 1977b; Munda and Kremer, 1977) to be maintained by variation in internal carbohydrate and amino acid levels. None the less inorganic ions are also implicated in osmotic maintenance, since Zimmerman and Steudle (1971) have shown that cell turgor of *Chaetomorpha linum* was dependent on adequate potassium supply in the medium, independent of the latter's osmotic potential.

The effect of wide ionic variations in estuary water at low salinity is particularly poorly understood and should be a fruitful field for future research.

4. *Altered Biotic Relationships*

Lowered diversity in estuaries resulting in reduced competition has been implicated, earlier in this work, in broadening of vertical algal zones in estuaries. In addition, the biotic factor of grazing needs to be considered. Conover (1958) has stated that grazing is increased in brackish water but in oxygen-deficient polluted estuaries restriction of animals may reduce grazing. Wilkinson *et al.* (1976) suggested that *Melosira nummuloides* was dominant in the upper reaches of the polluted Clyde and Wear estuaries partly because of the absence of grazing littorinids. Jorde and Klavestad (1959) suggested that *Stictyosiphon* was the most abundant alga in the inner part of a fjord because of the absence of competition which, combined with favourable salinity and temperature, enabled it to produce large summer forms there, although absent in summer from the open coast. This emphasizes that biotic and abiotic factors must be considered together.

5. *Heterotrophic Potential of the Algae*

High turbidity in estuaries gives low light penetration for photosynthesis combined with high availability of organic substrates from natural detritus accumulation, characteristic of estuaries, and from organic effluents. Therefore, algae with very low light requirements and/or wide heterotrophic abilities could be at an advantage. Light requirements of estuarine macroalgae are not accurately known, but Wilkinson *et al.* (1976) have suggested that the wide heterotrophic ability of benthic diatoms (Lewin, 1963) in general, and of *Melosira nummuloides* (Hellebust, 1970) in particular, may partly account for abundance of *Melosira* in polluted estuaries such as the Clyde.

6. *Turbidity and Sedimentation*

Turbidity has been considered in the previous section above. The sediment itself has been suggested as limiting distribution and form of *Fucus ceranoides* (Gillman, 1957; Chater, 1927) and of modifying the composition of vertical zonation patterns (Nienhuis, 1975). Russell (1972) ascribed the modification of the normal marine three-zone shore to a two-zone one at the mouth of the Cheshire Dee to turbidity and sedimentation; this conclusion has also been reached for the Severn estuary by Cox (1977a).

7. *Nature of the Substratum*

Modification of the substratum by sedimentation has already been discussed. Also to be considered is the physical nature of firm substrata. Tittley and Price (1977) have demonstrated considerable differences in the Thames estuary in species presence and species zonation on brick and concrete walls. By contrast, Wilkinson (1973b) did not find the zonation patterns in the Clyde estuary to vary on different substrata. One possible explanation is that the particularly resistant species which can colonize estuaries are less sensitive than open coast species to desiccation and other factors connected with the substratum, particularly when competition is reduced, but that particular species found in certain estuaries and extreme types of substrata still have an effect. The high suspended load of estuaries, by encouraging formation of sediment-binding turfs, may enable algae to overcome desiccation on non-porous rocky substrata. This is an extension of the suggestion of Dawes *et al.* (1978), mentioned earlier, that turf-forming by *Cladophora* was protective in mangrove swamps.

Much work remains to be done on the effect of factors in limiting distributions along estuaries. The imbalance of the lengths of the sections above on salinity and on other factors is merely a reflection of the lack of work on the other factors. Within the distribution range of a species, the estuarine environment may still exert profound effects on the life of algae, as shown in the next section.

EFFECTS OF THE ESTUARINE ENVIRONMENT

1. Introduction

The previous section has demonstrated how various factors in the estuarine environment can limit the distribution of different species to different extents. Within a species' distribution range, various estuarine factors can make modifications in the morphology, structure, reproductive behaviour and chemical composition of that species which are profound compared with modifications occurring between open coast situations. The extent of modification in estuarine species is partly linked to the ability of the species to colonize a narrower or wider range, according both to Jorde and Klavestad (1963) and to von Wachenfeldt's four distribution groups of species in the Baltic (described earlier). These workers were concerned with relatively stable salinity environments, and it is possible that in the less stable conditions of true estuaries a greater proportion of species will be affected.

2. Morphology and Structure

Changes can be seen by observation of field populations and by variation of conditions in laboratory experiments.

In general, field observations show that as algae penetrate into estuaries they become smaller. For marine species this has been shown in fucoids (Alexander *et al.*, 1935; den Hartog, 1967; Powell, 1972; Jordon and Vadas, 1972), *Stilophora* (Conover, 1958), Delesseriaceae (Waern, 1965) and *Callithamnion* (von Wachenfeldt, 1969). Freshwater species, by contrast, become smaller the further downstream they grow, e.g. *Lemanea* (Wood and Straughan, 1953). In general, brown algae were not reduced under a low relatively stable salinity of 11 ‰ in the Baltic, although red algae were reduced (Kristiansen, 1978). Reduction of size in *Fucus ceranoides* appears to be greater in estuaries with high sediment loads (Chater, 1927; Cotton, 1912). Besides size, actual morphology may be altered. Branching patterns are shown to have been modified in *Enteromorpha* (Burrows, 1959; Klugh, 1922), in *Fucus vesiculosus* (Jordan and Vadas, 1972) and in *Stilophora* (Conover, 1958). Coloration, and hence possibly pigment density and response to light intensity, has been found to vary with environmental gradients in brackish populations of *Cladophora glomerata* (Wallentinus, 1976) and of *Pilayella littoralis* (Munda, 1972c). The morphology of the antheridial cluster varies in *Vaucheria compacta* along estuaries (Simons, 1974). As with distributional data reviewed earlier, apparent conflicts exist in the literature. For example, Jordan and Vadas (1972) found increased vesiculation in *Fucus vesiculosus* going upstream, while vesiculation was reduced according to Alexander *et al.* (1935) and den Hartog (1967). The reasons for this are not known. Under brackish conditions, loose-lying populations of plants have been reported, e.g. in Delesseriaceae (Waern, 1965) and in *Pilayella* (Russell, 1967). Estuarine modifications have been recognized in distinctly described forms in various species, e.g. in *Rhodochorton purpureum* (= *Audouinella purpurea*) (Knaggs, 1966, 1967), in *Blidingia minima* (den Hartog, 1967) and in *Pilayella littoralis* (Russell, 1963).

Experimental investigations have enabled cytological and fine structural effects and differences between generations to be seen and particular factors to be investigated. von Wachenfeldt (1969) had reported from field observations that cell size of many algae apparently decreased with decreased salinity, and this has been confirmed experimentally by Ogata and Schramm (1971) for *Porphyra umbilicalis*. The only fine structural effect so far reported is a rearrangement of the thylakoids at low salinity in *Bangia* (Sheath and Cole, 1978). Most culture work has been done on *Enteromorpha*. The production of highly branched "bottle-brush" forms was attributed to temperature shock by Moss and Marsland (1976) but to salinity shock by Reed and Russell (1978a). Possibly more than one factor may directly cause the same effect or alternatively, since "bottle-brush" forms can result either from branching or from *in situ* germination, different factors may bring about the same apparent effect by influencing different processes. In *Enteromorpha salina* Kütz., Kapraun (1970) found that salinity modification of growth was different in male and female plants, while Stam and Holleman (1975) found that salinity modification was greater in fresh water than in marine isolates of *Phormidium*. Munda (1964) has used field transplant experiments as a sort of field-culture investigation to determine the morphological effects on fucoids described earlier.

Since algal taxonomy is largely based on morphology such profound modifications could be expected to have taxonomic implications. The extent of estuarine variation is so great as to obscure distinctions between species in *Enteromorpha* (Burrows, 1959), *Monostroma* (Cotton, 1912) and *Fucus* (Munda, 1964). Culture investigations of salinity tolerances and effects have suggested that marine and freshwater species separately recognized in two genera are really conspecific, namely *Rhizoclonium riparium* and *R. hieroglyphicum* (Nienhuis, 1975) and *Bangia fuscopurpurea* and *B. atropurpurea* (den Hartog, 1972).

3. Reproduction and Life-history

In estuaries, various parts of the reproductive process may be suppressed, giving increased importance to fragmentation as a means of propagation, and the seasonal timing of the life-history may also be altered.

Conover (1958) suggested that sterility of marine algae was common in brackish waters below 26 ‰. Sexual reproduction is the particular process normally inhibited, e.g. in *Rhizoclonium* (Nienhuis, 1974) and in *Ectocarpus* (Conover, 1958; Russell, 1971). Similarly, freshwater algae in estuaries may have sex repressed, e.g. *Zygnema* (Doty, 1946) and *Lemanea* (Wood and Straughan, 1953). Increased sediment load has been correlated with decreased sexual reproduction in *Fucus ceranoides* (Chater, 1927), but there has not been any experimental investigation of causal factors in any other algae.

As with morphological modification, reproductive modification can cause taxonomic problems, e.g. by increased hybridization between *Fucus* species (Russell, 1971). In the absence of sexual reproductive processes, plants must rely on other means of reproduction. For some algae (e.g. many brown algae) sexual reproduction is possible (Russell, 1971), but some (e.g. *Fucus* spp.) have no alternative organized method. As a consequence, fragmentation may become important and has been described in the maintenance of estuarine populations of *Pilayella* (Russell, 1967), *Codium* (Malinowski and Ramus, 1973) and *Laurencia* and *Digenea* (Conover, 1964).

In estuaries, the seasonal timing of reproduction may be altered. Penniman (1977) has reported that sexual and tetrasporic reproduction of *Gracilaria foliifera* occur earlier in the Great Bay estuary system than on the surrounding open coast. Edwards (1972) discovered that in the Tyne, Tees and Wear estuaries, north-east England, *Prasiola* and *Rosenvingiella*, normally annual on the nearby coast, were perennial.

4. Chemical Composition

As with the two preceding types of estuarine effect, some species show variation in chemical composition along estuaries, whilst others do not. Much of the available information comes from work on various fucoids by Munda (1963, 1964, 1972, 1977b), Munda and Garrasi (1978) and Munda and Kremer (1977). By means of (i) analysis of field samples from natural populations, (ii) transplants between different ecological situations, and (iii) laboratory culture under specific conditions, they have shown that some components decrease with decreasing salinity while some increase with decreasing salinity. Those which decreased were alginic acid, β-carotene, mannitol, chloride, dry weight and ash content. Those which increased were calcium, magnesium and total nitrogen. Changes in electrolytes and mannitol were short-term and easily reversed by changing the salinity regime, but changes in the other components were longer term. Munda suggested that mannitol could be involved in osmoregulation, but since mannitol biosynthesis did not appear to be influenced by salinity the correlation between mannitol level and salinity must be indirect. One possible cause could be the rapid use of mannitol as a respiratory substrate in the elevated levels of respiration at low salinity. Levels of sorbitol and of the amino acid proline have been correlated with salinity in *Stichococcus bacillaris* (Brown, 1977) and also suggested to function like mannitol in osmotic regulation. Munda also found a correlation between an amino acid and salinity; in this case the acid was glutamic acid. She noted that the levels of total nitrogen in fucoids were not only inversely related to salinity but that the difference between levels in marine and brackish populations was greater in more euryhaline fucoids; the highest total nitrogen content occurred in the brackish-water species *F. ceranoides*. The bulk of the variation in nitrogen content between species and between populations within species was due to glutamic acid levels. Unlike *S. bacillaris*, the correlation with salinity was inverse and no osmotic function was proposed for glutamic acid.

There has been little attempt to clarify the particularly confused taxonomy of estuarine algae by using chemotaxonomic methods. Cheney and Mathieson (1977) have analysed amino acids of *Chondrus* by electrophoresis. More variation was found between estuarine and nearby open coast populations than between geographically distant coastal populations. Brown and Hellebust (1977) have suggested that the osmoregulatory ability of Ulotrichales, employing amino acid or other substrates, could have chemotaxonomic importance. So far, neither of these lines of research have been reported as being completed and chemotaxonomy of estuarine algae remains a ripe field for investigation.

EFFECTS OF POLLUTION

To determine effects of any type of pollution on the vegetation requires comparison to be made between polluted and unpolluted situations. The idea of using one estuary as an unpolluted control against which to judge another has been criticized by Gray (1976), because every estuary is to some extent hydrographically unique. The alternatives are to examine changes along a gradient of pollution away from an effluent source to compare the same site at different times when the degree of pollution was different. Neither of these is wholly satisfactory. The former may be complicated by other factors changing along the gradient, while the latter, discussed further in

Wilkinson and Tittley (1979), is usually hampered by lack of acceptable early records. Despite all these problems, the following short account is synthesized from a combination of these approaches.

Edwards (1972) and Mathieson and Fralick (1973) have both demonstrated a reduction in number of algal species in polluted estuaries compared with less polluted ones. Bokn (1977) has described long-term changes in the Oslofjord with gradually increasing pollution; these included the loss of *Ascophyllum nodosum*, *Fucus vesiculosus* and *F. serratus*, the introduction of *F. distichus*, and the spread of *F. spiralis*. Peussa and Ravanko (1975) recorded the loss of *Dictyosiphon* and *Chorda* and the appearance of *Capsosiphon* with increasing pollution in part of the Baltic. Price and Tittley (1972) have described the contrasting situation, the reappearance of fucoids in the Thames estuary following abatement of pollution. Algae characteristic of sewage-polluted brackish water have been discussed by Anger (1975), Edwards (1972), Gillham (1957), Grenager (1957), L. Lindgren (1975), P. Lindgren (1965), Munda (1967), Nilsson (1975) and Sundene (1953). In general, larger brown algae were replaced by green algae or (in severe cases) by blue-green algae around outfalls and in polluted areas. Attempts have been made by Hayren (1923), Munda (1967) and Grenager (1957) to apply modifications of the saprobic system of Kolkwitz and Marsson (1908) to brackish waters. Unfortunately, the apparent pollution tolerance of particular species differed between localities, suggesting that interaction of pollution with other factors is more important in the complex brackish environment. An alternative approach to pollution indication is the use of species-composition of the microepiphyte community; this was shown by Sundene (1953) to be characterized by *Erythrotrichia*, *Acrochaetium* and *Calothrix* in polluted parts of the Oslofjord. The epiphytes were also found to be pollution-sensitive in a land-locked fjord by Klavestad (1957), who showed that *Gracilaria* was devoid of epiphytes when sewage pollution caused hydrogen sulphide formation in the water, but was covered with them when this did not happen. Gillham (1957) commented that benthic euglenoids were common around sewage outfalls; the unpublished observations of the present author also suggest that these organisms could form the basis for an index of water quality.

Little is known about the mechanism by which pollution affects the algae. Sewage has been regarded (Doty and Newhouse, 1954;

Knight and Johnston, in press; Sundene, 1953) as having its major effect through increased sediment-loading, resulting in increased turbidity and substrata. Nutrients from sewage would be expected to have an effect, but surprisingly little is known on this from brackish water. Burrows (1971) has shown that growth of *Ulva* is stimulated by sewage-derived nutrients, while Norin and Waern (1973) have found experimentally that seasonal ammonium enrichment in the Baltic induces a small dark form of *Cladophora glomerata*. Biotic factors can also be involved, since Bokn (1977) has suggested that the replacement of other fucoids by *F. distichus* has occurred in the Oslofjord because *F. distichus* reproduces earlier and its germlings therefore have time to become established before the other fucoid germlings become out-competed by the rapidly growing summer carpet of green algae stimulated by sewage nutrients. Pollution interactions also modify abiotic factors. For example, the discrepancies between the saprobic classifications mentioned earlier have been explained by Grenager (1957) on the basis of greater pollution tolerance at higher salinity; similarly, P. Lindgren (1965) has reported a raising of the salinity penetration limit for some algae under polluted conditions. This also agrees with Lein *et al.* (1974) who believed that pollution rather than salinity set fucoid distribution limits in the Oslofjord. In contrast is the finding of Pekkari (1973) that the salinity limit for *Fucus vesiculosus* was extended further into the Baltic under polluted conditions. Various authors (e.g. Munda, 1967) have indicated that *Melosira nummuloides* is more abundant under polluted conditions but none has previously reported the extreme dominance of *M. nummuloides* seen by Wilkinson *et al.* (1976) in the polluted Clyde and Wear estuaries. Possibly this is an example of local conditions, not necessarily directly concerned with pollution, interacting with pollution to make the final choice of dominants from a range of pollution-tolerant species. Intensive algal surveys of estuaries have been so rarely coupled with serious chemical surveys that it is too early to reach rigid conclusions about algal distribution in relation to pollution.

As with salinity effects, so pollution has further effects on algae within their modified tolerance limits. Size-reduction due to sewage pollution has been described in *Enteromorpha* (Munda, 1967) *Cladophora glomerata* (Norin and Waern, 1973) and *Chara* (Pekkari, 1973; Peussa and Ravanko, 1975). More intensive colouring has been reported in *C. glomerata* by Norin and Waern and in *Enteromorpha* by Wallentinus (1976). Edwards (1975) has reported that the summer presence of *Prasiola stipitata* (unusual, in that it is a winter annual on the nearby coast) is most marked in the Tyne estuary around sewage outfalls, suggesting that this seasonal modification might be a sewage effect. As with general estuarine conditions, so sewage pollution also influences chemical composition of the algae. Munda (1967) demonstrated a decrease in the mannitol level of fucoids transplanted from less polluted to more polluted parts of a fjord, but found no changes in other constituents. Since mannitol has been possibly implicated in rapid respiration at low salinities or in maintenance of osmotic equilibrium (see earlier discussion), this may provide a means by which to study the modification of salinity limits by sewage. The only other chemical effect detected is an increase, with pollution, of the nitrogen content of *Enteromorpha* (Wallentinus, 1976).

Sewage stimulation of estuarine green algae has been reported as having effects on higher trophic levels. For example, Perkins and Abbott (1972) have shown that macrobenthic animal populations in Ardmore Bay, in the Clyde estuary, have declined due to augmented reducing conditions resulting in the sediment from smothering by green algal blooms.

So far, this discussion of pollution effects has been concerned with sewage. Few other pollutants have been investigated with regard to algae specifically in brackish environments. There has, however, been some work on heavy metal effects. von Wachenfeldt (1969) has suggested that the elevated levels of copper in sewage effluents from Malmø are responsible for the disappearance from the area of many species, including sewage-tolerant algae such as *Blidingia* and *Ulva*, which would be expected to be abundant. The use of algae as trace metal indicators has been reviewed by Phillips (1977) who, like Bryan and Hummerstone (1977), pointed out that the algae are sensitive to, and indicate, dissolved levels, whilst particulate levels of the metals affect filter feeding animals such as mussels, also regarded as good indicators. Bryan and Hummerstone (1973) examined changes in metal accumulation by estuarine algae under a variety of conditions and concluded that variations in metal content with height on shore largely reflected the stratification of dissolved metal levels in the water column and therefore, to some extent, whether their input was in less saline or in more saline water.

This short account of estuarine algae in relation to pollution demonstrates how little is known in detail, despite the predominance of worst aquatic pollution being in estuaries. A final example of this is provided by the distributions of two species which have been suggested as pollution indicators.

Within the one fjord, Munda (1967) found that *Phormidium corium*, thought to be oligosaprobic, was present in two contrasting situations, in the cleanest parts of the fjord and near the outfalls, although being absent in between. Such a bimodal distribution has been reported on a wider geographical basis for *Capsosiphon fulvescens*. Records of its distribution have been given by Chihara (1967), Cotton (1912), den Hartog (1959), Klavestad (1957), Kristiansen (1978), Nienhuis (1967), Munda (1967, 1978a), Pedersen (1973), Peussa and Ravanko (1975), Ravanko (1968), Waern (1952) and Wilkinson (unpublished records). It does *not* appear bimodal with respect to salinity, having been reported from tidal fresh water right through to full sea water, but *is* bimodal with respect to:

(i) height on shore, and
(ii) pollution.

In many situations, *Capsosiphon* occurs in completely submerged water conditions, while in others it is at the upper levels of the intertidal zone. In most cases, it is reported from grossly polluted waters but has also been recorded from a small number of localities thought to be particularly free of sewage or other pollution. The use of a species as an indicator requires that not only should its distribution be well-known but that the causal factors and explanations of any apparent inconsistencies (such as bimodal distributions) should also be known. To these ends, much work remains to be done.

INTRASPECIFIC VARIATION

The preceding sections have shown that some algae have a wide distribution range in relation to estuarine conditions and that some vary morphologically and physiologically along this range. Certain authors have considered whether the causes of this variation are genetic or merely due to phenotypic modification. As pointed out by von Wachenfeldt (1969), there are also species which show no differences within their distribution range.

Variation is continuous in some species, e.g. the reduction in size of fucoids described earlier, while in others there are quite distinct morphological types characteristic of the estuarine environment and of the open coast, e.g. *Stilophora* (Conover, 1958), *Sphacelaria arctica* Harv. (Jorde and Klavestad, 1960), *Antithamnion* (Sundene, 1959), *Pilayella* (Russell, 1963), *Eugomontia sacculata* (Wilkinson, 1974) and *Rhodochorton* (= *Audouinella*) (Knaggs, 1966, 1967).

Similarly, physiological criteria show that separate physiological races may exist in some estuarine species and not in others. Different salinity tolerances for growth have been found in ecologically different isolates of *Caloglossa* and *Bostrychia* (Yarish *et al.*, 1977), *Eugomontia* (Wilkinson, 1974), *Ectocarpus* (Russell and Bolton, 1975), *Pilayella* (Bolton, 1979), *Enteromorpha* (Reed and Russell, 1978b), and various fucoids (Munda, 1963, 1977a); experiments have shown that salinity profoundly modifies the growth pattern of *Asterocytis ornata* (C. Ag.) Hamel [= *Chroodactylon ornatum*] (Lewin and Robertson, 1971), producing different forms. Different races with respect to photosynthetic performance have been found in *Gracilaria* (Dawes *et al.*, 1978) and in *Delesseria* (Nellen, 1966). By way of contrast, Simons (1974) could not find any races differing in salinity tolerance in the widely distributed euryhaline species, *Vaucheria compacta*, even though there was a morphological modification of the antheridial cluster. Norton and South (1969) concluded that *Saccorhiza* and *Chorda* in Britain were physiologically the same as in the Baltic Sea since they showed the same tolerance to low salinities in experiments, even though such tolerance would not be so necessary in the habitats occupied by these species in Britain. Particularly interesting is the finding of Black (1971) that there are no races differing in salinity tolerance in *Enteromorpha intestinalis*; this directly contradicts the finding of Reed and Russell (1978b). While an explanation for this might be in the use by these different authors of populations from environments where salinity stresses would be of a different nature (i.e. open coast and estuarine), this example indicates that confusion is to be found in work on intraspecific variation as in other fields of work on estuarine algae; thus, further studies are needed.

Black (1971) concluded from tolerance experiments that his populations of *Enteromorpha* were genetically similar, but inability to eradicate physiological differences by acclimation or by culture through several generations in uniform conditions has suggested that the differences are genetic in the examples of Russell (1963), Russell and Bolton (1975), Bolton (1979), Reed and Russell (1978b) and Yarish *et al.* (1977). The races were intersterile in *Antithamnion* (Sundene, 1959), also suggesting genetic differences. Probably continuous variation is phenotypic, since Munda (1963) has shown its reversal in fucoids by transplant experiments; distinct variation types may be genetic. The maintenance of genetic differences should be aided in those estuarine populations which show suppression of sexual, but not asexual, reproduction (see earlier). Genetic differences may not be so easily maintained in estuaries in those species which reproduce by fragmentation if there is immigration into the estuary of drift fragments from further downstream; these re-establish populations of short-lived algae which periodically die out.

Further study of intraspecific variation in estuarine algae could be important, because it may indicate the reasons why some species are euryhaline while others are not. It is tempting to believe that species are euryhaline because they consist of several physiologically different populations, but the present rather meagre evidence suggests that this may not always be so.

SUMMARY OF INFORMATION ON ESTUARINE MICROBENTHIC ALGAE

This review is not intended to be comprehensive for the microbenthic algae. However, they are included since certain species (e.g. *Melosira nummuloides*) form an indispensable part of the macroalgal communities and, since closely related to the larger algae, some aspects of their biology might fill in the gaps in information on the latter. A more comprehensive review on the diatoms is that of Round (1971).

The two ecologically most important groups of estuarine benthic microalgae appear to be diatoms and euglenoids. Hustedt (1959), among others, has commented on their association on estuarine flats. This review is restricted to these two groups. There are four principal habitat groups: epiphytic forms on other algae and higher plants, epilithic forms on rocks and hard substrata, epipelic forms on the surface of mud and epipsammic forms which burrow into mud. Epilithic and epiphytic communities have been found to have similar species composition (Main and McIntire, 1974; Moore and

McIntire, 1977) and have been sampled indirectly using artificial substrata such as oyster spat collectors (Bacon and Taylor, 1976), PVC (McIntire and Overton, 1971) and plexiglass (Welsh *et al.*, 1972). Bacon and Taylor indicated the need for caution in that community change on samplers could be due to succession of the colonizing community rather than to seasonal effects.

Baudrimont (1967) recognized three community types, freshwater, brackish and marine, along the Trieux estuary; in a smaller inflow, he noted a well-marked set of distributions of *Melosira* species, each dominant in one of these types. The epiphytic and epilithic communities have similar composition in the Yaquina estuary, Oregon, with no host specificity for the epiphytes (Main and McIntire, 1974). Distributions varied seasonally in the Yaquina estuary, since the apparently important ecological boundary for the diatoms at $5\,^0/_{00}$ salinity moved along the river with seasonal changes in freshwater flow. None the less, the wide tolerance of some diatoms was shown by the discovery of freshwater forms at a relatively marine site in the Mersey estuary (Ghazzawi, 1933). Larger populations were found on sand than on silt (Riznyk and Phinney, 1972b).

As to vertical distribution, an intertidal zonation pattern on hard substrata was described by Hopkins (1964b). Cox (1977a) reported that epilithic diatoms showed brackish-water submergence and that the vertical distribution at an outer site in the Severn estuary could be correlated with distribution pattern variation as one passed upstream (Cox, 1977b). Riznyk and Phinney (1972b) found the greatest biomass of sediment-living diatoms in the top 1 cm in the Yaquina estuary; Hopkins (1963) demonstrated this for the top 2 cm in the Sussex Ouse estuary. Viable cells penetrated to 18 cm depth in the Yaquina estuary, suggesting a possible heterotrophic mode of nutrition. The biomass decreased with tidal height in the Yaquina estuary, although the concentration towards the sediment surface increased, probably because of increased time for vertical migration between tides. Bracher (1929) noted that diatoms in the Bristol Avon concentrated in sediment furrows, whilst euglenoids concentrated on the ridges between. Gillham (1957) found euglenoids to be most conspicuous near sewage outfalls in the Exe estuary. Both diatoms and euglenoids migrate vertically in the sediment, coming to the surface in the light when the tide is out and descending in the dark and/or when the tide comes in (Bracher, 1919, 1929; Leach, 1970; Palmer and Round, 1965; Round and Palmer, 1966). This appears to be a diurnal rhythm which can be maintained on a daily periodicity in the laboratory when the tidal influence is removed, but which has a second tidal rhythm overlying it in the field (Bracher, 1919). Palmer and Round reached similar conclusions to those of Bracher and suggested that turbidity from the incoming tide has the effect of bringing about the same dark reaction. Perkins (1960) found only a light/dark diurnal rhythm in the Eden estuary and attributed this to exceptional water clarity.

Many environmental factors are known to influence presence and distribution of the estuarine microbenthic algae.

Light requirements for growth of some sediment-living forms may be high, since Admiraal (1977a) has shown the optimum intensity for some estuarine diatoms to be just below levels in the sea and Bracher (1929) reported that several hours of emersion was needed for active photosynthesis by the euglenoids. Sun/shade adaptations of microbenthic algae (Gargas, 1971) may affect populations. Main and McIntire (1974) found that the epiphytic forms had distributions partly determined by vertical isolation gradients. Considering nutrients as a factor, Admiraal (1977c) found that natural phosphate levels in Dutch estuaries were not limiting to growth, but he also found that enrichment of ammonium nitrogen by pollution might inhibit estuarine diatom photosynthesis (Admiraal, 1977d). For sediment-living forms, Admiraal (1977b) found a wide salinity tolerance as compared with phytoplankton, whilst Amspoker and McIntire (1977) found that salinity together with sediment was a major factor in horizontal distribution. Main and McIntire (1974) also found salinity important in limiting distributions of epibenthic forms. Amspoker (1977) found that sediment type had a greater effect on epipsammic and epipelic forms than on epiphytic forms, and Hopkins (1963) found greater number of cells and concentration nearer the surface in finer sediments. Diatoms required a higher (110–114%) water content than euglenoids (88–99%) in the sediment and both could be limited by this factor (Bracher, 1929). Sediment and substratum factors are probably more important than nutrients in determining distribution (Admiraal, 1977c). Hopkins (1964b) found great differences in diversity and variability of composition between concrete, wood, chalk and other algae, as substrata, and

Cox (1977b) stressed the need for hard substrata for tube-dwelling forms. Desiccation resistance was shown to be an important factor in vertical distribution of non-sediment dwelling forms (Hopkins, 1964a; Main and McIntire, 1974).

The interaction of the major factors in horizontal and vertical distribution of littoral diatoms has been studied in a laboratory model ecosystem (Wulff and McIntire, 1972). Variation of light intensity, desiccation, salinity and temperature were studied in relation to developing diatom assemblages and it was found that the vertical distribution was more closely related to light and desiccation in the summer than in the winter. McIntire (1978) believes that simpler tolerance experiments on single factors and single species are of little value; an alternative approach to the model ecosystem, which he has also used, is to seek correlations between factors and factor combinations on the one hand and community structure of diatoms on the other, by means of sophisticated multivariate mathematical techniques, after intensive field-surveys of both plants and environmental conditions (McIntire, 1973, 1978). McIntire found that there was a horizontal continuum of marine and brackish-water littoral diatom taxa which shifted along the estuary with seasonal hydrographic changes. Vertical clustering showed three separate desiccation-resistant communities, each dominated by different taxa, on the upper shore at different points in the estuary. While distributions were strongly correlated with physical factors in the winter, there was some evidence in summer of biotic relationship with macroalgae.

Seasonal changes in abundance were reported for *Euglena* and diatoms by Bracher (1920), with a minimum density in winter and maximum in April/May; Riznyk and Phinney (1972b), however, found an absence of seasonal fluctuations in mud-dwelling forms as compared with epiphytic ones. They suggest this was due to efficient nutrient supply through recycling in the sediment.

Production studies have been carried out only on microalgae in truly estuarine environments, and these studies have even then been restricted to sediment-living forms. It is difficult to make comparisons between the relatively few studies made, due to problems with methods. Some authors have measured rates of carbon fixation in the field, while others have inferred production from laboratory measurements of photosynthetic oxygen exchange. With regard to field measurements, Riznyk *et al.* (1978) have suggested that low tide values may be an overestimate, while Darley *et al.* (1976) have warned against submerging the plants, since they are active when the tide is out, and have suggested the use of gas analysis on air-exposed sediments. For work in the laboratory or using isolated cores in the field, the necessity of obtaining intact cores without disturbing the sediment and associated algae has been stressed by Marshall *et al.* (1971). Darley *et al.* have shown that taking of intact cores does not disturb rates of oxygen exchange measured the following day, provided that the diurnal rhythm of vertical migration back to the surface is first permitted to occur.

No attempt has here been made to place significance on a comparison of published measurements of rates because insufficient data are available. The most important point about available information is that the rates show a higher level of production by the microbenthos than by the phytoplankton (Grontved, 1960). It would therefore be interesting to determine what further contribution is made by the filamentous algae, for which truly estuarine data are lacking. This is particularly important, as Josselyn (1977) has shown that 40% of the annual input of detritus to the Great Bay estuary system derives from fucoids.

Higher rates were recorded from coarse than from fine sediments (Riznyk and Phinney, 1972a; Riznyk *et al.*, 1978). Rates were found to be similar under flooded and exposed conditions (Leach, 1970), but low production occurred near a flood channel, presumably due to disturbance of the sediment (Riznyk *et al.*, 1978). Riznyk *et al.* also found that autumn and spring peaks could be correlated with high nitrate and phosphate levels and that areas of high production had more invertebrates, suggesting that grazing increased the production rate.

This review has outlined a number of apparent conflicts in the published information relating to estuarine algae. These have probably arisen from two sources. First, they are a reflection of the smaller volume of work on estuarine relative to open coast algae. Secondly, they may also have arisen from inadequate acknowledgement by more floristically-inclined phycologists of the much greater physical and chemical complexity of the estuarine environment compared with the open coastal environment. This emphasizes the need for more positive attention to be paid by phycologists to measurement of the physical and chemical environment. Particularly fruitful fields for future research should be the effects of estuarine conditions on algal taxonomy and morphology, the effects of water chemistry on algal growth and distribution in estuaries, and the role of intraspecific variation in adaptation of algae to estuarine conditions. Problems may be more easily solved by an integrated approach to both macrobenthic and microbenthic algae in estuaries.

ACKNOWLEDGEMENT

The author is indebted to the Carnegie Trust for the Universities of Scotland for financial assistance towards a survey of British estuarine algae which, although as yet unpublished, has done much to crystallize the opinions expressed in this review.

REFERENCES

Admiraal, W. (1977a). Influence of light and temperature on the growth rate of estuarine benthic diatoms in culture. *Mar. Biol., Berl.* **39**, 1–9.

Admiraal, W. (1977b). Salinity tolerance of benthic estuarine diatoms as tested with a rapid polarographic method of photosynthesis. *Mar. Biol., Berl.* **39**, 11–18.

Admiraal, W. (1977c). Influence of various concentrations of orthophosphate on the division rate of an estuarine benthic diatom, *Navicula arenaria*, in culture. *Mar. Biol., Berl.* **42**, 1–8.

Admiraal, W. (1977d). Tolerance of estuarine benthic diatoms to high concentrations of ammonia, nitrite ion, nitrate ion and orthophosphate. *Mar. Biol., Berl.* **42**, 307–315.

Alexander, W. B. (1932). The natural history of the Firth of Tay. *Trans. Proc. Perth. Soc. nat. Sci.* **9**, 35–42.

Alexander, W. B., Southgate, B. A. and Bassindale, R. (1935). Survey of the River Tees. Part II. The estuary – chemical and biological. D.S.I.R., London. (*Tech. Pap. wat. Poll. Res.* No. 5).

Amspoker, M. C. (1977). "The distribution of intertidal diatoms associated with the sediments in Yaquina estuary, Oregon". Ph.D. thesis, Oregon State University, Corvallis.

Amspoker, M. C. and McIntire, C. D. (1977). A multivariate analysis of the distribution of sediment associated diatoms in Yaquina estuary, Oregon. *J. Phycol.* **13** (Suppl.), 4.

Anger, K. (1975). On the influence of sewage pollution on inshore benthic communities in the south Kiel Bay. Part 1. Qualitative studies on indicator species and communities. *Merentutkimuslait. Julk./Havsforskningsinst. Skr.* **239**, 116–122.

Bacon, G. B. and Taylor, A. R. A. (1976). Succession and stratification in benthic diatom communities colonizing plastic collectors in a Prince Edward Island estuary. *Botanica mar.* **19**, 231–240.

Baudrimont, R. (1967). Quelques observations sur les diatomées du Trieux (Côtes-du-Nord) et de l'Aber de Roscoff (Nord Finistère). *Botaniste* **50**, 17–32.

Behre, K. (1961). Die Algenbesiedlung der Unterweser unter berucksichtigung ihre Zuflusse. *Veröff. Inst. Meeresforsch. Bremerh.* **7**, 71–263.

Biebl, R. (1952). Ecological non-environmental constitutional resistance of the protoplasm of marine algae. *J. mar. biol. Ass. U.K.* **31**, 307–315.

Black, D. R. (1971). Distribution and ionic relationships of *Enteromorpha intestinalis* (L.) Link. *Br. phycol. J.* **6**, 268.

Black, D. R. and Weeks, D. C. (1972). Ionic relationships of *Enteromorpha intestinalis. New Phytol.* **71**, 119–127.

Bokn, T. (1977). Pollution effects on the fucoids in the inner Oslofjord. *J. Phycol.* **13** (Suppl.), 7.

Bolton, J. J. (1979). Estuarine adaptation in populations of *Pilayella littoralis* (L.) Kjellm. (Phaeophyta, Ectocarpales). *Estuar. cst. mar. Sci.* **9**, 273–280.

Boney, A. D. (1964). Growth and viability of sporelings of red algae under various experimental conditions. *Br. phycol. Bull.* **2**, 392–393.

Bové, J. M., Bové, C., Whatley, F. R. and Arnon, D. I. (1963). Chloride requirement for oxygen evolution in photosynthesis. *Z. Naturf.* **18b**, 683–688.

Boyle, M. and Doty, M. S. (1949). The tolerance of stenohaline forms to diluted sea-water. *Biol. Bull. mar. biol. Lab. Woods Hole* **97**, 232.

Bracher, R. (1919). Observations on *Euglena deses. Ann. Bot.* **33**, 93–108.

Bracher, R. (1920). The ecology of the Avon banks at Bristol. *J. Ecol.* **17**, 36–81.

Breivik, K. (1958). Observations on the macroscopic algal vegetation in the Fjords near Stavanger, Norway. *Nytt Mag. Bot.* **6**, 19–37.

Brown, L. M. (1977). Osmoregulatory mechanisms of a euryhaline alga, *Stichococcus bacillaris* (Chlorophyceae). *J. Phycol.* **13** (Suppl.), 9.

Brown, L. M. and Hellebust, J. A. (1977). Comparative osmoregulation and other new taxonomic characters in the Ulotrichales. *J. Phycol.* **13** (Suppl.), 10.

Bryan, G. W. and Hummerstone, L. G. (1973). Brown seaweed as an indicator of heavy metals in estuaries in south-west England. *J. mar. biol. Ass. U.K.* **53**, 705–720.

Bryan, G. W. and Hummerstone, L. G. (1977). Indications of heavy metal contamination in the Looe estuary (Cornwall) with particular regard to silver and lead. *J. mar. biol. Ass. U.K.* **57**, 75–92.

Burrows, E. M. (1959). Growth, form and environment in *Enteromorpha. J. Linn. Soc.* (Bot:) **56**, 204–206.

Burrows, E. M. (1964). Ecological experiments with species of *Fucus. Proc. int. Seaweed Symp.* **4**, 166–170.

Burrows, E. M. (1971). Assessment of pollution effects by the use of algae. *Proc. R. Soc.* B **177**, 295–306.

Cardinal, A. and Villalard, M. (1971). Inventaire des algues marines benthiques de l'estuaire du Saint Laurent (Québec). *Naturaliste can.* **98**, 887–904.

Chapman, A. R. O. (1973). A critique of prevailing attitudes towards the control of seaweed zonation on the seashore. *Botanica mar.* **16**, 80–82.

Chater, E. H. (1927). On the distribution of larger-brown algae in Aberdeenshire estuaries. *Trans. Proc. bot. Soc. Edinb.* **29**, 362–380.

Cheney, D. P. and Mathieson, A. C. (1977). Genetic variation and population differentiation in *Chondrus crispus*. *J. Phycol.* **13** (Suppl.), 13.

Chihara, M. (1967). Developmental morphology and systematics of *Capsosiphon fulvescens*. *Bull. natn. Sci. Mus. Tokyo* **10**, 163–170.

Christie, A. O. and Shaw, M. (1968). Settlement experiments with zoospore of *Enteromorpha intestinalis* (L.) Link. *Br. phycol. Bull.* **3**, 529–534.

Conover, J. T. (1958). Seasonal growth of benthic marine plants as related to environmental factors in an estuary. *Pub. Inst. mar. Sci. Univ. Tex.* **5**, 97–147.

Conover, J. T. (1964). The ecology, seasonal periodicity and distribution of benthic plants in some Texas lagoons. *Botanica mar.* **7**, 4–41.

Cotton, A. D. (1912). Marine algae. *In* "A Biological Survey of Clare Island in the County of Mayo, Ireland and of the Adjoining District" (R. L. Praeger, ed.). *Proc. R. Ir. Acad.* **31** (15), 1–178.

Cox, E. J. (1977a). The tube-dwelling diatom flora at two sites in the Severn estuary. *Botanica mar.* **20**, 111–119.

Cox, E. J. (1977b). The distribution of tube-dwelling diatom species in the Severn estuary. *J. mar. biol. Ass. U.K.* **57**, 19–27.

Darley, W. M., Dunn, E. L., Holmes, S. and Larew III, H. G. (1976). A ^{14}C method for measuring epibenthic microalgal productivity in air. *J. exp. mar. Biol. Ecol.* **26**, 207–217.

Dawes, C. J., Moon, R. E. and Davis, M. A. (1978). The photosynthetic and respiratory rates and tolerances of benthic algae from a mangrove and salt-marsh estuary: a comparative study. *Estuar. cst. mar. Sci.* **6**, 175–185.

Donze, M. (1968). The algal vegetation of the Ria de Arosa (N.W. Spain). *Blumea* **16**, 159–192.

Doty, M. S. (1947). The marine algae of Oregon. I. Chlorophyta and Phaeophyta. *Farlowia* **3**, 1–65.

Doty, M. S. and Newhouse, J. (1954). The distribution of marine algae into estuarine waters. *Am. J. Bot.* **41**, 508–515.

Droop, M. R. (1958). Optimum relative and actual ionic concentrations for growth of some euryhaline algae. *Verh. int. Verein. angew. Limnol.* **13**, 722–730.

Druehl, L. D. (1978). The distribution of *Macrocystis integrifolia* in British Columbia as related to environmental parameters. *Can. J. Bot.* **56**, 69–79.

Eaton, J. W., Brown, J. G. and Round, F. E. (1966). Some observations on polarity and regeneration in *Enteromorpha*. *Br. phycol. Bull.* **3**, 53–62.

Edwards, P. (1972). Benthic algae in polluted estuaries. *Mar. Poll. Bull.* **3**, 55–60.

Edwards, P. (1975). Evidence for a relationship between the genera *Rosenvingiella* and *Prasiola* (Chlorophyta). *Br. phycol. J.* **10**, 291–297.

Edwards, P. and Kapraun, D. F. (1973). Benthic marine algal ecology in the Port Aransas, Texas area. *Contrib. mar. Sci. Univ. Tex.* **17**, 15–52.

Eppley, R. W. (1958). Sodium exclusion and potassium retention by the red marine alga, *Porphyra perforata. J. gen. Physiol.* **41**, 901–911.

Eppley, R. W. and Cyrus, C. C. (1960). Cation regulation and survival of the red alga *Porphyra perforata* in diluted and concentrated sea-water. *Biol. Bull. mar. biol. lab. Woods Hole* **118**, 55–65.

Fromageot, M. C. (1923). Influence de la concentration en sels de l'eau de mer sur l'assimilation des Algues vertes. *C. r. hebd. Séanc. Acad. Sci., Paris* **177**, 779–780.

Gayral, P. and de Mazancourt, J. S. (1958). Algues microscopiques nouvelles provenant d'un sol d'estuaire (Oued Bou Regreb, Maroc) *Bull. Soc. bot. Fr.* **105**, 344–350.

Gargas, E. (1971). Sun-shade adaptation in microbenthic algae from the Oresund. *Ophelia* **9**, 107–112.

Gessner, F. (1969). Photosynthesis and ion loss in the brown algae *Dictyopteris membranacea* and *Fucus virsoides. Mar. Biol., Berl.* **4**, 349–351.

Gessner, F. and Hammer, L. (1968). Exosmosis and "free-space" in marine benthic algae. *Mar. Biol., Berl.* **2**, 88–91.

Gessner, F. and Schramm, W. (1971). Salinity – plants. *In* "Marine Ecology Vol. I. Environmental Factors Part 2" (O. Kinne, ed.), pp. 705–802. Wiley-Interscience, London.

Ghazzawi, F. M. (1933). The littoral diatoms of the Liverpool and Port Erin shores. *J. mar. biol. Ass. U.K.* **19**, 165–176.

Gillham, M. E. (1957). Vegetation of the Exe estuary in relation to water salinity. *J. Ecol.* **45**, 735–756.

Gray, J. (1976). Are marine baseline surveys worthwhile? *New Scientist* **70**, 219–221.

Grenager, B. (1957). Algological observations from the polluted area of the Oslofjord. *Nytt Mag. Bot.* 5, 41–60.

Grieve, J. and Robertson, D. (1864). On the distribution of marine algae on the C.L.T. buoys in the Clyde. *Proc. Glasg. phil. Soc.* 5, 121–126.

Grøntved, J. (1960). On the productivity of microbenthos and phytoplankton in some Danish fjords. *Meddr Danm. Fisk. og Havunders.* N.S., **3**, 55–92.

Hammer, L. (1968). Salzgehalt und Photosynthese bei marine Pflanzen. *Mar. Biol., Berl.* **1**, 185–190.

Hanisak, M. D. (1979). Growth patterns of *Codium fragile* ssp. *tomentosoides* in response to temperature, irradiance, salinity and nitrogen source. *Mar. Biol., Berl.* **50**, 319–332.

den Hartog, C. (1959). The epilithic algal communities occurring along the coast of the Netherlands. *Wentia* **1**, 1–241.

den Hartog, C. (1960). Comments on the Venice-system for the classification of brackish waters. *Int. Rev. ges. Hydrobiol. Hydrog.* **45**, 481–485.

den Hartog, C. (1967). Brackish water as an environment for algae. *Blumea* **15**, 31–43.

den Hartog, C. (1968). The littoral environment of rocky shores as a border between the sea and the land and between the sea and the fresh-water. *Blumea* **16**, 374–393.

den Hartog, C. (1970). Some aspects of brackish water biology. *Comm. biol. Soc. Scient. fenn.* **31**(9), 1–15.

den Hartog, C. (1971). The border environment between the sea and the fresh-water with special reference to the estuary. *Vie Milieu* (Supp.) **22**, 739–751.

den Hartog, C. (1972). The effect of the salinity tolerance of algae on their distribution as exemplified by *Bangia*. *Proc. int. Seaweed Symp.* 7, 274–276.

Hayren, E. (1923). Fororenigen och strandvegetationen i Helsingfors Hamnområde. *Svensk bot. Tidskr.* **17**, 62–68.

Hellebust, J. (1970). The uptake and utilisation of organic substances by marine phytoplankters. *In* "Organic Matter in Natural Waters" (D. W. Hood, ed.), pp. 225–256. University of Alaska Press, Alaska.

Hoffman, C. (1959). Études ecologiques de quelques algues de la mer Baltique. *Coll. int. Cont. natn. Rech. Scient.* **81**, 205–216.

Holmes, E. M. (1888). Marine algae in the Blackwater estuary. *Essex Nat.* **2**, 248–249.

Hopkins, J. T. (1963). A study of the diatoms of the Ouse estuary, Sussex. I. The movement of the mud-flat diatoms in response to some chemical and physical changes. *J. mar. biol. Ass. U.K.* **43**, 653–663.

Hopkins, J. T. (1964a). A study of the diatoms in the Ouse estuary, Sussex. II. The ecology of the mud-flat diatom flora. *J. mar. biol. Ass. U.K.* **44**, 333–341.

Hopkins, J. T. (1964b). A study of the diatoms of the Ouse estuary, Sussex. III. The seasonal variation in the littoral epiphyte flora and the shore plankton. *J. mar. biol. Ass. U.K.* **44**, 613–644.

Hustedt, F. (1959). Die diatomeenflora det Unterweser von der Lesummünding bis Bremerhaven mit Berücksichtigung des Unterlaufs de Hunte and Geeste. *Veröff. Inst. Meeresforsch. Bremerh.* **6**, 13–175.

Jordan, A. J. and Vadas, R. L. (1972). Influences of environmental parameters on interspecific variation in *Fucus vesiculosus*. *Mar. Biol., Berl.* **14**, 248–252.

Jorde, I. and Klavestad, N. (1959). Observations on *Ectocarpus*, *Feldmannia*, *Pylaiella* and *Stictyosiphon* in Hardangerfjord, West Norway. *Nytt Mag. Bot.* **7**, 145–156.

Jorde, I. and Klavestad, N. (1960). On the Sphacelariales of a fjord area in West Norway. *Nytt Mag. Bot.* **8**, 89–102.

Jorde, I. and Klavestad, N. (1963). The natural history of the Hardangerfjord. 4. The benthonic algal vegetation. *Sarsia* **9**, 1–99.

Josselyn, M. N. (1977). The significance of seaweeds to the estuarine detrital pool. *J. Phycol.* **13** (Suppl.), 33.

Kapraun, D. F. (1970). Field and cultural studies of *Ulva* and *Enteromorpha* in the vicinity of Port Aransas, Texas. *Contrib. mar. Sci. Univ. Tex.* **15**, 205–285.

Kjeldsen, C. K. and Phinney, H. K. (1972). Effects of variations in salinity and temperature on some estuarine macro-algae. *Proc. int. Seaweed Symp.* **7**, 301–308.

Klavestad, N. (1957). An ecological study of the vegetation in Hunnebunnen, an old oyster poll in South eastern Norway. *Nytt Mag. Bot.* **5**, 63–100.

Klugh, A. B. (1922). Ecological polymorphism in *Enteromorpha crinita. Rhodora* **24**, 50–55.

Knaggs, F. W. (1966). *Rhodochorton purpureum* (Lightf.) Rosenv. I. Observations on the relationship between morphology and environment. *Nova Hedwigia* **10**, 499–513.

Knaggs, F. W. (1967). A review of the world distribution and ecology of *Rhodochorton purpureum* (Lightf.) Rosenv. *Nova Hedwigia* **14**, 549–570.

Knight, S. [J. T.] and Johnston, C. S. (in press). Effects of pollution on the seaweed distribution in the Firth of Forth. *Proc. int. Seaweed Symp.* **8**.

Knutzen, J. (1973). Marine species of *Vaucheria* (Xanthophyceae) in South Norway. *Norw. J. Bot.* **20**, 163–181.

Kolkwitz, R. and Marsson, M. (1908). Ökologie der pflanzlichen Saprobien. *Ber. dt. bot. Ges.* **26**, 505–519.

Kristiansen, A. (1972). A seasonal study of the marine algae in Tuborg harbour, The Sound, Denmark. *Bot. Tidsskr.* **67**, 201–244.

Kristiansen, A. (1978). Marine algal vegetation in shallow water around the Danish island of Saltholm, The Sound. *Bot. Tidsskr.* **72**, 203–226.

Leach, J. H. (1970). Epibenthic algal production in an intertidal mudflat. *Limnol. Oceanogr.* **15**, 514–521.

Legendre, R. (1921). Influence de la salinité de l'eau de mer sur l'assimilation chlorophyllienne des algues. *C. r. Séanc. Soc. Biol.* **85**, 222–224.

Lein, A., Rueness, J. and Wiik, O. O. (1974). Algologische observasjoner i Iddefjorden og Singlefjorden. *Blyttia* **32**, 155–168.

Lepailleur, H. (1971). Contribution a l'étude de la végétation algal dans l'estuaire de l'Orne (France). *Vie Milieu* (Suppl.) **22**, 233–241.

Lersten, N. R. and Voth, P. D. (1960). Experimental control of zoid discharge and rhizoid formation in the green alga *Enteromorpha. Bot. Gaz.* **122**, 33–45.

Lewin, R. A. and Robertson, J. A. (1971). Influence of salinity on the form of *Asterocytis* in pure culture. *J. Phycol.* **7**, 236–238.

Lewin, J. C. (1963). Heterotrophy in marine diatoms. *In* "Symposium on Marine Microbiology" (C. H. Oppenheimer, ed.), pp. 227–235. Charles C. Thomas, Springfield, Illinois.

Lindgren, L. (1975). Algal zonation on rocky shores outside Helsinki as a basis for pollution monitoring. *Merentutkimuslait. Julk./Havsforskningsinst. Skr.* **239**, 344–347.

Lindgren, P. E. (1965). Coastal algae off Göteborg in relation to gradients of salinity and pollution. *Acta phytogeogr. Suecica* **50**, 92–96.

McIntire, C. D. (1973). Diatom association in Yaquina estuary, Oregon: A multivariate analysis. *J. Phycol.* **9**, 254–259.

McIntire, C. D. (1978). The distribution of estuarine diatoms along environmental gradients: canonical correlation. *Estuar. cst. mar. Sci.* **6**, 447–457.

McIntire, C. D. and Overton, W. S. (1971). Distributional patterns in assemblages of attached diatoms from Yaquina estuary, Oregon. *Ecology* **52**, 758–777.

McIntire, C. D. and Wulff, B. L. (1969). A laboratory method for the study of marine benthic diatoms. *Limnol. Oceanogr.* **14**, 667–678.

McIntosh, R. P. and Dawes, C. J. (1978). Low salinity tolerance and the effect of spring water on the distribution of *Borstrychia binderi* (Rhodophyta) in Floridian estuaries. *J. Phycol.* **14** (Suppl.), 38.

Main, S. P. and McIntire, C. D. (1974). The distribution of epiphytic diatoms in Yaquina estuary, Oregon. *Botanica mar.* **17**, 88–89.

Malinowski, K. C. and Ramus, J. (1973). Growth of the green alga *Codium fragile* in a Connecticut estuary. *J. Phycol.* **9**, 102–110.

Marshall, N., Oviatt, C. A. and Skauen, D. M. (1971). Productivity of the benthic microflora of shoal estuarine environments in southern New England. *Int. Rev. ges. Hydrobiol. Hydrog.* **56**, 947–956.

Mathieson, A. C. (1978). The distribution, composition and phenology of New England estuarine seaweeds. *J. Phycol.* **14** (Suppl.), 26.

Mathieson, A. C. and Dawes, C. J. (1974). Ecological studies of Floridian *Eucheuma* (Rhodophyta, Gigartinales). II Photosynthesis and respiration. *Bull. mar. Sci. Gulf Caribb.* **24**, 274–285.

Mathieson, A. C. and Fralick, R. A. (1972). Investigations of New England marine algae. V. The algal vegetation of the Hampton-Seabrook estuary and the open coast near Hampton, New Hampshire. *Rhodora* **74**, 406–435.

Mathieson, A. C. and Fralick, R. A. (1973). Benthic algae and vascular plants of the lower Menimack River and adjacent shoreline. *Rhodora* **75**, 52–64.

Mathieson, A. C. and Fuller, S. W. (1969). A preliminary investigation of the benthonic marine algae of the Chesapeake Bay region. *Rhodora* **71**, 524–534.

Milligan, G. M. (1965). The seaweeds of the Blackwater estuary with a complete list of marine algae recorded from Essex. *Essex Nat.* **31**, 309–327.

Milne, A. (1940). The ecology of the Tamar estuary. IV. The distribution of the fauna and flora on buoys. *J. mar. biol. Ass. U.K.* **24**, 69–87.

Moore, W. W. and McIntire, C. D. (1977). Spatial and seasonal distribution of littoral diatoms in Yaquina estuary, Oregon, U.S.A. *Botanica mar.* **20**, 99–109.

Moss, B. and Marsland, A. (1976). Regeneration of *Enteromorpha. Br. phycol. J.* **11**, 309–313.

Munda, I. (1963). The influence of salinity on the chemical composition, growth and fructification of some Fucaceae. *Proc. int. Seaweed Symp.* **4**, 123–126.

Munda, I. (1964). Observations on variation in form and chemical composition of *Fucus ceranoides* L. *Nova Hedwigia* **14**, 519–548.

Munda, I. (1967). Observations on the benthic marine algae in a land-locked fjord (Nordåsvàtnet) near Bergen, Western Norway. *Nova Hedwigia* **14**, 519–548.

Munda, I. (1969). Differences in the algal vegetation of two Icelandic fjords, Dyrafjördur (West Iceland) and Reydafjördur (East Iceland). *Proc. int. Seaweed Symp.* **6**, 255–261.

Munda, I. (1972a). The effect of different chlorinities on the survival of three freshwater species: *Cladophora fracta* (Müll. ex Vahl) Kützing, *Vaucheria geminata* Heering and *Tribonema vulgare* Pascher. *Razpr. Slov. Akad Znan. Umet.* **15**, 1–33.

Munda, I. (1972b). General features of the benthic algal zonation around the Icelandic coast. *Acta nat. islandica* **21**, 1–34.

Munda, I. (1972c). On the chemical composition, distribution and ecology of some common benthic marine algae from Iceland. *Botanica mar.* **15**, 1–45.

Munda, I. (1977a). Combined effects of temperature and salinity on growth rates of germlings of three *Fucus* species from Iceland, Helgoland and the Adriatic Sea. *Helgoländer wiss. Meeresunters.* **29**, 302–310.

Munda, I. (1977b). Differences in amino acid composition of estuarine and marine fucoids. *Aquatic Bot.* **3**, 273–280.

Munda, I. (1978a). Survey of the algal vegetation of the Dýrafjördur, north-west Iceland. *Nova Hedwigia* **29**, 281–403.

Munda, I. (1978b). Salinity dependent distribution of benthic algae in estuarine areas of Icelandic fjords. *Botanica mar.* **21**, 451–468.

Munda, I. M. and Garrasi, C. (1978). Salinity induced changes of nitrogenous constituents in *Fucus vesiculosus* (Phaeophyceae). *Aquatic Bot.* **4**, 347–351.

Munda, I. M. and Kremer, B. P. (1977). Chemical composition and physiological properties of fucoids under conditions of reduced salinity. *Mar. Biol., Berl.* **42**, 9–15.

Nellen, U. R. (1966). Uber den einfluss des Salzgehaltes auf die photosynthetische Leistung verschiedenen Standort-formen von *Delesseria sanguinea* und *Fucus serratus. Helgoländer wiss. Meeresunters.* **13**, 288–313.

Nelson-Smith, A. (1965). Marine biology of Milford Haven: The physical environment. *Fld Stud.* **2**, 155–188.

Nelson-Smith, A. (1967). Marine biology of Milford Haven: The distribution of littoral plants and animals. *Fld Stud.* **2**, 407–434.

Niemeck, R. A. and Mathieson, A. C. (1976). An ecological study of *Fucus spiralis* L. *J. exp. mar. Biol. Ecol.* **24**, 33–48.

Nienhuis, P. H. (1967). *Capsosiphon fulvescens* (C. Ag.) Setch. et Gardn. in Zuidwest Nederland. *Gorteria* **3**, 149–155.

Nienhuis, P. H. (1974). Variability in the life-cycle of *Rhizoclonium riparium* (Roth) Harv. (Chlorophyceae: Cladophorales) under Dutch estuarine conditions. *Hydrobiol. Bull.* **8**, 172–178.

Nienhuis, P. H. (1975). "Biosystematics and Ecology of *Rhizoclonium riparium* (Roth) Harv. (Chlorophyceae: Cladophorales) in the estuarine areas of the Rivers Rhine, Meuse and Scheldt". Thesis, University of Groningen, Bronder Offset B.V. Rotterdam.

Nilsson, J. P. (1975). En algologisk undersøkelse fra Sondeledfjorden ved Risor – en "land-locked" fjord som er saelig utsatt ved firurensing. *Blyttia* **33**, 17–26.

Norin, L. -L. and Waern, M. (1973). The zone of low algal standing crop near Stockholm. *Oikos* (Suppl.) **15**, 179–184.

Norton, T. A. and South, G. R. (1969). Influence of reduced salinity on the distribution of two laminarialean algae. *Oikos* **20**, 320–326.

Ogata, E. and Matsui, T. (1965). Photosynthesis in several marine plants of Japan as affected by salinity, drying and pH with attention to their growth habits. *Botanica mar.* 8, 199–217.

Ogata, E. and Schramm, W. (1971). Some observations on the influence of salinity on growth and photosynthesis in *Porphyra umbilicalis. Mar. Biol., Berl.* **10**, 70–76.

Ogata, E. and Takada, H. (1968). Studies on the relationship between the respiration and the changes in salinity in some marine plants in Japan. *J. Shimonoseki Univ. Fish.* **16**, 67–88.

Ohno, M. (1969). A physiological ecology of the early stage of some marine algae. *Rep. Usa mar. biol. Stn Kochi Univ.* **16**, 1–46.

Ohno, M. (1976). Some observations on the influence of salinity on photosynthetic activity and chloride ion loss in several seaweeds. *Int. Rev. ges. Hydrobiol. Hydrog.* **61**, 665–672.

Palmer, J. D. and Round, F. E. (1965). Persistant vertical migration rhythms in benthic microflora. I. The effect of light and temperature on the rhythmic behaviour of *Euglena obtusa. J. mar. biol. Ass. U.K.* **95**, 567–582.

Parke, M. and Dixon, P. S. (1976). Check-list of British marine algae – third revision. *J. mar. biol. Ass. U.K.* **56**, 527–594.

Pedersen, P. M. (1973). Preliminary note on some marine algae from South Greenland. *Bot. Tidsskr.* **68**, 145–149.

Pekkari, S. (1973). Effects of sewage water on benthic vegetation. *Oikos* (Suppl.) **15**, 185–188.

Penniman, C. A. (1977). Seasonal chemical and reproductive changes in *Gracilaria foliifera* (Forssk.) Børg. from Great Bay, New Hampshire, U.S.A. *J. Phycol.* **13** (Suppl.), 53.

Perkins, E. J. (1960). The diurnal rhythm of littoral diatoms of the R. Eden estuary, Fife. *J. Ecol.* **48**, 725–728.

Perkins, E. J. and Abbott, O. J. (1972). Nutrient enrichment and sand-flat fauna. *Mar. Poll. Bull.* **3**, 70–72.

Peussa, M. and Ravanko, O. (1975). Benthic macroalgae indicating changes in the Turku sea area. *Merentutkimuslait Julk./Havsforskningsinst. Skr.* **239**, 339–343.

Phillips, D. J. H. (1977). The use of biological indicator organisms to monitor trace metal pollution in marine and estuarine environment – a review. *Envir. Poll.* **13**, 281–317.

Phillips, J. (1972). Chemical processes in estuaries. *In* "The Estuarine Environment" (R. S. K. Barnes, ed.), pp. 35–50. Applied Science Publishers, London.

Powell, H. T. (1972). The ecology of the macroalgae in sea-lochs in Western Scotland. *Proc. int. Seaweed Symp.* **7**, 273.

Prange, R. K. (1978). An autecological study of *Blidingia minima* var. *subsalsa* (Chlorophyceae) in the Squamish estuary (British Columbia). *Can. J. Bot.* **56**, 170–179.

Price, J. H. and Tittley, I. (1972). The marine flora of the County of Kent and its distribution 1597–1972. *Br. phycol. J.* **7**, 282–283.

Price, J. H., Tittley, I. and Honey, S. I. (1977). The benthic marine flora of Lincolnshire and Cambridgeshire: a preliminary survey. Part I. *Naturalist, Hull* **102**, 3–20.

Priou, M. -L. and Serpette, M. (1954). Sur les associations algales des anses vaseuses du sud de la Bretagne. *Revue algol.* **1**, 25–28.

Ravanko, O. (1968). Macroscopic green brown and red algae in the southwestern archipelago of Finland. *Acta bot. fenn.* **79**, 1–50.

Reed, R. H. and Russell, G. (1978a). Salinity fluctuations and their influence on "bottle-brush" morphogenesis in *Enteromorpha intestinalis* (L.) Link. *Br. phycol. J.* **13**, 149–153.

Reed, R. H. and Russell, G. (1978b). Salinity tolerances in *Enteromorpha intestinalis* (L.) Link. *Br. phycol. J.* **13**, 205.

Rhodes, R. G. (1972). Studies on the biology of brown algae on the Atlantic coast of Virginia. I. *Porterinema fluviatile* (Porter) Waern. *J. Phycol.* **8**, 117–119.

Riznyk, R. Z. and Phinney, H. K. (1972a). Manometric assessment of interstitial microalgae production in two estuarine sediments. *Oecologia* **10**, 193–203.

Riznyk, R. Z. and Phinney, H. K. (1972b). The distribution of intertidal phytopsammon in an Oregon estuary. *Mar. Biol., Berl.* **13**, 318–324.

Riznyk, R. Z., Edens, J. I. and Libby, R. C. (1978). Production of epibenthic diatoms in a southern California impounded estuary. *J. Phycol.* **14**, 273–279.

Round, F. E. (1971). Benthic marine diatoms. *Oceanogr. mar. Biol. Ann. Rev.* **9**, 83–139.

Round, F. E. and Palmer, J. D. (1966). Persistant vertical migration rhythms in benthic microflora. II. Field and laboratory studies on diatoms from the banks of the River Avon. *J. mar. biol. Ass. U.K.* **46**, 191–214.

Rueness, J. (1973). Pollution effects on littoral algal communities in the inner Oslofjord, with special reference to *Ascophyllum nodosum. Helgoländer wiss. Meeresunters.* **24**, 446–454.

Russell, G. (1963). A study in populations in *Pilayella littoralis. J. mar. biol. Ass. U.K.* **43**, 469–483.

Russell, G. (1967). The ecology of some free-living Ectocarpaceae. *Helgoländer wiss. Meeresunters.* **15**, 155–162.

Russell, G. (1971). Marine algal reproduction in two British estuaries. *Vie Milieu* (Suppl.) **22**, 219–230.

Russell, G. (1972). Phytosociological studies on a two-zone shore. I. Basic pattern. *J. Ecol.* **60**, 539–545.

Russell, G. and Bolton, J. J. (1975). Euryhaline ecotypes of *Ectocarpus siliculosus* (Dillw.). Lyngb. *Estuar. cst. mar. Sci.* **3**, 91–94.

Russell, G. and Fielding, A. H. (1974). The competitive properties of marine algae in culture. *J. Ecol.* **62**, 689–698.

Schramm, W. and Ohno, M. (1973). Some observations on the influence of salinity on biological activity of *Fucus vesiculosus. Bull. Jap. Soc. Phycol.* **21**, 81–85.

Schwenke, H. (1958). Über einige zellphysiologische Faktoren der Hypotonieresistenz mariner Rotalgen. *Kieler Meeresforsch.* **14**, 130–150.

Sheath, R. G. and Cole, K. (1978). Salinity adaptations of a recent migrant into the Great Lakes, *Bangia atropurpurea* (Rhodophyta). *J. Phycol.* **14** (Suppl.), 23.

Simons, J. (1974). *Vaucheria compacta*, a euryhaline estuarine algal species. *Acta bot. neerl.* **23**, 613–626.

Simons, J. (1975). *Vaucheria* species from the estuarine areas in the Netherlands. *Neth. J. Sea Res.* **9**, 1–23.

Simons, J. and Vroman, M. (1973). *Vaucheria* species from the Dutch brackish inland ponds, "de putten". *Acta bot. neerl.* **22**, 177–192.

Söderström, J. (1963). Studies in *Cladophora. Bot. Gothoburgensia* **1**, 1–147.

Stam, W. T. and Holleman, H. C. (1975). The influence of different salinities on growth and morphological variability of a number of *Phormidium* strains (Cyanophyceae) in culture. *Acta bot. neerl.* **24**, 379–390.

Stewart, W. D. P. and Pugh, G. J. F. (1963). Blue-green algae of a developing salt-marsh. *J. mar. biol. Ass. U.K.* **43**, 309–317.

Sundene, O. (1953). The algal vegetation of Oslofjord. *Skr. norske Vidensk.-Akad. mat.-nat. Kl.* 1953(2), 1–245.

Sundene, O. (1959). Form variation in *Antithamnion plumula.* Experiments on Plymouth and Oslofjord strains in culture. *Nytt Mag. Bot.* **7**, 181–187.

Tittley, I. and Price, J. H. (1977). The marine algae of the tidal Thames. *Lond. Nat.* **56**, 10–17.

Townsend, C. and Lawson, G. W. (1972). Preliminary results on factors causing zonation in *Enteromorpha* using a tide simulating apparatus. *J. exp. mar. Biol. Ecol.* **8**, 265–276.

von Wachenfeldt, T. (1969). Aktuella problemstallningar. II. Sympunkter po algflora i Oresund. *Bot. Notiser* **122**, 427–434.

Waern, M. (1952). Rocky-shore algae in the Öregrund archipelago. *Acta phytogeogr. Suecica* **30**, 1–298.

Waern, M. (1965). A vista on the marine vegetation. *Acta phytogeogr. Suecica* **50**, 15–27.

Wallentinus, I. (1976). Environmental influences on benthic macro-vegetation in the Trosa-Asko area, Northern Baltic proper. I. Hydrographic and chemical parameters and the macrophyte communities. *Contr. Asko Lab.* **15**, 1–138.

Welch, E. B., Emery, R. M., Matsuda, R. I. and Dawson, W. A. (1972). The relation of periphytic and planktonic algal growth in an estuary to hydrographic factors. *Limnol. Oceanogr.* **17**, 731–737.

Wildish, D. J. (1971). A preliminary account of the ecology of the Medway estuary. *Trans. Kent Fld Club* **3**, 237–246.

Wilkinson, M. (1973a). The distribution of attached intertidal algae in estuaries with particular reference to the River Wear. *Vasculum* **58**, 22–28.

Wilkinson, M. (1973b). A preliminary survey of the intertidal benthic algae of the Clyde estuary. *Western Nat.* **2**, 59–69.

Wilkinson, M. (1974). Investigations on the autecology of *Eugomontia sacculata* Kornm., a shell-boring alga. *J. exp. mar. Biol. Ecol.* **16**, 19–27.

Wilkinson, M. (1975). Intertidal algae of some estuaries in Galloway. *Western Nat.* **4**, 42–50.

Wilkinson, M. (1977a). Distributions of macroscopic algae in estuaries. *Br. phycol. J.* **12**, 123.

Wilkinson, M. (1977b). Species distributions in British estuaries. *J. Phycol.* **13** (Suppl.), 74.

Wilkinson, M. and Roberts, C. (1974). Intertidal algae of the estuary of the River Add, Argyllshire. *Western Nat.* **3**, 73–82.

Wilkinson, M. and Tittley, I. (1979). The marine algae of Elie, Scotland: a reassessment. *Botanica mar.* **22**, 249–256.

Wilkinson, M., Henderson, A. R. and Wilkinson, C. (1976). Distribution of attached algae in estuaries. *Mar. Poll. Bull.* **7**, 183–184.

Wood, R. D. and Straughan, J. (1953). Time–intensity tolerance of *Lemanea fucina* to salinity. *Am. J. Bot.* **40**, 381–384.

Wulff, B. L. and McIntire, C. D. (1972). Laboratory studies of assemblages of attached estuarine diatoms. *Limnol. Oceanogr.* **17**, 200–214.

Yarish, C., Casey, S. and Edwards, P. (1977). Ecotypic differentiation of two estuarine red algae from New Jersey. *J. Phycol.* **13** (Suppl.), 75.

Yarish, C., Casey, S. and Edwards, P. (1978). Acclimation responses to salinity of three estuarine red algae from New Jersey. *J. Phycol.* **14** (Suppl.), 27.

Zimmerman, M. S. and Livingston, R. J. (1976). Seasonality and physicochemical ranges of benthic macrophytes from a North Florida estuary (Apalachee Bay). *Contrib. mar. Sci. Univ. Tex.* **20**, 33–45.

Zimmerman, U. and Steudle, E. (1971). Effects of potassium concentration and osmotic pressure of sea-water on the cell turgor pressure of *Chaetomorpha linum*. *Mar. Biol., Berl.* **11**, 132–137.

5 | Niche and Community in the Inshore Benthos, with emphasis on the Macroalgae

J. H. PRICE

Department of Botany, British Museum (Natural History), London, England

Abstract: The concept of *niche* or *species niche* is of great importance in community ecology and evolutionary studies but, at least so far as plants are concerned, remains somewhat elusive in framework and definition and is often confused in application. The term and concept, as such, have therefore been relatively little used in botany and less so in marine benthic macroalgal studies. Reasons for the latter extreme neglect are examined in detail, being worthy in themselves of study. Important amongst them is a paucity of information on biological aspects of individuals, of populations and of whole species, particularly in terms of reproductive patterns and inter/intraspecific population interactions. The significance and definition of "community" in the inshore benthos are also considered, since this unit is fundamental to niche studies. For the inshore benthic macroalgae, the lack of data occasionally creates great difficulty in the distinguishing of *niche* factors from *habitat* factors, and of either from factors of *range* (distribution area); all three are in any case clearly and closely related. The advantages of data organization on the basis of the niche concept and the probable need to apply the term *ecotope* (niche + habitat; *sensu* Whittaker, Levin and Root, 1973) in many macroalgal inshore benthic situations are considered in detail. The nature of benthic inshore marine communities and the complexity of obtaining required information in many cases cause this term and concept *ecotope* to be of considerable utility now and, in some conditions, for the foreseeable future. Niche dimensions relating to marine macroalgae are considered in an Appendix, as are mathematical models and information sources covering measures applied in niche quantification and delimitation.

Systematics Association Special Volume No. 17(b), "The Shore Environment, Vol. 2: Ecosystems", edited by J. H. Price, D. E. G. Irvine and W. F. Farnham, 1980, pp. 487–564, Academic Press, London and New York.

INTRODUCTION

Resource partitioning studies have become a major movement in both theoretical and practical approaches to ecology and evolution; this has been especially evident within very recent years (e.g. Benayahu and Loya, 1977; Connell, 1975; Dayton, 1971, 1973b; Paine, 1971a; J. Porter, 1976; Rastetter and Cooke, 1979; Roughgarden, 1976; Sale and Dybdahl, 1978; Schoener, 1974; Smith and Tyler, 1972, 1975; Stewart and Levin, 1973; Talbot *et al.*, 1979; Underwood, 1976; these are merely examples of a veritable multitude of papers). From perhaps the 1940s onwards ever increasing numbers of studies have been carried out, becoming gradually more detailed, on various of the factors affecting development and persistence of patterns in distribution, abundance and diversity of organisms in rocky marine intertidal areas (e.g. Burrows and Lodge, 1950; Castenholz, 1961; Connell, 1974; Dayton, 1971; Emerson and Zedler, 1978; Fahey, 1953; Haven, 1973; Hoshiai, 1960; Jones, 1948; Lodge, 1948; May *et al.*, 1970; Niell, 1979; Paine, 1966, 1977; J. Porter, 1974; Pyefinch, 1943; Southward, 1953, 1956, 1964; other examples are given in more specific contexts later). Such studies are essentially concerned with resource partitioning. Even more recently, similar studies have been initiated in subtidal conditions, although the logistics of these latter studies are necessarily more complex and therefore time-consuming (Field *et al.*, 1977; Hiscock, 1979; Kain, 1962–1977, 1975; Jones and Kain, 1967; Prentice and Kain, 1976; Velimirov *et al.*, 1977; Velimirov and Griffiths, 1979; amongst many others). All such approaches require, or develop the need for, very detailed knowledge of the potentials of constituent species in terms of individuals, populations, or other supposedly interacting groups. Directionalization (i.e. a firm idea of the purpose and methods to be adopted) is a prime requisite of the process of gaining this latter knowledge and necessitates strict marshalling of concepts before, during and after appropriate fieldwork. One aspect of that marshalling is *niche theory*, particularly important in studies at the level of the biological population (Colwell and Futuyma, 1971). In rocky coastal ecology, the *niche* is very rarely invoked by *name* although in practice often approached as a *concept*. It has been rightly said in respect of some forms of the concept (Whittaker *et al.*, 1973) that the niche is merely a theoretical construct; this in no sense invalidates the approach. A recent attempt (Kroes, 1977) to redefine and establish fresh limits for the application of the term and concept *niche* may remove at some levels the need to consider niche as merely a theoretical construct. This is fully discussed later.

The emphasis given in the title to plant life is intentional but does not imply a total neglect of the importance of animals in the benthic marine ecosystem. This importance applies especially in the context of definition of *niche axes* (see later); any neglect would therefore be wholly improper in that so many studies have firmly demonstrated the extent of interactions in both intertidal and subtidal. The title places emphasis on plant life only in the sense that the prime concern is with what the approach reveals about the marine algae, animals having obvious importance but being of themselves secondary, for the present purposes. The primary stimulus to the framing of this paper, essentially a review, has been the realization of the extent to which workers on shore (including Price, 1978!) have

(i) employed the terms niche and microniche in contexts that could lead to two or more different definitions of the terms, some wider than others;
(ii) been equivocal and inconsistent in use of the term, even throughout the same work;
(iii) not used the term at all where they could well have done, since more or less fully employing the background concepts; or
(iv) merely ignored the fact that such an approach might well stimulate constructive thinking.

Throughout the paper, I have maintained the deliberate policy of citing only those references that derive from the last ten or so years, unless there are classic studies that have no subsequent counterparts and have been required for the reasoning process adopted at that point in the text. The older literature can in most cases easily be traced by checking through the more recent studies.

HISTORY OF THE CONCEPT "NICHE"

The history of the niche concept is too well known or documented to require more than summarized reiteration here. Much greater detail is available in Whittaker and Levin (1975) and in Hutchinson

(1978), the latter in Chapter 5 of his "An Introduction to Population Ecology". Suffice it to say now that the employment of the term in its earlier years was predominantly zoological, for example its initial application to lady beetles (Johnson, 1910; Gaffney, 1975). Hutchinson (1978) suggested this latter was merely an example of the figurative use of an essentially architectural term and that Johnson was not establishing a theory of the niche. The increasingly technical use of the term came through studies by Grinnell (1914) and Taylor (1916), a process carried yet further by Grinnell himself (1917, 1924) and by Elton (especially in 1927). Apart from these, efforts in refining and rationalizing the concept can be attributed to relatively few people. The dimensional formulation with which all niche theory is of late fundamentally concerned was first presented by Hutchinson in 1958, although he was careful to acknowledge debt to many others. This formulation leads to some difficulty in discussing the niche conceptually without becoming rather mathematical, a pitfall that I shall hope generally to avoid here. Hutchinson's Cold Spring Harbour redefinition gave to each measurable feature of the environment, recognizable at that time or not, one coordinate in an infinitely (n-) dimensional (hyper-) space. Within that conceptual environment (hyperspace), the portion(s) within which in turn the "fitness of the individual was positive was called that individual's niche". MacArthur, whose (1968) words are quoted here, was a distinguished student of Hutchinson and responsible, before his untimely death, for interesting development of the niche concept; especially noteworthy is "The Theory of the Niche" (in Lewontin, 1968), a fascinating but rather heavily mathematical paper in which MacArthur concluded that *niche* and *phenotype* were in some views almost identical.

In omitting a host of interesting papers between then and the most interesting and useful compendium of earlier papers and connective explanatory comment by Whittaker and Levin (1975), I do many workers an injustice; the extent of that injustice can be gauged from Hutchinson (1978). It is not possible, however, to omit mention of the principally verbal and yet detailed and precise presentation by Whittaker *et al.* (1973); the importance of the latter will emerge clearly from the following pages. Whittaker and Levin indicated in 1975 that they were acutely aware of the subjectivity of their choices as to whose articles to include and whose to omit, many of the latter having at least equal claim, yet by the nature of their product, the detail was much fuller than is possible here and, with Hutchinson's (1978) recent book, will give very useful baseline coverage for anyone who wishes for a more complete background. Aspects of the history of the concept *niche* are also considered briefly in Kroes (1977), a new departure in some senses of definition and approach, and at somewhat greater length in both Vandermeer (1972) and Diamond (1978).

THE CONCEPTS OF "NICHE" AND "COMMUNITY"

1. General

> We might . . . regard niche theory as the quantification of methods that were intuitively employed by the early natural historians.
>
> (Vandermeer, 1972)

The question "what is a niche?" (Hutchinson, 1978) is simple; the answer is not, factually, conceptually or semantically. Human communication, verbal or mathematical, has always to some extent been bedevilled by misunderstandings through failure to define, or failure to define adequately. Ecological theory is a prime example of this (Lubchenco, 1978; Lewin and Enright, 1978; Lubchenco, 1979). The semantics involved in definition are not the whole problem, moreover. Conceptual confusion and confusion in application also often exist. It is true that "One simple solution to this problem would be for every author to specify what is meant in any particular situation" (Lubchenco, 1979), and equally that "Almost all attempts at definitions have been ignored. (Witness the concepts of *niche, competition, community* and *succession*)" (Lubchenco, 1979). There is certainly no generally accepted definition, despite wide usage, of the term *niche* (Kroes, 1977). Writing of the extant loosely-applied terminology for communications about ecological phenomena, Lidicker (1979) suggested that "Some would claim that such flexibility is a desirable attribute of an active field of intellectual activity, serving to inhibit premature solidification of concepts into precise definitions", but indicated that he personally felt "there now seems to be ample basis for some improvement in the current state of luxurious fluidity". I shall later outline what I consider the currently most useful and productive definitions for the inshore marine benthic situations.

The general concept of niche can be introduced, in its recently most usual form, by reference to the statement that opens Whittaker and Levin's Benchmark Volume on "Niche Theory and Application" (1975: Introduction, p. 1). Quoting briefly:

> A familiar definition in ecology is that of the community as an assemblage of organisms living together in a particular environment. No one is very happy with this definition. The word "assemblage" in particular misses the idea of the community as a functional system of interacting populations and ignores the questions of how this system of species is organized, how the various species are interrelated and fit together into the whole, and the place of each species in the functional whole. This place or role of a species in this system is termed the *niche* . . . [and we need to] understand how niches are conceived, defined, and measured; how the niches of different species relate to one another; and how they are to be placed in an evolutionary context. It is characteristic of this area of study that it links observation with theory by way of mathematics.

Essentially similar are the opinions expressed in Connell's (1975) introduction. Clarification of that linkage (from which detailed mathematical treatment will here be largely omitted, although sources of expressions are presented in Appendix II) requires the establishment of a few basic definitions for this paper, especially in view of the previous failures in this direction (see above) and of the residual disagreements despite definition. Subsections a–d of Section 2 (pp. 499–506) present these data.

Niche and *habitat* have often been used imprecisely to overlap with each other, or even consciously as alternatives. Whittaker and Levin (1975) indicated their belief that there could be no possible justification for two such equivalent terms, save for that which arises from loose thinking; with this view I concur, since the resultant situation is merely confusing. If they are deemed equivalent, one should be reduced to the "synonymy" of the other. However, Whittaker *et al.* (1973) have amply demonstrated that their separate application on a rational basis without confusion is entirely feasible, given a modicum of the acceptance of which Lubchenco (1979; see earlier) has deplored the absence.

Whittaker *et al.* (1973), with some amplification in Whittaker and Levin (1975), have suggested that use of the term *niche*, previous to their studies, was in several contrasting senses:

(i) The position or role of a species *in* a given community. (The *functional concept: niche* as such, in their view.)

(ii) The distributional relationship of a species to a range of environments and communities (i.e. to environmental gradients). (The *niche as habitat*, the place niche: *niche* = *habitat*.)

(iii) To include both intra- and inter-community factors. (Niche including habitat: *niche* = *habitat* + *niche*.)

Alternatives (ii) and (iii) above are, in these authors' views, undesirable since they are said to obscure the role of the species in a community. In my own view, alternative (iii) need not do so consistently, or even at all if used carefully. It is, however, true to say that there is some chance that evolutionary relationships may be obscured by lumping between communities in this latter alternative. The functional concept is correctly stated by Whittaker, Levin and Root to include genetic characteristics evolved *relative to other species* in the community; habitat difference involves evolutionary response to gradients of environmental factors external to "though often modified by" the community. Niche differentiation among species "within-habitat" (= intra-community) is *within-habitat* or *α-diversity*; the product of habitat differentiation is *between-habitat* or *β-diversity*. *γ-diversity*, that of an entire landscape, is the combination between α and β and relates to the *ecotope* (Peet, 1974); ecotope is defined at length later. At this point, it would be very easy to become embroiled in long debate of the concepts involved in species diversity theory. Although obviously only artificially set aside when matters such as niche breadth (see later) are considered, species diversity requires more detailed consideration than can be given here; any debate below that concerns the topic therefore does so incidentally to the main themes of this chapter. Differentiation of resources used *within* the community is usually referred to as *niche breadth* (see later and Appendix II) and is suggested by Whittaker *et al.* (1973) not necessarily to be based on the same mechanisms (ecotypic and subspecific differentiation; clone selection, and so on) as are responsible for habitat amplitude, as expressed in the habitat range (that is, *interpopulation* differences).

Kroes (1977) concluded that the prime reason for the extremely confused situation in the niche concept lay with a current failure to discriminate adequately between *attributes of the species* and *attributes of the ecosystem.* His short but interesting paper suggested the need for what he called the species *ecopotential*, a "new concept" (his phrase) although elsewhere in his paper (p. 323) almost directly equated to the *fundamental niche* of Hutchinson (1958) and other workers. Changes of both terminology and definition are proposed by Kroes. *Ecopotential* (defined as the aspects of the "average genotype" of a species that determine the ecological characteristics that develop or may develop in individual members of the species) and *species niche* (defined as the basic ecosytem building-block or functioning component and consisting of one species population only; based on a unique "ecological program", the species ecopotential) both have primary dependence on the "average genotype" of the species. The other Kroes categories are *primary niches* (groups of species populations that are either all producers, all consumers, or all decomposers, forming part of the structure of an ecosystem and functioning in energy and matter flow) and *intermediate niches* (e.g. plankton; tree-dwelling monkeys; macrobenthic seaweeds; shore-living invertebrates; these are components of the primary niche that become more ecosystem-specific "as finer distinctions are applied" but have similar "functions" in the ecosystem). These other categories, however necessary for Kroes' reasoning as to the non-dependence of ecosystem characteristics or components on an integrated single information source or programme (the genotype), add little in a meaningful functional way for the [species] niche concept itself. Kroes admits the equivalence or near equivalence of *ecopotential* with *fundamental niche* and of *species niche* with *realized niche.* He suggests that whilst it is not clear whether Hutchinson's (1958) *fundamental niche* is an attribute of just the species or also of the environment, it *is* clear that the *realized niche* does not include the species population itself, being the total of relations between population and environment. These Hutchinson concepts have been extended, tightened and clarified by many authors, including Whittaker *et al.* (1973) and Whittaker and Levin (1975), of whose efforts to distinguish intra- (niche) and inter- (habitat) community characteristics of species populations Kroes commented do "not seem to clarify the situation". A somewhat similar, if less extreme, opinion was expressed by Kulesza (1975), who considered that the Whittaker *et al.* (1973) distinctions would probably promote standardization of terms but would detract from utility in some contexts.

As I indicate elsewhere, my view of the refined concept of realized niche is that it could never be assumed from the recent attempts at understanding only to be constrained within the fundamental niche by aspects of competition. Kroes (pp. 323–324) complained that Hutchinson's realized niche suggested this. Realization in fact or concept of the fundamental niche or of its constrained manifestation on shore or in other environments *requires* that there be taken into consideration all factors constraining to the level considered. It is, to my mind, almost by definition clear that the fundamental niche reflects principally the capabilities of the species; that level of the niche will, in any meaningful form, of course always be affected in any factual or conceptual manifestation other than the absolute genotype by the ambient internal and external morphogenetic environment during organism (or population) growth and differentiation.

The ecopotential presents some difficulties; its underlying concept cannot now (and probably never will) be defined, except in relation to those environments within which populations (however small*) of the species manifestly occur. It may be possible for the species to occur in other conditions which would widen what we think of its ecopotential, but until that does happen how do we know? The ecopotential must then go unperceived as to limits, which will in any case doubtless be dynamic, because currently not fully expressed in nature, for whatever reason. This concept is therefore theoretically satisfying but of no immediate practical use whatsoever.

The same tends to apply to this "average genotype" that Kroes finds as the basis for ecopotential; there can be no "average genotype", at least not in any consistent form that is expressible. Since *species niche* (*sensu* Kroes) depends on *ecopotential* and species niche varies with individual population, the significances of both ecopotential and "average genotype" are expressible only in terms of an attribute that is never the same twice. In other words, this seems to me to be a rather over-elaborate way of making the statement that as a result of its genotype ("average genotype") this species has the ability to form populations in those conditions in which we observe it occurring; which conditions, of course, will vary from population to population across communities. This is

*This has to be viewed with some caution, since population size, aside from its inherent effect on persistence through reproductive element reservoir, may also affect the overall genetic properties and therefore population competitive abilities (Pielou, 1977).

fundamentally unchallengeable but not specially constructive. Rather more constructive along similar lines were Makarewicz and Likens (1975) who, defining the term niche to include some measure of population response to environmental variables, commented: "for it is the response of the range of genotypes in the population to the complex of environmental variables that is of concern".

Maguire's (1973) definition of niche is as the genetically (evolutionarily) determined *capacity* (range of tolerance) and *pattern of biological response* of an individual, a species population, or the whole species to environmental conditions. He indicated that it can be directly related to an individual's genome and to the gene pools of species' populations and of whole species. Environmental conditions are considered to include all physico-chemical and biological characteristics of the surroundings in which species, population, or individual lives and interacts. Habitat, by contrast, refers to some particular combination of environmental characteristics (including normal temporal fluctuation) in a particular geographical location. These points he developed further in his 1973 review, showing the method's heuristic utility and analytical power. Maguire's concept of *niche* is therefore an amalgam of *ecopotential, fundamental niche, realized niche*, and *ecotope*, as these are accepted here, i.e. it is the equivalent of Kroes's (1977) *ecopotential* plus the Whittaker *et al.* (1973) *ecotope*. His concept of *habitat* also shows change from the Whittaker *et al.* full concept that bears the same name. The latter authors identify habitat variables as *extensive* in that they change, by gradient (usually) or more abruptly/discontinuously (less often) from place to place, the habitat therefore representing the kinds of environmental balances a species can accept for at least temporary existence. If Maguire's indication is, as I believe it to be, that his *habitat* is tied to one community and its ambience, biotic and abiotic, at one particular location, then it is the direct statement of Whittaker *et al.*'s *community habitat* or *environment*, i.e. *biotope*, but not of the species' habitat in the sense of the range of conditions/communities in which that species will be found to occur.

Grubb (1977), in an interesting paper on the "regeneration niche", presented aspects of the niche concept with great clarity but somewhat awkward terminology. I tend to agree with his comment that most botanists find difficulty in the idea that every species in a high-diversity plant community occupies a different niche, this since autotrophic plants have the common requirements of light, CO_2, H_2O, and mineral nutrients. He attributes this difficulty in part to overlooking of regeneration in existing communities and its effect in introducing replacement plants of different species. His definitions of the niche terminology reorganize the niche concept *sensu* Whittaker *et al.* (1973); *niche* in his view includes those aspects the latter authors call *habitat*, that is, niche expresses (as in the views of Richards (1969), and Wuenscher (1969, 1974)) the total relationship of plant to environment, be it physico-chemical or biotic, within or between communities. Although I prefer the terminology as applied by Whittaker and his colleagues, this definition raises few problems of equivalence and none of comprehension. However, Grubb goes on to utilize precisely the same term "niche" in subsequent subdivision of the overall niche; his four major component niches, the habitat niche, the life-form niche, the phenological niche and the regeneration niche, are merely niche dimensions (axes) in the sense expressed first by Hutchinson (1958) and detailed further in the definitions section later in the present paper. These dimensions deal respectively with physico-chemical habitat tolerance, including fluctuation stimulus; with life-form (including size and annual productivity); with seasonality; and with the determinants of replacement of a mature individual by another one of the same species. All these phenomena are covered in slightly different combination and circumscription under the dimensional outlines in Appendix I.

I see little purpose in replacement of an easily understandable terminology that does *not* employ the same term at different hierarchical levels, and therefore is rather less confusing, by one that potentially confuses by that multi-level usage, even when prefixes do express the theme of that subdivision. Although different hierarchical levels are involved, the potential confusion is of a similar type to that deriving from Kroes' primary, intermediate and species niches (see above). With Whittaker, Levin and Root, I believe clarity is best served by retaining *niche* (or *species niche*) for the totality of that species population intra-community environmental relations, including those between individuals of the same species and therefore including the population addressed, and *for that hierarchical level alone.* I confess to a sneaking liking for Grubb's equating of habitat dimension to address (although I would contend that address is rather an amalgam of the isolable non-biotic parts of all the niches occupied); life-form and phenology dimensions to profession (although I would widen this for the benthic macroalgae to include several of the suggested dimension characteristics from Appendix I, then applying the preferred overall term "life-style"); and regeneration dimension to include, in agreement with Grubb, elements of all the above.

In extension of all this recent debate, therefore, and as a preliminary to presenting firm definitions that appear in the next section, I am inclined:

(i) to accept *ecopotential*, as the unexpressed individual-, or breeding group-, or local population-potentiality in ecological matters, often, as stated by Kroes (1977), more or less the equivalent of the full potential of the genotype;

(ii) to accept *fundamental niche* as the unconstrained expression of that ecopotential in the presence of only those limitations that derive from interactions between the ambient physical environment and the population, however small, of the species under consideration;

(iii) to accept *realized niche* as the totally constrained (but therefore dynamic) living relationships of the [algal] population within its (artificially or naturally) delimited community.

The fundamental and realized niches cannot be sensibly delimited in the exclusion of the population to which the exercise is being addressed. The further concepts of *habitat* and *ecotope* I accept in the definitions presented by Whittaker, Levin and Root (1973) and Whittaker and Levin (1975). I see no purpose in coupling the term "niche" to the suggested *primary* and *intermediate* levels distinguished by Kroes. Their truths are self-evident and do not need this kind of terminological juxtaposition in order for the relationships to be understood. The tendency is to complicate an already sufficiently complex background to the use of the term *niche*.

With the sole doubtful exception of *ecopotential*, it is *not* possible to define these concepts other than in relation to the ecosystem of which they reflect human perception. *Ecopotential* and *fundamental niche* will probably never be more than useful constructs, although they can be conceptually distinguished from each other. The *realized species niche* can have practical importance in the senses defined later; it is also a useful theoretical construct in other less clear conditions. *Habitat* has obvious practical importance, provided that its defined limits are strictly adhered to in its use. *Ecotope*, in the inshore marine benthos, seems likely to be of considerable to overriding practical importance because of current difficulties in distinguishing niche factors from habitat factors in some conditions.

2. *Definitions and Comments*

> Our [1973] article was written because of our feeling that confused usage threatened the useful life of the term 'niche'. We do not seek the enshrinement of particular definitions, but we feel that science would be poorly served if individual users simply chose whatever definitions suited them; such a practice would only compound confusion.
>
> (Whittaker *et al.*, 1975)

> Definition of the nature of scientific constructs can play as important a role in science as the original elaboration of an idea . . . [to] eliminate confusion and lead to the construct's proper application.
>
> (Peters, 1976)

But:

> *Niche* is one of those concepts that should not be defined too rigidly, but, roughly, a niche consists of the resources a species uses, where it finds them, and the strategy by which it harvests them.
>
> (Diamond, 1978)

The following subsections outline accepted definition, usage and background discussion of terms as employed in this paper.

(a) [Species] niche. The role of species within the community, that is, the way a particular species population fits into a given community is an evolved attribute of that population. With *habitat* and *range*, it forms the whole set of relationships of species to environment. Whether the niche referred to is the *theoretical possible* (i.e. *fundamental*) or the *realized* niche, it can equally be described as *n*-dimensional in the sense that everything around and within and pertaining to the existence, behaviour and interrelationships of that species, at the level concerned or within its community, is a dimension of its niche. Thus, the niche space is constructed by assuming a Cartesian coordinate system of relevant variables (Hutchinson, 1965; Shugart and Patten, 1972). Despite this horrendous, even frightening, number of potential dimensions, the study of ecological or other differences between species is a comparative

matter that can as yet usually be conducted in a niche space outlined by two or three dimensions (Hutchinson, 1978; see also Appendix I). These critical dimensions are neither necessarily nor always food resources; in the cases of photosynthetic benthic plants, of course, they never are (Wuenscher, 1969, 1974), unless critical illumination levels are involved for a particular community (cf. Wilce, 1967; Healey, 1972; Connell, 1978). Certain elements (e.g. nitrogen: Chapman, 1976; Jackson, 1977; Hansiak, 1979b) may be seasonally limiting.

Since the overall available niche space for a community represents primarily a conceptual resource matter and is not just positional space in the usual sense, it is usually referred to as *hyperspace* (Euclidean space), and the niche portion within which conditions for the existence of a particular species are satisfied forms that *species' niche hypervolume*, either:

fundamental (*potential* or *preinteractive*; Vandermeer, 1972; Connell, 1975):

unaffected by the modifying influences of predation, competition, parasitism and the like;

or *realized* (*actual* or *postinteractive*; Vandermeer, 1972; Connell, 1975):

the resultant from all interacting restraints;

as the case may be. Theoretically, these could be the same but are doubtfully ever so in practice.

Hyperspace has the same relationship to actual space as hypervolume has to actual volume – hyperspace is essentially the conceptual projection of all combinations of actual space, time, and resources, in circumstances in which:

(i) insufficient is known about the delimitation and realization of the actual measures and their combinations to permit formulation and meaningful use in any hypothesis, explanation, or other reasoning pattern, even though required for furtherance of theory or research; and/or

(ii) the human mind is not capable of comprehending the result of that delimitation due to excessive dimensionality, even if the data *are* available.

Wuenscher (1974) pointed out that the early zoological history of the niche and the fact that the application of the term there was mostly based on the nutritional role of an animal in its ecosystem (i.e. food and relations) (Weatherley, 1963) meant that the niche concept was hardly applicable to plants until the advent of the hyperspace concept that utilized *all* variables, of whatever nature. Since plants function in their ecosystems and relations to food/enemies only as primary producers, food sources, or decomposers, the earlier terms of reference were insufficiently specific to define plant niches.

Within niche dimensions (axes), measures delimiting the hyperspace for particular populations of a species within given communities are usually referred to as:

Niche breadth (= *niche width*): the extent of occupation by a species along a niche axis (dimension) (Hutchinson, 1978); e.g. the niche breadth in temperature is that range permitting survival for the requisite life-history phase(s) of a marine alga over the period necessary to maintain the local population. The appropriateness of species diversity data at this point is not denied, but not debated further here (see elsewhere and Appendix II).

Niche overlap: the extent to which competition between populations of two or more species in the same hyperspace for a given resource is direct; or, the joint use of resources by several coexisting species (Harner and Whitmore, 1977).

Species packing: the number of species that a given niche hyperspace can contain (Hutchinson, 1978); the elaboration into extra planes presented by Yoshiyama and Roughgarden (1977) is of interest. By analogy with the "species clouds" much debated in some sections of the literature, species packing must be affected by population response to the niche axes, so that in the areas of hyperspace less suited to the species the resources available there will be less demanded by that species as fewer individuals will make up that portion of the population concerned. Theoretically, at least, in those circumstances peripheral to the optimal parts of the available niche hyperspace, "niche overlap" will be freer and possibly species diversity richer. The extent to which the latter is borne out in practice and in the predictions by models or reasoning process is not pertinent to the aims of this paper, but has been a subject of continuing controversy; reference to standard texts will provide more detail.

Fine-grained/coarse-grained species (MacArthur and Levins, 1964): a different approach to the competitive aspects of the niche; how species may replace each other or co-exist in stable combinations (Hutchinson, 1978). Primarily (but not only) applicable to animals. If two co-occurring species both eat, possibly in different proportions, the same two renewable resources (foods), they are referred to as *fine-grained*. If subsequently selection favoured avoidance of competition by giving up that food used in smaller proportion and specializing in the other food, species so reacting would ultimately become *coarse-grained*. Morphologically similar species specialized in seeking optimal habitats but feeding in much the same way as competitors would be *fine-grained* (e.g. most plants, so far as applicable, including the benthic macroalgae; animals that spend much time searching for food and then eat it as soon as found). Morphologically specialized species feeding in an efficient way on a limited range of food sought over a wide range of habitats would be *coarse-grained* (e.g. animals that spend much time pursuing easily located prey). This therefore roughly represents the distinction between generalists and specialists (Blondel and Bourlière, 1979).

It should be appreciated that terms such as niche breadth, niche width, niche dimension and niche overlap have themselves been applied in an imprecise and variable manner, such that their boundaries of application have been blurred, or with firmly differing ideas as to the concepts to which the several terms individually relate. Thus, "niche width" for example has been defined as given above; as the *variety* of resources exploited by a population (few = narrow; many = wide); as the variability range of morphological characteristics taken as representative of the group of phenotypes(genotypes) delimiting dimension or whole niche. For more details, see the debates in most specialist texts on the niche; those in Roughgarden (1972; 1974) and in Vuilleumier (1979) are representative. Some of the measures outlined above remain largely inapplicable to plants. For mathematical expressions relating to the measures, see Appendix II. Quantifying the measures for particular populations in particular communities is never very easy and mostly time-consuming; ecological profiles and analysis by ordination are often involved.

Niche variables (i.e. dimensions, = axes) are *intensive* in that they change *within* a given community and at a particular place on the earth's surface; they are also intensive in that the term *niche* is most usefully applied exclusively to the intracommunity role of the species.

Connell (1975), writing partly on the basis of his experience with marine communities, and Vandermeer (1972) have both suggested that the distinctions drawn between *fundamental* and *realized niches* make the concept a very useful one; Vandermeer considered this the most important principle derivable from Hutchinson's original (1958) formalization. Grubb (1977) has indicated that the pre-interactive/postinteractive difference could be applied individually to dimensions (his various subsidiary niches), but since these are interactive axes of the overall species niche such separation could lead to misrepresentation or misappreciation of the overall situation. If, as is usually accepted, communities are organized by interactions, then the manner and degree of that organization will be reflected in the differences between the sizes and shapes of realized and fundamental niches, when these can be formalized.

In commenting on the distinctions between the fundamental and realized niches, Vandermeer (1972) introduced another possibly interesting and useful concept into the overall theory. This is the *partial niche*, i.e. the developmental stages of the niche as the development or evolution from unaffected fundamental to "completely" constrained realized niche of the "mature" community occurs. Thus, there is a theoretical continuum of niche types as a population, or patches within it, evolves in parallel with or out of phase with its containing community. This continuum, commencing in virgin territory with the fundamental niche but unlikely, save in clearance experiments, ever in practice to be in that particular state on a shore, passes through first partial, second partial, to *m*th partial niche (= the realized niche), the latter also unlikely ever to be identifiable easily or for long as a "final" stage of the development.

We come here to what is basically the area of *equilibrium* and *stability* concepts. All these attempt to formalize in a static manner what is essentially a mosaically dynamic situation that will vary from place to place and time to time within the same population within the single community. It is unlikely that *stability* represents any more than an artificially convenient discussion point, in which it is joined by *equilibrium*. Connell (1972), quoting Den Boer (1968), concluded similarly in stating "heterogeneity and/or instability must be recognized as fundamental features of a natural situation". The whole of ecological study is dealing with situations that are never precisely the same for even micro-seconds (admittedly an extreme *reductio ad absurdum*). The overall picture in a zone, belt, band or community on the shore may over large areas represent a similar balance for even years at a time; however, the detail of its constituent parts will vary markedly, regularly or irregularly in phasing, from one time to another. Except in a very general way, the formalization of species niche and its dimensions is also bound to represent a static presentation of a thoroughly dynamic situation. Huston (1979) has interestingly debated this and allied points, commenting that "Constant competitive coefficients may well be meaningless except in uniform stable environments which never exist in nature".

(b) Habitat. The species distributional response to inter-community environmental factors and therefore essentially the kind(s) of environmental balances or communities in which a species is capable, temporarily or permanently, of existence. Its quantification is therefore the reflection of a combination of data from the fundamental niches. The *m*-variables (dimensions) of physical and chemical environment that form spatial gradients in an area define as axes a *habitat hyperspace*. The part of this hyperspace a given species occupies is its *habitat hypervolume*. The species' population response to habitat variables within the hypervolume (as expressed in a population measure) describes its habitat. The environment of a particular community in the landscape is a *community habitat* or *biotope*. Habitat (English) and biotope (European) tend to be used interchangeably, although occasionally there are attempts at distinguishing between them (e.g. as in Blondel and Bourlière, 1979).

Habitat variables are *extensive* (cf niche variables) in that they change from place to place on the earth's surface and, in some cases, form well-defined spatial gradients – e.g. tidal gradients. As a result of spatial gradients, it is more usual for an area to be covered by communities blending into one another than by a collection of discrete communities.

Blondel and Bourlière (1979), quoting from personal communication with C. Ferry, presented an illustration of the habitat–niche relationship, likening it to that between lock and key. The lock (habitat) is formed of a series of biotic and abiotic factors over which the species has no control and must therefore accept; the niche (key), representing the potential of the population, can be more or less well adapted to opening that lock. Certain locks are very simple and open with all keys, and certain populations have very flexible genomes accommodating to very varied habitats: they are the generalists. High security locks open only with very sophisticated keys special only to them, and certain populations are finely adapted to only one habitat: these are the hyperspecialists. Although this is a generally attractive analogy, it fails to take sufficient account of the evolutionary adaptive characteristics that could alter the position with time.

(c) Range (area). The third primary aspect of the species' environmental relationships is its *area* – its geographic range. This is a clear, comparatively uncomplicated, concept, but the extent to which peripheral areas of a range may show variations from optimal (central) areas of that range in niche and habitat characteristics for the species concerned has sometimes to be fully appreciated.

It should be emphasized that Whittaker *et al.* (1973) indicate that these environmental relationships of a species form a complete whole; there is often no sharp distinction between *niche* and *habitat*, or between *habitat* and *area*, a given environmental factor being involved in all three. In the state of knowledge of benthic macroalgae, their populations and communities, it is often difficult to distinguish the level and direction of activity of the factor; another pointer towards the view expressed later.

(d) Ecotope. The species' full range of adaptations to external factors of both species niche (a) and habitat (b). The name *ecotope* is here accepted from Whittaker, Levin and Root (1973); variables of habitats and niches may be combined, defining as axes an $(m + n^1)$-dimensional *ecotope hyperspace.* The n^1 symbol relates to the n niche axes for particular communities extended to the full range of communities. The part of this hyperspace to which a given species is adapted is its *ecotope hypervolume.* When a population measure is superimposed on this hypervolume, the ecotope of the species is defined.

As with niche and habitat, so ecotope has been equated to habitat, biotope, microlandscape, biogeocoenosis, and so forth, all of which are equally inappropriate synonyms. The only reservation in use in the above framework has to lie with possible confusion created; ecotope has not been frequently employed and (so far as I am aware) never in benthic marine studies. It therefore represents little problem in possible terminological confusion and can be of considerable utility.

THE TERM OR CONCEPT "NICHE" IN INSHORE BENTHIC ECOLOGY: RELATIONSHIP TO "COMMUNITY"

> where it is possible to measure directly the dynamic relations between organisms and their physical and biological environment, this is to be preferred to . . . indirect methods . . . [such as mathematical models]. Such direct measurement is difficult in most habitats, but it is possible in a few. The marine rocky intertidal is one of these.
>
> (Connell, 1972)

> Rocky intertidal and shallow subtidal regions in temperate latitudes have proved to be ideal 'natural laboratories' in studying the role of competition in structuring communities.
>
> (Menge, 1979)

The intertidal, by its being directly and consistently affected by tidal fluctuation, is one of the more stressful of environments. Jackson (1977) observes that this peripheral environment contains a very small percentage of the world's marine hard substrata and that there must presumably be a "trade-off" between the advantage in occupying such a stressful environment and the maintenance of superior competitive ability for space in physically less stressful subtidal environments. Since it is still logistically easier to deal with, the more stressful intertidal remains ecologically rather better known than the less stressful subtidal. Much of the information used in the sections that follow therefore derives from the intertidal. It is probably generally true to say that invasion of the intertidal pools and channels by competitively superior plant species from the subtidal is not as successful as it otherwise might be because they have thus entered a more stressful situation which they are less well-equipped to deal with. By contrast, subtidal incursion by otherwise intertidal species is rarely a real competitive success and usually occurs under conditions of unusual and excessive stress in the intertidal (e.g. massive freshwater effects such as layering in sea-lochs; ice-scour;

excessive insolation). There is usually morphological change in individuals associated with the subtidal incursion, although growth when submerged in the absence of competition is good in all tested species (Edwards, 1977), with the exception of certain upper intertidal fucoids. Benthic macroalgae, then, are able to effect such translocations, and do so, when the combinations of spore reservoir, spore viability, general environmental tolerance and environmental pressure are all adequate. These factors have to be borne in mind when utilizing for research purposes the advantages of the inshore benthos, outlined above. Because the advantages have been recognized and of late exploited, there is considerable background data to be considered as regards the concept "community".

1. Community

> a deep knowledge of the natural history and environmental physiology of the organisms involved will be needed to arrive at a satisfactory description of a community and its physical environment.
>
> (Roughgarden, 1979b)

The concept of "niche" as envisaged by Whittaker, Levin and Root (1973) is inescapably bound up with the concept of "community" ("an assemblage of organisms living together in a particular environment"), and neither is especially simple to define to a standard acceptable to all for inshore benthic situations, despite the longevity and depth of knowledge available for the latter (Connell, 1972). Since not frequently applied directly as a term in such conditions, niche has hardly been used enough to do more than strongly hint that understanding of it varies widely from person to person consequent upon animal/plant group studied, location of study, aims, and a whole host of other characteristics. This is therefore an appropriate point at which to consider if standardization is possible for the inshore benthos, thus reflecting the strongly felt need that led to the "Benchmark" work of Whittaker and Levin (1975), as well as to the more recent redefinitions by Kroes (1977) and by Grubb (1977).

It should be emphasized that the consideration of *community* presented below concerns only the ecologist's view of the concept, not the view of the palaeontologist. Boucot (1978) has published a stimulating review of community evolution, in which he emphasized the high degree of behavioural, structural and (of kinds) numerical conservatism of communities throughout geologic time. He concluded that the very narrow constraints on allopatric speciation dictate its extensive occurrence generally *only* after significant changes in the environment, which correlate on a broad regional or global basis with major brief time-intervals of extermination, changes in provincialism, changes in rate of cladogenesis, and change in total number of communities. Correlation also commonly occurs with physical changes such as in land mass relations or major climatic variation. The geological record suggests that relative environmental uniformity does not encourage generation or occupation of new niches, adaptive zones, or habitats at a continuous rate, but that the spasmodic physical changes tend to do so. Boucot (1978) commented that "The realized capacity of particular environments . . . remains about constant". This palaeontological view of lengthy periods of constancy in taxa and relative abundance contrasts with the ecological view, which is over an essentially human time-scale that comprehends all the vagaries of recruitment and death, seasonal biotic change, local physical and biotic catastrophies, transitory changes in physical environment, and so on. These "change, both slowly and rapidly, the taxic contents and relative abundances occurring on any one patch of ground through time" (Boucot, 1978). Therefore, despite (i) the importance of the other view to both sets of workers (Boucot, 1978; Laporte, 1977) and (ii) the fact that although short-term dynamic changes are often dramatic they fluctuate between such relatively fixed limits that the fossil record remains largely unchanged over geologically significant time, only the human time-scale of recorded history is referred to here.

Community is frequently, loosely, and often very conflictingly applied in benthic ecological studies, its implied (relatively infrequently defined) meaning often varying widely in works by the same author at different times, even between parts of the same work; the more predicable variation between workers is a commonplace. There are, however, *some* very carefully framed definitions based on the intertidal levels (e.g. Dayton, 1971 and other data; Connell, 1975; Mills, 1969; Menge, 1976, 1979; Connell and Slatyer, 1977), probably as a reflection of the ease with which both visual estimates can be made and inshore benthic populations can be experimentally manipulated in the field and compared with nearby controls derived from essentially the same circumstances (Connell, 1972).

Menge (1976), for example, understood community as "a directly or indirectly interacting assemblage of organisms occupying a particular habitat". This was elsewhere in the work indicated to include *all* species (except the microorganisms, although these should not be excluded) from primary producers to top predators, and therefore differs from usage in "bird communities" and "plant communities", which are strictly *guilds* (i.e. groups of species that exploit the same class of environmental resource in a similar way; this groups species without regard to taxonomic position on the basis of significant overlap in niche requirements).

The rationale for necessary inclusion of the often overlooked, misunderstood or ignored microorganisms in any study of marine benthic (epibenthic, epibiotic) community structure was presented with considerable clarity by Sieburth (1976):

> If it were not for the bacteria which solubilize particulate organic matter and utilize soluble organic matter, and the bacteria-eating protozoa and larger forms that feed upon them, the "waste products" resulting from excretion, defecation, and death could be considered a loss to the food pyramid . . . . But bacteria and bacteria-eating forms are present in considerable numbers throughout the lengths and depths of the seas and occur as indispensable components in all five ecosystems [neuston; plankton; epibios (= epibenthos); benthos; fecal-seston]. The bacterial-protozoan partnership that utilizes dissolved organic carbon (DOC) and particulate organic carbon (POC) is not separate from "the mainstream of trophodynamics" . . . but is a mechanism for keeping DOC and POC in the mainstream of trophodynamics by connecting the ecosystems and maintaining the long-term steady state of life in the sea.

Hoppe (1978) indicated similarly that "almost all uptake of dissolved organic substances in the sea is to be attributed to bacteria". Sieburth (1976) went on to describe the initial attachment and sequences of development on both inanimate and living surfaces, passing in his account from the initial reversible absorption of some bacterial types, through irreversible absorption of other types, according to nature of the surface colonized, which then plateaus after a few days and gives way as dominant biomass to protozoa, then diatoms, followed by spores and larvae of seaweeds and invertebrates. The presence of bacteria has been shown in culture to be necessary to "normal" growth in many seaweeds, whilst others carry a surface seasonal microbial cover that they control chemically or by cuticle sloughing.

Menge's (1976) understanding of community differs from the usage in studies such as that of Lindstrom and Foreman (1979); community as specified there represents an association of organisms, recognized by "dominant" growth forms/species, without any implication of functional interrelationships amongst the species. Equally recently, Connell (1975) and Connell and Slatyer (1977), the latter in a detailed and useful analysis of changes in species composition during succession,* based in large part on benthic marine situations, defined *community* as "the set of organisms that occur together and that significantly affect each other's distribution and abundance. It is the interactions that make a community a unit worthy of study". Woodin (1978), working on refuges and disturbance in a soft-bottom community (sand-flat), concluded that it is feasible to view communities as "compilations of species successfully exploiting refuges in space and/or time". Since the agents of disturbance cited throughout the work included crabs, fish, shrimps, shorebirds and the like, Woodin was clearly dealing with biological interactions as well as with physical disturbance patterns. Perhaps the most complete statement of the nature of the benthic marine community is still that presented by Connell (1972), in commenting on the Paine (1966) and Dayton (1971) notion of grazing or predation as "biological disturbance". Connell stated that:

> the community consists of a set of animals, plants, and microorganisms which, in living together, have evolved various adaptations to each other; and so grazers or predators cannot be regarded as causing "disturbance" or "delaying" the "normal" succession. Having evolved with the rest of the species in the community, they are an essential part of it at any stage in its history; and to regard their activities as disturbance relegates them to a special category for which there is little or no basis.

A more succinct statement which, despite his (1976) exclusion of microorganisms, can be taken to cover more or less the same ground as Connell (*vid. supr.*) was given by Menge (1979): the community is "a group of cooccurring interacting species at all trophic levels in a particular habitat".

---

*Connell and Slatyer (1977) presented a scheme outlining three models of mechanisms of species succession; this scheme was also reproduced in Chapman (1979). The topic *per se* is not pursued here.

From all available evidence, it is clear that although *community structure* (static) or *community organization* (dynamic) (these being distinguished apart by Menge, 1976, a source of some of the evidence; his distinctions have been accepted by other workers, e.g. Keough and Butler, 1979) are strongly affected by biological interactions, yet there has to be a greater or lesser overriding admixture of physical factors in virtually all cases (Woodin, 1974; Connell, 1975; Glynn, 1976; Osman, 1977; Sutherland and Karlson, 1977; Menge, 1978a,b; Peterson, 1979). Lewis (1977b) commented that "The ultimate primacy of physical factors is irrefutable". Viewing the bands or zones of intertidal seaweeds as communities, although there appear to be good reasons why one should do so only with circumspection (Russell, 1972, 1973; Boudouresque and Lück, 1972; see also later), those studies by Connell (1972, 1975), Paine (1974), Grant (1977), Menge (1976), Schonbeck and Norton (1978) and Underwood (1978) indicate that both upper limits of such bands and, within the high intertidal, community structure, tend to be determined by responses to physical variables and to intraspecific competition. Neither predation nor interspecific competition had significant influence on patterns of upper intertidal space utilization in the New England areas examined by Menge. The lower limits of "zones" appeared to be more strongly affected by interspecific competition for space and by predation, including grazing (Paine, 1974; Connell, 1972, 1975; Menge, 1976; Underwood, 1978).

Exposed shore mid-intertidals apparently were structured primarily by interspecific competition in which *Mytilus edulis* L. outcompeted *Balanus balanoides* (L.) for space, although on vertical surfaces the rate of replacement was slow, with *B. balanoides* taking two years to be outcompeted by *M. edulis* (Menge, 1976). Whilst predators had no controlling effect on space utilization in the exposed areas, in sheltered areas the mid-intertidal primary space utilization was determined largely by predators – *Thais* overrode everything, obscuring even the interspecific *M. edulis*/*B. balanoides* competition. For the algae, it appeared that *Fucus* spp. survival was inhibited by *Mytilus* and enhanced by *Balanus* in three-way competition, suggesting that even the scarcity of fucoids in exposure may be partly caused by competition with *Mytilus*.

These and other practical experiments and observations indicate that what may appear at first sight perhaps to be distinctions between factors in the niche and factors in the habitat (biological as opposed to physico-chemical) are not wholly clear in practice. Nevertheless, as Caswell (1976) observed, models all concur in giving biological interactions a major role in determination of community structure in general and species diversity in particular; he used "neutral" (random) models from cybernetics, from control theory, and from niche theory in arriving at this conclusion, all these theoretical approaches concurring. It is still curious that Caswell found on back-comparisons with actual community structure across gradients of importance in biological interactions (successional *vs* climax; high variation *vs* low variation environment; temperate *vs* tropics) in birds, fish, trees and insects, that results contradicted some widely held theories of community structure. Biological interactions (e.g. competition and predation: cf. Menge and Sutherland, 1976; Glasser, 1978, 1979) are often predicted to generate greatest increase in species diversity, whilst neutral model analysis showed lower diversity than would have been expected even in the absence of such interactions. However, predation and physical disturbances, when intense, can also directly reduce species richness (Paine and Vadas, 1969b; Dayton, 1971; Vance, 1979). Whether predation and competition, the latter commonly for the resources of space (Connell, 1972; Dayton *et al.*, 1974) or space and light (Dayton, 1975a,b; Pearse and Hines, 1979), are complementary or contradictory theories in their effects as mechanisms on species diversity and how these processes affect both diversity and community structure are elegantly debated by Menge and Sutherland (1976). Preferential predation on a dominant competitor, at sites protected from strong water-movement (Menge, 1976, 1978a,b; Paine, 1974; Peterson, 1979), often counteracts the general effects of the competitive efficiency, resulting in co-existence of a number of species greater than would otherwise have occurred (Paine, 1969; Hastings, 1977, 1978; Caswell, 1978; Glasser, 1979; Teramoto *et al.*, 1979). According to Sutherland and Karlson (1977), it is an "emerging paradigm" of macrobenthic community organization that, in the absence of such predation or physical disturbances, there exist competitive hierarchies in which one or a few species "wins" (as e.g. in Price and John, 1978).

All these comparatively recent comments and definitions tend to break away, as has much of the more recent detailed inshore macrobenthic ecological work, from the earlier and more classically descriptive approach that applied when plant communities were being examined on shore. The earlier descriptions largely looked at seaweeds as zonational organisms in the intertidal – entirely valid but of restricted application beyond a certain point of detail. Much of this background was examined by Chapman in an analysis (1974) of the ecology of macroscopic marine algae, during which he drew a firm distinction between community ecology and population biology, at the same time admitting that this was for convenience only, arbitrary subdivisions of the subject in ecology being neither easy nor ever completely valid. All the aspects considered by Chapman under his population biology section and some of those recognized in community ecology fall within the coverage of the niche concept as understood here and by Whittaker, Levin and Root (1973). It is therefore somewhat strange that Chapman did not at any point refer to the term *niche*, the more so when one notes the care he took to state precisely the two major views of community structure. These are the *individualistic* (effectively closed in some significantly restrictive way) and the *continuum* (open-ended), the view adopted here and generally implied by zonational approaches. Whittaker, Levin and Root (1973) have inclined to the view that generally, but by no means only, the acceptance of a high degree of community individualism can be more productive of an effective approach. Hence the distinction they are able to draw between niche and habitat, whilst still realizing the justification on some occasions for combining both into ecotope. The point is considered further later and in the Discussion and Conclusions section. Dayton (1971, 1972, 1975a,b) has produced a perceptive and detailed series of benthic studies in which *community* is accurately defined, for example in his 1971:352 statements. The remarks and their outcome need not be repeated in detail here, except to indicate that he stated, of a particular set of sites and their communities in Washington State: "This community is open ended since much of the primary productivity and decomposition occur elsewhere; however, all communities are open ended in an energetic sense .... Most of the changes in populations in this community, therefore, occur as predictable responses to other populations in the intertidal community". Lewis (1977a) and Kussakin (1977) have also emphasized the open-endedness of marine benthic populations.

Two matters emerge immediately from all the above:

(i) Any individualistic view of community distinctness is arbitrary, however useful – in a continuous medium with unknown but generally effective viability and distribution of reproductive elements or fragments, it is probably false to improper to regard communities on any basis other than as a continuum, with species independently distributed along environmental gradients and within that affected mainly by local interactions. Communities, therefore, must be based on more than a few dominants, even though considerable community control rests with them once they have established (Connell, 1972).

(ii) It is exceedingly important to acquire as much information as possible about the energy flow patterns within and between communities and the seasonal chemical changes that occur, whatever the eventual aim of the investigations (Pamatmat, 1977). Studies such as those of Jeffries (1979), Johnson *et al.* (1977), Mann (1972a,b, 1973, 1977), Miller and Mann (1973), Niell (1977, 1979), Paine (1971b), Velimirov *et al.* (1977), and of Littler and his colleagues (Littler, 1971, 1973a,b,c, 1976; Littler and Murray, 1974, 1975, 1977, 1978; Littler and Doty, 1975; Murray and Littler, 1978; Seapy and Littler, 1978) are therefore of great importance to any investigations of communities and have eventually as much relevance to the subject of the individual plant's or animal's use of energy as to the subject of energy use at community, population, or inter-community levels. In the last analysis, all are clearly dependent on what "strategies" of energy use are adopted at individual plant/animal levels.

The clear importance of chemical relations at community level is interestingly and cogently debated by Whittaker and Feeny (1971), although not in a specifically benthic marine context. They indicate the versatility with which evolution has produced both chemical agents for functions and combinations of those functions within the same chemical product. Ecosystem study demonstrates how chemical interactions may be essential, even the principal, aspects of species niche differentiation within communities and of the community organization. This is certainly true for many benthic marine plants and colonial animals, in both of which production of allelochemicals* is a characteristic important in spatial competition (Fletcher, 1975; Jackson and Buss, 1975; Green, 1977; Jackson, 1977; Choat and Black, 1979; Hughes, 1980). It is also true in some solitary animals, where employment of substances incidentally acquired is known to be effective defence against being eaten (Kinnel *et al.*, 1979; see details later).

Whittaker and Feeny provide a fitting summary to this section on community aspects. To quote briefly from their own final section (1971):

> Ecologists consider that ecosystems are given functional unity by transfer of energy, inorganic nutrients, and foods between environment and organisms. To these two classes of materials in community transfer, inorganic nutrients and foods, should be added the third, allelochemics.* An intricate pattern of exchanges of materials of all three classes relates the organisms of a community to the environment and to one another. If the inorganic and organic nutrients provide the essential fabric of this pattern, the allelochemics provide much of the color and detail of its design.

2. *Niche*

What does all the above debate imply for the benthic application of species niche concept, with which I started? On whatever basis of consideration, it is clearly very firmly tied into community organization, which in this medium would seem difficult to impossible to regard in any other light than as a variable continuum. With current levels of knowledge and on this basis, ecotope (*sensu* Whittaker *et al.*, 1973) would seem to be the more logical, useful and safer concept commonly to apply, for the present at least.

And how do the plant's or animal's overall "life strategies", or individual constituent strategies within the overall pattern, relate to and lie within this framework? And what, indeed, about this word *strategy*? Does it carry overtones which indicate that (in any context that may carry or manifestly result, as the niche does, in microevolutionary implications) it should be avoided? According to Louw (1979) this is certainly the case:

---

*Allelochemics(= allelochemicals): chemicals (excluding foods) by which organisms of one species affect the growth, health, behaviour or population biology of organisms of another (Whittaker and Feeny, 1971: 757).

> can you imagine a group of barnacles convening a meeting to decide on which of a set of isoenzymes to use so that their metabolism could become temperature-independent? The term [strategy] is therefore semantically quite incorrect . . . [and] philosophically grossly misleading, as it implies that a process has occurred which is the very antithesis of the evolutionary concept of chance and necessity.

Personally, I shall go on using the word strategy, for which in this context there is no immediately suitable replacement, but with an occasional careful look over the shoulder!

Even on the basis of only the restricted number of critical niche dimensions commonly thought necessary to the study of differences between two species (Hutchinson, 1978) or between groups (populations) of the same "species" in two different communities, considerations of niche characteristics within the primarily acceptable physical ambience (fundamental niche) requires several factors to be taken into account as fully as possible. Competitive limitations (especially light and space, in the inshore benthic macroalgae: "Space on which to live is often the most important limiting resource in marine hard substratum environments" Jackson (1977)); predation (although it is hardly applicable to the herbivore–plant relationship included here for convenience, one tenable view of predation in other forms is as an extreme form of interference competition, or an evolutionary development from it, wherein competition for a (food) resource exploited by two organisms has resulted in interference, demonstrating to the interferer the greater attraction, availability, or ease of processing, as food-source, of the interfered with than of the originally-sought food-source); the effects of or requirement for parasitism, epiphytism, symbiosis, epizoism and the like; effectiveness of reproductive strategies; seasonality; all these and more provide important examples of potentially limiting factors. Summaries of the latter are given by Menge and Sutherland (1976) and by Levandowsky and White (1977), amongst others. Limiting factors are not always easy to perceive, establish or investigate. The demonstration beyond doubt of the structuring effect on community and/or the existence of the dimension in niche, for example, has been suggested to require a five- (Reynoldson and Bellamy, 1971) or six- (Menge, 1979) step regime of unequivocal establishment in an ideal study. The significance of interspecies (interference or exploitation) competition, and indeed the actual balance of its detailed nature (Case and Gilpin, 1974), in structuring communities and in affecting niche width has been the subject of continuing debate. The general views for (Diamond, 1978) and against (Wiens, 1977) the overriding importance of competition as a factor have recently been summarized in very readable essay form. Appendix I (this chapter) generalizes a number of niche dimensions customarily found to be of importance to benthic marine macroalgal (realized) niche delimitation. Some of the suggested dimensions are predominantly *scenopoetic* (physically based), some *bionomic* (relating to biological interactions); most are, or represent the resultant reaction to, a varying mixture of these two characteristics.

For the inshore benthos, determinant niche axes for a species are usually at least primarily of the physical environment (scenopoetic); at a secondary level, bionomic axes predominate. This, like almost all else in this subject, is a generalization and oversimplification, since the nature of determinant factors (axes) is not always so readily deduced. The microenvironment in which a parasite or epiphyte appears (its niche), for example, is at first sight determined as to axes by its "host" or "substrate", another plant or animal; but which aspects of the microenvironment being so provided are really the primary determinants – the chemistry of the host's exterior mucilage or internal cell structure? The local salinity pattern? The shading pattern as the host moves or is moved? The protection from being eaten? Shelter from direct effects of wave-beat on a plant that, if attached to resistant rock rather than flexible algal surface, would be intolerably stressed? In the vast majority of cases, we simply do not know and the terms scenopoetic and bionomic have therefore currently only importance in classifying the possible factors, not in delimiting their direct or inter-actions in specific cases in the present state of our knowledge. A further point is that, unless the axes are to be so generally drawn (verbalized) as to be unhelpful or so finely drawn as to be unrealizable, overlaps in the verbal framing of the individual dimensions (axes) are inevitable; examples can be easily noted in Appendix I. Non-sexual reproduction, indeterminate growth and allelochemical production, for example, are important characteristics in spatial competition (Jackson, 1977) but individually relate to different dimensional heads in that Appendix. This overlap is a normal phenomenon in any human attempt to classify essentially non-isolable characteristics.

With the last few years, much important practical and theoretical work has been done on mutual strategies and adaptations (co-evolution) within prey–predator and other competitive relationships (including here herbivores and algae); these form a highly significant niche dimension. Theoretical models have been provided by, for example, Lomnicki (1974), Holt (1977), Rosenzweig and Schaffer (1978), Roughgarden (1976, 1977, 1979a,b), Schaffer and Rosenzweig (1978), and Wilcox and MacCluer (1979). In the field, or on that aspect, the extremely interesting work by Vadas (1977) on sea urchins, by Zimmerman *et al.* (1979) on amphipods, by Connell (see e.g. 1974) and by Paine (see e.g. 1977), and the useful stimulating review by Colwell and Fuentes (1975), *inter alia* warrant reference. Vadas, without employing the term *niche* or *species niche*, started from the premise of a statement of dimension – the presumption that feeding behaviour is a requisite vital to the survival of the species and that therefore preferential feeding leads to efficient exploitation of prey, contributes to long-term (evolutionary) survival, and forms an adaptive feature of the species.

Comparisons between theoretical feeding preferences and empirical data are few (Menge, 1972a,b; Menge and Menge, 1974; Lubchenco and Menge, 1978; Stenseth, 1978) but do tend to show that existing use of models needs much further refinement. Predictions, in many cases, have not been wholly borne out in practice. Existing models are largely based on abundances and energy values of potential prey items and include either market demand curves (strategic analysis) or stochastic theory. Vadas (1977), using a subtidal situation (San Juan Island, Washington), analysed the ecological interactions and evolutionary adjustments between sea urchins and benthic algae at the species level, taking careful account also of the importance of predation and other factors on community organization. The whole paper is worth reading, but the important points here are that species of *Strongylocentrotus* demonstrated feeding behaviour that was a compromise between preferences and algal availability. *Nereocystis*, the preferred diet (27–40% of feeding observations), was selected despite its adverse physiognomy and low abundance. Lesser feeding on *Laminaria saccharina* (L.) Lamour. also seemed to be adaptive. Ulvoids (*Monostroma* and *Ulva*) showed high field feeding (24–28%), despite being low in preferences in the laboratory, thus indicating choice because of easy availability. Intermediate preference algae (*Alaria; Laminaria groenlandica* Rosenv.; *L. complanata* (Setch. et

Gardn.) Setch.) showed feeding in nature primarily based on their availability. *Costaria* was highly preferred but taken in proportion to availability, in the field. Most algae available (*Agarum; Opuntiella*) were avoided, suggesting chemical evolution that has reduced browsing (see section on allelochemicals, earlier). Adaptations and strategies shown by the algae, then, were as shown in Table I.

Table I

r-selection[a] (*opportunistic mode*)	*K*-selection[a] (*perennial mode*)
Escape (time or space) dominant or important subtidal algae, especially those highly preferred.	*Defence* dominant or important subtidal algae, especially those *not* preferred by urchins.
chemically attractive; short life-history; patchy growth; high reproductive potential – *Nereocystis*.	physical defence – calcareous greens and reds.
very available; short life-history; dense patches; high reproductive potential – Ulvoids; *Alaria*.	chemical defence – *Agarum*; *Opuntiella*.
(Vadas found that the long-lived *Laminaria* spp. represent something of a problem – despite their long life, they are grazed where available.)	

[a]On the general topic of *r* and *K* strategies and selection, not dealt with in detail here, see: MacArthur and Wilson 1967; Pianka, 1970, 1972; King and Anderson, 1971; Gadgil and Solbrig, 1972; Peters, 1976; Southwood and Comins, 1976; Berry, 1977; Levandowsky and White, 1977; Stenseth, 1978; Blondel and Bourlière, 1979; Chapman, 1979.

Studies elsewhere, to demonstrate whether or not similar strategies (niche dimensions or variables) are present to the same degree or in the same or similar balance in other populations of these organisms, are now highly desirable. It seems likely that this will prove to be the general case, at least in principle. Stenseth (1978: 302–303) has generalized that in *r*-selected species (short lives; low survival from birth to maturation; often "big-bang" reproducers; *or* early maturation and reproductive peak soon after) grazing is more likely to maximize plant fitness than in *K*-selected species (the slow developers, perennials, well-adapted to more or less stable environment). Therefore, annuals should be more palatable than perennials in any community. Presuming the relative gain (η) to be independent of successional stage, this means early successional plants should be more palatable to grazers than later successional plants; this is true even when young of dominants succeed in establishing early (Connell, 1972). The earlier stages tend to be dominated by grazing food chains, the later ones by detritus food chains. The more susceptible early plants of the finally large perennials will also be preferred, the larger young plants and adults possessing a refuge in size if they are protected from natural grazers by the predators of the latter or by some physical event. These considerations make the statements by Seeliger and Edwards (1977), in their study of benthic macroalgae as metal-concentrating agents, appear as not inaccurate but far too over-generalized; these latter authors indicated that "in most coastal waters the benthic algae are largely unconsumed and their organic matter is passed along the food web as detritus and dissolved organic matter". This certainly happens to some extent (Laycock, 1974; Moebus and Johnson, 1974; Fankboner and De Burgh, 1977; Penhale and Smith, 1977; De Burgh and Fankboner, 1978), although it has been demonstrated (Zimmerman *et al.*, 1979) that the characteristics of becoming detritus and being consumed are not mutually exclusive. Certain Gammaridean amphipods feed exclusively or facultatively on small particle detritus from seagrasses and algae.

Vadas (1977) further showed that, in the sea urchins he was studying, optimization of the food was based not primarily on the obviously important food value of the algae, but more on differences in absorption efficiencies and feeding rates. Selection was of the algae more rapidly ingested, more efficiently absorbed, and therefore providing greatest nutritional value. It is clear from a survey of available studies (see Appendix I) that the algal population being subject to grazing is by no means always on balance adversely affected by that niche dimension.

The extent to which there remains profound need for further data on every aspect of potential or known interactions between individuals, populations or larger groups of every constituent of the inshore benthic biota will be abundantly clear from consideration above. It will also be apparent that the deeper penetrates the investigation of particular interrelationships, the more interactive elements there are revealed at hitherto unsuspected levels of involvement. A particularly apposite illustration of this is presented by Kinnel *et al.* (1979)

in their investigation of the allelochemicals* (in this case, antifeedant substances) of *Aplysia brasiliana* Rang. This algal browser was found to be unacceptable as food, in the main, when proffered to sharks and smaller fishes; the only acceptable portion, consistently, was the buccal muscular mass. It had previously been noted in the field that the animal was avoided as food even when readily available. At least a major element in the distastefulness of the tissues was traced as two halogenated cyclic ethers, brasilenyne and *cis*-dihydrorhodophytin. Both these substances are related to the known algal metabolite rhodophytin; they, together with obtusenyne (another brasilenyne, and therefore rhodophytin, relative), have been isolated from the tissues of algae known to co-exist with, and in some cases in captivity to be consumed by, *A. brasiliana.* Since the animal itself does not synthesize the substances concerned, none of which incidentally is present in the consumed buccal mass, there seems little doubt that the compounds are sequestered by the animals from the algae that they eat. Not only, then, has coevolution resulted in the more obvious aspects of browser–browse balance but there has also been subtle, perhaps originally accidental, development by selection pressure of the use of otherwise alien chemical substances that came into the biochemical ambit of the consuming organism. The number of species niche dimensions, for both chemical source and consumer, that this interrelationship materially affects can be appreciated from what has been discussed earlier and from data presented in Appendix I.

DISCUSSION AND CONCLUSIONS

1. General Summary of Use of Niche in Marine Benthic Macroalgal Ecology

Niche has hitherto been used much more often in connection with marine benthic zoology than with the botany of that ecosystem. Chiefly, this is probably because of the greater ease and clarity with which competition, predation and reproductive characteristics are deduced and reflected in the anthropomorphic derivation of animal "strategies". It is, however, also a result of the tradition of approach, in that the marine benthic macroalgae have long been viewed on an

*The general topic of allelochemicals is treated earlier in this chapter.

intertidal basis principally as zone-forming organisms, the concept of niche having largely been by-passed in the persisting tradition of the zonation being all-important. Although it would be short-sighted to deny importance to zonation patterns, they do not represent the most productive approach for the current views of population ecology. Within the modern approaches of the last 30 years, the terms community, range, habitat and the like have been used very widely, variably and often imprecisely, all of them at some stage or other being so applied as to include factors (dimensions; axes) that legitimately fall within that outlining of the niche concept presented in Whittaker *et al.* (1973) and, more recently, by Hutchinson (1978). Menge (1976) may well be right in suggesting that, although the pioneers of community structure study were plant ecologists who tended to ignore the role of animals, the studies then produced were largely descriptive, probably due in part to the envisaged difficulty of manipulating the components of most plant associations. Without this manipulation, the deepening and broadening of studies from population to community level, accompanied by the change in emphasis from simple description to comparative and experimental analyses of interactions between component populations and between populations and the physical environment, characteristic of many more recent intertidal and some subtidal (primarily zoological) investigations, can simply not be achieved. Yet applications of this kind fundamentally involving both plants and animals in communities of the intertidal (principally) and subtidal (to a lesser extent) are now much more frequent. This is especially true of recent North American and European studies such as those of Menge, Lubchenco, Littler, Lewis, Murray, Paine, Dayton, Connell, Vadas, Foster (1975a,b), W. E. Jones and his colleagues (Jones *et al.*, 1975; Fletcher *et al.*, 1975, 1976; Jones *et al.*, 1978, 1979a,b,c, 1980), and many others of similar style. Cautious optimism that at least the more productive directions of study are now recognized would therefore not be out of order.

2. *The Future*

> despite a large and growing body of question-oriented research, a major task remaining before us is to determine the relative roles played by biotic and abiotic agents in structuring both populations and communities.
>
> (Menge, 1979)

> The basic question in evolutionary community ecology is to understand how the simultaneous action of natural selection in each of several interacting populations shapes the overall community consisting of those populations . . . . What is needed are comparative data on the community structure of comparable independently coevolved communities . . . [and] data on community structure obtained from the perspective of an evolutionist and biogeographer . . . . [also, conceptually] We lack a definition of what it means for two communities to be qualitatively identical to one another. It is trivially obvious that few places on earth are the same in terms of the physical characteristics of the environment. As a result, the ecological communities at different places almost surely exhibit some quantitative differences. Yet we may want to speak of the communities at two different places as being in some sense qualitatively the same even though they do exhibit quantitative differences. To speak in this way we need some objective procedures to evaluate the quantitative differences which are detected between two communities. We need to know how, in principle, to compare communities.
>
> (Roughgarden, 1979b)

There are still very few communities in rocky marine inshore conditions for which data are sufficiently detailed and long-term to be revealing of precise and repeated relationships within the community. I, amongst many others, have elsewhere (Price, 1973) indicated the need and the rationale for long-term studies of such marine communities. Those of the latter so well-known as most closely to approach the degree of detail required (chiefly in northwest Europe and on western and eastern coasts of U.S.A.) are thus far documented over too short a term and principally then on largely zoological grounds. Algae/animal interrelationships have certainly *been* documented, but even the admirable studies of those workers detailed at the end of Section 1 above do not concern themselves *directly* with the expression of integrated niche characteristics for the plants. Such data are naturally reflected in the studies to some degree because of the depth and care taken with their organization. Understanding in any full sense of the confines of species niche for any benthic macroalgae remains to be achieved, being unrealized (save by the plants!) for populations of even such well-known organisms as the fucoids. Perhaps "observations of niche segregation" in nature are even now in many circles "shunned as a menial activity devoid of respectability or scientific sex appeal" (Diamond, 1978).

What must then be asked in relation to inshore marine benthic communities is: have they sufficient stability and constancy to permit the niche concept to have any meaningful long-term application, or are the plasticity, seasonal variability, mutational and other changes in organisms, organization, and environment (Lewis, 1977a) such that (i) the amount of information needed for reasonable assessment of niche for species certainly far exceeds our present knowledge and may for any foreseeable future do so; (ii) the requirements of individual plant species within the pattern of community relationships are so much less fixed or circumscribed than those of animals that, because of that flexibility and of the chances of distribution in a continuous marine medium, the niche concept can in relatively few cases (either on animal/animal, plant/animal, or plant/plant basis) be disentangled from the general term ecotope?

Even in these potentially restrictive circumstances, in my view the retention of the concept *niche* (species niche) has much to recommend it. It may lead to directed and more orderly thought in situations where it is all too easy to fail to distinguish clearly causes and events, just as much as it is to fail to reintegrate data for evaluation purposes after establishment outside the overall system. The species niche concept is, being integral with community and a reflection of ecological potential, of both autecological and synecological significance; the particular bias depends on the objectives of an investigation. Apart from the purely ecological data spin-off, there are other advantages of looking at species, species groups, populations, communities, or individual interrelationships in the light of even the presently unrefined state of the niche concept.

Comparison of particular species niches between different communities could be instrumental in indicating present microevolutionary trends. These could perhaps amount to a speciation trend in plants that on all available classical taxonomic grounds would be attributed to the same specific taxon (as e.g. in Fenical and Norris, 1975; Crews *et al.*, 1977). Whittaker and Levin (1975: ix) have cogently commented that' "the most essential role of the niche concept lies in the interpretation of the way species evolve and relate to one another in communities". A fairly gross marine macroalgal example could be changes in or preferential extensions to substrata not normally associated with particular species, e.g. the detection of epiphyte or parasite hitherto associated with particular "hosts" on other substrata, the usually preferred one not, or not then, being exploited (as in Harlin, 1973a). As a field example, there would seem to be some occasional tendencies thus in *Polysiphonia lanosa* (L.) Tandy, normally expected on *Ascophyllum nodosum* (L.) Le Jol. but occasionally to be found only on *Fucus vesiculosus* L. or *F. serratus* L. in the available presence of *Ascophyllum.* This could, equally, be read as either poor available data/ observations on the species, or a residual tendency in an epiphyte elsewhere specialized towards the single "host" species *Ascophyllum.* As to whether this represents irreversible genetic change, reversible or irreversible change within the physiological potential of the genotype of a local population, seasonal availability of host, or other events, is not always clear.

There are also potential taxonomic overtones. Detailed knowledge of the niche tendencies of species populations in different communities may well provide indications of field evidence for the taxonomic treatment of morphologically confusing or intractable entities that are currently "genres diaboliques". Even where there is apparent interfertility, as shown for example by Rueness (1973, 1978) and others in such problem genera as *Ceramium*, consistent appearance of certain forms in certain definite and definable sets of conditions (including host preferences or obligations) may well indicate a level of evolutionary pattern with sufficient validity for ecological if not taxonomic recognition. This recognition at ecological level may lead to more firmly-founded taxonomic distinction when either the entity so wills or when humanity has the further ability to gather sufficient detailed data to demonstrate what is already there. Formation of sterility barriers is clearly often a progressive matter. Pursuing confirmation or denial of separate taxonomic status through the niche patterns in such cases can focus attention more firmly on the potential of characteristics that may otherwise be overlooked; for example, does the same predator feed equally on both the "species" populations or is one strongly preferred or even only that one eaten? Boucot (1978) has summarized this point in stating "Efforts to determine speciation mechanisms *must* be oriented ecologically, in the community sense".

Knowledge of this kind can lead to a considerably more profound and precise set of statements about individual or complexed species in Floras. The efficacy of such a product must depend on the parity and depth of data on species reactions over long periods in individual communities, as well as on the experimental application of data garnered from all available fields of study. As things now stand, in few to no cases do the ecological statements (regarding, say, habitat preferences) in Flora volumes represent a reflection of more than a patchy, mosaic overall view that is often locally unreliable in the extreme. In no sense does the available information represent any well-rounded statement of niche relationships of a particular species. The present patchwork-quilt entries of information regarding hosts, seasonality, substrata preferences, reproductive "strategies" and the like have the principal function of pointing to the inadequacies of our data. Characteristics that could reflect some aspects of the species niche in particular communities are lumped together with characteristics of different aspects from other communities, and often none of this is fully assessed as to its status or its relationships to such matters as distribution range. The data therefore often reflect an amalgam that would variously apply, with the definitions accepted earlier, to *species niche*, to *habitat*, or to *range*, without in the conjunction presented succeeding in clarifying any of these. We therefore *need* much more detailed and *very* long-term studies of individual inshore benthic communities, much as emphasized by Lewis (1978a,b) and Wiens (1977) for different eventual end-points. If the studies also contribute to monitoring for pollution effects or conservation management, so much the better.

The niche concept approach can thus assume paramount importance both ecologically and taxonomically. If we are ever to be in a position to make significant use of a vast fund of potential characteristics, large amounts of data from field conditions over virtually the whole community-type range exploited by any marine organism need to be available to us. Currently they are not, and the complexities of acquiring them over both space and time are well enough emphasized and known not to require further labouring here.

Amongst the intra-community range of characteristics, those of the physical environment remain relatively the easier to demonstrate in field or laboratory than those of interspecific or interpopulation reactions. Our present rather simplistic views of the levels of interspecies reactions therefore are unlikely to reflect fully the realities of detailed effects between species in the field. Culture conditions, however valuable the data so acquired, automatically isolate from the harsh realities of field growth, although they may demonstrate certain aspects of the latter (Fletcher, 1975); they more usually test specific gross physical or chemical environmental characteristics in an artificial medium aimed at optimum growth of the research organism, rather than at understanding the precise field conditions in which it was growing. The investigation, for example, of the relationships between real algal parasite and real host has been much neglected, even though its importance in ecological, physiological, evolutionary and taxonomic terms has long been recognized. Although now such workers as Evans and his group, Nonomura, Goff, Harlin, Peyrière, and others (for details, see Appendix I) are looking in depth at the evidence for "parasitism", and therefore at the realities of the parasite/host relationship in the macroalgae, we are still far from understanding fully the significance, in both present and evolutionary terms, of the relationship.

If the current trend (see Discussion and Conclusions, Section 1) towards more comprehensive experimental analyses in field and laboratory continues and is more fully taken up elsewhere than in western Europe and North America, a meaningful trend in turn towards application of the species niche concept directly to benthic macroalgae should gradually represent less of a problem. The perhaps less satisfactory, less stimulatory, and certainly less precise ecotope concept will be required less and less. Yet there will always be some problems of conceptual overlap and probable disagreement (see earlier). It is interesting that Menge (1976) found it necessary to offer definitions of terms such as community, community structure, community organization, guild, and so on "Because various ecological terms used . . . often mean different things to different workers" on the inshore benthos. I suspect that most of us have felt this problem to a high degree at times, yet few do more than merely to use terms for convenience, rarely attempting to evolve definitions precise enough for others at least to evaluate critically when necessary.

Currently, then, the species niche concept remains, on the whole, only stimulatory and of theoretical (directive) value, rather than of immediately practical value. It could be much more than that; it deserves to be much more than that, in both mathematical and verbal frameworks; in due course, perhaps it will be. It is potentially of the utmost importance as the only really complete framing of the physiological and whole-plant biological relationships as they occur in the environment within which the plant is evolving. All these factors on which we place so much importance when demonstrated in the laboratory, and the extent to which they have any real significance in the life of the plant/population/species, can only be assessed in the last analysis in the living population. The application of the species niche concept does at least help to indicate the direction for what is logical consideration of the really significant manifestations (for both ecologists and taxonomists) in the normal life of the plant. The time-scale likely in the future practical refinement of the species niche concept is at least debatable. If it accords with the reservations and comments of Glass (1979), thus following the general trend of our knowledge as to the laws of nature then, given the present astounding rate of growth in the latter, "In one or two centuries we should know"! (Glass, 1979). In some senses, at least, the niche concept currently is to benthic macroalgal, and indeed to all, ecological studies what taxonomy is to all biological studies. Fundamentally necessary, it nevertheless has to take account of advances in all other fields and is, withal, despised by many of those who, did they but realize it, need it most. At best neglected, it is often wholly ignored; most probably, this is because its aims are rather poorly understood outside the initiates. In the final analysis, the niche represents the conceptual expression of the whole evolutionary pattern and history of the species population under consideration; Whittaker and Levin (1975: 30) called it "the end product of an evolutionary search for an optimal way of life", whilst Blondel and Bourlière (1979: 366) commented that: "La niche écologique optimale peut ainsi être considérée comme le meilleur compromis entre énergie investie pour la survie de l'organisme et l'énergie investie pour son propre remplacement." When we can understand enough about enough populations and communities, the data assembled may support the same conceptual expression for, who can say, whole races, species, or possibly even genera.

In the absence of the *term* niche, however, would anything be lost beyond recall or simply escape the framing of a concept? It is doubtful if this is the case, although as yet we cannot be sure. Margalef (1968) even went so far as to state: "the concept of ecological niche will probably turn out to be unnecessary". Peters (1976: 5–7) suggested that the Hutchinsonian niche is merely a tautology. I cannot find immediate sympathy with so extreme a view as the former, whilst the latter does not necessarily invalidate the use of term or concept, although I am prepared to debate the need for the *term* niche or species niche. Certainly, the many detailed papers recently forthcoming on both sides of the Atlantic (see the references for details) have generally succeeded in coping, directly or indirectly, with complex issues of ecological relationships amongst the inshore benthos without having markedly failed to convey their meanings. In few to no cases has the *term niche* been directly employed, despite the fact of those papers largely dealing with factors falling within the constructs of niche axes. I find myself more in sympathy with Vuilleumier (1979) in his comments that

> une analogie existe entre la notion d'espèce dite biologique et la notion de niche dite multidimensionnelle: ni l'une ni l'autre de ces notions n'est définissable de manière qui plaise à tous, mais toutes les deux possèdent une valeur heuristique; ces notions nous forcent donc, non seulement à penser, mais encore à penser clairement et surtout logiquement, que ce soit pour prouver qu'elles sont valables, ou pour demontrer qu'elles ne valent rien.

The principal *raison d'être* of the *term niche*, then, and its primary justification, must lie with the pattern and stimulus that it gives to organization and comprehensiveness of thought-process and data presentation about the *concept niche*; these are major aspects of its overall heuristic value. This justification is of no small importance; very little of moment has ever been achieved in any scientific field, or its achievement ever been fully appreciated, without much constructive background thought and the introduction of an evocative terminology. *Niche* as a *term* may aid but little the initiated; it *can be* a very convenient peg for those attempting to join the initiated. In some circumstances, as is often the case with data available on benthic macroalgae, quality and quantity of information for species or species populations are such that only *ecotope* can as yet legitimately be used. Although of lower precision, this concept/term is also a useful peg on or around which to coordinate information.

In poetic summary, I requote lines with which some may already be familiar. They bear reiteration in the present context, since previously published in places where marine botanists would probably rarely have cause to look (Geisel, 1955; Levin, 1970; Whittaker and Levin, 1975).

And NUH is the letter I use to spell Nutches
Who live in small caves, known as Nitches, for hutches.
These Nutches have troubles, the biggest of which is
The fact there are many more Nutches than Nitches.
Each Nutch in a Nitch knows that some other Nutch
Would like to move into his Nitch very much.
So each Nutch in a Nitch has to watch that small Nitch
Or Nutches who haven't got Nitches will snitch.

(Geisel, Dr Theodor Seuss, 1955)*

It would be difficult to find a better summary of some of the main aspects of nitch (niche) theory!

ACKNOWLEGEMENTS

I thank Dr M. Gibby for reading and commenting on the manuscript. Dr J. D. Taylor discussed various points and helped considerably with information on zoological literature. The text was also read from different viewpoints, wholly or partly, by Mr J. F. M. Cannon and Dr E. N. Arnold, to whom I am grateful. Random House Publishing Co. Inc., New York, is acknowledged for permission to publish the extract from "On Beyond Zebra".

APPENDIX I

Research themes and suggested generalized species–niche dimensions[a] of importance to the distinguishing of ecological differences (1) between species of benthic marine macroalgae or (2) between morphologically identical "species" in different communities

Dimension characteristic[b]	Important aspects; thematic research questions requiring initial or further addressing	Recent works that have contributed important data/comment
1.[c] Light	Photosynthetic aspects: photosynthetic morphology; pigments; function (including chemistry); requirements; correlation with environment? Where and in what conditions is the energy balance positive?	14;[d] 15; 16; 17; 18; 27; 28; 37; 39; 44; 45; 46; 48A; 52; 58; 63; 77; 87; 88; 95; 96; 98; 99; 100; 103; 107; 108; 109; 110; 116; 119; 120; 128; 136; 138; 142A; 143; 155; 156; 159; 159A; 163A; 164; 174; 184; 187; 188; 189; 190; 193; 205; 211; 211A; 215; 219; 225; 226; 227; 228; 229; 230; 231
2. Mechanical tolerance and response	Morphological -flexibility; -tolerance; growth form; -resistence; -adaptation. How much wave-beat or water-motion of whatever kind does the alga withstand or require?	4; 6; 10; 25; 27; 37; 46; 47; 56; 58; 58A; 63; 64; 110A; 111; 119; 120; 137; 147; 148; 151; 158; 159; 181; 192; 195B; 201; 203; 204; 204A; 208; 211; 217; 218
3. Physical tolerance and response	Ability to withstand desiccation or other environmental extremes. Where and when does the alga grow best? On what substratum type? In what temperature/salinity? With what, if any, consequent seasonality?	10; 21; 22; 25; 27; 28; 31; 38; 43; 46; 52; 57; 58; 58A; 75; 77; 82; 84; 86; 89; 102; 106; 108; 110A; 111; 120; 125; 130; 131; 133; 137; 138; 139; 142; 153; 156; 158; 159; 181; 184; 192; 193; 195A; 195B; 196; 201; 203; 204; 204A; 209; 211
4. Reproduction ("Sex has always been an embarrassment to population biologists"; Bell, 1978).	Reproductive strategies manifest. Opportunist (*r*) or perennial (*K*)? Contribution from non-sexual and vegetative forms of reproduction? Range phenomena? Relations to physical environment? Length of breeding period?	4; 6; 9; 10; 11; 19C; 26; 28; 33; 34; 51; 58A; 59; 64A; 75; 76; 77; 90; 101; 105; 106; 106A; 108; 110A; 120; 122; 125; 128; 133A; 137; 138; 139; 149; 151; 163; 171; 172; 177; 183; 193A; 195B; 202; 213; 214; 217; 220; 221; 222; 223; 223A

Appendix I (Continued)

Dimension characteristic[b]	Important aspects; thematic research questions requiring initial or further addressing	Recent works that have contributed important data/comment
5. General susceptibility	Which are the most environmentally tolerant/susceptible life-history phases? To which factors are they susceptible? How does this affect recruitment rates and patterns? Or rate of growth after settlement? Or life expectancy? Or life-history in the field?	4; 8; 9; 10; 20; 20A; 23; 24; 30; 32; 34; 35; 41; 42; 58A; 59; 76; 77; 79; 80; 81; 117; 119; 120; 128; 151; 152; 153; 168; 186; 193A; 203; 204; 204A; 210; 211; 217
6. Predation; refuges; competition	What eats or otherwise affects the alga, and why? What form does the grazing/eating take – herbivory or detritivory; microphagy or macrophagy? What is the effect on the alga? What is the effect on the survivors, from indirect effects on the community as a whole? Any seasonal variation? Are there refuges (including time; the eventual size of the alga)? Is the alga an efficient competitor and how does it compete (growth/reproductive rates; allelochemicals)?	2; 5; 12; 13; 18A; 19; 19A; 26A; 28A; 29; 30; 31; 32; 40; 40A; 41; 41A; 46; 49; 53A; 55B; 57; 58; 60; 61; 64; 89; 91; 92; 93; 94; 96; 97; 113; 114; 117; 118; 119; 120; 121; 123; 124; 125; 126; 134; 135; 139A; 139B; 140; 141; 142; 146A; 153; 154; 154A; 159; 160; 161; 162; 165; 166; 167; 169; 170; 173; 178; 179; 180; 182; 185; 204A; 211B; 213A; 214; 215A; 216; 217; 224; 232
7. Obligate relations	Any obligate biological relationships? Parasitism? Symbiosis? Epiphytism? Epizoism? Obligatory successional patterns?	1; 3; 20C; 31; 36; 48; 53; 54; 55; 65; 66; 67; 68; 69; 70; 71; 72; 73; 74; 83; 85; 108; 110A; 112; 115; 117; 157; 175; 191; 195; 197; 206; 207; 212; 220
8. Growth and life-history strategies	General growth strategy – canopy/erect/underflora/crustose/boring/epiphyte/endophyte habit? Annual or perennial? Dimorphic (pleomorphic) life-history?	4A; 19C; 20A; 31; 40A; 41; 44; 45; 55A; 55C; 62; 96; 117; 119; 120; 124; 176; 177; 181; 195B; 221; 222
9. Incipient speciation[e] (evolution)	Known interfertility or sterility barriers showing differences between morphological species (apparent) and delimitable breeding populations?	7; 19B. 20B; 50; 58A; 104; 127; 129; 132; 144; 145; 146; 150; 176; 177; 194; 195; 195B; 198; 200; 221; 222

Appendix I (Continued)

[a]According to Fenchel (1978), writing on fauna: "the three main dimensions of the ecological niche . . . [are] habitat, time, and food resources". For marine benthic macroalgae, this should read "space on appropriate substrata, light, temperature, and time", so far as major themes are concerned. Not all these are expressible as a simple single dimension; there are too many overtones. Time, for example, is a major factor in the generalized dimensions 3–6 and 8–9 in this Appendix.

[b]See text for comments on separation and distinctness of dimensions.

[c]Strict order of importance of the dimensions is not here implied; ranking of dimensions requires too much knowledge of the order and progress of evolutionary patterns yet to be feasible. All dimensions contribute to present-day niche, habitat and range characteristics, but their evolutionary history is with few exceptions (cf. Olson, 1978) insufficiently known and may, in fact, be indicated more strongly when firmer and increased data on the characteristics themselves are available. The fundamental step for the evolution of autotrophic life concerned the development of chlorophyll *a* and its subsequent evolution in a common ancestor for mitochondria, aerobic non-photosynthetic bacteria, photosynthetic bacteria, blue-green algae (Cyanobacteria), and chloroplasts (Olson, 1978) through to the present sophistications of chlorophyll/protein bioenergetic processes. In that sense and for that reason, the Appendix has been opened with the photosynthetic aspects. In terms of active effect on present biology, evolutionary patterns, and therefore ecology/taxonomy, the dimension outlined in entry 9 (breeding barriers) undoubtedly has the most impact. Russell (1978) has recently suggested invoking the deme terminology for situations in the benthic brown macroalgae that may reflect at least incipient breeding barriers, or the potential for their occurrence; these situations involve consistent appearance in known conditions of phenotypic (phenodeme) and ecotypic (ecodeme) variation patterns, and may indicate future isolation of a gamodeme. Gregorius (1979) very recently provided mathematical models to establish differences for demes that persist as opposed to those that do not, at the same time outlining thereby differences between the intraspecific (deme) population interactions and the corresponding mode of interspecific population interactions.

[d]It is, of course, impossible to cite all sources because so many papers have merely passing reference to characteristics of great importance. References given here therefore represent a selection of recent papers containing considerable data pertinent to the suggested niche dimension or thematic question, either in general terms or more specific to the benthic macroalgae. Older literature, save for the few earlier classical important papers listed, is generally traceable through the more recent works. Few of the studies cited are sufficiently long-term or adequately-detailed individually to go far towards niche definitions for particular axes (dimensions) in particular populations within particular communities. Other important references are referred to in the text where that was more appropriate; they are in general *not* repeated in this Appendix. See terminal references for details of works to which the numbers given relate.

[e]This dimension cannot strictly be judged solely on a niche basis, since it requires comparisons between communities across habitat type; it is, nevertheless, of great potential importance to the niche concept and its realization for particular populations of "species".

APPENDIX II: SELECTED SOURCES OF DATA ON MATHEMATICAL EXPRESSIONS (= MODELS) AND BACKGROUND INFORMATION FOR CHARACTERISTICS ASSOCIATED WITH THE SPECIES NICHE

> The fact that ecology is essentially a mathematical subject is becoming ever more widely accepted. (Pielou, 1969, 1977)

> Only with the development of mathematical niche models in the late 1950s and 1960s could niche studies be related to quantitative theory and hence rise above lowly scientific status. (Diamond, 1978)

> All ecologists are uncomfortably aware of the numerous simplifying assumptions that underlie most models . . . [but] their usefulness is great and it consists *not in answering questions but in raising them*.
> (Pielou, 1977)

> les modèles en emploi courant ne peuvent fonctionner, mathématiquement, qu'avec des limitations strictes. . . . comment définir en pratique les dimensions de la niche . . . comment déterminer que plusieurs dimensions sont indépendantes les unes des autres? Comment mesurer (définir) la forme de la courbe d'utilisation des ressources? Comment mesurer l'équilibre biologique d'une communauté naturelle? Autant de questions sans réponse, et qui rendent en grande partie illusoire le passage direct des modèles au monde réel. (Vuilleumier, 1979)

1. Species Diversity

Species diversity is considered by many as an important function of niche breadths and niche overlaps, although Grubb (1977) and others conclude that species diversity has more to do with requirements for regeneration (i.e. adaptive changes in reproductive characteristics) than with partitioning of the adult's habitat dimensions of the niche. There is variety in the mathematical expressions used; see Hutchinson (1978) for some debate.

Sources: MacArthur (1972); Pianka (1975).
Validity: discussed by Pianka (1975: 301).

$$D_s \cong \frac{D_r}{D_u}(1 + C\bar{\alpha}) \longrightarrow$$

D_s = species diversity; D_r = diversity of resources used by entire community; D_u = diversity of utilization (niche breadth) of each species; C = number of potential competitors; $\bar{\alpha}$ = mean competition coefficient [mean niche overlap].

See also: Hurlbert (1971); Whittaker (1972); Peet (1974); May (1975); Pielou (1975); May (1976); Pielou (1977); Connell (1978); Hutchinson (1978); Huston (1979); Vuilleumier (1979).

2. Niche Breadths (= widths)

Sources: for list of earlier techniques, see Pianka (1975: 302–303); see Simpson's (1949) "Index of Diversity" and Pianka (1975) for expression below. Levins (1968), who originated the measure, cites the same expression in its alternative forms.

$$B = \frac{1}{\sum P^2 i[h]} \longrightarrow$$

B = niche breadth; Pi = proportion of the ith species or resource category; h = length along axis, in slightly expanded expression and explanation in Levins (1968) and Hutchinson (1978).

See also: McNaughton and Wolf (1970); Colwell and Futuyma (1971); Pielou (1972, 1977); Shugart and Patten (1972); Vandermeer (1972); Sabath and Jones (1973); May (1976); Cohen (1978); Hanski (1978); Blondel and Bourlière (1979); Hastings (1979); Lamotte (1979); Sabo and Whittaker (1979); Petraitis (1979). Debate on the efficacy of current measures appears in Petraitis (1979).

3. Niche Overlaps

There are many contrasting suggested expressions for this measure; debate on efficacy of expressions appears in many texts; e.g. Blondel and Bourlière (1979); Petraitis (1979). See the latter for suggested changes; comments on broad classification of overlap appear under Section 5 in this Appendix.

Sources of expression given below: MacArthur and Levins (1967); Levins (1968).

Expression improved by: Pianka (1975).

See also, for contributory data: Colwell and Futuyma (1971); Pielou (1972, 1977); Shugart and Patten (1972); Sabath and Jones (1973); May (1974, 1975, 1976); McMurtrie (1976); Abrams

(1976, 1977); Harner and Whitmore (1977); Wiens (1977); Connell (1978); Hanski (1978); Hurlbert (1978); Nisbet *et al.* (1978); Nold (1979); Sabo and Whittaker (1979); Blondel and Bourlière (1979); Vuilleumier (1979); Lamotte (1979).

Expression:

$$\alpha_{jk} = \alpha_{kj} = \frac{\sum_{i}^{n} Pij\,Pik}{\sqrt{\sum_{i}^{n} P^2ij \sum_{i}^{n} P^2ik}} \longrightarrow$$

Pij = proportion of ith resource used by jth species. Pik = proportion of ith resource used by kth species.

Relationship between competition coefficients (α) and niche breadth/niche overlaps: *see* Colwell and Futuyma (1971); Vandermeer (1972); Pianka (1974a,b); Abrams (1975); Pianka (1976); Wiens (1977); Hutchinson (1978); Lane (1978); Bierbaum and Zischke (1979); Menge (1979); Nold (1979).

Niche overlap as function of environmental variablility: *see* May and MacArthur (1972); Abrams (1976); Nisbet *et al.* (1978); Turelli (1978).

4. *Species Packing: Fine-grained and Coarse-grained Species*

Sources of complex debate and proofs: MacArthur and Levins (1964); MacArthur (1970); May and MacArthur (1972); Vandermeer (1972); May (1976); Yoshiyama and Roughgarden (1977); Connell (1978); Hutchinson (1978); Nisbet *et al.* (1978); Vuilleumier (1979).

5. *Average Ecological Distance*

Root mean square of resource measures on five resource axes, expressed in half-change units.

See: Sabo and Whittaker (1979) – specific to this measure; Pielou (1977) – general background to distance measures; Petraitis (1979) – relationship of distance measures to niche overlap and to other classes of overlap; these latter are association indices, correlation coefficients and information measures.

REFERENCES

(Numbers that follow many of the references relate to use in Appendix I)

Abrams, P. A. (1975). Limiting similarity and the form of the competition coefficient. *Theor. Pop. Biol.* 8, 356–375.

Abrams, P. A. (1976). Niche overlap and environmental variability. *Math. Biosci.* 28, 357–372.

Abrams, P. A. (1977). Density-independent mortality and interspecific competition: a test of Pianka's niche overlap hypothesis. *Am. Nat.* **111**, 539–552.

Adey, W. H. and Sperapani, C. P. (1971). The biology of *Kvaleya epilaeve*, a new parasitic genus and species of Corallinaceae. *Phycologia* **10**, 29–42. [1.

Adey, W. H. and Vassar, J. M. (1975). Colonization, succession and growth rates of tropical crustose coralline algae (Rhodophyta, Cryptonemiales). *Phycologia* **14**, 55–69. [2.

Adey, W. H., Masaki, T. and Akioka, H. (1974). *Ezo epiyessoense*, a new parasitic genus and species of Corallinaceae (Rhodophyta, Cryptonemiales). *Phycologia* **13**, 329–344. [3.

Allender, B. M. (1977). Ecological experimentation with the generations of *Padina japonica* Yamada (Dictyotales: Phaeophyta). *J. exp. mar. Biol. Ecol.* **26**, 225–234. [4.

Ardré, F. (1977). Sur le cycle du *Schizymenia dubyi* (Chauvin ex Duby) J. Agardh (Nemastomacée, Gigartinale). *Revue algol.* N.S., **12**, 73–86. [4A.

Barrales, H. L. and Lobban, C. S. (1975). The comparative ecology of *Macrocystis pyrifera*, with emphasis on the forests of Chubut, Argentina. *J. Ecol.* **63**, 657–677. [5.

Bell, G. (1978). The evolution of anisogamy. *J. theor. Biol.* **73**, 247–270. [6.

Benayahu, Y. and Loya, Y. (1977). Space partitioning by stony corals soft corals and benthic algae on the coral reefs of the northern Gulf of Eilat (Red Sea). *Helgol. wiss. Meeresunters.* **30**, 362–382.

Berry, R. J. (1977). "Inheritance and Natural History". Collins, London.

Bierbaum, T. J. and Zischke, J. A. (1979). Changes in barnacle population structure along an intertidal community gradient in the Florida Keys. *Mar. Biol., Berl.* **53**, 345–351.

Blondel, J. and Bourlière, F. (1979). La niche ecologique, mythe ou réalité? *Terre et Vie* **33**, 345–374.

Bolwell, G. P., Callow, J. A., Callow, M. E. and Evans, L. V. (1977). Cross-fertilisation in fucoid seaweeds. *Nature, Lond.* **268**, 626–627. [7.

Boney, A. D. (1975). Mucilage sheaths of spores of red algae. *J. mar. biol. Ass. U.K.* **55**, 511–518. [8.

Boney, A. D. (1978a). The liberation and dispersal of carpospores of the red alga *Rhodymenia pertusa* (Postels et Rupr.) J. Ag. *J. exp. mar. Biol. Ecol.* **32**, 1–6. [9.

Boney, A. D. (1978b). Survival and growth of alpha-spores of *Porphyra schizophylla* Hollenberg (Rhodophyta: Bangiophyceae). *J. exp. mar. Biol. Ecol.* **35**, 7–29. [10.

Bonneau, E. R. (1978). Asexual reproductive capabilities in *Ulva lactuca* L. (Chlorophyceae). *Botanica mar.* **21**, 117–121. [11.

Boucot, A. J. (1978). Community evolution and rates of cladogenesis. *Evolutionary Biol.* **11**, 545–655.

Boudouresque, C. -F. and Lück, H. B. (1972). Recherches de bionomie structural au niveau d'un peuplement benthique sciaphile. *J. exp. mar. Biol. Ecol.* **8**, 133–144.

Breen, P. A. and Mann, K. H. (1976a). Changing lobster abundance and the destruction of kelp beds by sea urchins. *Mar. Biol., Berl.* **34**, 137–142. [12.

Breen, P. A. and Mann, K. H. (1976b). Destructive grazing of kelp by sea urchins in Eastern Canada. *J. Fish. Res. Bd Can.* **33**, 1278–1283. [13.

Brinkhuis, B. H. (1977a). Seasonal variations in salt-marsh macroalgae photosynthesis. I. *Ascophyllum nodosum* ecad *scorpioides*. *Mar. Biol., Berl.* **44**, 165–175. [14.

Brinkhuis, B. H. (1977b). Seasonal variations in salt-marsh macroalgae photosynthesis. II. *Fucus vesiculosus* and *Ulva lactuca*. *Mar. Biol., Berl.* **44**, 177–186. [15.

Brinkhuis, B. H. (1977c). Comparisons of salt-marsh fucoid production estimated from three different indices. *J. Phycol.* **13**, 328–335. [16.

Brinkhuis, B. H. and Jones, R. F. (1974). Photosynthesis in whole plants of *Chondrus crispus*. *Mar. Biol., Berl.* **27**, 137–141. [17.

Brinkhuis, B. H., Tempel, N. R. and Jones, R. F. (1976). Photosynthesis and respiration of exposed salt-marsh fucoids. *Mar. Biol., Berl.* **34**, 349–359. [18.

Brock, R. E. (1979). An experimental study on the effects of grazing by parrotfishes and role of refuges in benthic community structure. *Mar. Biol., Berl.* **51**, 381–388. [18A.

Burrows, E. M. and Lodge, S. M. (1950). A note on the inter-relationships of *Patella, Balanus* and *Fucus* on a semi-exposed coast. *Ann. Rep. mar. Biol. Stn Pt Erin* **62**, 30–34, 1949.

Burrows, E. M. and Lodge, S. M. (1951). Autecology and the species problem in *Fucus*. *J. mar. biol. Ass. U.K.* **30**, 161–175. [19A.

Burrows, E. M. and Lodge, S. M. (1953). Culture on *Fucus* hybrids. *Nature, Lond.* **172**, 1009. [19B.

Caram, B. (1977). Quelques observations nouvelles sur le cycle de reproduction du *Cutleria adspersa* (Mert.) De Notaris (Pheophycées, Cutlériales) des côtes Françaises. *Revue algol.* N.S., **12**, 87–99. [19C.

Case, T. J. and Gilpin, M. E. (1974). Interference competition and niche theory. *Proc. natn. Acad. Sci., U.S.A.* **71**, 3073–3077.

Castenholz, R. W. (1961). The effect of grazing on marine littoral diatom populations. *Ecology* **42**, 783–794.

Caswell, H. (1976). Community structure: a neutral model analysis. *Ecol. Monogr.* **46**, 327–354.

Caswell, H. (1978). Predator mediated coexistence: a non-equilibrium model. *Am. Nat.* **112**, 127–154.

Chamberlain, A. H. L. and Evans, L. V. (1973). Aspects of spore production in the red alga *Ceramium*. *Protoplasma* **76**, 139–159. [20.

Chamberlain, Y. M. (1978). Investigation of Taxonomic Relationships amongst Epiphytic, Crustose Corallinaceae. *In* "Modern Approaches to the Taxonomy of Red and Brown Algae" (D. E. G. Irvine and J. H. Price, eds), pp. 225–246. Academic Press, London and New York. [20C.

Chapman, A. R. O. (1974). The ecology of macroscopic marine algae. *Ann. Rev. Ecol. Syst.* 5, 65–80.

Chapman, A. R. O. (1976). Nitrate-nitrogen and the seasonal growth of *Laminaria. Br. phycol. J.* **11**, 192–193.

Chapman, A. R. O. (1978). Experimental and numerical taxonomy of the Laminariales: a review. *In* "Modern Approaches to the Taxonomy of Red and Brown Algae" (D. E. G. Irvine and J. H. Price, eds). pp. 423–432. Academic Press, London and New York. [20B.

Chapman, A. R. O. (1979). "Biology of Seaweeds Levels of Organization". University Park Press, Baltimore, Md; Edward Arnold, London. [20A.

Chapman, A. R. O. and Craigie, J. S. (1977). Seasonal growth in *Laminaria longicruris*: relations with dissolved inorganic nutrients and internal reserves of nitrogen. *Mar. Biol., Berl.* **40**, 197–205. [21.

Chapman, A. R. O. and Craigie, J. S. (1978). Seasonal growth in *Laminaria longicruris*: relations with reserve carbohydrate storage and production. *Mar. Biol., Berl.* **46**, 209–213.

Charters, A. C., Neushul, M. and Coon, D. A. (1972). Effects of water motion on spore attachment. *Proc. int. Seaweed Symp.* 7, 243–247. [23.

Charters, A. C., and Neushul, M. and Coon, D. A. (1973). The effect of water motion on algal spore adhesion. *Limnol. Oceanogr.* **18**, 884–896. [24.

Cheney, D. P. and Dyer, J. P., III. (1974). Deep-water benthic algae of the Florida Middle Ground. *Mar. Biol., Berl.* **27**, 185–190. [25.

Cheney, D. P. and Mathieson, A. C. (1978). On the ecological and evolutionary significance of vegetative reproduction in seaweeds. *J. Phycol.* 14, (Suppl.), 27. [26.

Choat, J. H. and Black, R. (1979). Life histories of limpets and the limpet-Laminarian relationship. *J. exp. mar. Biol. Ecol.* **41**, 25–50.

Chock, J. S. and Mathieson, A. C. (1979). Physiological ecology of *Ascophyllum nodosum* (L.) Le Jolis and its detached ecad *scorpioides* (Hornemann) Hauck (Fucales, Phaeophyta). *Botanica mar.* **22**, 21–26. [27.

Clayton, M. N. (1976). Complanate *Scytosiphon lomentaria* (Lyngbye) J. Agardh (Scytosiphonales: Phaeophyta) from southern Australia: the effects of season, temperature, and daylength on the life history. *J. exp. mar. Biol. Ecol.* **25**, 187–198. [28.

Clokie, J. J. P. and Boney, A. D. (1980). The assessment of changes in intertidal ecosystems following major reclamation work: framework for interpretation of algal-dominated biota and the use and misuse of data. *In* "The Shore Environment, Vol. 2: Ecosystems" (J. H. Price, D. E. G. Irvine and W. F. Farnham, eds). Systematics Association Special Volume No. 17(b). Academic Press, London and New York. [28A.

Cohen, J. E. (1978). "Food Webs and Niche Space". University Press, Princeton, N.J.

Colwell, R. K. and Fuentes, R. E. (1975). Experimental studies of the niche. *Ann. Rev. Ecol. Syst.* **6**, 281–310.

Colwell, R. K. and Futuyma, D. J. (1971). On the measurement of niche breadth and overlap. *Ecology* **52**, 567–576.

Connell, J. H. (1961). Effects of competition, predation by *Thais lapillus* and other factors on natural populations of the barnacle *Balanus balanoides*. *Ecol. Monogr.* **31**, 61–104. [29.

Connell, J. H. (1971). On the role of natural enemies in preventing competitive exclusion in some marine animals and in rain forest trees. *In* "Dynamics of Populations" (P. J. Den Boer and G. R. Gradwell, eds), pp. 298–312. Proc. Advcd Study Inst. Dynam. Numbers Population, Oosterbeek, 1970. Centre for Agric. Publ. Documentation, Wageningen. [30.

Connell, J. H. (1972). Community interactions on marine rocky intertidal shores. *Ann. Rev. Ecol. Syst.* **3**, 169–192. [31.

Connell, J. H. (1974). Ecology: field experiments in marine ecology. *In* "Experimental Marine Biology" (R. N. Mariscal, ed.), pp. 21–54. Academic Press, New York and London.

Connell, J. H. (1975). Some mechanisms producing structure in natural communities: a model and evidence from field experiments. *In* "Ecology and Evolution of Communties" (M. L. Cody and J. M. Diamond, eds), pp. 460–490. Belknap Press of Harvard University Press, Cambridge, Mass. [32.

Connell, J. H. (1978). Diversity in tropical rain forests and coral reefs. *Science, N.Y.* **199**, 1302–1310.

Connell, J. H. and Slatyer, R. O. (1977). Mechanisms of succession in natural communities and their role in community stability and organization. *Am. Nat.* **111**, 1119–1144.

Conway, E. and Cole, K. (1973). Observations on an unusual form of reproduction in *Porphyra*. *Phycologia* **12**, 213–225. [33.

Conway, E. and Cole, K. (1977). Studies in the Bangiaceae: structure and reproduction of the conchocelis of *Porphyra* and *Bangia* in culture (Bangiales, Rhodophyceae). *Phycologia* **16**, 205–216. [34.

Coon, D. A., Neushul, M. and Charters, A. C. (1972). The settling behaviour of marine algal spores. *Proc. int. Seaweed Symp.* **7**, 237–242. [35.

Court, G. J. (1977). The symbiotic association of the red algae *Janczewskia gardneri* and *Laurencia spectabilis* (Ceramiales, Rhodophyceae). *J. Phycol.* 13 (Suppl.) 14. [36.

Crews, P., Campbell, L. and Heron, E. (1977). Different chemical types of *Plocamium violaceum* (Rhodophyta) from the Monterey Bay region, California. *J. Phycol.* **13**, 297–301.

Dahl, A. L. (1973). Surface area in ecological analysis: quantification of benthic coral-reef algae. *Mar. Biol., Berl.* **23**, 239–249. [37.

Daly, M. A. and Mathieson, A. C. (1977). The effects of sand movement on intertidal seaweeds and selected invertebrates at Bound Rock, New Hampshire, U.S.A. *Mar. Biol., Berl.* **43**, 45–55. [38.

Dawes, C. J., Stanley, N. F. and Moon, R. E. (1977). Physiological and biochemical studies on the i-carrageenan producing red alga *Eucheuma uncinatum* Setchell and Gardner from the Gulf of California. *Botanica mar.* 20, 437–442. [39.

Dayton, P. K. (1971). Competition, disturbance, and community organization: the provision and subsequent utilization of space in a rocky intertidal community. *Ecol. Monogr.* **41**, 351–389. [40.

Dayton, P. K. (1972). Toward an understanding of community resilience and the potential effects of enrichments to the benthos at McMurdo Sound, Antarctica. *In* "Proceedings of the Colloquium on Conservation Problems in the Antarctic" (B. C. Parker, ed.), pp. 81–95. Allen Press.

Dayton, P. K. (1973a). Dispersion, dispersal, and persistence of the annual intertidal alga, *Postelsia palmaeformis* Ruprecht. *Ecology* 54, 433–438. [40A.

Dayton, P. K. (1973b). Two cases of resource partitioning in an intertidal community: making the right prediction for the wrong reason. *Am. Nat.* **107**, 262–270.

Dayton, P. K. (1975a). Experimental evaluation of ecological dominance in a rocky intertidal algal community. *Ecol. Monogr.* **45**, 137–159. [41.

Dayton, P. K. (1975b). Experimental studies of algal canopy interactions in a sea otter-dominated kelp community at Amchitka Island, Alaska. *Fishery Bull. Fish. Wildl. Serv. U.S.* **73**, 230–237. [41A.

Dayton, P. K., Robilliard, G. A., Paine, R. T. and Dayton, L. B. (1974). Biological accommodation in the benthic community at McMurdo Sound, Antarctica. *Ecol. Monogr.* **44**, 105–128.

De Burgh, M. E. and Fankboner, P. V. (1978). A nutritional association between the bull kelp *Nereocystis leutkeana* and its epizoic bryozoan *Membranipora membranacea. Oikos* **31**, 69–72.

Den Boer, P. J. (1968). Spreading of risk and stabilization of animal numbers. *Acta Biotheor.* **18**, 165–194.

Devinny, J. S. and Volse, L. A. (1978). Effects of sediments on the development of *Macrocystis pyrifera* gametophytes. *Mar. Biol., Berl.* **48**, 343–348. [42.

De Wreede, R. E. (1978). Growth in varying culture conditions of embryos of three Hawaiian species of Sargassum (Phaeophyta, Sargassaceae). *Phycologia* **17**, 23–31. [43.

Diamond, J. M. (1978). Niche shifts and the rediscovery of interspecific competition. *Am. Sci.* **66**, 322–331.

Digby, P. S. B. (1977a). Growth and calcification in the coralline algae, *Clathromorphum circumscriptum* and *Corallina officinalis*, and the significance of pH in relation to precipitation. *J. mar. biol. Ass. U.K.* **57**, 1095–1109. [44.

Digby, P. S. B. (1977b). Photosynthesis and respiration in the coralline algae, *Clathromorphum circumscriptum* and *Corallina officinalis* and the metabolic basis of calcification. *J. mar. biol. Ass. U.K.* **57**, 1111–1124. [45.

Drew, E. A. (1974). An ecological study of *Laminaria ochroleuca* Pyl. growing below 50 metres in the Straits of Messina. *J. exp. mar. Biol. Ecol.* **15**, 11–24. [46.

Dring, M. J. and Lüning, K. (1975). Induction of two-dimensional growth and hair formation by blue light in the brown alga *Scytosiphon lomentaria. Z. Pflanzenphysiol.* **75**, 107–117. [47.

Ducker, S. C. and Knox, R. B. (1978). Alleloparasitism between a seagrass and algae. *Naturwissensch.* **65**, 391–392. [48.

Duncan, M. J. (1973). *In situ* studies of growth and pigmentation of the phaeophycean *Nereocystis leutkeana*. *Helgol. wiss. Meeresunters.* **24**, 510–525. [48A.

Ebert, T. A. (1977). An experimental analysis of sea urchin dynamics and community interactions on a rocky jetty. *J. exp mar. Biol. Ecol.* **27**, 1–22. [49.

Edwards, P. (1970). Attempted hybridization in the red algal genus *Polysiphonia*. *Nature, Lond.* **226**, 467–468. [50.

Edwards, P. (1973). Life history studies of selected British *Ceramium* species. *J. Phycol.* **9**, 181–184. [51.

Edwards, P. (1977). An investigation of the vertical distribution of selected benthic marine algae with a tide-simulating apparatus. *J. Phycol.* **13**, 62–68. [52.

Elton, C. S. (1927). "Animal Ecology". Sidgwick and Jackson, London.

Emerson, S. E. and Zedler, J. B. (1978). Recolonization of intertidal algae: an experimental study. *Mar. Biol., Berl.* **44**, 315–324.

Ernst, C. H. and Norris, J. N. (1978). Observations on the algal genus *Basicladia* and the red-bellied turtle, *Chrysemys rubriventris*. *Estuaries* **1**, 54–57. [53.

Estes, J. A., Smith, N. S. and Palmisano, J. F. (1978). Sea otter predation and community organization in the western Aleutian Islands, Alaska. *Ecology* **59**, 822–833. [53A.

Evans, L. V., Callow, J. A. and Callow, M. E. (1973). Structural and physiological studies of the parasitic red alga *Holmsella*. *New Phytol.* **72**, 393–402. [54.

Evans, L. V., Callow, J. A. and Callow, M. E. (1978). Parasitic red algae; an appraisal. *In* "Modern Approaches to the Taxonomy of Red and Brown Algae" (D. E. G. Irvine and J. H. Price, eds), pp. 87–109. Academic Press, London and New York. [55.

Fahey, E. M. (1953). The repopulation of intertidal transects. *Rhodora* **55**, 102–108.

Fankboner, P. V. and De Burgh, M. E. (1977). Diurnal exudation of ^{14}C-labelled compounds by the large kelp *Macrocystis integrifolia* Bory. *J. exp. mar. Biol. Ecol.* **28**, 151–162.

Farnham, W. F. and Fletcher, R. L. (1976). The occurrence of a *Porphyrodiscus simulans* Batt. phase in the life history of *Ahnfeltia plicata* (Huds.) Fries. *Br. phycol. J.* **11**, 183–190. [55A.

Farrow, G. E. and Clokie, J. [J. P.] (1979). Molluscan grazing of sublittoral algal-bored shells and the production of carbonate mud in the Firth of Clyde, Scotland. *Trans. Roy. Soc. Edinb.* **70**, 139–148. [55B.

Feldmann, J. (1967). Les types biologiques d'Algues marines benthiques. *Mém. Soc. bot. Fr.* 1966, 45–60. [55C.

Fenchel, T. M. (1978). The ecology of micro- and meiobenthos. *Ann. Rev. Ecol. Syst.* **9**, 99–121.

Fenical, W. and Norris, J. N. (1975). Chemotaxonomy in marine algae: chemical separation of some *Laurencia* species (Rhodophyta) from the Gulf of California. *J. Phycol.* **11**, 104–108.

Field, J. G., Jarman, N. G., Dieckmann, G. S., Griffiths, C. L., Velimirov, B. and Zoutendyk, P. (1977). Sun, waves, seaweed and lobsters: the dynamics of a West Coast kelp-bed. *S. Afr. J. Sci.* **73**, 7–10. [56.

Fishelson, L. (1977). Stability and instability of marine ecosystems, illustrated by examples from the Red Sea. *Helgol. wiss. Meeresunters.* **30**, 18–19. [57.

Fitzgerald, W. J., Jr. (1978). Environmental parameters influencing the growth of *Enteromorpha clathrata* (Roth) J. Ag. in the intertidal zone on Guam. *Botanica mar.* **21**, 207–220. [58.

Fjeld, A. and Løvlie, A. (1976). Genetics of multicellular marine algae. *In* "The Geneties of Algae" (R. A. Lewin, ed.), pp. 219–235. Blackwell Scientific Publications, Oxford, London, Edinburgh, Melbourne. [58A.

Fletcher, A., Jones, W. E., Hiscock, K. and Thorburn, I. (1975). "The Second Report of the Coastal Surveillance Unit. Species changes from March 1974 to February 1975". Marine Science Laboratories, Univ. Coll. N. Wales, Menai Bridge, Anglesey.

Fletcher, A., Jones, W. E., Logan, S. J., McConnell, B. J. and Richards, A. V. L. (1976). "The Third Report of the Coastal Surveillance Unit. Species changes from March 1975 to February 1976". Marine Science Laboratories, Univ. Coll. N. Wales, Menai Bridge, Anglesey.

Fletcher, R. L. (1975). Heteroantagonism observed in mixed algal cultures. *Nature, Lond.* **253**, 534–535.

Forbes, M. A. and Hallam, N. D. (1978). Gamete structure and fertilization in the brown alga *Hormosira banksii* (Turner) Decaisne. *Br. phycol. J.* **13**, 299–310. [59.

Forbes, M. A. and Hallam, N. D. (1979). Embryogenesis and substratum adhesion in the brown alga *Hormosira banksii* (Turner) Decaisne. *Br. phycol. J.* **14**, 69–81.

Foreman, R. E. (1977). Benthic community modification and recovery following intensive grazing by *Strongylocentrotus droebachiensis*. *Helgol. wiss. Meeresunters.* **30**, 468–484. [60.

Foster, M. S. (1975a). Algal succession in a *Macrocystis pyrifera* forest. *Mar. Biol., Berl.* **32**, 313–329.

Foster, M. S. (1975b). Regulation of algal community development in a *Macrocystis pyrifera* forest. *Mar. Biol., Berl.* **32**, 331–342.

Fretter, V. and Manly, R. (1977). Algal associations of *Tricolia pullus, Lacuna vincta* and *Cerithiopsis tubercularis* (Gastropoda) with special reference to the settlement of their larvae. *J. mar. biol. Ass. U.K.* **57**, 999–1017. [61.

Gadgil, M. and Solbrig, O. T. (1972). The concept of *r*- and *K*-selection: evidence from wild flowers and some theoretical considerations. *Am. Nat.* **106**, 14–31.

Gaffney, P. M. (1975). Roots of the niche concept. *Am. Nat.* **109**, 490.

Garbary, D. J. (1976). Life-forms of algae and their distribution. *Botanica mar.* **19**, 97–106. [62.

Geisel, T. S. (Dr. Seuss). (1955). "On Beyond Zebra". Random House, New York.

Gerard, V. A. and Mann, K. H. (1979). Growth and production of *Laminaria longicruris* (Phaeophyta) populations exposed to different intensities of water movement. *J. Phycol.* **15**, 33–41. [63.

Gerwick, W. H. and Lang, N. J. (1977). Structural, chemical and ecological studies on iridescence in *Iridaea* (Rhodophyta). *J. Phycol.* **13**, 121–127. [64.

Giesel, J. T. (1976). Reproductive strategies as adaptations to life in temporally heterogeneous environments. *Ann. Rev. Ecol. Syst.* **7**, 57–79. [64A.

Glass, B. (1979). Milestones and rates of growth in the development of biology. *Q. Rev. Biol.* **54**, 31–53.

Glasser, J. W. (1978). The effect of predation on prey resource utilization. *Ecology* **59**, 724–732.

Glasser, J. W. (1979). The role of predation in shaping and maintaining the structure of communities. *Am. Nat.* **113**, 631–641.

Glynn, P. W. (1976). Some physical and biological determinants of coral community structure in the eastern Pacific. *Ecol. Monogr.* **46**, 431–456.

Goff, L. J. (1976a). The biology of *Harveyella mirabilis* (Cryptonemiales; Rhodophyceae). V. Host responses to parasite infection. *J. Phycol.* **12**, 313–328. [65.

Goff, L. J. (1976b). Solitary bodies (S-bodies) in the parasitic red alga *Harveyella mirabilis* (Choreocolacaceae, Cryptonemiales). *Protoplasma* **89**, 189–195. [66.

Goff, L. J. (1979a). The biology of *Harveyella mirabilis* (Cryptonemiales, Rhodophyceae). VI. Translocation of photoassimilated ^{14}C. *J. Phycol.* **15**, 82–87. [67.

Goff, L. J. (1979b). The biology of *Harveyella mirabilis* (Cryptonemiales, Rhodophyceae). VII. Structure and proposed function of host-penetrating cells. *J. Phycol.* **15**, 87–100. [68.

Goff, L. J. and Cole, K. (1973). The biology of *Harveyella mirabilis* (Cryptonemiales, Rhodophyceae). I. Cytological investigations of *Harveyella mirabilis* and its host, *Odonthalia floccosa*. *Phycologia* **12**, 237–245. [69.

Goff, L. J. and Cole, K. (1975). The biology of *Harveyella mirabilis* (Cryptonemiales, Rhodophyceae). II. Carposorophyte development as related to the taxonomic affiliation of the parasitic red alga, *Harveyella mirabilis*. *Phycologia* **14**, 227–238. [70.

Goff, L. J. and Cole, K. (1976a). The biology of *Harveyella mirabilis* (Cryptonemiales, Rhodophyceae). III. Spore germination and subsequent development within the host *Odonthalia floccosa* (Ceramiales, Rhodophyceae). *Can. J. Bot.* **54**, 268–280. [71.

Goff, L. J. and Cole, K. (1976b). The biology of *Harveyella mirabilis* (Cryptonemiales, Rhodophyceae). IV. Life history and phenology. *Can. J. Bot.* **54**, 281–292. [72.

Grant, W. S. (1977). High intertidal community organization on a rocky headland in Maine, U.S.A. *Mar. Biol., Berl.* **44**, 15–25.

Green, G. (1977). Ecology of toxicity in marine sponges. *Mar. Biol., Berl.* **40**, 207–215.

Gregorius, H. -R. (1979). The effect of genetic incompatibility of demes on total population development. *Theor. Pop. Biol.* **16**, 1–12.

Grinnell, J. (1914). An account of the mammals and birds of the Lower Colorado Valley. *Univ. Calif. Publ. Zool.* **12**, 51–294.

Grinnell, J. (1917). The niche-relationships of the California thrasher. *Auk* **34**, 427–433.

Grinnell, J. (1924). Geography and evolution. *Ecology* **5**, 225–229.

Grubb, P. J. (1977). The maintenance of species-richness in plant communities: the importance of the regeneration niche. *Biol. Rev.* **52**, 107–145.

Guiry, M. D. (1974). The occurrence of the red algal parasite *Halosacciocolax lundii* Edelstein in Britain. *Br. phycol. J.* **9**, 31–35. [73.

Guiry, M. D. (1975). *Halosacciocolax kjellmanii* Lund parasitic on *Palmaria palmata* forma *mollis* (S. et G.) Guiry in the eastern North Pacific. *Syesis* **8**, 113–117. [74.

Hansen, J. E. (1977). Ecology and natural history of *Iridaea cordata* (Gigartinales, Rhodophyta) growth. *J. Phycol.* **13**, 395–402. [75.

Hansen, J. E. and Doyle, W. T. (1976). Ecology and natural history of *Iridaea cordata* (Rhodophyta; Gigartinaceae): population structure. *J. Phycol.* **12**, 273–278. [76.

Hansiak, M. D. (1979a). Growth patterns of *Codium fragile* ssp. *tomentosoides* in response to temperature, irradiance, salinity, and nitrogen source. *Mar. Biol., Berl.* **50**, 319–332. [77.

Hansiak, M. D. (1979b). Nitrogen limitation of *Codium fragile* ssp. *tomentosoides* as determined by tissue analysis. *Mar. Biol., Berl.* **50**, 333–337. [78.

Hanski, I. (1978). Some comments on the measurement of niche metrics. *Ecology* **59**, 168–174.

Hardy, F. G. (1978). Attachment and development of *Halidrys siliquosa. Br. phycol. J.* **13**, 201. [79.

Hardy, F. G. and Moss, B. L. (1978). The attachment of zygotes and germlings of *Halidrys siliquosa* (L.) Lyngb. (Phaeophyceae, Fucales). *Phycologia* **17**, 69–78. [80.

Hardy, F. G. and Moss, B. L. (1979). Attachment and development of the zygotes of *Pelvetia canaliculata* (L.) Dcne et Thur. (Phaeophyceae, Fucales). *Phycologia* **18**, 203–212. [81.

Harlin, M. M. (1973a). "Obligate" algal epiphyte: *Smithora naiadum* grows on a synthetic substance. *J. Phycol.* **9**, 230–232. [82.

Harlin, M. M. (1973b). Transfer to products between epiphytic marine algae and host plants. *J. Phycol.* **9**, 243–248. [83.

Harlin, M. M. (1974). The surfaces seaweeds grow on may be a clue to their control. *Maritimes* (*Univ. R. I. Grad. Sch. Oceanogr.*) **18**, 7–8. [84.

Harlin, M. M. and Craigie, J. S. (1975). The distribution of photosynthate in *Ascophyllum nodosum* as it relates to epiphytic *Polysiphonia lanosa. J. Phycol.* **11**, 109–113. [85.

Harlin, M. M. and Lindbergh, J. M. (1977). Selection of substrata by seaweeds: optimal surface relief. *Mar. Biol., Berl.* **40**, 33–40. [86.

Harner, E. J. and Whitmore, R. C. (1977). Multivariate measures of niche overlap using discriminant analysis. *Theor. Pop. Biol.* **12**, 21–36.

Hastings, A. (1977). Spatial heterogeneity and the stability of predator prey systems. *Theor. Pop. Biol.* **12**, 37–48.

Hastings, A. (1978). Spatial heterogeneity and the stability of predator-prey systems: predator-mediated coexistence. *Theor. Pop. Biol.* **14**, 380–395.

Hastings, H. M. (1979). Stability considerations in community organization. *J. theor. Biol.* **78**, 121–127.

Hata, M. and Yokohama, Y. (1976). Photosynthesis-temperature relationships in seaweeds and their seasonal changes in the colder region of Japan. *Bull. Jap. Soc. Phycol.* **24**, 1–7. [87.

Hatcher, B. G., Chapman, A. R. O. and Mann, K. H. (1977). An annual carbon budget for the kelp *Laminaria longicruris*. *Mar. Biol., Berl.* **44**, 85–96. [88.

Haven, S. B. (1973). Competition for food between the intertidal gastropods *Acmaea scabra* and *Acmaea digitalis*. *Ecology* **54**, 143–151.

Healey, F. P. (1972). Photosynthesis and respiration of some Arctic seaweeds. *Phycologia* **11**, 267–271.

Himmelman, J. H. and Carefoot, T. H. (1975). Seasonal changes in calorific value of three Pacific Coast seaweeds and their significance to some marine invertebrate herbivores. *J. exp. mar. Biol. Ecol.* **18**, 139–151. [89.

Hiscock, K. (1979). Systematic surveys and monitoring in nearshore sublittoral areas using diving. *In* "Monitoring the Marine Environment" (D. Nichols, ed.), pp. 55–74. Institute of Biology, Symp. No. 24, London.

Holt, R. D. (1977). Predation, apparent competition, and the structure of prey communities. *Theor. Pop. Biol.* **12**, 197–229.

Hoppe, H. -G. (1978). Relations between active bacteria and heterotrophic potential in the sea. *Neth. J. Sea Res.* **12**, 78–98.

Hoshiai, T. (1960). Synecological study on intertidal communities III. An analysis of interrelation among sedentary organisms on the artificially denuded rock surface. *Bull. mar. Biol. Stn Asamushi* **10**, 49–56.

Hoyle, M. D. (1978). Reproductive phenology and growth rates in two species of *Gracilaria* from Hawaii. *J. exp. mar. Biol. Ecol.* **35**, 273–283. [90.

Hughes, R. N. (1980). Predation and community structure. *In* "The Shore Environment, Vol. 1: Methods" (J. H. Price, D. E. G. Irvine and W. F. Farnham, eds), Systematics Association Special Volume No. 17(a). Academic Press, London and New York. [91.

Hurlbert, S. H. (1971). The non-concept of species diversity: a critique and alternative parameters. *Ecology* **52**, 577–586.

Hurlbert, S. H. (1978). The measurement of niche overlap and some relatives. *Ecology* **59**, 67–77.

Huston, M. (1979). A general hypothesis of species diversity. *Am. Nat.* **113**, 81–101.

Hutchinson, G. E. (1958). Concluding remarks. *Cold Spring Harb. Symp. Quant. Biol.* **22**, 415–427, 1957.

Hutchinson, G. E. (1965). "The Ecological Theater and the Evolutionary Play". Yale University Press, New Haven, Conn.

Hutchinson, G. E. (1978). "An Introduction to Population Ecology". Yale University Press, New Haven, Conn. and London.

Jackson, G. A. (1977). Nutrients and production of giant kelp. *Macrocystis pyrifera*, off southern California. *Limnol. Oceanogr.* **22**, 979–995. [92.

Jackson, J. B. C. (1977). Competition on marine hard substrata: the adaptive significance of solitary and colonial strategies. *Am. Nat.* **111**, 743–767.

Jackson, J. B. C. and Buss, L. (1975). Allelopathy and spatial competition among coral reef invertebrates. *Proc. natn. Acad. Sci. U.S.A.* **72**, 5160–5163.

Jeffries, H. P. (1979). Biochemical correlates of seasonal change in marine communities. *Am. Nat.* **113**, 643–658.

John, D. M. and Price, J. H. (1979). The marine benthos of Antigua (Lesser Antilles) I. Environment, distribution and ecology. *Botanica mar.* **22**, 313–326. [93.

Johnson, D. L. and Richardson, P. L. (1977). On the wind-induced sinking of *Sargassum. J. exp. mar. Biol. Ecol.* **28**, 255–267. [94.

Johnson, R. H. (1910). Determinate evolution in the color pattern of the lady-beetles. *Carnegie Inst. Wash. Publns* **122**, 104 pp.

Johnson, W. S., Gigon, A., Gulmon, S. L. and Mooney, H. A. (1974). Comparative photosynthetic capacities of intertidal algae under exposed and submerged conditions. *Ecology* **55**, 450–453. [95.

Johnston, C. S., Jones, R. G. and Hunt, R. D. (1977). A seasonal carbon budget for a laminarian population in a Scottish sea-loch. *Helgol. wiss. Meeresunters* **30**, 527–545. [96.

Jones, N. S. (1948). Observations and experiments on the biology of *Patella vulgata* at Port St Mary, Isle of Man. *Proc. Trans. Lpool Biol. Soc.* **56**, 60–77.

Jones, N. S. and Kain, J. M. (1967). Subtidal algal colonization following the removal of *Echinus. Helgol. wiss. Meeresunters.* **15**, 460–466. [97.

Jones, W. E., Fletcher, A., Hiscock, K. and Hainsworth, S. (1975). "The First Report of the Coastal Surveillance Unit. February–July 1974". Marine Science Laboratories, Univ. Coll. N. Wales, Menai Bridge, Anglesey.

Jones, W. E., Fletcher, A., Bennell, S. J., McConnell, B. J., Mack Smith, S., Mitchell, J. and Roberts, C. M. (1978). "The Fourth Report of the Coastal Surveillance Unit. Species changes from March 1974 to February 1977". Marine Science Laboratories, Univ. Coll. N. Wales, Menai Bridge, Anglesey.

Jones, W. E., Fletcher, A., Bennell, S. J., McConnell, B. J. and Mack Smith, S. (1979a). Changes in littoral populations as recorded by long term surveillance. I. Selected examples of cyclic changes. *In* "Cyclic Phenomena in Marine Plants and Animals" (E. Naylor and R. G. Hartnoll, eds), pp. 93–100. Pergamon Press, Oxford and New York.

Jones, W. E., Fletcher, A., Bennell, S. J., McConnell, B. J., Richards, A. V. L. and Mack-Smith, S. (1979b). Intertidal surveillance. *In* "Monitoring the Marine Environment" (D. Nichols, ed.), pp. 1–23. Institute of Biology, Symp. No. 24, London.

Jones, W. E., Bennell, S. J., Beveridge, C. M., Cooke, F. P., Fletcher, A., McConnell, B. J., Mack Smith, S. and Mitchell, J. S. (1979c). "The Fifth Report of the Coastal Surveillance Unit". Marine Science Laboratories, Univ. Coll. N. Wales, Menai Bridge, Anglesey.

Jones, W. E., Bennell, S., Beveridge, C., Fletcher, A., McConnell, B. J., Mack Smith, S. and Mitchell, J. S. (1980). Methods of data collection and processing in rocky intertidal monitoring. *In* "The Shore Environment, Vol. 1:

Methods" (J. H. Price, D. E. G. Irvine and W. F. Farnham, eds), Systematics Association Special Volume No. 17(a). Academic Press, London and New York.

Kageyama, A. and Yokohama, Y. (1974). Photosynthetic properties of marine benthic brown algae from different depths in coastal area. *Bull. Jap. Soc. Phycol.* **22**, 119–123. [98.

Kageyama, A. and Yokohama, Y. (1977). Pigments and photosynthesis of deep-water green algae. *Bull. Jap. Soc. Phycol.* **25**, 168–175. [99.

Kageyama, A., Yokohama, Y., Shimura, S. and Ikawa, T. (1977). Function of siphonaxanthin in a deep-growing green alga. *Plant Cell Physiol.* **18**, 447–480. [100.

Kain, J. M. (1962–1977). [Aspects of] The biology of *Laminaria hyperborea. J. mar. biol. Ass. U.K.* I. Vertical distribution. **42**, 377–385, 1962. II. Age, weight and length. **43**, 129–151, 1963. III. Survival and growth of gametophytes. **44**, 415–433, 1964. IV. Growth of early sporophytes. **45**, 129–143, 1965. V. Comparison with early stages of competitors. **49**, 455–473, 1969. VI. Some Norwegian populations. **51**, 387–408, 1971. VII. Reproduction of the sporophyte. **55**, 567–582, 1975. VIII. Growth on cleared areas. **56**, 267–290, 1976. IX. Growth patterns of fronds. **56**, 603–628, 1976. X. The effect of depth on some populations. **57**, 587–607, 1977.

Kain, J. M. (1975). Algal recolonization of some cleared subtidal areas. *J. Ecol.* **63**, 739–765. [101.

Kain, J. M. (1977). The biology of Laminaria hyperborea. X. The effect of depth on some populations. *J. mar. biol. Ass. U.K.* **57**, 587–607. [102.

Kain, J. M., Drew, E. A. and Jupp, B. P. (1976). Light and the ecology of *Laminaria hyperborea* II. *In* "Light as an Ecological Factor: II" (G. C. Evans, R. Bainbridge and O. Rackham, eds), pp. 63–92. Blackwell, Oxford. [103.

Kapraun, D. F. (1977a). The genus *Polysiphonia* in North Carolina, USA. *Botanica mar.* **20**, 313–331. [104.

Kapraun, D. F. (1977b). Asexual propagules in the life history of *Polysiphonia ferulacea* (Rhodophyta, Ceramiales). *Phycologia* **16**, 417–426. [105.

Kapraun, D. F. (1978a). Field and cultural studies on selected North Carolina *Polysiphonia* species. *Botanica mar.* **21**, 143–153. [106.

Kapraun, D. F. (1978b). Field and culture studies on growth and reproduction of *Callithamnion byssoides* (Rhodophyta, Ceramiales) in North Carolina. *J. Phycol.* **14**, 21–24. [106A.

Keast, J. F. and Grant, B. R. (1976). Chlorophyll A:B ratios in some siphonous green algae in relation to species and environment. *J. Phycol.* **12**, 328–331. [107.

Keough, M. J. and Butler, A. J. (1979). The role of asteroid predators in the organization of a sessile community on pier pilings. *Mar. Biol., Berl.* **51**, 167–177.

Kilar, J. A. and Mathieson, A. C. (1978). Ecological studies of the annual red alga *Dumontia incrassata* (O. F. Müller) Lamouroux. *Botanica mar.* **21**, 423–437. [108.

King, C. E. and Anderson, W. W. (1971). Age-specific selection. II. The interaction between *r* and *K* during population growth. *Am. Nat.* **105**, 137–159.

King, R. J. and Schramm, W. (1976a). Determination of photosynthetic rates for the marine algae *Fucus vesiculosus* and *Laminaria digitata*. *Mar. Biol., Berl.* **37**, 209–213. [109.

King, R. J. and Schramm, W. (1976b). Photosynthetic rates of benthic marine algae in relationship to light intensity and seasonal variations. *Mar. Biol., Berl.* **37**, 215–222. [110.

Kinnel, R. B., Dieter, R. K., Meinwald, J., Van Engen, D., Clardy, J., Eisner, T., Stallard, M. O. and Fenical, W. (1979). Brasilenyne and *cis*-dihydrorhodophytin: antifeedant medium-ring haloethers from a sea hare (*Aplysia brasiliana*). *Proc. natn. Acad. Sci. U.S.A.* **76**, 3576–3579.

Knoepffler-Péguy, M. (1977). Polymorphisme et environnement chez les *Feldmannia* (Ectocarpacées). *Revue algol.* N.S., **12**, 111–128. [110A.

Koehl, M. A. R. and Wainwright, S. A. (1977). Mechanical adaptations of a giant kelp. *Limnol. Oceanogr.* **22**, 1067–1071. [111.

Kroes, H. W. (1977). The niche structure of ecosystems. *J. theor. Biol.* **65**, 317–326.

Kugrens, P. and West, J. A. (1973). The ultrastructure of an alloparasitic red alga *Choreocolax polysiphoniae*. *Phycologia* **12**, 175–186. [112.

Kulesza, G. (1975). Comment on "niche, habitat, and ecotope". *Am. Nat.* **109**, 476–479.

Kussakin, O. G. (1977). Intertidal ecosystems of the seas of the USSR. *Helgol. wiss. Meeresunters.* **30**, 243–262.

Lamotte, M. (1979). La niche ecologique, des concepts theoriques aux utilisations pratiques. *Terre et Vie* **33**, 509–520.

Lane, P. A. (1978). Zooplankton niches and the community structure controversy. *Science, N.Y.* **200**, 458–461.

Lang, C. and Mann, K. H. (1976). Changes in sea urchin populations after the destruction of kelp beds. *Mar. Biol., Berl.* **36**, 321–326. [113.

Laporte, L. F. (1977). Paleoenvironments and paleoecology. *Am. Scient.* **65**, 720–728.

Lawrence, J. M. (1975). On the relationship between marine plants and sea urchins. *Oceanogr. mar. Biol. ann. Rev.* **13**, 213–286. [114.

Laycock, R. A. (1974). Detrital food chain based on seaweeds. 1. Bacteria associated with surface of *Laminaria* fronds. *Mar. Biol., Berl.* **25**, 223–232.

Lee, I. K. and Kurogi, M. (1978). *Neohalosacciocolax aleutica* gen. et sp. nov. (Rhodophyta), parasitic on *Halosaccion minjaii* I. K. Lee from the north Pacific. *Br. phycol. J.* **13**, 131–139. [115.

Levandowsky, M. and White, B. S. (1977). Randomness, time scales, and the evolution of biological communities. *Evolutionary Biol.* **10**, 69–161.

Levin, S. A. (1970). Community equilibria and stability, and an extension of the competitive exclusion principle. *Am. Nat.* **104**, 413–423.

Levins, R. (1968). "Evolution in a Changing Environment: Some Theoretical Explorations". University Press, Princeton.

Lewey, S. A. (1978). Variation in the pigment composition of *Sargassum muticum*. *Br. phycol. J.* **13**, 203. [116.

Lewin, R. and Enright, J. T. (1978). Browsers and their browse. *Nature, Lond.* **276**, 10.

Lewis, J. R. (1976). Long-term ecological surveillance: practical realities in the rocky littoral. *Oceanogr. mar. Biol. Ann. Rev.* **14**, 371–390. [117.

Lewis, J. R. (1977a). Rocky foreshores. *In* "The Coastline . . . ." (R. S. K. Barnes, ed.), pp. 147–158. Wiley, London, New York, Sydney, Toronto.

Lewis, J. R. (1977b). The role of physical and biological factors in the distribution and stability of rocky shore communities. *In* "Biology of Benthic Organisms" (B. F. Keegan, P. Ó. Céidigh and P. J. S. Boaden, eds), pp. 417–424. Pergamon Press, London and New York. (*Proc. European Symp. mar. Biol.* **11**).

Lewis, J. R. (1978a). The implications of community structure for benthic monitoring studies. *Mar. Pollut. Bull.* **9**, 64–67.

Lewis, J. R. (1978b). Benthic baselines – a case for international collaboration. *Mar. Pollut. Bull.* **9**, 317–320.

Lewis, J. R. and Bowman, R. S. (1975). Local habitat-induced variations in the population dynamics of *Patella vulgata* L. *J. exp. mar. Biol. Ecol.* **17**, 165–203. [118.

Lidicker, W. Z. Jr. (1979). A clarification of interactions in ecological systems. *BioSci.* **29**, 475–477.

Lindstrom, S. C. and Foreman, R. E. (1979). Seaweed associations of the Flat Top Islands, British Columbia: a comparison of community methods. *Syesis* **11**, 171–185, 1978.

Littler, M. M. (1971). Standing stock measurements of crustose coralline algae (Rhodophyta) and other saxicolous organisms. *J. exp. mar. Biol. Ecol.* **6**, 91–99.

Littler, M. M. (1973a). The population and community structure of Hawaiian fringing-reef crustose Corallinaceae (Rhodophyta, Cryptonemiales). *J. exp. mar. Biol. Ecol.* **11**, 103–120.

Littler, M. M. (1973b). The distribution, abundance, and communities of deep-water Hawaiian crustose Corallinaceae (Rhodophyta, Cryptonemiales). *Pacific Sci.* **27**, 281–289.

Littler, M. M. (1973c). The productivity of Hawaiian fringing-reef crustose Corallinaceae and an experimental evaluation of production methodology. *Limnol. Oceanogr.* **18**, 946–952.

Littler, M. M. (1976). Calcification and its role among the macroalgae. *Micronesica* **12**, 27–41. [119.

Littler, M. M. and Doty, M. S. (1975). Ecological components structuring the seaward edges of tropical Pacific reefs: the distribution, communities and productivity of *Porolithon*. *J. Ecol.* **63**, 117–129.

Littler, M. M. and Murray, S. N. (1974). The primary productivity of marine macrophytes from a rocky intertidal community. *Mar. Biol., Berl.* **27**, 131–135.

Littler, M. M. and Murray, S. N. (1975). Impact of sewage on the distribution, abundance and community structure of rocky intertidal macro-organisms. *Mar. Biol., Berl.* **30**, 277–291.

Littler, M. M. and Murray, S. N. (1977). "Influence of Domestic Wastes on the Structure and Energetics of Intertidal Communities near Wilson Cove, San Clemente Island". California Water Resources Center, contribution no. 164. Davis, California: University of California.

Littler, M. M. and Murray, S. N. (1978). Influence of domestic wastes on energetic pathways in rocky intertidal communities. *J. appl. Ecol.* **15**, 583–595.

Lobban, C. S. (1978). The growth and death of the *Macrocystis* sporophyte (Phaeophyceae, Laminariales). *Phycologia* **17**, 196–212. [120.

Lodge, S. M. (1948). Algal growth in the absence of *Patella* on an experimental strip of foreshore, Port St. Mary, Isle of Man. *Proc. Trans. Lpool Biol. Soc.* **56**, 78–85. [121.

Lomnicki, A. (1974). Evolution of the herbivore-plant, predator-prey, and parasite-host systems: a theoretical model. *Am. Nat.* **108**, 167–180.

Louw, G. (1979). Biological 'strategies'. *Science, N.Y.* **203**, 955.

Løvlie, A. and Bryhni, E. (1978). On the relation between sexual and parthenogenetic reproduction in haplo-diplontic algae. *Botanica mar.* **21**, 155–163. [122.

Lowe, E. F. and Lawrence, J. M. (1976). Absorption efficiencies of *Lytechinus variegatus* (Lamarck) (Echinodermata: Echinoidea) for selected marine plants. *J. exp. mar. Biol. Ecol.* **21**, 223–234. [123.

Lubchenco, J. (formerly Menge, J. Lubchenco) (1978). Plant species diversity in a marine intertidal community: importance of herbivore food preference and algal competitive abilities. *Am. Nat.* **112**, 23–39. [124.

Lubchenco, J. (1979). Consumer terms and concepts. *Am. Nat.* **113**, 315–317.

Lubchenco, J. and Menge, B. A. (1978). Community development and persistence in a low rocky intertidal zone. *Ecol. Monogr.* **48**, 67–94. [125.

Lundberg, B. and Lipkin, Y. (1979). Natural food of herbivorous Rabbitfish (*Siganus* spp.) in Northern Red Sea. *Botanica mar.* **22**, 173–181. [126.

Lüning, K. (1975). Kreuzungsexperimente an *Laminaria saccharina* von Helgoland und von der Isle of Man. *Helgol. wiss. Meeresunters.* **27**, 108–114. [127.

Lüning, K. and Neushul, M. (1978). Light and temperature demands for growth and reproduction of Laminarian gametophytes in Southern and Central California. *Mar. Biol., Berl.* **45**, 297–309. [128.

Lüning, K., Chapman, A. R. O. and Mann, K. H. (1978). Crossing experiments in the non-digitate complex of *Laminaria* from both sides of the Atlantic. *Phycologia* **17**, 293–298. [129.

Luther, G. (1976a). Bewuchsuntersuchungen auf Natursteinsubstraten im Gezeitenbereich des Nordsylter Wattenmeeres. *Helgol. wiss. Meeresunters.* **28**, 145–166. [130.

Luther, G. (1976b). Bewuchsuntersuchungen auf Natursteinsubstraten im Gezeitenbereich des Nordsylter Wattenmeeres; Algen. *Helgol. wiss. Meeresunters.* **28**, 318–351. [131.

MacArthur, R. H. (1968). The theory of the niche. *In* "Population Biology and Evolution" (R. C. Lewontin, ed.), pp. 159–176. Syracuse University Press, Syracuse, N.Y.

MacArthur, R. H. (1970). Species packing and competitive equilibrium for many species. *Theor. Pop. Biol.* **1**, 1–11.

MacArthur, R. H. (1972). "Geographical Ecology: Patterns in the Distribution of Species". Harper and Row, New York.

MacArthur, R. H. and Levins, R. (1964). Competition, habitat selection, and character displacement in a patchy environment. *Proc. natn. Acad. Sci. U.S.A.* **51**, 1207–1210.

MacArthur, R. H. and Levins, R. (1967). The limiting similarity, convergence, and divergence of coexisting species. *Am. Nat.* **101**, 377–385.

MacArthur, R. H. and Wilson, E. O. (1967). "The Theory of Island Biogeography". University Press, Princeton.

McLachlan, J., van der Meer, J. P. and Bird, N. L. (1977). Chromosome numbers of *Gracilaria foliifera* and *Gracilaria* sp. (Rhodophyta) and attempted hybridizations. *J. mar. biol. Ass. U.K.* **57**, 1137–1141. [132.

McMurtrie, R. (1976). On the limit to niche overlap for nonuniform niches. *Theor. Pop. Biol.* **10**, 96–107.

McNaughton, S. J. and Wolf, L. L. (1970). Dominance and the niche in ecological systems. *Science, N.Y.* **167**, 131–139.

Magne, F. (1974). Peuplement d'un substrat calcaire dans la zone intercotidale. *Bull. Soc. phycol. France* **19**, 121–128. [133.

Magne, F. (1977). La reproduction sexuée chez l'*Acrochaetium asparagopsidis* (Chemin) Papenfuss, Rhodophycée. *Revue algol.* N.S., **12**, 61–72. [133A.

Maguire, B., Jr. (1973). Niche response structure and the analytical potentials of its relationships to the habitat. *Am. Nat.* **107**, 213–246.

Maguire, B., Jr. (1976). Analysis and modeling of evolutionary dynamics with the response structure/environmental structure approach. *Evolutionary Biol.* **9**, 365–407.

Makarewicz, J. C. and Likens, G. E. (1975). Niche analysis of a zooplankton community. *Science, N.Y.* **190**, 1000–1003.

Mann, K. H. (1972a). Ecological energetics of the seaweed zone in a marine bay on the Atlantic coast of Canada. I. Zonation and biomass of seaweeds. *Mar. Biol., Berl.* **12**, 1–10.

Mann, K. H. (1972b). Ecological energetics of the seaweed zone in a marine bay on the Atlantic coast of Canada. II. Productivity of the seaweeds. *Mar. Biol., Berl.* **14**, 199–209.

Mann, K. H. (1973). Seaweeds: their productivity and strategy for growth. *Science, N.Y.* **182**, 975–981.

Mann, K. H. (1977). Destruction of kelp-beds by sea-urchins: a cyclical phenomenon or irreversible degradation? *Helgol. wiss. Meeresunters.* **30**, 455–467. [134.

Mann, K. H. and Breen, P. A. (1972). The relation between lobster abundance, sea urchins and kelp beds. *J. Fish. Res. Bd Can.* **29**, 603–609. [135.

Mann, K. H. and Chapman, A. R. O. (1975). Primary production of marine macrophytes. *In* "Photosynthesis and Productivity in Different Environments" (J. P. Cooper, ed.), pp. 207–223. University Press, Cambridge. [136.

Margalef, R. (1968). "Perspectives in Ecological Theory". University Press, Chicago.

Mathieson, A. C. and Burns, R. L. (1975). Ecological studies on economic red algae. V. Growth and reproduction of natural and harvested populations of *Chondrus crispus* Stackhouse in New Hampshire. *J. exp. mar. Biol. Ecol.* **17**, 137–156. [137.

Mathieson, A. C. and Norall, T. L. (1975). Physiological studies of subtidal red algae. *J. exp. mar. Biol. Ecol.* **20**, 237–247. [138.

Mathieson, A. C., Shipman, J. W., O'Shea, J. R. and Hasevlat, R. C. (1976). Seasonal growth and reproduction of estuarine fucoid algae in New Hampshire. *J. exp. mar. Biol. Ecol.* **25**, 273–284. [139.

Mattison, J. E., Trent, J. D., Shanks, A. L., Akin, T. B. and Pearse, J. S. (1977). Movement and feeding activity of red sea urchins (*Strongylocentrotus franciscanus*) adjacent to a kelp forest. *Mar. Biol., Berl.* **39**, 25–30. [139A.

May, R. M. (1974). On the theory of niche overlap. *Theor. Pop. Biol.* **5**, 297–332.

May, R. M. (1975). Some notes on estimating the competition matrix, α. *Ecology* **56**, 737–741.

May, R. M. (ed.). (1976). "Theoretical Ecology: Principles and Applications". Blackwell, Oxford; W. B. Saunders, Philadelphia and Toronto.

May, R. M. and MacArthur, R. H. (1972). Niche overlap as a function of environment variability. *Proc. natn. Acad. Sci., U.S.A.* **69**, 1109–1113.

May, V., Bennett, I. and Thompson, T. E. (1970). Herbivore-algal relationships on a coastal rock-platform (Cape Banks, N.S.W.). *Oecologia, Berl.* **6**, 1–14. [139B.

Menge, B. A. (1972a). Foraging strategy of a starfish in relation to actual prey availability and environmental predictability. *Ecol. Monogr.* **42**, 25–50.

Menge, B. A. (1972b). Competition for food between two intertidal starfish species and its effect on body size and feeding. *Ecology* **53**, 635–644.

Menge, B. A. (1976). Organization of the New England rocky intertidal community: role of predation, competition, and environmental heterogeneity. *Ecol. Mongr.* **46**, 355–393.

Menge, B. A. (1978a). Predation intensity in a rocky intertidal community. Relation between predator foraging activity and environmental harshness. *Oecologia, Berl.* **34**, 1–16.

Menge, B. A. (1978b). Predation intensity in a rocky intertidal community. Effect of an algal canopy, wave action and desiccation on predator feeding rates. *Oecologia, Berl.* **34**, 17–35. [140.

Menge, B. A. (1979). Coexistence between the seastars *Asterias vulgaris* and *A. forbesi* in a heterogeneous environment: a non-equilibrium explanation. *Oecologia, Berl.* **41**, 245–272. [141.

Menge, B. A. and Sutherland, J. P. (1976). Species diversity gradients: synthesis of the roles of predation, competition and temporal heterogeneity. *Am. Nat.* **110**, 351–369. [142.

Menge, J. L. and Menge, B. A. (1974). Role of resource allocation, aggression, and spatial heterogeneity in coexistence in two competing intertidal starfish. *Ecol. Monogr.* **44**, 189–209.

Merrill, J. E. and Waaland, J. R. (1979). Photosynthesis and respiration in a fast growing strain of *Gigartina exasperata* (Harvey and Bailey). *J. exp. mar. Biol. Ecol.* **39**, 281–290. [142A.

Miller, R. J. and Mann, K. H. (1973). Ecological energetics of the seaweed zone in a marine bay on the Atlantic coast of Canada. III. Energy transformations by sea urchins. *Mar. Biol., Berl.* **18**, 99–114.

Mills, E. L. (1969). The community concept in marine zoology, with comments on continua and instability in some marine communities: a review. *J. Fish. Res. Bd Can.* **26**, 1415–1428.

Mizusawa, M., Kageyama, A. and Yokohama, Y. (1978). Physiology of benthic algae in tide pools I. Photosynthesis-temperature relationships in summer. *Jap. J. Phycol.* **26**, 109–114. [143.

Moebus, K. and Johnson, K. M. (1974). Exudation of dissolved organic carbon by brown algae. *Mar. Biol., Berl.* **26**, 117–125.

Müller, D. G. (1976). Sexual isolation between a European and an American population of *Ectocarpus siliculosus* (Phaeophyta). *J. Phycol.* **12**, 252–254. [144.

Müller, D. G. (1977). Sexual reproduction in British *Ectocarpus siliculosus* (Phaeophyta). *Br. phycol. J.* **12**, 131–136. [145.

Müller, D. G. (1978). Locomotive responses of male gametes to the species specific sex attractant in *Ectocarpus siliculosus* (Phaeophyta). *Archiv Protistenk.* **120**, 371–377. [146.

Murdoch, W. W. (1979). Predation and the dynamics of prey populations. *In* "Population Ecology Symposium Mainz, May 1978" (U. Halback and J. Jacobs, eds). *Fortschritte der Zoologie* 25(2–3), 295–310. Gustav Fischer Verlag, Stuttgart and New York. [146A.

Murray, S. N. and Dixon, P. S. (1973). The effect of light intensity and light period on the development of thallus form in the marine red alga *Pleonosporium squarrulosum* (Harvey) Abbott (Rhodophyta: Ceramiales). I. Apical cell division – main axes. *J. exp. mar. Biol. Ecol.* **13**, 15–27. [147.

Murray, S. N. and Dixon, P. S. (1975). The effects of light intensity and light period on the development of thallus form in the marine red alga *Pleonosporium squarrulosum* (Harvey) Abbott (Rhodophyta: Ceramiales). II. Cell enlargement. *J. exp. mar. Biol. Ecol.* **19**, 165–176. [148.

Murray, S. N. and Littler, M. M. (1978). Patterns of algal succession in a perturbated marine intertidal community. *J. Phycol.* **14**, 506–512.

Nakahara, H. and Nakamura, Y. (1973). Parthenogenesis, apogamy and apospory in *Alaria crassifolia* (Laminariales). *Mar. Biol., Berl.* **18**, 327–332. [149.

Nakahara, H. and Yamada, I. (1974). Crossing experiments between four local forms of *Agarum cribrosum* Bory (Phaeophyta) from Hokkaido, northern Japan. *J. Fac. Sci. Hokkaido Univ.*, ser. V (Botany) **10**, 49–54. [150.

Neushul, M. (1972). Functional interpretation of benthic marine algal morphology. *In* "Contributions to the Systematics of Benthic Marine Algae of the North Pacific . . ." (I. A. Abbott and M. Kurogi, eds), pp. 47–73. Japanese Society of Phycology, Kobe, Japan. [151

Neushul, M., Coon, D. A. and Charters, A. C. (1972). Direct observation of algal spores under neutral conditions. *Proc. int. Seaweed Symp.* **7**, 231–236. [152

Neushul, M., Foster, M. S., Coon, D. A., Woessner, J. W. and Harger, B. W. W (1976). An *in situ* study of recruitment, growth, and survival of subtidal marine algae: techniques and preliminary results. *J. Phycol.* **12**, 397–408. [153.

Nicotri, M. E. (1977). Grazing effects of four marine intertidal herbivores on the microflora. *Ecology* 58, 1020–1032. [154.

Nicotri, M. E. (1980). Factors involved in herbivore food preference. *J. exp. mar. Biol. Ecol.* **42**, 13–26. [154A.

Niell, F. X. (1977). Rocky intertidal benthic systems in temperate seas: a synthesis of their functional performance. *Helgol. wiss. Meeresunters.* **30**, 315–333.

Niell, F. X. (1979). Structure and succession in rocky algal communities of a temperate intertidal system. *J. exp. mar. Biol. Ecol.* **36**, 185–200. [155.

Niemeck, R. A. and Mathieson, A. C. (1978). Physiological studies of intertidal fucoid algae. *Botanica mar.* **21**, 221–227. [156.

Nisbet, R. M., Gurney, W. S. C. and Pettipher, M. A. (1978). Environmental fluctuations and the theory of the ecological niche. *J. theor. Biol.* **75**, 223–237.

Nold, A. (1979). Competitive overlap and coexistence. *Theor. Pop. Biol.* **15**, 232–245.

Nonomura, A. M. (1979). Development of *Janczewskia morimotoi* (Ceramiales) on its host *Laurencia nipponica* (Ceramiales, Rhodophyceae). *J. Phycol.* **15**, 154–162. [157.

Norton, T. A. (1975). Growth-form and environment in cave-dwelling plants of *Plumaria elegans*. *Br. phycol. J.* **10**, 225–233. [158.

Norton, T. A., Hiscock, K. and Kitching, J. A. (1977). The ecology of Lough Ine XX. The *Laminaria* forest at Carrigathorna. *J. Ecol.* **65**, 919–941. [159

Nultsch, W. and Pfau, J. (1979). Occurrence and biological role of light-induced chromatophore displacements in seaweeds. *Mar. Biol., Berl.* **51**, 77–82. [159A.

O'Connor, R. J., Seed, R. and Boaden, P. J. S. (1979). Effects of environment and plant characteristics on the distribution of Bryozoa in a *Fucus serratus* L. community. *J. exp. mar. Biol. Ecol.* **38**, 151–178. [160.

Ogden, J. C. (1976). Some aspects of herbivore-plant relationships on Caribbean reefs and seagrass beds. *Aquatic Bot.* **2**, 103–116. [161.

Ogden, J. C. and Lobel, P. S. (1978). The role of herbivorous fishes and urchins in coral reef communities. *Env. Biol. Fish.* **3**, 49–63. [162.

Okuda, T. (formerly Sawada, T.) (1975). Reproduction of Ulvaceous Algae with special reference to the periodic fruiting II. Fruiting of *Ulva pertusa* during the neap tides in Okayama. *J. Fac. Agr., Kyushu Univ.* **19**, 149–157. [163.

Olson, J. M. (1978). Precambrian evolution of photosynthetic and respiratory organisms. *Evolutionary Biol.* **11**, 1–37. [163A.

Oohusa, T., Araki, S., Sakurai, T. and Saitoh, M. (1978). Diurnal variations of the photosynthetic pigments, total nitrogen and total nitrogen/total carbohydrate ratio of cultivated *Porphyra* thalli and their relationships to the quality of dried Nori. *Jap. J. Phycol.* **26**, 185–187. [164.

Osman, R. W. (1977). The establishment and development of a marine epifaunal community. *Ecol. Monogr.* **47**, 37–63.

Paine, R. T. (1966). Food web complexity and species diversity. *Am. Nat.* **100**, 65–75. [165.

Paine, R. T. (1969). The *Pisaster-Tegula* interaction: prey patches, predator food preference and inter-tidal community structure. *Ecology* **50**, 950–961. [166.

Paine, R. T. (1971a). A short-term experimental investigation of resource partitioning in a New Zealand rocky intertidal habitat. *Ecology* **52**, 1096–1106.

Paine, R. T. (1971b). The measurement and application of the calorie to ecological problems. *Ann. Rev. Ecol. Syst.* **2**, 145–164.

Paine, R. T. (1974). Intertidal community structure: experimental studies on the relationship between a dominant competitor and its principal predator. *Oecologia, Berl.* **15**, 93–120. [167.

Paine, R. T. (1977). Controlled manipulations in the marine intertidal zone, and their contributions to ecological theory. *In* "The Changing Scenes in Natural Sciences, 1776–1976". *Acad. Nat. Sci., Spec. Publ.* **12**, 245–270.

Paine, R. T. (1979). Disaster, catastrophe, and local persistence of the Sea Palm *Postelsia palmaeformis. Science, N.Y.* **205**, 685–687. [168.

Paine, R. T. and Vadas, R. L. (1969a). Calorific values of benthic marine algae and their postulated relation to invertebrate food preference. *Mar. Biol., Berl.* **4**, 79–86. [169.

Paine, R. T. and Vadas, R. L. (1969b). The effects of grazing by sea urchins, *Strongylocentrotus* spp., on benthic algal populations. *Limnol. Oceanogr.* **14**, 710–719. [170.

Pamatmat, M. M. (1977). Benthic community metabolism: a review and assessment of present status and outlook. *In* "Ecology of Marine Benthos" (B. C. Coull, ed.), pp. 89–111. University of South Carolina Press, Columbia, S. Carolina. Belle, W. Baruch Library in Marine Science, No. 6.

Parker, G. A., Baker, R. R. and Smith, V. G. F. (1972). The origin and evolution of gamete dimorphism and the male-female phenomenon. *J. theor. Biol.* **36**, 529–553. [171.

Pearlmutter, N. L. and Vadas, R. L. (1978). Regeneration of thallus fragments of *Rhodochorton purpureum* (Rhodophyceae, Nemalionales). *Phycologia* **17**, 186–190. [172.

Pearse, J. S. and Hines, A. H. (1979). Expansion of a central California kelp forest following the mass mortality of sea urchins. *Mar. Biol., Berl.* **51**, 83–91. [173.

Peet, R. K. (1974). The measurement of species diversity. *Ann. Rev. Ecol. Syst.* **5**, 285–307.

Penhale, P. A. and Smith, W. O., Jr. (1977). Excretion of dissolved organic carbon by eelgrass (*Zostera marina*) and its epiphytes. *Limnol. Oceanogr.* **22**, 400–407.

Pentecost, A. (1978). Calcification and photosynthesis in *Corallina officinalis* L. using the $^{14}CO_2$ method. *Br. phycol. J.* **13**, 383–390. [174.

Peters, R. H. (1976). Tautology in evolution and ecology. *Am. Nat.* **110**, 1–12.

Peterson, C. H. (1979). The importance of predation and competition in organizing the intertidal epifaunal communities of Barnegat Inlet, New Jersey. *Oecologia, Berl.* **39**, 1–24.

Petraitis, P. S. (1979). Likelihood measures of niche breadth and overlap. *Ecology* **60**, 703–710.
Peyrière, M. (1977). Ultra-structure d'*Harveyella mirabilis* (Cryptonemiales, Rhodophycée) parasite de *Rhodomela confervoides* (Ceramiale, Rhodophycée): origine des synapses secondaires entre cellules de l'hôte et du parasite et entre cellules du parasite. *C.r. hebd. Séanc. Acad. Sci. Paris*, sér. D **285**, 965–968. [175.
Pianka, E. R. (1970). On *r* and *K* selection. *Am. Nat.* **104**, 592–597.
Pianka, E. R. (1972). *r* and *K* selection or *b* and *d* selection? *Am. Nat.* **106**, 581–588.
Pianka, E. R. (1974a). "Evolutionary Ecology". Harper and Row, New York.
Pianka, E. R. (1974b). Niche overlap and diffuse competition. *Proc. natn. Acad. Sci. U.S.A.* **71**, 2141–2145.
Pianka, E. R. (1975). Niche relations of desert lizards. *In* "Ecology and Evolution of Communities", pp. 292–314. Belknap Press of Harvard University Press, Cambridge, Mass. and London.
Pianka, E. R. (1976). Competition and niche theory. *In* "Theoretical Ecology: Principles and Application" (R. M. May, ed.), pp. 114–141. W. B. Saunders Co., Philadelphia.
Pielou, E. C. (1972). Niche width and niche overlap: a method of measuring them. *Ecology* **53**, 687–692.
Pielou, E. C. (1975). "Ecological Diversity". Wiley-Interscience, New York.
Pielou, E. C. (1977). "Mathematical Ecology" (2nd edn). Wiley, New York, London, Sydney, Toronto. (Largely replaces 1st edn of 1969).
Polanshek, A. R. and West, J. A. (1975). Culture and hybridization studies on *Petrocelis* from Alaska and California. *J. Phycol.* **11**, 434–439. [176.
Polanshek, A. R. and West, J. A. (1977). Culture and hybridization studies on *Gigartina papillata* (Rhodophyta). *J. Phycol.* **13**, 141–149. [177.
Porter, J. W. (1974). Community structure of coral reefs on opposite sides of the Isthmus of Panama. *Science, N.Y.* **180**, 543–545. [178.
Porter, J. W. (1976). Autotrophy, heterotrophy, and resource partitioning in Caribbean reef-building corals. *Am. Nat.* **110**, 731–742.
Porter, K. G. (1976). Enhancement of algal growth and productivity by grazing zooplankton. *Science, N.Y.* **192**, 1332–1334. [179.
Potts, D. C. (1977). Suppression of coral populations by filamentous algae within damselfish territories. *J. exp. mar. Biol. Ecol.* **28**, 207–216. [180.
Prentice, S. A. and Kain, J. M. (1976). Numerical analysis of subtidal communities on rocky shores. *Est. cst. mar. Sci.* **4**, 65–70.
Price, J. H. (1973). Advances in the study of benthic marine algae since the time of E. M. Holmes. *Bot. J. Linn. Soc.* **67**, 47–102.
Price, J. H. (1978). Ecological determination of adult form in *Callithamnion*: its taxonomic implications. *In* "Modern Approaches to the Taxonomy of Red and Brown Algae" (D. E. G. Irvine and J. H. Price, eds), pp. 263–300. Syst. Ass. Spec. Vol. 10. Academic Press, London and New York. [181.
Price, J. H. and John, D. M. (1978). Subtidal ecology in Antigua and Ascension:

a comparison. *Prog. in underw. Sci.* **3**, (*Rep. underw. Ass.*, N.S.), 111–133. [182.

Price, J. H., Tittley, I. and Richardson, W. D. (1979). The distribution of *Padina pavonica* (L.) Lamour. (Phaeophyta: Dictyotales) on British and adjacent European shores. *Bull. Br. Mus. nat. Hist.* (Bot.) **7**, 1–67. [183.

Pyefinch, K. A. (1943). The intertidal ecology of Bardsey Island, North Wales, with special reference to the recolonization of rock surfaces, and the rock-pool environment. *J. Anim. Ecol.* **12**, 82–108.

Quadir, A., Harrison, P. J. and De Wreede, R. E. (1979). The effects of emergence and submergence on the photosynthesis and respiration of marine macrophytes. *Phycologia* **18**, 83–88. [184.

Raffaelli, D. (1979). The grazer-algae interaction in the intertidal zone on New Zealand rocky shores. *J. exp. mar. Biol. Ecol.* **38**, 81–100. [185.

Ramon, E. (1973). Germination and attachment of zygotes of *Himanthalia elongata* (L.) S. F. Gray. *J. Phycol.* **9**, 445–449. [186.

Ramus, J. (1978). Seaweed anatomy and photosynthetic performance: the ecological significance of light guides, heterogeneous absorption and multiple scatter. *J. Phycol.* **14**, 352–362. [187.

Ramus, J., Beale, S. I. and Mauzerall, D. (1976). Correlation of changes in pigment content with photosynthetic capacity of seaweeds as a function of water depth. *Mar. Biol., Berl.* **37**, 231–238. [188.

Ramus, J., Lemons, F. and Zimmerman, C. (1977). Adaptation of light-harvesting pigments to downwelling light and the consequent photosynthetic performance of the eulittoral rockweeds *Ascophyllum nodosum* and *Fucus vesiculosus*. *Mar. Biol., Berl.* **42**, 893–903. [189.

Ramus, J., Beale, S. I., Mauzerall, D. and Howard, K. L. (1976). Changes in photosynthetic pigment concentration in seaweeds as a function of water depth. *Mar. Biol., Berl.* **37**, 223–229. [190.

Rastetter, E. B. and Cooke, W. J. (1979). Responses of marine fouling communities to sewage abatement in Kaneohe Bay, Oahu, Hawaii. *Mar. Biol., Berl.* **53**, 271–280.

Rawlence, D. J. (1972). An ultrastructural study of the relationship between rhizoids of *Polysiphonia lanosa* (L.) Tandy (Rhodophyceae) and tissue of *Ascophyllum nodosum* (L.) Le Jolis (Phaeophyceae). *Phycologia* **11**, 279–290. [191.

Reed, R. H. and Russell, G. (1978). Salinity fluctuations and their influence on "bottle brush" morphogenesis in *Enteromorpha intestinalis* (L.) Link. *Br. phycol. J.* **13**, 149–153. [192.

Reynoldson, T. B. and Bellamy, L. S. (1971). The establishment of interspecific competition in field populations, with an example of competition in action between *Polycelis nigra* (Mull.) and *P. tenuis* (Ijima) (Turbellaria, Tricladida). *In* "Dynamics of Populations" (P. J. Den Boer and G. R. Gradwell, eds.), pp. 282–297. Proc. Advcd Study Inst. Dynam. Numbers Population, Oosterbeek, 1970. Centre for Agric. Publ. Documentation, Wageningen.

Richards, P. W. (1969). Speciation in the tropical rain forest and the concept of the niche. *Biol. J. Linn. Soc.* **1**, 149–153.

Robertson, A. and Pearson, H. W. (1979). Physiological studies on the effects of water stress in certain intertidal and subtidal algae. *Br. phycol. J.* **14**, 127. [193.

Rosenthal, R. J., Clarke, W. D. and Dayton, P. K. (1974). Ecology and natural history of a stand of giant kelp, *Macrocystis pyrifera*, off Del Mar, California. *Fishery Bull. Fish. Wildl. Serv. U.S.* **72**, 670–684. [193A.

Rosenzweig, M. L. and Schaffer, W. M. (1978). Homage to the Red Queen. II. Coevolutionary response to enrichment of exploitation ecosystems. *Theor. Pop. Biol.* **14**, 158–163.

Roughgarden, J. (1972). Evolution of niche width. *Am. Nat.* **106**, 683–718.

Roughgarden, J. (1974). Niche width: biogeographic patterns among *Anolis* lizard populations. *Am. Nat.* **108**, 429–442.

Roughgarden, J. (1976). Resource partitioning among competing species – a coevolutionary approach. *Theor. Pop. Biol.* **9**, 388–424.

Roughgarden, J. (1977). Coevolution in ecological systems: results from 'loop analysis' for purely density-dependent coevolution. *In* "Measuring Selection in Natural Populations" (F. D. Christiansen and T. M. Fenchel, eds), pp. 499–517. Springer-Verlag, New York. Vol. 19 in Lecture Notes in Biomathematics.

Roughgarden, J. (1979a). "Theory of Population Genetics and Evolutionary Ecology, An Introduction". MacMillan Publishing Co., New York.

Roughgarden, J. (1979b). A local concept of structural homology for ecological communities with examples from simple communities of West Indian *Anolis* lizards. *In* "Population Ecology Symposium Mainz, May 1978". (U. Halbach and J. Jacobs, eds). *Fortschritte der Zoologie* **25**(2–3), 149–157. Gustav Fischer Verlag, Stuttgart and New York.

Rueness, J. (1973). Speciation in *Polysiphonia* (Rhodophyceae, Ceramiales) in view of hybridization experiments: *P. hemisphaerica* and *P. boldii. Phycologia* **12**, 107–109. [194.

Rueness, J. (1978). Hybridization in Red Algae. *In* "Modern Approaches to the Taxonomy of Red and Brown Algae" (D. E. G. Irvine and J. H. Price, eds), Syst. Ass. Spec. Vol. 10. Academic Press, London and New York. [195.

Russell, G. (1972). Phytosociological studies on a two-zone shore. I. Basic pattern. *J. Ecol.* **60**, 539–545.

Russell, G. (1973). The "litus-line": a re-assessment. *Oikos* **24**, 158–161.

Russell, G. (1978). Environment and Form in the Discrimination of Taxa in Brown Algae. *In* "Modern Approaches to the Taxonomy of Red and Brown Algae" (D. E. G. Irvine and J. H. Price, eds), Syst. Ass. Spec. Vol. 10. Academic Press, London and New York. [195B.

Russell, G. and Bolton, J. J. (1975). Euryhaline ecotypes of *Ectocarpus siliculosus* (Dillw.) Lyngb. *Est. cst. mar. Sci.* **3**, 91–94. [195A.

Russell, G. and Morris, O. P. (1973). Ship-fouling as an evolutionary process. *Proc. int. Congr. mar. Corr. Fouling* **3**, 719–730. [196.

Russell, G. and Wareing, A. -M. (1979). The *Herponema velutinum – Himanthalia elongata* coincidence. *Br. phycol. J.* **14**, 128. [197.

Sabath, M. D. and Jones, J. M. (1973). Measurement of niche breadth and overlap: the Colwell-Futuyma method. *Ecology* **54**, 1143–1147.

Sabo, S. R. and Whittaker, R. H. (1979). Bird niches in a subalpine forest: an indirect ordination. *Proc. natn. Acad. Sci., U.S.A.* **76**, 1338–1342.

Saito, Y. (1972). On the effects of environmental factors on morphological characteristics of *Undaria pinnatifida* and the breeding of hybrids in the genus *Undaria*. *In* "Contributions to the Systematics of Benthic Marine Algae of the North Pacific". (I. A. Abbott and M. Kurogi, eds), pp. 117–130. Japanese Society of Phycology, Kobe, Japan. [198.

Saito, Y. Yoneta, T. and Yoshikawa, M. (1977). The relationships of parasite and host in the red algae *Janczewskia tokidae* and *Laurencia nipponica*. *Bull. Jap. Soc. Phycol.* **25**(Suppl.), 311–317. [199.

Sale, P. F. and Dybdahl, R. (1978). Determinants of community structure for coral reef fishes in isolated coral heads at lagoonal and reef slope sites. *Oecologia, Berl.* **34**, 57–74.

Sanbonsuga, Y. and Neushul, N. (1978). Hybridization of *Macrocystis* (Phaeophyta) with other float-bearing kelps. *J. Phycol.* **14**, 214–224. [200.

Santelices, B. (1977). Water movement and seasonal algal growth in Hawaii. *Mar. Biol., Berl.* **43**, 225–235. [201.

Sawada, T. and Watanabe, T. (1974). Reproduction of Ulvaceous Algae with special reference to the periodic fruiting I. Semilunar rhythmicity of *Ulva pertusa* in Northern Kyushu. *J. Fac. Agr., Kyushu Univ.* **18**, 81–88. [202.

Schaffer, W. M. and Rosenzweig, M. L. (1978). Homage to the Red Queen. I. Coevolution of predators and their victims. *Theor. Pop. Biol.* **14**, 135–157.

Schoener, T. W. (1974). Resource partitioning in ecological communities. *Science, N.Y.* **185**, 27–39.

Schonbeck, M. W. and Norton, T. A. (1978). Factors controlling the upper limits of fucoid algae on the shore. *J. exp. mar. Biol. Ecol.* **31**, 303–318. [203.

Schonbeck, M. W. and Norton, T. A. (1979a). An investigation of drought avoidance in intertidal fucoid algae. *Botanica mar.* **22**, 133–144. [204.

Schonbeck, M. W. and Norton, T. A. (1979b). Drought-hardening in the upper-shore seaweeds *Fucus spiralis* and *Pelvetia canaliculata*. *J. Ecol.* **67**, 687–696. [204A.

Seapy, R. R. and Littler, M. M. (1978). The distribution, abundance, community structure, and primary productivity of macroorganisms from two central California rocky intertidal habitats. *Pacific Sci.* **32**, 293–314.

Seeliger, U. and Edwards, P. (1977). Correlation coefficients and concentration factors of copper and lead in seawater and benthic algae. *Mar. Poll. Bull.* **8**, 16–19.

Sheath, R. G., Hellebust, J. A. and Sawa, T. (1977). Changes in plastid structure, pigmentation and photosynthesis of the conchocelis stage of *Porphyra leucosticta* (Rhodophyta, Bangiophyceae) in response to low light and darkness. *Phycologia* **16**, 265–276. [205.

Shugart, H. H., Jr. and Patten, B. C. (1972). Niche quantification and the concept of niche pattern. *In* "Systems Analysis and Simulation in Ecology", Vol. II (B. C. Patten, ed.), pp. 283–327. Academic Press, New York and London.

Sieburth, J. McN. (1976). Bacterial substrates and productivity in marine ecosystems. *Ann. Rev. Ecol. Syst.* **7**, 259–285.

Simpson, E. H. (1949). Measurement of diversity. *Nature, Lond.* **163**, 688.

Smith, C. L. and Tyler, J. C. (1972). Space resource sharing in a coral reef fish community. *Nat. Hist. Mus. Los Angeles Cty. Sci. Bull.* **14**, 125–170.

Smith, C. L. and Tyler, J. C. (1975). Succession and stability in fish communities of dome shaped patch reefs in the West Indies. *Am. Mus. Novitates* **2572**, 1–18.

Southward, A. J. (1953). The ecology of some rocky shores in the south of the Isle of Man. *Proc. Trans. Lpool Biol. Soc.* **59**, 1–50.

Southward, A. J. (1956). The population balance between limpets and seaweeds on wave beaten rocky shores. *Rep. mar. Biol. Stn Port Erin* **68**, 20–29.

Southward, A. J. (1964). Limpet grazing and the control of vegetation on rocky shores. *In* "Grazing in Terrestrial and Marine Environments" (D. J. Crisp, ed.), pp. 265–273. Blackwells, Oxford.

Southwood, T. R. E. and Comins, H. N. (1976). A synoptic population model. *J. Anim. Ecol.* **45**, 949–965.

Stebbing, A. R. D. (1973a). Competition for space between the epiphytes of *Fucus serratus* L. *J. mar. biol. Ass. U.K.* **53**, 247–261. [206.

Stebbing, A. R. D. (1973b). Observations on colony overgrowth and spatial competition. *In* "Living and Fossil Bryozoa" (G. P. Larwood, ed.), pp. 173–183. Academic Press, London and New York. [207.

Steneck, R. S. and Adey, W. H. (1976). The role of environment in control of morphology in *Lithophyllum congestum*, a Caribbean algal ridge builder. *Botanica mar.* **19**, 197–215. [208.

Stenseth, N. C. (1978). Do grazers maximize individual plant fitness? *Oikos* **31**, 299–306.

Stewart, F. M. and Levin, B. R. (1973). Partitioning of resources and the outcome of interspecific competition: a model and some general considerations. *Am. Nat.* **107**, 171–198.

Strömgren, T. (1977). Short-term effects of temperature upon the growth of intertidal Fucales. *J. exp. mar. Biol. Ecol.* **29**, 181–195. [209.

Sutherland, J. P. and Karlson, R. H. (1977). Development and stability of the fouling community at Beaufort, North Carolina. *Ecol. Monogr.* **47**, 425–446.

Suto, S. (1950). Studies on shedding, swimming and fixing of the spores of seaweeds. *Bull. Jap. Soc. Sci. Fish.* **16**, 1–9. [210.

Talbot, F. H., Russell, B. C. and Anderson, G. R. V. (1979). Coral reef fish communities: unstable, high-diversity systems? *Ecol. Monogr.* **48**, 425–440, 1978.

Taylor, W. P. (1916). The status of the beavers of Western North America, with a consideration of the factors in their speciation. *Univ. Calif. Publ. Zool.* **12**, 413–495.

Teramoto, E., Kawasaki, K. and Shigesada, N. (1979). Switching effect of predation on competitive prey species. *J. theor. Biol.* **79**, 303–315.

Terry, L. A. (1979). The effect of irradiance and temperature on the early development of some species of Fucaceae. *Br. phycol. J.* **14**, 128. [211.

Todd, C. D. (1978). Changes in spatial pattern of an intertidal population of the nudibranch mollusc *Onchidoris muricata* in relation to life-cycle, mortality and environmental heterogeneity. *J. Anim. Ecol.* **47**, 189–203. [211B.

Towle, D. W. and Pearse, J. S. (1973). Production of the giant kelp, *Macrocystis*, estimated by *in situ* incorporation of ^{14}C in polyethylene bags. *Limnol. Oceanogr.* **18**, 155–159. [211A.

Turelli, M. (1978). Does environmental variability limit niche overlap? *Proc. natn. Acad. Sci., U.S.A.* **75**, 5085–5089.

Turner, C. H. C. and Evans, L. V. (1978). Translocation of photoassimilated ^{14}C in the red alga *Polysiphonia lanosa*. *Br. phycol. J.* **13**, 51–55. [212.

Umamaheswara Rao, M. (1976). Spore liberation in *Gracilaria corticata* J. Agardh growing at Mandapam. *J. exp. mar. Biol. Ecol.* **21**, 91–98. [213.

Underwood, A. J. (1976). Food competition between age-classes in the intertidal neritacean *Nerita atramentosa* Reeve (Gastropoda: Prosobranchia). *J. exp. mar. Biol. Ecol.* **23**, 145–154.

Underwood, A. J. (1978). A refutation of critical tidal levels as determinants of the structure of intertidal communities on British shores. *J. exp. mar. Biol. Ecol.* **33**, 261–276.

Underwood, A. J. (1979). The ecology of intertidal gastropods. *Adv. mar. Biol.* **16**, 111–210. [213A.

Vadas, R. L. (1977). Preferential feeding: an optimization strategy in sea urchins. *Ecol. Monogr.* **47**, 337–371. [214.

Vallespinos, F. (1976). Comunidades bentónicas de sustrate duro del litoral NE español. III: pigmentos y producción. *Investigación pesq.* **40**, 515–532. [215.

Vance, R. R. (1979). Effects of grazing by the sea urchin, *Centrostephanus coronatus*, on prey community composition. *Ecology* **60**, 537–546. [215A.

Vandermeer, J. H. (1972). Niche theory. *Ann. Rev. Ecol. Syst.* **3**, 107–132.

Van Valen, L. (1974). Predation and species diversity. *J. theor. Biol.* **44**, 19–21. [216.

Velimirov, B. and Griffiths, C. L. (1979). Wave-induced kelp movement and its importance for community structure. *Botanica mar.* **22**, 169–172. [217.

Velimirov, V., Field, J. G., Griffiths, C. L. and Zoutendyk, P. (1977). The ecology of kelp bed communities in the Benguela upwelling system. Analysis of biomass and spatial distribution. *Helgol. wiss. Meeresunters.* **30**, 495–518. [218.

Vuilleumier, F. (1979). La niche de certains modelisateurs: parametres d'un monde real ou d'un univers fictif? *Terre et Vie* **33**, 375–423.

Wassman, R. and Ramus, J. (1973). Seaweed invasion. *Nat. Hist.* **82**, 24–36. [219.

Weatherley, A. H. (1963). Notions of niche and competition among animals, with special reference to freshwater fish. *Nature, Lond.* **197**, 14–17.

West, J. A. (1979). The life history of *Rhodochorton membranaceum*, an endozoic red alga. *Botanica mar.* **22**, 111–115. [220.

West, J. A., Polanshek, A. R. and Guiry, M. D. (1977). The life history in culture of *Petrocelis cruenta* J. Agardh (Rhodophyta) from Ireland. *Br. phycol. J.* **12**, 45–53. [221.

West, J. A., Polanshek, A. R. and Shevlin, D. E. (1978). Field and culture studies on *Gigartina agardhii* (Rhodophyta). *J. Phycol.* **14**, 416–426. [222.

Whittaker, R. H. (1972). Evolution and measurement of species diversity. *Taxon.* **21**, 213–251.

Whittaker, R. H. and Feeny, P. P. (1971). Allelochemics: chemical interactions between species. *Science, N.Y.* **171**, 757–770.

Whittaker, R. H. and Levin, S. A. (1975). "Niche Theory and Application". Dowden, Hutchinson and Ross, Inc, Stroudsburg, Pennsylvania. Benchmark Papers in Ecology, No. 3.

Whittaker, R. H., Levin, S. A. and Root, R. B. (1973). Niche, habitat and ecotope, *Am. Nat.* **107**, 321–338.

Whittaker, R. H., Levin, S. A. and Root, R. B. (1975). On the reasons for distinguishing "niche, habitat, and ecotope". *Am. Nat.* **109**, 479–482.

Whittick, A. (1977). The reproductive ecology of *Plumaria elegans* (Bonnem.) Schmitz (Ceramiaceae: Rhodophyta) at its northern limits in the western Atlantic. *J. exp. mar. Biol. Ecol.* **29**, 223–230. [223.

Whittick, A. (1978). The life history and phenology of *Callithamnion corymbosum* (Rhodophyta: Ceramiaceae) in Newfoundland. *Can. J. Bot.* **56**, 2497–2499. [223A.

Wiens, J. A. (1977). On competition and variable environments. *Am. Scient.* **65**, 590–597.

Wilce, R. T. (1967). Heterotrophy in Arctic sublittoral seaweeds: an hypothesis. *Botanica mar.* **10**, 185–197.

Wilcox, D. L. and MacCluer, J. W. (1979). Coevolution in predator-prey systems: a saturation kinetic model. *Am. Nat.* **113**, 163–183.

Woodin, S. A. (1974). Polychaete abundance patterns in a marine soft-sediment environment: the importance of biological interactions. *Ecol. Monogr.* **44**, 171–187. [224.

Woodin, S. A. (1978). Refuges, disturbance, and community structure: a marine soft-bottom example. *Ecology* **59**, 274–284.

Wuenscher, J. E. (1969). Niche specification and competition modeling. *J. theor. Biol.* **25**, 436–443.

Wuenscher, J. E. (1974). The ecological niche and vegetation dynamics. *In* "Handbook of Vegetation Science: Part VII Vegetation and Environment" (B. R. Strain and W. D. Billings, eds), pp. 37–45. Dr. W. Junk, b.v., The Hague.

Yarish, C., Edwards, P. and Casey, S. (1979). Acclimation response to salinity of three estuarine red algae from New Jersey. *Mar. Biol., Berl.* **51**, 289–294. [225.

Yokohama, Y. (1973a). Photosynthetic properties of marine benthic green algae from different depths in the coastal area. *Bull. Jap. Soc. Phycol.* **21**, 70–75. [226.

Yokohama, Y. (1973b). Photosynthetic properties of marine benthic red algae from different depths in coastal area. *Bull. Jap. Soc. Phycol.* **21**, 119–124. [227.

Yokohama, Y. (1973c). A comparative study on photosynthesis-temperature relationships and their seasonal changes in marine benthic algae. *Int. Revue ges. Hydrobiol.* 58, 463–472. [228.

Yokohama, Y., Kageyama, A., Ikawa, T. and Shimura, S. (1977). A carotenoid characteristic of Chlorophycean seaweeds living in deep coastal waters. *Botanica mar.* **20**, 433–436. [229.

Yoshiyama, R. M. and Roughgarden, J. (1977). Species packing in two dimensions. *Am. Nat.* **111**, 107–121.

Zavodnik, N. (1973). Seasonal variations in rate of photosynthetic activity and chemical composition of the littoral seaweeds common to North Adriatic, Part I: *Fucus virsoides* (Don.) J. Ag. *Botanica mar.* **16**, 155–165. [230.

Zavodnik, N. (1975). Effects of temperature and salinity variations on photosynthesis of some littoral seaweeds of the North Adriatic Sea. *Botanica mar.* **18**, 245–250. [231.

Zimmerman, R. Gibson, R. and Harrington, J. (1979). Herbivory and detritivory among Gammaridean amphipods from a Florida seagrass community. *Mar. Biol., Berl.* 54, 41–47. [232.

6 | Southern California Rocky Intertidal Ecosystems: Methods, Community Structure and Variability

MARK M. LITTLER

Department of Ecology and Evolutionary Biology, University of California, Irvine, California, U.S.A.

Abstract: No comparable spectrum of rocky intertidal systems has previously been examined to the level of sampling effort and synoptic overview provided herein. The scope of this work is such that temporal and spatial variations of the macroinvertebrate and macrophyte species have been assessed in terms of tidal location, cover, frequency, density, wet weight, dry weight, ash-free dry weight, species diversity, evenness, richness and cluster analysis. These descriptive parameters were used at each of 12 representative sites during four separate quarters of 1976–1977 to characterize a spectrum of intertidal systems and to relate important aspects of distribution and abundance to possible causal (biotic and abiotic) features of the environment.

Many of the methods employed were newly developed and have not been treated in detail in the scientific literature. In particular, the undisturbed sampling method, utilizing permanently-marked sampling locations, provides a powerful tool for quantification of seasonal and yearly biological differences and this is what we have emphasized. This procedure has the advantage of being rapid and simple to use, thus enabling a greater number of samples to be taken per unit of time. When used with infrared film, the technique permits the quantification of blue-green algae, the predominant cover organisms in most rocky intertidal habitats. This system also permits a high degree of quality control because photo-samples scored by various individuals can be reviewed

Systematics Association Special Volume No. 17(b), "The Shore Environment, Vol. 2: Ecosystems", edited by J. H. Price, D. E. G. Irvine and W. F. Farnham, 1980, pp. 565–608, Academic Press, London and New York.

by the total research staff, including senior taxonomic personnel, to ensure standardization and accuracy in the quantification process. The infrared photographs also emphasize unhealthy thalli with reduced chlorophyll contents that are often masked by accessory pigments; these would otherwise not be visible by color photography or to the unaided eye. Another important feature of the technique is that permanent historic data sets (i.e. photo-samples) are obtained which depict the status of the biota at a given point in time; these may become useful at a future date for purposes not originally intended. Additionally, changes (e.g. due to human disturbance) can easily be documented by direct comparison of photo-samples taken of the same quadrats at different times. Seasonality can also be demonstrated by direct comparisons of photo-samples taken of the identical quadrats over different sampling periods.

The broad range of environmental variability within the Bight results in a complex intermingling of physical conditions that is reflected in the diversity and complexity of intertidal and other biological systems. The present data, and those from the 1975–1976 study (Littler, 1980), strongly suggest that local or even site-specific conditions tend to predominate most often and to obscure broad overall effects. Numerous workers (Emery, 1960; Schwartzlose, 1963; Jones, 1971) have emphasized that the Southern California Continental Borderland is a very unusual region located within the overlapping boundaries of two major biogeographic regions, which results in a complex biological regime. Throughout the Bight, there exists a mosaic of temporally and spatially changing water temperatures, substrate types and slopes, upwelling conditions, wave exposures, water transparencies, levels of natural and human-induced stresses and nutrient concentrations. Therefore, it was not surprising that the different systems showed a high degree of site-specific autonomy.

Overall, water temperature mediated by oceanic current systems accounts for much of the large-scale biogeographic pattern exhibited by rocky intertidal ecosystems in Southern California. Operating at a less coarse level are factors such as wave action and coastal upwelling, moderate levels of which lead to richer intertidal communities. A still finer (site-specific) level of organization would seem to be controlled by such parameters as stability of the substrate, sand inundation, beach slope, desiccation stress, substrate type, level of human disturbance and unpredictable disturbances (e.g. floods or storms). Within this framework, predation and competition among the biotic elements themselves have been shown (Paine, 1966; Connell, 1972; Dayton, 1971, 1975) to be important in fine-tuning of the community structure.

The highly epiphytized, compact turf morphology, characterized by algal populations having relatively great surface-to-volume ratios, large reproductive capacities, high growth rates, simple thallus forms and mechanisms for short and simple life-histories is suggested to be characteristic of communities in stressed environments. As substantiated by the community-recovery data, such populations may in fact be extremely useful in identifying intermediate seral communities maintained in subclimax by lack of environmental constancy or by some form of stress.

PREFACE

This chapter summarizes the second year (1976–1977) biological baseline studies for the rocky-intertidal portion of the Southern California Islands and mainland. The purpose of the 3.8-year (July 1975–April 1979) program was to provide the scientific and resource management communities with a description of the major biological elements present and their variation in space and time throughout the Outer Continental Shelf (OCS) region. Such research constitutes an essential first step towards understanding community dynamics and is critical to the development of future experimental studies.

Sufficient data have now been accumulated and analyzed to provide a reasonable basis for comparisons with conditions at some future date, presumably during petroleum resource development. Knowledge of other variables, such as biogeographic patterns, is being enhanced through additional (1977–1978 and ongoing) rocky-intertidal assessments, while others remain relatively intractable due to their great variability and limitations in analytical resolution. Moreover, the erratic change in weather experienced during the 1977–1978 year of study (i.e. extremely heavy rainfall) may force reassessment of some patterns and conclusions presented here. Nevertheless, we have reached a point where experimental studies designed to elucidate the fundamental processes governing major ecological phenomena have become necessary, and several are under way. The purpose of such studies is to generate predictive capabilities for environmental managers and to focus on key or indicator aspects of the rocky intertidal systems during future monitoring programs.

INTRODUCTION

The Southern California Outer Continental Shelf (Fig. 1) is defined as the triangular area bounded by Point Conception, Tanner and Cortez submarine banks (about 200 km west of San Diego) and the U.S./Mexico International Border. This region is one of the most physiographically intriguing and well-studied continental terraces of the world's oceans. Sheppard and Emery (1941) aptly labelled this area the Southern California Borderland, recognizing its similarity

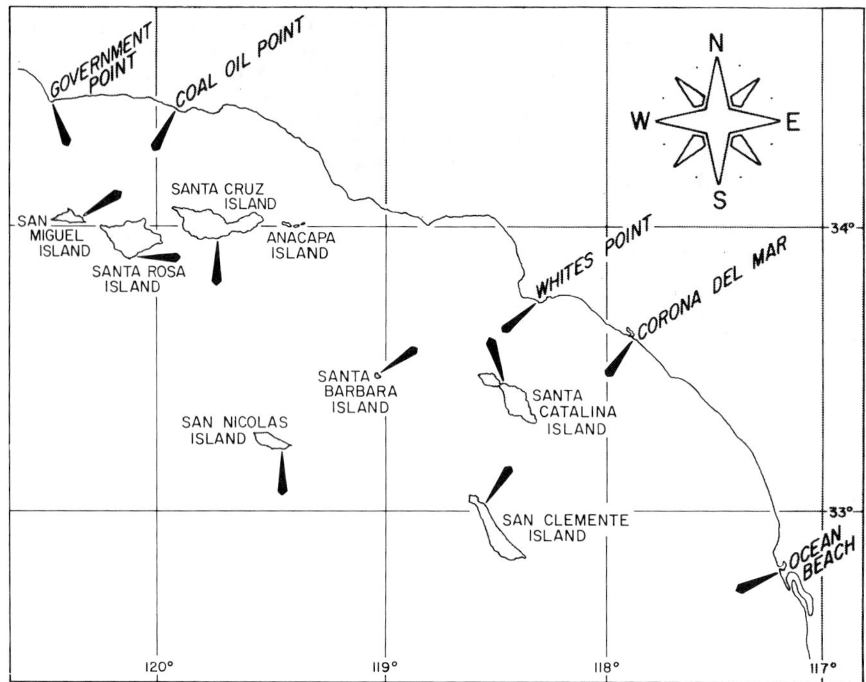

Fig. 1. Location of study sites.

to the adjoining coast. However, due to the concavity of the shoreline south of Point Conception, this region has more recently been referred to as the Southern California Bight (SCCWRP, 1973). Much is known about the climatology of this system (Kimura, 1974); however, published biological information is extremely scarce. Cockerell (1939) has emphasized that the Southern California Bight is unusual because of the effects of both cold and warm water mixing and in certain respects is comparable to such diverse regions as the Galapagos Islands. The changing climatic patterns result in a complex intermingling of physical conditions that are reflected in the broad spectrum and variability of the biological systems within the Bight.

The predominant driving force of water circulation in the Southern California Bight is the cold California Current. This system, a portion of the eastern limb of the clockwise North Pacific gyre, originates in north-west North America and flows southerly along the western coast of the United States. At Point Conception, the northern boundary of the Southern California Outer Continental Shelf (OCS), the coastline turns to the east deflecting the California Current to the south-east. Off northern Baja California, the system divides into two branches, one which curves towards the coast then north through the Channel Islands (forming the Southern California Countercurrent), while a second branch continues south along the coast of Baja California. The north-west flow of the Southern California Countercurrent is a reasonably permanent feature of the circulation pattern (Schwartzlose, 1963), being well developed in the winter but weaker during the spring. In addition to the southerly flowing California Current, the area is influenced by a deep (200 m) undercurrent, the Davidson Current, that also flows north-west along the coast. During late fall and early winter, when northerly winds are weak, the Davidson Current rises to the surface along the coast as far south as the tip of Baja California and flows north past Point Conception (Reid *et al.*, 1958). This system transports warm, highly-saline water great distances along the coast and is in evidence as far north as the state of Washington. While both the Davidson and California Currents include complex systems of eddies and gyres, each flows with moderate speeds of 12–25 cm/s at the surface (5–10 cm/s at 200 m) maintaining net water transport in the two directions.

Apparently neither current system completely dominates the other, although the effect of the Davidson Current diminishes as it submerges during part of the year. However, the deflection of the California Current as it impinges on Point Conception results in the formation of a strong counter-clockwise gyre (most pronounced during the winter months) between the mainland and the northern Channel Islands geographic group (Schwartzlose, 1963). This pattern of surface water circulation has also been substantiated by Hendricks (1977) and a satellite thermal imagery overview is presented in Fig. 2.

Another hydrographic feature is the pattern of wind-driven upwelling. In Southern California this process occurs along both mainland and island shores where strong, steady winds displace surface water in a southerly direction; this surface water is replaced by deep offshore water containing high levels of nutrients. In Southern

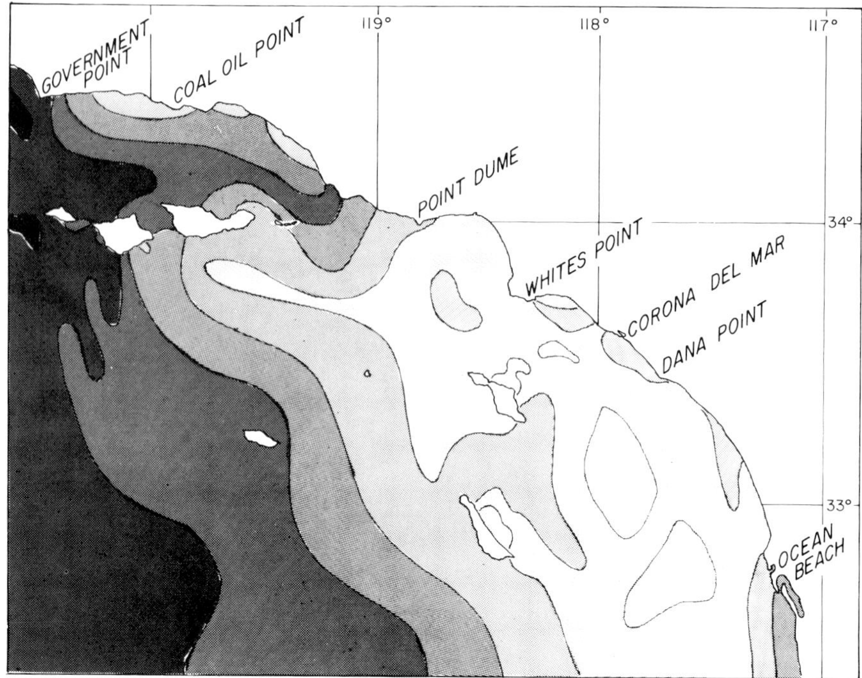

Fig. 2. Distribution of surface water temperatures within the Southern California Bight based on remote sensing (redrawn from the 23 June 1976 NOAA-3 satellite imagery in Hendricks, 1977). Darkest tones represent coldest temperatures with 1.4°C increases for each successively lighter tone.

California, upwelling is most intense in April, May and June; occasionally, wind conditions result in cases of non-seasonal upwelling (Jones, 1971). Upwelling is most intense south of capes and points (e.g. Point Conception) that extend into nearshore current streams (Reid *et al.*, 1958). Such upwelling of deep nutrient-laden water may partially account for the high productivity and richness of the Southern California Bight's biological components. Wind conditions are also important in that major reversals occur (Kimura, 1974) predominantly throughout late fall and winter. This results in strong, hot and dry "Santa Ana" winds from the inland desert regions at the time of low tides during the daylight hours, thereby causing extreme heating and desiccation stress to intertidal organisms.

An important ecological factor related to water movement on

the Southern California OCS is the protection of certain mainland shores and the mainland sides of islands from open ocean swell and storm waves. This leads to a higher wave-energy regime on the unprotected outer island shores with marked effects on their biological communities. Nearly all of the Southern California mainland coastline is protected to some degree by the outlying islands (Ricketts *et al.*, 1968). The only mainland sites receiving direct westerly swell are near the cities of Los Angeles and San Diego. The combination of prevailing currents and their associated eddies and gyres, the deflection of currents and swell by island land masses, and wind-driven coastal upwelling results in complex intermixings of distinct water masses, each with its particular hydrographic features.

Rocky shorelines occur throughout the entire coastal area of the Southern California Bight. The rocky-intertidal habitat is found interspersed at irregular intervals with sandy beaches and inlets to lagoons or estuaries. The 12 study sites sampled under this program (Fig. 1) are divided between islands (7) and mainland(5) and, less clearly between north (north-west) and south (south-east). The northern Channel Islands (San Miguel, Santa Rosa, Santa Cruz and Anacapa) form a discrete geographic group with some affinity to the northern mainland sites of Government Point and Coal Oil Point. Similarly, the southern islands (San Nicolas, Santa Barbara, Santa Catalina, San Clemente) together with the three sites to the south of Santa Monica Bay (Whites Point, Corona del Mar and Ocean Beach) may be considered a discrete unit. However, the trend of increasing water temperatures to the south is partially offset by exposure of the outermost islands (San Miguel and San Nicolas) to the eastern margin of the cold California Current system (Fig. 2), so that a division of island sites into northern and southern on the basis of geographic location related to temperature regime is not accurate.

A number of substrate types were represented among the 12 rocky intertidal habitats sampled (Table I), ranging from hard, irregular flow breccia to smooth sandstone or siltstone. Some sites (especially Coal Oil Point and San Nicolas Island) are heavily inunda[illegible] a yearly basis by sand, which scours and removes organisms completely buries them. Sand appears to be consistently these two sites in the upper intertidal, eliminating an

Table I. Physiographic attributes of the 12 rocky-intertidal habitats studied

Study areas	Latitude & Longitude	Water temperature	Substrata	Tidal range (m)	Wave exposure	Disturbance source	Sand cover
Government Point	34°26′35″N 120°27′06″W	cold	Monterey shale/siltstone	− 0.3 to + 2.1	exposed (heavy)	oil seeps	mid-intertidal
Coal Oil Point	34°24′27″N 119°52′40″W	cold (moderate)	Monterey shale/siltstone	− 0.6 to + 0.9	exposed (moderate)	oil seeps	(extensive)
Whites Point	33°43′11″N 118°19′39″W	warm to intermediate	Diatomaceous Monterey shale and Unstable boulders	− 0.3 to + 0.9	exposed (moderate)	domestic wastes	upper intertidal cobbles
Corona del Mar	33°35′14″N 117°51′54″W	warm to intermediate	Unstable granitic boulders on sandstone/ siltstone	− 0.3 to + 0.9	exposed (moderate)	human usage (extensive)	upper intertidal
Ocean Beach	32°44′35″N 117°15′15″W	warm to intermediate	Poorly consolidated friable sandstone	+ 0.3 to + 4.0	exposed	none	none
San Miguel Island	34°02′55″N 120°20′08″W	cold	Irregular volcanic flow breccia	− 0.3 to + 2.7	exposed (moderate)	none	lower intertidal
Santa Rosa Island	33°53′31″N 120°06′31″W	cold (moderate)	Smooth sandstone	+ 0.3 to + 3.4	exposed (moderate)	none	lower intertidal
Santa Cruz Island	33°57′43″N 119°45′16″W	intermediate	Irregular volcanic breccia	+ 0.3 to + 4.0	surge	none	none
Santa Barbara Island	33°28′43″N 119°01′36″W	intermediate	Vesicular volcanic rock	+ 0.3 to + 3.7	surge (heavy)	none	none
Santa Catalina Island	33°26′47″N 118°29′04″W	warm	Vesicular volcanic rock	− 0.6 to + 3.0	protected	none	none
San Nicolas Island	33°12′54″N 119°28′22″W	cold	Sandstone	− 0.3 to + 1.5	exposed (moderate)	none	extensive
San Clemente Island	33°00′06″N 118°33′03″W	warm	Stable granitic boulders	− 0.3 to + 2.1	protected	none	none

component from the biota. The presence of extensive loose boulder fields (e.g. Whites Point and Corona del Mar) constitutes another form of environmental instability limiting community development. The existence of such natural disturbances in rocky intertidal habitats has important implications in interpreting changes associated with petroleum exploration and development.

The Southern California Bight contains a mixture of relatively low temperature and low salinity water transported from the north by the California Current system and higher temperature and salinity water brought north by the Davidson Current (Maloney and Chan, 1974). Added to this are the effects of seasonal upwelling and the concomitant input of cold nutrient-rich deep water. The mean monthly surface water temperatures on the Southern California OCS range from a low of 13°C in March and April to 20°C in August and September. Although the area over the continental shelf undergoes considerable mixing from differential currents and waves, the system becomes extensively stratified throughout the summer months with the depth of the thermocline rarely exceeding 50 m (Jones, 1971).

Intertidal habitats in Southern California, although little studied, are unique in the U.S.A. owing to their large usage by an exceptionally dense, recreation-oriented, human population. This intensive usage makes the intertidal zone particularly sensitive to additional forms of environmental stresses. The effects of environmental deterioration and general lack of adequate baseline information have posed severe problems, particularly during the past 10 years when attempts have been made to assess the immediate effects of specific pollutants on Southern California coastal organisms. Problems were obvious in the attempts to evaluate the impacts of the Santa Barbara oil spills of 1969 (see Nicholson and Cimberg, 1971; Straughan, 1971; Foster, *et al.*, 1971).

Previous reviews of existing information on intertidal macrophytes (Murray, 1974) and of macroinvertebrates (Bright, 1974) in the Southern California Bight have pointed to the paucity of information on the ecology of this region. The most widely used information has been that of Dawson (1959, 1965) on marine algae. Dawson noted reductions in species numbers ranging from 50 to 70% at sites near sewage outfalls. Others (Nicholson and Cimberg, 1971; Widdowson, 1971; Thom, 1976; Thom and Widdowson, 1978) have since measured further declines in macrophyte species numbers at many of the same areas studied by Dawson. These workers attributed such declines to human influence but presented only circumstantial evidence as documentation. The declines do not seem to have been instantaneous (Nicholson, 1972), but probably are the result of human pressures that have been increasing markedly since the turn of the century. With further expansion of the human population in Southern California, even the marine communities on some of the relatively inaccessible offshore Channel Islands (e.g. Anacapa Island) are being altered (Littler, 1978).

The marine ecosystems of the Southern California Channel Islands have received relatively little scientific attention. Although limited taxonomic lists have been published for Santa Catalina Island (Dawson, 1949; Nicholson and Cimberg, 1971), Santa Cruz Island (Hewatt, 1946), Anacapa Island (Dawson and Neushul, 1966; Neushul *et al.,* 1967) and San Clemente Island (Sims, 1974; Seapy, 1974), quantitative data concerning the ecology of intertidal organisms are available only for San Nicolas Island (Caplan and Boolootian, 1967) and San Clemente Island (Littler and Murray, 1974, 1975, 1978; Murray and Littler, 1978a; Kindig and Littler, 1980).

The research reported here was responsive to the specifications and requirements determined by the Bureau of Land Management. Study sites were selected to cover a broad spectrum of habitats, with the majority located near lease tracts that might have a high probability of being affected by oil development operations. The primary objective was the quantification of biological variability as well as the relation of any variation to possible causal mechanisms. This paper is the synthesis of the first two years (1975–1976 and 1976–1977) of comprehensive investigations along the lines of the following programs: (1) taxonomic and systematic studies of the macroepibiota, (2) determinations of the seasonal distribution and abundance patterns of macrophyte and macroinvertebrate standing stocks and (3) temporal and spatial analyses of variation in community organization.

MATERIALS AND METHODS

The intertidal study of mainland and island rocky shores consisted of several approaches including: (1) determinations of the spatial and temporal variability of dominant intertidal populations at 12 sites; (2) the responses of intertidal communities to natural catastrophic events (such as storms, high surf conditions and floods); (3) recovery rates and patterns of various communities at different times of the year at contrasting tidal heights following artificial disturbance (harvesting), as well as specialized studies undertaken during 1977–1978 concerning (4) assessments of the role of possible key species populations and (5) the synoptic surveying of all island intertidal communities during daytime low tides by means of helicopter overflights and mapping techniques. This last study gives us considerable confidence that our 12 sites are indeed representative of major intertidal systems within the Southern California Bight. We have also developed methods for use in examining the ecological effects of anthropogenic disturbances including: (6) comparative studies of growth rates following transplantation, (7) measurements of primary productivity for dominant rocky intertidal macrophytes (Kindig and Littler, 1980) and (8) calorific investigations of dominant producer and consumer populations (Littler and Murray, 1978). The last two provide energetic data of value for analyzing community function. Although we have extensively used all of these methods over the last several years, only the methods and data resulting from the 1976–1977 baseline analysis of standing stock will be presented here because of space limitations.

1. Standing Stock Sampling and Analysis

Much of our knowledge of benthic marine organisms is based upon subjective observations, although some studies have employed "quasi-quantitative" methods. Among such methods are those in which diagrammatic sketches within sample units are made and subsequently used to obtain estimates of abundance (e.g. Manton, 1935; Abe, 1937), the use of transect lines to estimate cover (e.g. Nicholson and Cimberg, 1971; Widdowson, 1971) and the utilization of metal grids (e.g. Caplan and Boolootian, 1967) to assess the abundance of organisms. Such *in situ* assessments are usually time-consuming and often physically exhausting, thereby severely limiting the number of samples that can be taken within the field time available (e.g. during the low-tide cycle). A significant problem with all of these visually based *in situ* techniques is that of parallax (due to movement of the observer and organisms relative to the sampling devices) which has been shown (Littler, 1971) to be an unsatisfactorily large source of error when measuring the cover of space-occupying organisms.

The principal method of sampling the intertidal biota during this study was a photogrammetric technique of undisturbed sampling (modified from Littler, 1968, 1971) which yields parallax-free samples that can be used to generate precisely detailed and highly-reproducible quantitative information, i.e. cover, density (number of individual organisms per unit area) and frequency (percentage of sample plots in which a given species occurs). Two to four belt transects, 4 to 70 m apart as dictated by the steepness of the shoreline and topography, were laid perpendicular (by means of a sighting compass) to the waterline at each study site from immediately above the high-water level of intertidal organisms to just below the waterline at low tide thus providing locations for a minimum of 40 samples. The general location of each study area was determined by consulting aerial photographs and maps of the region. After extensive reconnaissance of each area, the precise location of the upper end of each transect was determined (by consensus of several experienced marine biologists) along a biologically representative part of the shoreline. To provide permanent sample locations, holes were drilled and eyebolts cemented into the substrate at the upper and lower ends of the transect lines; this enabled the precise replacement of the transects during seasonal studies. A sampling optimization analysis by the Poisson statistic (Wilson, 1976) revealed that at least 30, 0.15 m^2, samples were required to assess adequately a typical rocky intertidal site. Therefore, approximately 40 rectangular quadrats, 30 cm × 50 cm (0.15 m^2), and 40 square quadrats, 1.0 m × 1.0 m (1.0 m^2), were placed along the transect lines at 1.0 to 3.0-m levels (depending upon the steepness of the shoreline), thereby providing permanent, stratified plots for sampling temporal and spatial distributions of organisms. To furnish statistically-adequate numbers, no fewer than four replicate quadrats of each size were represented in a given 0.3-m tidal interval, whenever possible. This was done after the first site visit by adding quadrats to the immediate right and left sides (in some cases upper and lower sides) of quadrats known to be at tidal heights that were "under-sampled". The 1.0 m^2 quadrats were used to sample large macrophytes and the rarer forms of large invertebrate species. Quadrat locations were permanently marked with metal studs, stainless steel nails, epoxy putty or eyebolts set in "hard-rock" cement. Totals of approximately 2000 0.15 m^2 and 2000 1.0 m^2 quadrats were analyzed during 1976–1977 and compared with the data set from about the same number taken in 1975–1976.

Relative vertical tidal heights for each quadrat were measured from permanent reference points by means of a stadia rod and a standard (20-power) surveyor's transit. A permanent reference point was established at each of the study sites for surveying the tidal heights on the individual quadrats. The height of this reference point was determined in relation to mean lower low water (MLLW) by measuring, at six or more places along the shoreline on successive days, the midpoint between low and high wave peaks at the time of the predicted (U.S. Department of Commerce Tide Tables, 1976, 1977) low tides. Repeatability of measurements checked on different site visits was $< \pm 0.1$ m.

Throughout the program, considerable care was taken to minimize trampling and other forms of disturbance to the biotic communities under study.

Physical descriptions of each study site (including date, time, tidal stages, wave heights, air and water temperature, cloud cover and salinity) were recorded at the time of each visit. Oceanographic literature and climatological data were used, where available, to characterize further the respective environmental features of each study site (Table I).

(a) Undisturbed samples. Data were obtained by photographing the numbered quadrats perpendicular to the substrate with two cameras equipped with electronic flash units. Each quadrat contained a grey plastic label affixed to the upper left corner that was marked with a wax pencil to identify permanently each of the photosamples. One camera contained 35-mm Kodachrome-64 slide film and the other contained Ektachrome infrared (IR) slide film.

In the laboratory, the developed pairs of transparencies were projected simultaneously (the IR below the color) through a panel of glass (45 x 55 cm) onto two sheets (each 21 x 28 cm) of white bristol paper taped and glued to the glass. The paper contained a grid pattern of dots at 2.0-cm intervals on the side of the transmitted light; this has been shown (Littler and Murray, 1975) to be an appropriate density (i.e. 1.0 per cm^2) for consistently reproducible estimates of cover. Red dots were found to contrast best with the biological detail shown by the projected color transparencies; black dots were used in conjunction with the IR transparencies. The transparencies were aligned and focused on to the paper from the side opposite the field of dots (out of view) to assure unbiased assessments. The number of dots superimposed on each species was then scored twice (i.e. replicated after movement of the grid) with the percentage cover values expressed as the number of "hits" for each species divided by the total number of dots contained in the quadrats. Reproducibility was high and seldom varied more than ± 5% for a given species. Species that were not abundant enough to be scored by the replicated grid of point intercepts were assigned a cover value of 0.1%.

The IR transparency was found to be essential in the delineation of the various species of primary producers (e.g. blue-green algae are dominant forms that can only be discerned reliably on dark, wet substrate by use of IR photography) and in assessing the status of their health. Each species fluoresces differently in the infrared band, according to its chlorophyll content and health (the percentage of dead branches on an algal thallus can be seen more clearly in IR). In cases of multi-layered communities, more than one photograph per quadrat was taken to quantify each stratum after upper strata had successively been moved aside, often yielding total biotic cover of greater than 100%. The only organisms removed from the permanent undisturbed quadrats were very small samples taken occasionally for taxonomic purposes.

Two miniature tape recorders and plastic (polypropylene) coated paper were used as a rapid method of taking field notes on the contents of the photo-samples. For every disturbed and undisturbed sample, a taxonomist recorded the taxa, counted the individual macroinvertebrates and visually estimated the cover of each species in a detailed section-by-section format (each quadrat was subdivided into 20 equal sections). It is worthwhile noting that most previous studies stopped at this level of quantification (by estimation *in situ*). We found that such approximations usually could not be repeated precisely (i.e. often exceeding ± 25% for dominant organisms) because of parallax problems and differences between and within observers. Observer differences were influenced by varying degrees of field distractions and stresses, which were especially pronounced during heavy surf and night-time low-tide conditions. Recorded *in situ* information was transcribed in the laboratory and used for density counts of small animals and to minimize taxonomic and other problems encountered while interpreting undisturbed samples (i.e. IR and colour transparencies) in the laboratory.

The method as applied here does not allow for the quantification of microalgae, small epifauna or infauna when they occur in low abundances. We realize that these may be metabolically very active, but their analysis requires special techniques and expertise, which latter comprise separate problems in themselves. For this reason, our measurements were restricted to macro-epibiota that could be discerned in the field with the unaided eye. However, we did quantify microbiota (e.g. turfs of filamentous algae) when it occurred in high abundances, and most of the residual infaunal organisms from disturbed sampling have been identified and retained for future analyses. These latter samples never exceeded 1.0% of the biomass in a given quadrat.

These undisturbed methods were used at a total of 12 different habitats over the two years of study, including re-assessments following catastrophic disturbances (e.g. flooding and storm surf) at two of these sites.

(b) Disturbed samples. Biomass measurements of the standing stock yield information contributing to community description and provide an additional set of variables to be examined with time; we used the wet weight, dry weight and organic dry weight values in the same manner as the cover, density and frequency data from the undisturbed method. The disturbed quadrats were selected for their biological similarity to the undisturbed photo-quadrats; the organisms within each were harvested quantitatively by means of nylon or metal scrapers and fixed in formalin for subsequent sorting in the laboratory. All portions of algae having holdfasts within a given quadrat were taken. If most of the holdfast of an alga was outside the quadrat, it was not harvested. Organisms half-in and half-out of a quadrat were harvested only from the left and upper margins of the quadrat. Disturbed plots ($0.15\,m^2$ for complexes of small organisms and $1.0\,m^2$ for larger organisms) were photographed and harvested within the high, middle and lower intertidal levels. Approximately 12 plots of each size were taken per

visit at each intertidal site, yielding a total of ~1400 disturbed samples from 1975–1977.

In the laboratory, the harvested specimens were identified, packaged and catalogued for determinations of wet, dry and ash-free biomass. After sorting to species, the samples were rinsed quickly in distilled water and weighed in aluminum foil containers of known weight. The samples were then dried to constant weight at 50°C, wrapped and sealed in heavy-duty aluminum foil, cooled to room temperature in desiccators and weighed to 0.001 g. For those organisms having large inorganic components (such as calcium carbonate), ash-free dry weights were determined following 24 h of combustion at 400°C in a muffle furnace. We feel that ash-free dry weight is the best measure of biomass, but because of time constraints only representative calcifying species have been combusted. All fleshy organisms (such as frondose algae) were analyzed for wet and dry weight. Consequently, the results of this study expressed as organic dry weight included ash-free dry weights for organisms with hard parts (e.g. crabs, bivalves, coralline algae) and dry weights for non-calcareous species.

All biomass data were considered on the basis of 0.3-m tidal intervals to formulate an overall picture of the distribution of standing stocks for each study site. Mean wet and dry organic biomass were averaged for every species in each tidal interval and the wet and dry organic weights per square meter for all species were summed to yield a distributional pattern of biomass as a function of tidal height. Values over all of the various tidal heights were averaged to produce a mean standing stock number (in wet and dry organic weight) per average square meter of substrate; these values were then used to compare the 12 study sites.

(c) Collection of floristic and faunistic data. Additional representative organisms were collected in duplicate, curated, and archived as permanent taxonomic voucher specimens. These were listed by site for disturbed samples, undisturbed samples and collections outside the study quadrats. An effort was made to relate variations in environmental and biological conditions to changes in the composition and organization of intertidal associations. These specimens have been deposited in the Smithsonian Institution's National Natural History Museum, Washington, D.C., U.S.A.

(d) Analyses of data. Information obtained by the photogrammetric sampling method (undisturbed) and by the harvest method (disturbed) provided quantitative information on the distribution of standing stocks in relation to tidal height. These data were summed and averaged to interpret differences in intertidal populations and communities between sites and seasonally within sites. Species cover frequency and density fluctuations have been calculated for 0.3-m vertical intervals throughout the intertidal zone. Biomass data were computed each season for wet weight (including hard parts) and organic dry weight (minus hard parts) in grams per square meter of substrate.

Diversity measurements have been widely used by those responsible for assessing the effects of human stresses on biotic communities. Species diversity is often measured by indices that include components of both richness and equitability. The problem with any single index is that both components of diversity are confounded. Many diversity indices also contain the underlying assumption that the ecological importance of a given species is proportional to its abundance. We attempted to avoid these problems by using the standardly-applied Shannon and Weaver (1949) index (H') (incorporating both richness and evenness) along with separate indices for richness [counts of taxa, Margalef's (1968) D'] and evenness [Pielou's (1975) J']. These were calculated for the cover data using natural logarithms and used as supplementary information to quantify seasonal changes in compositional patterns of the biota at each site and to provide between-site comparisons of community structure. Poole (1974) has indicated that, regarding the Shannon-Weaver Index, the base of the logarithms is very much open to choice; however, in most ecological cases natural logarithms should be used. By simply multiplying our H'_e diversity values by the factor 1.443, interested readers can obtain H'_2 numbers.

To characterize objectively natural between-site groupings in an unbiased manner, the yearly undisturbed cover data at every site for each macrophyte and macroinvertebrate species were subjected to hierarchical cluster analyses (flexible sorting) by the Bray and Curtis (1957) percentage distance statistic (Smith, 1976). This produced a dendrogram of assemblages that were then interpreted according to their environmental affinities and used to map the prevalent biogeographical patterns for the various sites.

2. *Community Recovery and Development Studies*

These methods are presented in considerable detail by Murray and Littler (1978b) and only a general overview will be presented here. The biomass harvesting procedures employed during the 1975–1976 and 1976–1977 programs permitted the subsequent analysis of community recovery from the mechanically disturbed plots. Macroorganisms occupying the rock surfaces were photographed and then harvested from the substrate with the aid of knives and scraping tools; all portions of macrophytes or macroinvertebrates that were attached within the quadrats were removed. Generally, the experimental procedures were effective in producing disturbed plots devoid of macroorganisms with the exception of the encrusting forms (particularly the encrusting algae). Following the harvesting procedures, study plots were marked and reference points were established, from which compass triangulations were recorded, to aid in future sample relocation. During subsequent visits, the colonizing populations were assessed using the undisturbed sampling procedures described above.

Generally, 12 experimental (disturbed) quadrats were cleared of biota during each of the four 1975–1976 visits to each study site (see Littler, 1980). Analyses were carried out for periods approximating 3, 6, 9 and 12 months following plot harvesting for all the intertidal sites except Government Point and Santa Rosa Island, where the research program was newly begun in 1976–1977, and for Corona del Mar, where substrate instability prevented the relocation of harvested plots.

The pre-harvest and post-harvest samples for each site were grouped by 0.6 m tidal heights beginning with the − 0.3 to + 0.3 m interval and species abundance values (cover, frequency and density) were separately determined. This method facilitated comparisons of species abundances between periods before and after the mechanical removal. The Bray and Curtis (1957) index was used to measure the percentage similarity between the pre-harvest and post-harvest values.

RESULTS AND DISCUSSION

1. *Species Composition*

A total of 414 taxa was recorded during the year from all 12 of the study areas (Table II). The number of macrophyte taxa (197) was

Table II. Numbers of taxa by major taxonomic groups in quadrats at all 12 sites

Major groups		Numbers of taxa collected
Macrophytes		
Bacillariophyta		1
Chlorophyta		20
Cyanophyta		3
Phaeophyta		41
Rhodophyta		130
Spermatophyta		2
Total		197
Macroinvertebrates		
Annelida	– Polychaeta	8
Arthropoda	– Crustacea	24
Cnidaria	– Anthozoa	4
Cnidaria	– Hydrozoa	5
Chordata	– Ascidiacea	8
Echinodermata	– Asteroidea	6
Echinodermata	– Echinoidea	1
Echinodermata	– Holothuroidea	1
Ectoprocta (Bryozoa)		6
Mollusca	– Bivalvia	17
Mollusca	– Cephalopoda	1
Mollusca	– Gastropoda	104
Mollusca	– Polyplacophora	12
Porifera	– Calcarea	2
Porifera	– Demospongiae	18
Total		217

about equal to the number of macroinvertebrate taxa (217). Over half the number of macrophyte taxa were representative of the Rhodophyta; however, Phaeophyta (especially *Egregia menziesii*)* provided the major contribution to biomass. Of the macroinvertebrates, gastropods represented the most taxa (104), but *Mytilus californianus* Conrad was by far the biomass dominant. Taxa occurring in all 12 study sites were the same ubiquitous forms recorded during 1975–1976 (Littler,

*Names and authorities for benthic macroalgae follow those employed in Abbott and Hollenberg (1976).

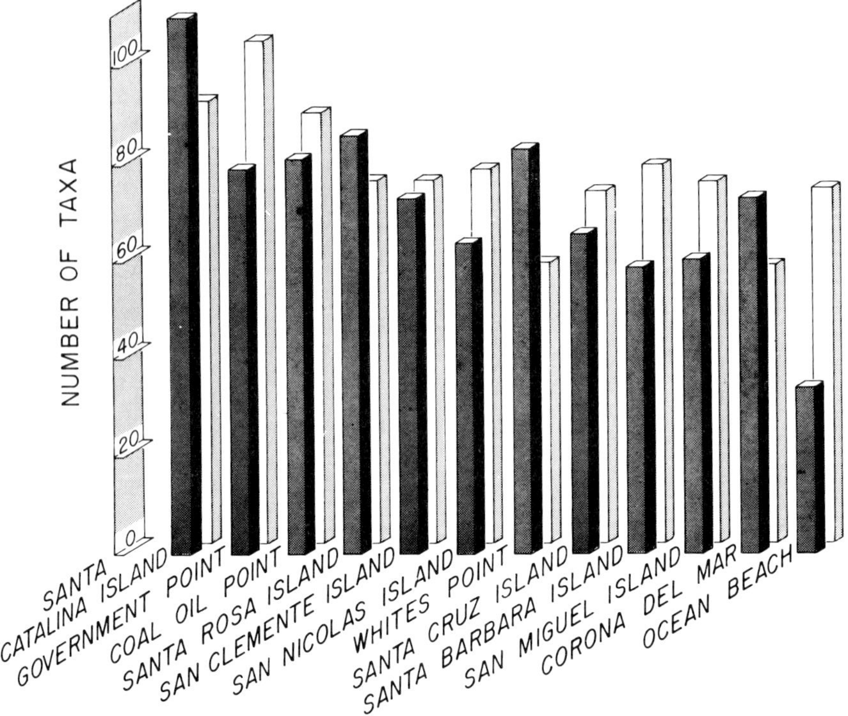

Fig. 3. Mean annual numbers of macrophyte taxa (histograms in rear) and macroinvertebrate taxa (dark histograms in front) found in quadrats.

Table III. Taxa common to all 12 sites

Macrophytes	Macroinvertebrates
Benthic diatoms	*Acmaea* (*Collisella*) *conus* Test
Blue-green Algae	*Acmaea* (*Collisella*) *digitalis* Rathke
Bossiella orbigniana ssp. *dichotoma*	*Acmaea* (*Collisella*) *limatula* Carpenter
Ceramium eatonianum	*Acmaea* (*Collisella*) *pelta* Rathke
Corallina officinalis var. *chilensis*	*Acmaea* (*Collisella*) *scabra* Gould
Corallina vancouveriensis	*Acmaea* (*Collisella*) *strigatella* (Carpenter)
Egregia menziesii	*Anthopleura elegantissima*
Gelidium coulteri	*Chthamalus fissus/dalli*
Gelidium pusillum	*Cyanoplax hartwegii* (Carpenter)
Gigartina canaliculata	*Littorina planaxis* Philippi
Gigartina spinosa	*Mytilus californianus* Conrad
Lithophyllum proboscideum	*Pachygrapsus crassipes* Randall
Carpopeltis rugosum	*Pugettia producta* (Randall)
Pterocladia capillacea	*Tetraclita squamosa rubescens*
Pterosiphonia dendroidea	

1980; Table III), except that *Pterocladia capillacea*, *Gigartina spinosa* and *Gelidium pusillum* were not as widespread in the 1975–1976 samples. The Government Point site (Fig. 3) included a unique community made up of a mixture of warm and cold water macrophytes; therefore, it is not surprising that this site contained by far the greatest number of plant taxa.

2. Abundance of Populations

Because space and light are considered (Connell, 1972) to be limiting resources in the rocky intertidal, cover is of primary ecological importance. Cover is also an aspect of structural heterogeneity; e.g. greater than 100% cover indicates vertical layering of canopy species above the understory components. Such structural complexity represents an important attribute of intertidal communities because it contributes to microhabitat diversity and is thus related to the number of species that a given site can accommodate. Major macrophytic cover throughout the 12 stations was provided by the blue-green algae (overall mean of 34% cover), the coralline algae *Corallina officinalis* var. *chilensis* and *C. vancouveriensis* (9% cover each), the red alga *Gigartina canaliculata* (6%), the tracheophytes *Phyllospadix* spp. (3%), and the phaeophyte *Egregia menziesii* (3%). This pattern is quite similar to that recorded for 1975–1976, except that blue-green and coralline algal values increased considerably. The lowest yearly mean macrophyte cover was present at Whites Point (72%), followed by Coal Oil Point (78%), San Nicolas Island (89%), and San Miguel Island (89%, Table IV). All but the last of these are under some form of environmental stress.

The dominant macroinvertebrates throughout the Bight in terms of cover were *Chthamalus fissus* Darwin/*dalli* Pilsbry (4%), *Anthopleura elegantissima* (Brandt) (3%), *Phragmatopoma californica* (Fewkes) (3%), *Mytilus californianus* (2%), *Dodecaceria fewkesi* Berkeley et Berkeley (1%) and *Tetraclita squamosa rubescens* Darwin (1%). This represents increases over the 1975–1976 values (Littler, 1980), shown by *C. fissus/dalli, P, californica, D. fewkesi* and *T. squamosa rubescens*. The habitats with the greatest macroinvertebrate cover (Table V) were those that contained large stands of either *A. elegantissima* or *M. californianus*. Minimal macroinvertebrate cover was again registered at Corona del Mar (4%), Whites Point (6%), and San Clemente Island (6%).

Table IV. Seasonal and mean yearly macrophyte % cover; comparisons between sites

Sites	Months				
	MJJA	SON	DJ	FMA	Mean
Government Point	125	107	100	119	113
Ocean Beach	111	106	102	113	108
Santa Barbara Island	99	106	106	109	105
San Clemente Island	113	111	94	103	105
Corona del Mar	110	111	94	98	103
Santa Cruz Island	99	100	98	101	100
Santa Rosa Island	100	100	98	98	99
Santa Catalina Island	94	99	91	97	95
San Nicolas Island	100	94	95	66	89
San Miguel Island	94	88	84	89	89
Coal Oil Point	86	78	73	74	78
Whites Point	74	73	67	75	72
Means	100	98	92	95	96

Table V. Seasonal and mean yearly macroinvertebrate % cover; comparisons between sites

Sites	Months				
	MJJA	SON	DJ	FMA	Mean
San Nicolas Island	33	30	29	26	30
Santa Rosa Island	31	32	30	26	30
Government Point	26	30	29	28	28
San Miguel Island	24	24	22	24	24
Santa Barbara Island	16	14	15	17	16
Coal Oil Point	18	17	19	9	16
Ocean Beach	15	12	15	12	14
Santa Cruz Island	10	11	12	11	11
Santa Catalina Island	9	10	8	8	9
Whites Point	7	6	6	6	6
San Clemente Island	6	7	6	7	6
Corona del Mar	5	2	3	5	4
Means	17	16	16	15	16

Frequency is a useful parameter for denoting the breadth of distribution of the various taxa. Of the macrophytes, blue-green algae occurred in the greatest number of samples throughout 1976–1977 (87%) followed by *Corallina officinalis* var. *chilensis* (46%), Ralfsiaceae (41%) and *Gigartina canaliculata* (40%). Widespread macroinvertebrates were *Chthamalus fissus/dalli* (44% frequency), *Anthopleura elegantissima* (41%), *Acmaea* (*Collisella*) *scabra* Gould (33%) and *Littorina planaxis* Philippi (31%).

Macroinvertebrates with the highest mean densities averaged over all 12 of the study sites were *Chthamalus fissus/dalli* with 1730 individuals/m^2 followed by *Phragmatopoma californica* (262/m^2) and *Littorina planaxis* (216/m^2).

Organic dry weight (ODW) is also an ecologically important parameter as it represents the bound food energy available to higher trophic levels. *Egregia menziesii* was by far the predominant organism with an overall mean of 119 g/m^2 ODW followed by *Phyllospadix scouleri* Hook. (86 g/m^2), *Pelvetia fastigiata* (63 g/m^2), *Gigartina canaliculata* (50 g/m^2), *Eisenia arborea* (45 g/m^2) and *Phyllospadix torreyi* S. Watson (44 g/m^2). This depicts considerable increases in *Phyllospadix* over the previous year's values, due mainly to its dominance at the two new sites (Santa Rosa Island and Government Point), and makes *Phyllospadix*, as a genus, the dominant biomass organism throughout the 12 sites. *Eisenia arborea* replaced *Halidrys dioica* as an important contributor of organic dry weight relative to 1975–1976 findings. For all 12 sites, macroinvertebrate biomass was comprised mainly of *Mytilus californianus* (49 g/m^2 ODW), *Anthopleura elegantissima* (29 g/m^2), *Pseudochama exogyra* (Conrad) (6 g/m^2) and *Tetraclita squamosa rubescens* (4 g/m^2). This represents important gains over 1975–1976 values by *M. californianus*, *P. exogyra* and *D. fewkesi*. The sites with the lowest biotic standing stocks (ODW, Fig. 4), were Corona del Mar (331 g/m^2), Santa Cruz Island (342 g/m^2), Ocean Beach (395 g/m^2), and San Clemente Island (509 g/m^2). All of these sites lack considerable standing stocks of the larger brown algal macrophytes, with the exception of San Clemente Island which was extremely depauperate in macroinvertebrate biomass. In terms of organic dry weight, the macrophytes overshadowed the macroinvertebrates at all sites. Macrophytes had their dry organic biomass maxima at Santa Catalina Island (1340 g/m^2), Government Point (1011 g/m^2), San Nicolas Island (784 g/m^2) and

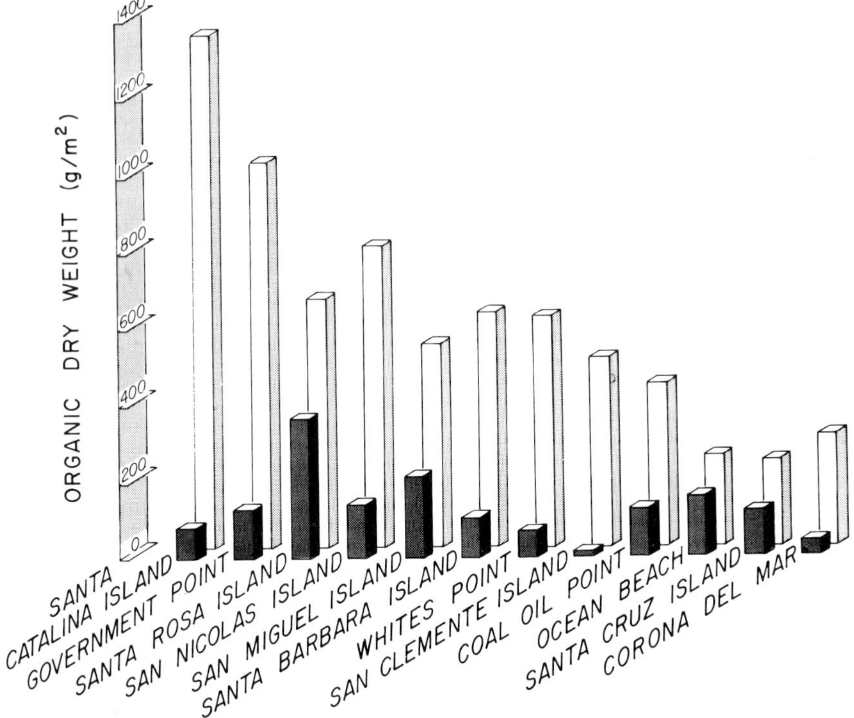

Fig. 4. Mean annual dry organic biomass of macrophytes (histograms in rear) and macroinvertebrates (dark histograms in front) for the entire intertidal zones sampled.

Santa Rosa Island (651 g/m^2). The first two of these sites were dominated by larger brown algal stocks while the last two contained a large biomass of *Phyllospadix*. Santa Rosa Island (370/m^2) and San Miguel Island (210 g/m^2) had the largest organic dry biomass of macroinvertebrates, due mainly to *M. californianus*. The lowest macroinvertebrate organic dry weights were recorded from San Clemente Island (16 g/m^2), Corona del Mar (39 g/m^2), and Whites Point (69 g/m^2); all of these are exposed to varying degrees of disturbance, except in the case of San Clemente Island which is enigmatic in regard to its depauperate animal populations.

3. Biogeography

(a) Cluster analysis. All 12 sites were subjected to statistical cluster analysis based on the combined overall mean cover values for both

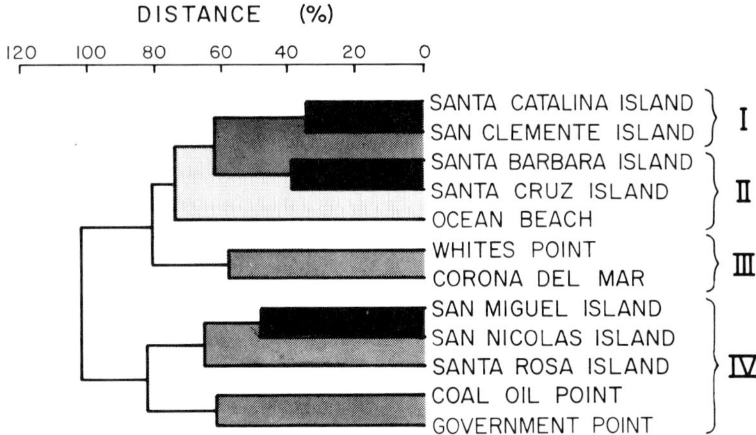

Fig. 5. Dendrogram display of differential clustering for all 12 study sites using combined macrophyte and macroinvertebrate mean cover data. Degree of shading indicates level of similarity (Bray–Curtis % distance).

macrophyte and macroinvertebrate populations (Fig. 5). These results were more clearly displayed by overlaying the cluster groupings on a map showing the 12 Southern California Bight stations (Fig. 6). Cover was chosen as the most significant and revealing biogeographic parameter because, as mentioned, intertidal organisms compete for the limiting resources of space and light using their cover and because our cover data are based on a maximum number of samples (i.e. the undisturbed quadrats). The dendrogram (Fig. 5) revealed groupings that agreed closely with our predictions (based on hydrographic information) regarding the affinities between sites. For example, the sites most strongly influenced by the cold California Current system (i.e. San Miguel Island, San Nicolas Island, Santa Rosa Island, Coal Oil Point and Government Point) formed a group broadly separated from sites exposed to predominantly warmer water systems (cf. Figs 2 and 6). Within these two broad assemblages, the island sites containing the warmest-water elements and exposed to the warmer current systems (i.e. Santa Catalina and San Clemente) were most tightly clustered. The predicted intermediate water sites, Santa Barbara and Santa Cruz Island, formed a second close grouping with the mainland Ocean Beach site, which latter was less tightly grouped. Of the warm-water sites, Whites Point and Corona del Mar

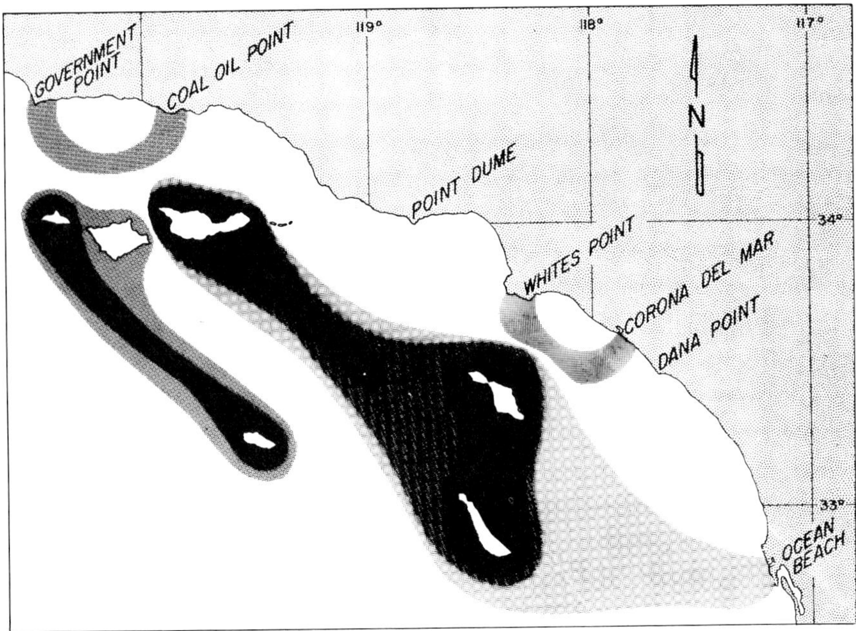

Fig. 6. Map overlay of cluster results (Fig. 5) using Bray–Curtis distance. Degree of shading indicates level of similarity.

formed a distinct pairing, no doubt related to the degree of human-induced and other disturbances to which these two habitats are exposed. They are both dominated by subclimax communities comprised of fine filamentous turfs. Both of the northernmost mainland sites (i.e. Government Point and Coal Oil Point) showed close affinities as did San Miguel and San Nicolas Islands, all of which are strongly influenced by the cold California Current system. Santa Rosa Island clustered less strongly with these last two sites. The above patterns are quite similar to those determined during 1975–1976 (Littler, 1980) from the cover data set and are also basically similar to those recently determined independently from binary (presence/absence) data for the island macrophytes (Murray, Littler and Abbott, 1980) and macroinvertebrates (Seapy and Littler, 1980).

(b) Islands vs. *mainland comparisons*

(i) Lower shore. It is instructive and quite revealing to compare island with mainland rocky intertidal habitats. First, a direct comparison

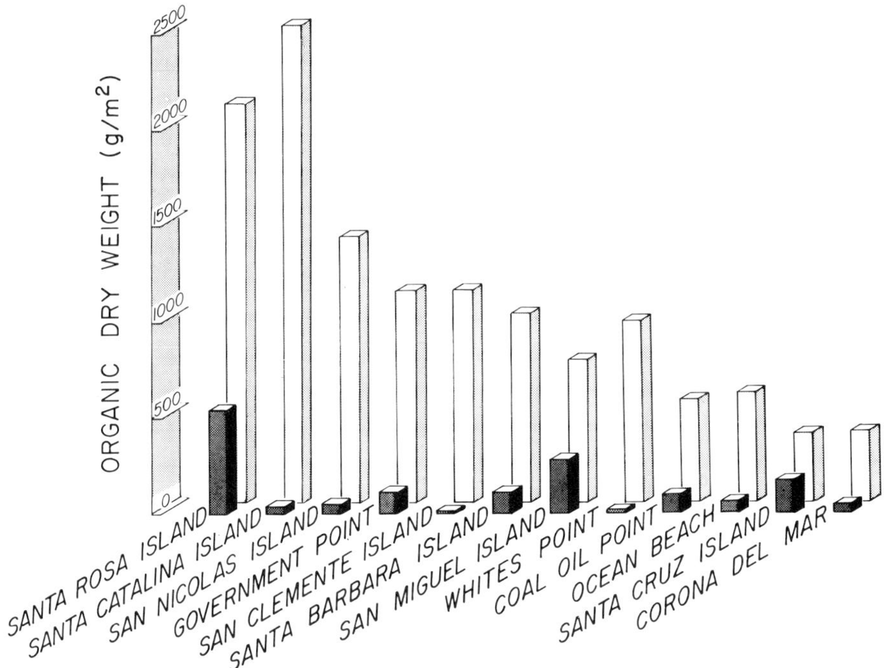

Fig. 7. Mean annual dry organic biomass of macrophytes (histograms in rear) and macroinvertebrates (dark histograms in front) for the lowest three 0.3-m intervals sampled.

was made between sites considering only the lower portions of the shoreline. This form of comparison was made so as to place all sites on an equal basis, because three of the five mainland sites do not contain an upper intertidal, whereas six of the seven island sites do. The means for the lowest three 0.3 m intervals that could be sampled throughout the year were determined for each site and are presented in Figs 7 and 8. The average lower intertidal dry organic biomass for islands (1495 g/m^2) was nearly double that for mainland sites (786 g/m^2), as had been the case for the 1975–1976 data set (Fig. 7). The bulk of this biomass was contributed by macrophytes (1313 and 712 g/m^2 for island and mainland sites, respectively) and mostly resided in the larger brown algae (e.g. *Egregia*, *Halidrys*, *Eisenia*) and surf grasses (*Phyllospadix torreyi*, *P. scouleri*). The same tendency was evident for island *vs* mainland macroinvertebrate biomass (177 *vs* 74 g/m^2 ODW).

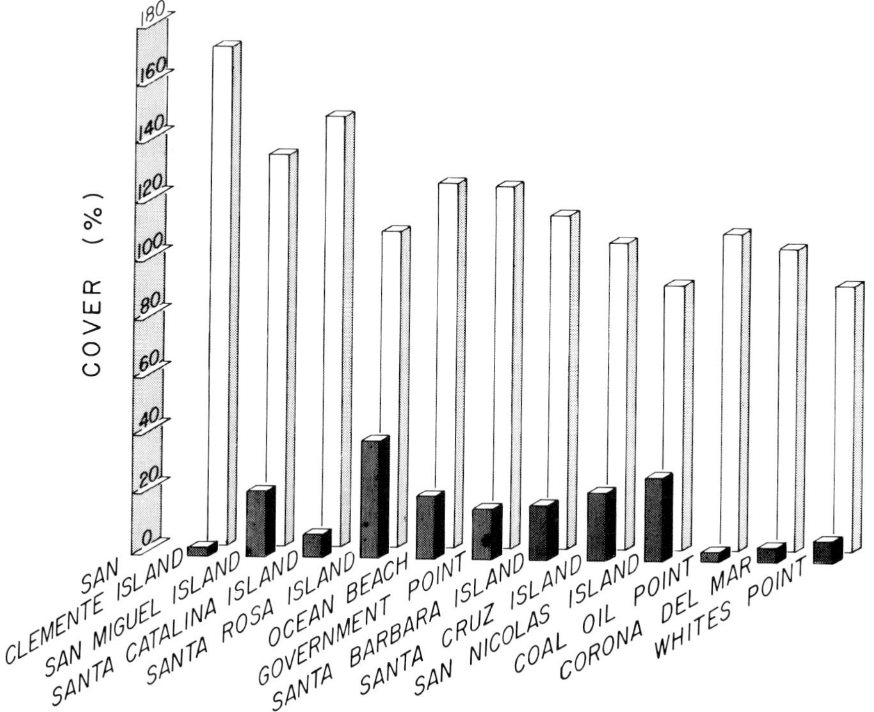

Fig. 8. Mean annual cover of macrophytes (histograms in rear) and macroinvertebrates (dark histograms in front) for the lowest three 0.3-m intervals sampled.

Similar trends held for comparisons between cover (Fig. 8); for example, island mean cover was 144%, while mainland cover was only 120%. Differences between island and mainland macrophytic cover (i.e. 124 *vs* 109%) were not pronounced. However, island mean macroinvertebrate cover was nearly double that of the mainland (20 *vs* 11%). These patterns are similar to those described for the 1975–1976 data set (Littler, 1980) and are possibly attributable to human disturbances that have occurred increasingly along the populated portions of the Southern California mainland (Widdowson, 1971; Thom and Widdowson, 1978). When one compares values at the two sites near the extreme ends of the Southern California mainland (i.e. Government Point and Ocean Beach), it becomes apparent that the biomass and cover of standing stocks at these two sites approach the levels exhibited by island sites (Fig. 4 and Tables IV and V). Although the relatively depauperate Corona del Mar and Whites Point sites are subjected to considerable natural disturbances as well, this leads one to speculate that human influence has played a major role in reducing mainland intertidal standing stocks, in terms of both biomass and cover, near heavily-populated areas.

(ii) Total intertidal. Samples could not be obtained from the upper intertidal zones at one of the island sites (i.e. San Nicolas Island) and three of the five mainland sites (i.e. Coal Oil Point, Whites Point, and Corona del Mar) because of consistent sand or boulder inundation of the upper solid substrate. On the assumption that these sites, as well as the eight others, are representative of major habitats (based on data from our ongoing 1977–1978 island survey studies, we are reasonably confident of this), we felt that comparisons of trends (e.g. between mainland and island sites) would be interesting. In other words, it was important that mainland rocky intertidal systems which often have their upper shorelines inundated by sand and gravel, and are thereby poor in upper intertidal fauna, be documented. Similarly, it was just as essential to represent major island intertidal systems, with stations having well-developed high intertidal faunal assemblages. The grand totals and means of all parameters measured were summed and averaged for the seven island sites and five mainland sites, respectively (Table VI). The islands had higher values than mainland sites in nearly every respect. One definite trend shown by the data is that mainland sites contained lower stocks than island sites. For example (Table VI), islands averaged 809 dry organic g/m^2 (663 g/m^2 macrophytes and 146 g/m^2 macroinvertebrates), while mainland sites averaged only 617 g/m^2 ODW (513 g/m^2 macrophytes and 104 g/m^2 macroinvertebrates). These comparisons of dry organic weights point to a considerable discrepancy between the sizes of the brown-algal standing stocks in the lower intertidal (i.e. *Egregia menziesii*, *Eisenia arborea* and *Halidrys dioica*) which were relatively depauperate and patchy at nearly all mainland sites near heavily populated areas (although they still dominated the biomass there). This apparent reduction of mainland brown-algal biomass is likely to be attributable to environmental stress; the data of Littler and Murray (1975) showed a comparable reduction in stocks of large brown algae, near

Table VI. Island and mainland overall yearly means for all of the parameters measured

Parameters	Means		Difference (%)
	Islands	Mainland	
Number of taxa			
Macrophytes	77	76	1.3
Macroinvertebrates	74	70	5.7
Cover (%)			
Macrophytes	97	95	2.1
Macroinvertebrates	18	14	28.6
Macroinvertebrate Density/m^2	3054	3421	−12.0
Biomass (g/m^2)			
Lower 3 intervals			
Wet weight			
Macrophytes	1318	712	85.1
Macroinvertebrates	177	74	139.2
Organic dry weight			
Macrophytes	124	109	13.8
Macroinvertebrates	20	11	81.8
Entire intertidal			
Wet weight			
Macrophytes	3481	3041	14.5
Macroinvertebrates	1979	1121	76.5
Organic dry weight			
Macrophytes	663	513	29.2
Macroinvertebrates	146	104	40.4
Diversity			
Richness (D$'$)	20.02	17.01	17.7
Evenness (J$'$)	0.56	0.59	−5.4
Shannon–Weaver (H$'$)	2.57	2.56	0.4

a sewage outfall on San Clemente Island, directly correlated with sewage-induced environmental stress. Thom and Widdowson (1978) arrived at similar conclusions for mainland communities, while North *et al.* (1972) and Kindig and Littler (1980) have provided relevant data on the physiological responses to domestic effluents of sewage tolerant *vs* intolerant macrophytes. This trend in biomass reduction is also emphasized when the mean total biomass values for the

Government Point and Ocean Beach sites, which are removed from the more heavily populated Los Angeles and Orange Counties, are compared. These two sites averaged 768 g/m² ODW (624 g/m² macrophytes and 144 g/m² macroinvertebrates), values intermediate between mainland and island sites.

Similar trends are also indicated by the cover data extracted from Tables IV and V. For example (Table VI), biological cover on islands was 115 *vs* 109% for mainland (97 *vs* 95% for macrophytes, 18 *vs* 14% for macroinvertebrates). This difference is slightly more pronounced than that reported during 1975–1976. Again, while extensive algal turf communities were prevalent in the middle to low intertidal zones at nearly all sites, the island turfs were comprised of larger, more robust populations with epiphytes primarily of medium-sized frondose algae. However, mainland turf communities near populated areas again were characterized by smaller and simpler forms, had more compact structures, and often were heavily coated with a predominance of fine, filamentous epiphytes similar to those documented (Littler and Murray, 1975; Murray and Littler, 1978a) from a sewage-perturbated community on San Clemente Island. The two mainland sites removed from human population centers (Government Point and Ocean Beach) had algal turf communities which more nearly approximated those of the island systems.

4. Physical Factors

(a) Substrate disturbance. Island sites tended to be dominated by the larger perennial species characteristic of mature communities. The sand-influenced San Nicolas Island site was unusual in that subclimax and mature communities co-occurred throughout the study area. In places where sand scouring was frequent, opportunistic organisms associated with pioneer stages of community development occurred; by contrast, slightly raised areas not inundated by sand were occupied by relatively mature assemblages. Santa Rosa Island also contained a highly variable zone, below + 0.9 m, which appeared to be affected by sand deposition. The three mainland sites that were subjected to a high degree of disturbance (Corona del Mar, Whites Point and Coal Oil Point) were distinguished by opportunistic species assemblages.

(b) Wave shock. Contrary to the previous year, there tended to be fewer macroinvertebrate taxa in samples from sites having heavy wave exposure (Fig. 3) while the highest number of macroinvertebrates was encountered on Santa Catalina Island, a relatively sheltered habitat. As in 1975–1976, macrophyte species showed increased numbers at sites with prominent surge or swell, possibly due to less desiccation stress above MLLW (Fig. 3), allowing a greater number of normally subtidal species to inhabit higher regions. The Ocean Beach community seemed to be relatively constant (Table IV) but lacked the large brown seaweeds usually found in other mature communities. The absence of these species is probably related to the high degree of wave shock that this site receives and to the friable nature of the sandstone substrate; furthermore, it was observed that the large seaweeds and barnacles were easily torn loose during periods of high wave activity.

5. Species Diversity

As was the case during the previous year, richness indices gave information that closely paralleled the counts of total taxa (cf. Figs 3 and 9). Santa Catalina Island (D′ = 25.69), one of the more environmentally benign sites, was considerably richer than the other sites.

The sites high in evenness (Fig. 9) were generally low in richness (e.g. San Miguel Island and Government Point). Conversely, Ocean Beach and Coal Oil Point were among the lowest in terms of richness but showed only moderate evenness values. Santa Cruz Island and Santa Rosa Island were moderately rich but disproportionately low in evenness. As was pointed out during 1975–1976 (Littler, 1980), evenness indices do not appear to be particularly indicative of environmental disturbance.

The three sites lowest in H′ (Fig. 9) were heavily dominated by mussels and because of their low evenness values showed lower diversity than any of the other 12 sites. As mentioned for evenness (J′), the data do not show a clear relationship between the levels of environmental disturbance observed and Shannon–Weaver diversity.

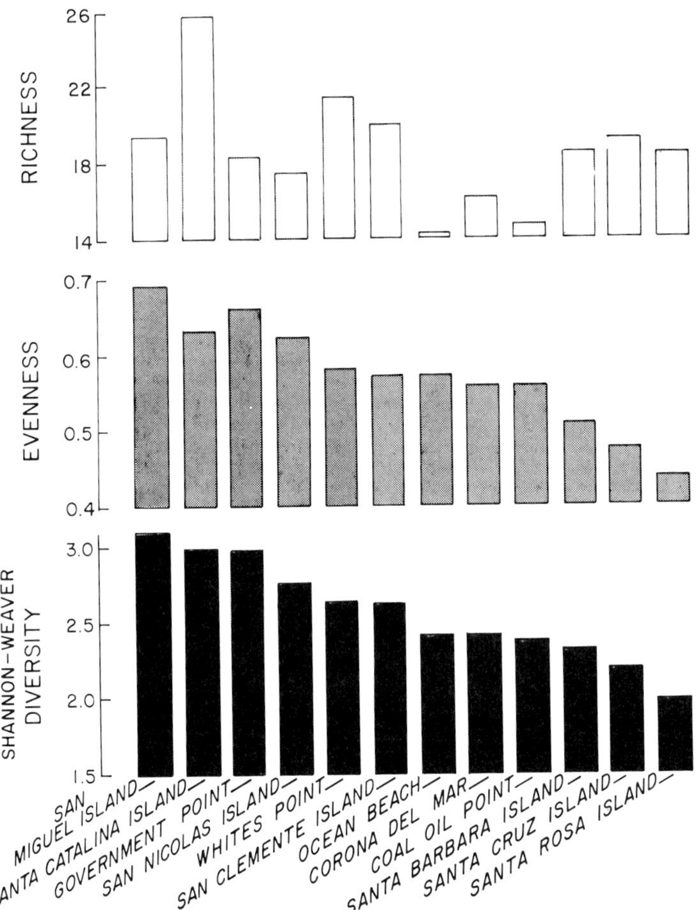

Fig. 9. Mean annual richness (D_e'), evenness (J_e'), and Shannon–Weaver diversity (H_e'), using macrophyte and macroinvertebrate mean cover.

6. *Temporal Variation*

The 1975–1976 study was characterized by a general lack of widespread or consistent temporal patterns except for (i) a slight lowering of most parameters at all sites following the winter months and (ii) recruitment of barnacles and several other macroinvertebr[illegible]s at several sites during the winter through spring period. The o[illegible] lack of consistent seasonal tendencies strongly suggested tha[illegible] or even site-specific conditions tended to predominate most often and to obscure broad climatic effects. This agrees with other descriptions (Stephenson and Stephenson, 1972) of rocky intertidal systems that also have a high degree of autonomy. In the present investigation, all 12 sites displayed seasonality in macrophyte cover (mean range of 14% seasonal difference, Table IV), except for Santa Cruz and Santa Rosa Islands which had annual ranges of only 3% and 2%, respectively. Sites showing the greatest seasonal range (San Nicolas Island, range of 34%; Government Point, range of 25%) had large decreases in cover at times of sand-inundation. In general, the winter months were the times of minimum macrophyte cover (an average of 8% less), much of which was due to die-back following the late fall to winter periods of daytime low tides with concomitant desiccation, heat and insolation stress. As was the case during 1975–1976, the general tendency for many of the macrophytes (in particular, turf species, turf epiphytes, *Phyllospadix* and the large brown, lower-intertidal seaweeds, especially *Egregia menziesii*) was to increase throughout spring and summer, reaching their peak in fall and then showing marked declines associated with the stressful daytime low tide periods of late fall and winter. This trend may have been particularly pronounced during the drought years of 1975–1976 and 1976–1977, when winter desiccating ("Santa Ana") wind conditions prevailed, coinciding with early afternoon low tides. Cover increases over 1975–1976 values (Table IV) ranged from 11% to 32% and occurred at all of the sites except Whites Point (no change), Coal Oil Point (decrease of 1%) and Santa Catalina Island (decrease of 5%).

Table V illustrates macroinvertebrate cover (seasonal and annual) for all sites. The mean overall intertidal macroinvertebrate cover for the 10 sites sampled during 1975–1976 was slightly greater (1.5%) than for the same sites during 1976–1977. Coal Oil Point no longer supported the greatest cover of macroinvertebrates (decrease of 12%), as had been the case for 1975–1976. All other sites remained about the same as during 1975–1976 in terms of total macroinvertebrate cover (ranging from a decrease of 2% to an increase of 4%). Seasonal change was slight among the 12 sites, being prominent only at Coal Oil Point (average range of 10%) and San Nicolas Island (annual range of 7%), both of which experienced important sand-inundation effects. Several of the sites showed a late winter to early

Table VII. Seasonal and mean yearly macroinvertebrate density (no./m²); comparisons between sites

Sites	Months				
	MJJA	SON	DJ	FMA	Mean
Santa Rosa Island	8577	7160	6698	6468	7226
Government Point	6242	7322	6468	6580	6653
Coal Oil Point	3959	4527	5484	1676	3912
Santa Barbara Island	3500	2853	2816	3583	3188
San Nicolas Island	3270	3351	3042	2652	3079
Ocean Beach	3583	1823	2130	2056	2398
Corona del Mar	824	420	1221	5997	2116
San Clemente Island	2795	1853	1539	2076	2066
Whites Point	4971	1168	694	1266	2025
Santa Cruz Island	2942	1399	1572	2129	2010
Santa Catalina Island	1960	1961	2038	1846	1951
San Miguel Island	1865	1916	1863	1784	1857
Mean	3707	2979	2964	3176	3207

spring increase in macroinvertebrate cover associated with the recruitment of juvenile barnacles.

Seasonality in macroinvertebrate density occurred at all sites (Table VII). The winter months tended to be the times of minimal density (an average of 734 individuals/m^2 less than in summer months). Three sites showed striking annual ranges in numbers of individuals/m^2 (Corona del Mar, range of 5173/m^2; Whites Point, range of 4277/m^2; Coal Oil Point, range of 3808/m^2). These dramatic fluctuations in macroinvertebrate densities were associated with substrate instability and seasonal influxes of sand. Four sites showed marked increases in mean macroinvertebrate densities compared to 1975–1976 (Corona del Mar, increase of 1535/m^2; Whites Point, + 531/m^2; San Nicolas Island, + 403/m^2; Coal Oil Point, + 302/m^2), while two sites underwent considerable decreases (San Miguel Island, decrease of 441/m^2 and Santa Catalina Island, 331/m^2 fewer). Also, richness (D′) tended to increase slightly through recruitment during the winter months at many sites; this was presumably a result of stressful conditions, caused by daytime low tides, which in turn decreased the abundances of certain dominant canopy species.

7. *Response of Intertidal Communities to Natural Disturbances*

During the present investigation, two of the study sites were subjected to natural disturbances. Corona del Mar became flooded by an unusually heavy rainfall in May 1977, while Santa Catalina Island was disturbed by a large storm during May 1976. Such natural events are disturbing factors recurrent in biological communities (Connell, 1978) and their effects have not been adequately documented. The unpredictable occurrences of storms or high waves have been correlated with subtidal standing-stock fluctuations in the tropics (Doty, 1971), in which seasonality was obscured. Studies of the responses of intertidal communities to natural perturbations may give information on the recoverability of different components and thus provide one method of measuring community stability (resilience).

At the Corona del Mar study site, the encrusting algae *Hydrolithon decipiens*, blue-green algae, and the red algae *Gelidium coulteri/pusillum*, showed declines of 1.3%, 7.8%, and 5%, respectively. following the flood. However, several macrophyte taxa characteristic of disturbed environments, *Ulva californica/Enteromorpha* sp. and Ectocarpaceae, showed sizable increases in mean cover (mean increases of 14.6% and 8.9%, respectively) after the disturbance. The most striking effect of the storm was on the purple sea urchin, *Strongylocentrotus purpuratus* (Stimpson). This species decreased dramatically from about 2.0% cover to less than 0.1% in the lower intertidal (MLLW to + 0.3 m) and disappeared entirely from the + 0.3 to 0.6 m interval. Belt transects in the flooded area recorded an average of 90.5% urchin mortality (19 recently killed out of 21 urchins) while a census of the total area between the two permanent transect lines revealed 93.6% mortality (52 dead out of 54 urchins). A comparable area just beyond the flooded region (20 m north of the north transect line) contained only 1.1% mortality of *S. purpuratus* (6 dead out of 539 urchins). These observations indicate that freshwater inundation of the intertidal due to severe rainstorms can have highly localized catastrophic effects on intertidal populations, which may have important implications for subsequent interpretations of [illegible]nity changes.

[illegible]n, abundance and community structure of the [illegible]and site were studied one month after a large storm [illegible]a. The storm lasted for three days (13–15 April 1976).

During this period, the combination of extreme high tides and heavy westerly swells resulted in waves striking the bluff surface + 6.5 m above MLLW. The storm caused a dramatic thinning of the kelp beds immediately seaward of the study area and broke away a large portion of the bluff that rises 3.0 m above the west and center transect lines. In addition, the substrate along the center transect line showed evidence of abrasion due to the seaward transport of broken rubble. One of the immediate outcomes of the storm was a reduction in standing stocks. Macrophyte cover was reduced by 8.7% with dramatic decreases in cover of the articulated coralline alga *Corallina officinalis* var. *chilensis* and of the canopy-forming brown algae *Egregia menziesii* and *Eisenia arborea*. Decreases were also determined for the red alga *Gelidium purpurascens* and the encrusting coralline alga *Lithophyllum proboscideum* along the lower shoreline, where they had developed beneath the brown algal canopies prior to the storm. The larger canopy-forming algae were probably removed from their anchorage by the strong wave action, while the shade-acclimated *G. purpurascens* and *L. proboscideum* may have suffered from increased insolation received in the absence of a canopy.

Drift seaweed biomass consisting predominantly of the larger kelps increased (Zobell, 1971) on Southern California beaches during the period of most frequent storms (November through February). A strong positive correlation was noted (Zobell, 1971) between the quantity of seaweed on shores and wave height, as well as wind velocity, thereby providing additional evidence of the significance of storm conditions to seaweed communities.

The decreases in abundance of these dominant algal populations were partially offset by cover increases in opportunistic seaweed species. *Scytosiphon dotyi*, *Enteromorpha* sp., *Colpomenia sinuosa* and benthic diatoms were most abundant on disturbed surfaces after the storm and showed large increases over their previous cover values. These species are known (O. Wilson, 1925; Emerson and Zedler, 1978; Murray and Littler, 1978a) readily to occupy vacated patches within relatively mature biotic communities.

An overall 24.5% decrease in macroinvertebrate density occurred due to the storm. Suspension feeding organisms such as barnacles and tube-forming mollusks suffered the greatest decreases. These sessile species were presumably killed by abrasion and dislodgement from the substrate. Many members of the grazing guild were reduced in numbers following the storm although, of the dominants, only *Littorina planaxis* suffered a large (35.8%) decrease. Overall, the short-term effects of the storm resulted in abrupt localized declines in several of the abundant organisms, whereupon newly vacated space became occupied by short-lived opportunistic species of algae. Large-scale changes in overall community patterns did not result, nor were they interpreted as likely to occur over a longer term since abundances of the dominants showed little change beyond normal seasonal variability.

8. Recovery of Disturbed Quadrats

The successional study was designed to determine biological recovery rates in fixed quadrats following severe mechanical disturbances, i.e. the removal of all fleshy and upright organisms. A primary objective was to identify sensitive species which would be slow to re-establish. While this research did not directly address the potential effect of oil on natural intertidal communities, certain effects of oil are highly mechanical (e.g. smothering; Crapp, 1971) and the resultant mortality suffered by populations provides free space such as that produced by natural physical disturbances.

Generally, intertidal macrophytes were effective at rapidly re-establishing their overall cover on disturbed surfaces, while the macroinvertebrate populations recovered much more slowly. All of the sites (except Santa Cruz Island and Santa Catalina Island) re-attained their pre-harvest mean macrophyte cover values after 12 months, whereas none of the macroinvertebrate species attained pre-harvest levels of cover and overall pre-harvest densities were matched only at Whites Point. After 12 months, an average of only 55.4% of the pre-harvest densities and 64.4% Bray–Curtis cover similarity was recorded at the nine sites.

Certain species showed a high degree of resilience and quickly re-established on the disturbed areas. The articulated coralline algae (e.g. *Corallina officinalis* var. *chilensis*) showed remarkably rapid recovery rates from remnant basal-crust portions, particularly where they had previously formed a dense turf. Certain of the frondose forms such as *Gigartina canaliculata* also showed rapid recovery following plot clearance. *Egregia menziesii* began to recolonize disturbed surfaces soon after harvesting at several sites; however, sites subjected to other disturbances (such as Whites Point, Coal Oil Point and Corona del Mar) were not readily recolonized by *Egregia*. Filamentous algae (e.g. rhodophycean turf at Coal Oil Point) showed rapid re-establishment to pre-harvest levels. Among the macroinvertebrates that appeared to be most rapid in recolonizing disturbed surfaces were the tube worms *Phragmatopoma californica* and *Dodecaceria fewkesi*.

Several populations of macrophytes and macroinvertebrates were very slow to recover at all sites and are, thus, heavily impacted by disturbance. The upper intertidal rockweeds *Hesperophycus harveyanus* and *Pelvetia fastigiata* consistently failed to re-establish. These species were generally abundant adjacent to the disturbed plots; however, vegetative encroachment by them or by other large frondose seaweeds such as *Halidrys dioica* and *Prionitis lanceolata* was also extremely slow, particularly at the island sites. Populations of sessile bivalves were similarly quite slow to recover. For example, the mussels *Mytilus californianus*, *M. edulis* L., *Septifer bifurcatus* (Conrad) and *Brachidontes adamsianus* (Dunker) all revealed virtually negligible recovery after 12 months, as did the rock oyster *Pseudochama exogyra*.

ACKNOWLEDGEMENTS

This project would have been impossible without the high level of skills, dedication and perseverance shown by such individuals as: Keith E. Arnold, Rebecca L. Baugh, Martin J. Byhower, Joyce E. Cook, Charles A. Currie, Jr., Cally A. Curtis, Sally L. Dean, William M. Dunstan, Steven R. Fain, Steven D. Gaines, Phyllis Y. Ha, Roxanna R. Hager, Mark E. Hay, John N. Heine, Maurice L. Hill, Jeff F. Karnes, Richard A. Kendall, Andrew C. Kindig, Robert E. Kleban, Diane S. Littler, Greg S. MacKay, Donn L. Marrin, David R. Martz, Martina M. McGlynn, Wayne N. McMahon, Ronald K. Mizusawa, Lisa J. Morgan, Jane B. Norman, Shirlianne Ouimette, Debra S. Printy, Michael S. Rios, Greg T. Ruggerone, Sally A. Russell, Mark P. Schildhauer, Robert H. Sims, Lawrence H. Solomon, Frank M. Sweeney, Edward R. Tomasek, Peggy J. Trabue, Lynnette L. Vesco, Deborah J. Wilson, William F. White, Susan A. Yamada, Karen K. Yoshihara and John R. Ysais.

Andrew C. Kindig participated very ably as coordinator of the overall field and laboratory efforts while Diane S. Littler served as administrative and materials organizer as well as project illustrator. Special acknowledgements are given to my colleagues Dr Steven N. Murray and Dr Roger R. Seapy, who identified macrophyte and macroinvertebrate specimens, respectively, throughout the project and also provided technical and scholarly expertise which contributed immeasurably to overall quality control. The credibility of the information gathered was elevated greatly through the efforts of Dr Isabella A. Abbott, who annotated and confirmed most of our algal identifications. Special thanks are given to the following people for verification and identification of macroinvertebrate species: Dr Gerald Bakus (Porifera), Dr Gilbert Jones (Mollusca and Crustacea), and Dr Charles Lambert (Ascidiacea). We are indebted to Cecil W. Robinson for the time and care he spent characterizing the samples of substrate. Funding for this research was provided by the Bureau of Land Management, U.S. Department of the Interior through Contract No. AA 550-CT6-40 awarded to Science Applications, Inc.

REFERENCES

Abbott, I. A. and Hollenberg, G. J. (1976). "Marine Algae of California". Stanford University Press, Stanford, California.

Abe, N. (1937). Ecological survey of Iwayama Bay, Palao. *Palao Trop. Biol. Stn Stud.* **1**, 217–324.

Bray, J. R. and Curtis, J. T. (1957). An ordination of the upland forest communities of southern Wisconsin. *Ecol. Monogr.* **27**, 325–349.

Bright, D. B. (1974). Benthic invertebrates. *In* "A Summary of Knowledge of the Southern California Coastal Zone and Offshore Areas, Vol. II" (M. D. Dailey, B. Hill and N. Lansing, eds), pp. 10–1 to 10–29. U.S. Department of the Interior, Bureau of Land Management, Washington, D.C.

Caplan, R. I. and Boolootian, R. A. (1967). Intertidal ecology of San Nicolas Island. *In* "Proceedings of the Symposium on the Biology of the California Islands" (R. N. Philbrick, ed.), pp. 201–217. Santa Barbara Botanic Gardens, Santa Barbara, California.

Cockerell, T. D. A. (1939). The marine invertebrate fauna of the Californian islands. *Proc. 6th Pac. Sci. Congr.* **3**, 501–504.

Connell, J. H. (1972). Community interactions on marine rocky intertidal shores. *Ann. Rev. Ecol. Syst.* **3**, 169–192.

Connell, J. H. (1978). Diversity in tropical rain forests and coral reefs. *Science, N.Y.* **199**, 1302–1310.

Crapp, G. B. (1971). The ecological effects of standard oil. *In* "The Ecological Effects of Oil Pollution on Littoral Communities" (E. B. Cowell, ed.), pp. 181–207. Applied Science Publications, Essex, England.

Dawson, E. Y. (1949). "Contributions toward a Marine Flora of the Southern California Channel Islands, I–III". Allan Hancock Foundation Occasional Paper No. 8. University of Southern California, Los Angeles, California.

Dawson, E. Y. (1959). A primary report on the benthic marine flora of southern California. *In* "Oceanographic Survey of the Continential Shelf Area of Southern California", pp. 169–264. California State Water Pollution Control Board Publ. No. 20. Sacramento, California.

Dawson, E. Y. (1965). Intertidal algae. *In* "An Oceanographic and Biological Survey of the Southern California Mainland Shelf", pp. 220–231, Appendix

351–438. California State Water Control Board Publ. No. 27. Sacramento, California.

Dawson, E. Y. and Neushul, M. (1966). New records of marine algae from Anacapa Island, California. *Nova Hedwigia* **12**, 173–187.

Dayton, P. K. (1971). Competition, disturbance, and community organization: the provision and subsequent utilization of space in a rocky intertidal community. *Ecol. Monogr.* **41**, 351–389.

Dayton, P. K. (1975). Experimental evaluation of ecological dominance in a rocky intertidal algal community. *Ecol. Monogr.* **45**, 137–159.

Doty, M. S. (1971). Antecedent event influence on benthic marine algal standing crops in Hawaii. *J. exp. mar. Biol. Ecol.* **6**, 161–166.

Emerson, S. E. and Zedler, J. B. (1978). Recolonization of intertidal algae: an experimental study. *Mar. Biol., Berl.* **44**, 315–324.

Emery, K. O. (1960). "The Sea off Southern California; a Modern Habitat of Petroleum". Wiley, New York.

Foster, M., Neushul, M. and Zingmark R. (1971). The Santa Barbara oil spill, part 2: initial effects on intertidal and kelp bed organisms. *Environ. Pollut.* **2**, 115–134.

Hendricks, T. J. (1977). Satellite imagery studies. *In* "Coastal Water Research Project, annual report for the year ended 30 June 1977", pp. 75–78. Southern California Coastal Water Research Project. El Segundo, California.

Hewatt, W. G. (1946). Marine ecological studies on Santa Cruz Island, California. *Ecol. Monogr.* **16**, 187–208.

Jones, J. H. (1971). "General Circulation and Water Characteristics in the Southern California Bight". Southern California Coastal Water Research Project. El Segundo, California.

Kimura, J. C. (1974). Climate. *In* "A Summary of Knowledge of the Southern California Coastal Zone and Offshore Areas, Vol. II" (M. D. Dailey, B. Hill and N. Lansing, (eds), pp. 2–1 to 2–70. U.S. Department of the Interior, Bureau of Land Management. Washington, D.C.

Kindig, A. C. and Littler, M. M. (1980). Growth and primary productivity of marine macrophytes under exposure to domestic sewage effluents. *Mar. Environ. Res.* **3**, 81–100.

Littler, M. M. (1968). Development of reef-building crustose coralline algae measurement techniques. *Western Society of Naturalists 49th Meeting Abstracts* **17**.

Littler, M. M. (1971). Standing stock measurements of crustose coralline algae (Rhodophyta) and other saxicolous organisms. *J. exp. mar. Biol. Ecol.* **6**, 91–99.

Littler, M. M. (1978). "Assessments of Visitor Impact on Spatial Variations in the Distribution and Abundance of Rocky Intertidal Organisms on Anacapa Island, California". U.S. National Parks Service, Washington, D.C.

Littler, M. M. (1980). Overview of the rocky intertidal systems of Southern California. *In* "The California Islands: Proceedings of a Multidisciplinary Symposium" (D. M. Power, ed.). Santa Barbara Museum of Natural History, Santa Barbara, California.

Littler, M. M. and Murray, S. N. (1974). The primary productivity of marine macrophytes from a rocky intertidal community. *Mar. Biol., Berl.* **27**, 131–135.

Littler, M. M. and Murray, S. N. (1975). Impact of sewage on the distribution, abundance and community structure of rocky intertidal macro-organisms. *Mar. Biol., Berl.* **30**, 277–291.

Littler, M. M. and Murray, S. N. (1978). Influence of domestic wastes on energetic pathways in rocky intertidal communities. *J. appl. Ecol.* **15**, 583–595.

Maloney, N. J. and Chan, K. M. (1974). Physical oceanography. *In* "A Summary of Knowledge of the Southern California Coastal Zone and Offshore Areas, Vol. I" (M. D. Dailey, B. Hill and N. Lansing, eds), pp. 3–1 to 3–65. U.S. Department of the Interior, Bureau of Land Management, Washington, D.C.

Manton, S. M. (1935). Ecological surveys of coral reefs. *Scient. Rep. Gt. Barrier Reef Exped.* **3**, 273–312.

Margalef, R. (1968). "Perspectives in Ecological Theory". University of Chicago Press, Chicago.

Murray, S. N. (1974). Benthic algae and grasses. *In* "A Summary of Knowledge of the Southern California Coastal Zone and Offshore Areas, Vol. II" (M. D. Bailey, B. Hill and N. Lansing, eds), pp. 9–1 to 9–61. U.S. Department of the Interior, Bureau of Land Management, Washington, D.C.

Murray, S. N. and Littler, M. M. (1978a). Patterns of algal succession in a perturbated marine intertidal community. *J. Phycol.* **14**, 506–512.

Murray, S. N. and Littler, M. M. (1978b). Analysis of the patterns of recovery of intertidal and subtidal communities. *In* "The Annual and Seasonal Ecology of Southern California Rocky Intertidal, Subtidal and Tidepool biotas. Southern California baseline study, year two, final report, Vol. III, rept. 1.1" (M. M. Littler, ed.), pp. III–1.1.20–1 to III–1.1.20–226. U.S. Department of the Interior, Bureau of Land Management, Washington, D.C.

Murray, S. N., Littler, M. M. and Abbott, I. A. (1980). Biogeography of the California marine algae with emphasis on the southern California Islands. *In* "The California Islands: Proceedings of a Multidisciplinary Symposium" (D. M. Power, ed.). Santa Barbara Museum of Natural History, Santa Barbara, California.

Neushul, M., Clarke, W. D. and Brown, D. W. (1967). Subtidal plant and animal communities of the Southern California Islands. *In* "Proceedings of the Symposium on the Biology of the California Islands" (R. N. Philbrick, ed.), pp. 37–55. Santa Barbara Botanic Garden, Santa Barbara, California.

Nicholson, N. L. (1972). The Santa Barbara oil spills in perspective. *Calif. Mar. Res. Comm., CalCOFI Report* **16**, 130–149.

Nicholson, N. L. and Cimberg, R. L. (1971). The Santa Barbara oil spill of 1969: post-spill survey of the rocky intertidal. *In* "Biological and Oceanographic Survey of the Santa Barbara Channel oil spill 1969–1970, Vol. I" (D. Straughan, ed.), pp. 325–399. Allan Hancock Foundation, University of Southern California, Los Angeles, California.

North, W. J., Stephens, G. C. and North, B. B. (1972). Marine algae and their relations to pollution problems. *In* "Marine Pollution and Sea Life" (M. Ruivo, ed.), pp. 330–340. F.A.O. Fishing News (Books) Ltd., London.

Paine, R. T. (1966). Food web complexity and species diversity. *Am. Nat.* **100**, 65–75.

Pielou, E. C. (1975). "Ecological Diversity". Wiley, New York.

Poole, R. W. (1974). "An Introduction to Quantitative Ecology". McGraw-Hill, New York.

Reid, J. L., Jr., Roden G. I. and Wyllie, J. G. (1958). Studies of the California Current System. *Calif. Mar. Res. Comm., CalCOFI Report* **6**, 27–56.

Ricketts, E. F., Calvin, J. and Hedgpeth, J. W. (1968). "Between Pacific Tides" (4th edn.). Stanford University Press, Stanford, California.

Schwartzlose, R. A. (1963). Nearshore currents of the western United States and Baja California as measured by drift bottles. *Calif. Mar. Res. Comm., CalCOFI Report* **9**, 15–22.

Seapy, R. R. (1974). Macro-invertebrates. *In* "Biolgocal Features of Intertidal Communities near the U.S. Navy sewage Outfall, Wilson Cove, San Clemente Island, California" (S. N. Murray and M. M. Littler, eds), pp. 19–22. Naval Undersea Center Technical Paper 396, San Diego, California.

Seapy, R. R. and Littler, M. M. (1980). Biogeography of rocky intertidal macro-invertebrates. *In* "The California Islands: Proceedings of a Multidisciplinary Symposium" (D. M. Power, ed.). Santa Barbara Museum of Natural History, Santa Barbara, California.

Shannon, C. E. and Weaver, W. (1949). "The Mathematical Theory of Communication". University of Illinois Press, Urbana.

Sheppard, F. P. and Emery, K. O. (1941). Submarine topography off the California coast: canyons and tectonic interpretations. Geological Society of America, Special Paper 31.

Sims, R. H. (1974). Macrophytes. *In* "Biological Features of Intertidal Communities near the U.S. Navy sewage Outfall, Wilson Cove, San Clemente Island, California" (S. N. Murray and M. M. Littler, eds), pp. 13–17. Naval Undersea Center Technical Paper 396, San Diego, California.

Smith, R. W. (1976). "Numerical analysis of ecological survey data". Ph.D. Dissertation, University of Southern California, Los Angeles.

Southern California Coastal Water Research Project. (1973). "The Ecology of the Southern California Bight: Implications for Water Quality Management". Southern California Coastal Water Research Project, Technical Report 104. El Segundo, California.

Stephenson, T. A. and Stephenson, A. (1972). "Life between Tidemarks on Rocky Shores". W. H. Freeman, San Francisco.

Straughan, D. (ed.) (1971). "Biological and Oceanographical Survey of the Santa Barbara Channel oil spill 1969–70. Vol. I. Biology and Bacteriology". Allan Hancock Foundation, University of Southern California, Los Angeles, California.

Thom, R. M. (1976). "Changes in the intertidal flora of the southern California mainland". M. A. Thesis, California State University, Long Beach, California.

Thom, R. M. and Widdowson, T. B. (1978). A resurvey of E. Yale Dawson's 42 intertidal algal transects on the southern California mainland after 15 years. *Bull. S. Calif. Acad. Sci.* **77**, 1–13.

U.S. Department of Commerce (1976). "Tidal Tables 1976, West Coast of North and South America". National Ocean Survey, Rockville, Maryland.

U.S. Department of Commerce (1977). "Tidal Tables 1977, West Coast of North and South America". National Ocean Survey, Rockville, Maryland.

Widdowson, T. B. (1971). Changes in the intertidal algal flora of the Los Angeles area since the survey by E. Yale Dawson in 1956–1959. *Bull. S. Calif. Acad. Sci.* **70**, 2–16.

Wilson, J. L. (1976). Data synthesis. *In* "Southern California Baseline Study, final report, Vol. III, rep. 5.2". U.S. Department of the Interior, Bureau of Land Management, Washington, D.C.

Wilson, O. T. (1925). Some experimental observations of marine algal successions. *Ecology* **6**, 303–311.

Zobell, C. E. (1971). Drift seaweeds on San Diego County beaches. *Beih. Nova Hedwigia* **32**, 269–314.

7 The Assessment of Changes in Intertidal Ecosystems Following Major Reclamation Work: Framework for Interpretation of Algal-dominated Biota and the Use and Misuse of Data

J. J. P. CLOKIE

University Marine Biological Station, Millport, England

and

A. D. BONEY

Department of Botany, University of Glasgow, Glasgow, Scotland

Abstract: Observations have been made over a number of years in and around the area of the construction site of the Hunterston Iron-Ore Terminal in the Firth of Clyde. This includes a jetty ending in a water depth of 40 m and a reclaimed area. In the course of this work, the area around the site has been used both to assess the validity and increase the effectiveness of questions and answers on the present and future environmental impact of overall construction and associated industrial activities. The value of intertidal macroalgae for monitoring purposes has been a principal question. The actual processes whereby algae-dominated facies are built up are considered from inoculum source to the mature state. The actual or possible effect of human activity on each partitioning process is considered. Data on inocula sources are reviewed in the context

Systematics Association Special Volume No. 17(b), "The Shore Environment, Vol. 2: Ecosystems", edited by J. H. Price, D. E. G. Irvine and W. F. Farnham, 1980, pp. 609–675, Academic Press, London and New York.

of the total Firth of Clyde flora, past and present. Propagule input is described in relation to plant/plant and plant/animal interactions, and to entry into established communities.

We have used our data to consider some of the fundamental problems involved in the use of macroalgae for monitoring purposes in the field. The most important stages in value judgements include: the assessment of seral stage; the community sequencing; use of exegetes (interpretable phenomena) and indicators. These incorporate information at the highest level of complexity, thus enabling characterization of what is "normal".

INTRODUCTION

The industrialization of the central part of the Firth of Clyde has been in progress for about 100 years. This started with large-scale sewage dumping, has continued with the building of two nuclear power stations, and was followed by the construction of a major iron ore and coal terminal, a direct reduction works and land reclamation. We have had the opportunity to observe algal-dominated intertidal and subtidal zones over a number of years and thus of detecting whether changes have occurred. Rounsefell (1972) has reviewed likely effects of reclamation. Whilst collecting data, we have asked a number of other questions on the effectiveness of and rationale for shore monitoring. As a vehicle for these questions we will describe aspects of the intertidal, leaving aside most of our subtidal observations. The overall site is shown in Fig. 1 and is detailed further in Fig. 2. The risks to the local biota from the ore terminal include presence of the physical structure, oil from bilges, iron ore released during off-loading or released from the storage area, and coal dust and effluent deriving from the direct reduction plant. As would be expected, all normal precautions will be taken to minimize these effects. At the site between Fairlie and the Hunterston power station infall, there has been a reduction of sandy beach from 341 ha to 205 ha.

We review work which has sought to extend the methods of interpreting the benthic marine algal communities and give examples of the data types collected, suggesting whether or not they are useful. By deciding on the process-indicating value or "exegetic

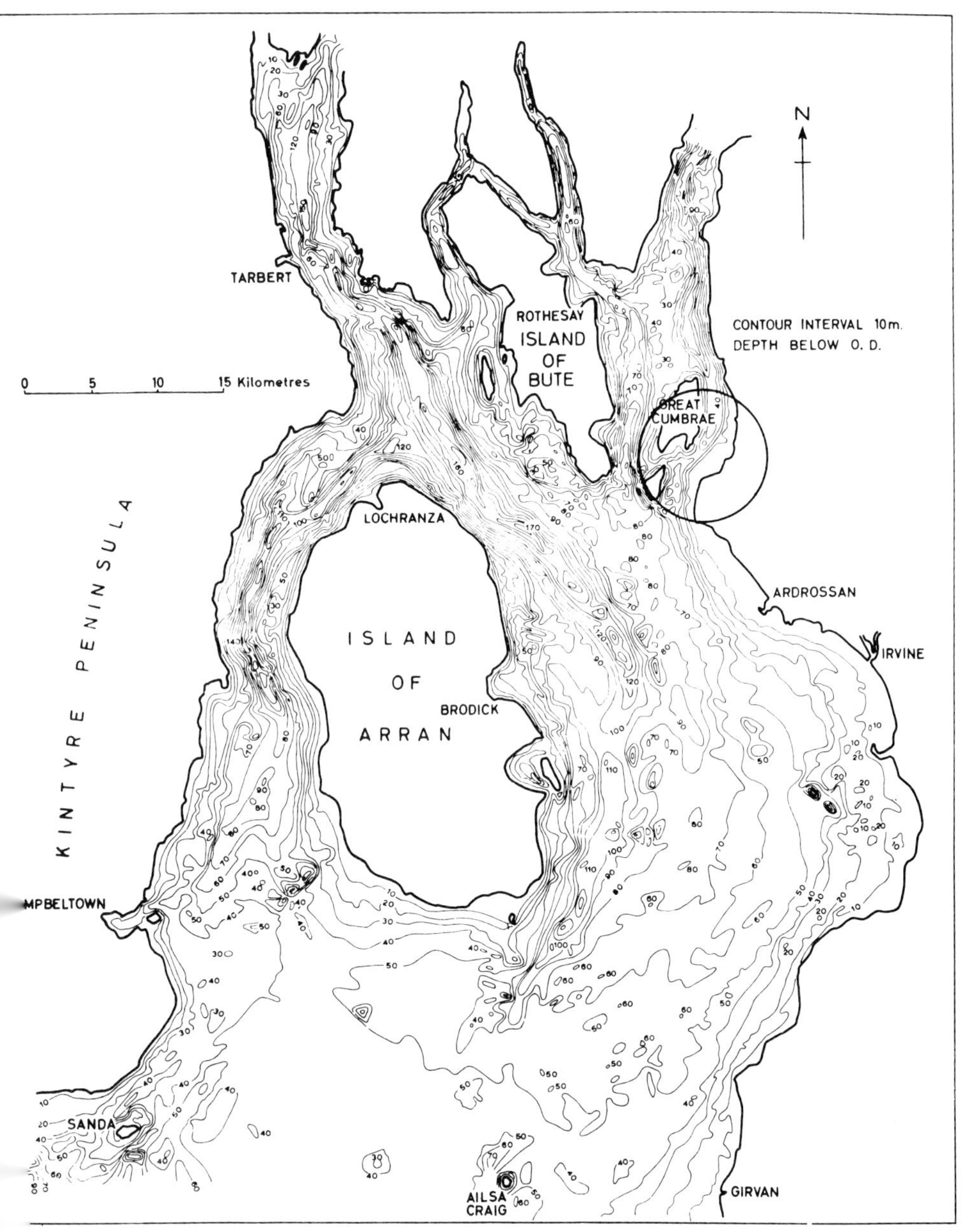

Fig. 1. The Firth of Clyde with region of industrial development circled.

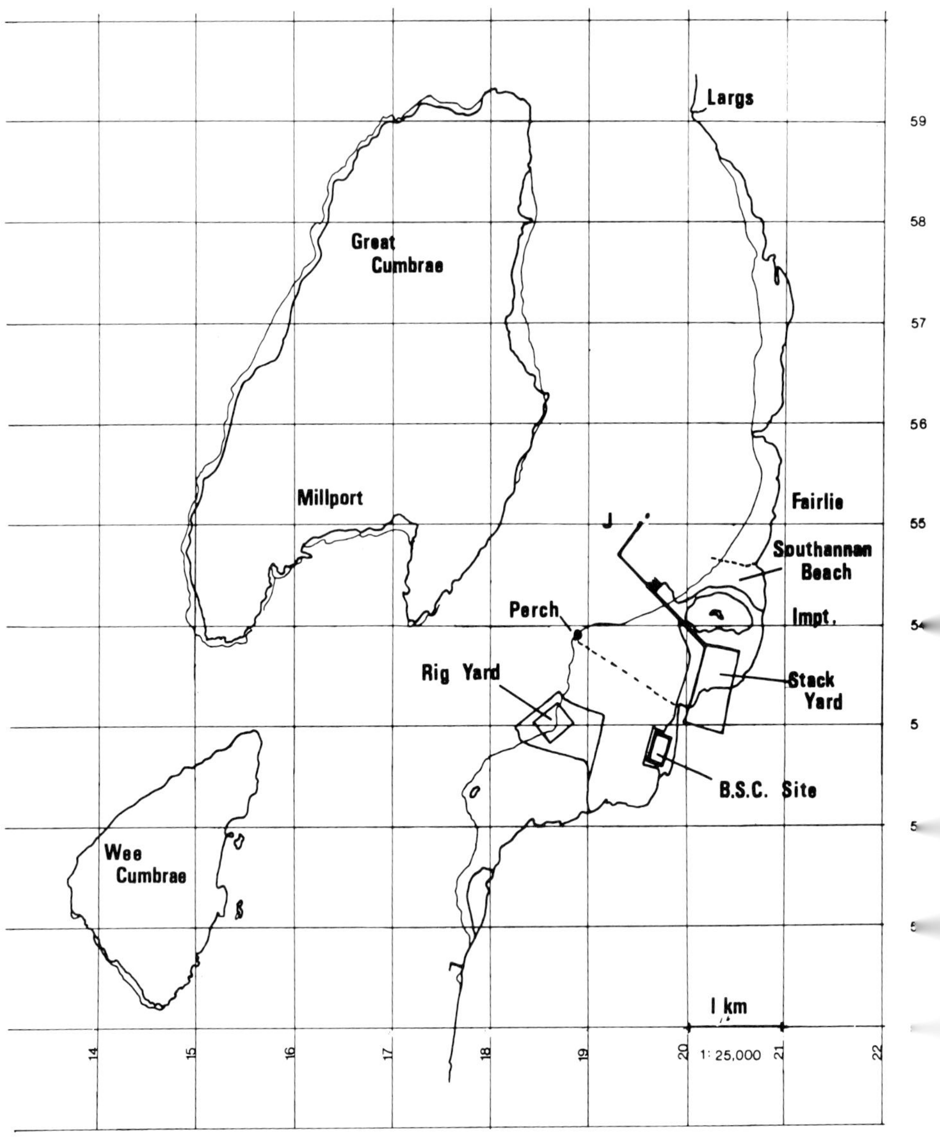

Fig. 2. The Fairlie Channel with industrial sites.

value"* of recognizable ecological phenomena, we hope to argue for their more frequent or routine use. Some of the broader aspects of monitoring are reviewed elsewhere in these volumes and in, e.g. Baker (1976a, b). We have asked very simple questions and have aimed for the simplest pragmatism in their answers. Can one convince the future pollution monitor that he should be spending more time looking at the algae than he actually does? If changes in intertidal environments are but a pale reflection of a changed factor, then he would be justified in using only chemical monitoring. To be cost-effective requires a more subtle approach in interpreting macroalgal communities. It is not sufficient to consider that they are useful as a matter of faith or because a few species have already received attention in the past.

Our approach has not been original. We have set up a series of experiments to see where the most sensitive links occur in the development of a mature facies. The process consists of formalizing the biologist's intuition about a locality. The features which enable one to make intuitive judgements derive from a synopsis of the whole milieu and the designation – the normal flora – permeates this synopsis. If, after months of work and critical assessment, there is still an interpretative value judgement to be made on a facies one should consider whether there are other ways of arriving at that same value judgement.

One of the main problems in the exegetic and indicator use of the macroalgae is that, except where major environmental change has occurred, most changes are too long-term for the "noise" to be separated from the effect. A reason for this is that most monitoring is carried out in what even now are fairly unpolluted milieux (cf. Sládaček, 1972, 1973), and small differences are not easily classified (Pearson and Rosenberg, 1978). For this reason, the plea is made for a more flexible use of process-indicating (exegetic) language. It is probable that much of what is known of the effects of pollutants on the processes controlling the appearance of a beach has been reported only in the "grey area" literature that is for the most part inaccessible.

---

*We use the word *exegete* (*exegetic*) to encompass *process indicating phenomena* or *process indicating species*. The word *indicator species* will be used in its classical (Clements) sense, as one on the basis of which a particular community can be characterized at natural stage or climax.

SYNOPSIS OF THE QUESTIONS

1. Are the Intertidal Macroalgae of Value for Monitoring Purposes?

In retrospect, our consideration of the deeper-growing subtidal algae, with a view to selecting species for a precise determination of the lower limit of the photic zone, has proved most useful (Clokie and Boney, 1980), (Fig. 3). However, the impetus for monitoring has often been provided by local concern about a deteriorating beach, or concern at the threat of onshore pollution, and then most consideration is given to the intertidal. Giving consideration to the flora alone, it may be seen that the Clyde marine benthic flora neatly straddles the chart datum line (Table I), over 75% of the species actually crossing it.

Quick inspection of the communities shows the narrowness of the viewpoint that any ecosystem of monitoring value exists on the beach alone. A more valid question, seldom asked, is whether intertidal species are too ecologically robust to be much use for monitoring purposes.

A feature of permanent transects set up for monitoring purposes is that a very rigorous selection for very atypical beaches is often made. Attempts to promote inter-beach comparability lead to omission of many physical features which help in algal ecosystem interpretation. The beaches selected often give evenly-sloping short transects which are unusual and of little use if large scale assessment of a locality is needed. There is no point in ignoring boulder beaches or sandflats.

2. Is the Work purely Academic?

Having bracketed off a section of the Firth where changes might occur, how did we frame the work? What we aimed for was a data collection which could be used quite independently to assess the impact of a given activity, either now or at any time in the future. We have thus worked from the general to the specific, whilst keeping the observations as broad as possible, and have attempted to be sure that the biological context within which our site is found is known. Because the emphasis has been to erect a quasi-legal data suite for purposes as diverse as being able to answer a short-term question on

Table I. Distribution of algal species with depth (Firth of Clyde)

	+ 100	90	80	70	60	50	40	30	20	10	0	− 10	− 20	− 30	− 40	− 50	− 60	− 70
100	×																	
90	3	×																
80	3	1	×															
70	2	0	1	×														
60	0	0	0	0	×													
50	4	1	1	0	0	×												
40	0	0	3	0	0	0	×											
30	0	0	0	0	0	0	0	×										
20	2	1	3	1	1	2	0	0	×									
10	3	3	0	6	2	2	0	1	0	×								
0	5	1	2	2	5	11	0	10	7	4	×							
− 10	1	3	2	1	3	10	2	3	7	42	10	×						
− 20	0	0	0	1	0	2	0	1	2	13	18	3	×					
− 30	0	0	0	0	0	1	0	0	1	11	5	7	1	×				
− 40	0	0	0	0	0	1	0	0	0	1	2	4	0	2	×			
− 50	1	1	1	0	0	0	0	1	0	3	3	4	1	0	0	×		
− 60	0	0	0	0	0	0	1	0	0	1	0	1	0	0	0	0	×	
− 70	0	0	0	0	0	0	0	0	0	0	0	0	0	0	0	0	0	×
− 80	0	0	0	0	0	0	0	0	0	0	0	1	1	0	0	0	0	0
− 90	0	0	0	0	0	0	0	0	0	0	0	0	0	0	0	0	0	0
− 100	1	0	0	0	0	0	0	0	0	0	0	0	0	1	0	0	0	0

The horizontal axis represents the upper limit of a species and the vertical the lower limit. Upper limit is the percentage of mean high water of spring tides and the lower limit the greatest depth at which a species has so far been found as a percentage of the depth of the photic limit defined by "*Conchocelis*". The box encloses species which straddle the chart datum line, thus showing that there are few truly intertidal or truly sublittoral algae. The data are derived from a limited number of transects and will in due course require amendment; presentation now outlines areas for productive consideration of competitive effects. The single entity indicated as present from + 100% to − 100% is "*Conchocelis*", not a discrete species. The original data are presented in Clokie and Boney (1979 and 1980).

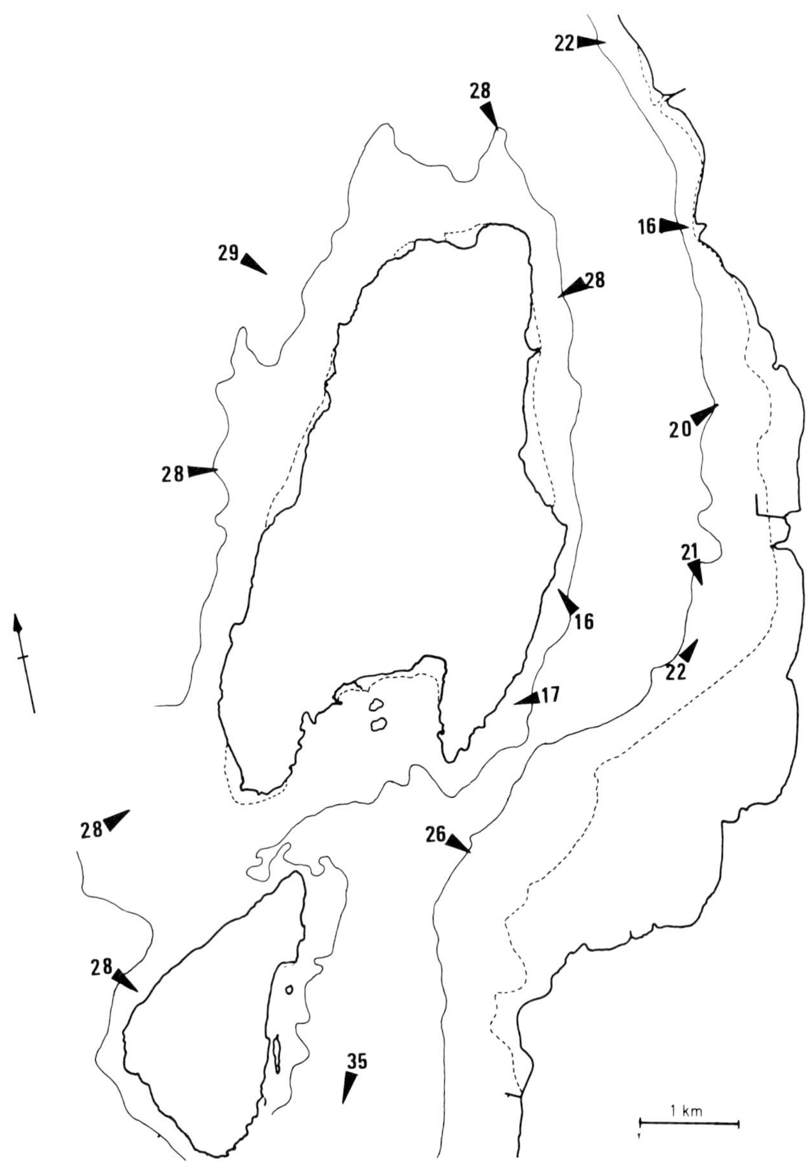

Fig. 3. The lower limit of the photic zone as defined by *Conchocelis* occurrence near the Hunterston Iron Ore and Coal Terminal. The limit is shallower within the Largs channel than outside in the main channel. Values increase in the Firth of Clyde from 0 m to 5 m at the head of the Firth, to 28 m to the west of Great Cumbrae, and to over 40 m around the outer parts of the Firth (Sanda). The lower limit is a fundamental and easily measured feature, and is of significance in base-line studies. The offshore contour is at 30 m.

change or being able to make long-term observations, the work was assuredly not purely academic. Predictive and descriptive intertidal interpretations are, however, so few that very often one needs to side-track to obtain the simplest explanation.

3. Before and after Studies?

The information sought by a buyer generally includes a requirement for "before and after" studies. Long-term changes (10 years or longer?) are unlikely to be found, except from the historical side of floristic work. In the Clyde we have examined older records, especially those of the green algae. Subtidally, we have compared changes in the "maerl" bank areas, which were described 100 years ago, and within the flora in the Saltcoats and Ardrossan area. There are indications that changes of emphasis have taken place, with a general deterioration over the last 100 years. These long-term changes, discussed under a later heading, are as difficult to pin down here as, for example, on the north-east coast of England or in the Firth of Forth (Wilkinson and Tittley, 1979). In terms of approach, it is difficult to improve on photographs and well-described permanent quadrats.

4. Predictive Aspects?

Predictive intertidal studies are less well-advanced than for terrestrial environments (O'Connor, 1974). In our experience there has been a keen interest in knowing what a given area of beach will eventually look like, especially in the early stages of rejuvenation of the succession when changes were very marked. One should not be misled into dealing only with the algae. In one instance a rapid increase in *Zostera noltii* Hornem. occurred at Southannan Beach. Most other predictions we have made behaved as forecast. Predictive work is still almost an art-form but we consider that it could become much more clearly defined. In some cases it is only possible to predict that change in progress is likely to continue.

5. Trouble-shooting?

An understanding of the succession and factors maintaining the mature facies explained a group of changes which occurred early in the construction phase of the site. A change of wave-regime enabled a climax community of a sandy/shelly beach at Southannan to rejuvenate. The result was a spectacular increase in algae, which continued for several years until the climax facies were approached. Some details of this are given later. Explanation of these events in terms of the general ecology of the area seemed satisfactory, both to the operator of the terminal and to local residents. This undoubtedly is a subject area where we could have misused our knowledge of the site either inadvertently, in convincing ourselves, or intentionally, in influencing the local residents. As it turned out, predictions we made at the time were later largely justified, and no other group of organisms could have been more relevant than the algae.

6. *Management of Beaches?*

Management of beaches will inevitably become more necessary as public opinion becomes more informed, concomitant with the increasing world-wide loss of intertidal amenity. Successional interpretation will show where a facies will develop and we have found no lack of support when advice to prevent visible deterioration has been given. Examples of the latter situation include requests from interested parties for data on the effects of major movements of beach material, or in showing where damage is being done by cockle grubbing, lugworm digging, and movements of machinery. The legal side of beach management is so complex that much caution has to be exercised. The noteworthy *Mercenaria* decision* and the N.C.C. ideas on limitation of bait-digging should be reviewed in the light of damage being done to beaches, demonstrable by rejuvenation of the succession.

7. *Whitewashing?*

It is probable that no industrialist would be so naïve these days as to pay for research to be done outside his organization in expectation of a particular result. There are examples in the literature where

---

*"Public Enquiry concerning several orders for Marchwood foreshore held at Southampton in 1971". Lucas Newtown Oyster Co, Isle of Wight.

surprising conclusions have been reached. A risk which is never fully admitted is that contracted research organizations may wish to keep a low profile and may choose to ignore for obvious reasons certain aspects of a site where there has been a deterioration. Work carried out within organizations may tend to be exonerative. This is obviously far from satisfactory. Literature reports on specific instances of pollution and algal communities are extremely rare (Borowitza, 1972), one of the best examples being the description of the inshore at Wylva (Hoare and Hiscock, 1974). An alternative approach is to say that some organization (not paying for the work) makes greater impact than the research funder. In our case, we have looked at a number of polluted sites for comparative purposes, in the quest for indicators and exegetes, for instance the shores near the Hunterston power station and in Troon harbour.

8. Framework for Description?

Finally, is a more formal framework needed than a standard cover/abundance description? The methods of continental limnologists and their criticisms are reviewed by Sládaček (1973, 1977). He justifies the methodology by showing that the essence of the methods is to select trophic and seral changes. Many of his comments are relevant here. To extract from the macroalgae the sort of answers one seeks requires a full comprehension of the community behaviour. Assessment of the impact at a sensitive stage in the development and maintenance of a mature facies may then be framed more effectively.

The synthesis of data from these observations can be used to define what is normal at any one locality. There is nothing to stop this being modelled, but so far this has not been done. If one can tell whether a community is advancing through seral succession, has stopped or is mosaicing, then simple answers can be given. The use of species diversity or indicator species in the simple sense is hazardous.

In essence, commenting on one milieu requires knowledge of many others before comparisons can be drawn. Succession is the key to interpretation of processes on the beach (Appendix I).

PARTITIONING THE SETTLEMENT SEQUENCE AND COMMUNITY SEQUENCING

To increase the exegetic use of macroalgae we considered the general ecology of as many species or process-indicating phenomena (exegetes) as possible. As the flora of the Firth of Clyde is restricted and that of the intertidal even more so, it is not unreasonable to partition the processes leading to successful colonization. Some parts of these processes are independent of the impact of a pollutant or changing environment. To see which phases are most susceptible (i.e. to identify the weakest links), the same set of questions has been asked for many species. This is followed by an assessment of the way mature facies, which are often stands predominantly of a single species, are maintained.

The data are being collected purely for interpretative work and to assess whether a community is at the most likely climax for a particular habitat. Inhibition of climax implies disturbance, and the cause of the disturbance can then be sought. If the community is at the climax then the factors required to prevent regression should be known. By asking these questions one can get practical answers to otherwise intractable or ill-defined problems.

The processes may be partitioned as shown in Fig. 4, which summarizes the natural history of a species. The stages are "if" clauses and form part of the framework for the more formal description required. Clearly each step is the sum of the preceding. Community sequencing continues from the final stage.

Stage 1: Available Stock

A requirement is to be able to fit the flora of the Hunterston site with that of the surrounding area, and with the flora for the geographical region (Table II, Fig. 5). The flora is restricted for two main reasons, habitat limitation and the already polluted nature of the central parts of the Firth. The former we think to be the more important. A general characteristic of the Hunterston site was that, overall, species numbers increased for a while after disturbance and then steadily reduced. The species were all representative of Firth of Clyde flora. This sequence is a feature of the juvenile part of the succession. Data from settlement studies are discussed below.

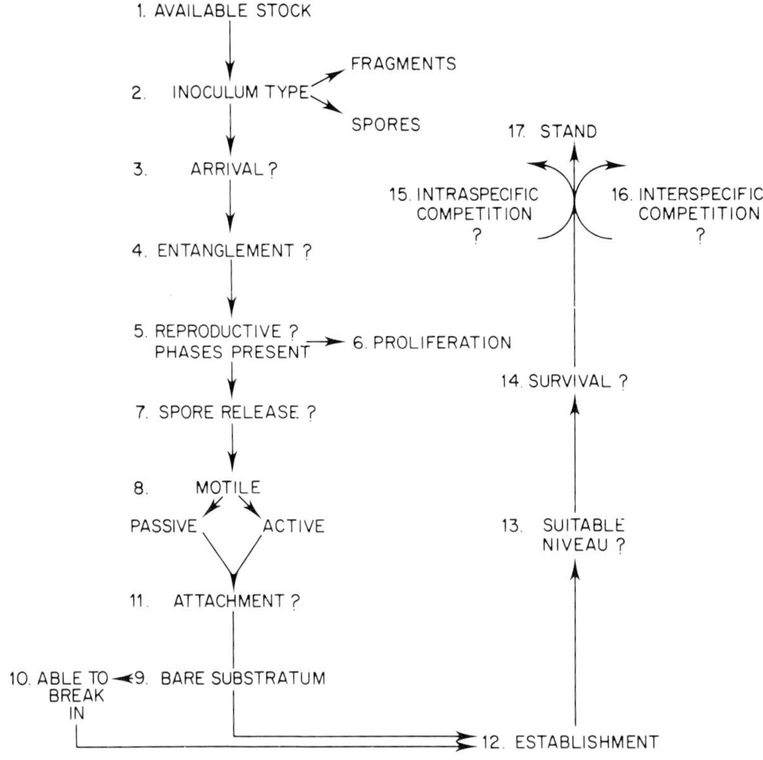

Fig. 4. The natural history of a species (see description in text).

Table II. Comparisons of species numbers

	Red algae	Brown algae	Green algae[a]	Total
U.K. flora	334	197	134	665
Clyde flora	136	75	64	275
Fairlie Channel flora	113	66	62	241

[a]Excluding the Volvocales.

Historical comparisons should assist in the overall placing of the flora in its context. In some areas of the Firth of Clyde, there appear to have been gross changes over the past 100 years. In a historical/literary comparison the authors (Clokie and Boney, 1979) suggested that the descriptions made by Landsborough in 1849 could be used to show that there had been a great reduction of diversity at Saltcoats

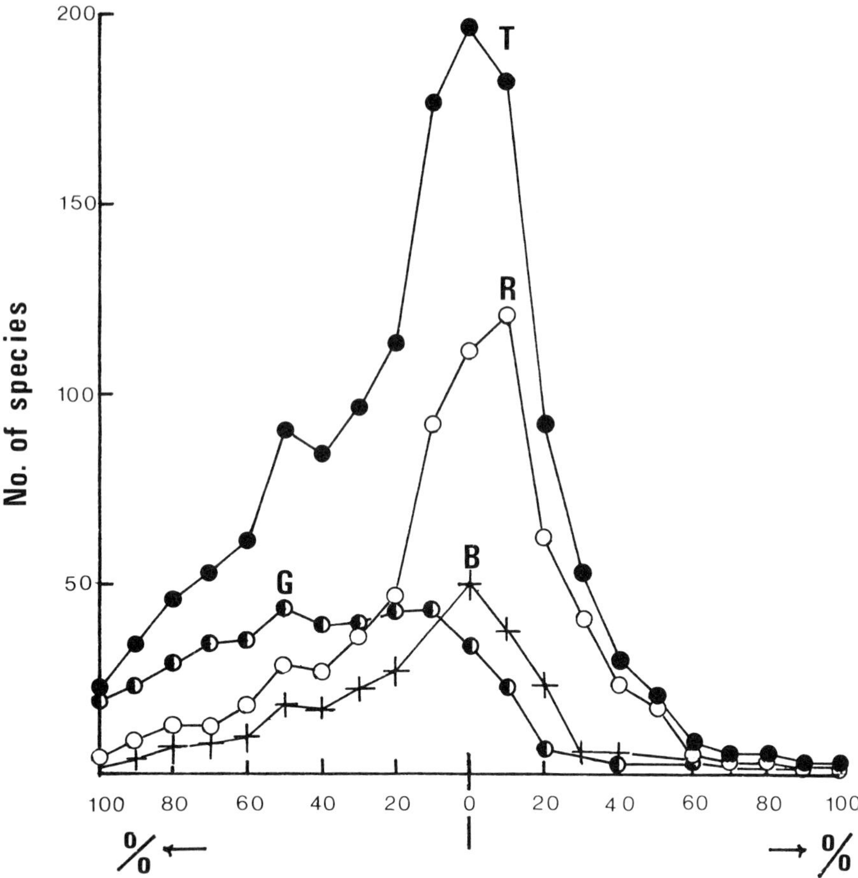

Fig. 5. Frequency diagram of Firth of Clyde marine algal flora, showing number of species at any one depth. T = total spp. of brown, green and red algae. B = brown algae; G = green algae; R = red algae. Percentage figures are as defined for Table I, with percentage of the height of MHWS to the left and percentage of photic limit depth to the right.

(15 miles to the south of the site) over the period (Table III). The same descriptions could be used to show that certain species having a clinal distribution along the Firth have always had this.

For various localities in the Firth of Clyde it has always seemed that the species number increases down a pollution gradient until the grazing level increases sufficiently to reduce it. Adequate demonstration of the effect is not easy except on a small scale. Studies in

Table III. Possible species losses at Saltcoats (Ayrshire) between 1850 and 1979

	1850	1979	on both lists	missing
Florideophyceae	85	43	35	50
Bangiophyceae	6	8	5	1
Phaeophyceae	48	19	18	30
Chlorophyceae	21	28	16	5

The number of missing species could be reduced still further by other exclusions and adjustments. Offshore sublittoral material cannot be included in the modern comparisons because of the distance away from the effects of inshore pollution. Similar sites in the Firth of Clyde would have a much richer flora.

the literature would suggest factors controlling species diversity in the algae are still poorly known; some factors are discussed below. From the standpoint of monitoring, deletions are as important as presences.

Stage 2: Inoculum Source

Proximity of inoculum stock to the surface to be colonized is unlikely to be affected by pollution. Literature dealing with the problem includes work at Surtsey (Fridriksson, 1975) and earlier work by Rees (1940), Gessner (1957) and others. Data are conflicting under this heading. Some species do spread with difficulty. Because of preemption of an available surface, late arrivals may not in any case enter until the initial cover begins to break up.

Stage 3: Arrival Phase

From experiments we have done, algae can travel equally well or better as fragments than as spores. At the Hunterston site this was particularly noticeable where a beach was scraped at the request of local residents (Fig. 6). About 1500 m^2 was treated in this way before it could be stopped. After a time, adult fucoids had returned with much the same density as before, rafting-in pebbles with their attached flora (cf. Grieve, 1881).

The low diversity of species in the early phases of colonization does not seem to be caused by lack of input of available propagula. Input quantity need not be high; some algae which are spread as fragments need no further accessions when once established (e.g. *Dumontia incrassata** and *Gigartina stellata* spreading from a persistent crustose base), whilst algae such as *Ascophyllum* are both long-lived and rather widely-spaced when adult. In the one well-documented example we have of *Ascophyllum* input, though, the density of young plants was high and these plants only occurred when the previous canopy began to break up.

Studies on the drift at Southannan beach show that much of the cast material is of local origin. Environmental problems were caused by the drift rotting. Management policies for abatement rest more with careful tutelage on how to look after the beach than on active methods of removal. Physical removal is very expensive. The relative abundance of drift weed at Southannan beach is shown in Table IV.

Table IV. Seasonal composition of driftweed at Southannan Beach, Fairlie

	Phanerogamic debris (%)	Fucoid material (%)	*Enteromorpha/ Urospora* (%)	*Enteromorpha* (%)
Winter	60	30		10
Spring	33	33	33	
Summer		10		90
Autumn	10	40		50

On some areas of the site, mobile communities are almost entirely composed of algae which have drifted in carrying their substrata. This is particularly the case in chart datum fringe communities, with the algae often attached to *Ensis* and other bivalves; this allows a species-rich community to come and go. Permanent surveyors' pegs near these sites do not undergo the same species number changes. In lagoons, the low species numbers could be as much a function of reduced input as of habitat limitation.

Stage 4: Entanglement

This is a critical phase in the early stages of colonization. Entrapping can be physical or biological, when the flora already present can

*Nomenclature and authorities for the macrobenthic marine algae follow the data presented in Parke and Dixon (1976).

Fig. 6. Effects of removal of surface sand from Southannan Beach. (a) August 1977 (2 months after sand removal); (b) May 1978.

entrap other species which can sporulate or proliferate. Examples often seen at the Hunterston site are entrapment of *Gigartina* or *Gelidium* in *Blidingia* or *Enteromorpha* canopies, either of which can completely cover a beach in the early stages. The entanglement phase is affected by pollution only in so far as previous settlement might effect subsequent settlement. Physical entrapment can occur on rocks or amongst badly littered beaches, where reinforcing bars and iron pieces have been left in waste concrete. The species-poor nature of buoys and piles could be a reflection of the lack of anything to hold an adult plant long enough to release spores. It was regularly noticed that well-developed covers of filamentous green algae on sandy beaches could be produced by drifting fragments being trapped basally in *Arenicola* burrows but continuing to grow outside (e.g. *Urospora bangioides* and *Enteromorpha clathrata*).

To test the availability of algal fragments, some experiments were carried out with bristle brush impingers (a 6 cm x 4 cm bottle brush). One set out daily for a month collected 25% of the available flora (Fig. 7). A previous experiment using ten impingers per day collected 96 species in 5 days, i.e. about a third of the available flora. In most cases the material was alive and would have been capable of providing spores or continuing growth if conditions were suitable. Spore release was demonstrated in some cases.

Stage 5: Presence of Reproductive Phase

We thought at first that a prime categorization for an area would be on the basis of fertility data. Events during the life of an alga are generally tied closely to the climate but are difficult to pin down and characterize on a routine basis. Over geographic zones comparisons may be made. The information is a requirement for a calendar predicting or explaining arrivals, and details the features underlying temporal partition (see below).

Even where differences might be expected none has been shown, e.g. with the hot water effluent area at the Hunterston power station, no earlier development of *Ascophyllum* gametes has been found when making comparisons with material from elsewhere; the peaks of fertility seem to vary from beach to beach, cf. Barnett (1971) and the behaviour of certain invertebrates.

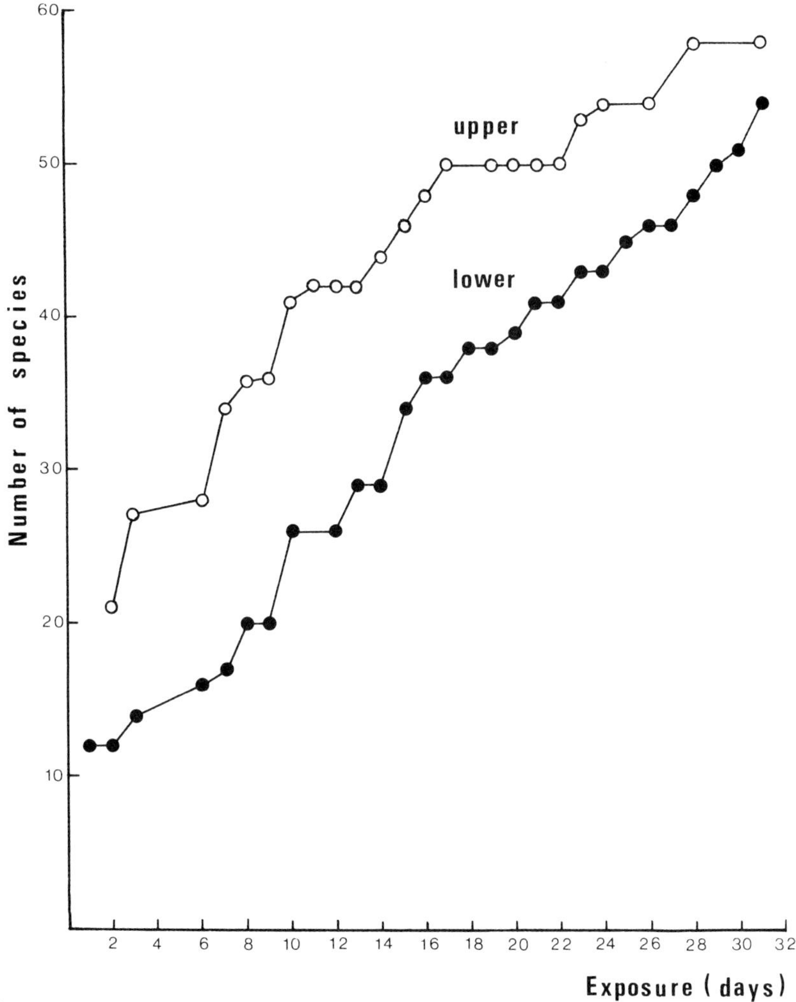

Fig. 7. Cumulative numbers of species collected as fragments by bottle brush impingers (see text).

Delay of reproduction or its complete suppression in eutrophic milieux has long been reported in the literature, and the phenomenon is of great indicator value. Comparative studies at Troon, Ayr and Leith show that early colonists which become very large are suppressing spore production, as in the cases of *Rhizoclonium*, *Prasiola* and ulvoid algae, and *Porphyra*.

Stage 6: Proliferation

A characteristic of many filamentous algae is their ability to proliferate and re-attach. In the interpretation of data on diversity, this may be significant. Some taxa (*Gelidium*, "*Trailliella*") are presumably recruited by this method. Ring phenomena amongst the green algae could be produced in this way on sandy beaches. Figure 8 shows a cross-section of an *Enteromorpha* clump on a sandy beach. This phenomenon is probably very common, but is not easily seen in the field.

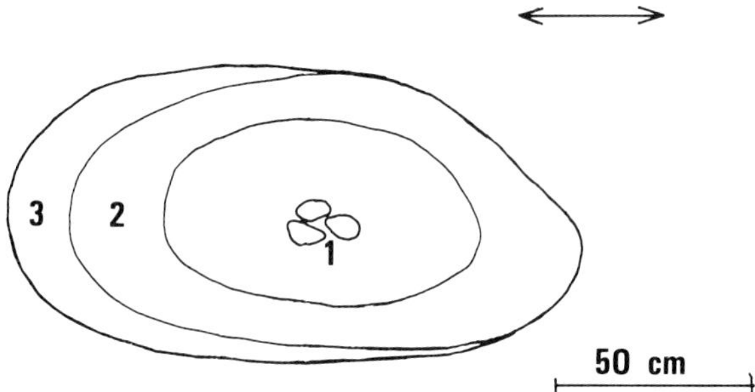

Fig. 8. Ring formation by green algae; cross-section of *Enteromorpha* clump on unshelved sandy beach at Hunterston. 1, Pebbles with *Enteromorpha intestinalis*. 2, *E. prolifera* (active over winter at high levels and in low salinities). 3, *E. clathrata* (more active in summer when salinities are high). Arrow indicates main directions of water flow (May 1978).

Stage 7: Inducement of Spore Release

Direct action of known pollutants on these processes has been described (Boney, 1968); reference to the latter work will provide further data.

Stage 8: Motility/Mobility of Spreading Phases

As for stage 7, though this is clearly easily affected by the presence of a dissolved pollutant.

Stage 9: Bare Substratum

Many algae are not capable of breaking into an already existing mature canopy. Settlement space results from innumerable causes that are often described in the literature. These range from newly constructed beaches to new algal surfaces for epiphyte utilization, loss of canopy from rock peeling or physical impact damage, grazing phenomena or seasonal die-off. At Hunterston, new substrata have been created by all these. The long-term effects on the community are very characteristic and their understanding vital for full comprehension. For example, increase in length of hard rock shoreline from 4 to 12 km has provided a range of rocky shore types. Non-porous vertical surfaces such as epoxytar-painted steel or well-filled concrete seem to recruit noticeably fewer species than on more normal surfaces. Table V gives a list of typical examples. These are typical of juvenile rather than of colonist communities. Many of the differences ascribed to surface quality are in fact linked to the maintenance of a damp surface, as shown by transects of pervious or impervious rock. Modification of steel structures by cathodic protection impressed current is now commonplace and preliminary observations show that communities develop in a less disturbed manner than on non-protected structures (Table VI).

Table V. Intertidal algae typical of new concrete and epoxy tar-painted surfaces

Rhodophyta	Phaeophyta	Chlorophyta
Audouinella purpurea	*Ectocarpus* spp.	*Blidingia marginata*
Bangia atropurpurea	*Fucus spiralis*	*B. minima*
Ceramium rubrum	*F. vesiculosus*	*Bryopsis plumosa*
Lomentaria clavellosa	*F.* hybrids	*Capsosiphon fulvescens*
Palmaria palmata	*Giffordia* spp. (some)	*Chaetomorpha linum*
Phycodrys rubens	*Laminaria digitata*	*"Codiolum gregarium"*
Polysiphonia brodiaei	*L. saccharina*	*Enteromorpha intestinalis* (forms)
P. elongata	*Petalonia fascia*	*E. linza*
P. urceolata	*Pilayella littoralis*	*E. prolifera*
Porphyra leucosticta	*Sphacelaria radicans*	*Monostroma fuscum*
P. linearis	*Waerniella lucifuga*	*M. wittrockii*
P. umbilicalis		*Prasiola crispa*
		P. stipitata
		Pseudendoclonium submarinum (and other green *Pseudendoclonium*-like basal forms)
		Rhizoclonium riparium
		Spongomorpha arcta
		Ulva lactuca
		Ulva sp.
		Urospora (all species)

Table VI. Preliminary data on effects on flora of impressed current cathodic protection

Species	Site					
	1	2	3	4	5	6
Rhodophyta						
Antithamnium floccosum	–	–	–	–	+	–
Audouinella purpurea	–	+	+	+	+	–
A. secundata	–	–	–	+	–	–
Bangia atropurpurea	–	+	+	–	–	–
Callithamnium hookeri	–	+	–	+	–	–
Ceramium rubrum	–	+	–	+	–	–
C. shuttleworthianum	–	–	–	–	+	–
"Conchocelis"	–	+	–	+	+	–
Erythrotrichia carnea	–	+	–	–	+	–
Gigartina stellata	–	–	–	+	+	–
Lomentaria clavellosa	–	–	–	–	+	–
Membranoptera alata	–	–	–	–	+	–
Polysiphonia urceolata	–	–	–	–	+	–
Porphyra umbilicalis	–	+	+	–	+	–
Phaeophyta						
Ectocarpus siliculosus	–	–	–	–	+	–
Elachista fucicola	–	+	–	–	+	–
F. serratus hybrid	–	+	+	+	+	+
F. vesiculosus hybrid	–	–	–	+	+	–
F. serratus hybrid	–	+	–	+	+	–
Laminaria digitata	–	–	–	–	+	–
Pilayella littoralis	–	–	–	+	+	+
Ralfsia clavata	–	–	–	+	–	–
Chlorophyta						
Blidingia marginata	+	–	+	–	–	+
B. minima	–	+	+	+	+	–
Bryopsis plumosa	–	–	–	–	+	–
Capsosiphon fulvescens	+	–	+	–	–	–
Cladophora albida	–	+	–	+	+	–
Enteromorpha compressa	–	+	–	+	–	+
E. compressa sp. A	+	+	–	+	+	+
E. compressa sp. B	–	+	–	+	–	–
E. compressa corn.	–	+	–	–	–	+
Monostroma wittrockii	–	+	–	+	–	–
Prasiola crispa	+	+	+	+	+	+
P. stipitata	–	+	+	+	–	+

Table VI (*continued*) . . .

Species	Site					
	1	2	3	4	5	6
Pseudendoclonium (forms)	+	+	+	+	+	+
Spongomorpha arcta	—	—	—	—	—	+
Ulothrix speciosa	—	+	—	—	—	—
Ulva lactuca	—	—	+	+	+	—
Urospora bangioides	+	+	+	—	—	—
TOTALS 39	6	22	12	21	24	10

Site 1 = unprotected pile, Fairlie pier; Sites 2–5 = Leith Dock; 2 = cathodic protected by impressed current; 3 = concrete dock wall; 4 = armoured inner mole; 5 = armoured outer side of mole; 6 = outer mole near fertilizer factory; + = present; — = absent.

Deletion in 1 due to flaking of surface; in 2 lack of suitable microhabitat; in 3 uniformity of substratum; in 4 by competition; in 5 by competition in mature but polluted area; in 6 by solid waste.

Sediment movements regularly cause removal of established flora from rocks in winter and this is always readily seen by the summer cover where species diversity is increased. These "scrubbed off" areas have communities typical of the younger stages of succession. At the Hunterston site, one previously sandy beach was altered by the winnowing away of some of the fine sediment, which caused the previously buried shell material to recruit an algal cover. This seral rejuvenation was dramatic. A much larger area was affected than might have been due to extensive bait digging bringing shell material to the surface.

It is well known that the time when bare substratum occurs is of critical importance. Settlement studies have been made at various times and it appears that the details are far from simple. In essence, however, although there are about 200 species (Table I) of algae capable of intertidal life, the broad picture may approximate to that in Fig. 9. Such background data are necessary to account for the later appearance of a community. There is usually a requirement for following through the succession and critical statements on the "most likely settling" time are time-consuming to collect (Fig. 10). The settlement in this part of the Firth of Clyde seems to follow this sequence, except where there is interference by external influences.

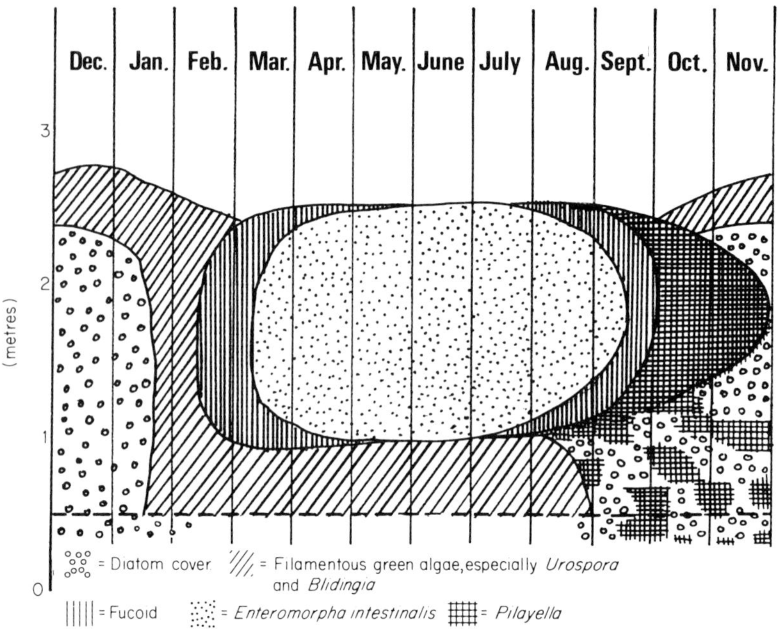

Fig. 9. Outline diagram of the most probable settling organisms in the Fairlie Channel at various times of the year. Data from observations made over a period of years; provide a rough guide to the starting points for successions.

The preemption of available space is referred to here as "temporal partitioning" and we have numerous examples, in the area, wherein major differences in algal cover have this as their cause. It is even possible to encounter two different fucoid canopies so-caused on a single beach, as is shown by Table VII. Temporal parititioning is only one aspect controlling the appearance of intertidal communities.

Other colonization results have merely posed more questions. For example the flora on about 60 concrete block tops was scored for *Enteromorpha* or fucoid cover and no explanation can so far be advanced for the initial mosaic settlement which occurred under identical conditions. Trials with settlement on panels have shown that these stages and temporal partitioning together are instrumental in giving quite different appearances to populations or communities

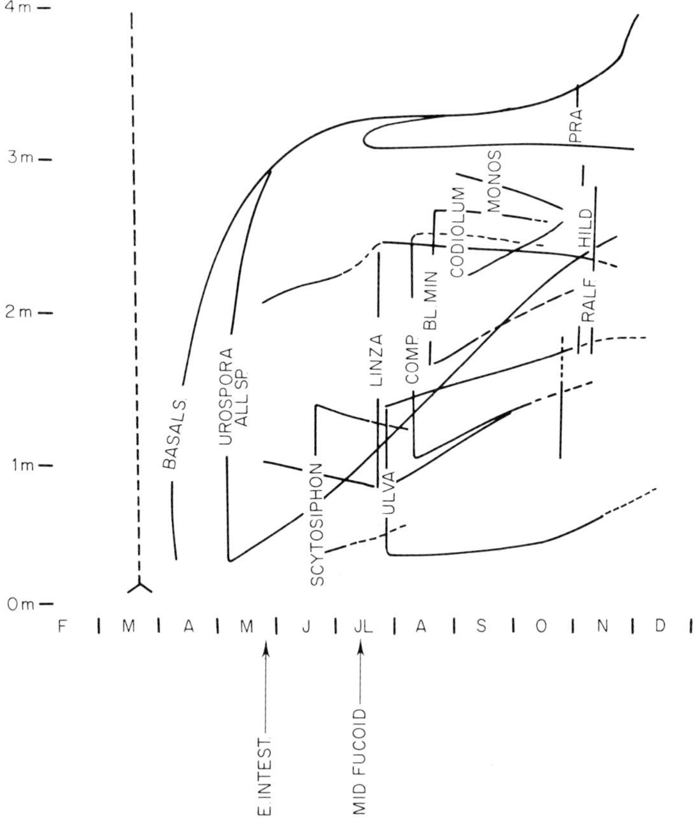

Fig. 10. Dominant arrivals on the Marine Station boat slip, first stripping. Dotted vertical line marks the data of clearance with formalin. Some organisms settle and spread outwards; others are outcompeted and their area of occurrence contracts. Basic arrival calendars are a requirement for trouble-shooting type monitoring. Key: Basal S = basal structures of various green algae; *Urospora* = mainly *Urospora bangioides* and *U. penicilliformis*; *Linza* = *Enteromorpha linza*; *Ulva* = all spp. of *Ulva*; *Comp* = *Enteromorpha compressa*; *Bl min* = *Blidingia minima*; *Codiolum* = "Codiolum gregarium"; *Hild.* = *Hildenbranchia rubra* *Monostr* = *Monostroma wittrockii; Ralf* = *Ralfsia* spp.; *Pr* = *Prasiola stipitata.*

on otherwise similar habitats (Table VIII). Further elaboration of the results is presented in the legend to Table VIII. Some experiments are in progress in which is utilized an open substrate that allows competition in the upper parts of the thallus but not in the lower part; so far, these have not shown much success.

Table VII. Effect of temporal partitioning on fucoid settlements

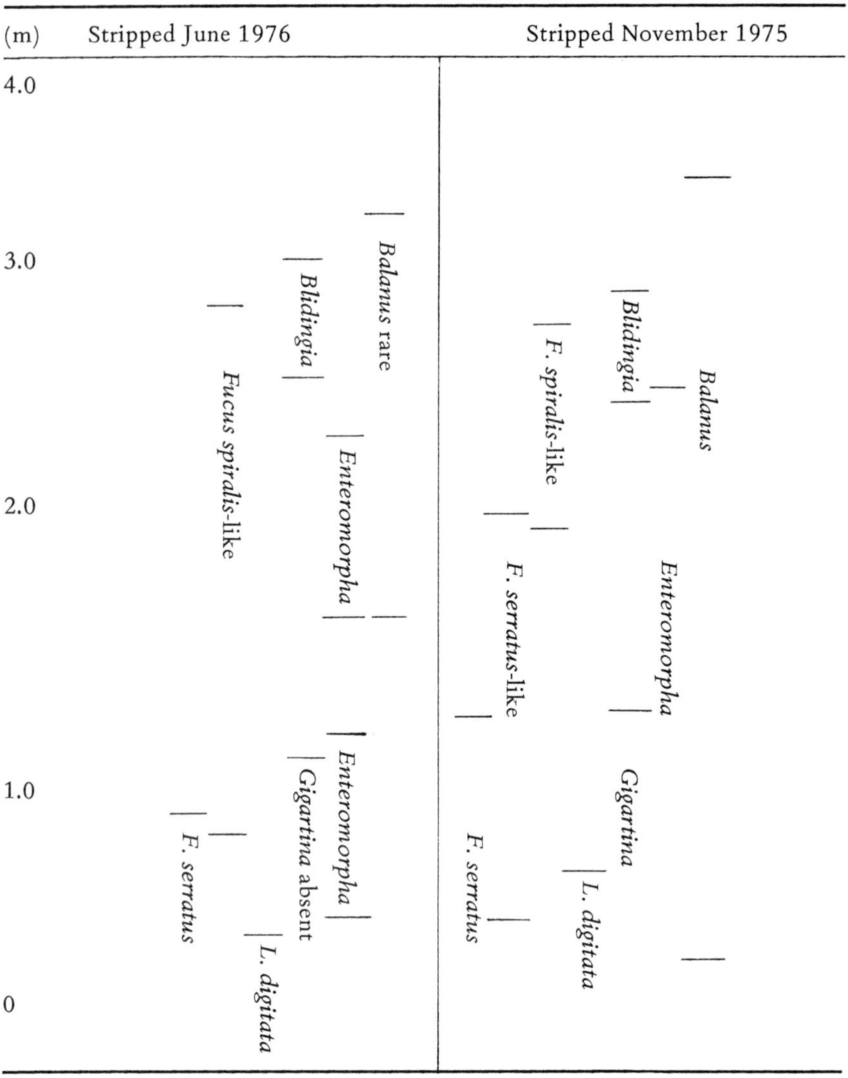

(m)	Stripped June 1976	Stripped November 1975
4.0		
		Balanus
3.0	*Balanus* rare; *Blidingia*; *Fucus spiralis*-like	*Blidingia*; *F. spiralis*-like
	Enteromorpha	
2.0		*F. serratus*-like; *Enteromorpha*
	Enteromorpha	
1.0	*Gigartina* absent; *F. serratus*	*Gigartina*; *F. serratus*; *L. digitata*
	L. digitata	
0		

The vertical axis represents metres above chart datum (CD) and the two vertical halves of the diagram represent the two sides of the concrete boat slipway at Keppel. Upper and lower limit of species are indicated by the horizontal short lines. On reading date (August, 1977), there was marked difference in the fucoid canopy on the two sides of the inclined slipway. The difference in *Balanus* cover was probably caused by (i) the left-hand side's picking up the last of the spatfall in 1976 and (ii) the density of the algae in the second year being too great to allow much recruitment. The cover on the right permitted a 1976 spatfall. The algae also manifest degrees of temporal partitioning.

Table VIII. Temporal partitioning in the early stages of succession

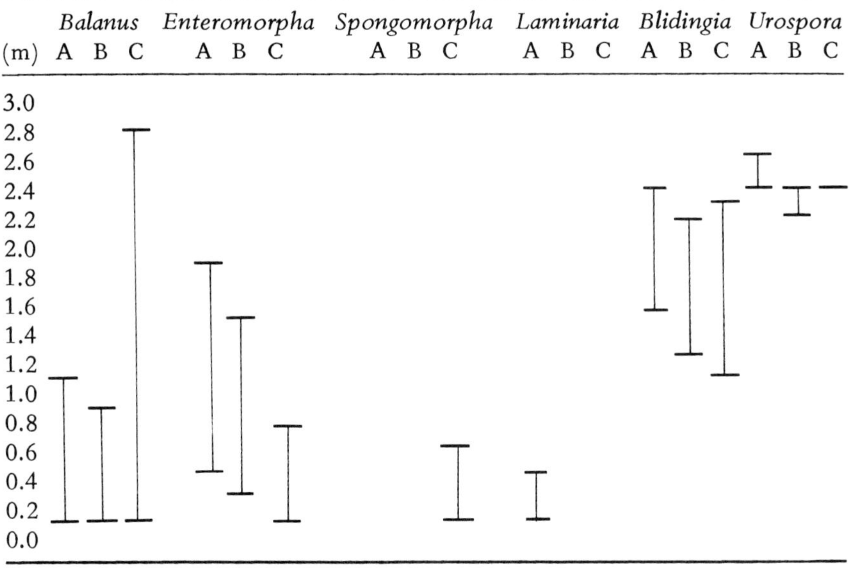

	Balanus			*Enteromorpha*			*Spongomorpha*			*Laminaria*			*Blidingia*			*Urospora*		
(m)	A	B	C	A	B	C	A	B	C	A	B	C	A	B	C	A	B	C
3.0																		
2.8																		
2.6																		
2.4																		
2.2																		
2.0																		
1.8																		
1.6																		
1.4																		
1.2																		
1.0																		
0.8																		
0.6																		
0.4																		
0.2																		
0.0																		

Wooden battens were put in the sea and fixed at the depth shown (metres above chart datum). The battens were facing the shore and about 25 m from it. Sampling was in August, the battens being put out in March (A), May (B) and June (C). Presence at time of sampling is shown. *Balanus* colonized successfully on the June battens but was still prevented from entering the canopy of *Urospora*, *Enteromorpha* and *Blidingia*, this canopy being already present on the March and May battens. Thus, *Balanus* was less common on the March and May battens than on the June battens. In May, *Spongomorpha* was virtually prevented from penetrating the *Enteromorpha* canopy, the latter already growing on the March batten and then entirely excluding *Spongomorpha*. Competition immediately after settling, or absence of propagule input, also prevented *Spongomorpha* development, in June. *Urospora* was excluded, after canopy growth and development, from all but the uppermost parts of the battens, although it was still capable of competition where the *Blidingia* canopy was weakest.

Many species colonized the surface so well that further settlement did not take place until the first canopy broke up. First canopies therefore can affect subsequent settlement for long periods. Because the succession may be so easily side-stepped, interpretation of successional data must not be too rigid; there are always different options available. The uppermost parts of the shore (2.5–3.4 m) are easier to interpret (Fig. 12) because of the small number of species present.

Temporal or spatial "shuttering" by the algae causes many familiar boundaries. For instance, a good feature by which to identify mature communities is the occurrence of a break in the barnacle cover in the upper part of the barnacle zone. This break lies either within the *Balanus* zone or between the *Balanus* and *Chthamalus* zones at about

Table IX. Temporal partitioning of communities caused by differing toxicities of substrata. This experiment utilizes analogues of toxic substrata, as e.g. slag, used for reclamation. Various chemicals or mixtures of chemicals were soaked into nylon rope and species numbers present thereon assessed after 5 months. There was a gradation of effect from permitted development of mature fairly diverse communities to limitation to juvenile communities. Cover and development state of communities both derive from subjective visual assessment. The causal factor is assumed to be the time over which each chemical exerted its toxic effects. Overall diversity is dependent on chance as well as space. Species habitually spreading as fragments are sporadic, whilst *Scytosiphon* has been able to break in at any stage (cf. Fletcher and Chamberlain, 1975)

	Treatment										
	1	2	3	4	5	6	7	8	9	10	11
Appearance											
Well mixed cover	+	+	+	+	+	+	+	+			
Large green algae		+	+								
Small green algae				+	+	+					
Green algal sporelings							+	+			
Filamentous brown algae								+			
Abundant diatoms					+		+	+	+	+	+
Bare substratum											+
Macrophyte cover (%)	100	80	90	80	20	40	80	80	1	1	1
Animals											
Jassa spp.	+	+	+	+	+	+		+			
Mytilus edulis	+	+	+		+	+	+	+			
Hydroids	+			+						+	
Algae											
Bryopsis plumosa					+						
Chaetomorpha capillaris		+	+			+					
Cladophora sericea		+					+				
Enteromorpha intestinalis (i)	+	+	+		+	+	+				
(ii)	+	+	+		+		+	+			
(iii)				+							
Monostroma fuscum							+				
Spongomorpha arcta					+						
Ulva lactuca	+	+	+	+	+	+	+				
Ectocarpus fasciculatus					+						
Giffordia granulosa		+	+		+		+				
G. sandriana											+
G. secunda	+			+				+			
G. spp.?											+

Table IX (*continued*) . . .

	Treatment										
	1	2	3	4	5	6	7	8	9	10	11
Laminaria saccharina	+		+	+	+			+			+
Petalonia fascia	+										
Scytosiphon lomentaria	+	+	+				+	+	+	+	+
Antithamnion cruciatum						+					
A. floccosum			+		+						
Audouinella caespitosa	+		+		+	+					
A. secundata[a, b]	+	+		+							
Callithamnion hookeri[a]				+							
Ceramium rubrum	+	+	+	+	+	+	+	+			
Erythrotrichia carnea[b]	+	+	+	+	+	+	+				
Nitophyllum punctatum[b]					+						
Polysiphonia elongata	+		+			+	+				
P. urceolata[c]							+				
P. violacea[b]	+						+				
Porphyra leucosticta	+										
Rhodomela confervoides	+										
No. algal species	15	10	12	8	13	8	12	5	1	1	4

Chemicals (vertical columns)
1 = Control; 2 = "Diuron"; 3 = TTD (Tetramethylthiuram disulphide); 4 = Zinc pentachlorophenate; 5 = Tributyl tin fluoride + TTD; 6 = Copper pentachlorophenate; 7 = "Monuron"; 8 = Tributyl tin fluoride; 9 = Tributyl tin oxide + TTD; 10 = Tributyl tin oxide; 11 = Tributyl tin oxide + TTD + "Monuron".

[a]epizoic population
[b]epiphytes
[c]input as fragments
+ = present
no symbol = absent

the level of + 2.9 m. It is caused by a winter covering of *Urospora* spp. and of Cyanophyta that prevents settlement of the cyprid stage. *Blidingia* is a frequent preempter, as is also the diatom film lower down on the beach in spring. Fucoid cover can prevent smaller species from growing, although this of course could result from action later in the settlement sequence. Another commonly seen mosaic is that of *Prasiola* and *Blidingia*. Shuttering by barnacles and *Mytilus* may also occur. Simple experiments using a paint which subsequently flakes off can be used to mimic the effect. Fouling experiments with adjuvents of differing toxicities (Table IX) provide other analogies to the "natural" situation in which temporal partitioning is a response to differing toxicities of substrara; see Table IX legend for further explanation.

Fine sediment coating the surface of rocks certainly inhibits early settlement, as was shown by some preliminary observations at Hunterston on a site affected by silt movements from the construction of a nearby rig yard. A similar result could be possible were iron ore release to occur.

Preemption by a slick of oil or sediment or an established stand is a common cause of mosaicing in disturbed habitats. Temporal or spatial shuttering phenomena are a most important line of evidence in assessing community age and hence long-term stability. Many familiar boundaries are caused and persist in old communities.

It seems that the effects from shuttering persist for different periods at different heights on the beach. In environments with the heaviest environmental stress, the species diversity will in any case be low. In the long-term development of species diversity this factor is critical. Areas already polluted sufficiently to reduce or remove grazing activity will frequently allow greater establishment of algal cover than non-polluted ones.

Stage 10: Ability to break in

An attribute of some species is that they first appear amongst an already-growing stand. The commonest example is that of *Enteromorpha intestinalis* and mid-shore fucoids. The abundance of either is a function of spore release timing, as given in Fig. 9; subsequent conditions control the long-term survival of either.

The partial shuttering by other algae in open cover is a frequent occurrence at lower levels on the beach. *Scytosiphon* is a notable example. This also occurs with *Pilayella* and low-growing *Ectocarpus* and *Giffordia* spp.

The time-scale of maturation of the succession varies widely. Some examples of the build-up are discussed below. Table X shows details of transects around the edge of a slot, cut in a fucoid canopy, which enabled a diatom settlement to preempt the surface; this caused changes which were persistent for at least 3 years after the damage. This is an effect which could be picked up after a pollution incident only affecting a small area.

Climax communities which allow for very little entry are characteristic of both tidal and subtidal areas. Whether exclusion occurs at cellular level or through the activities of herbivores working almost synergistically will not be dealt with here.

Stage 11: Attachment

Though there are well-known data in the literature on spore attachment, e.g. Linskens (1966) and Luther (1976), these data are not much use for facies interpretation because of the narrow range of species considered.

It seems that many pollutants act at the attachment stage, either by predisposing an already present flora to prevent break in by a species (e.g. *Urospora* cover will prevent most other species) or by coating the surface. Oil prevented all but the *Urospora* and *Monostroma wittrockii* from settling at Troon in the more heavily-oiled parts of the harbour, and low levels of diesel oil as a film prevented the development of all but juvenile phases of the succession at a temporary harbour during the construction phase at Hunterston. As soon as construction ceased so did the succession advance.

Stage 12: Establishment

Several experiments have been carried out in an attempt to increase the exegetic use of the earlier parts of the settlement processes. The literature would suggest that the regular placing of panels (*vide* Chapter 13, this volume) could provide an easily controlled and operated pollution-monitoring method, assessed for oil monitoring with *Mytilus* for example. Logistical problems preclude their use in low-budget work, although such experimental data are necessary for understanding the processes as a whole.

Stage 13: Presence at Suitable Niveaux

This includes processes leading to active selection of level on the beach. This is restricted to spore-bearing fragments being stranded or entangled near the normal level. The significance of rapid spore adhesion needs more study. The topic also includes all normal physiological requirements which might become more restricting

Table X a, b. Transects traversing both diversity increase at slot margin and effects of preempted space

(a) runs from silt/diatom cover to fucoid cover in shelter from wave-action

Sample	1	2	3	4	5	6	7	8	9	10
Cladophora albida	1	1	1	–	2	5	3	7	3	–
Polysiphonia nigrescens	–	1	–	–	–	–	–	–	–	–
Enteromorpha intestinalis	–	1	–	–	–	–	–	–	–	–
Pilayella littoralis	–	–	1	–	–	–	–	1	–	–
Ceramium rubrum	–	–	–	1	–	–	1	–	–	–
Monostroma wittrockii	–	–	–	1	1	–	–	–	–	–
Spongomorpha arcta	–	–	–	1	–	–	–	–	–	–
Ulva sp. A	–	–	–	1	1	1	–	–	–	–
Spacelaria radicans	–	–	–	–	3	–	–	–	–	–
Gigartina stellata	–	–	–	–	–	1	–	–	–	–
Polysiphonia urceolata	–	–	–	–	–	2	3	–	–	–
Membranoptera alata	–	–	–	–	–	–	2	–	5	–
Ulva lactuca	–	–	–	–	–	–	1	–	1	1
Porphyra leucosticta	–	–	–	–	–	–	–	1	–	–
Audouinella floridula	–	–	–	–	–	–	–	1	1	–
Chondrus crispus	–	–	–	–	–	–	–	–	–	3
Fucus hybrids	–	–	–	–	–	–	–	–	–	6
Total algal cover	1	3	2	4	7	9	10	10	10	10
Diatom silt cover	9	7	8	6	3	1	0	0	0	0
No. of taxa	1	3	2	4	3	4	5	4	4	3

(b) runs from silt/diatom cover to fucoid cover seawards (towards greater exposure to wave-action)

Sample	1	2	3	4	5	6	7	8	9	10
Scytosiphon lomentaria	1	–	–	–	–	–	–	–	–	–
Audouinella floridula	1	–	–	–	–	–	–	–	–	–
Cladophora albida	–	–	–	1	–	1	1	1	1	–
"Conchocelis"	–	–	–	1	–	1	1	1	1	–
Ulva sp. A	–	–	–	1	–	–	–	–	–	–
Pilayella littoralis	–	–	–	–	2	1	1	6	1	1
Ceramium rubrum	–	–	–	–	–	1	–	–	–	–
Polysiphonia nigrescens	–	–	–	–	–	4	5	–	–	–
Bryopsis plumosa	–	–	–	–	–	–	1	–	–	–
Monostroma wittrockii	–	–	–	–	–	–	1	–	–	–
Polysiphonia urceolata	–	–	–	–	–	–	–	1	4	1
Ulva rigida	–	–	–	–	–	–	–	1	–	–

Table X (b) (*continued*) . . .

Sample	1	2	3	4	5	6	7	8	9	10
Fucus hybrids	–	–	–	–	–	–	–	–	1	8
Petalonia fascia	–	–	–	–	–	–	–	–	1	–
Ulva lactuca	–	–	–	–	–	–	–	–	1	–
Total algal cover	2	0	0	3	2	8	10	10	10	10
Diatom/sand cover	8	10	10	7	8	2	0	0	0	0
No. of taxa	2	0	0	3	1	5	6	5	7	3

Algae scored for abundance (1–10) at 5 cm intervals; sample size 2 cm^2. Species in order of occurrence. Original settlement on this horizontal surface of a concrete block at mean tide level was dense cover of fucoid hybrids. The slot (size 0.5 m × 1.0 m) was cut in July 1976 by scraping and application of formalin. Present data from March 1979. Further fucoid regeneration has not occurred. After cleaning, a diatom/sand carpet developed; into this *Sphacelaria radicans* and *Audouinella floridula* later penetrated from centres of development. Just after scraping, dredging offsite caused high suspended-solid loadings in the surrounding water and maintenance of the slot was probably partly caused by this. The slot shows the time for which effects of damage may persist and be recognized. If canopy conditions were suitable in a year to allow fucoid input, an additional 5 years (2 for the first input to develop, with break-up beginning in the third year and the community becoming of uneven age by the fifth year, thus resembling typical unevenly-aged mature stands) would be necessary for the slot to merge with the surrounding vegetation. The sequence of species across the transects reflects aspects of the succession. A gradation of species across the boundaries seems a standard feature which has considerable potential.

under polluted conditions, or which have a greater bearing under conditions of competition, discussed below (Russell and Fielding, 1974).

Stage 14: Survival

This is one of the most useful links in the settlement process. In general initial colonization of all species occurs over a much wider band than their usual mature occurrence. Zone accuracy is thus a prime indicator of community age and is of great predictive value. In some cases, it has been noticed that on an alternative substratum algae characteristic of one zone may be found in another. For example in undisturbed habitats *Prasiola*, so characteristic of the extreme HWM, can also occur epiphytically near the chart datum line. Many other species have been seen to do this and the phenomenon is particularly common with fine filamentous deep-water species.

At the limit of their depth tolerance they tend to grow epiphytically rather than epilithically. Seasonality can have the same effect. For instance in *Bangia*, which may regularly be found on the low shore in spring as well as in its more usual HWM habitat.

In general, most of the intertidal algae are found outside their zone in juvenile and disturbed communities. It seems to be accepted that the tolerance range of the majority of species is wide enough to mean that factors external to the organism are responsible for the precise zonation of most species.

Stage 15: Intra- and Interspecific Plant Reactions

Intraspecific reactions, although of obvious importance in forming the ultimate appearance of a community, have not so far yielded much of exegetic significance. Certain species form a continuous basal substratum where lack of mutual competition must be an advantage in preventing entry of other species, e.g. primarily, as in *Gigartina, Dumontia* or *Hildenbrandia*, or secondarily, as in *Enteromorpha compressa* or *Pseudendoclonium*. Interspecific reactions have, however, provided a rich vein of exegetes owing to the vertical environmental cline in the intertidal. Interpretation is at present still poor since the situation is very complex, and many reactions are barely explained. The potential full range of a species is very seldom achieved. Normally competition limits the range; knowing the type and nature of the competitors leads one to indications of the age and stability of the community. As a community ages, one would expect to get more and more closely defined zones. Zone sharpness itself is shown to occur in many species from Keppel slip and in the Hunterston site data. An interdigitating horizontal boundary implies either a perfectly matched species pair or a young or disturbed (i.e. rejuvenated) community. A linear horizontal boundary implies that several generations of continuity have passed. One must watch out for other causes of clear-cut horizontal limits, for example, temporal partition development of the high shore "winter exploitation zone", or the few cases where a physiological requirement lets a species come to its limit without a contact. Such examples show that one has to know the exact tolerances and limits of the species concerned. Some species (often the rare ones) are always overrun, others always survive. In stressed (high shore) environments, the *Pelvetia/Fucus spiralis*, *Pelvetia/Porphyra*, *Porphyra/Blidingia* contacts are all boundaries to watch for. In medium-stress milieux contacts of *Ascophyllum/Gigartina*, both plants are characteristic of late maturity in the succession, whilst *Gigartina/Phymatolithon polymorphum* contacts are all indicators of age. Polluted environments with reduced species-range can have species pairs with clear-cut horizontal boundaries, as such delayed seral stage communities with their juvenile community species range could have been developing for sufficient time for sharpness to have occurred, though with a smaller number of species.

The essential experiments here are at present only in progress; this should be an area for wider general examination. One requires a comparison between very gently sloping beaches and vertical beaches which would provide observations on zone sharpening through competition. Clearly, sharpening between a species pair should be better developed in the first rather than in the second type of beach. This would also help to explain unanswered problems of lower diversity on horizontal beaches.

Zone sharpening is clearly the other aspect of zone width. Zone width is of high exegetic value in the detection of disturbance. Young communities in the intertidal zone have wide zones, generally through preemption of settlement space. Thus Pielou's (1975) description of the process has a strongly applied side. Numerous cases of apparent migration have been described in the past (e.g. by Rees, 1940) and most instances of this are caused by competitive pressure forcing a less able species up or down a beach (Figs 10 and 11) except in instances of a moving fertility band following seasonal environmental change (e.g. in *Dumontia*). Any disturbance prevents this from happening. For example, *Porphyra* generally can settle in winter over the whole intertidal. In older communities it is found to retreat, or be pushed upwards or downwards off the intertidal. Grazing pressure prevents it being common downwards and so it occupies a narrow band at the top. Disturbed (and ungrazed) communities may have a continuous *Porphyra* cover, which may even be persistent. At Southannan beach *Porphyra* was only present at the extreme low or high water marks, except at disturbed or new areas. An example was on the mid-shore shell bank, which behaved as a new surface for algal settlement, or in ruts in a shingle beach caused by sewer-extending operations.

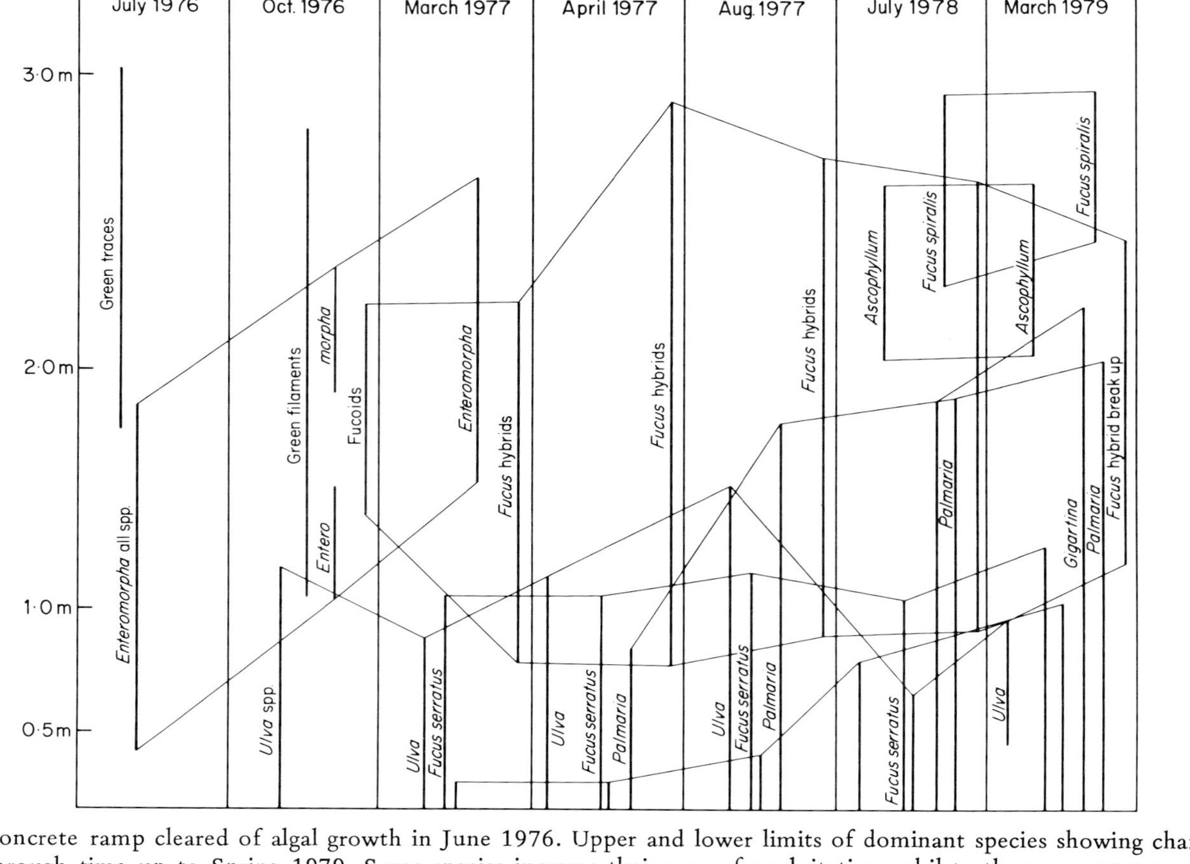

Fig. 11. Concrete ramp cleared of algal growth in June 1976. Upper and lower limits of dominant species showing changes through time up to Spring 1979. Some species increase their area of exploitation, whilst others are outcompeted. Seasonal effects are superimposed.

Porphyra persisted until outcompeted by *Enteromorpha* species on the shell bank, or outgrazed by littorinids on the track marks.

Further illustrations of this are easily observed; *Pelvetia*, for example, is pushed upwards until it occupies a narrow fringe. This takes about 4 years to complete. Examples (as in sea lochs) where it occupies a wider band are probably caused by disturbance from the effects of fresh water. *Blidingia* is pushed downwards or upwards by *Porphyra*, up by fucoids or *Gigartina*, or itself can push *Urospora* upwards (Fig. 12).

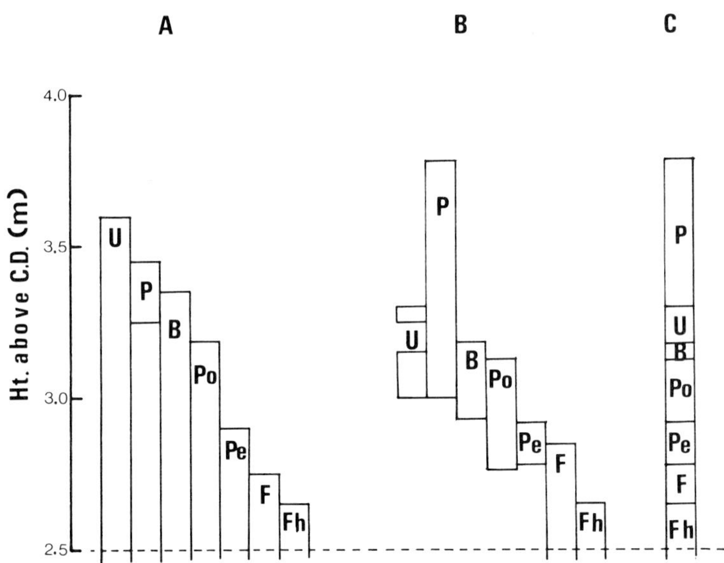

Fig. 12. Exegetic values of zone widths and zone sharpening at Hunterston. A, Original or subsequent settlement limits over 4 years (from July 1975). B, Species present in February 1979. C, Present dominant species at levels given. Zonation pattern has same limits at Keppel pier. Except in *Prasiola*, the zones have narrowed and sharpened as stability increased, with some species pushed back to their physical limits where they become poor competitors (*Porphyra*, *Pelvetia*). Other species are restricted above and below by competitors. This epitomizes one dimension of the potential and realized niches achieved by the species concerned. Data for south side of Hunterston causeway. Key: U = *Urospora bangioides*; P = *Prasiola stipitata*; B = *Blidingia minima*; Po = *Porphyra umbilicalis*; Pe = *Pelvetia canaliculata*; F = *Fucus spiralis*; Fh = Fucoid hybrids.

Table XI. Increase in species diversity as the succession advances

		Keppel Slip No. of spp. per quadrat (0.1 m²)								Old Pier Max. No. per level shown within climax		
		Stripped June 1976					Stripped Nov. 1975			Grazed	Climax	
Months of age		2	4	10	14	33	17	21	40	?	?	
at date: months		8	10	3	8	3	3	8	3	7	2	
at date: year	[19]	76	76	77	77	79	77	77	79			
Q	*Ht.*											
1												
2							1					
3		0	0	1	0	1	—	0	1			MHWS
4		0	0	1	0	1	1	0	2	0	2	
5		0	0	2	0	2	2	0	2	5	14	
6		0	0	2	0	3	2	0	2			
7		0	0	2	0	2	2	0	2			
8	3 m	0	0	4	0	2	3	0	2	3	5	
9		1	3	5	0	1	4	0	3			
10		3	4	5	3	5(2)	5	2	4			MHWN
11		4	4	6	4	5(3)	4	4	5			
12		—	9	7	6	5	—	6	5	2	5	
13		—	7	5	2	4(3)	—	6	5	2	5	
14		—	7	3	7	8(4)	—	4	4			
15		5	6	4	6	7(4)	—	3	4			
16		—	6	4	4	7(3)	—	3	6			
17		—	8	3	6	6	—	4	6			MSL
18	2 m	—	3	9	6	9(6)	—	4	7	2	5	
19		—	5	4	5	9	—	3	12			
20		6	6	5	4	9	5	4	10			
21		5	5	7	5	8	8	4	13			
22		—	4	7	8	8	—	8	—	2	5	
23		6	4	6	—	14	—	5	—			
24		—	4	—	5	—	—	12	12	5	10	
25		—	6	7	—	—	11	5	15			MLWN
26	1 m	—	5	14	11	11	14	—	15	11	15	
27		—	—	7	—	—	15	—	16			
28		6	—	10	—	21	12	14	18	14	—	
29		—	—	8	15	—	18	17	25	—	—	MLWS
30	0.5	4	—	8	—	18	—	—	24	29	30	
31		—	—	12	—	15	—	15	15			
32		—	—	16	—	17	—	—	10			
33		—	—	12	—	27	—	—	17			
34		—	—	—	—	—	—	—	12			

In summary, a wide zone implies a short period for competition and a narrow one a long period. Fixing the time limits for these depends on the natural history of the algae concerned. Generally, it may be said that high stress environments have zones which reach their minimum width in a season and low stress environments may require a number of years.

Another exegete concomitant with competition is the steady loss of species in older communities. Settlement data almost always show this. At Millport, communities with greatest overall diversity appear at about 1 year for the upper shore and 2 or 3 for the lower (Table XI). Some subtidal communities (Table XII) do not conform. Lower shore communities which remain diverse are often kept so by normal environmental disturbance. Very low diversity may indicate the presence of some overriding stress factor as, for example, at the beach at Hunterston power station. Diversity, as pointed out earlier, is also controlled by microhabitat range and species stock, size and life-form, and its use as an exegete needs to be handled with great care.

There are many reasons for diversity to increase as a community matures. One is for epiphyte numbers to increase. The response of epiphytes as a pollution monitor has been used in the past, but it is

---

The table compares species numbers on an inclined boat slip with those on a vertical pier wall bearing an intensely-grazed community. The quadrats on the slip were stripped, using formalin, in June 1976 and November 1975. All the quadrats were scored for overall appearance, but only a representative sample of plants was identified. The values on the right show the number of species in a 10 cm-wide band down the vertical wall in an attempt to provide comparable figures. The ages of the sampled communities at the sampling dates appear above appropriate columns. Figures under Q and *Ht* respectively represent 0.1 m^2 quadrats that are 1 m apart on the Keppel Slip, and the exact heights relative to CD at convenient intervals.

On the slip, the total number of species reduces in summer on the upper parts of the section. In the middle section, the numbers have started to reduce (parentheses indicate number in grazed areas of the quadrats). On the lowest parts environmental instability prevents much reduction, although the cover of the understory is very low. As the succession advances, the species-ranges, with composition and abundance, change. The quadrat lines on the slip were 1 m apart (see Table VII for different fucoid cover). By 1979, the first settlement of fucoids was depauperate and breaking-up; *Ascophyllum nodosum* had successfully settled between Q18 and Q12.

On the vertical pier wall the number of species also increased in winter, especially where just out of the range of grazing molluscs.

The details of the build-up and loss of species is a valuable source of basic information on the individual behaviour of the species concerned. Unless the attributes of the species in a particular area are known, it is difficult to make field interpretations at sites whose previous history is not available. No amount of simplification into mathematical abstraction can give a clearer picture.

Table XII. Total number of species settling on bricks placed at the limit of foliose algae in the sublittoral. It was expected that, as no complete canopy would be formed at the depth used, temporal partitioning would not occur. However, there was a strong element of that partitioning; it seemed to be caused by silting and diatom growth, which prevented development by subsequent arrivals. The succession at this depth is very similar to that on the upper part of the beach in the "winter exploitation zone"; there, in the time available (summer) for growth, species numbers increase quite rapidly and then undergo reduction again, with very few surviving the winter. No further samples were taken and the remaining bricks have been left for settlement by crustose algae

	J	F	M	A	M	J	Jy	A	S	O	N	D	J
D	1		0	5		7	?	10		9	8	7	1
J			0	8		14	13	15		10	4	5	10
F													
M				2		9	9	12		9	7	12	1
A						6	6	8		10	9	6	7
M													
J							3	6		1	8	4	4
Jy								0		0	0	0	0
A										0	0	0	0
S													
O											0	0	0
N												0	1
D													0

not the case that epiphyte loadings automatically decrease towards a pollutant source. Some pollution probably causes an increase and this may be a good indicator of seral interruption either *per se* or at the base of a zone where a species is debilitated, e.g. *Pelvetia*. If standing stock is also decreasing then so will epiphytism. The full use of epiphyte flora has remained unresolved for exegetic purposes. One reason for this is the complex nature of the data collected. Table XIII shows the use of epiphyte relationships for interpretive purposes and Table XIV suggests intricate relationships between epiphyte loads and fucoid hybrids.

Experiments to see whether the age of the community is associated with greater epiphytism have not yet proved conclusive, even though it seems clear that this is so. So much depends on the number of species, the number of commoner preferred host plants, and the succession of those host plants.

A potentially useful area for indicators is in the assessing of the

Table XIII a. Epiphytism and other interspecific contacts

In order to increase the monitoring value of inter-algal contacts, they may be reviewed along the following lines.

(1) Neutral physical contact
  Intertwining, e.g. *Chaetomorpha capillaris* on *Cladophora sericea*
  Abutment, e.g. *Hildenbrandia crouanii* and *H. rubra*

(2) Effect causing reaction
  Repulsion at a distance, e.g. *H. rubra* and *Pseudendoclonium submarinum*
  Lifting, e.g. *Ralfsia verrucosa* and blue-green algae
  Smothering and debilitating
    Epiphytic facultative, e.g. *Pilayella littoralis* on *C. sericea*
    Epiphytic obligate, e.g. *Audouinella secundata*
    Parasitic facultative, e.g. *Streblonema* phases on fucoids
    Endophytic obligate, e.g. *Codiolum petrocelidis* in *Petrocelis cruenta*
  Passive penetration, e.g. *Chaetomorpha melagonium* through *Phymatolithon polymorphum*
  Hypertrophy inducing penetration, e.g. *Ralfsia* spp. within *Lithophyllum incrustans*

effects of sedimentary pollution. Boney (1978) showed that algae have different abilities as collectors of iron ore dust. Good collectors would, if debilitated, be less able to reject epiphytes. The suggestion that debilitated state of a host plant enhances the collection of epiphytes by that host could be made in view of the easily verified result of partially killing some of the larger intertidal algae such as *Fucus* or *Gigartina.* A low concentration of formalin causes a normal succession to start on either of these. This presumably is the reason behind the occasionally considerable epiphyte cover on fucoids growing in eutrophic environments (e.g. river mouths). Restricting observations to a handful of epiphyte collectors might be an easier approach to their exegetic use.

One great value in assessing epiphyte loads is that the community may be sequenced according to which of a species pair "wins" under which sets of conditions. The community as one finds it is thus more easily interpreted (Fig. 13).

Other aspects of behaviour between two species may be of use for community sequencing. Many crustose and some filamentous algae lie over one another. A matrix of contacts showing these relationships is of value in community sequencing. Furthermore, if two

Table XIII b. Lattice diagram of epiphytic and other inter-algal relationships

	A. secundata	*C. hookeri*	*C. roseum*	*C. diaphanum*	*C. albida*	*C. rupestris*	*E. intestinalis*	*E. compressa*	*E. prolifera*	*E. carnea*	*G. pusillum*	*I. sphaerophora*	*P. littoralis*	*R. riparium*	*S. arcta*	a	b	c
Audouinella secundata	×	0	0	0	1	1	1	1	1	0	1	0	1	0	1	8	0	6
Callithamnion hookeri	0	×	0	0	1	1	0	0	0	0	1	2	0	2	0	3	2	9
C. roseum	0	0	×	0	1	1	0	0	0	0	1	2	0	2	0	3	2	9
Ceramium diaphanum	0	0	0	×	0	0	0	0	0	0	0	0	0	2	0	0	1	13
Cladophora albida	2	2	2	0	×	0	0	0	0	2	0	2	2	2	0	0	7	7
C. rupestris	2	2	2	0	0	×	0	0	0	2	0	2	2	2	0	0	7	7
Enteromorpha compressa	2	0	0	0	0	0	×	0	0	0	0	0	0	2	0	0	2	12
E. intestinalis (tubul.)	2	0	0	0	0	0	0	×	0	0	0	0	0	2	0	0	2	12
E. prolifera	2	0	0	0	0	0	0	0	×	0	0	0	0	2	0	0	2	12
Erythrotrichia carnea	0	0	0	0	1	1	0	0	0	×	1	0	1	0	1	5	0	9
Gelidium pusillum	2	2	2	0	0	0	0	0	0	2	×	0	2	2	0	6	0	8
Isthmoplea sphaerophora	0	1	1	0	1	1	0	0	0	0	0	×	0	0	1	5	0	9
Pilayella littoralis	2	0	0	0	1	1	0	0	0	2	1	0	×	2	0	3	3	8
Rhizoclonium riparium	0	1	1	1	1	1	1	1	1	0	1	0	1	×	1	11	0	0
Spongomorpha arcta	2	0	0	0	0	0	0	0	0	2	0	2	0	2	×	0	4	10

The species shown have been scored for epiphytic contact; sample size 20 cm^2. There are 120 potential contacts of interest and each could be scored, as could rarity of occurrence and nature of contact. In this example, recording was restricted to these first order reactions. This enables one to gauge the success of the species concerned, the age of the community and the impact of a pollutant. Examples of the conclusions which may be drawn include: (1) The succession is mid-term, or a delayed stage; some host species have multiple generations of epiphytes, whilst others have only new arrivals. Low numbers of epiphytes imply early stages. (2) Some epiphytes are much more successful than others, e.g. *R. riparium* which, being aggressively competitive, finds conditions more usually exploitable than does, e.g. *P. littoralis*, probably even as regards the occasional inundations of fresh water. (3) Conversely others are less successful than they might be. *P. littoralis* when very aggressive tends to indicate very limiting conditions (e.g. communities oiled by diesel oil). *E. carnea*, if not too early in its life-history, would in general be more frequently found epiphytic. (4) Some species are at risk from being outcompeted; an example here is *G. pusillum*. *Gigartina stellata* might already have been lost through being outcompeted.

The populations were growing adjacent to a waste pipe discharging sea water and occasional fresh water, but little else.

Lattice diagrams give a picture of the dynamic relationships and summarize the net result of competition or growth attributes. The relationships depend on factors such as rarity or season, as well as on direct biological attributes of their competitive ability in the presence or absence of debilitating environmental factors.

Key: 1 = left to right reaction; 2 = right to left reaction; 0 = no reaction in this class of observation; a = total for left to right; b = total for right to left; c = total for no reaction.

Table XIV. Epiphytes on fucoid hybrids. A small sample of older plants was collected from a 3-year-old stand at MTL and scored for epiphyte cover and morphology of host. The data suggest that some hybrids are more susceptible to being epiphytized than others and that this extra load leads to their more rapid removal by water movements. In older communities, one does not very often see heavily epiphytized fucoid adults; this may be a way of observing that the community is still in the early part of the succession. Hybrids are eventually replaced by plants more like the classical species

Nearest name	length	epiflora 1	2	scored	V	T	S	St
Spir/Vesic	31	2	2	L	+	+	–	–
Spir/Vesic	29	2	2	L	+	+	–	–
Spir/Vesic	35	2	2	L	–	+	–	–
Spir/Vesic	35	7	3	H	–	+	–	–
Spir/Vesic	33	2	2	L	–	–	–	–
Spir/Vesic	29	5	4	H	+	+	–	+
Spir/Vesic	39	9	4	H	+	+	–	+
Serr	28	1	1	L	–	+	+	nf
Serr	39	3	4	L	–	–	+	nf
Spir/Serr	17	9	2	H	–	+	+	–
Spir/Serr	17	5	1	H	–	+	+	–
Spir/Serr	29	9	2	H	–	+	+	+
Spir/Serr	25	9	1	H	–	+	+	+
Spir/Vesic	30	9	3	H	–	+	+	–
Spir/Vesic	30	1	1	L	+	–	+	–
Spir/Vesic	42	0	0	L	+	–	+	–
Spir/Vesic	31	0	0	L	–	–	–	–
Vesic/Serr/Vesic	34	2	2	L	+	+	–	–
Vesic/Serr/Vesic	24	6	2	H	–	+	+	+
Vesic/Serr/Vesic	40	0	0	L	–	+	+	–

Key: Spir = *Fucus spiralis*; Vesic = *F. vesiculosus*; Serr = *F. serratus*.
Length = Length of whole adult.
Col 1 = Cover abundance of epiphytes on adult plant, scored 1–10; 2 = Number of epiphyte species, excluding blue-green algae.
Scored = Subjective summary of epiphyte abundance, col. 1 + col. 2: L = low, H = high.
V = presence of vesicles; T = twisted thallus; S = serrations > 0.2 mm long; St = sterile band on receptacle.

species in the same geographic range occupy similar niches then the ascendancy of one over the other should tell us much about the nature of the influence pushing the reaction to one side or the other. We are only in the early stages of assessing the exegetic significance of this. Frequently, in the sublittoral, a species overlaps others in the central part of its range but is itself overlapped outside (Fig. 14).

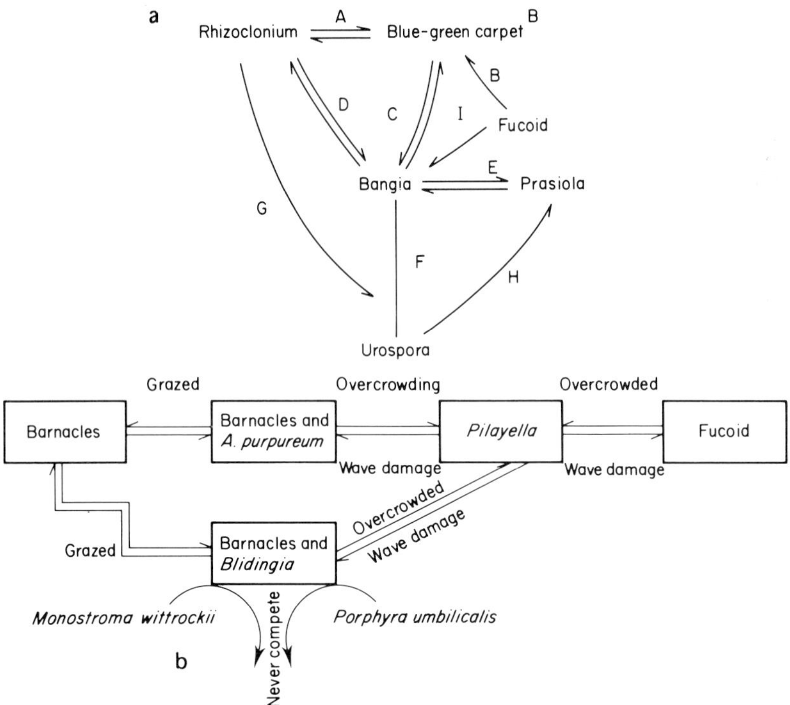

Fig. 13a. Interalgal competition on a pier pile in shadow. The algae present have been considered in pairs from field observations. The nature of the boundaries or the contacts may be then assessed, as an aid to sequencing. (A) Equally matched; competition depends on new input and desiccation. (B) Upper limit of fucoid outcompetes blue-green carpet, shelters herbivores which sharpen the blue-green border; boundary thus moves up. (C) *Bangia* outcompetes blue-green carpet, but this survives summer better. (D) Can mix, both nutrient-enhanced; *Rhizoclonium* only higher because of shadow. (E) Often separated by temporal partition. (F) *Urospora* outcompetes *Bangia*; often found together in polluted places. (G) *Rhizoclonium* more desiccation-resistant under these conditions. (H) *Prasiola crispa* outcompeted and forced downwards. (I) *Bangia* has the advantage on harder substrata. *Deletions*: one would expect *Audouiniella purpurea* and *Waerniella lucifuga* at this level (3.4 m); as they are absent, it is likely that they have been outcompeted and this implies at least twelve months of competition. The community is at climax and similar examples have not been seen to occur within 5 years.

Fig. 13b. Copy of field notebook entry; midshore, Leith mole, 20279, Station 6. The technique can give a rapid summary of major behavioural attributes in the field. Grazers generally low – enables *Monostrome* and others to enter. The community is highly disturbed, zonation weak, mosaicing very common, and species number very low.

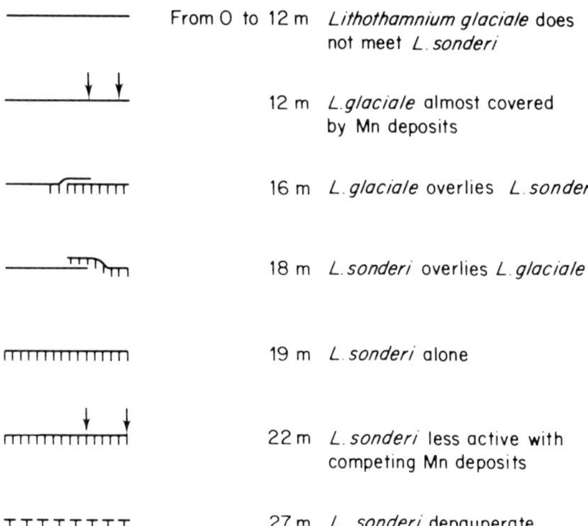

Fig. 14. The behaviour of *Lithothamnium glaciale* and *L. sonderi* down water column. N.B. Limit of the photic zone as defined by *Conchocelis* is 28 m on this transect.

Stage 16: Interspecific Reactions Animal/Plant

The control of mature communities by grazing reactions is well known. The use of these features for interpretation is still at an elementary stage. One result of an onshore pullutant is to remove grazers in an overgrazed community. Most colonization work or before-and-after studies are organized to show that recolonization occurs. This seems never in doubt. The minutie of the events and the interplay between grazers and behavioural attributes of their algal food source are of the highest significance in the search for algal exegetes. The "normal" beach appearance is dependent on grazing and, in turn, thus highly dependent on the requirements of both the grazed crop and the behaviour of the grazer. It is the nature of the equilibrium that we need to typify.

As the algal component of a community ages so does the animal component. Very young communities have no resident grazing population and algal cover reaches a peak which is never later regained. This sequence has been observed at both the Keppel slip and Southannan beach and there is an obvious dependence on nearness of potential input for both the grazing animals and the plants. At the slip, littorinids migrated back after clearance whereas, on the causeway area, input was clearly mostly via the planktonic phase. When the biota were badly out of balance, there was a considerable problem with cast weed at Southannan beach, as discussed above; later on, this was reduced. Further examples of the interplay are zone sharpness (e.g. *Porphyra* being excluded from open but mature communities); *Blidingia* surviving lower on the beach than normal because the slope prevented littorinids from sheltering; maintenance of open glades for long periods. Microtopographical features can lead to some grazing boundaries being persistent over many years (Fig. 15). Community mosaicing in mature low-species-number stands (e.g. cf. *Gigartina*) requires a resident population of herbivores maintaining the open areas but presumably requiring the shelter of the canopy. Both the mature community and the general pattern of the normal beach are conceived to be almost devoid of algal growth, especially on more exposed or abraded areas. Much of the small-scale patterning or mosaicing in the mature community has a microtopographical origin. Other aspects include the maintenance of freedom from epiphytes in mature fucoid and *Gigartina* stands. All these are exegetes of community age and thus of freedom from disturbance. The usual sorts of time-scale range from 3 to 5 years for *Patella* immigration at the causeway to a year for littorinid incursion. One could expect viviparous littorinids to take longer to immigrate. They have not yet entered the causeway area. Low shore limpets seem of significance only in the maintenance of small-scale patterning, e.g. as *Acmaea tessulata*,* or in the maintenance of crust morphology, as with *Acmaea virginea*.

Where disturbance is so strong as to destroy the herbivores present then delayed succession communities appear. Typical examples include freshwater or high nutrient affected areas (Fig. 16 at Erskine ferry, where zonation is poorly developed). Very little is known of practical exegetic use of the modifications of food organisms by pollutants or their nutrient uptake. Grazers may be debilitated by low level pollutants, but it is difficult to transfer the abundant laboratory data in the literature back into the field. Some examples

*Nomenclature and authorities for marine animals mentioned follow the data presented in the Plymouth Marine Fauna (Marine Biological Association, 1957).

we have looked at include a heavily-oiled site at Troon harbour and a site at Leith, where heavy suspended solid loadings have inhibited virtually all grazers.

Stability of the substratum is necessary before any sort of equilibrium is reached. Canopies which often break up may provide poor cover for grazing organisms, as for instance on the shell bank at Southannan (Fig. 17a, b).

Sandy beaches and mudflat areas probably have a number of rather unexpected organisms actively engaged in removing algae.

Management of grazing organisms in the intertidal can be achieved in a number of ways, either by modifying the substratum or by the addition of the animals themselves (Table XV). As a trial, 1100 kg of littorinids were introduced at two sites on the Southannan beach, which then showed a marked enhancement of grazer activity, at the points of introduction. The trial seemed to suggest that a reasonable technique would be to augment the natural number of herbivores or to prevent their being collected from areas which carry too large an algal cover. Figure 18 shows littorinids after the above introduction. So far as we are aware, no one has collected data on the impact of large-scale littorinid removal, although some beaches around the Firth of Clyde appear to have above normal macrophyte cover due to littorinid removal. Certain features of the experimental introduction were unexpected. One case occurred where *Mytilus* byssus threads tied down the littorinids and prevented their feeding (Fig. 19). Other cases occurred where mutual grazing was insufficient to keep the shells free from algae and the animals were then cast up. We considered that these occurrences were the result of low density of littorinids, but were unable further to study the problem. These two phenomena could be used exegetically to characterize low littorinid densities. Even though *Littorina littorea* is a very well-known animal, there are many features not well enough known to allow predictive statements to be made with certainty.

Other techniques for beach management include provision of armouring of a type which allows animals to move from one block to another. Very large armouring is unsuitable for littorinids (they fall between the blocks and cannot climb back) and very small pieces are too mobile. One area which we were able to specify was lined with pebbles; these we considered would be a compromise. There is at present in the UK very little possibility of ensuring that

(a)

(b)

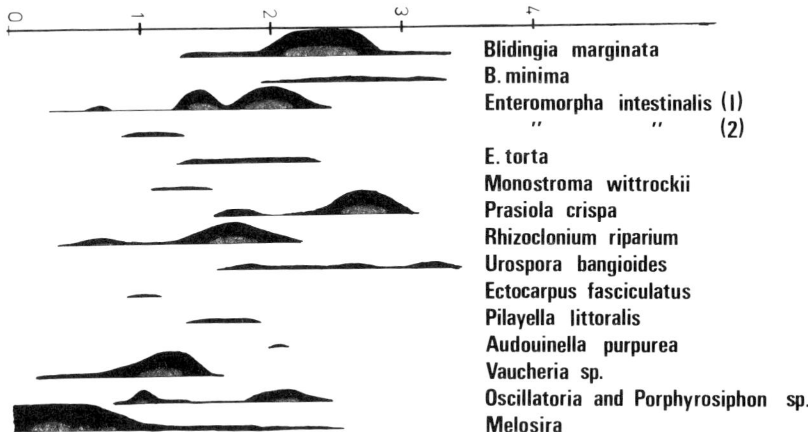

Fig. 16. Delayed-succession communities at Erskine Ferry, R. Clyde. Heights given are relative to arbitrary datum line. Zonation is weakly defined in these types of highly polluted community.

intertidal reclaimed areas are constructed in such a way as to lead to the development of normal rocky shore communities.

Stage 17: The Mature Stand

The key to all the preceding sections lies in locating and interpreting the exegetes to define where the community is in the succession (cf. Murray and Littler, 1978). At maturity, the climax community is the sum of all the preceding stages. There is no consensus for a reasonable definition of the intertidal climax, nor one which would be a guide to knowing whether the overgrazed aspect of most beaches is a climax or a derived or displaced climax. Other problems are to be

---

Fig. 15. Persistence of zonal boundaries near to the Marine Station slipway. (a), 1908. (b), 1979. The boundary on the block with pipe (centre) has now gone. On the boulder next left, the boundary is near where it was, as it is on the boulder behind the pipe. The generally darker appearance of the upper and middle beach at present seems to be caused by blue-green algae and other upper shore algae; it may reflect a local nutrient enhancement.

(a)

found in arguments of whether the single species stand is a worthwhile abstraction, or even as to how ecosystems may be divided.

From the preceding, it must be considered normal for communities to mosaic, for their zonation to sharpen, for normal seasonal changes to take place and so on. What has to be separated off is the behaviour of these exegetes when "normality" is disturbed. It is probable that some of the very robust organisms are themselves potentially inefficient in such cases, and there is no easy way of establishing whether those that are more robust are in fact the key organisms.

To assist in the comprehension of maintenance processes, we rather arbitrarily suggested that communities could be sequenced. We simply set down the contacts between the adjacent species in an interrogative fashion and tried to account by small-scale experimentation or observation for the success of the main species. Community-sequencing diagrams, when drawn and verified, can be used to predict either what would happen if a deletion occurred or if a break in the sequence were to happen. Figure 20 a, b shows the situation in the Firth of Clyde for high-grazed and low-grazed *Gigartina*-dominated communities. The same will apply for any other species.

Appendix I is a summary of the processes, occurring on the beach, that are considered to have exegetic significance; when ascertained, these can be used in conjunction with Appendix II, itself to be used in making the value judgements.

Fig. 17a, b. Shell banks and algal cover at Southannan Beach. The succession (Fig. 17a) advances on *Mytilus* or exposed shell patches. The *Mytilus* shows dark in the photograph. The algal mosaic thus formed is dependent upon the survival of the *Mytilus*; when this mosaic breaks up, either because of anoxic conditions forming under the algal blanket or because of wave damage, the succession regenerates. Wash-outs are formed as seen in the foreground. In the distance may be seen wash-outs caused by bait-digging, better seen in Fig. 17b, and shell debris heaps start again at an early stage of the succession. The surface structure of beaches such as these is fragile by virtue of the buried shell layer and the effect is persistent for at least two years. Larger grazing animals cannot become established under such conditions although, as the whole area did slowly become less juvenile floristically, one must assume that other grazing animals such as harpacticoids, nematodes and polychaetes become increasingly important. Little seems to have been published on these groups and their consumption of macrophytes.

Table XV. Increase in numbers of algal entities across a grazing boundary. Imprecise taxonomic or non-taxonomic groups have also been included, since these may be of utility in assessment of age and grazing intensity. Sample size is 1 cm^2. The transect runs from dense filamentous algae into heavily-grazed crustose forms. The column for 0 cm represents the visually-assessed centre of the boundary strip. The community to the left of centre (30; 20; 10) is multistratose, although predominantly long-lived and attached or short-lived and epiphytic. Certain filamentous species (e.g. *C. albida*) show grazing resistance. A number of species extremely sensitive to grazing occur centrally (column 0); these are presumably either out of reach of, or protected by taller species from, grazing pressure from the right. The right-hand columns (10; 20; 30) include forms adapted to withstand grazing by molluscs. Comments on significance and recognition of such boundaries are presented in Table X.

	Grazing pressure ⟶						
Distance from boundary "centre" (cm)	30	20	10	0	10	20	30
Audouinella purpurea	+	+	+	+	—	—	—
Chaetomorpha capillaris	+	+	—	—	—	—	—
Cladophora albida	+	—	—	+	+	—	—
C. sericea	+	+	—	—	—	—	—
Enteromorpha intestinalis (cornucop)	+	+	+	—	—	—	—
E. intestinalis (prolif)	+	+	+	+	+	—	—
E. intestinalis (tubular)	+	—	+	+	—	—	—
Erythrotrichia carnea	+	+	+	—	—	—	—
Gigartina stellata (upper part)	+	+	+	+	+	—	—
Pilayella littoralis	+	+	—	—	—	—	—
Porphyra leucosticta	+	—	—	—	—	—	—
Rhizoclonium riparium	+	+	—	+	—	—	—
Sphacelaria radicans	+	+	+	—	—	—	—
Streblonemoid forms	+	+	+	—	—	—	—
Callithamnion hookeri	—	+	—	—	—	—	—
Gigartina stellata (base)	—	+	+	+	+	+	+
Spongomorpha arcta	—	+	—	—	—	—	—
Audouinella secundata	—	—	+	+	—	—	—
Blidingia marginata	—	—	—	+	—	—	—
"*Conchocelis*"	—	—	—	+	+	+	+
Cyanophytes	—	—	—	+	+	+	+
Monostroma wittrockii	—	—	—	+	—	—	—
Pseudendoclonium submarinum	—	—	—	+	+	—	—
Rosenvingiella polyrhiza	—	—	—	+	—	—	—
Urospora bangioides	—	—	—	+	—	—	—
Urospora (base)	—	—	—	+	—	—	—
Phymatolithon lenormandii	—	—	—	—	—	—	+
Number of taxa (excluding *Balanus*)	14	14	10	16	7	3	4
Balanus balanoides	—	—	—	+	+	+	+

Diversity indices are probably too abstract to be used routinely on algal communities, unless over very small areas. Also, techniques involving randomizing run the risk of confusing boundaries. To illustrate this point, simple minimal area curves have been drawn for the communities on the Old Pier at Millport (Fig. 21). In each, there is a gentle climb as one transgresses the boundaries of the small-scale patterning. With approximately 120 species to be found along a few yards of wall, it is hardly surprising that this patterning is on a very small scale.

Mapping of the geographical extent of individual species shows that the Hunterston site is very close to the boundary where there is a marked discontinuity. Although there are suitable substrata on either side of the boundary, some very obvious species do not survive in the Channel (e.g. *Laminaria hyperborea*, *Ptilota plumosa*, *Plocamium cartilagineum*).

Some indicator species are to be found in the algal flora. Most of the species regarded as such are also indicators of succession. Indicator species include well-known plants such as *Fucus ceranoides* (marking the freshwater input region); *Enteromorpha clathrata* (marking the more saline areas); *E. prolifera* (marking less saline areas); *Vaucheria* spp. (in less-oxygenated areas of the environmental lake). For other indicators of succession, see Clokie and Boney (1979). It is noticeable that species missing in the Fairlie Channel seem to be from around the Chart Datum line.

Many species show morphological changes (under different conditions) which may be used for interpreting processes, e.g. *Gigartina stellata* in the stressed area near the Hunterston Power Station outfall or adjacent to any sewer pipe where colour, morphology and strength change with increase in distance. *Ascophyllum nodosum* shows the same effects; at the hot water outfall mentioned above, it has become increasingly changed and has disappeared from quite large areas. This topic was reviewed by Russell (1978) and is of great importance for interpretative purposes.

CONCLUSION

Details of the changes at Hunterston have been discussed throughout the text as examples of the data classes being sought. Communities on new sea walls behaved more or less within the framework of

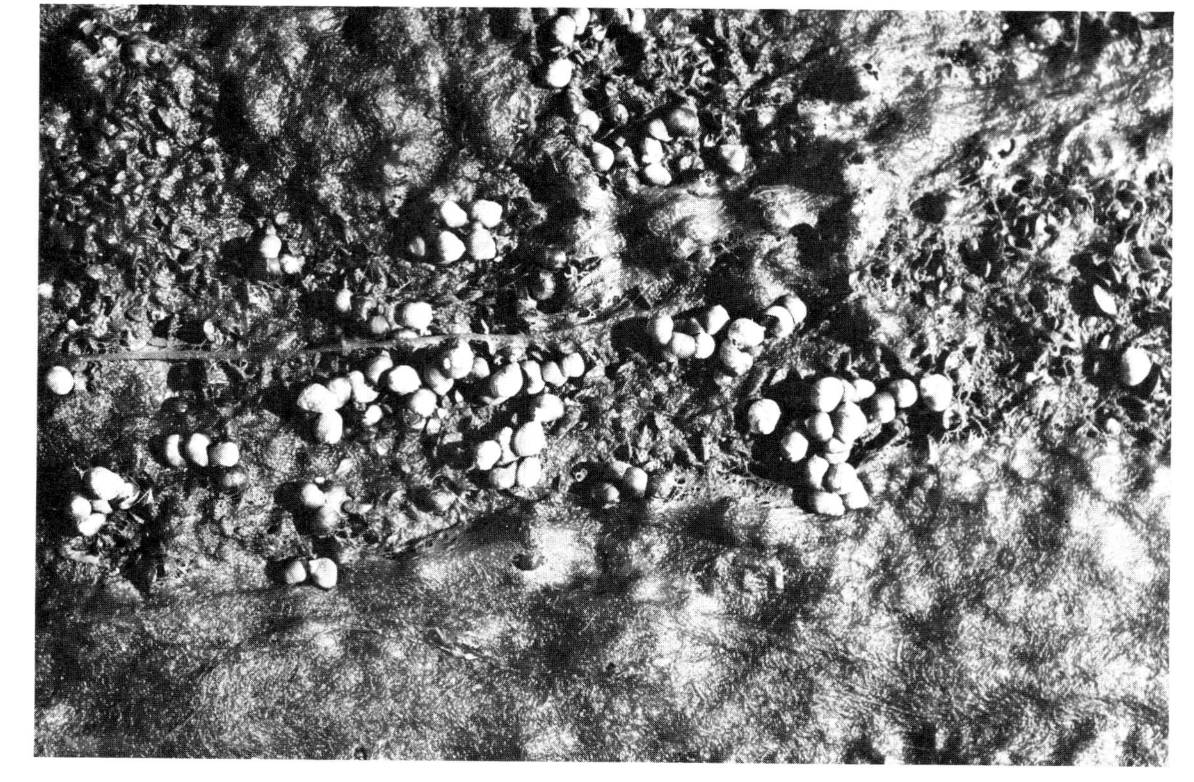

Fig. 18. *Littorina* spp. one week after introduction. Young *Mytilus* have been exposed by removal of filamentous *Enteromorpha*, including *E. intestinalis* varieties and *E. clathrata*. Survival seems good, so long as the populations are at a sufficiently high density.

Fig. 19. *Littorina* spp. trapped by *Mytilus* byssus threads. These were fastened into the *Mytilus* bed and the phenomenon seems to be one of the side effects of low density populations. Another is excessive growth of epizoic algae, which are not removed by mutual grazing, causing their removal by water movements.

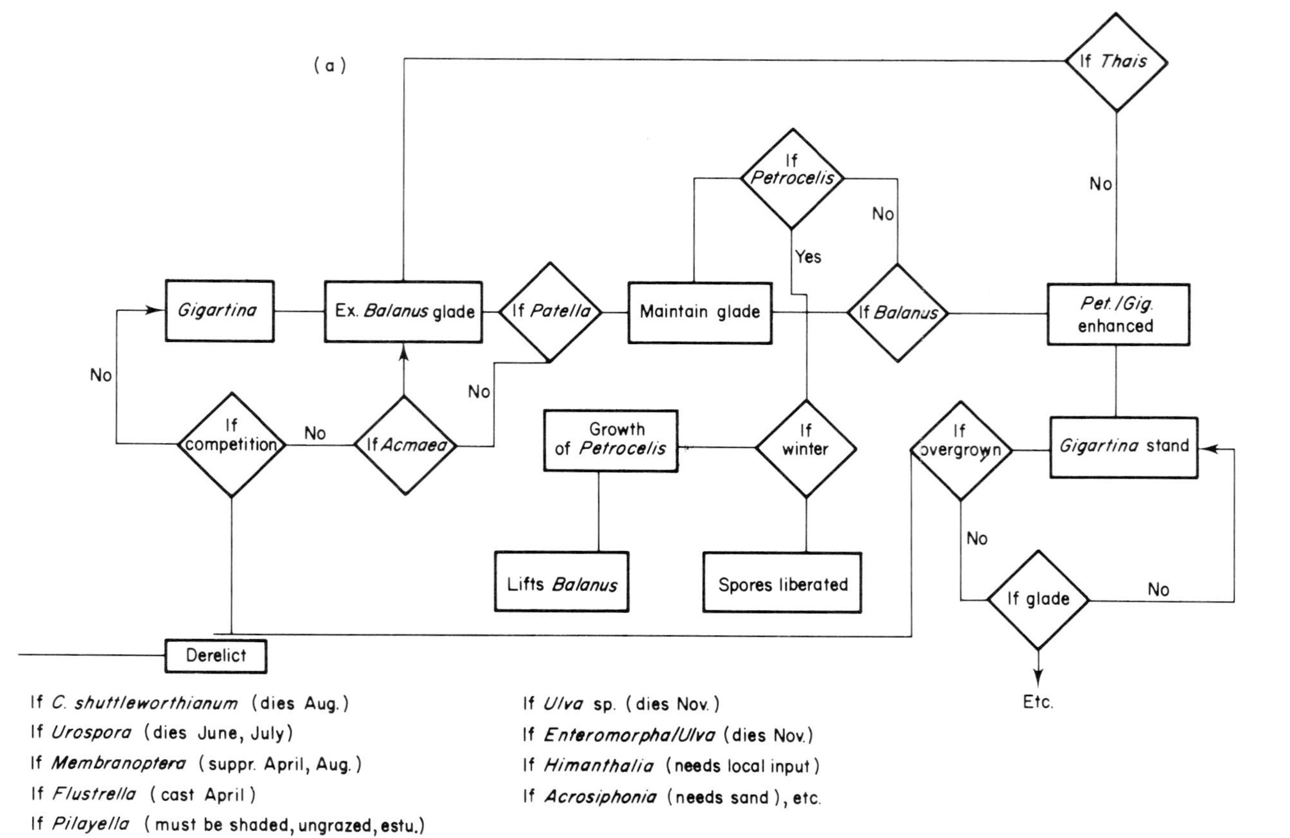

(a)
Gigartina
Ex. Balanus glade
If Patella
Maintain glade
If Petrocelis
Yes
No
If Balanus
Pet./Gig. enhanced
If Thais
No
No
If competition
No
If Acmaea
No
Growth of Petrocelis
If winter
Lifts Balanus
Spores liberated
If overgrown
Gigartina stand
No
If glade
No
Etc.
Derelict
If C. shuttleworthianum (dies Aug.)
If Urospora (dies June, July)
If Membranoptera (suppr. April, Aug.)
If Flustrella (cast April)
If Pilayella (must be shaded, ungrazed, estu.)
If Ulva sp. (dies Nov.)
If Enteromorpha/Ulva (dies Nov.)
If Himanthalia (needs local input)
If Acrosiphonia (needs sand), etc.

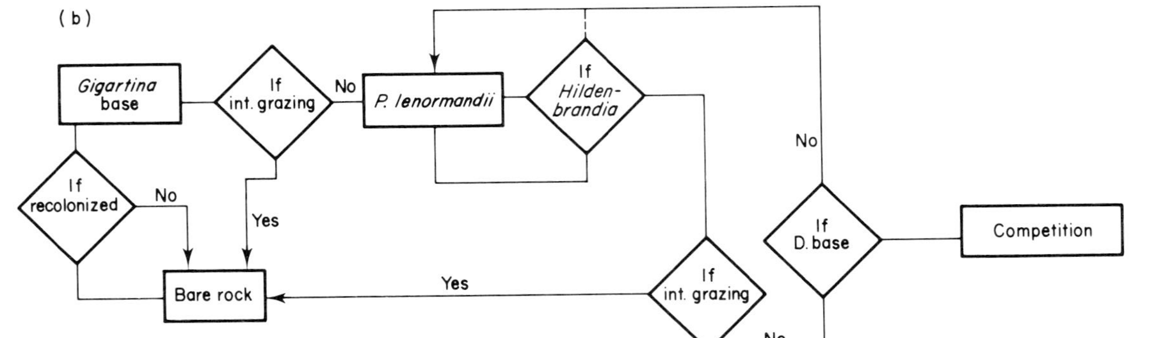

Fig. 20a, b. Heavily and lightly grazed *Gigartina* communities. Community-sequencing attempts to set out the controlling features of a species. In the case of *Gigartina stellata*, which is the typical dominant intertidal alga of the mid-part of the Firth of Clyde, grazing and competition exert most of the control. Each link may be verified by small-scale experimentation or field assessment; each link may be affected in a different way by the presence of a pollutant or artificial influence. (a) represents the situation in lightly-grazed communities and (b) in heavily-grazed communities. When the overall biology of the species at any particular site under assessment is sufficiently known, then the indicator value and exegetic value of associated phenomena can be more fully exploited.

Fig. 21. (a) (above) Photograph of the north side of the "Old Pier" at Millport, detailed in (b). (b) (below) Exegetic value of zone widths. Over 120 spp. may be found over the year in the compass of a few yards. Zones are ill-defined and overlap. Larger algae are outcompeted, overgrazed or inhibited. Plots are cumulative species numbers and actual species numbers for a sequence of 10 samples ($0.5\,m^2$) taken at 2 cm intervals and selected from the best homogeneous stands available. Diversity in most cases continues to increase with sample size, due to the cutting across of species boundaries. This zone-mixing and high diversity is typical of areas with moderate eutrophication. Key: A = Upper shore *Pilayella*-dominated; B = Upper shore *Waerniella lucifuga*- and *Audouinella purpurea*-dominated; C = Mid-shore heavily grazed; D = low shore heavily grazed; E = species-rich low shore; F = *Gigartina*-dominated, high diversity, ungrazed; G = *Gigartina* outcompeted (and therefore depauperate) by limited range of green algae; H = green algae alongside stairway, physical damage; I = rejuvenated sere caused by trampling and cleaning of stairway; x ——— x′ line along which data were taken to demonstrate species-diversity increase over a grazing boundary.

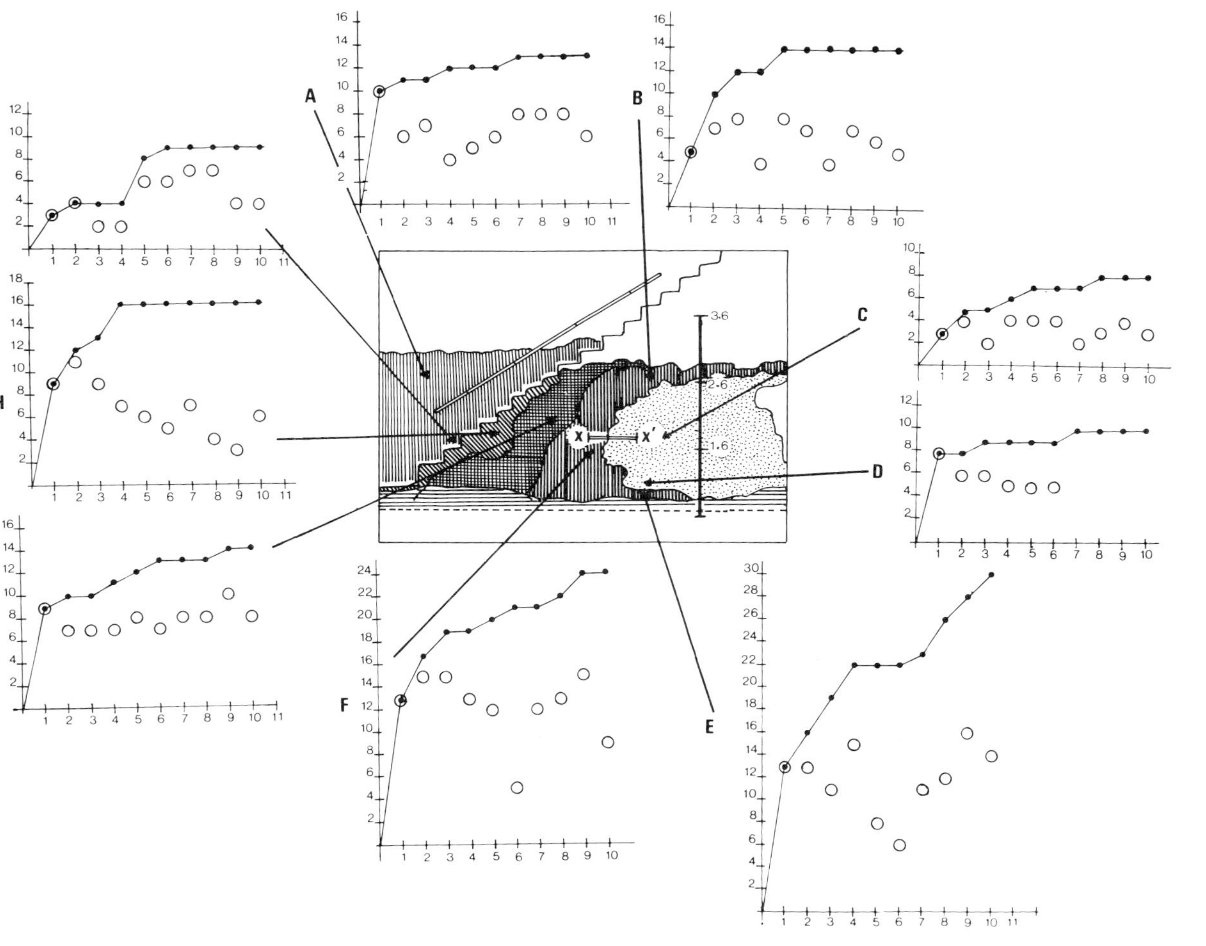

A
B
C
D
E
F
G
H
I
X
X′
3.6
2.6
1.6

previous data, except where building operations caused disturbance. The communities are not yet mature and emphasize the long maturation period. Areas nearby were greatly affected, as would have been expected, through the shelter provided by the structure. This allowed complete renewal of the succession and caused a great imbalance of producers and consumers, which in turn led to local problems with cast algae. Recycling of the communities has continued due to local sediment movements and extensive bait-digging.

Other areas of the site have also become more sheltered with similar, although less well-developed, effects involving slight rejuvenation even at a distance. South of the site, the impact of a nuclear power station's thermal discharge completely outweighs any physical effect of the structures.

It seems that the intertidal should not be studied without reference to the subtidal communities and that no group of organisms can tell one more about the changes occurring. Selection of a single species or group of species, or of one aspect such as cover/abundance, for this purpose seems to be a highly questionable art, and the criticism that the whole community is too time-consuming to deal with is irrelevant if the processes are interpreted rather than the standing-stock quantified minutely. It would be much better to select exegetes and indicators such as those considered and to use them to show the overall processes. Whether impact of the future activities at the site will be picked up remains to be seen. If they are not observed because the net has been too coarse, then we have been wasting our time.

ACKNOWLEDGEMENTS

Grant support for J.J.P.C. for the study came in the first instance from the Natural Environment Research Council. In more recent years, the work has been supported by British Steel. We gratefully acknowledge the support given. Our thanks also to the Leith Port Engineer, Mr D. Mieras, for assistance with regard to both access and collection of material. Professor P. S. Dixon (University of California, Irvine) and Mr W. Halcrow (Forth River Purification Board) are thanked for helpful criticism.

APPENDIX I

SOME EXEGETES ASSOCIATED WITH SUCCESSION

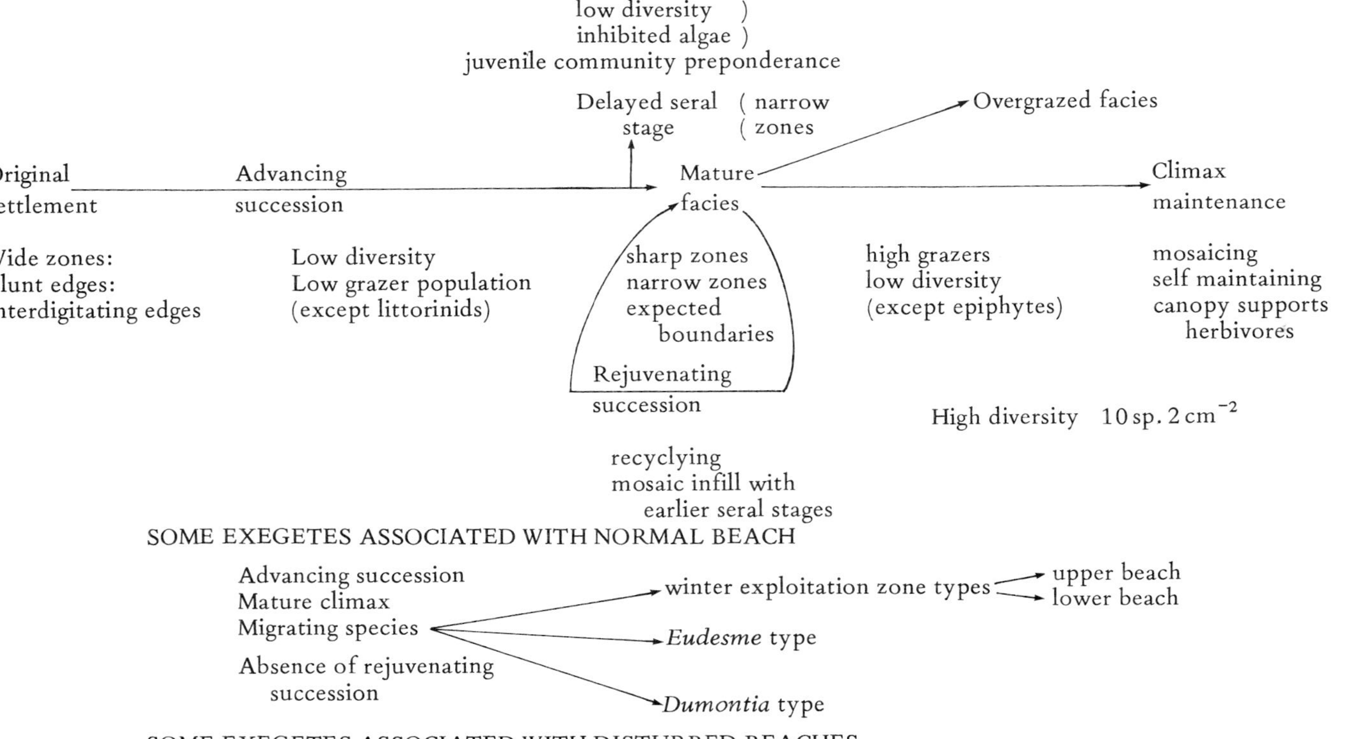

SOME EXEGETES ASSOCIATED WITH NORMAL BEACH

SOME EXEGETES ASSOCIATED WITH DISTURBED BEACHES

Rejuvenating succession
Presence of colonists in mature communities
Species outside their zone

APPENDIX II: FRAMEWORK FOR DESCRIPTION AND ASSESSMENT OF NORMALITY

(1) Limits of stock and local overall diversity.

(2) Significance of deletions.

(3) Successional position of various levels on beach.

(4) An assessment for these levels from the attributes of indicator species and indicator pairs ("community dissection").

APPENDIX III: TERMINOLOGY

It will be noted that the terminology used throughout the text includes few of the more recent technical terms. As it was the authors' intention to provide examples of the data types which were collected and to comment on whether they are of use for the practical purpose of assessing change, the aim was to keep the language as direct and lacking in jargon as possible. Studies on the assessment and documentation of change using the benthic macroalgae are so lamentably ill-developed that the collector of such data is forced to retain an almost Tansleyan terminology, on to which may be grafted such terms as seem readily applicable. It is hoped that the ideas here will not be seen as the attempts to re-vamp elegant syntheses (e.g. those of Lewis, 1964, and of the Stephensons, 1949), but rather to re-direct and increase the use of macroalgae as simple and standard monitoring tools. If such proofs as have been used in the present text are scientifically deficient, then this reflects only the complexities of the details of succession and a requirement for rather more fundamental data than are readily obtainable from the literature.

J. J. P. Clokie

APPENDIX IV: AN EXAMPLE OF THE USE OF THE BENTHIC MICROALGAE FOR TROUBLE-SHOOTING

1. Situation: One finds a 25 cm^2 area at MTL with *Blidingia marginata*, *Callithamnion hookeri*, *Capsosiphon fulvescens*, *Enteromorpha intestinalis* (flat morph) and *Gigartina stellata*

2. Deductive process:

Taxa	Epiphytic relations	Check first	Conclude	
B. marginata	–	basal crust?	If no, then input within 4 months;	X
			If yes, then perennial, either development inhibited through slope, or hard material, or external factors.	
C. hookeri	on *Gigartina*	even aged plants	If no, then at least 2 years need be added to host plant age;	X
			If yes, could be a few months if parental plants nearby.	
C. fulvescens	–	rare	Could be a function of slot-cutting by, e.g. littorinids.	X
		common	Nutrient-rich or freshwater, as well as space for settlement and low grazing. (rare or common within 2 months)	
E. int. flat	–	basal layer	If yes, (rarely) peculiarity of habitat;	
			If no, input over winter; moderate to no grazing.	X
G. stellata	–	basal layer	If yes, input over at least 5 years, probably much longer;	X
			If no, input could be 3 or more years.	
		colour	If dark, then high nutrient.	X
		size	If large and lax, then f.w. influence.	

3. Conclusion: Hence, from these five species alone it is possible to conclude that the community is over 5 years old, probably over 7, is subjected to rather high nutrient-loading; is continually under some stress; was damaged in May or June by either grazer-incursion or (more likely) physical and external factors.

APPENDIX V: SIGNIFICANT HERBIVORES FOUND IN THE FIRTH OF CLYDE: THEIR EFFECTS ON ALGAL COMMUNITIES, AS AN AID TO INTERPRETATION (pp. 673–674)

Class	Taxon	Main food type	Ecological significance
Nematoda	–(some)	early succession spp.	Weakening of alga.
Polychaeta	*Arenicola*	early succession spp.	Pulls filamentous forms down burrows, where they lodge.
Copepoda	Harpacticoids	early succession spp.	Loss of input.
Malacostraca	*Jassa*	–	Smothers smaller species.
	Gammarids	epiphytes	? Removes or inhibits epiphytes.
Lamellibranchia	*Mytilus*	filamentous spp.	Removes sporelings with foot, causing mosaicing.
Polyplacophora	*Lepidochitona*	sporelings	Cleans off shells; allows borer growth; keeps crustose algal margins smooth; shows age of community.
	Lepidopleurus	"*Conchocelis*" and other borers	Cuts windows in inorganic and algal blanket; allows borer growth.
Gastropoda	*Patella*	all short algae except crusts	Increases marginal diversity; cuts and maintains slots.
	Patina	laminarians	Loss of adults.
	Acmaea tessulata	diatoms and surface film	Allows growth of crusts; causes typical crust boundaries; important in maintenance of lower shore communities.
	A. virginea	calcareous crusts and shells with borers	Cuts holes in crusts; aids smallest middle succession crusts, e.g. *Fosliella*, or soft red crusts; enables "*Conchocelis*" and other borers to penetrate to the photic limit.
	Gibbula	? sporelings	Maintains mature appearance.

APPENDIX V (*Continued*) . . .

Class	Taxon	Main food type	Ecological significance
Gastropoda (continued)	*Lacuna vincta*	adult algae esp. *Gigartina Dilsea*, and thinner ulvoids	Causes loss of adult alga, by fragmenting; excludes some mid-succession spp.
	Littorina littorea	driftweed, and all attached algae	Reduces diversity, when population is dense. Maintains beach appearance.
	L. saxatilis	sporelings	Removes all algae, except some crusts from typical upper shore.
	L. neritoides	blue-green algae	Pushes blue-green crust up the shore in winter.
	L. littoralis	epiphytes, meristoderm of fucoids, ? *Porphyra*	Weakens adults, part of mechanism for removal of epiphytes.
	Hydrobia	? blue-green algae and filamentous forms	Prevents blanket growth on mud flats.
	Trivia	diatoms	Surface cleaner; helps crustose spp.
Echinodermata	*Echinus*	all algae (except *Phycodrys* and a few others) that encrust animals like barnacles and tubeworms; any subtidal object they can break	Major controller of the sublittoral; sharpens lower limit of intertidal species, esp. *Gigartina*; causes gaps in animal cover for new input.
	Psammechinus	most drift algae; filamentous algae on the more hidden parts of boulders	Maintains downward margin of some algae; helps the harder crustose corallines.
Diptera	larvae of various spp.	*Enteromorpha* and other filamentous algae	Break up of the canopy by weakening; major importance in polluted, less saline, milieux.
Pisces	*Mullus*	(whilst searching for animals)	Removes *Enteromorpha*, *Petalonia*, and other mid-succession algae from piles and buoys.

REFERENCES

Baker, J. M. (1976a). Biological monitoring – principles methods and difficulties. *In* "Marine Ecology and Oil Pollution" (J. M. Baker, ed.), pp. 41–54. Applied Science Publishers, Barking.

Baker, J. M. (1976b). Investigations of refinery effluent effects through field surveys. *In* "Marine Ecology and Oil Pollution" (J. M. Baker, ed.), pp. 201–226. Applied Science Publishers, Barking.

Barnett, P. R. O. (1971). Some changes in intertidal sand communities due to thermal pollution. *Proc. Roy. Soc. London.* B **177**, 353–364.

Boney, A. D. (1968). Experiments with some detergents and certain intertidal algae. *Fld Stud.* **2** (Suppl.), 55–72.

Boney, A. D. (1978). Marine algae as collectors of iron ore dust. *Mar. Poll. Bull.* **9**, 175–180.

Borowitzka, S. (1972). Intertidal algal species diversity and the effect of pollution. *Aust. J. mar. Freshwat. Res.* **23**, 73–84.

Clokie, J. J. P. and Boney, A. D. (1979). Check-List of marine algae in the Firth of Clyde. *Scott. Fld Stud.* **1**, 3–13.

Clokie, J. J. P. and Boney, A. D. (1980). *Conchocelis* distribution in the Firth of Clyde: estimates of the lower limits of the photic zone. *J. exp. mar. Biol. Ecol.* **46**, 111–125.

Fletcher, R. L. and Chamberlain, A. H. L. (1975). Marine fouling algae. *In* "Microbial Aspects of the Deterioration of Materials" (R. J. Gilbert and D. W. Lovelock, eds), pp. 59–81. Academic Press, London and New York.

Fridriksson, S. (1975). "Surtsey, Evolution of Life on a Volcanic Island". Butterworth, London.

Gessner, F. (1957). "Meer und Strand". VEB. Deutscher Verlag der Wiss., Berlin.

Grieve, S. (1881). Physical changes brought about by the floating power of seaweed. *Trans. bot. Soc. Edinb.* **1881**, 72–77.

Hoare, R. and Hiscock, K. (1974). An ecological survey of the rocky coast adjacent to a bromine extraction works. *Est. cst. mar. Sci.* **2**, 329–348.

Lewis, J. R. (1964). "The Ecology of Rocky Shores". English Universities Press, London.

Linskens, H. F. (1966). Ädhäsion von Fortpflanzungzellen Benthontischer Algen. *Planta* **68**, 99–110.

Luther, G. (1976). Bewuchsuntersuchungen auf Naturstein Substraten im Gezeitbereich des Nordsylter Wattenmeeres. *Helgoländer wiss. Meeresunters.* **28**, 145–166; 318–351.

Marine Biological Association (1957). "Plymouth Marine Fauna" (3rd edn.). Mar. Biol. Ass. U.K., Plymouth.

Murray, S. N. and Littler, M. M. (1978). Patterns of algal succession in a perturbated marine intertidal community. *J. Phycol.* **14**, 506–512.

O'Connor, F. B. (1974). The ecological basis for conservation. *In* "Conservation in Practice" (A. Warren and F. B. Goldsmith, eds), pp. 57–72. Wiley, London and New York.

Parke, M. W. and Dixon, P. S. (1976). Check-list of British marine algae – third revision. *J. mar. biol. Ass. U.K.* **56**, 527–594.

Pearson, T. H. and Rosenberg, R. (1978). Macrobenthic succession in relationship to organic enrichment and pollution in the marine environment. *Oceanogr. mar. Biol. ann. Rev.* **16**, 229–311.

Pielou, E. C. (1975). "Ecological Diversity". Wiley, New York.

Rees, T. K. (1940). Algal colonization at Mumbles Head. *J. Ecol.* **28**, 403–437.

Rounsefell, G. A. (1972). Ecological effects of offshore construction. *J. mar. Sci.* **2**, 1–80 + appendix 1–119.

Russell, G. (1978). Environment and form in the discrimination of taxa in brown algae. *In* "Modern Approaches to the Taxonomy of Red and Brown Algae" (D. E. G. Irvine and J. H. Price, eds), pp. 339–361. Systematics Association Special Volume No. 10. Academic Press, London and New York.

Russell, G. and Fielding, A. H. (1974). The competitive properties of marine algae in culture. *J. Ecol.* **62**, 689–698.

Sládaček, V. (1972). The structure of saprobic communities. *Int. Rev. ges. Hydrobiol.* **57**, 361–366.

Sládaček, V. (1973). System of water quality from the biological point of view. *Arch. Hydrobiol. Beih. Ergebn. Limnol.* **7**, 1–218.

Sládaček, V. (1977). Einfurhung in die quantitative Saprobiologie. *Arch. Hydrobiol. Beih. Ergebn. Limnol.* **9**, 65–78.

Stephenson, T. A. and Stephenson, A. (1972). "Life between Tide Marks on Rocky Shores". W. H. Freeman, San Francisco.

Wilkinson, M. and Tittley, I. (1979). The marine algae of Elie – a reassessment. *Botanica mar.* **22**, 249–256.

8 | Fish–Algal Relations in Temperate Waters

ALWYNE WHEELER

Department of Zoology, British Museum (Natural History), London, England

Abstract: Algae and marine fishes interact in several ways, some by direct association but none in an obligate sense. The indirectness of most of the associations is such that few studies have even touched upon the relationship and those so doing have stressed the underlying complexity of the situation.

Compared with those of tropical waters, very few temperate marine fishes feed on algae or other plant material. There are even fewer, if any, fish that rely solely on algae for food in cool waters, but some species do consume algae in partial fulfilment of their diet, by accident, or as a result of unusual habitats. The major contribution of algae to the diet of fishes seems to lie in increasing the available habitats for those invertebrates on which the fish mainly rely.

The degree of algal cover in intertidal situations affects the composition of the fish fauna. In certain extreme conditions, the presence of fish may be dependent on the prior presence of algae. The total biomass of fish in intertidal and sublittoral habitats may well be related to the extent of algal cover, but direct comparisons can rarely be made due to the complicating factors of species diversity, wave exposure and level on the shore of intertidal habitats.

The most direct association between fish and algae lies in the provision by the latter of a suitable environment for certain nest-building and crevice-spawning fish to breed. Here, the presence of adequate algal cover is essential to the maintenance of some of the littoral fish populations. In a sense, this is a specialized extension of the general additional cover that algae provide for cryptic and thigmotactic species. In some cases, the association has progressed towards adaptation of colour and body form to produce protective resemblance.

Systematics Association Special Volume No. 17(b), "The Shore Environment, Vol. 2: Ecosystems", edited by J. H. Price, D. E. G. Irvine and W. F. Farnham, 1980, pp. 677–698, Academic Press, London and New York.

However, in temperate waters examples of protective resemblance are fewer and less dramatic than those of tropical situations.

INTRODUCTION

That plants play a fundamental role in the ecology of both freshwater and marine ecosystems is accepted as a generality by all ecologists and lies at the root of much fishery science. Despite this, the relations between fish and plants have only been touched on tangentially in studies which were directed at exploring other aspects of fish biology or the ecology of certain temperate plant communities. Direct relationships might well be postulated, however, in that fishes feed directly on plants, find animal food in the invertebrate herbivores dependent on the vegetation, live in plant cover, use plant shelter for their eggs, and while young use vegetation as a nursery habitat.

In fresh water, these associations are well documented and examples of each could be cited, although the number of fish which eat plant material exclusively, the most direct association possible, are few. In tropical seas, associations between fishes and plants are well established in all aspects of the relationship and in various habitats there is a large number of herbivorous fishes, many of which are specialized as browsers or grazers on algae. In contrast with the position in tropical seas there are relatively few temperate marine fish which depend on plants for food, an interesting situation in view of the wealth of algal growth in many littoral and sublittoral temperate regions.

In temperate seas, the more important relationships between fishes and algae seem to be that the latter provide an enhanced habitat with greater food resources in the form of herbivores, especially crustaceans, and by sheltering other invertebrates and fishes. So far as food is concerned the relationship is thus largely indirect. However the cover provided by algae, especially in the littoral and immediately sublittoral zones, is an important factor in reducing predation on fishes in general, and in certain areas algal beds act as nursery grounds for the young of fishes which as adults live further offshore. The importance of the cover provided by algae is demonstrated by the numerous species of fish which can adapt their general coloration to merge with the algae dominant in the area they inhabit. In a few cases modification of body form produces a closer resemblance to algae and marine plants, an association which is often heightened by the behaviour of the fish. In general, however, such associations appear to be less common, or perhaps less observed, in temperate seas than they are in tropical waters.

The provision of cover for fish has in some cases been extended to the specialized function of acting as nesting sites. A number of littoral fishes build nests in algae; some use fragments of algae in the construction of the nest. A more intimate relationship is provided by those species which lay their eggs, and guard them, beside or even within hollow holdfasts.

These associations between fish and algae are discussed in greater detail here and the opportunity is taken to make comparisons with similar associations in tropical seas. The relationships between fish and algae are complex and by no means fully explored; it is hoped that this summary will stimulate further enquiry into the topic.

EFFECT OF ALGAE ON THE DISTRIBUTION AND ABUNDANCE OF FISHES

The presence of a substantial algal cover can be predicted to have a considerable effect on the fish fauna both in qualitative and quantitative assessments. However, in the littoral zone the association between fish and algae is one of a considerable complexity on account of other parameters, amongst them the effects of the geological formation of the shore, exposure, vertical distribution, and size of water-filled pools which affect both the algae and the fish. Gibson (1972), in a study of vertical distribution and feeding relationships of intertidal fishes on the French Atlantic coast, found in an attempt to correlate the number of fish in a pool with (a) the level of the pool on the shore, (b) percentage cover and (c) surface area, that when area and level were eliminated there appeared to be a correlation with cover in sheltered shores, although on exposed shores the number of fish per pool was correlated with both cover and surface area. However, the attempted statistical treatment of the situation in this study was possibly inadequate to interpret the complexity of the situation. One immediate objection is that the data were derived from collections made in pools in low tide conditions and as the fish fauna is mobile at high tide some species may have owed their presence in the pool to relatively random movements.

The assessment of "cover" was moreover based solely on algal cover and made no allowance for the anfractuosities of the pool bed; these make an important contribution to cover for thigmotactic species. The importance of surface rugosity as a factor in species richness of the fish fauna on a coral reef has recently been demonstrated by Luckhurst and Luckhurst (1978), and Emery (1978) has also commented on the importance of boulders as cover for fishes in Arctic marine habitats. There seems to be no reason to doubt that similar factors affect fishes in temperate littoral waters. For these reasons, as well as from the indefinite nature of the results obtained, it is necessary to regard with some reservations the conclusions concerning the effect of algal cover on fish distribution in Gibson's otherwise excellent study.

The interesting work of Marsh *et al.* (1978) on the clinid fishes in intertidal rock pools in South Africa does indeed suggest that the cover provided by algae is a significant factor in species richness. In this study the clinids were captured, identified, weighed and measured from a series of pools; all algae were removed from the pool, were quantified, and the pools were measured. A second sampling was made 12 weeks after the pools were denuded and again all fish were captured. In no case were there more fish at the second sampling than the first, although in some of the pools algal cover had regenerated completely. Only in these pools had the clinid community regained its former abundance. However, the recolonized pools contained relatively smaller fish and it is suggested that colonization was effected by younger, sexually maturing fish which had not hitherto established territories. Marsh *et al.* concluded that "some measure of cover appears to be the best, or only significant, predictor of species richness, abundance and biomass of clinids in the pools investigated". It is clear from their results that in this context algae make a significant contribution to this cover.

At a very simple level, evaluation of the importance of algal cover to fish in intertidal situations can be illustrated by the example of a collection made by the author on the sandy shore at Mundesley, Norfolk, on the North Sea coast of England. Along this coast the foreshore is virtually unrelieved sand or shingle. To limit longshore drift of the sand, groynes made of iron tubing set vertically in the sand and fastened to girders have been constructed in zig-zag fashion down the shore. Pools of standing water had formed at the bases of these groynes between LWN and ELWS tide levels and the iron pillars supported growths of acorn branches and green algae. Collections made in these pools in autumn 1961 revealed fish fauna which was in the main typical of the sandy shore with the two notable additions of several specimens of the blenny, *Lipophrys pholis** and of the gadoid five-bearded rockling, *Ciliata mustela*. Both these species are more usually found on rocky shores, either in intertidal pools or, in the case of the rockling, under rock cover. Undoubtedly their occurrence in this atypical habitat was at least partly the result of green algae providing cover in low-tide conditions, although this blenny feeds on acorn barnacles as well as on algae. Other cases could be cited of the similar occurrence of species, normally associated with rocky shores and algal cover, in intertidal and sublittoral situations on coastlines composed mainly of sand or mud.

In British seas there are some 48 species of fish which are found in littoral or immediately sublittoral situations on both rocky shores and soft shores (sand, mud or both, including shores with a small quantity of shells or pebbles). Gravel shores are not inhabited by benthic fishes. This figure excludes those casual species (such as the bass, *Dicentrarchus labrax*, sprat, *Sprattus sprattus*, and anchovy, *Engraulis encrasicolus*) which are found from time to time in the littoral zone in pools, presumably as a result of being trapped by the falling tide. A list is presented in Table I, where indications are given of the normal habitat of the species, based on the entirely arbitrary division between rocky shores and soft shores. This tabulation also shows features of the biology of the fishes – those which burrow into the surface (E), those which are strongly inclined to seek shelter in rock crevices or under inorganic material (B), and those which are normally found in heavy algal cover (A). It should be emphasized that these divisions are subjective assessments of the normal biology of the species and cover observations on littoral fishes from the Channel Islands to Shetland made by the author between 1955 and 1975; exceptions to all divisions and categories will be found but these do not represent normal behaviour.

On rocky shores some 31 species have been encountered. Of these,

---

*Citations of most names and authorities throughout this paper accord with those presented in Wheeler (1969, 1978) and in Bailey *et al.* (1970).

Table I. Species of fish occurring in the littoral and immediate sublittoral on rocky and soft substrata in the British Seas.

Species	Normal habitats					
	Rocky shores			Soft shores		
	A	B	C	D	E	F
Eel *Anguilla anguilla*	—	+	—	—	+	+
Conger eel *Conger conger*	—	+	—	—	—	—
Small-headed clingfish *Apletodon microcephalus*	+	—	—	—	—	—
Two-spotted clingfish *Diplecogaster bimaculata*	+	—	—	—	—	—
Shore clingfish *Lepadogaster lepadogaster*	+	+	—	—	—	—
Saithe *Pollachius virens*	+ juv.	—	+	+	—	—
Shore rockling *Gaidropsarus mediterraneus*	+	+	—	+	—	—
Five-bearded rockling *Ciliata mustela*	+	+	—	+	—	+
Northern rockling *Ciliata septentrionalis*	+	+	—	+	—	—
Viviparous blenny *Zoarces viviparus*	—	+	—	—	+	+
Sand-smelt *Atherina presbyter*	—	—	+	—	—	+?
Stickleback *Gasterosteus aculeatus*	+	—	—	—	—	—
Fifteen-spined stickleback *Spinachia spinachia*	+	—	—	—	—	—
Nilsson's pipefish *Syngnathus rostellatus*	—	—	—	—	—	+
Deep-snouted pipefish *Syngnathus typhle*	—	—	—	—	—	+
Worm pipefish *Nerophis lumbriciformis*	+	+	—	+	—	—
Sea scorpion *Taurulus bubalis*	+	+	—	+	—	—
Lumpsucker *Cyclopterus lumpus*	+ juv.	+	—	+	—	—
Sea-snail *Liparis liparis*	—	+	—	+	—	+
Montagu's sea-snail *Liparis montagui*	?	+	—	—	—	—
Thick-lipped Grey mullet *Chelon labrosus*	—	—	+ juv.	—	—	+
Ballan wrasse *Labrus bergylta*	+ juv.	—	—	+	—	—
Goldsinny *Ctenolabrus rupestris*	+	—	—	+	—	—
Corkwing wrasse *Crenilabrus melops*	+	—	—	+	—	—
Lesser Weever *Echiichthys vipera*	—	—	—	+	+	+
Tompot blenny *Parablennius gattorugine*	+	+	—	+	—	—
Shanny *Lipophrys pholis*	+	+	—	+	—	+
Montagu's blenny *Coryphoblennius galerita*	+	+	—	—	—	—
Yarrell's blenny *Chirolophis ascanii*	—	+	—	?	—	—
Butterfish *Pholis gunnellus*	+	+	—	+	—	—
Sandeel *Ammodytes tobianus*	—	—	—	—	+	+
Dragonet *Callionymus lyra*	—	—	—	—	+	—
Giant goby *Gobius cobitis*	+	—	—	—	—	—
Rock goby *Gobius paganellus*	+	+	—	—	—	—
Black goby *Gobius niger*	—	—	—	—	—	+
Leopard-spotted goby *Thorogobius ephippiatus*	—	+	—	—	—	—

Table I. (Continued)

Species	Normal habitats					
	Rocky shores			Soft shores		
	A	B	C	D	E	F
Two-spotted goby *Gobiusculus flavescens*	+	—	+	—	—	—
Common goby *Pomatoschistus microps*	—	—	+	+	—	+
Painted goby *Pomatoschistus pictus*	—	—	+	—	—	+
Sand goby *Pomatoschistus minutus*	—	—	+	+	—	+
Brill *Scophthalmus rhombus*	—	—	+	+	+	+ juv.
Turbot *Scophthalmus maximus*	—	—	+	+	+	+ juv.
Topknot *Zeugopterus punctatus*	—	+ juv.	—	+	—	—
Plaice *Pleuronectes platessa*	—	—	+	+	+	+ juv.
Flounder *Platichthys flesus*	—	—	+	+	+	+ juv.
Dab *Limanda limanda*	—	—	+	+	+	+ juv.
Sole *Solea solea*	—	—	+	+	+	+ juv.

Key: A, Mainly associated with algae; B, mainly in crevices and under inorganic shelter; C, free-swimming; D, shows strong adaptive coloration; E, burrows in substrata; F, present regularly.

four can be classed as free-swimming, three of which, *Atherina presbyter, Pollachius virens*, and *Chelon labrosus*, either breed in the intertidal zone or use it as a nursery area, while the fourth, *Gobiusculus flavescens*, is strongly associated with algae (as is *Pollachius virens* on coastlines in the north of the British Isles). The remaining 27 species can be grouped into three categories: those found both in association with algae and in crevices or under rocks (total of 12), those dependent on inorganic cover (total of 8), and those dependent on algal cover alone (total of 10). This simple analysis suggests that algal cover is of considerable significance in contributing to the species richness of the intertidal fish fauna.

The species which are associated particularly with algae represent several systematic groups and the significance of their associations varies. The most abundant (both in terms of species represented and in individual occurrence) are the gadiform rocklings, especially

Gaidropsarus mediterraneus and *Ciliata mustela*; the sticklebacks, *Gasterosteus aculeatus* (especially in the north of the British Isles) and *Spinachia spinachia*; the wrasses, particularly *Crenilabrus melops*; the blennies, particularly *Lipophrys pholis*; and the gobies, particularly *Gobius paganellus*. The cottid *Taurulus bubalis* is extremely widespread in the British Isles, particularly on algal-rich shores, but is the only representative of the group to be common littorally, although *T. lilljeborgi* is occasionally found on rocks at ELWS (Dunne, 1972) and *Myoxocephalus scorpius* is locally common on soft bottoms just below this level.

It is important to point out that such essentially rocky-shore and algal-associated species as *Ciliata mustela* and *Lipophrys pholis* which are recorded in Table I on soft shores have only been found in situations, such as those described above on the Norfolk coast, where transient growth of green algae is found on artificial hard surfaces. Elsewhere on soft shores these species have been encountered amongst algae growing on broken sea walls and moorings, and on occasional natural rock outcrops in otherwise sandy shores.

These species apart, the fish fauna of the littoral and immediately sublittoral zones on soft bottoms can be seen from this table to be sparse and highly specialized in that most of the species either burrow or are cryptically coloured. The total number of species listed for soft shores is 19, which is considerably less than the 31 found on rocky shores, and includes the two species (mentioned above) that are dependent on algae. This total also includes *Atherina presbyter*, which has been found free-swimming in exceptional areas of open water tide pools that may be nursery areas for the young, and is dependent on sparse algal or other plant growth. Of the remainder, most burrow into the substratum, at least when the tide is low and in many cases most of the time. This is particularly well-developed behaviour in the weever, *Echiichthys vipera*, the sandeels, *Ammodytes* spp., the dragonet, *Callionymus lyra*, and all the flat-fishes (Pleuronectiformes), although the latter tend to lie close to the surface with only a slight covering of sand or mud on them, in contrast to the total burrowing of the sandeels and the almost complete covering of the weever and dragonet. Both the weever and the flat-fishes have very well-developed cryptic coloration. This latter feature is also highly developed in the gobies, especially the pomatoschistine species. These small fish do not burrow, but are extremely common in intertidal situations on sand and mud and adapt their dorsal coloration to match their surroundings almost perfectly, relying on this and their quick darting swimming to avoid predators.

This extensive analysis of the British shore-fish fauna illustrates the importance of algal cover as a factor influencing the number of species represented. The comparison of total numbers of fish species on rocky shores *versus* soft shores shows a clear advantage in favour of the former. However, the most numerous group on soft substrates, the flat-fishes, all inhabit the sublittoral fringe as juveniles, and the number of species of fish which occur regularly as adults or sub-adults is very few (at most 15 species, several of which are uncommon). The presence of algae is thus a major factor for the species represented in the littoral zone. The precise nature of the association between fish and algae varies from species to species of fish and will be discussed later.

The general association between the ichthyofauna and marine algae can be seen in a number of specialized faunas. Possibly best known is the distinctive fauna of the giant kelp, *Macrocystis* spp., on the Californian coast and northwards in varying abundance along the Pacific coast of North America. Of interest in this connection is Quast's (1968b) conclusion that "standing crop estimates of resident fishes in kelp beds are close to median values from the literature for lakes and coral reefs"; this worker's studies into the intricate relations between the larger fishes and the kelp beds suggest that the species-richness of the fish fauna is also enhanced by the presence of kelp. The extremely rich cottid fauna of the Pacific coast of North America, which comprises at least 78 species (Bailey *et al.*, 1970), contains many species which live in tide pools and shallow water (Bolin, 1944) and in close association with algae (Hart, 1973). This is also true of many of the numerous stichaeid fishes, 25 species of which are recorded by Bailey *et al.* (1970). The clinid fauna of the southern tip of Africa, for which the work of Marsh *et al.* (1978) has already been mentioned, was studied by Penrith (1969, 1970). Of the 33 species of the family present, all of which are endemic, 14 are more or less exclusively intertidal and a further nine occur both inter- and subtidally (Penrith, 1970). No fewer than nine of the total are specialized for living amongst algae; several species of *Pavoclinus* appear to show a wide preference for beds of the alga *Caulerpa filiformis* (Suhr) Hering, while *Gymutoclinus rotundifrons* (Barnard) appeared to be confined to kelp. It is clear from Penrith's excellent studies of this fascinating group that the presence of algae has played some part in the evolution of this fauna in association with the relatively few representatives of the families Blenniidae and Gobiidae, which tend to dominate the littoral fauna in other temperate regions.

ALGAE AS A FOOD RESOURCE

Possibly the most direct relationship between fish and algae is when the latter form a major, if not the sole, source of food for fish. In tropical waters a large part of the fish fauna depends on algae for food, but in temperate seas this appears not to be the case.

In their classic study of ecological relationships of fish and coral reefs in the Marshall Islands, Hiatt and Strasburg (1960) have shown that a substantial proportion of the fish biomass is composed of herbivores. The fish families which dominate in this group are the surgeon fishes (Acanthuridae), rabbit fishes (Siganidae), parrot fishes (Scaridae), and damsel fishes (Pomacentridae), most of which show dental and other morphological modifications associated with their diet. Randall (1967), in a study of the food habits of fishes on West Indian reefs, showed that benthic algae were the major food of surgeon fishes and parrot fishes, as well as of the rudder-fishes or sea chubs (Kyphosidae), while a number of blennies (Blenniidae) were also herbivores. Partial herbivores included a number of damsel fishes, sea breams (Sparidae), trigger fishes (Balistidae) and gobies (Gobiidae). Only the larger herbivores and omnivores ate large, coarse algae; the remainder fed on filamentous green algae. The parrot fishes here, as in the Marshall Islands, also fed on the algae in dead coral and contributed greatly to erosion of the coral reef and the build-up of coral sand. The effect of grazing and browsing by marine fishes was also studied by Randall (1961) in the Hawaiian Islands and he demonstrated that in the immediately sublittoral zone algal abundance was strongly affected by the presence of herbivorous fish, particularly the surgeon fishes and parrot fishes.

In contrast to this strongly herbivorous community in tropical waters relatively few fish in temperate seas eat algae. It is significant in the first place that, of the families which are shown to be major herbivores in tropical waters, only blennies and gobies are represented in any numbers in temperate areas. The dominant herbivores, the surgeon fishes and rabbit fishes, are not represented at all, and the parrot fishes occur very sparsely in the warmer parts of the temperate zone.

In his study of the food of littoral fishes on the Atlantic coast of France, Gibson (1972) showed that of the 13 species examined only five species ate algae in any quantity. Of these it was an important constituent of the diet in only two, the blenny, *Lipophrys pholis*, and the giant goby, *Gobius cobitis*. In the Mediterranean, Gibson (1968) had earlier shown that of 19 species of littoral fish examined only two, the blenny, *Parablennius gattorugine*, and the giant goby, ate significant quantities of algae. In these studies *Parablennius gattorugine* appears to be the only species which was dependent on algae as a major source of food. However, my own observations (Wheeler, 1969, and unpublished) on the giant goby in both British and French intertidal pools suggest that its dependence on green filamentous algae for food may be partly a consequence of its habit of living in pools near EHWS, in which invertebrates are generally scarce. In such cases the algae therefore often represent the major food resource available to the fish.

Fishes which are usually encountered sublittorally in the temperate eastern Atlantic appear to include even fewer alga-eaters than the littoral species. Even the wrasses (Labridae), which are mostly strongly associated with algal cover or rocks with algae, appear to feed very little on plant matter. Quignard (1966) analysed the diet of 17 Mediterranean species and in no case did he list algae in the remains within the gut. A more recent study by Dipper *et al.* (1977) of the diet of the ballan wrasse, *Labrus bergylta*, has shown that algae comprised only 4% by volume of the gut contents in 139 fish with food; this broadly confirms what can be established from Quignard's more general analysis. However, Gibson (1972) found algae in a number of *Crenilabrus melops* examined, so algal eating has some significance in this group.

Other fishes which eat algae include the grey mullets (Mugilidae), which ingest filamentous green algae in some quantity, together with diatoms and other benthic organisms (Hickling, 1970). Approximately half of Hickling's sample of 96 specimens of *Chelon labrosus* contained filamentous green algae, but as this fish is an indiscriminate benthos feeder which also grazes on algae covering stones and pier pilings it seems that ingestion of algae may to some extent be accidental. Other European species which feed on algae to a greater or less extent include several sea breams (Sparidae), which are most abundant in the Mediterranean and the eastern Atlantic but unknown or very scarce north of Biscay. The species *Boops boops, Sarpa salpa,* and *Puntazzo puntazzo* (Gmelin) all possess incisiform front teeth, characteristically notched in the former two and strongly protruding in *Puntazzo.* Teeth with broad similarity in shape can be seen in the obligate algal eaters such as surgeon fishes and rabbit fishes in tropical seas. Tortonese (1975), in his general work on Italian fishes, indicates that all three are omnivorous, with algae or higher plants featuring prominently in their diet. Information on the diet of *Sarpa salpa* in South African waters is available from the study of Christensen (1978). He found that this species ingests harpacticoid copepods when young, diatoms and red algae as large juveniles, and red and green algae as adults. There remains, however, some doubt as to whether the algae are digested even though there is substantial comparative lengthening of the gut as the fish increases in size.

In his study of the fishes of the kelp beds of California, Quast (1968c) found that of the extensive fish fauna relatively few species actually ate algae. The three species which were heavily dependent on algae, the opaleye, *Girella nigricans*, halfmoon *Medialuna californiensis*, and the zebra perch, *Hermosilla azurea*, are members of the family Kyphosidae which, as Randall (1967) showed, are all herbivorous fishes. Interestingly, as most other algal eaters consume filamentous green algae, Quast found that the opaleye was actually feeding on *Macrocystis* and other brown algae as well as coralline algae, although young fish (up to 32 mm length) have a mixed plant and animal diet. Despite these observations there is evidence that a purely algal diet does not sustain the opaleye over a period of one month, and no trace of alginase activity was detectable in the gut of a fresh specimen. As Quast pointed out, this suggests that animal materials may be the principal nutrient in the diet despite the bulk of algae in the gut. Other fishes, such as the damsel fishes *Chromis punctipinnis* and *Hypsypops rubicunda*, the wrasses *Halichoeres semicinctus* and *Oxyjulis californica*, and the greenling *Oxylebius pictus*, were found to contain algae in the gut. However, it appears from observation of the remainder of the diet that algae occupy a very minor place in the nutritional order of these species. It is indeed very possible that it was ingested either with animal food, or on account of encrusting animal matter on the algae.

Such general conclusions as can be drawn from these observations suggest that, outside tropical reef areas, algae do not play an important role as food for fish. Even in the *Macrocystis* beds of Pacific North America, where a distinctive fauna exists in close association with algae, the members of only one family of fishes are confirmed herbivores and although other species eat algae it is only incidental to preferred animal diet.

ALGAE AS A HABITAT FOR FOOD ORGANISMS

As so few of the fishes living in association with algae utilize the latter as a major food source, the role of algae as a habitat for food organisms needs to be examined. The food of algal-associated fishes is basically invertebrate, although a few piscivorous fishes lie in concealment amongst algal fronds, for example the California halibut, *Paralichthys californicus*, in *Macrocystis* beds (Quast, 1968c). Of the food-forming invertebrates some sessile forms, such as bryozoans and tunicates, may actually grow on the algal fronds and some lamellibranch molluscs may also attach themselves, but at most their association with algae is that of deriving shelter in low tide situations. The majority of these animals are mobile and enjoy varied relationships in the algal community. It thus seems that the major role played by the algae is to provide invertebrates with protection from desiccation in low tide situations, but provision of shelter from predators is also important. Some invertebrates, however, feed directly on algae.

The food of algal-associated fishes varies with species and with location, so that it is not practicable here to discuss the biology of more than a few examples. Amongst the 13 littoral species studied by Gibson (1972), the most important groups of food-organisms were gastropods, polychaetes, amphipods, copepods, ostracods, isopods and brachyuran decapods. For the Californian *Macrocystis* beds, Quast (1968c) found that the animal groups most frequently eaten were, in order of priority, amphipods, crabs, shrimps and isopods. Although the biology of the individual species within these groups will vary from taxon to taxon, it can be suggested that at least some are abundant in the algae because they feed on the plants. Thus, the members of the isopod genus *Idotea* are known to eat algae (Naylor, 1955), and these crustaceans were heavily predated by at least one of the kelp-associated fishes, the clinid *Heterostichus rostratus*, in Quast's study. Dipper *et al.* (1977) found that *Idotea neglecta* G. O. Sars and *I. granulosa* Rathke, although of secondary importance, were eaten by the ballan wrasse. The abundant intertidal isopod *Ligia oceanica* (L.) is also found with some frequency in the gut of *Gobius cobitis* (Gibson, 1970; and personal observation) and according to Nicholls (1931) it feeds mainly on *Fucus vesiculosus* L., although other fucoids and *Laminaria* are eaten.

Certain groups of crabs eat algae to a greater or lesser extent. Although, in northern European littoral zones, the most abundant crab is the shore crab (*Carcinus maenas* (L.)) this species apparently eats relatively little algae and Ropes (1969) quantified the algal contribution to its diet at about 12% of frequency of occurrence. Nevertheless, with such an abundant animal on rocky, algal-covered shores, this represents a considerable quantity of algal material. The shore crab features in the diet of a number of littoral and sublittoral fishes, including the giant goby, *Gobius cobitis* (Gibson, 1970; Wheeler, 1969) and the ballan wrasse, *Labrus bergylta* (Dipper *et al.*, 1977).

Other crabs are more positively herbivorous. Hartnoll (1963) showed that algae are an important food for several species of spider crab (Majidae) in the Irish Sea and, it may be presumed, elsewhere. Several shore-dwelling grapsid crabs and xanthids are algivorous, including the European wrinkled crab, *Xantho incisus* Leach (Warner, 1977), but relatively few species of these groups occur in temperate waters and of those that do occur none seems to be recorded in the fish diets which have been studied.

Most other crustaceans which feature in the diet of algal-associated fishes have less direct dependence on algae for food. Thus, copepods are mainly diatom feeders, barnacles are filter feeders, and amphipods and shrimps in general are scavengers, eating algae mainly in the form of detritus.

A community of littoral and sublittoral molluscan browsers exists in the limpets, chitons, periwinkles and topshells which contribute to the diet of a number of fishes. Thus *Lipophrys pholis* is recorded as eating *Littorina* and small specimens of *Patella* (Gibson, 1972), and *Littorina* appears to be its diet abundantly throughout the year (Dunne, 1977); *Labrus bergylta* feeds on *Patina pellucida* (L.), which is closely associated with *Laminaria*, as well as on *Littorina* spp. (Dipper *et al.*, 1977). This molluscan fauna, which is characterized by feeding on algae, forms probably the most important indirect connection between algae and fishes.

In general, it seems that algae provide food for some of the prey organisms of inshore fishes but only in fishes with relatively specialized diets can the algae be said to contribute significantly, if indirectly, to fish diet. The most significant contribution appears to be that algae provide shelter and a three-dimensional habitat which is occupied by prey organisms that depend only partly on the algae for food. The contribution of algae as a habitat for food organisms is thus complex but must be regarded as of considerable importance to the fish fauna, since the latter derives very little food directly from the algae.

ALGAE AS PROTECTION FOR FISHES

An aspect of the enhanced fish fauna of algal-rich communities is that the fish derive a positive advantage from living within the cover. The most obvious such advantage would be a reduction of predator pressure by resemblance in coloration or body form of the fish to the surrounding algae. Advantageous also is the effectiveness this resemblance bestows on the fish as a predator.

In tropical waters, both freshwater and marine, several examples have been described of protective resemblance between fish and algae. Randall and Randall (1960) gave a review of examples of mimicry and protective resemblance in tropical marine fishes and cited several cases where close resemblance to algae in shape and coloration has been observed. Some examples include juvenile *Kyphosus sectatrix* resembling *Sargassum*, and the wrasse *Novaculichthys taeniourus* resembling floating green algae, while the so-called sargassum fish, *Histrio histrio*, which is totally adapted to a life within *Sargassum* clumps, is a frequently cited example of extreme protective resemblance.

In temperate waters, there appear to be few cases of modification of body form so extreme as to afford protective resemblance. General resemblance in coloration can, however, be seen in a wide range of species in littoral and sublittoral habitats in European seas. Thus, *Taurulus bubalis* usually has a dull olive-green back with lighter sides when found amongst fucoid algae, but individuals caught on red algae or juveniles amongst *Corallina* are invariably reddish in colour on the back and sides, offering a close match with their surroundings. As can be seen from Table I, a number of other north European algal-living shore fish show strong adaptive coloration. This is particularly noticeable with the juvenile saithe, *Pollachius virens*, which are common in tide pools in Scotland and Orkney, have distinctly olive backs and yellowish sides, and prove very difficult to distinguish from the fronds of *Laminaria* and *Fucus* amongst which they hide. The colouring of adults which do not live amongst algae is very different. The general colouring of most of the blennies and wrasses is also very variable according to the background colour of the algae amongst which the individual is living.

The worm pipefish, *Nerophis lumbriciformis*, is possibly the most highly developed mimic of algae. Although it is also found under rocks and amongst *Fucus* spp., in Guernsey (Wheeler, 1970) and elsewhere I have found it particularly abundant in *Bifurcaria bifurcata* Ross, to the stems of which its elongate, rounded body bears a remarkable resemblance. Its colour is variable with the background; often, under stones, it appears dark slaty green or black, but in *Bifurcaria* its coloration assumes the medium brown tone of the algae. This is the most notable example that I have encountered in European seas of protective resemblance to algae.

In his study of the fish fauna of the *Macrocystis* beds, Quast (1968a) defined several groups of fishes which were closely associated with algae at various levels in the community. On the sea bed, living among "flabellate and coralline red algae", were various cottid species and the spotted kelpfish, *Gibbonsia elegans*, all cryptically coloured and difficult to see. Another group inhabited the holdfasts of the kelp and this group also showed cryptic coloration. The most extreme resemblances in coloration and morphological adaptation were observed in the group of fishes that inhabits the kelp stipes and fronds in the kelp forest. In particular, the clinid species, the giant kelpfish, *Heterostichus rostratus*, and the striped kelpfish, *Gibbonsia metzi*, the kelp pipefish, *Syngnathus californiensis*, and the kelp clingfish, *Rimicola muscarum*, are all markedly cryptically coloured. The two clinids are elongate, with compressed bodies, and the clingfish is relatively long and slender when compared with other members of the family; all therefore display considerable modification of body form towards protective resemblance to the algae in which they live. This is also true of the pipefish, although in this family as a whole cryptic coloration, morphology and life-style are well developed. In the *Macrocystis* community in general, many of the active, free-swimming species such as the kelp bass, *Paralabrax clathratus*, the black perch, *Embiotoca jacksoni*, and the kelp perch, *Brachyistius frenatus*, tend to possess cryptic coloration.

Fishes living amongst algae therefore tend to develop cryptic coloration but the degree to which this occurs depends on the life-style of the species. Those that are relatively sedentary show the greatest adaptation. Changes in body form are less pronounced, but are nevertheless detectable. In general, it can be concluded that algae offer considerable protection for the small and inactive fish species, or for the young of larger free-swimming species, which respond by producing some degree of protective resemblance.

ALGAE AS SHELTER FOR BREEDING AND AS NURSERY AREAS

It has already been observed that juvenile specimens of fish which are normally free-swimming inshore species as adults are found in algal-rich shore environments (Table I). To what extent this is due to a deliberate selection of the algal environment or merely random distribution of young fish in search of living space is arguable. However, in the case of such active species as *Atherina presbyter, Pollachius virens* and *Chelon labrosus*, which are often found in intertidal pools, it seems certain that there is either a selection of nursery ground or that pools are used for egg-laying.

In the case of *Atherina presbyter*, there is a strong assumption that the eggs, which are equipped with distinct adhesive filaments, are at least occasionally attached to algae in tide pools in Great Britain (Miller, 1962; Wheeler, 1970). Attachment of the eggs by means of these filaments is common amongst the fishes of this family (Atherinidae) in both freshwater and marine habitats, although some species utilize higher plants rather than algae and others appear not to exercise selection of plants for spawning, the eggs being shed over stones or flotsam (Breder and Rosen, 1966). The saithe, however, breeds offshore and juveniles found in intertidal situations must be present as a result of inshore drifting of postlarvae. Those specimens must therefore be using algal-rich intertidal pools, as well as sublittoral habitats, as nurseries.

Possibly the best-known nest-builders in algae are the sticklebacks, particularly the fifteen-spined stickleback, *Spinachia spinachia* and (along the northern sea board of northern Europe, virtually from Scotland northwards) the three-spined stickleback, *Gasterosteus aculeatus.* Both species build nests composed mainly of plant (principally algal) fragments under algal cover. *Spinachia* builds in clumps of *Fucus* spp. or of *Halidrys*, while *Gasterosteus* nests are usually built in low tufts of algae, in rock crevices, or on bare rock (Wootton, 1976), although I have found one nest built of *Enteromorpha* near to clumps of this alga in an otherwise algal-deficient pool on the north-west coast of Scotland. The related tubesnout, *Aulorhynchus flavidus*, which is widely distributed from Baja California to Alaska, shares the habit of nest building of the other Gasterostiformes. The male tubesnout constructs a nest out of *Macrocystis* fronds bound together with an adhesive secretion, although the eggs are not laid *in* the nest but rather on the algae near the nest's upper surface (Breder and Rosen, 1966). Nest-building in the alga *Desmarestia aculeata* (L.) Lamour. was reported in the Friday Harbour area of Washington (Hart, 1973).

Members of the family Labridae exhibit striking differences in their spawning. Most of the tropical species, which are very numerous, appear to produce pelagic eggs; many of the Old World temperate wrasses, by contrast, construct nests and lay demersal, adhesive eggs. Members of the genus *Labrus* and many *Crenilabrus* species build nests in algae in the low intertidal or the subtidal, most of them also using algae in the construction of the nest (Wheeler, 1978; Breder and Rosen, 1966). Certain inshore species of the family Cottidae also lay eggs in clumps amongst low tufted seaweed, but nests are rarely constructed. In one example, the European sea scorpion *Taurulus bubalis*, a nest is built and the male is reported to guard the clump of eggs (Wheeler, 1978). Most members of the family attach their eggs to crevices, lay them inside shells, or on bare rock. In this family, internal fertilization and parental care are also well developed.

At least some of their relatives in the family Agonidae, such as *Agonus cataphractus*, the European hooknose or pogge, also utilize algae for the deposition of clumps of eggs. In the latter species, the eggs are laid between the branching holdfasts of kelp, or occasionally on the upper surfaces of the discoid holdfasts of fucoid algae, but spawning is very uncommon in the intertidal zone (Wheeler, 1978). Similarly, some members of the family Clinidae, e.g. the Mediterranean *Clinitrachus argentatus* (Risso) (Breder and Rosen, 1966), are said to construct nests in algae whilst other species lay their eggs in sponges; in many, fertilization is internal, and viviparity is widespread. The order Gobiesociformes includes species which usually lay and guard their eggs inside crevices, in mollusc shells, or beneath boulders. The European small-headed clingfish (*Apletodon microcephalus*), however, both lays its eggs and guards them within the hollow holdfasts of *Laminaria*; very probably other members of this family make similar use of algae, but in general the biology of these tiny cryptic fishes is little known.

The use of algae as nest sites is therefore widespread amongst bony fishes, several fish families being involved. Most of them, however, belong to groups which generally spawn in crevices or under rocks and the laying of eggs amongst or inside algal holdfasts, and even nest-building within algal clumps, can be seen as elaborations of the normal breeding behaviour of the group.

Very few elasmobranch fishes use algae as a habitat in which to deposit eggs, although the two inshore scyliorhinid dogfishes of Europe lay their egg-cases tangled in sublittoral algae. The paucity of algal associations with elasmobranchs is a reflection of the carnivorous, generally active-swimming, lifestyles of the latter and of the considerable degree of viviparity that they exhibit.

Algal cover also serves as a nursery area for some active, pelagic species more usually found as adults in open water. The number of instances in which this has been demonstrated, however, is relatively small and the algal fish community is composed mainly of benthic thigmotactic species.

SUMMARY

There is considerable indirect evidence that algae influence fishes in a number of ways. The most direct association is that of provision of shelter to fish communities that would otherwise be confined to the sea bed, as their life-styles are benthic and thigmotactic. This is particularly true of the littoral fish fauna, for which algal cover also provides protection against both non-aquatic predators and desiccation. Sublittorally too, the presence of kelp increases the living space available to an otherwise mainly benthic community. The stipes and fronds of kelp create a three-dimensional environment for small cryptic species, whilst for active-swimming fish they provide cover and points of reference between the surface and the sea bed. Where extensive kelp beds exist, as on the Pacific coast of North America, the fish fauna has evolved a high degree of endemism.

The value of the protection offered by algae is reflected in the extent to which fishes associated with them adopt protective resemblances in both colour and form. While the examples cited for temperate water are less extreme than those described from tropical marine or freshwater habitats, there are nevertheless sufficient of them to suggest that algal cover is a significant factor in the maintenance of a diverse inshore fish fauna. The provision of cover by algae leads to a number of fish species adopting a nest-building reproductive behaviour, in which the algal fronds are either used directly as nests or in building nests, or the eggs are laid in clumps close to algal holdfasts.

Algae seem to be of minor importance as food in temperate waters, a striking contrast to the situation in tropical seas. However, there is little doubt that invertebrates utilizing the algae as a base for attachment or for food and shelter provide a major source of food for the fishes that also inhabit the algal community.

It can reasonably be stated, therefore, that algae contribute considerably to the diversity of the littoral and sublittoral fish community and increase the biomass of fishes in areas where they are well represented.

REFERENCES

Bailey, R. M., Fitch, J. E., Herald, E. S., Lachner, E. A., Lindsey, C. C., Robins, C. R. and Scott, W. B. (1970). A list of common and scientific names of fishes from the United States and Canada (3rd edn.). *Spec. Publ. Am. Fish. Soc.* 6, 1–149.

Bolin, R. L. (1944). A review of the marine cottid fishes of California. *Stanford ichth. Bull.* 3(1), 1–135.

Breder, C. M. and Rosen, D. E. (1966). "Modes of Reproduction in Fishes". Natural History Press, New York.

Christensen, M. S. (1978). Trophic relationships in juveniles of three species of sparid fishes in the South African marine littoral. *Fishery Bull. natn ocean. atmos. Adm.* **76** (2), 389–401.

Dipper, F. A., Bridges, C. R. and Menz, A. (1977). Age, growth and feeding in the ballan wrasse *Labrus bergylta* Ascanius 1767. *J. Fish Biol.* **11**, 105–120.

Dunne, J. (1972). Some interesting fish recorded from Galway Bay and adjacent areas during 1970 and 1971. *Scient. Proc. R. Dubl. Soc.* (B) **3** (12), 159–163.

Dunne, J. (1977). Littoral and benthic investigations on the west coast of Ireland – VII the biology of the shanny, *Blennius pholis* L. (Pisces) at Carna, Connemara. *Proc. R. Ir. Acad.* **77** B (12), 207–226.

Emery, A. R. (1978). The basis of fish community structure: marine and fresh-water comparisons. *Env. Biol. Fish.* **3**, 33–47.

Gibson, R. N. (1968). The food and feeding relationships of littoral fish in the Banyuls region. *Vie Milieu* (A) **19** (2A), 447–456.

Gibson, R. N. (1970). Observations on the biology of the giant goby *Gobius cobitis* Pallas. *J. Fish Biol.* **2**, 281–288.

Gibson, R. N. (1972). The vertical distribution and feeding relationships of intertidal fish on the Atlantic coast of France. *J. Anim. Ecol.* **41**, 189–207.

Hart, J. L. (1973). Pacific fishes of Canada. *Bull. Fish. Res. Bd Canada* **180**, 1–740.

Hartnoll, R. G. (1963). The biology of Manx spider crabs. *Proc. zool. Soc. Lond.* **141**, 423–496.

Hiatt, R. W. and Strasburg, D. W. (1960). Ecological relationships of the fish fauna on coral reefs of the Marshall Islands. *Ecol. Monogr.* **30** (1), 65–127.

Hickling, C. F. (1970). A contribution to the natural history of the English grey mullets (Pisces, Mugilidae). *J. mar. biol. Ass. U.K.* **50**, 609–633.

Luckhurst, B. E. and Luckhurst, K. (1978). Analysis of the influence of sub-strate variables on coral reefs fish communities. *Mar. Biol., Berl.* **49**, 317–323.

Marsh, B., Crowe, T. M. and Siegfried, W. R. (1978). Species richness and abundance of clinid fish (Teleostei; Clinidae) in intertidal rock pools. *Zoo-logica afr.* **13**, 283–291.

Miller, P. J. (1962). Evidence for the breeding in Manx waters of the sand smelt, *Atherina presbyter* C. & V. *Rep. mar. biol. Stn Port Erin* **74**, 27–28.

Naylor, E. (1955). The diet and feeding mechanisms of *Idotea*. *J. mar. biol. Ass. U.K.* **34**, 347–355.

Nicholls, A. G. (1931). Studies on *Ligia oceanica*. Part II The process of feeding, digestion and absorption, with a description of the structure of the foregut. *J. mar. biol. Ass. U.K.* **17**, 675–707.

Penrith, M. -L. (1969). The systematics of the fishes of the family Clinidae in South Africa. *Ann. S. Afr. Mus.* **55** (1), 1–121.

Penrith, M. -L. (1970). The distribution of the fishes of the family Clinidae in southern Africa. *Ann. S. Afr. Mus.* **55** (2), 135–150.

Quast, J. C. (1968a). 5. Fish fauna of the rocky inshore zone. *Fish Bull. Calif.* **139**, 35–55.

Quast, J. C. (1968b). 6. Estimates of the population and the standing crop of fishes. *Fish Bull. Calif.* **139**, 57–79.

Quast, J. C. (1968c). 8. Observations on the food of the kelp-bed fishes. *Fish Bull. Calif.* **139**, 109–142.

Quignard, J. -P. (1966). Recherches sur les Labridae (Poissons Téléostéens Perciformes) des Côtes Européennes systématique et biologie. *Naturalia monspel. ser. Zool.* **5**, 1–247.

Randall, J. E. (1961). Overgrazing of algae by herbivorous marine fishes. *Ecology, Brooklyn* **42** (4), 812.

Randall, J. E. (1967). Food habits of reef fishes of the West Indies. *Stud. trop. Oceanogr.* **5**, 665–847.

Randall, J. E. and Randall, H. A. (1960). Examples of mimicry and protective resemblance in tropical marine fishes. *Bull. mar. Sci. Gulf Caribb.* **10** (4), 444–480.

Ropes, J. W. (1969). The feeding habits of the green crab, *Carcinus maenas* (L.). *Fishery Bull. Fish. Wildl. Serv. U.S.* **67** (2), 183–203.

Tortonese, E. (1975). Osteichthyes (Pesci Ossei) Parte seconda. *Fauna d'Italia* **11**, 1–636.

Warner, G. F. (1977). "The Biology of Crabs". Elek Science, London.

Wheeler, A. (1969). "The Fishes of the British Isles and North West Europe". MacMillan, London.

Wheeler, A. (1970). Notes on a collection of shore fishes from Guernsey, Channel Islands. *J. Fish Biol.* **2**, 323–328.

Wheeler, A. (1978). "Key to the Fishes of Northern Europe". F. Warne, London.

Wootton, R. J. (1976). "The Biology of the Sticklebacks". Academic Press, London and New York.

9 | Predation and Community Structure

ROGER N. HUGHES

Department of Zoology, University College of North Wales, Bangor, Gwynedd LL5D 2UW, Wales

Abstract: Predators may have two levels of effect on communities. The first level encompasses the possible consequences of reduced prey densities due to predation. This level may influence the species richness and stability properties of the community. The second level includes the behavioural and evolutionary consequences of the predator–prey arms race. This level may influence the genetic, phenotypic, behavioural or life-history properties of predators and prey. Both levels may influence the species composition of the community.

Competition for space is an almost universal phenomenon among rocky shore communities, and competition for space or food may be important on many sedimentary shores. Potential dominants will tend to exclude species below them in competitive hierarchies unless competition is interrupted. Such interruption may be caused by predation in the more benign physical environments and in the trophically more complex communities. For predation to have the effects of promoting species richness and avoiding instability, individual prey species must be neither over-exploited nor under-exploited. Special features of predator–prey systems such as density-dependent predation rates, density-dependent prey preferences, search images, prey refuges, are potentially stabilizing effects operating on an ecological time-scale. On an evolutionary time-scale, the development of anti-predator defence mechanisms will tend to reduce the number of potential enemies of certain prey species. In such cases, the co-evolution of specialized predators able to break through the preys' defences may have the important effect of checking the prey population densities, so preventing competitive exclusions within the prey trophic level.

Intertidal predator–prey systems are examined in the above context. Herbivorous and carnivorous predators are seen to prevent competitive exclusion

Systematics Association Special Volume No. 17(b), "The Shore Environment, Vol. 2: Ecosystems", edited by J. H. Price, D. E. G. Irvine and W. F. Farnham, 1980, pp. 699–728, Academic Press, London and New York.

among prey species in certain shore environments. Some invertebrate predators appear to have complex foraging behaviours which may stabilize community structure. The study of foraging methods of intertidal predators is an almost virgin field which holds great promise for the understanding of intertidal community dynamics.

INTRODUCTION

In an ecological context, predation can be taken to include both herbivory and carnivory, the only real difference between the two being the trophic level of the prey. Such a broad definition will include a bewildering diversity of predatory forms, so an elementary classification of basic types may be useful. We may thus distinguish between grazers, which eat only part of each prey item without killing it, and predators which kill each prey item. The killers may be subdivided into ambushers which rely on the movement of prey towards them, searchers which actively forage for prey but spend relatively little time chasing individual prey (handling time short relative to search time) and pursuers which indulge in long and tenacious pursuits of individual prey (handling time long relative to search time). As with all arbitrary biological classifications, it will be difficult to place some organisms in particular categories. The categories should be regarded as extremes in a continuum.

On an ecological time scale, predation may have important effects on community structure by limiting prey population densities. The dynamics of predator–prey systems are still not well understood, even though five decades have elapsed since Lotka and Volterra produced the first substantial theoretical treatments on the subject. It is now known however, that even a simple, single predator and prey system can exhibit an impressive repertoire of dynamical behaviour depending on the relative magnitudes of predator/prey intrinsic rates of increase, generation times, resource limitation of prey population density and the response of predator attack rate and population growth rate to changes in prey density (May, 1976). When multiple predator–prey systems are considered together with spatial and temporal environmental heterogeneity, the picture becomes bewildering. Fortunately, empirical studies, especially on intertidal communities, have begun to suggest some simple generalizations about the influence of predation on community structure. The most fundamental theme seems to be that uninterrupted competition within a community will usually result in the progressive exclusion of poorer competitors by superior competitors until only one or a few competitive dominants remain to monopolize the resources, with a consequent reduction in species richness of the community. By interrupting competition, predation, in common with other possible forces, may prevent competitive exclusions and so have the effect of promoting community species richness (Paine, 1966).

Potential competitors within a community cannot always be arranged in a hierarchy of competitive ability; for example Lubchenco and Menge (1978) found that the competitive success of sessile organisms of the low intertidal zone of rocky shores in New England depends on unpredictable temporal and spatial effects on settlement, so that relative competitive abilities are not static. Nevertheless, competitive hierarchies are sufficiently widespread to justify their use as a paradigm for discussing general community structure.

The effect of predation on competitive hierarchies is most readily seen where the competitive processes themselves are easily understood. Not surprisingly, therefore, it is the effect of herbivores on terrestrial plant communities and the effect of herbivores and carnivores on communities of littoral sedentary organisms which have been well documented, for in both cases the prey organisms clearly compete for space and associated resources.

However, in addition to its possible effect on community species richness, predation may also have equally important effects on prey population dynamics and spatial distribution which in turn will affect community structure and function. To understand these effects, it is necessary to know how the predators forage and how their population dynamics are coupled with those of their prey. Because it is amenable to experimental analysis and because it does not necessarily involve very long-term observations, the study of foraging methods has recently emerged as a promising line in our quest for an understanding of community function (Krebs, 1978).

The first part of the following discussion will explore current knowledge of foraging methods in littoral predators. This will lead on to an examination of the predator–prey arms race taking place on an evolutionary time-scale and involving feedback between predation tactics and prey defence mechanisms. Such coevolution will tend to reduce both the number of predator species per prey species and the diet widths of the predators feeding on these prey, and therefore may have important effects on community structure and stability. Finally, field studies on the effects of predation on intertidal community structure will be reviewed and some promising lines for future research suggested.

THE KINDS OF LITTORAL PREDATORS

Substratum-type, exposure to wave action and geographical latitude will have distinct but overlapping effects on the taxonomy of predators and prey. Only the broadest generalizations will be considered here.

Cool-temperate rocky shores are dominated by fucoid algae in sheltered to moderately exposed places and by barnacles and mussels in very exposed places. Fucoid thalli are grazed by a few specialized prosobranch gastropods while their microscopic sporelings, together with unicellular algae, are grazed by a much wider range of prosobranchs including chitons, limpets, trochids and littorinids. Barnacles and mussels are eaten by muricid gastropods, a few nudibranchs, asteroids, crabs, blennies, wrasses and a few birds. Grazing gastropods are eaten by crabs, fish and birds. On many rocky shores solitary or colonial sea anemones are important carnivores. The lower boundary of the rocky littoral zone is dominated by kelps which are grazed by a few specialized gastropods and, in many parts of the world, by sea urchins. Sea urchins are eaten by large decapod crustaceans, asteroids and certain vertebrates.

Cool-temperate sedimentary shores are dominated by deposit and filter feeding polychaetes, bivalves, gastropods, amphipods and isopods. All are eaten by fish, birds and decapod crustaceans. Polychaetes are also eaten by other polychaetes, while bivalves are eaten by certain gastropods.

Warm-temperate and tropical cliff-like shores are often dominated by barnacles and microalgae or turf-forming algae, with the addition of colonial vermetid gastropods, serpulid polychaetes and zoanthid anemones when there is adequate wave action. In these habitats, and in the more complex reef–lagoon system commonly found in the tropics, algal grazers are represented by more diverse taxa than in cool-temperate regions, with the notable addition of grapsid crabs and a variety of fish which migrate onshore with the tide. There is also a greater taxonomic variety of carnivores, especially among molluscs, crabs and fish.

Tropical sedimentary shores have rather similar infauna to temperate shores but have the conspicuous addition of ocypodid crabs, some of which are detritus feeders, but others of which are important carnivores.

On a world-wide scale, the predominant predatory taxa on shores are anthozoans, gastropods, decapod crustaceans, asteroids, echinoids, fish and birds. Among these taxa are found the whole continuum of predator types outlined in the introduction. Specific examples are illustrated in Fig. 1.

FORAGING METHODS

The conceptual study of foraging methods has taken two roads, one leading to the study of prey choice (optimal diets), the other leading to the study of choice of feeding locations (optimal foraging). Both avenues of approach are sometimes grouped under the general heading of "optimal foraging" (Pyke *et al.*, 1977; Krebs, 1978). Only the dietary aspects of foraging have thus far received much attention by littoral biologists, but the study of spatial aspects of foraging offer a promising topic for the future.

1. Optimal Diets

Nearly all theoretical developments in this area have been built upon the "energy maximization premise" which states that predators should choose prey items so as to maximize their rate of energy intake. For a particular predator, each prey type will have a characteristic dietary "value" defined as the ratio of energy yield to handling time. Handling time includes all the events from perception of the prey item to the resumption of searching for more prey. According to the type of predator, handling time might therefore include events such as pursuit, attack, subduing, ingestion, digestive pause. It is assumed that the predator can rank all prey items in order of their prey values and that it can use this ranking to decide whether encountered prey should be eaten or not. Simple models predict that (1) the highest ranking prey should always be eaten when encountered, and (2) lower ranking prey should only be eaten

Fig. 1. Predator types. Herbivorous grazers: periwinkle, limpet, grapsid crab. Carnivorous grazers: dorid nudibranch, aeolid nudibranch, cowrie. Ambushers: sea anemone. Searchers: shore crab, sea scorpion (sculpin), errant polychaete. Pursuers: gastropods of the families Naticidae, Conidae, Muricidae, and starfish.

when better prey are too scarce to meet the energy requirements of the predator, irrespective of their own relative abundance. As the highest ranking prey become scarce, progressively lower ranking prey should be included sequentially into the diet. The lower ranking prey should be dropped from the diet in the reverse order as preferred prey become more abundant. One facet of this second prediction, that diets should expand or contract according to the availability of preferred prey, is intuitively rather obvious and has been recorded many times in nature. But the second facet, that the abundance of lower ranking prey should not influence their inclusion in the diet, is less obvious and has rarely been recorded. However, modifications to the simple models which allow for the possibilities of significant time intervals taken by the predator to evaluate each prey item and of the predator's ability to reduce handling times with increased experience of particular prey types, alter the prediction so that lower ranking prey should be included in the diet when sufficiently abundant, even if preferred prey are plentiful (Hughes, 1979). The learning component in the model also leads to the possibility of switching, whereby the predator changes from a specialized diet on one prey type to that on another. This is caused by two prey types being transposed in rank as their respective handling times are altered by the predator's experience (Hughes, 1979).

Although the energy maximization premise probably has fairly general applicability, it will be overriden in those cases where predators can only assess the dietary values of different prey types by sampling them from time to time (Westoby, 1974) and where nutrients rather than energy are limiting (Pulliam, 1975). Nevertheless, there is considerable evidence that predator diets often do conform to the prediction of the energy maximation premise and this evidence will now be reviewed for littoral predators, taking the major categories of predators in turn.

(a) Grazers. These are either herbivores feeding on algae, or carnivores feeding on sedentary invertebrates. The herbivores are, however, likely to ingest newly settled invertebrates larvae. Diet widths in herbivores tend to be broad, but there is often a marked sequence of preferences for particular prey species. The sea urchins *Strongylocentrotus droebachiensis* (O. F. Müller) and *S. franciscanus* eat over a dozen algal species on Californian shores, but in the laboratory

they show marked prey preferences which are correlated with the absorption efficiencies for the different algae (Vadas, 1977). The most efficiently absorbed and therefore the most preferred alga, *Nereocystis luetkeana* (Mert.) Post. et Rupr., is always eaten when encountered, but its availability depends on dislodged plants being washed inshore. Consequently, the availability of *Nereocystis* is never sufficient to meet the dietary requirements of the urchins which have, therefore, to feed also on less preferred algae. The latter species are eaten in proportion to their abundances in the field, except for *Opuntiella californica* (Farl.) Kyl. which is avoided owing to its herbivore-repellent chemicals. Although by no means a rigorous test of optimal diet theory, the preferences shown by the urchins for particular algae in the laboratory and the composition of their natural diets are certainly consistent with theoretical predictions.

The dietary values of algae may not depend simply on their absolute energy content but will also depend on physical or chemical properties which affect the rate of ingestion and efficiency of absorption by the grazers. Whereas the preferences shown by *Strongylocentrotus* spp. were correlated with absorption efficiencies, they were not correlated with the energy content of the algal tissues (Vadas, 1977). Similarly, the chiton *Katherina tunicata* (Wood) prefers *Hedophyllum sessile* (C. Ag.) Setch. to *Iridaea cordata* (Turn.) Bory (Himmelman and Carefoot, 1975). *Hedophyllum* tissue has a lower energy content than that of *Iridaea*, but in feeding trails *Katherina* was found to ingest *Hedophyllum* three times as fast as *Iridaea.* Evidently the radular teeth of *Katherina* are better able to cope with the fleshy constitution of *Hedophyllum* than with the limper material of *Iridaea* (Himmelman and Carefoot, 1975). Whether algal grazers can recognize the value of individual plants by olfaction or whether they need to ingest some tissue in order to evaluate the prey item, is not known. It will be important to find this out, because if prey evaluation depends on the ingestion of a sample of the algal tissue, then the time invested in sampling will, in theory, tend to widen the diet. When sampling time, or prey recognition time, is important, the energy maximization premise predicts that sub-optimal prey should be eaten according to their relative abundances (Hughes, 1979), as was the case with *Strongylocentrotus* spp. (Vadas, 1977).

The energy maximization premise may not be applicable to all predators all of the time. On British Columbian shores the isopod *Ligia pallasii* (Brandt) prefers *Nereocystis luetkeana* and *Ulva* spp., neither of which grow in its immediate habitat (Carefoot, 1973). *Ligia pallasii* does not therefore feed on algae simply in proportion to their availability. However, the preferences for *Nereocystis* and *Ulva* seem to be based on different criteria, since the rate of energy intake from *Nereocystis* is less than a quarter of that from *Ulva*. Carefoot (1973) suggests that the high water content of *Nereocystis*, which depresses its energy yield, may be a valuable resource for *Ligia*, whereas *Ulva* is valuable for its energy yield.

Diet widths in carnivorous grazers tend to be narrower than in herbivores, some species feeding only on single prey species. Such specialized diets are likely to be the result of coevolution between predator and prey. Toxic chemicals have been found very frequently among sedentary invertebrates (Jackson and Buss, 1975) and it is not surprising, therefore, that only the relatively few predators coevolved to withstand these defence mechanisms commonly feed on such prey. Each colony of a sedentary animal presents to the predator a patch of similarly sized polyps or zooids, or in the case of sponges, a homogeneous patch of tissue. There will be very little variation in prey value at different points within the food patch. Carnivorous grazers therefore encounter very monotonous arrays of prey items and consequently optimal diet theory is less applicable to them than it is to predators with wider choices of prey types. Optimal patch use theory may be more relevant to specialized carnivorous grazers.

(b) Predators on discrete food items. This group could include those herbivores which feed on unicellular algae, since each prey item is destroyed when attacked. However, such herbivores have conventionally been regarded as grazers and there is perhaps some justification for retaining this view because many patches of algal cells, whether benthic diatoms or planktonic phytoflagellates, will consist of clones. A predator cropping a fraction of the genetically identical cells in a clone is analogous to a predator grazing part of a multicellular plant. The precise classification is, however, of minor importance since it is irrelevant to the application of optimal diet theory. Prey choice among littoral herbivores feeding on benthic unicellular algae has scarcely been studied. Differences in radular morphology

and body size among gastropods will cause different species to graze the substratum to different depths, so that their diets are likely to differ, but such mechanisms have evolved as a result of interspecific competition rather than in response to selection for optimal foraging. Because handling times per prey item are vanishingly small, specialized diets would theoretically not be expected in grazers on unicellular algae.

Some of the most successful applications of optimal diet theory have been those concerned with intertidal carnivores feeding on discrete prey items. Preferences for prey items with the highest dietary value, defined as the ratio of energy yield to handling time, have been demonstrated for a number of littoral predators. These include the starfish *Asterias rubens* L. feeding on the bivalve *Macoma balthica* L. (Anger *et al.*, 1977), the starfish *Leptasterias hexactis* (Stimpson) feeding on a variety of gastropods and barnacles (Menge, 1972), the shore crab *Carcinus maenas* (L.) feeding on mussels *Mytilus edulis* L. (Elner and Hughes, 1978), the dogwhelk *Thais lapillus* (L.) feeding on *Mytilus edulis* (Bayne and Scullard, 1978), the dogwhelk *Acanthina punctulata* (Sowerby) feeding on winkles *Littorina* spp. (J. L. Menge, 1974), the dogwhelk *Thais emarginata* (Deshayes) feeding on barnacles *Balanus glandula* Darwin (Emlen, 1966), the fifteen-spined stickleback *Spinachia spinachia* (L.) feeding on mysids *Neomysis integer* (Leach) and *Praunus flexuosus* (O. F. Müller) (Kislalioglu and Gibson, 1976), the redshank *Tringa totanus* (L.) feeding on the amphipod *Corophium volutator* (Pallas) and polychaetes (Goss-Custard, 1977a,b), the oystercatcher *Haematopus ostralegus* L. feeding on cockles *Cerastoderma edule* (L.) (O'Connor and Brown, 1977), and the black oystercatcher *H. bachmani* Audubon feeding on mussels, *Mytilus californianus* Conrad, and limpets, *Acmaea* spp. (Hartwick, 1976).

Among the most extensive applications of optimal diet theory to date are those concerned with shore crabs, redshanks and oystercatchers, as summarized below. When fed on mussels scattered haphazardly on the floor of laboratory aquaria, shore crabs were found to select mussel sizes close to those predicted from experimental determinations of dietary value, and optimal mussel size was found to increase with increased size of the crab (Elner and Hughes, 1978). Feeding sequences showed that the differential size-specific predation was not merely due to a passive mechanical phenomenon,

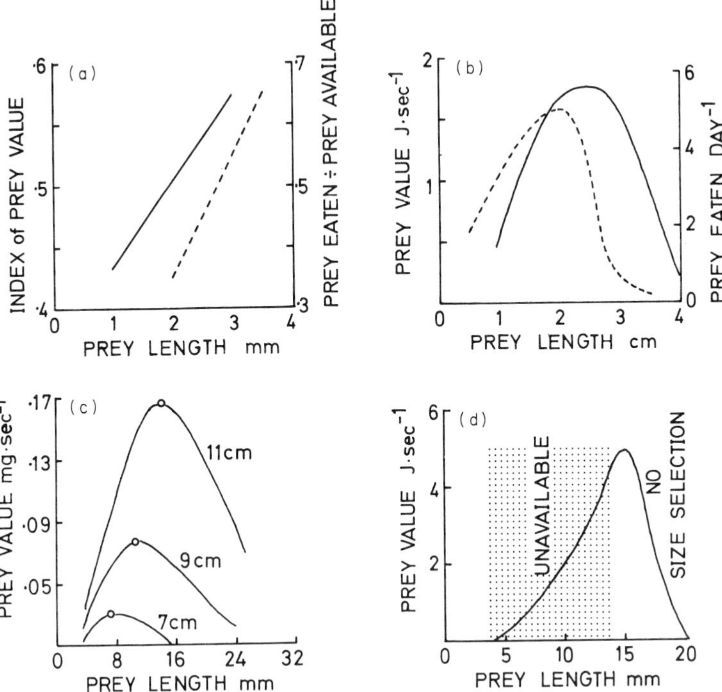

Fig. 2. Prey values and preferences of the predators. (a) *Balanus glandula* eaten by *Thais emarginata* (Emlen, 1966). Solid line = prey value; dashed line = prey preference. (b) *Mytilus edulis* eaten by *Carcinus maenas* (Elner and Hughes, 1978). Solid line = prey value; dashed line = prey preference. (c) *Praunus flexuosus* eaten by *Spinachia spinachia* (Kislalioglu and Gibson, 1972). Prey value curves for sticklebacks of 7, 9 and 11 cm in length respectively. Open circles = mean preferred prey sizes. (d) *Thais lapillus* eaten by *Carcinus maenas* (Hughes and Elner, 1979). Solid line = prey value.

but resulted from the active acceptance or rejection of individual mussels by the crabs. The precise mechanisms enabling the crabs to evaluate mussels in this way are as yet unknown. When optimally sized mussels became depleted, the crabs expanded their diets to include less valuable mussels, both smaller and larger than the optimum. Even when optimally sized mussels were plentiful, less valuable mussels were still taken in small numbers when they too were abundant. Because shore crabs locate and identify prey items by smell and touch, it is likely that significant prey-recognition times are involved, in which case theory predicts that suboptimal prey should be taken in proportion to their relative abundance (Hughes, 1979).

A rather different foraging method is used by shore crabs feeding on dogwhelks. Adult dogwhelks are too robust for shore crabs to crack, while the fragile juveniles live beneath stones or in crevices where they are inaccessible to crabs. Consequently, only subadult dogwhelks of a narrow size range are available as prey to shore crabs. Not only are sub-adult dogwhelk relatively scarce, but owing to individual variability in shell strength, the time required for a crab to crack them is rather unpredictable. Therefore, it is unlikely that shore crabs would use on dogwhelks such a finely-tuned optimal diet selection mechanism as they do on mussels which are abundant and have predictable prey values. When fed on dogwhelks in the laboratory, shore crabs were found to use a constant persistence time, whereby all encountered dogwhelks, irrespective of size, were attacked for up to about three minutes and abandoned if not opened by this time (Hughes and Elner, 1979).

Black oystercatchers foraging on an exposed rocky shore near Vancouver Island fed preferentially on mussels, concentrating on sizes somewhat larger than the model size for the mussel population (Hartwick, 1976). Only mussels of the preferred size and the largest available limpets were transported to the nestlings some distance from the mussel bed, whereas the adults included in their own diets smaller mussels and a few of the smaller limpets which were very abundant on the mussel beds. The larger handling costs associated with feeding prey to the chicks evidently caused the parents to be more selective in their choice of prey items for the chicks than for their own diets, as would be expected from optimal diet theory.

Redshanks foraging on estuarine mudflats populated by the amphipod *Corophium volutator* (Pallas) and the polychaete *Nereis diversicolor* O. F. Müller have been observed to feed preferentially on *Corophium*, the number of polychaetes taken being independent of their own relative abundance but dependent only on the density of *Corophium* (Goss-Custard, 1977a). The absolute dietary value of *Corophium* is less than that of *Nereis*, but the higher attack success rate for *Corophium* gives the latter prey a higher expected dietary value. On mudflats populated mainly by polychaetes *Nereis diversicolor* and *Nephthys hombergi* Lamarck, redshanks were found to select the largest size classes of worm, which have the highest dietary value. Again the rate of consumption of less preferred, smaller worms was found to depend only on the density of the preferred sizes of worm (Goss-Custard, 1977b).

The applications of optimal diet theory considered thus far have all assumed that prey handling times are constant for a predator feeding on a given prey type. It is possible, however, that handling times, recognition times and attack success rates may be altered by experience and thus might be functions of the encounter rate with each prey type. It will be very important to establish whether such is the case because, when handling times are allowed to be functions of encounter rates with the prey, the optimal diet model predicts that the dietary values of prey may become transposed in rank, so that the predator might switch from a specialized diet on one prey type to that on another (Hughes, 1979). Switching of diets would have community-stabilizing properties if it prevented particular prey types from being exploited to local extinction. It could also be a mechanism for apostatic selection when the alternative prey types are different morphs of the same species. This subject has scarcely been explored, but there is scattered evidence that the feeding behaviour of some littoral predators may become modified with experience. Oyster drills *Urosalpinx cinerea* (Say), fed for a while on barnacles *Balanus balanoides* (L.), react more strongly to water which has flowed over barnacles than others which have not recently fed on barnacles (Pratt, 1974). Dogwhelks *Thais lapillus* fed for a time on mussels *Mytilus edulis* attack this prey more efficiently than those previously fed on barnacles (Morgan, 1972). The crown of thorns starfish *Acanthaster planci* (L.) normally reacts strongly to extract from the tissues of certain corals, but gradually suppresses the response after continued presentation of the extract on plaster tablets. The starfish evidently learns to associate the olfactory stimuli with "prey" of zero dietary values (Huxley, 1976). Ghost crabs *Ocypode ceratophthalmus* (Pallas) apparently use vision to locate their bivalve prey *Donax faba* Gmelin on East African shores and prey differentially on certain colour morphs (Smith, 1975). It is not known if *Ocypode* can form search images but it would seem capable of learning. Another visual predator, the redshank, concentrates increasingly on *Corophium* as the latter increases in density, a response which may involve the development of a search image (Goss-Custard, 1977a). The actual switching of diets has only twice been recorded for littoral predators. Murdoch (1969) found that the dogwhelk *Acanthina spirata* (Blainville) switched from a diet of mussels (*Mytilus californianus*) to one of barnacles (*Balanus glandula*) as their relative abundance were altered. The switch could be reversed by training to the alternative prey type. Switching in a Scottish population of 0-group plaice *Pleuronectes platessa* L. was noted by Trevallion *et al.* (1970) who found that plaice diets contained almost exclusively *Tellina tenuis* da Costa siphons or polychaetes, depending on which were most abundant. We should expect the modification of foraging methods by learning wherever special attack methods or recognition stimuli are associated with particular prey types.

2. *Optimal Patch Use*

The energy maximization premise can be applied to a predator's allocation of foraging time among different environmental patches, each containing certain prey mixtures and prey densities. Predictions analogous to those of optimal diet theory are produced: the predator should concentrate on the richest patches and stay in them until their net rate of energy intake in these patches falls to the average intake for the habitat. This, of course, requires the predator to commit some of its foraging time to sampling other patches for comparison. Useful reviews of the subject may be found in Pyke *et al.* (1977) and Krebs (1978).

Although very relevant to the study of intertidal predator–prey systems and community structure, optimal patch use theory has not yet been adequately tested in the marine context. Two notable exceptions are both concerned with birds. O'Connor and Brown (1977) demonstrated very elegantly how oystercatchers foraging for cockles in Strangford Lough, Northern Ireland, concentrate on the most profitable patches, i.e. those with the highest densities of second-winter cockles, until the prey become so depleted that it is more profitable to move on to other patches which previously would have had poorer stocks of cockles. The oystercatchers apparently assess pitch quality as they fly over the area and perceive the local densities of the anvils where cockles are smashed open. A similar concentration on the most profitable patches was observed in redshanks foraging for *Corophium* in the Ythan estuary, Scotland (Goss-Custard, 1970).

Application of optimal patch use theory to littoral invertebrate predators will be a promising area for development. The way in which predators, such as dogwhelks foraging over a mosaic of mussels and barnacles, or nudibranchs feeding among patches of sessile colonial invertebrates, exploit local patches of prey is likely to have important effects on prey spatial distribution and hence community structure. A predator conforming to the predictions of optimal patch use theory should have the effect of evening-out prey density among different patches rather than causing local extinctions of prey.

3. The Limits of Diet Width

Optimal diet theory predicts how a predator should choose its diet from a given set of alternative prey types, but does not tell us how large such a set may be. The size of the prey set, i.e. whether a predator is a specialist or a generalist, was given theoretical treatment by MacArthur (1972). Other things being equal, ambush predators such as sea anemones should have very wide diets since they cannot influence the rates of encounter with different prey types; whereas pursuers, such as many fish and muricid gastropods which use lengthy stalking or attack procedures, should have specialized diets, feeding only on relatively large, energy-rich prey which repay the cost of the chase. Searchers like the shore crab, which forage but do not extensively pursue individual prey, should have flexible diets which contract or expand according to the nature of the available prey. Overlying these considerations will be the effects of coevolution. Anti-predator defence mechansims will cause selection for certain predators to develop counterattack mechanisms, but this will require specialized techniques, often including modifications to morphology and behaviour so that the predator becomes able to feed efficiently only on the coevolved prey species. Nudibranchs are examples of such specialized predators.

THE DYNAMICS OF PREDATION

Optimal foraging theory deals with the predator's choice of prey types and foraging sites. However, the intensity of predation on chosen prey types will depend on the way in which the attack rate per predator changes with prey density, the so-called functional response, and the way in which predator density changes with prey density, termed the numerical response. The functional and numerical responses can, at least in theory, affect the stability of predator–prey systems according to whether they are positively density-dependent (potentially stabilizing), negatively density-dependent (destabilizing) or, in the case of the numerical response, operating with appreciable time lags (destabilizing).

1. Functional Response

When the attack rate per predator is plotted against prey density, a variety of curves may be obtained depending on the nature of the predator and prey, but three distinct shapes of curve are customarily used as reference points. Type 1 is a line of constant slope terminated by an upper threshold prey density beyond which the attack rate does not change, and possibly by a lower threshold prey density below which attack rate decreases rapidly; such a functional response requires a negligible prey-handling time and it has been found only among filter feeders. Type 2 is a curve with slope decreasing monotonically to zero at an upper asymptote; the slope decreases because the time taken to handle prey accounts for an increasing proportion of available foraging time, so that the attack rate becomes limited by the handling of prey items rather than by prey density; such a functional response has been found among many invertebrates, including the helmet shell *Cassis tuberosa* (L.) feeding on sea urchins *Echinometra lucunter* (L.) (Hughes and Hughes, 1971) and among certain vertebrates, e.g. redshanks feeding on *Corophium* and polychaetes (Goss-Custard, 1976). Type 3 is a sigmoid curve, the inflexion point usually occurring in the lower range of prey densities. Below the inflexion, the slope increases due to an increase in attack efficiency which may be due to a variety of causes such as reduced handling time, development of a search image, or improved attack method, all of which involve forms of learning. Above the inflexion, the slope decreases to zero because of the effect of handling time, as in the Type 2 functional response. Because learning is sometimes thought to require a rather sophisticated nervous system, Type 3 functional responses have been thought more likely to occur among vertebrates than among invertebrates. Recent work, however, has shown that

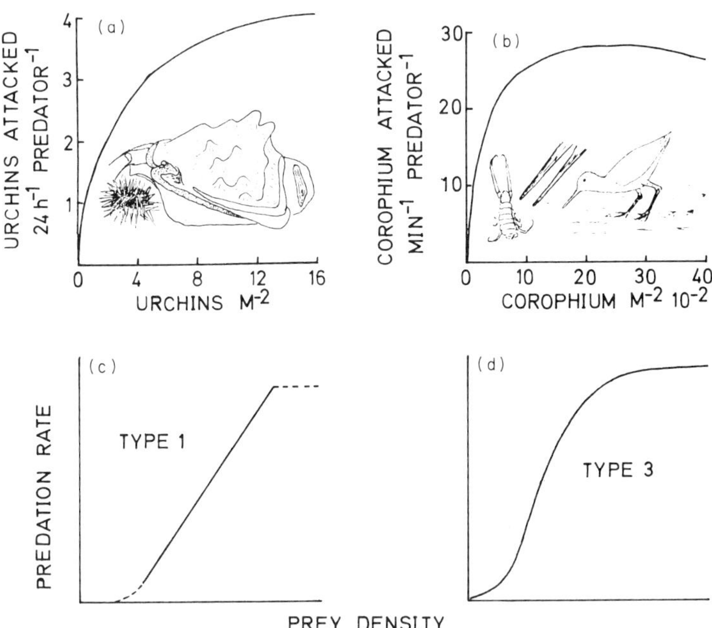

Fig. 3. Functional response curves. (a) Type 2 response of *Cassis tuberosa* feeding on *Echinometra lucunter* (Hughes and Hughes, 1971). (b) Modified type 2 response of *Tringa totanus* feeding on *Corophium volutator* (Goss-Custard, 1976). The decline in attack rate at high prey densities remains unexplained. (c) Hypothetical type 1 response, e.g. filter feeder. (d) Hypothetical type 3 response, showing inflexion at low prey densities caused for example by learned behaviour which modifies attack efficiency or reduces handling time.

increases in attack-efficiency over very low ranges of prey density do occur in a variety of invertebrate predators, suggesting that some of the recorded Type 2 responses would have had inflexions if sufficiently low prey densities had been used (Hassell *et al.*, 1977). Type 3 functional responses have not yet been found among littoral predators, but this is no doubt because of the very few investigations made to date.

As far as stability is concerned, the Type 1 functional response is density-independent and therefore not stabilizing, Type 2 is negatively density-dependent and destabilizing, while Type 3 is positively density-dependent below the inflexion and therefore stabilizing, but negatively density-dependent above the inflexion. The stabilizing effect of the Type 3 response therefore depends on whether the predators are able to keep the prey density below the inflexion. Since the inflexion usually occurs at very low prey densities, it is unlikely that the Type 3 functional response could have any stabilizing effect in nature. A more interesting corollary of the Type 3 response is that the changes in attack-efficiency causing the inflexion will automatically result from learned behaviour such as modifications of handling time or the development of search images, which are prerequisites for switching diets as discussed above under optimal diet. We should therefore expect predators capable of switching to have Type 3 functional responses. Because of the importance of switching in maintaining polymorphisms among prey by apostatic selection, and perhaps in preventing the local extinctions of certain prey types, functional responses among littoral predators would repay detailed investigation.

2. *Numerical Response*

(a) Aggregative numerical response. The numerical response refers to the way in which predator density changes as a function of prey density, and may incorporate two quite different phenomena. Over the short-term, predators may tend to aggregate in local patches of high prey density. This may involve a variety of behavioural mechanisms and has been termed the aggregative numerical response. Examples include the sea urchin *Strongylocentrotus franciscanus*, which clusters around kelp forests by decreasing its locomotory activity once kelp have been located, but increases locomotory activity when food supply runs low (Mattison *et al.*, 1977), and the oyster drill *Urosalpinx cinerea* (Say) which, when starved, is attracted to effluent from satiated conspecifics but repelled by effluent from other starved individuals. This mechanism is likely to attract *Urosalpinx* to local patches of high prey density (Pratt, 1976). Large feeding aggregations of starfish *Asterias rubens* and dogwhelks *Thais lapillus* have been noted on certain shores (Seed, 1969). In both cases, individuals are attracted by chemicals leaking from prey attacked by conspecifics, often leading to the multiple attack of a single prey item. Whether such behaviour is of mutual benefit to the individual predators remains unanswered, but single

Thais will often leave large mussels only partially consumed when isolated in the laboratory, so that sharing such a prey item then would not necessarily be disadvantageous (personal observation). Also, several *Asterias* will sometimes together open large *Cyprina islandica* (L.) (Anger *et al.*, 1977) or mussels (ap Rheinallt, personal communication) which could not have been opened by single starfish. Feeding aggregations of muricid snails have been described for Californian shores, involving *Ocenebra poulsoni* (Carpenter) and *Shaskyus festivus* Hinds feeding on the clams *Penitella penita* (Conrad) and *Parapholas californica* (Conrad) or on the trochid snail *Tegula ligulata* Menke [= *T. eiseni* Jordan] (Fotheringham, 1974).

Whatever the precise behavioural mechanism, an aggregative numerical response will tend to ensue if predators forage according to the predictions of optimal patch use theory, until the prey densities in different patches have been equalized. This is illustrated by the redshank which, when foraging on mudflats for *Corophium* and polychaetes, tends to concentrate its efforts on local patches of high prey density, with the effect that the overall predation rate is strongly density-dependent, even though the functional response is inversely density-dependent (Goss-Custard, 1976). By concentrating predation on patches of high prey density while alleviating predation pressure in patches of low prey density, the aggregative numerical response will tend to stabilize predator–prey systems. Aggregative responses have scarcely been investigated in marine predators but deserve further attention.

(b) Reproductive numerical response. Over a longer time-scale, predator density may track prey density by increased predator birth-rate with increased prey consumption. This has been termed the Reproductive Numerical Response and because of the long time-scale involved, has not received much empirical attention, certainly not with regard to intertidal communities. The time lag in any reproductive response, caused by the predator's generation time, will tend to impart instability, an effect which is aggravated when the generation time of the predator is much longer than that of the prey.

COEVOLUTION

Continued predation pressure generates selection for prey defence mechanisms, which in turn generates selection for predation mechanisms able to overcome the defences. This predator–prey arms race may have profound effects on the diet widths of predators, the kinds of predators present in a community and on the phenotypes, spatial distribution and productivity of the prey. Increased investment in specialized biological functions usually involves a trade-off with other biological functions. A predator which becomes perfected to combat the defences of a certain prey type may, because of its specialized morphology, become inefficient at dealing with most other prey types. The energy invested by a prey species in morphological or biochemical defences is unavailable for other aspects of somatic growth or reproduction. Coevolution should therefore be borne in mind in any detailed investigation of community structure and function.

The dogwhelk *Thais lapillus* provides a good example of selection for defence mechanisms generated by specific predators. On exposed shores where crabs are scarce, dogwhelks have relatively thin shells with short spires and wide mouths. On more sheltered shores heavily populated by the crabs *Carcinus maenas* or *Cancer pagurus* L., dogwhelks have much thicker shells with more elongated spires and narrower mouths. The thickened shell prevents crushing by crabs while the narrow mouth prevents insertion of the crab chaela (Hughes and Elner, 1980).

Biochemical defence mechanisms are widespread among sessile invertebrates. In addition to its defensive nematocysts, the sea anemone *Anemonia sulcata* (Pennant) contains toxic polypeptides which are lethal when injected into certain fish and crustaceans (Moller and Beress, 1975). The Red Sea sponge *Latrunculia magnifica* Keller contains a cholinesterase inhibitor (Neeman *et al.*, 1975) and in an extensive survey of sponge toxicity Green (1977) found that the proportion of species toxic to fish increases towards the tropics where fish predators are more numerous, and that it is those species exposed to fish predation, rather than those protected by microhabitats, which are toxic. The paucity of herbivores attacking fucoid algae and kelps in many parts of the world suggests that these plants possess special, probably biochemical, defence mechanisms. Whether or not large dominant algae are heavily grazed certainly has profound effects on community structure, as shown below, and the whole aspect of predator–prey coevolution among intertidal communities would repay further investigation.

COMMUNITY STRUCTURE

If, in a physically benign, unvarying environment, a set of species were allowed to compete uninterruptedly for a common resource, say space at a certain tidal height on the shore, then in many cases there would be a progressive exclusion of the poorer competitors, leading to eventual resource monopoly by the best competitor, the so-called potential dominant. Taking a wider range of levels on the shore, several species might be found to co-exist, each having evolved mechanisms for the more efficient exploitation of resources at a different position in the resource spectrum. At each of these positions in the resources spectrum there might be a set of potential competitors forming a competitive hierarchy, but after a long enough sequence of competition all except the species at the top of the hierarchy, the potential dominant, will have been excluded. Such a series of potential dominants is seen on many British shores dominated by fucoid algae, where *Pelvetia canaliculata* (L.) Dcne et Thur., *Fucus spiralis* L., *F. vesiculosus* L. or *Ascophyllum nodosum* (L.) Le Jol., and *F. serratus* L. form a replacement series from splash zone to sublittoral fringe, each species at its own shore level outcompeting those from higher levels. The number of co-existing potential dominants along such a resource spectrum depends on several possible factors such as the width of the resource spectrum, the taxonomy of the competitors, the harshness of the environment, the amplitude and predictability of environmental fluctuations. But for every potential dominant, usually there will be quite a number of species lower down in the competitive hierarchy whose presence in the community must depend either on local or temporary reversals in the outcome of competition, equivalent to transposing positions in the competitive hierarchy, or on the prevention of competitive exclusions by the interruption of competition. Reversals in the outcome of competition could, in theory, be caused by any temporal or localized alterations in environmental conditions which have differential adverse effects on the potential dominants or favourable effects on the subdominants. An example might be the presence of *Fucus serratus* in the middle of the *F. vesiculosus* zone due to a small drainage channel which creates local environmental conditions more favourable for *F. serratus*. Such environmental heterogeneity may often be quite important in promoting community species richness. However, competitive reversals are likely to be confined to small, localized patches of habitat and a more widespread co-existence within the community of competing species must depend on processes which interrupt competition and prevent competitive exclusions. Co-existence will be promoted by any factor which reduces the population densities of superior competitors sufficiently to free adequate resources for the maintenance of inferior competitors. This effect may be accomplished by physical factors, such as the dislodgement of a clump of mussels by wave action, or by biological factors such as predation. Of course, the disturbances must not be so indiscriminate as to affect adversely all species or so severe as to extinguish the populations of superior competitors. Ice-scraping and severe temperature or salinity fluctuations, for example, are likely to reduce rather than promote species richness. Predation, on the other hand, can have just the right properties to enhance co-existence among a set of competitors. Indeed, predation has been revealed as the key factor maintaining the species richness of a number of intertidal communities, as reviewed below. Predation will be most effective in preventing competitive exclusions when the predators prefer the potential dominants to the subdominants, but such predation must not be so heavy as to eliminate completely the potential dominants. The intensity of predation will depend on the predator population densities, so that maximum species richness can only be maintained if the predator population densities are under some kind of control which prevents them from becoming too low for effective depression of the prey population densities or too high for the survival of the prey populations. Switching of diets at threshold prey densities, foraging by optimal patch use and aggregative numerical responses will tend to prevent local prey extinctions, but their effects will be overridden when predator densities are persistently so high that all local patches become depleted of prey. Some of these points have been illustrated using a laboratory ecosystem containing marine algae together with herbivorous and carnivorous zooplankton, in which size and availability-dependent prey selection promoted co-existence of prey species (Glasser, 1978). Glasser also suggested that predation could promote prey species richness by reducing prey population densities so that more food resources become available per prey individual. In accordance with optimal diet theory, the prey should contract their diet widths in response to increased abundance of food and the reduced interspecific overlap in food-resource usage should allow co-existence. In this situation, optimal foraging reinforces the effect of lowered population densities in reducing interspecific competition.

The existence of competitive hierarchies among sessile rocky shore organisms and the promotion of co-existence among competitors by predation have been demonstrated a number of times since Paine's (1966) classic field experiments revealed how mussels, barnacles, limpets, chitons and others could co-exist on rocky shores of west North America when the potential dominant, *Mytilus californianus*, was cropped by the starfish *Pisaster ochraceus*. Dayton (1971) demonstrated more clearly the structure of the competitive hierarchy in Paine's (1966) community and showed how a physical disturbance factor, impact by wave-borne logs, could have similar effects on the community to those of a biological disturbance factor, predation by *Pisaster*. Algal species richness on the Washington coastline was found to be enhanced by sea urchins *Strongylocentrotus purpuratus* (Stimpson) which grazed the potential dominant brown alga *Hedophyllum sessile* (Dayton, 1975). Similar examples are reviewed in Paine (1977), while earlier works revealing the effects of grazers on intertidal algal communities are reviewed by Connell (1972).

More recent work has shown how the enhancement of species-richness by predation depends also on the intensity of predation, the position of the prey in the competitive hierarchy, the spatial heterogeneity and the physical harshness of the environment (Fig. 4). Whereas very light predation on competitive dominants will have no effect on species-richness, e.g. *Littorina obtusata* (L.) grazing on *Ascophyllum nodosum*, very intense predation may reduce species-richness. Sea urchins are notoriously capable of wiping out kelp populations (Lawrence, 1975), while Reise (1977) found that intense predation by juvenile shore crabs *Carcinus maenas*, shrimps *Crangon crangon* (L.) and gobies *Pomatoschistus microps* (Kröyer) reduced the infaunal species-richness of intertidal mudflats in the eastern North Sea. Predators with such potentially intense effects must fall under some kind of population control for species-richness to be maintained. Thus, the elimination of *Laminaria* spp. from large shallow sublittoral areas in Nova Scotia by the sea urchin *Strongylocentrotus droebachiensis* (Lang and Mann, 1976) is apparently due to overfishing

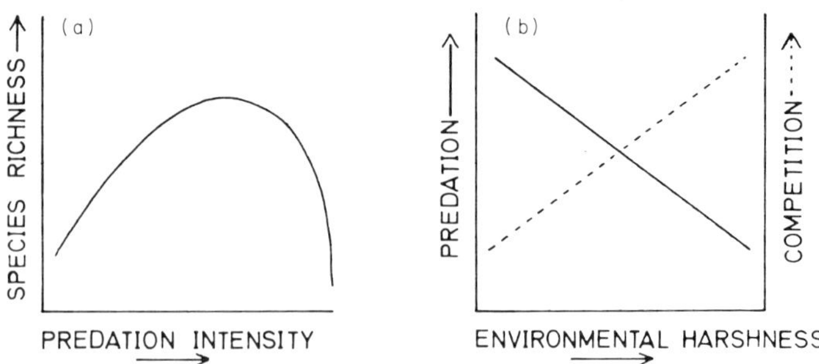

Fig. 4. (a) The effect of predation intensity on community species-richness. (b) The relative importances of predation (solid line) and competition (dashed line) in determining community structure along a gradient of environmental harshness.

of the lobster *Homarus americanus* Milne–Edwards which feeds on the urchins (Breen and Mann, 1976). Similarly, overhunting of the sea otter *Enhydra lutris* (L.) in the Aleutian Islands has allowed local populations of *Strongylocentrotus polyacanthus* A. Agassiz and H. L. Clark to become so dense as to eliminate the fleshy macroalgae (Estes *et al.*, 1978). The importance of predation intensity on species-richness is very nicely illustrated by Lubchenco's (1978) account of *Littorina littorea* (L.) grazing on the algae of New England shores. In tide pools, the competitive dominant is *Enteromorpha intestinalis* (L.) Link, which is also the preferred prey species of *L. littorea.* When *L. littorea* is rare, *Enteromorpha* monopolizes the tide pools through competitive exclusions, but when the *L. littorea* is present at moderate densities, the grazing reduces algal densities and prevents competititve exclusions, so that many ephemeral and perennial algal species coexist. At very high densities of *L. littorea* all edible algae are eaten, allowing monopoly of the substratum by the inedible, but competitively inferior *Chondrus crispus* Steckh.

The elimination of prey species by intense predation will, of course, be less likely if prey are able to escape in spatial refuges or by growing too large for the predators. For example, *Balanus glandula* has a spatial refuge at high shore levels where it escapes predation by *Thais emarginata* (Deshayes) (Connell, 1970), while *Mytilus californianus* eventually grows too large to be eaten by *Pisaster ochraceus* (Paine, 1976).

Lubchenco's (1978) work also illustrates how the promotion of species-richness depends on the level at which predation has its effect within the competitive hierarchy. In tide pools, *Littorina littorea* (L.) prefers the competitive dominant *Enteromorpha* so that grazing can interrupt the successional sequence of competitive exclusions. On emergent rock faces, however, the competitive dominants are the fucoids *F. vesiculosus, F. distichus* L. and *Ascophyllum nodosum. L. littorea* has a low preference for fucoids and so has a negligible effect on their population densities. Instead, *L. littorea* grazes preferentially on the set of about 14 understory species of green, brown and red algae so that as winkle density increases, grazing eliminates the understory species and algal species-richness declines.

Increased physical harshness of the environment seems to be correlated with the diminished importance of predation as a promoter of community species-richness (Fig. 4b). There is a marked contrast between the species-rich, trophically complex rocky shore communities of the Pacific coast of North America, in which predation plays a key role in facilitating co-existence among competing prey species, and the relatively species-poor trophically simple rocky shore communities of the Atlantic coast, in which competition rather than predation is a major force structuring the communities (Menge, 1976). Menge and Sutherland (1976) concluded that, owing to the more extreme climate of the eastern seaboard, the Atlantic coast is subject to greater temporal variability in temperature and correlated microhabitat variables, and that this physiologically more stressful environment reduces the number of species able to live intertidally. There are relatively few predator species and the prey consist of a small set of physiologically-robust sessile organisms whose populations are influenced more by competition than by predation (Fig. 5).

However, the spatial distribution and population age structures of sedentary organisms in these rather simple rocky shore communities depend not only on competition but also on mortality caused either by physical factors, such as the sloughing of local patches of mussels and barnacles (Grant, 1977) which become mechanically unstable through age, or by predation, as seen on the Yorkshire coast where mussels are devastated at low-tide level by periodic aggregations of *Asterias rubens* and are obliterated in

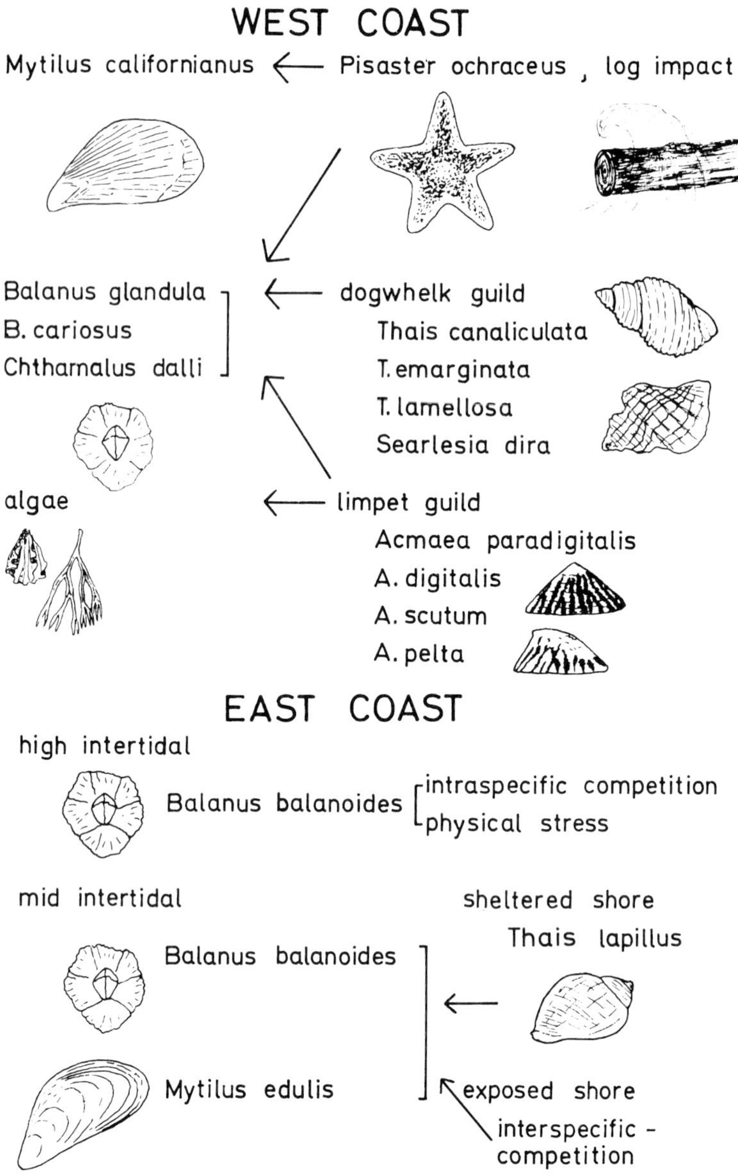

WEST COAST

Mytilus californianus ← Pisaster ochraceus, log impact

Balanus glandula
B. cariosus
Chthamalus dalli

← dogwhelk guild
Thais canaliculata
T. emarginata
T. lamellosa
Searlesia dira

algae ← limpet guild
Acmaea paradigitalis
A. digitalis
A. scutum
A. pelta

EAST COAST

high intertidal

Balanus balanoides [intraspecific competition, physical stress]

mid intertidal

Balanus balanoides
Mytilus edulis

← sheltered shore
Thais lapillus

exposed shore
interspecific - competition

Fig. 5. Determinants of community structure on the Washington coast of North America (Dayton, 1971) and on the New England coast of North America (Menge, 1976).

the vicinity of crevices by dogwhelks, *Thais lapillus*, which use the crevices for shelter (Seed, 1969). Empty barnacle tests are an important resource for a characteristic set of animals, notably small gastropods, bivalves and isopods, which use them for shelter. Predation of barnacles by dogwhelks may therefore have important effects on community structure by producing empty barnacle tests. These more subtle effects of predation on community structure deserve much more attention.

CONCLUSIONS

Although much can still be done by using predator exclusion experiments in elucidating the effects of predation on the species composition of littoral communities, a new class of exciting discoveries could be made by focussing attention on specific foraging techniques and on the coevolution of predators and prey. Invertebrate predators will probably turn out to show much more sophistication in their foraging methods than they are presently given credit for. Established theory on optimal diets and optimal patch use provides sets of predictions which could help to structure investigations of these foraging methods. We could ask whether important littoral predators such as blennies, crabs, dogwhelks and starfish are able to modify foraging behaviour in the light of experience. Do their foraging methods have stabilizing density-dependent properties such as switching diets, optimal patch use, aggregative numerical responses? How do these predators affect prey population structure and spatial distribution?

Distributions of prey phenotypes and the numbers of types of different predators attacking a particular prey species should be examined in the light of coevolution. We could, for example, look for chemical defences in those macroalgae which are mysteriously free of grazers, or set up experiments on the effectiveness of predation on polymorphic prey.

The application of optimal foraging theory offers an exciting, barely explored avenue of approach for littoral biologists.

REFERENCES

Anger, K., Rogal, U., Schriever, G. and Valentin, C. (1977). *In situ* investigations on the echinoderm *Asterias rubens* as a predator of soft bottom communities in the western Baltic Sea. *Helgoländer wiss. Meeresunters.* **29**, 439–459.

Bayne, B. L. and Scullard, C. (1978). Rates of feeding by *Thais* (*Nucella*) *lapillus* (L.). *J. exp. mar. Biol. Ecol.* **32**, 113–129.

Breen, P. A. and Mann, K. H. (1976). Changing lobster abundance and the destruction of kelp beds by sea urchins. *Mar. Biol., Berl.* **34**, 137–142.

Carefoot, T. H. (1973). Feeding, food preferences, and the uptake of food energy by the supralittoral isopod *Ligia pallasii*. *Mar. Biol., Berl.* **18**, 228–236.

Connell, J. H. (1979). A predator-prey system in the marine intertidal region. I. *Balanus glandula* and several predatory species of *Thais*. *Ecol. Monogr.* **40**, 49–78.

Connell, J. H. (1972). Community interactions on marine rocky intertidal shores. *Ann. Rev. Ecol. Syst.* **3**, 169–192.

Dayton, P. K. (1971). Competition, disturbance, and community organization: the provision and subsequent utilization of space in a rocky intertidal community. *Ecol. Monogr.* **41**, 351–389.

Dayton, P. K. (1975). Experimental evaluation of ecological dominance in a rocky intertidal algal community. *Ecol. Monogr.* **45**, 137–159.

Elner, R. W. and Hughes, R. N. (1978). Energy maximization in the diet of the shore crab, *Carcinus maenas*. *J. Anim. Ecol.* **47**, 103–116.

Emlen, J. M. (1966). "Time, energy and risk in two species of carnivorous gastropods". Ph.D. thesis, University of Washington, Seattle.

Estes, J. A., Smith, N. S. and Palmisano, J. F. (1978). Sea otter predation and community organization in the western Aleutian Islands, Alaska. *Ecology* **59**, 822–833.

Fotheringham, N. (1974). Trophic complexity in a littoral boulder field. *Limnol. Oceanogr.* **19**, 84–91.

Glasser, J. W. (1978). The effect of predation on prey resource utilization. *Ecology* **59**, 724–732.

Goss-Custard, J. D. (1970). The responses of redshank (*Tringa totanus* (L.)) to spatial variations in the density of their prey. *J. Anim. Ecol.* **39**, 91–113.

Goss-Custard, J. D. (1976). Variation in the dispersion of redshank, *Tringa totanus*, on their winter feeding grounds. *Ibis* **118**, 257–263.

Goss-Custard, J. D. (1977a). The energetics of prey selection by redshank, *Tringa totanus* (L.), in relation to prey density. *J. Anim. Ecol.* **46**, 1–19.

Goss-Custard, J. D. (1977b). Optimal foraging and size selection of worms by redshank, *Tringa totanus*, in the field. *Anim. Behav.* **25**, 10–29.

Grant, W. S. (1977). High intertidal community organization on a rocky headland in Maine, U.S.A. *Mar. Biol., Berl.* **44**, 15–25.

Green, G. (1977). Ecology of toxicity in marine sponges. *Mar. Biol., Berl.* **40**, 207–215.

Hartwick, E. B. (1976). Foraging strategy of the black oyster catcher (*Haematopus bachmani* Audubon). *Can. J. Zool.* **54**, 142–155.

Hassell, M. P., Lawton, J. H. and Beddington, J. R. (1977). Sigmoid functional responses by invertebrate predators and parasitoids. *J. Anim. Ecol.* **46**, 249–262.

Himmelman, J. H. and Carefoot, T. H. (1975). Seasonal changes in calorific value of three Pacific coast seaweeds, and their significance to some marine invertebrate herbivores. *J. exp. mar. Biol. Ecol.* **18**, 139–151.

Hughes, R. N. (1979). Optimal diets under the energy maximization premise: the effects of recognition time and learning. *Am. Nat.* **113**, 209–221.

Hughes, R. N. and Elner, R. W. (1980). Tactics of a predator *Carcinus maenas* and morphological responses of the prey, *Nucella lapillus*. *J. Anim. Ecol.* **49**, 65–78.

Hughes, R. N. and Hughes, H. P. I. (1971). A study of the gastropod *Cassis tuberosa* (L.) preying upon sea urchins. *J. exp. mar. Biol. Ecol.* **3**, 215–315.

Huxley, C. J. (1976). Response of *Acanthaster planci* (L.) to partial stimuli. *J. exp. mar. Biol. Ecol.* **22**, 199–206.

Jackson, J. B. C. and Buss, L. (1975). Allelopathy and spatial competition among coral reef invertebrates. *Proc. natn Acad. Sci. U.S.A.* **72**, 5160–5163.

Kislalioglu, M. and Gibson, R. N. (1976). Prey "handling time" and its importance in food selection by the 15-spined stickleback, *Spinachia spinachia* (L.). *J. exp. mar. Biol. Ecol.* **25**, 115–158.

Krebs, J. R. (1978). Optimal foraging: decision rules for predators. *In* "Behavioural Ecology: An Evolutionary Approach" (J. R. Krebs and N. B. Davies, eds), Blackwell Scientific Publications, Oxford.

Lang, C. and Mann, K. H. (1976). Changes in sea urchin populations after the destruction of kelp beds. *Mar. Biol., Berl.* **36**, 321–326.

Lawrence, J. M. (1975). On the relationship between marine plants and sea urchins. *Oceanogr. mar. Biol. ann. Rev.* **13**, 213–286.

Lubchenco, J. (1978). Plant species diversity in a marine intertidal community: importance of herbivor food preference and algal competitive abilities. *Am. Nat.* **112**, 23–39.

Lubchenco, J. and Menge, B. A. (1978). Community development and persistence in a low rocky intertidal zone. *Ecol. Monogr.* **48**, 67–94.

MacArthur, R. H. (1972). "Geographical Ecology: Patterns in the Distribution of Species". Harper and Row, New York.

Mattison, J. E., Trent, J. D., Shanks, A. L., Akin, T. B. and Pearse, J. S. (1977). Movement and feeding activity of red sea urchins (*Strongylocentrotus franciscanus*) adjacent to a kelp forest. *Mar. Biol., Berl.* **39**, 25–30.

May, R. M. (ed.) (1976). "Theoretical Ecology: Principles and Applications". Blackwell Scientific Publications, Oxford.

Menge, B. A. (1972). Foraging strategy of a starfish in relation to actual prey availability and environmental predictability. *Ecol. Monogr.* **42**, 25–50.

Menge, B. A. (1976). Organization of the New England rocky intertidal community: role of predation, competition, and environmental heterogeneity. *Ecol. Monogr.* **46**, 355–393.

Menge, B. A. and Sutherland, J. P. (1976). Species diversity gradients: synthesis of the roles of predation, competition, and temporal heterogeneity. *Am. Nat.* **110**, 351–369.

Menge, J. L. (1974). Prey selection and foraging period of the predaceous rocky intertidal snail, *Acanthina punctulata*. *Oecologia* **17**, 292–316.

Moller, H. and Beress, L. (1975). Effect on fishes of two toxic polypeptides isolated from *Anemonia sulcata*. *Mar. Biol., Berl.* **32**, 189–192.

Morgan, P. R. (1972). The influence of prey availability on the distribution and predatory behaviour of *Nucella lapillus* (L.). *J. Anim. Ecol.* **41**, 257–274.

Murdoch, W. W. (1969). Switching in general predators; experiments on predator specificity and stability of prey populations. *Ecol. Monogr.* **39**, 335–354.

Neeman, I., Fishelson, L. and Kashman, Y. (1975). Isolation of a new toxin from the sponge *Latrunculia magnifica* in the Gulf of Aquaba (Red Sea). *Mar. Biol., Berl.* **30**, 293–296.

O'Connor, R. J. and Brown, R. A. (1977). Prey depletion and foraging strategy in the oystercatcher *Haematopus ostralegus*. *Oecologia* **27**, 75–92.

Paine, R. T. (1966). Food web complexity and species diversity. *Am. Nat.* **100**, 65–75.

Paine, R. T. (1976). Size-limited predation: an observational and experimental approach with the *Mytilus – Pisaster* interaction. *Ecology* **57**, 858–873.

Paine, R. T. (1977). Controlled manipulations in the marine intertidal zone, and their contributions to ecological theory. *In* "The Changing Scenes in Natural Sciences, 1776–1976". Acad. Nat. Sci., Special Publication No. 12, 245–270.

Pratt, D. M. (1974). Attraction to prey and stimulus to attack in the predatory gastropod *Urosalpinx cinerea*. *Mar. Biol., Berl.* **27**, 37–45.

Pulliam, H. R. (1975). Diet optimization with nutrient constraints. *Am. Nat.* **109**, 765–768.

Pyke, G. H., Pulliam, H. R. and Charnov, E. L. (1977). Optimal foraging: a selective review of theory and tests. *Q. Rev. Biol.* **52**, 137–154.

Reise, K. (1977). Predator exclusion experiments in an intertidal mud flat. *Helgoländer wiss. Meeresunters.* **30**, 263–271.

Seed, R. (1969). The ecology of *Mytilus edulis* L. (Lamellibranchiata) on exposed rocky shores. I. Breeding and settlement. *Oecologia* **3**, 277–316.

Smith, D. A. S. (1975). Polymorphism and selective predation in *Donax faba* Gmelin (Bivalvia: Tellinacea). *J. exp. mar. Biol. Ecol.* **17**, 205–219.

Trevallion, A., Edwards, R. R. C. and Steele, J. H. (1970). Dynamics of a benthic bivalve. *In* "Marine Food Chains" (J. H. Steele, ed.). Oliver and Boyd, Edinburgh.

Vadas, R. L. (1977). Preferential feeding: an optimization strategy in sea urchins. *Ecol. Monogr.* **47**, 337–371.

Westoby, M. (1974). An analysis of diet selection by large generalist herbivores. *Am. Nat.* **108**, 290–304.

10 The Significance of Free-living Nematodes to the Littoral Ecosystem

H. M. PLATT

Department of Zoology, British Museum (Natural History), London, England

and

R. M. WARWICK

Institute for Marine Environmental Research, Plymouth, England

Abstract: The role played by free-living marine nematodes in the littoral ecosystem is assessed. Since little is known of the nematodes of rocky shores, this assessment is based mainly on the results of investigations of particulate shores. Nematodes are considered to be the most ubiquitous, abundant and diverse marine metazoan group. They are of major energetic importance, form a significant part of the diet of many other animals, play vital roles in facilitating decomposition and in influencing the physical stability of beaches, and are potentially important indicators of environmental conditions. The authors conclude that any general assessment of intertidal habitats is incomplete if the nematode fauna is not taken into consideration.

INTRODUCTION

Seventeen years ago, Christie (1962) published an obituary of the distinguished nematologist Dr Gotthold Steiner. It told of Steiner's

Systematics Association Special Volume No. 17(b), "The Shore Environment, Vol. 2: Ecosystems", edited by J. H. Price, D. E. G. Irvine and W. F. Farnham, 1980, pp. 729–759, Academic Press, London and New York.

emigration to the United States in 1921 to join Dr Nathan Cobb who at the time was engaged in a crusade to convince his sceptical colleagues of the economic importance of plant-parasitic nematodes – apparently with little success. When Cobb died in 1932, Steiner continued his efforts and was fortunate to live long enough to see their predictions come true and "even his most extravagent claims vindicated". This recognition had finally come rather indirectly through the introduction of nematicides in the 1940s, demonstrating increased yields when the nematode burden was controlled. Today, plant nematology is recognized as one of the most vital fields of agricultural research.

In an analogous way, a series of more or less speculative claims has been made over the years for the importance of free-living nematodes in the marine environment. These claims centre around the numerical abundance of the worms, their ubiquitous occurrence and their energetic importance in relation to their biomass. We will also argue that they play an important direct role as food for other organisms as well as indirectly influencing other processes. The uses of marine nematodes (i) as tools for investigating more theoretical biological problems such as diversity and bioenergetics and (ii) as indicators of environmental quality have also been hinted at, but as yet not fully evaluated on a practical level.

In this chapter we shall review some past and present studies on the ecology of intertidal nematodes in the context of these claims, with a view to increasing awareness of this field of study in non-nematodes-specialists interested in the shore ecosystem as a whole. Although this account will be necessarily based mainly on evidence taken from soft shores, perhaps many of the conclusions may well prove equally relevant to rocky shores when the nematode fauna of the latter has received the attention it properly deserves.

BASIC FIELD DATA

There is now a considerable body of nematological data testifying to the large number of both individuals and species which may be found on all types of shores. By virtue of their wide range of adaptations they have exploited all littoral habitats, including the potentially inhospitable mobile sand beaches, exposed rocky shores and the upper reaches of estuaries. On rocky shores, they are found in the interstices of holdfasts and in the more delicate seaweeds, on larger algae, among hydroids, bryozoans and so on, and wherever sediment accumulates.

1. Abundance

Whilst little is yet known of their absolute density on rocky shores (where numerical assessments are more difficult to obtain due to problems of sampling), they are known to be the most abundant metazoans of particulate shores (Table I). Although relatively few studies directly compare macrofaunal and meiofaunal densities in the same area, the literature comparing individual meiofaunal groups is more extensive (reviewed by McIntyre, 1969) and clearly demonstrates the dominance of nematodes.

Nematodes reach their highest densities in muddy estuaries and salt marshes, as highlighted by the data from Rees (1940), Teal and Wieser (1966) and Warwick and Price (1979), all of whom reported maximum numbers of individuals in the range 10–23 million/m^2. Densities are intermediate in muddy or silty sand, in the order of 1–5 million/m^2 (Perkins, 1958; Ott, 1972a; Platt, 1977a) and lowest on very exposed sandy shores, up to about 0.1 million/m^2 (Gray and Rieger, 1971; Warwick, 1968). However, although on more settled shores the majority are confined to the upper few centimetres, on well-oxygenated exposed shores nematodes can penetrate very deeply (McLachlan, 1977) so that many data reported from such habitats may be underestimates due to inadequate depths of coring.

Some of the gross morphological adaptations enabling nematodes to inhabit successfully the whole range of sediment habitats and giving some impression of the diversity of form are illustrated in Fig. 1. Contrary to popular opinion, marine nematodes do not "all look the same," and it is time that this myth was finally put to rest. In general, most nematodes of fine sediments are short burrowing forms, while in coarser sandy sediments the majority are interstitial, being either very small or very elongate and thin. Some of the largest nematodes are found in kelp holdfasts, where the interstices are relatively large (Moore, 1971).

In terms of biomass, nematodes are again normally a major component of the meiobenthos, although generally having a lower

Table I. Comparison of nematode, other meiofauna and macrofauna densities at mid-tide levels on various particulate shores (numbers per m^2)

Habitat	Location	Nematoda (% of total meiofauna)	Other meiofauna	Macrofauna	Source
Exposed sand	Algoa Bay South Africa	502 200 (31.0)	1 117 800	44	McLachlan (1977)
Sheltered sand	Algoa Bay South Africa	1 091 500 (59.0)	758 500	13	McLachlan (1977)
Exposed sand	Porto Novo, India	1 150 000 (58.7)	810 000	128	McIntyre (1968)
Sheltered sand	Porto Novo, India	3 240 000 (99.9)	4 025	2400[a]	McIntyre (1968)
Exposed sand	Firemore Bay, Scotland	105 000 (39.9)	158 200	945	McIntyre and Eleftheriou (1968) McIntyre and Murison (1973)
Sheltered sand	Swartkops Estuary, South Africa	526 000 (81.4)	120 000	28	Dye and Furstenberg (1978)
Sheltered mud	Bristol Channel, England	2 320 000 (91.7)	210 000	7120	Rees (1940)
Sheltered mud	Lynher Estuary, England	12 460 000 (93.5)	863 000	3849	Warwick *et al.* (1979)

[a]Station 5, just below mid-tide

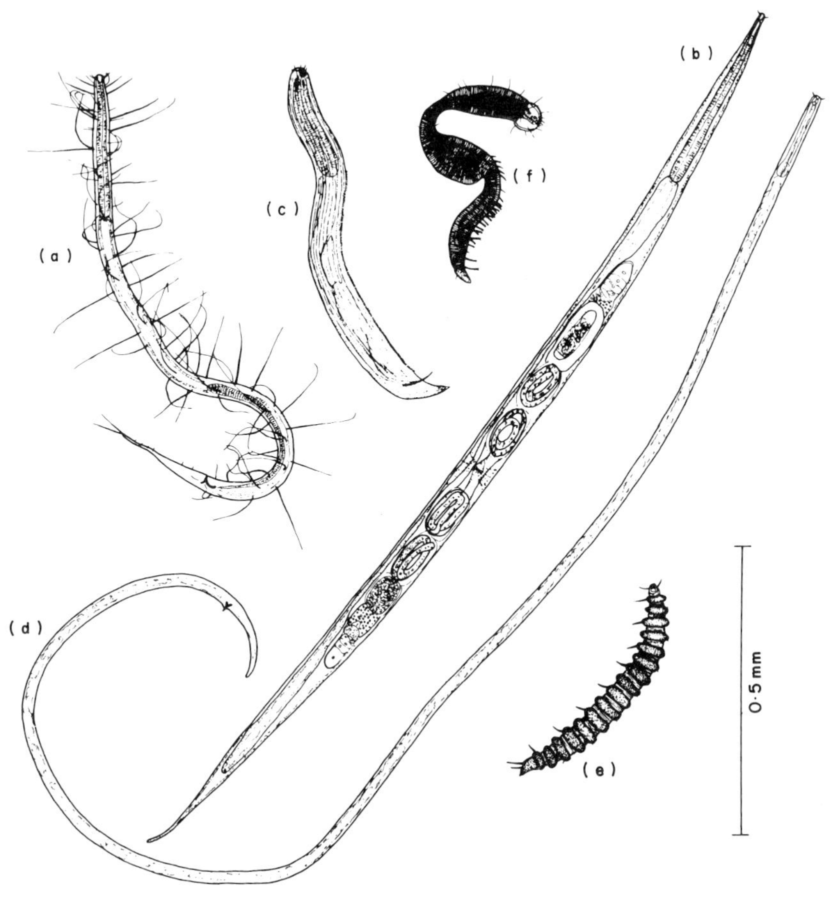

Fig. 1. Variety of form in marine nematodes. (a) *Trichotheristus mirabilis* (Stekhoven and De Coninck), a typical interstitial species the long body setae of which help maintain its position in mobile habitats. (b) *Anoplostoma viviparum* (Bastian), a viviparous species in which retention of the eggs until hatching affords protection in environments with widely fluctuating environmental conditions. (c) *Richtersia inaequalis* Riemann, a short fat burrower with numerous longitudinal files of short spines. (d) *Metalinhomoeus filiformis* (De Man), an extremely elongated form a common adaptation to interstitial habitats. (e) *Desmoscolex* sp., body annulations and bristles aid locomotion and perhaps afford protection. (f) *Dracograllus eira* (Inglis), distinctive body shape with ventral ambulatory bristles. (Figures original, scale line 0.5 mm.)

Table II. Comparison of nematode, other meiofauna and macrofauna biomass at mid-tide levels on various particulate shores (g ash-free dry weight per m^2)

Habitat	Location	Nematoda	Other meiofauna	Macrofauna	Source
Sheltered sand	Algoa Bay, South Africa	0.15	0.88	1.11	McLachlan (1977)
Exposed sand	Firemore Bay, Scotland	0.24	0.52	1.07	McIntyre and Eleftheriou (1968) McIntyre and Murison (1973)
Sheltered sand	Swartkops Estuary, South Africa	0.22	0.06	5.67	Dye and Furstenberg (1978)
Sheltered mud	Lynher Estuary, England	1.97	4.65	13.57	Warwick *et al.* (1979)

biomass than the macrofauna (Table II). Estimates vary, but intertidal meiofaunal biomass is generally from a fifth to half the total (i.e. meiobenthos plus macrobenthos) dependent upon substrate type, with nematodes accounting for a significant proportion of the total meiofaunal value. However, there are grounds for believing that many studies may underestimate the meiofaunal component through inefficient sampling and/or extraction techniques (Gerlach, 1971).

2. *Diversity*

An important feature of nematode populations, perhaps the most significant in understanding their ecological success, is the large number of species present in any one habitat – usually an order of magnitude greater than for any other major taxon. However, species-richness varies among habitats, being greatest in sandy sites, lower in estuaries and muddy sites (Table III). Diversity also tends to be lower in algal communities.

In all, about 4000 species of free-living marine nematodes, placed in some 450 genera, have been described to date. Despite this apparently daunting number, the difficulties involved in coming to terms with the taxonomy of the group are considerably eased by the fact that most of these species are rare or so poorly described that

Table III. Nematode diversity in various intertidal habitats

Habitat	Location	Number of Species	Source
Sand	Washington, USA	106	Wieser (1959)
Sand	Firemore Bay, Scotland	104	McIntyre and Murison (1973)
Fine sand	Wrightsville Beach, North Carolina	145	Ott (1972a)
Fine sand	Strangford Lough, N. Ireland	51–71	Platt (1977a)
Mud	Lynher Estuary, England	40	Warwick and Price (1979)
Mud	Blythe Estuary, England	37	Capstick (1959)
Kelp holdfasts	North Sea coast, England	61	Moore (1971)
Seaweeds	Plymouth, England	70	Wieser (1952)
Seaweeds	Rovinj, Yugoslavia	32	Ott (1967)

they may never be recognized again. In reality, a European marine nematologist can expect to have to deal regularly with only a few hundred common or characteristic species which invariably fall into about 50 of what might be termed key "genus-complexes" – equivalent to terms such as terebellids, spionids, cumaceans or limpets used in conventional macrofaunal ecology. Ecologically, the rarer forms can usually be ignored or lumped with a particular "genus-complex", since a great deal of useful information could be obtained simply through recognizing these key groupings.

The total number of species in any one habitat, then, is always relatively high. A more detailed community analysis further shows a variation among habitats in the degree of species dominance, as illustrated in Fig. 2. In general, seaweeds and low salinity muds have a relatively low number of species, but are dominated by a single or a few species, whereas sand and high salinity muds have more species with none totally dominating the assemblage.

Variation in the degree of dominance can be seen even within a single beach, as demonstrated by the assemblages from a high salinity sandflat (Fig. 3). An important factor correlating with these patterns of diversity appears to be the stability of the habitat in terms of short- or long-term fluctuations in the physical conditions (Ott, 1972b).

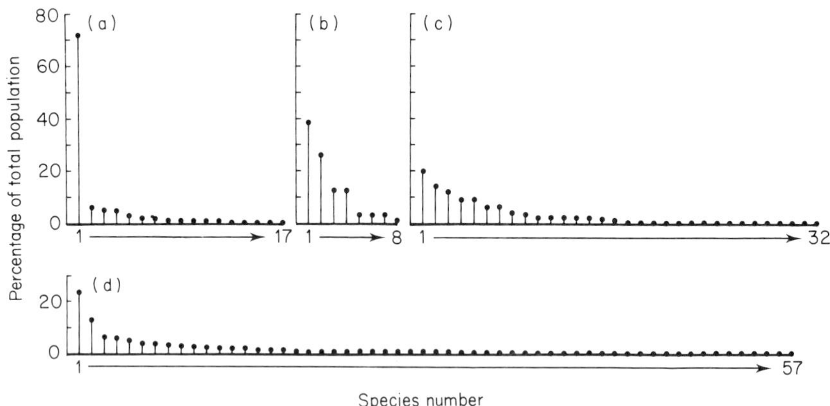

Fig. 2. Comparison of percentage species abundance in four habitats in the south-west of the United Kingdom. (a) Intertidal seaweed (*Corallina*), Isles of Scilly; (b) low salinity estuarine mud, MTL, Exe estuary, Devon; (c) high salinity estuarine mud, MTL, Lynher estuary, Cornwall; (d) beach sand, MLWST, Exmouth, Devon.

This high species diversity requires some explanation. It seems clear that nematodes are able to partition the environment extensively in various ways. Food partitioning seems to be the most crucial, and most nematodes appear to be highly selective feeders (Tietjen and Lee, 1973). Wieser (1953) devised a feeding classification scheme which, although almost certainly a gross simplification, has nevertheless withstood the test of time and is still accepted as a valuable analytical tool. He divided the nematodes into four main groups based upon the gross morphology of the buccal cavity (its size and degree of dentition) and suggested each of these groups fed in different ways. These groups are: 1A, selective deposit feeders; 1B, non-selective deposit feeders; 2A, epigrowth feeders; 2B, predators and omnivores. They are illustrated and further explained in Fig. 4 (a–d).

The relative proportions of each of these four feeding groups in any one community depend on the nature of the available food, which in turn is reflected by the nature of the sediment. For example, in the Exe estuary (Fig. 5), approximately similar proportions are found in mud. But in muddy-sand, non-selective deposit feeders equipped to injest larger particles dominate. However, in cleaner

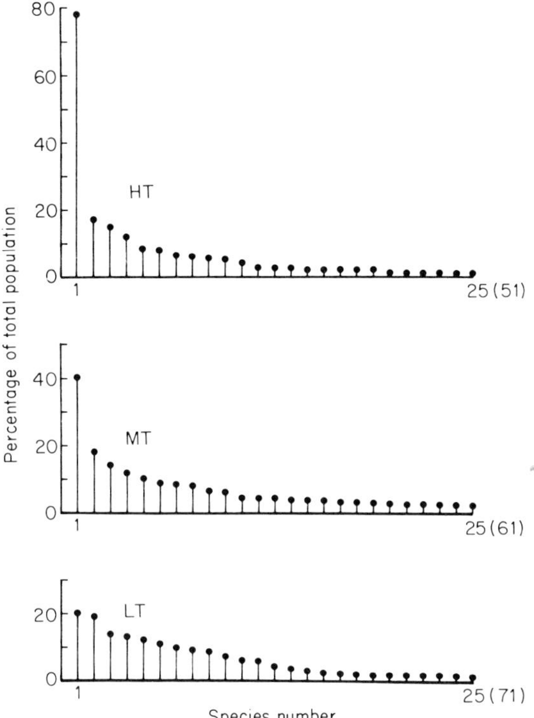

Fig. 3. Comparison of percentage species abundance of the 25 most common species at high (HT) mid (MT) and low (LT) tide levels on a high salinity sandflat (Strangford Lough, Northern Ireland). Total number of species at each site shown in parenthesis.

sandy areas, the numbers of all deposit feeders are reduced and forms dominate which are able to scrape food from surfaces, pierce other organisms to obtain their contents or act as predators.

Recently, the possible significance of selective digestion has been discussed by Tietjen and Lee (1977) who point out the limits to enzyme production imposed by having low numbers of secretory cells which also function in the absorption process. This is a probable factor leading to the evolutionary development of selective feeding behaviour. But although the diet of any one individual species may be limited, as a group nematodes feed on a wide variety of materials – on organic detritus, bacteria, diatoms, decomposing organisms and as carnivores on other organisms (including other nematodes).

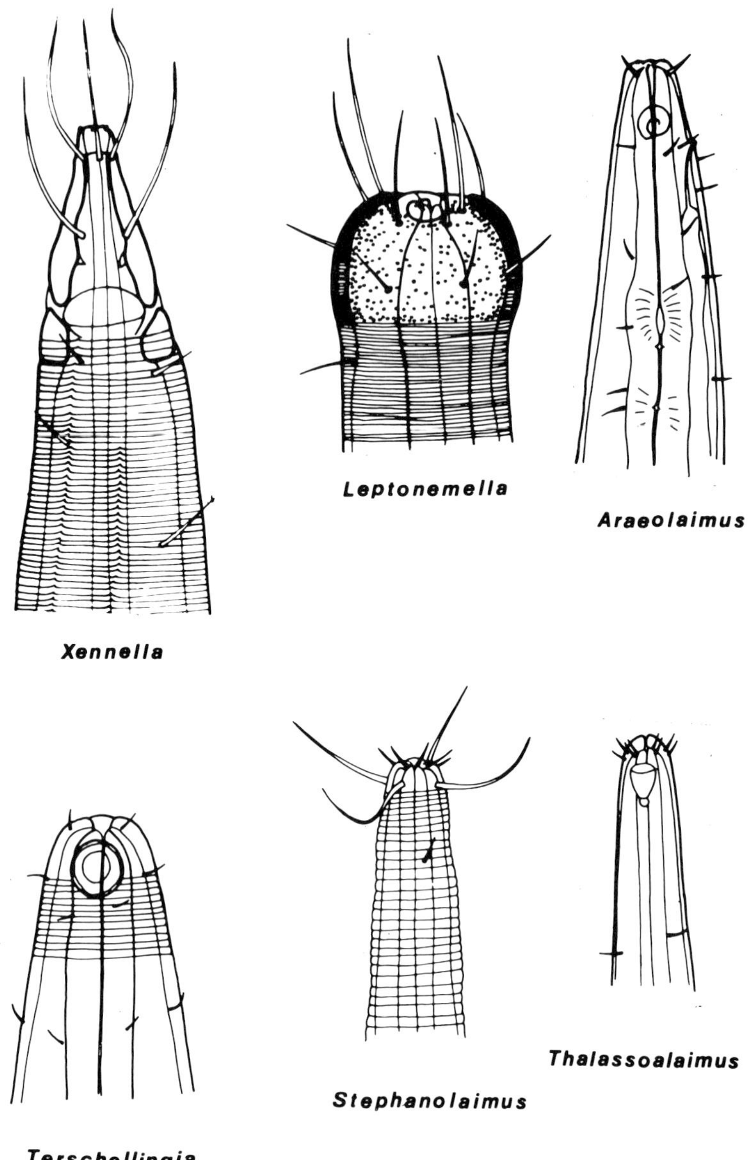

Fig. 4a–d. Genera representing the four feeding groups.

Fig. 4a. Selective deposit feeders: species without (or with a minute) buccal cavity only able to ingest small particles and/or fluid, therefore perforce selective.

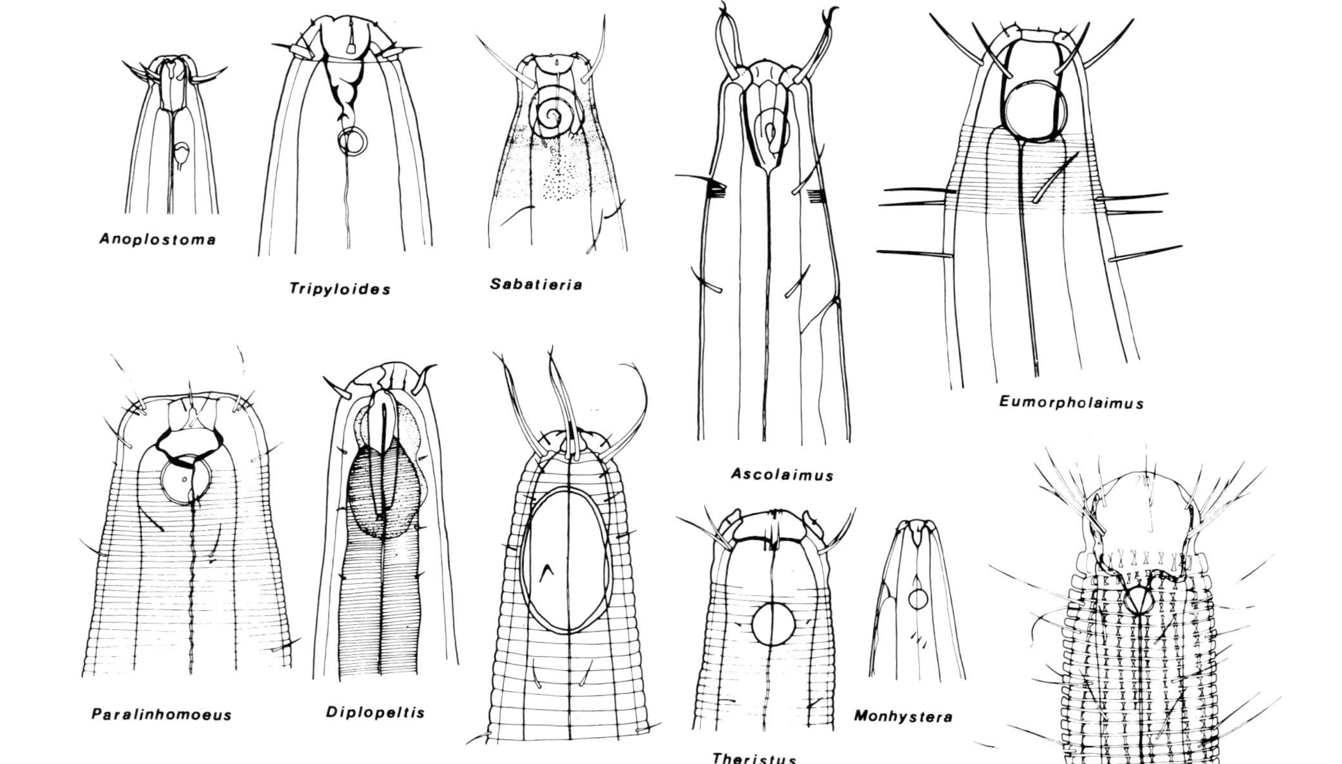

Fig. 4b. Non-selective deposit feeders: species with buccal cavity of varying degrees of development but lacking dentition, hence able to ingest particles of a wider size range.

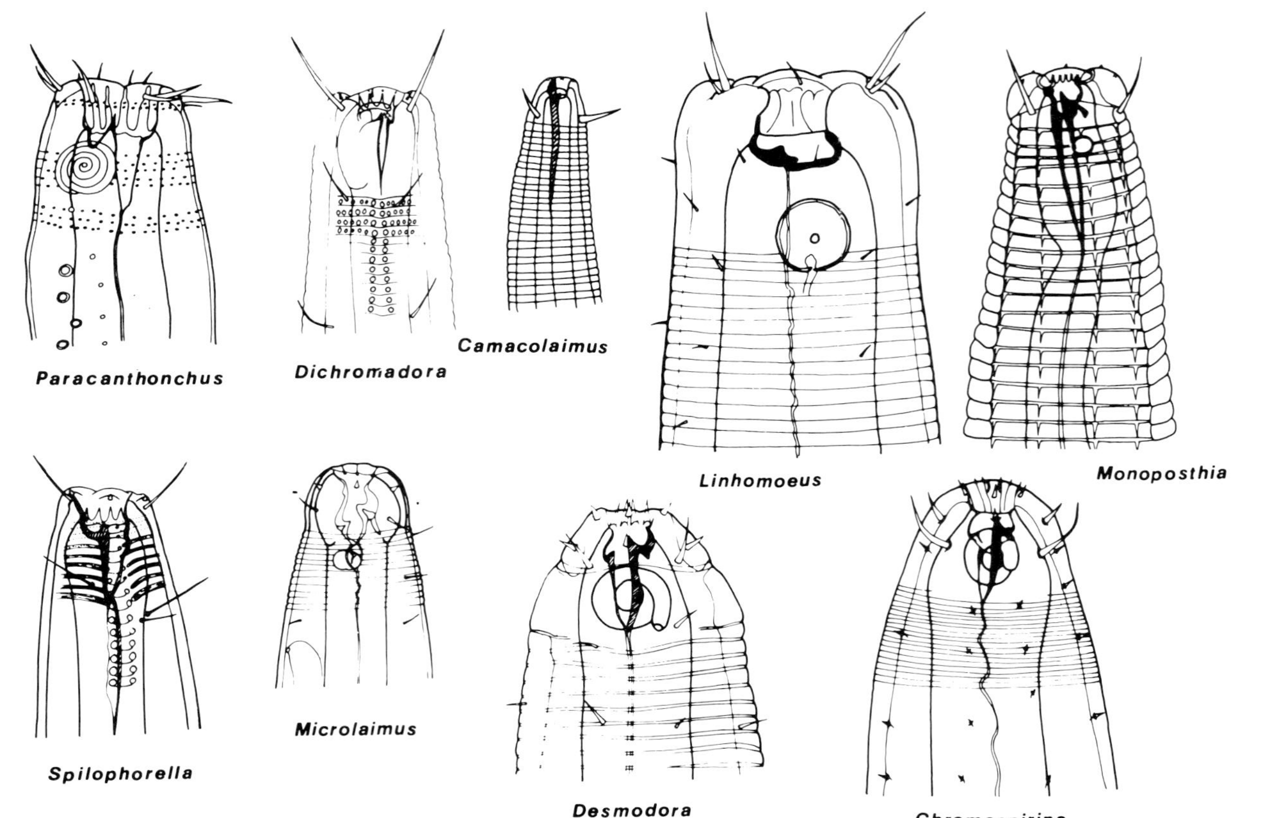

Fig. 4c. Epigrowth feeders: species with a buccal cavity containing teeth and/or denticles enabling cells to be pierced or objects to be scraped off surfaces.

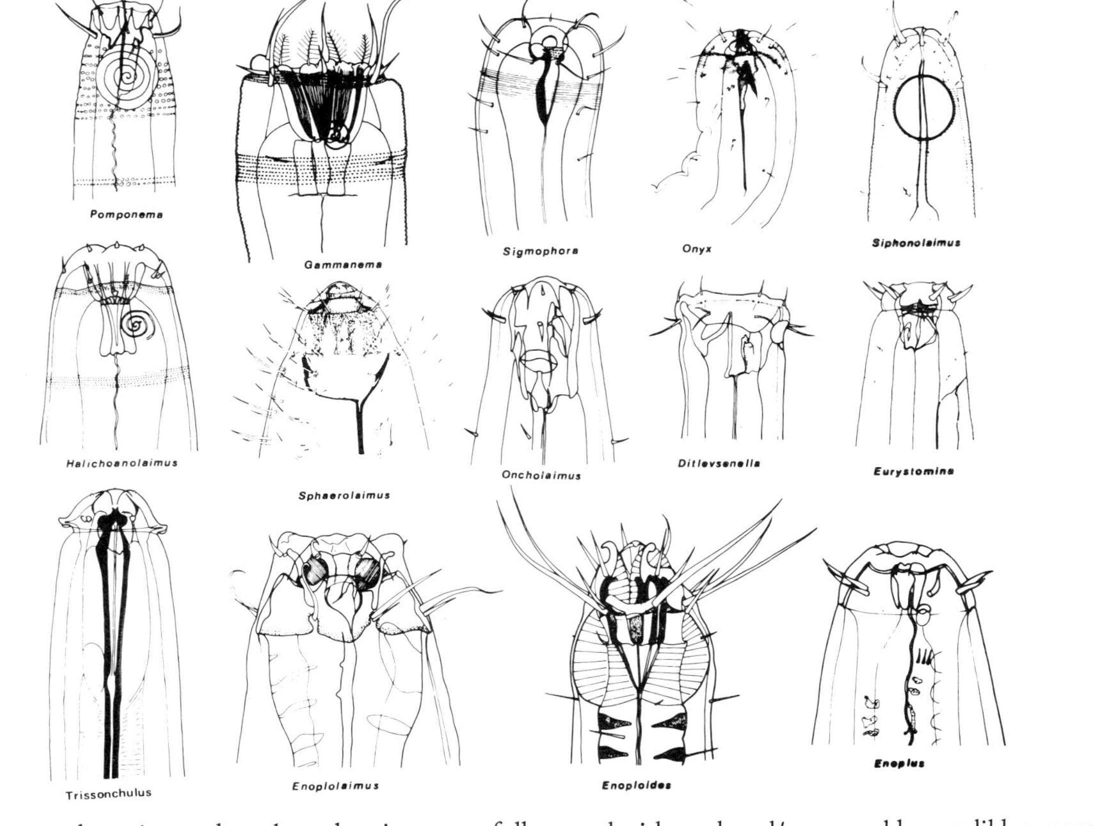

Fig. 4d. Predators and omnivores: large buccal cavity, powerfully armed with teeth and/or moveable mandibles, some feeding partly as epigrowth feeders but some also able to sieze and swallow prey or pierce and suck out their contents.

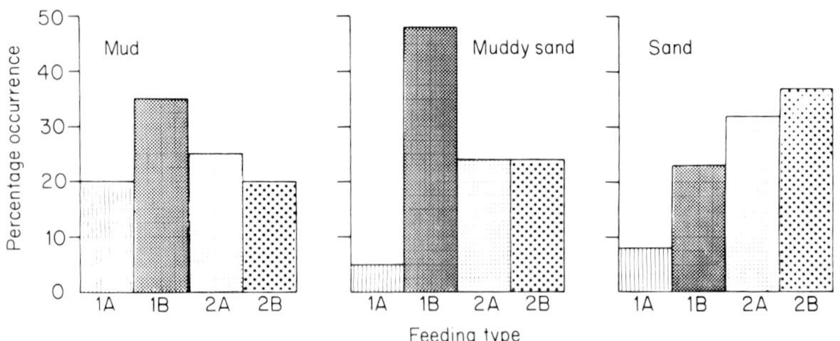

Fig. 5. Relative proportions of the four feeding groups in mud, muddy sand and clean sand from the Exe estuary, Devon.

Clearly, we are only at the beginning of our understanding of feeding in marine nematodes, as revealed in a stimulating account of the "mucus-trap hypothesis" by Reimann and Schrage (1978) who also discuss dissolved organic substances as a possible food source.

3. Distribution

Resource partitioning has led to behavioural and reproductive strategies enabling each species to make the most efficient use of the available food. This is reflected in the observed spatial and temporal partitioning by nematodes of the littoral and other habitats.

The "static" vertical and horizontal distribution on sediment shores, i.e. the snapshot impression revealed by discontinuous sampling, has been well documented (Warwick, 1971; Platt, 1977b; Boaden, 1977). Although many species tend to be concentrated at preferred depths in the sediment, there is now evidence to show that a number migrate vertically – perhaps to exploit diurnal diatom migrations or in response to the tide (Boaden and Platt, 1971; Rieger and Ott, 1971). Likewise, some species can migrate horizontally over short periods in response to a particular food source (Meyers and Hopper, 1966; Gerlach, 1971, 1977).

Spatial partitioning is also known from algal associations. Ott (1967) found that juveniles of a certain species were found at the tips of fronds whilst adults were only at the bases. He correlated this with a change in feeding habits – the juveniles being epigrowth

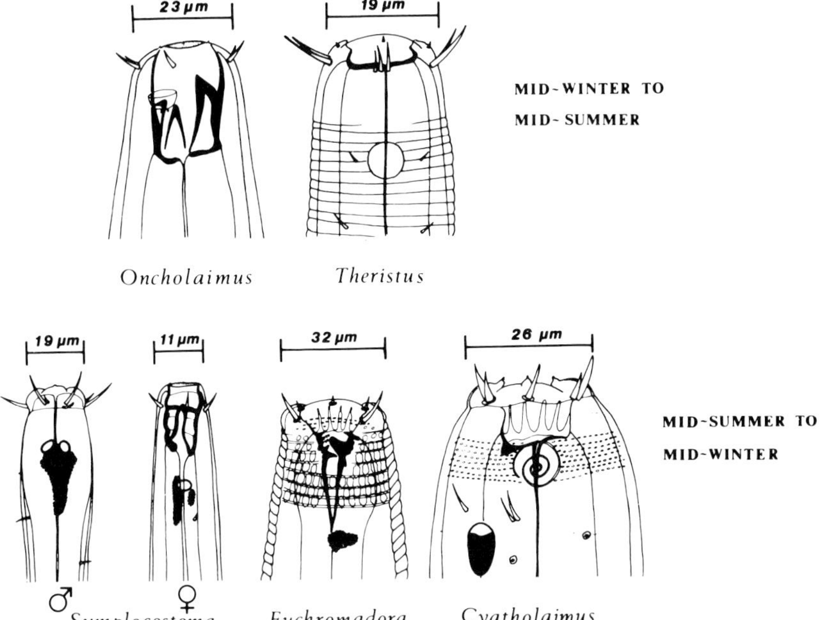

Fig. 6. Major components of Scilly Isles seaweed nematode fauna at different times of the year (from Warwick, 1977).

feeders, the adults predatory. Warwick (1977) found evidence that faunal composition can be directly related to the coarseness, texture and silt content of the seaweeds; probably associated with the specific epigrowths on different weeds upon which the worms preferentially feed.

Seasonal partitioning also occurs, with populations responding to temporal changes in the nature of the available food. This is possible only as a result of the short generation time of most species – in the order of one or two months in many instances (Hopper and Meyers, 1966; Gerlach and Schrage, 1971; Tietjen and Lee, 1973; Hopper *et al.*, 1973). For example, amongst the seaweed associations described by Warwick (1977), in spring and early summer carnivore/omnivores (2B) or deposit feeders (1A, 1B) dominated the fauna (Fig. 6). These forms had no preference for the tips of fronds and lacked any visual mechanisms. However, later in the year, epigrowth feeders (2A) increased and dominated the populations. These animals were able to scrape bacteria and unicellular algae from the fronds, or to pierce larger objects to suck out their contents, and possessed light-detecting mechanisms, presumably enabling them to position themselves near the frond tip where light intensity and hence epifloral density are both greater.

Even those species with longer generation times may have different food requirements at different life stages, which in part may be imposed passively by the gradually increasing size as the animals develop through the larval stages, or where the larvae are structurally different from the adults.

Finally, sexual partitioning of the food supply occurs in some groups. For example, in the genus *Symplocostoma* (Fig. 6), the male lacks the well developed buccal cavity of the female. Presumably the female needs to feed in order to satisfy the great energetic demands of egg production, whilst the male need only provide sperm. Thus it appears that the male sacrifices the prime food source to avoid competition with the female.

To summarize this section, we would argue that the data presented above substantiate the claim of nematodes to be *the most ubiquitous, abundant and diverse marine metazoan group.*

ENERGY FLOW THROUGH NEMATODE POPULATIONS

Despite the low biomass of nematodes in relation to the macrofauna, the metabolic activity per unit biomass is of course higher because of their small individual size. There have been several speculative attempts to convert numerical and mass data to energetic units, but only recently has more direct evidence been obtained to put these on a firmer footing. Some of this work will be discussed in terms of metabolism, production and consumption by the nematodes.

1. *Metabolism*

Warwick and Price (1979, Table 6) assembled estimates of mudflat and saltmarsh nematode population respiration rates ranging from 13 to 122 litres O_2/m^2/year (equivalent to a mean of 6 litres O_2/m^2/year per g wet weight at 20°C) – considerably higher than most values reported for macrofauna groups (McNeill and Lawton, 1970).

In the Lynher estuary, the annual nematode respiration per m^2

was equivalent to 11.2 g carbon metabolized, whilst the total for the entire macrofauna was only 21.6 g carbon (Warwick *et al.*, 1979). Since the nematode biomass is only about 15% of the macrofauna, this is a rate about 3.5 times higher than that of the macrofauna in terms of unit biomass. This confirmed earlier respiration estimates (on a unit biomass basis) such as those of Gerlach (1971), who suggested an overall metabolic rate for the meiofauna five times that of the macrofauna.

It is worth noting that in oxygen-deficient sediments there exists a significant number of anaerobically respiring meiofaunal groups, part of the thiobios (Boaden and Platt, 1971). Thus, the oxygen consumption alone may not be a true measure of total nematode metabolism. Obligate anaerobic nematodes form a characteristic fauna (Ott and Schiemer, 1973) and one species has been shown to perform better under oxygen-deficient conditions than in oxygen-rich (Wieser *et al.*, 1974). Some of Wieser's early experiments on anaerobic survival gave indications of this (Wieser and Kanwisher, 1961). Relative respiration rates of a large number of individual species have been discussed by Warwick and Price (1979). However, since little is yet known of the occurrence and relative importance of anaerobic metabolism, we cannot so far say by how much the total value of metabolism in low-oxygen habitats is underestimated.

2. Production

There are enormous problems in estimating the production of populations composed predominantly of species with overlapping generations. At the moment, many estimates are acknowledged to be little more than guesswork. Gerlach (1978) suggested a meiobenthic production to biomass (P/B) ratio of 10, which accords with an earlier estimate of McIntyre (1964). The P/B ratio of the nematode population in the Lynher estuary (Warwick and Price, 1979), was estimated from respiration data to be 8.4–8.7 and the total nematode production was significantly (about 1.2 times) greater than that of the entire macrofauna production (Warwick *et al.*, 1979). These estimates rely on several as yet unverified assumptions; thus far, there are no reliable estimates for any nematode species. However, if a P/B figure of 10 is assumed to be reasonably accurate for meiofauna and 2 for the macrofauna (Gerlach, 1978),

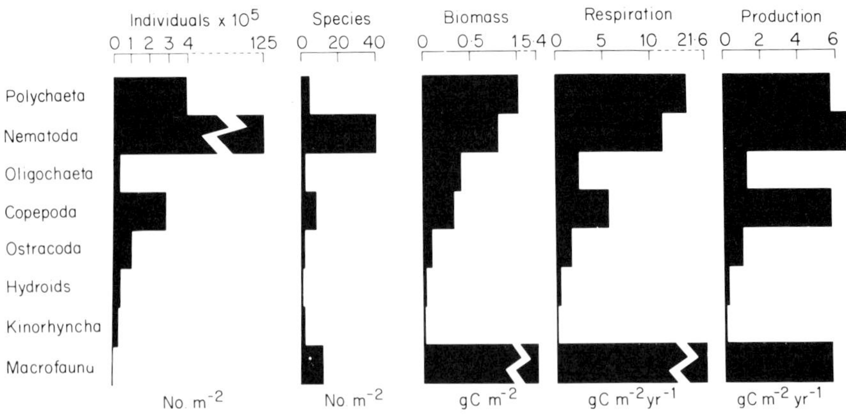

Fig. 7. Relative importance of nematodes compared with other meiofauna groups and the macrofauna in the Lynher estuary, Cornwall. Data based on Warwick *et al.* (1979), with subsequent refinements.

then for an intertidal meiofaunal biomass of 20% to 50% of the total (meio + macro), meiofaunal production would be from about equal to, to five times greater than, that of the macrofauna. The comparative production data from the Lynher estuary (Fig. 7) clearly support these speculative estimates and, since nematodes form a major proportion of the meiobenthos in many areas, the relationships shown may well prove to be fairly typical for most particulate shores.

3. Consumption

Since very little is known experimentally about the amount of food nematodes ingest, it can only be inferred indirectly. Warwick *et al.* (1979) estimated consumption from respiration and production data, assuming assimilation = production + respiration and an assimilation efficiency of 60%, and arrived at a consumption rate of 29.705 gC/m²/year. If the food had a similar water and carbon content to that of the nematodes, i.e. a dry weight/wet weight ratio of 0.25 (Wieser, 1960) and carbon comprises 40% of the dry weight (Steele, 1974), then this annual consumption rate would be equivalent to about 300 g/m²/year wet weight, almost 40 times their standing crop biomass (about 8 g/m² wet weight). This compares with a macrobenthos consumption of about 10 times their standing crop, i.e. only twice the total amount consumed by the nematodes alone.

However, the Lynher estuary nematode fauna is dominated by epigrowth and non-selective deposit feeders (about 70% of the total), which are probably mainly diatomivorous. Diatoms have a high ash content (about 50%) due to their siliceous tests, so that their carbon content is probably only about 20% of the dry weight (Vinogradov, 1953). Therefore, a more realistic figure for annual consumption may be 600 g/m^2/year wet weight.

The only experimental data concerning marine nematode ingestion rates are those of Tietjen and his co-workers (Tietjen *et al.*, 1970; Tietjen and Lee, 1973, 1977). Using a bacterial deposit feeder (*Rhabditis marina* Bastian) and a diatomivorous "epigrowth" feeder (*Chromadora macrolaimoides* Steiner) they demonstrated under laboratory conditions that the highest daily rates at which these animals would ingest food was from 10 times (for *Rhabditis* feeding on *Pseudomonas* sp.) to 50 times (for *Chromadora* feeding on *Nitzschia closterium* (Ehrenb.) W. Smith) their own body weight. Applying these results to the 8 g/m^2 Lynher population, and taking as an overall figure for the daily ingestion rate say 10 times body weight (i.e. biomass), then the annual wet weight consumption may be expected to be in the region of 30 000 g/m^2/year – 50 times the 600 g/m^2/year rate suggested from the production data. Even though the production-derived Lynher estimate ignores excretion, mucus production, and so on, an adjustment for these factors is hardly likely to compensate for this discrepancy. Clearly, a much lower feeding rate and/or a lower assimilation efficiency must pertain in the natural population if these differences are to be reconciled.

To emphasize a point made above, although as individuals they are highly selective feeders (by selective ingestion and/or digestion), nematodes as a whole exploit a very wide spectrum of food types. This factor enables both consumption and production to be continuously higher than in groups with a more restricted diet – perhaps the main explanation for the energetic importance of nematodes.

Although further work is needed, especially in non-sedimentary environments, we feel justified at this stage in describing nematodes in energetic terms as potentially *the most important single metazoan group in many shores ecosystems.*

NEMATODES AS FOOD FOR SECONDARY CONSUMERS

So far, we have only considered the energetic role of marine nematodes as primary consumers. They will now be evaluated as part of the diet of other organisms. Initially, nematodes and meiofauna in general were thought to be a trophic dead-end, acting either in competition with macrofauna for primary food sources or functioning as nutrient recyclers (McIntyre, 1969; Marshall, 1970; Heip and Smol, 1976). Smidt (1951), for example, suggested that, because nematodes were to be found undigested in the hindmost part of the fish's intestine, they were of little or no nutritive value, although presumably it could be argued that this was only the remnants of a much greater amount of ingested material which simply escaped the digestive processes. More recently, alternative arguments have been put forward to suggest that nematodes may indeed be consumed directly as food and their production thereby passed up the trophic chain (Elmgren, 1977). Some of the possible candidates for the role of nematode consumers will now be discussed (Fig. 8).

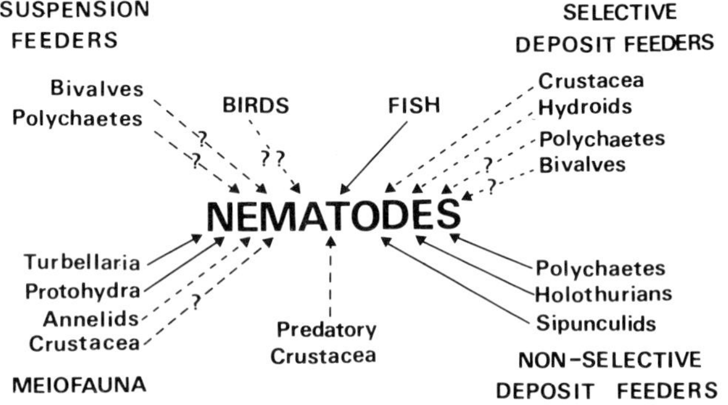

Fig. 8. Summary of known and potential nematophagous organisms. Continuous lines from known nematovores, broken lines from probable nematovores and queried broken lines from possible nematovores.

1. Consumption by Other Meiofauna

Among the meiofaunal carnivores known to be feeding on nematodes (other than carnivorous nematodes themselves) are *Protohydra* (Muus, 1966; Heip and Smol, 1976), many turbellarians (Remane, 1933;

Bilio, 1967; Elmgren, 1977) and the meiofaunal stages of annelids (Perkins, 1958). We would expect that in due course other groups will be shown to utilize nematodes, for part of their diet at least, possible candidates being copepods and the meiofaunal stages of certain other crustaceans.

2. Consumption by Macrobenthos

(a) Deposit feeders. Non-selective deposit feeders, such as some polychaetes, echinoids, holothurians and sipunculids, cannot avoid ingesting nematodes. But the questions to be answered are: are they digested and what proportion of the diet do they represent? Hansen (1978) has shown that food utilization in the guts of sediment-feeding sipunculids and holothurians was almost 100%, but although meiofauna (mainly nematodes) were utilized as food, they did not represent a significant part of the total food structure. However, this was in an area where 92% of the total calorific content of the sediment was provided by faecal pellets. Hylleberg (1975) also indicated that nematodes form only a small fraction of the food of *Abarenicola*: the same may be true for *Nephthys* (Warwick *et al.*, 1979) and *Pontoporeia* (Elmgren, 1977). Gerlach (1978) suggested that meiofauna (including Foraminifera) in subtidal sand contribute about 20% to the food of deposit-feeding macrofauna. As Gerlach points out, "bacterial biomass is not very much higher than meiofaunal biomass; therefore meiofauna automatically has to be considered as an important source of food, if the concept of non-selective feeding is valid".

If selective deposit feeders, such as terebellids and bivalves (e.g. *Scrobicularia*) do not make use of nematodes, they must be able to reject them (together with other meiofaunal components) before passing the sorted food, presumably diatoms and appropriately-sized inert particulate matter, to the mouth. Perhaps the activity of nematodes contributes to their being rejected, although the eggs of nematodes, which are produced in large quantities and are comparable in size to diatoms, could be available to such animals. However, hydroids have been shown to consume nematodes (Christensen, 1967) whilst other animals, such as crabs, may take in and crush meiofauna as a consequence of their normal feeding method (Teal, 1962).

(b) Suspension feeders. Resuspension of soft bottoms must play an important part in the nutrition of benthic filter-feeding organisms and in the dispersal of meiobenthos (Tenore 1977; Platt, 1979). Possibly the same arguments given above with respect to selective deposit feeding also hold true here, namely, that the activity of suspended nematodes enables them to avoid the various filter-feeding mechanisms.

(c) Carnivores. Any animal selectively taking nematodes (or any other component of the meiofauna) in a non-random way is, of course, a carnivore in the strict sense. Here again, very little direct evidence is available, but it seems that most predatory macrobenthic organisms, as adults, do not take nematodes.

Adult shrimps under laboratory conditions have been shown to be able to survive with free-living nematodes as food (Gerlach and Schrage, 1969) but since growth was impaired, they may not alone be an adequate diet. The role of nematodes in the diet of smaller mobile crustaceans, such as mysids and cumaceans, has yet to be fully assessed. Mauchline (1971a,b) examined the stomach contents of mysid species and found mainly harpacticoid copepods, dinoflagellates and unidentifiable fine particulate material. Depdolla (1916), however, showed that mysids would feed on pieces of "roundworm" thrown into an aquarium. Perhaps the reason for nematodes not being more frequently reported in the guts of various animals is because, once macerated, they are difficult to identify as such by the investigator. Crustaceans, we would speculate, may turn out to be major meiofaunal predators since their highly active delicate feeding mechansims seem theoretically able to manipulate the organisms. In terrestrial soils, nematodes are known to be fed on by arthropods (Nicholas, 1975) and perhaps crustaceans play a similar role in the marine environment, particularly as juveniles.

3. Consumption by Vertebrates

Fish, especially in their young stages, are known to take large quantities of meiofauna, including nematodes (McIntyre, 1969). Most often implicated are flat-fish (Bregnballe, 1961; Muus, 1967), gobies (Smidt, 1951) and mullet (Odum, 1970; Lassere *et al.*, 1976). Stomachs of mullet from the Plymouth area were found to be full of meiofauna, diatoms and sediment in roughly the same proportions as in the surface sediment – but no macrofauna. They were presumably feeding non-selectively on the surface mud, as their feeding marks would indicate. The mullet's stomach is followed by a muscular crushing gizzard which should successfully pulverise any organisms present in the sediment.

Shore-feeding birds, such as shellduck and small waders, feed selectively in sand and mudflats, but although such birds are known to take meiofaunal-sized oligochaetes and polychaetes (Evans, personal communication), the extent to which nematodes are ingested is unknown. Certainly there seem to be anomalies in the feeding of some of the birds, in that their stomach contents often fail to reveal the presence of the macrobenthic organisms that might be expected to form a part of their diet. Perhaps the ingestion of some of the larger meiofaunal animals, although not alone sufficient to sustain the birds, forms a "make-weight" whilst they are searching for the preferred but rarer organisms.

To summarize this section, would it not seem strange for the process to evolution not to have produced organisms able to make full use of such a relatively abundant food resource as the marine nematodes? Is it credible that nematodes in the guts of those animals in which the sediment is in any way ground up could survive such a treatment? Surely, the null hypothesis should be that nematodes do play a direct but as yet unquantified part in the diet of many animals in the shore environment. For non-selective feeders, this part may be roughly proportional to their contribution to the total benthic organic matter. For selective feeders, nematodes may be a more significant dietary component. Thus, we would expect that further evidence will substantiate the claim that nematodes form *a major part of the diet of many animals operating at higher trophic levels.*

OTHER ROLES PLAYED BY NEMATODES

In addition to their direct energetic involvement in the benthic food web, nematodes are potentially important in more indirect ways. The two functions to which we wish to draw attention are the part which nematodes play in facilitating decomposition and their influence on sediment stability.

1. Decomposition

The breakdown of dead organisms and detritus, and the consequent recycling of their constituent nutrients, is a vital role played by the bacterial flora. There is now evidence to show that this microbial activity is stimulated significantly by benthic organisms such as nematodes, as discussed recently by Gerlach (1978) and Tenore *et al.* (1977). Not only may burrowing and feeding activities improve the exchange of metabolites and provide essential nutrients for bacteria, but by they themselves feeding on bacteria the meiofauna thereby maintain the microorganisms in a "youthful" condition. In other words, they keep bacterial populations at the point of maximum growth (the log phase) or sustainable yield. Gerlach (1977) showed how certain nematodes are attracted to decaying organisms; large numbers of *Rhabditis* sp. are associated with rotting seaweeds; dead cumaceans (*Diastylis rathkei* (Krøyer)) in Swansea Bay have been found full of the nematode *Sabatieria breviseta* Stekhoven. In all these instances, it may be assumed that nematode–bacteria interaction enhances the rate of breakdown compared to that from bacterial activity alone. Further highlighting the importance of these mechanisms is the work of Billen (1978) on the sediments off the Belgian coast. His data on nitrogen recycling indicated that, in these shallow coastal zones, a major part of recycling occurs in the benthic phase rather than in the water column and suggested that the involvement of the benthos in these processes may confer some degree of stability to the ecosystem.

2. Sediment Stability

The burrowing of marine nematodes and its affect on microenvironments within sediments has recently attracted attention and indicated that nematodes play two opposing roles with regard to sediment stability. One is that they assist bioturbation, as shown by Cullen (1973), who observed the obliteration of surface tracks in controlled experiments where large organisms had been removed. The opposing suggestion is that, by producing a network of mucus-lined burrows, as Cullen (1973) himself noted and as also discussed by Riemann (1974) and Riemann and Schrage (1978), the sediment is rendered more stable. Clearly, nematodes at their highest densities of around

$1000/cm^3$ must have some effect on sediment habitats, but the exact balance between disturbance and stability needs further investigation.

So, although their prime importance in many shore environments may be their key position as primary consumers and as food for higher organisms, we would suggest that *nematodes play vital subsidiary roles in enhancing organic decomposition and in modifying the physical stability of sedimentary shores.*

USE OF NEMATODES AS AN INDICATOR GROUP

Without wishing to enter into the current controversies surrounding the practicalities of using marine organisms to monitor or test for environmental conditions (Gray, 1976; Lewis, 1978; Moore, 1978) we would like to evaluate briefly the nematodes in relation to several recent speculations on the possible usefulness of meiofauna (Arlt, 1975; Elmgren, 1975; Pequegnat, 1975; McIntyre, 1977; Newton *et al.*, 1979).

If the whole concept of biological indicators is viable, nematodes, we suggest, should prove ideal candidates, especially on particulate shores. Attention is drawn to the following points:

(i) because of their conservative reproductive strategies, nematode populations are inherently stable – thus, any alteration in population structure can more easily be related to some environmental perturbation;

(ii) short generation times and high diversity enable a nematode population to respond more quickly than macrofauna to alterations in the nature of the food supply;

(iii) nematodes span the whole range of polluted situations and are among the last to survive on grossly polluted shores (Bouwman, 1979; Heip, personal communication);

(iv) sampling for the numerically abundant nematodes is easier than for most other meiofauna groups or for the macrofauna; macrofauna require larger samples, creating greater habitat disturbance and logistic problems;

(v) the cost of nematode faunal analysis would be relatively low.

Nematodes do not appear to be useful indicators of specific inorganic pollutants: both Lorenzen (1974) and Tietjen (1977) failed to detect any faunistic differences attributable to titanium waste dumping and heavy metal pollution respectively. However, they do appear to be useful in other respects. Warwick and Gage (1975) showed that nematode distribution in Loch Etive reflected the integrated salinity conditions in the water column above over a period of time and, perhaps more importantly, detailed analysis of community structure has been shown to reflect the influence of abnormal sediment loads – conditions often associated with generally turbid and polluted coastal waters. This was demonstrated clearly by Moore (1971), in relation to the nematode fauna of kelp holdfasts.

Varying environmental conditions, in terms of the particulate load of the overlying water, are reflected in the trophic structure, i.e. the proportions of the various feeding groups, in the nematode population. Feeding behaviour is relatively easily deduced from the buccal cavity and oesophageal morphology – even by a non-nematode-specialist. Thus, the identification of individual species is not required, and here the argument that only easily identifiable animal groups can be used as environmental indicator organisms does not necessarily hold true. It is the distribution of functional types which may be of use, rather than that of the species themselves.

We hope that our arguments will stimulate others to consider using nematodes in pollution work. Only by such attempts can there be an ultimate refutation or substantiation of the claim that, if any group of marine animals can fulfil such a role then, potentially, *marine nematodes could be important biological indicators of environmental conditions.*

CONCLUSIONS

In the course of this chapter, we have put forward certain claims, some of which are admittedly based more on intuition than fact. Although evidence is slowly accumulating to substantiate these claims, a great deal of work remains to be done to convince the sceptics. But we feel the indications are now sufficiently clear to make a more concentrated effort worthwhile. Most studies to date have really only demonstrated a *potential* rather than an *actual* importance in the shore environment, and meiofaunal research in general needs much greater attention in the next decade or so, in order to place it firmly within the establishment of marine biology, stemming upwards from teaching at undergratuate level.

We hope that, in future, no general description of shore habitats will be thought of as complete if it excludes a consideration of one of its principal components – the nematode fauna. The authors wish to be spared the protracted frustrations of Drs Cobb and Steiner by seeing, in the not-too-distant future, the study of marine nematodes being viewed in its proper perspective.

REFERENCES

Arlt, G. (1975). Remarks on indicator organisms (meiofauna) in the coastal waters of the GDR. *Merentutkimuslait. Julk./Havsforskningsinst. Skr.* **239**, 272–279.

Bilio, M. (1967). Nahrungsbeziehungen der Turbellarien in Küstensalzwiesen. *Helgoländer wiss. Meeresunters.* **15**, 602–621.

Billen, G. (1978). A budget of nitrogen recycling in North Sea sediments off the Belgian coast. *Est. cst. mar. Sci.* **7**, 127–146.

Boaden, P. J. S. (1977). Thiobiotic facts and fancies (Aspects of the distribution and evolution of anaerobic meiofauna). *Mikrofauna Meereboden* **61**, 45–63.

Boaden, P. J. S. and Platt, H. M. (1971). Daily migration patterns in an intertidal meiobenthic community. *Thalassia jugosl.* **7**, 1–12.

Bouwman, L. A. (1979). Investigations on nematodes in the Ems-Dollart Estuary. *Annales Soc. r. Zool. Belg.* **108**, 103–105.

Bregnballe, F. (1961). Plaice and flounder as consumers of the microscopic bottom fauna. *Meddr. Danm. Fisk. og Havunders.* **3**, 133–182.

Capstick, C. K. (1959). The distribution of free-living nematodes in relation to salinity in the middle and upper reaches of the river Blyth estuary. *J. Anim. Ecol.* **28**, 189–210.

Christensen, H. E. (1967). Ecology of *Hydractinia echinata* (Hydroidea, Athecata). I. Feeding biology. *Ophelia* **4**, 245–275.

Christie, J. R. (1962). Steiner, Gotthold – In Memoriam. *Proc. Helm. Soc. Wash.* **29**, 94–96.

Cullen, D. J. (1973). Bioturbation of superficial marine sediments by interstitial meiobenthos. *Nature, Lond.* **242**, 323–324.

Depdolla, P. (1916). Biologische Notizen über *Praunus flexuosus* (Müller). *Zool. Anz.* **47**, 43–47.

Dye, A. H. and Furstenberg, J. P. (1978). An ecophysiological study of the meiofauna of the Swartkops estuary. 2. The meiofauna: composition, distribution, seasonal fluctuation and biomass. *Zoologia Africana* **13**, 19–32.

Elmgren, R. (1975). Benthic meiofauna as indicator of oxygen conditions in the northern Baltic proper. *Merentutkimuslait. Julk./Havsforskningsinst. Skr.* **239**, 265–271.

Elmgren, R. (1977). Baltic benthos communities and the role of the meiofauna. *Contr. Askö Lab.* **14**, 1–31.

Gerlach, S. A. (1971). On the importance of marine meiofauna for benthos communities. *Oecologia* **6**, 176–190.

Gerlach, S. A. (1977). Attraction to decaying organisms as a possible cause for patchy distribution of nematodes in a Bermuda beach. *Ophelia* **16**, 151–165.

Gerlach, S. A. (1978). Food-chain relationships in subtidal silty sand marine sediments and the role of meiofauna in stimulating bacterial productivity. *Oecologia* **33**, 55–69.

Gerlach, S. A. and Schrage, M. (1969). Freilebende Nematoden als Nahrung der Sandgarnele *Crangon crangon.* Experimentelle Untersuchungen über die Bedeutung der Meiofauna als Nahrung für das marine Makrobenthos. *Oecologia* **2**, 362–375.

Gerlach, S. A. and Schrage, M. (1971). Life cycles in marine meiobenthos. Experiments at various temperatures with *Monhystera disjuncta* and *Theristus pertenuis* (Nematoda). *Mar. Biol., Berl.* **9**, 274–280.

Gray, J. S. (1976). Are marine base-line surveys worthwhile? *New Scientist* **70**, 219–221.

Gray, J. S. and Reiger, R. M. (1971). A quantitative study of the meiofauna of an exposed sandy beach, at Robin Hood's Bay, Yorkshire. *J. mar. biol. Ass. U.K.* **51**, 1–19.

Hansen, M. D. (1978). Nahrung und Fressverhalten bei Sedimentfressern dargestellt am Beispiel von Sipunculiden und Holothurien. *Helgoländer wiss. Meeresunters.* **31**, 191–221.

Heip, C. and Smol, N. (1976). On the importance of *Protohydra leuckarti* as a predator of meiobenthic populations. *Proc. 10th Eur. mar. Biol. Symp. (Ostend)* **2**, 285–296.

Hopper, B. E. and Meyers, S. P. (1966). Aspects of the life cycles of marine nematodes. *Helgoländer wiss. Meeresunters.* **13**, 444–449.

Hopper, B. E., Fell, J. W. and Cefalu, R. C. (1973). Effect of temperature on life cycles of nematodes associated with the mangrove (*Rhizophora mangle*) detrital system. *Mar. Biol., Berl.* **23**, 293–296.

Hylleberg, J. (1975). Selective feeding by *Abarenicola pacifica* with notes on *Abarenicola vagabunda* and a concept of gardening in lugworms. *Ophelia* **14**, 113–137.

Lasserre, P., Renaud-Mornant, J. and Castel, J. (1976). Metabolic activities of meiofauna communities in a semi-enclosed lagoon. Possibilities of trophic competition between meiofauna and mugilid fish. *Proc. 10th Eur. mar. Biol. Symp. (Ostend)* 2, 393–414.

Lewis, J. R. (1978). The implications of community structure for benthic monitoring studies. *Mar. Poll. Bull.* **9**, 64–67.

Lorenzen, S. (1974). Die Nematodenfauna der sublitoralen Region der Deutschen Bucht, insbesondere im Titan-Abwassergebiet bei Helgoland. *Veröff. Inst. Meeresforsch. Bremerh.* **14**, 305–327.

McIntyre, A. D. (1964). Meiobenthos of sub-littoral muds. *J. mar. biol. Ass. U.K.* **44**, 665–674.

McIntyre, A. D. (1968). The meiofauna and macrofauna of some tropical beaches. *J. Zool., Lond.* **156**, 377–392.

McIntyre, A. D. (1969). Ecology of marine meiobenthos. *Biol. Rev.* **44**, 245–290.

McIntyre, A. D. (1977). Effects of pollution on inshore benthos. *In* "Ecology of Marine Benthos" (B. C. Coull, ed.), pp. 301–318. University of South Carolina Press, Columbia.

McIntyre, A. D. and Eleftheriou, A. (1968). The bottom fauna of a flatfish nursery ground. *J. mar. biol. Ass. U.K.* **48**, 113–142.

McIntyre, A. D. and Murison, D. J. (1973). The meiofauna of a flatfish nursery ground. *J. mar. biol. Ass. U.K.* **53**, 93–118.

McLachlan, A. (1977). Studies on the psammolittoral meiofauna of Algoa Bay, South Africa. II. The distribution, composition and biomass of the meiofauna and macrofauna. *Zoologica Africana* **12**, 33–60.

McNeill, S. and Lawton, J. H. (1970). Annual production and respiration in animal populations. *Nature, Lond.* **225**, 472–474.

Marshall, N. (1970). Food transfer through the lower trophic levels of the benthic environment. *In* "Marine Food Chains" (J. H. Steele, ed.), pp. 52–56. Oliver and Boyd, Edinburgh.

Mauchline, J. (1971a). The biology of *Praunus flexuosus* and *P. neglectus* (Crustacea, Mysidacea). *J. mar. biol. Ass. U.K.* **51**, 641–652.

Mauchline, J. (1971b). The biology of *Schistomysis kervillei* (Crustacea, Mysidacea). *J. mar. biol. Ass. U.K.* **51**, 653–658.

Meyers, S. P. and Hopper, B. E. (1966). Attraction of the marine nematode, *Metoncholaimus* sp., to fungal substrates. *Bull. mar. Sci. Gulf Caribb.* **16**, 142–150.

Moore, P. G. (1971). The nematode fauna associated with holdfasts of kelp (*Laminaria hyperborea*) in north-east Britain. *J. mar. biol. Ass. U.K.* **51**, 589–604.

Moore, P. G. (1978). Benthic monitoring studies. *Mar. Poll. Bull.* **9**, 194.

Muus, B. J. (1967). The fauna of Danish estuaries and lagoons. Distribution and ecology of dominating species in the shallow reaches of the mesohaline zone. *Meddr. Danm. Fisk. og Havunders.* **5**, 1–316.

Muus, K. (1966). Notes on the biology of *Protohydra leuckarti* Greef (Hydroidea, Protohydridae). *Ophelia* **3**, 141–150.

Newton, A. J., Henderson, A. R. and Holmes, P. J. (1979). Monitoring the effects of domestic and industrial wastes. *In* "Monitoring the Marine Environment" (D. Nichols, ed.), pp. 171–179. Institute of Biology, Symp. No. 24, London.

Nicholas, W. L. (1975). "The Biology of Free-living Nematodes". Clarendon Press, Oxford.

Odum, W. E. (1970). Utilization of the direct grazing and plant detritus food chains by the striped mullet *Mugil cephalus*. *In* "Marine Food Chains" (J. H. Steele, ed.), pp. 222–240. Oliver and Boyd, Edinburgh.

Ott, J. (1967). Vertikalverteilung von Nematoden in Beständen nordadriatischer Sargassaceen. *Helgoländer wiss. Meeresunters.* **15**, 412–428.

Ott, J. (1972a). Determination of fauna boundaries of nematodes in an intertidal sand flat. *Int. Rev. ges. Hydrobiol.* **57**, 645–663.

Ott, J. (1972b). Studies on the diversity of the nematode fauna in intertidal sediments. *In* "Fifth European Marine Biology Symposium" (B. Battaglia, ed.), pp. 275–285.

Ott, J. and Schiemer, F. (1973). Respiration and anaerobiosis of free living nematodes from marine and limnic sediments. *Neth. J. Sea. Res.* **7**, 233–243.

Pequegnat, W. E. (1975). Meiobenthos ecosystems as indicators of the effects of dredging. *In* "Estuarine Research", Vol. II. (L. E. Cronon, ed.), pp. 573–584. Academic Press, New York and London.

Perkins, E. J. (1958). The food relationships of the microbenthos, with particular reference to that found at Whitstable, Kent. *Ann. Mag. nat. Hist.* **13**, 64–77.

Platt, H. M. (1977a). Ecology of free-living marine nematodes from an intertidal sandflat in Strangford Lough, Northern Ireland. *Est. est. mar. Sci.* **5**, 685–693.

Platt, H. M. (1977b). Vertical and horizontal distribution of free-living marine nematodes from Strangford Lough, Northern Ireland. *Cah. Biol. Mar.* **18**, 261–273.

Platt, H. M. (1979). Sedimentation and the distribution of organic matter in a sub-Antarctic marine bay. *Est. cst. mar. Sci.* **9**, 51–63.

Rees, C. B. (1940). A preliminary study of the ecology of a mud-flat. *J. mar. Biol. Ass. U.K.* **24**, 185–199.

Remane, A. (1933). Verteilung und Organisation der benthonischen Mikrofauna der Kieler Bucht. *Wiss. Meeresunters. (Kiel)* **21**, 161–221.

Rieger, R. and Ott, J. (1971). Gezeitenbedingte Wanderungen von Turbellarien und Nematoden eines nordadriatischen Sandstrandes. *Vie Milieu* Suppl. **22**, 425–447.

Riemann, F. (1974). On hemisessile nematodes with flagelliform tails living in marine softbottoms and on micro-tubes found in deep sea sediments. *Mikrofauna Meeresboden* **40**, 1–15.

Riemann, F. and Schrage, M. (1978). The mucus-trap hypothesis on feeding of aquatic nematodes and implications for biodegradation and sediment texture. *Oecologia* **34**, 75–88.

Smidt, E. L. B. (1951). Animal production in the Danish Waddensea. *Meddr. Danm. Fisk. og Havunders.* **11**, 1–151.

Steele, J. H. (1974). "The Structure of Marine Ecosystems". Blackwell Scientific Publications, Oxford.

Teal, J. M. (1962). Energy flow in the salt marsh ecosystem of Georgia. *Ecology* **43**, 614–624.

Teal, J. M. and Wieser, W. (1966). The distribution and ecology of nematodes in a Georgia salt marsh. *Limnol. Oceanogr.* **11**, 217–222.

Tenore, K. R. (1977). Food chain pathways in detrital feeding benthic communities: a review, with new observations on sediment resuspension and detrital recycling. *In* "Ecology of Marine Benthos" (B. C. Coull, ed.), pp. 37–53. University South Carolina Press, Columbia.

Tenore, K. R., Tietjen, J. H. and Lee, J. J. (1977). Effect of meiofauna on incorporation of aged eelgrass, *Zostera marina*, detritus by the polychaete

Nephthys incisa. *J. Fish Res. Bd Can.* **34**, 563–567.

Tietjen, J. H. (1977). Population distribution and structure of the free-living nematodes of Long Island Sound. *Mar. Biol., Berl.* **43**, 123–136.

Tietjen, J. H. and Lee, J. J. (1973). Life history and feeding habits of the marine nematode, *Chromadora macrolaimoides* Steiner. *Oecologia* **12**, 303–314.

Tietjen, J. H. and Lee, J. J. (1977). Feeding behaviour of marine nematodes. *In* "Ecology of Marine Benthos" (B. C. Coull, ed.), pp. 21–35. University South Carolina Press, Columbia.

Tietjen, J. H., Lee, J. J., Rullman, J., Greengart, A. and Trompeter, J. (1970). Gnotobiotic culture and physiological ecology of the marine nematode *Rhabditis marina* Bastian. *Limnol. Oceanogr.* **15**, 535–543.

Vinogradov, A. P. (1953). "The Elementary Chemical Composition of Marine Organisms". Yale University Press, Sears Foundation for Marine Research.

Warwick, R. M. (1968). "The ecological distribution of free-living marine nematodes in some substrates in the Exe estuary". Unpublished Ph.D. Thesis, University of Exeter, England.

Warwick, R. M. (1971). Nematode associations in the Exe estuary. *J. mar. biol. Ass. U.K.* **51**, 439–454.

Warwick, R. M. (1977). The structure and seasonal fluctuations of phytal marine nematode associations on the Isles of Scilly. *In* "Biology of Benthic Organisms" (B. F. Keegan, P. Ó. Céidigh and P. J. S. Boaden, eds), pp. 577–585. Pergamon Press, Oxford.

Warwick, R. M. and Gage, J. D. (1975). Nearshore zonation of benthic fauna, especially Nematoda, in Loch Etive. *J. mar. biol. Ass. U.K.* **55**, 295–311.

Warwick, R. M. and Price, R. (1979). Ecological and metabolic studies on free-living nematodes from an estuarine mud-flat. *Est. cst mar. Sci.* **9**, 257–271.

Warwick, R. M., Joint, I. R. and Radford, P. J. (1979). Secondary production of the benthos in an estuarine environment. *In* "Ecological Processes in Coastal Environments" (R. L. Jeffries and A. J. Davy eds), pp. 429–450. Blackwell Scientific Publications, Oxford.

Wieser, W. (1952). Investigations on the microfauna inhabiting seaweeds on rocky coasts. IV. Studies on the vertical distribution of the fauna inhabiting seaweeds below the Plymouth Laboratory. *J. mar. biol. Ass. U.K.* **31**, 145–174.

Wieser, W. (1953). Die Beziehung zwischen Mundhöhlengestalt, Ernährungsweise und Vorkommen bei freilebenden marinen Nematoden. Eine ökologisch-morphologische Studie. *Ark. Zool.* **4**, 439–484.

Wieser, W. (1959). "Free-living Nematodes and Other Small Invertebrates of Puget Sound Beaches". University of Washington Press, Seattle.

Wieser, W. (1960). Benthic studies in Buzzards Bay. II. The Meiofauna. *Limnol. Oceanogr.* **5**, 121–137.

Wieser, W. and Kanwisher, J. W. (1961). Ecological and physiological studies on marine nematodes from a small salt marsh near Woods Hole, Massachusetts. *Limnol. Oceanogr.* **6**, 262–270.

Wieser, W., Ott, J., Schiemer, F. and Gnaiger, E. (1974). An ecophysiological study of some meiofauna species inhabiting a sandy beach at Bermuda. *Mar. Biol., Berl.* **26**, 235–248.

11 Invertebrate Epiphytes of Coastal Marine Algae

P. J. HAYWARD

Department of Zoology, University College of Swansea, Wales

Abstract: The familiar associations between coastal marine algae and a broad range of invertebrate animals have been shown to result from larval responses to the algal substrata, leading to selective settlement. Such responses are a feature of the settlement behaviour of both sessile and non-sessile species and may restrict populations of each species to a broader or narrower range of algal substrata. The basis of selection remains to be clarified, but appears to be related to a chemical recognition of particular surfaces by marine larvae. Algal epifaunas include both stenotopic and eurytopic species, the incidence of the latter varying according to the influence of physical environmental factors. Biological interactions within an epifaunal community include those between the epiphyte and the alga, which may lead to restricted distribution of the epiphyte on the algal thallus; those between different epiphytic species, which may lead to distinct zonation of each species, and interactions between specialized predators and their sessile prey species. Integration of the three levels of interaction is necessary to an understanding of community structure.

INTRODUCTION

Associations between marine invertebrates and algae have long been remarked upon by marine zoologists. Linnaeus (1767), for example, considered some such associations to be so typical that, for several

---

Systematics Association Special Volume No. 17(b), "The Shore Environment, Vol. 2: Ecosystems", edited by J. H. Price, D. E. G. Irvine and W. F. Farnham, 1980, pp. 761–787, Academic Press, London and New York.

bryozoan species, he felt able to define them partly by reference to their habitat, on "Fuci". Monographic works of the last century also noted the occurrence of invertebrate animals on marine algae, perhaps largely for practical reasons, enabling the organism to be located and collected quite easily. Certainly, the specificity of some of these associations does not seem to have been appreciated by all taxonomic specialists.

The study of the fauna of coastal seaweeds developed quite recently during the present century; the work of Colman (1940) is a well known example. He studied the fauna of eight species of seaweed along transects at Church Reef, Wembury, and identified 177 species of invertebrate. For each species of alga, at each sampling point, the population of invertebrate species was calculated per 100 g of damp weed. By calculating the mean weight of each alga per m^2 of rock surface, total invertebrate populations were estimated for each of the sites sampled. An indication of the range and numbers of animals recorded by Colman is given by Table I. This work allowed an immediate comparison with results from the developing study of shore zonation, but the emphasis was directed towards population studies, with little attention being given to specific associations. Similarly, Wieser (1952) conducted a quantitative survey of the fauna of eight species of algae at Plymouth but was largely concerned with the vertical zonation of invertebrate species. This approach has been followed by many workers but more recently emphasis has tended to be shifted towards an understanding of the composition and structure of epiphytic communities. For example, Hagerman (1966) carried out a detailed investigation of the epifauna of *Fucus serratus* L. in the Øresund, Denmark, and presented data on the abundance and seasonal occurrence of the fauna. Research into the behavioural adaptations of marine invertebrate larvae which result in localized settlement on particular substrata provides another important source of data on epiphytic communities. The literature is extensive but, although several good accounts are available, reviews have tended to be fairly broad-based (e.g. Meadows and Campbell, 1972; Scheltema, 1974) and a comprehensive review of those aspects of the field important to an understanding of algal epifaunas is still awaited.

Table I. Mean populations of invertebrates in seven species of algae and in *Lichina*: individuals per 100 g weed. From Colman (1940).

	Pelvetia canaliculata	*Fucus spiralis*	*Lichina pygmaea*	*Fucus vesiculosus*	*Ascophyllum nodosum* and *Polysiphonia lanosa*	*Fucus serratus*	*Gigartina stellata*	*Laminaria digitata* holdfasts
Porifera	—	—	—	—	—	—	—	8.3
Coelenterata	—	—	—	—	3.0	0.2	216.0	31.0
Turbellaria and Nemertinea	—	0.3	—	5.3	63.6	0.5	2.8	40.2
Nematoda	3.4	3.2	—	3.3	76.1	21.2	16.5	247.8
Polychaeta	—	0.8	—	—	72.6	0.6	73.8	2056.0
Oligochaeta	0.2	3.2	11.0	0.3	39.2	0.2	—	9.7
Sipunculoidea	—	—	—	2.0	—	0.3	10.8	1.5
Ostracoda	—	0.5	—	16.0	353.3	3.0	0.5	7.5
Copepoda	—	25.8	—	221.0	272.2	178.1	1676.2	54.0
Cirripedia	—	—	287.0	—	—	—	1.2	51.0
Tanaidacea	—	—	—	—	0.2	—	—	13.7
Isopoda	15.2	0.5	2886.0	4.3	30.0	8.1	32.2	6.3
Amphipoda	15.4	46.3	35.0	1.3	48.1	4.3	83.8	125.3
Decapoda	—	0.2	—	—	0.2	0.1	—	4.0
Pycnogonida	—	—	—	—	0.2	—	—	3.7
Acarina	—	3.2	436.0	135.7	222.4	75.6	758.8	7.3
Insecta	0.8	1.3	161.0	2.3	58.3	2.0	—	—
Pelecypoda	—	—	9447.0	—	14.8	0.8	42.0	96.2
Gastropoda	8.8	13.5	453.0	67.0	163.3	23.5	72.2	19.5
Bryozoa	—	—	—	—	0.2	6.1	158.2	73.5
Tunicata	—	—	—	—	—	—	—	7.8
Total	43.8	98.8	13,716.0	458.5	1417.7	324.6	3145.0	2864.3

THE EPIPHYTIC FAUNA

Marine algae provide a number of resources for exploitation by invertebrate animals. By their very abundance, they are important in supplying a greatly increased surface area for the attachment of sessile or non-sessile sedentary animals on most rocky shores. They also provide shelter, offering a refuge for vagile species during periods of low tide, but also supplying permanent habitats for less motile species. They may act as sediment traps, an added attraction for many animal species. Finally, algae are an important food source, either directly so in the case of algal browsing species, or indirectly so in the case of detrital feeders, or species grazing upon microbial films, the algal frond providing an ideal collecting and culturing surface.

The animal species occurring on algae may be utilizing one, two or all three of these resources and the term epiphyte, thus defined, is perhaps impossibly broad. Sedentary invertebrates attached to a particular alga will include eurytopic and stenotopic species; those settling on, in or beneath it will probably be largely eurytopic, and the browsers and grazers will include both specialized and euryphagic species. An interesting comparison may perhaps be made with certain other organisms known or inferred to modify the environment in which they live. For example, dense populations of tunicates such as *Ascidia* and *Ascidiella*, beds of bivalves, clumps of hydroids such as *Nemertesia* and *Tubularia*, and extensive populations of the bryozoans *Flustra* and *Pentapora* will each offer numerous opportunities for exploitation by sedentary and motile animals. In many cases, the species will be the same as those occurring in algal epifaunas. In view of this, many investigations into epiphytic communities have been directed towards demonstrating the modification of the fauna by environmental factors (e.g. Jones, 1973). Sloane *et al.* (1957) and Sloane *et al.* (1961) studied the epifauna of laminarian algae, and of the undergrowth algae beneath the laminarian canopy, in Lough Ine Rapids and showed that whereas some species were most abundant in areas of moderate to strong current, the majority declined in numbers as current strength increased. Similarly, Ryland and Nelson-Smith (1975) showed that populations of sessile epiphytes on *Laminaria* spp. in a rapids system in western Ireland varied in abundance according to the speed of flow through the rapids.

Among the sea lochs of the Western Isles numerous rapids systems occur where isolated, almost landlocked and completely sheltered bays are linked to the main body of sea water by narrow channels. Algal cover within the channels is luxuriant and the almost continuously flowing water enables immense populations of filter-feeding animals to develop. *Fucus serratus* L., which on a seashore of average exposure may be expected to support a fauna of perhaps ten epiphytic species, here supports an enormous assemblage of animals. The two common epiphytic bryozoans *Alcyonidium* and *Flustrellidra* compete for space with perhaps another six species, including heavily calcified species such as *Schizoporella unicornis* (Johnston in Wood) and *Umbonula littoralis* Hastings, which elsewhere are found only on hard substrata and cannot survive the constant flexing of an algal frond in even moderate wave surge. Hydroid species are similarly multiplied; two or three sponges occur, most frequently *Scypha ciliata* (Fabr.) and *S. compressa* (Fabr.), also several tunicates, and even species of sedentary bivalve, such as *Mytilus edulis* L. and *Modiolus modiolus* (L.). In these circumstances the age of the alga is also important, and presumably the complete lack of storm damage in such areas results in large, long-lived plants, enabling a dense population of epiphytes to develop.

Clearly, it is necessary to attempt a more precise definition of epiphytic species if the study of algal epifaunas is to result in ecological accounts of comparative use. Many studies of algal epifaunas are in reality studies of part of a marine habitat of which the alga is just one component. As such they produce lengthy lists of animal species but fail to pinpoint characteristic epiphytes or to reveal biological interactions. Norton's (1971) study of the fauna of *Saccorhiza polyschides* Batt. at Port Erin and Lough Ine resulted in a list of 89 species, almost all of which were eurytopic forms, and none of the species shown to be restricted to *Saccorhiza* at the two localities can be considered to be truly epiphytic.

An epiphytic species may be defined as one which is directly dependent upon an algal resource for at least the most significant stages of its life history. Such a species might be termed a primary, or obligate, epiphyte. Secondary epiphytes are purely opportunistic, eurytopic species which are able to make use of the alga over part of their habitat range but are neither restricted to nor dependent upon it. Primary epiphytes would include sessile species whose larvae display a faculty for discrimination at settlement, leading to a restricted distribution on one or a few algal species. Numerous examples may be found among tubeworms, bryozoans and hydroids. The definition would also embrace specialized algal browsers and grazers, such as the opisthobranch *Limapontia capitata* (Müller) and the gastropod *Patina pellucida* (L.), which spend the whole of their life cycle on one or a few algal species and whose larvae may need to select the appropriate substratum before successfully undergoing metamorphosis. The secondary epiphytes, which frequently constitute the majority of the epifauna, may of course be important ecologically; some may have a significant effect on the algal population, perhaps by sheer weight of numbers, but many probably have no effect at all. However, if the epifauna of an algal species is to be treated as an ecological community, two further groups of organisms must be considered besides the primary epiphytes. These are, those secondary epiphytes which can be shown to have a direct effect on the community, such as non-selective algal browsers, and those species which are not concerned with the alga at all, but which are dependent upon the primary epiphytes as a food source. The latter group might include many mites, pycnogonids and polychaetes, but is most usefully restricted to the specialized feeders, as exemplified by numerous opisthobranchs, the larvae of which, in some cases, will only achieve successful metamorphosis by settlement upon the favoured food organism. A selective list of apparent primary epiphytes is given in Table II.

The range of seaweeds utilized by invertebrate animals is large. Almost all intertidal species attract one or more characteristic epiphytes and this is probably true of subtidal species as well. Different species of algae vary in their attractiveness to epiphytes; the basis of attractiveness is not clearly understood but is probably attributable to a variety of factors. Physical factors would include the size of the plant, and consequently the surface area available for settlement and growth, and surface texture, including the degree of concavity and surface rugosity. On these points algae such as *Halidrys siliquosa* (L.) Lyngbye and *Ascophyllum nodosum* (L.) Le Jolis are probably to a large extent unattractive. The rigidity of the alga is also important, one reason, perhaps, why the majority of green algae seem to carry few sessile epiphytes. The quantities of mucus exuded by a plant may discourage epiphytes; Ryland (1959), for example, considered that the fruiting conceptacles of *Fucus serratus* were unattractive to bryozoan larvae for this reason. The vertical range of an alga may affect its epifauna; Miller (1961) stated that the opisthobranch *Hermaea bifida* (Montagu) occurs on the rhodophyte *Griffithsia flosculosa* (Ellis) Batt. only at ELWS and below, although the plant extends upshore as far as MTL, probably because the delicate slug is unable to withstand prolonged exposure and its attendant problem of desiccation. Similarly, Ryland (1959) showed that *Fucus spiralis* L. was quite acceptable as a substratum to settling bryozoan larvae, but never bore bryozoan epiphytes on the shore simply because the high tidal level at which the weed occurred was inimical to them.

Shore exposure is important both in regulating the relative proportions of algal species, and thereby restricting a larva's range of choice, and by its effect on the size and age structure of individual algal populations. On sheltered shores *Flustrellidra hispida* (Fabricius) and species of *Alcyonidium* (both ctenostomatous Bryozoa) are almost confined to *Fucus serratus*; where this alga is small and sparsely distributed, on more exposed shores, the same epiphytes occur principally on *Chondrus crispus* Stackh. and *Gigartina stellata* (Stackh.) Batt. The smaller rhodophytes seem to vary in attractiveness according to structural characteristics and to physical, environmental factors. The broad-fronded species seem to be preferred by sessile animals, while the filamentous types are attractive to small gastropods, nematodes and pycnogonids, for example. However, the suitability of filamentous red algae for *Rissoa* may be dependent upon their chance ability to filter and retain the sediment on which the snails feed, and the availability of sediment may vary with shore aspect and exposure.

In summary, green algae are generally attractive only to motile epiphytes, perhaps specialized herbivores. Brown algae, by virtue of their dominance on most shores, and of their broad, flat, rigid or semi-rigid fronds, are consistently favourable, whereas red algae are either second choice substrata in areas where brown algae are scarce, or attractive to a particular fauna of small, specialized feeders.

Not all portions of an algal plant are equally attractive to epiphytes; this will be discussed further under the appropriate heading, but some generalizations may be made here. Again, the variation may be attributed to inherent characteristics of the plant or to self-evident

Table II. Some examples of primary epiphytes in British waters, with their principal algal substrata

Epiphyte	Alga
Coelenterata	
Aglaophenia pluma	*Laminaria* spp.
	Halidrys siliquosa
Amphisbetia operculata	*Laminaria* spp.
Clava multicornis	*Ascophyllum nodosum*
	Fucus spp.
Dynamena pumila	*Laminaria* spp.
	Fucus spp.
Obelia geniculata	*Laminaria* spp.
Mollusca	
Elysia viridis	*Codium tomentosum*
	Cladophora spp.
Hermaea bifida	*Griffithsia flosculosa*
	Delesseria sanguinea
	Heterosiphonia plumosa
Hermaea dendritica	*Codium tomentosum*
	Bryopsis spp.
Lacuna pallidula	*Fucus serratus*
Lacuna vincta	*Fucus serratus*
	Laminaria spp.
	Halidrys siliquosa
Limapontia capitata	*Enteromorpha* spp.
	Cladophora spp.
Littorina obtusata	*Ascophyllum nodosum*
	Fucus serratus
Patina pellucida	*Laminaria* spp.
Rissoa parva	*Laurencia* spp.
	Lomentaria articulata
	Plumaria elegans
Polychaeta	
Pileolaria militaris	*Rhodymenia* spp.
	Calliblepharis ciliata
Spirorbis corallinae	*Corallina officinalis*
Spirorbis inornatus	*Laminaria digitata*
	Saccorhiza polyschides
	Himanthalia elongata
Spirorbis rupestris	*Phymatolithon* spp.
Spirorbis spirorbis	*Fucus serratus*
	Fucus vesiculosus
	Laminaria spp.
	Saccorhiza polyschides

Table II (*continued*) . . .

Epiphyte	Alga
	Chondrus crispus
	Gigartina stellata
Crustacea	
Idotea granulosa	*Ascophyllum nodosum*
	Polysiphonia lanosa
	Fucus serratus
	Cladophora spp.
Idotea pelagica	*Fucus* spp.
Bryozoa	
Alcyonidium hirsutum	*Fucus serratus*
	Chondrus crispus
	Gigartina stellata
Alcyonidium polyoum	*Fucus serratus*
Flustrellidra hispida	*Fucus serratus*
	Chondrus crispus
	Gigartina stellata
Membranipora membranacea	*Laminaria* spp.

physical factors. The apical areas of plants of many fucoids seem to be avoided by marine larvae. This may be a physical effect of, for example, mucus exuded by fruiting apices, or may be due to age-dependent gradients of attractiveness in the surface of the thallus, evidence for which is discussed below. The smooth, flexible frond of most *Laminaria* species is unacceptable to all but the most specialized epiphytes; the wrinkled frond of *L. saccharina* (L.) Lamour. usually has a higher epiphyte load than those of other species, but diversity is generally low. By contrast, the holdfast in all *Laminaria* species is a rich and complex microhabitat which has attracted a great deal of attention, both as a self-contained community and as a convenient sampling unit. Recent work has included studies of the composition and development of the holdfast fauna, and its modification by environmental factors (Jones, 1973; Moore, 1978), but community interrelationships remain understudied. The stipe of *Laminaria* may have a bryozoan epifauna often distinct from that of the holdfast, with a predominance of erect species, such as *Crisia* and *Scrupocellaria*, and an epiflora of small red algae which may themselves support populations of epiphytes.

The literature of epiphytic faunas includes numerous accounts of the distribution of particular animal groups. In many cases, the association between the epiphyte and its substratum was recognized as fairly narrowly defined, and the study established the range of substrata utilized by each animal species. For example, Rogick and Croasdale (1949) catalogued the bryozoan epiphytes of the Woods Hole area; 30 species were reported from 37 species of marine algae. The range of algal substrata colonized by each bryozoan species was given, together with the diversity of species observed on each alga. Further examples are those of Ryland (1962) on the bryozoan epiphytes of the north Wales coast, and Nishihira (1966) who noted the associations between epiphytic hydroids and their algal hosts at Tsuchiya, Japan. Such work continues to make interesting contributions, particularly in respect of little known coasts or algal species, but the most important contributions of recent years are those which have demonstrated that the observed associations could be related to larval settlement behaviour.

HABITAT SELECTION

The observed distributions of marine invertebrates are not the result of random processes, but rather the expression of precise behavioural patterns which lead to the selection of the habitat most suited to each species. In the case of sessile, or non-sessile sedentary, species the distribution of the adult is the result of a choice exhibited by the prospecting larva. The factors which influence the distribution of marine invertebrates have attracted a good deal of attention over the past two decades and several comprehensive reviews are available, the most notable being that of Meadows and Campbell (1972). Epiphytic species have been widely used in experimental work investigating environmental influences on larval behaviour.

The factors which influence the selection of substrata by marine invertebrate larvae are numerous, and it has been shown that responses to gravity, light and current are all important in narrowing the choice of prospecting larvae. However, for many species biological interactions are ultimately of the greatest importance. The role of biological interactions in settlement behaviour has recently been reviewed by Scheltema (1974). Perhaps the simplest type of biological influence is that exerted by the presence of surface films. Such films have been shown to influence the settlement of marine larvae on inorganic as well as organic surfaces although, as Scheltema (1974) has pointed out, the nature of the attraction is neither understood nor yet shown to be of universal importance. The larvae of *Spirorbis spirorbis* (L.) settle more readily on filmed surfaces than clean ones (Knight-Jones, 1951), and the attractiveness of the film varies according to the microorganisms which constitute it (Meadows and Williams, 1963). Conversely, some bryozoan larvae seem to be indifferent to surface films, or even to avoid them (Crisp and Ryland, 1960). This subject is of some interest in considering epiphytic species, because in certain cases it is clear that the attraction exerted by the algal substratum may be enhanced or depressed by other factors.

Whatever the nature of the initial factors determining the suitability of a surface for settlement, in most epiphytic species which have been studied the algal substratum has been shown to exert the most important influence. Knight-Jones (1951) showed that larvae of *Spirorbis spirorbis* displayed a predilection for *Fucus serratus*, but the larval responses were influenced also by other factors so that the importance of the algal substratum was not always clearly evident. In particular, a strong gregarious response was noted, although this tended to decrease with time (Knight-Jones, 1953). Subsequently, it was shown that the larvae would select *F. serratus* when offered a choice of algal substrata (Gross and Knight-Jones, 1957; De Silva, 1962), and Williams (1964) showed that the attraction lay in some inherent quality of the substratum; seawater extracts of *F. serratus*, when used to condition filmed settlement surfaces, resulted in greatly enhanced settlement of larvae. Similarly, Ryland (1959) demonstrated that larvae of a number of bryozoan species, when offered a range of algal substrata, settled in significantly higher numbers on the algal species upon which they occurred on the shore. Crisp and Williams (1960) found that extracts of fucoids would induce heavy settlement of bryozoan larvae when applied to inorganic surfaces. Nishihira (1967) investigated the association between the hydroid *Sertularella miurensis* Stechow and its algal substratum *Sargassum tortile* C. Ag. Field sampling of 19 species of algae demonstrated the association well; the hydroid occurred at consistently high numbers on *S. tortile*, although two other species of *Sargassum* bore significant numbers of the epiphyte in areas where the usual substratum was scarce or absent.

Table III. Settlement of *Sertularella miurensis* on five species of algae during a two week period. From Nishihira (1967).

Alga	Weight (g)	No. colonies	Colonies/100 g weed
Sargassum tortile	15.8	532	3367.0
S. hemiphyllum	6.7	102	1522.3
S. thunbergii	3.1	2	64.5
Rhodomela larix	27.0	1	3.7
Dictyopteris divaricata	5.2	0	0

Nishihira considered that physical factors resulting from the zoned distribution of the different algal species might be important in determining the distribution of the epiphyte, and so contrived an ingenious field experiment. Five plants each of five species of algae, including *S. tortile*, were wired to a grid and transplanted in a bed of *S. tortile* during the breeding season of the epiphyte. There were four replicates, each submerged for two weeks, and the results demonstrated conclusively the attraction of *S. tortile* over the other four species (Table III). Subsequently (Nishihira, 1968a), larvae of another hydroid, *Coryne uchidai* Stechow, were subjected to experiments similar to those performed by Ryland (1959). *C. uchidai*, which occurs most abundantly on *S. tortile*, *S. confusum* C. Ag., and *S. hemiphyllum* C. Ag., settled preferentially on the three *Sargassum* species when offered a choice of 15 algae. In later experiments (Nishihira, 1968b) it was shown that extracts of the different *Sargassum* species when added to dishes of larvae of *C. uchidai* promoted immediate settlement, whereas an extract of *Ulva pertusa* Kjellm. had no effect. When offered agar blocks previously soaked in *Sargassum* extract, the larvae again settled on these in preference to untreated controls; blocks treated with *U. pertusa* extract were not preferred to the control blocks.

The ability of larvae to select a particular algal substratum is not confined to sessile epiphytes. Barnes and Gonor (1973) studied larval settlement in the chiton *Tonicella lineata* (Wood) which, on the Oregon coast, occurs intertidally on the encrusting coralline algae which constitute its preferred food. The larvae of *T. lineata*, presented with a range of algal and inorganic substrata, settled preferentially on algae of the genera *Lithophyllum* and *Lithothamnion*. Seawater extracts of *Lithothamnion* successfully promoted settlement on inert surfaces, in preference to untreated controls; most importantly, it was found that metamorphosis of the larva would only proceed if it came into contact with the preferred substratum, or with a treated surface. A further example is that of Kiseleva (1967), quoted by Scheltema (1974), who demonstrated that the veligers of two species of small prosobranch gastropod settled preferentially on the algal species which constituted their main food sources.

Increasingly, then, experimental work is demonstrating that the observed distribution of epiphytic species results from the influence on larval settlement exerted by the algal substratum. However, in some cases the distribution of the alga and its epiphyte do not exactly coincide, and the epiphyte may occur on several species of algae, a fact which perhaps militated against an early recognition of the specificity of many associations. Gross and Knight-Jones (1957) found that larvae of the apparently eurytopic *Spirorbis spirorbis*, from populations in the Menai Straits, settled readily on a number of algal species but especially on *Fucus serratus* and *F. vesiculosus* L., on both of which it occurred naturally in the Menai Straits. Subsequently, larval settlement patterns of *S. spirorbis* for two localities on the South Wales coast were compared with those of the Menai Straits populations (Knight-Jones *et al.,* 1971). At Swansea, *S. spirorbis* occurs naturally on *F. serratus* and larvae from that population consistently selected *F. serratus* in preference to *F. vesiculosus*. At Abereiddy, where *F. serratus* is scarce or absent, the tubeworm occurs on *F. vesiculosus* and larvae of that population chose the latter alga on which to settle. Finally, larvae from adult *S. spirorbis* on *F. serratus* and on *F. vesiculosus*, from the Menai Straits, were independently offered a choice and again each group failed to discriminate between the two algae, suggesting that the influence of the parental substratum is less important than the inherent larval behaviour patterns of each population. The results of the three experiments are summarized in Fig. 1. Further evidence of this phenomenon, for other species of tubeworms, was discussed by E. W. Knight-Jones *et al.* (1975).

Doyle (1975) presented a theoretical model to describe habitat selection by marine larvae in situations where the relative proportions of different suitable substrata vary. The predictions of the model were tested by a field study of the occurrence of *Spirorbis spirorbis* on *Ascophyllum nodosum* and on three species of *Fucus* at five

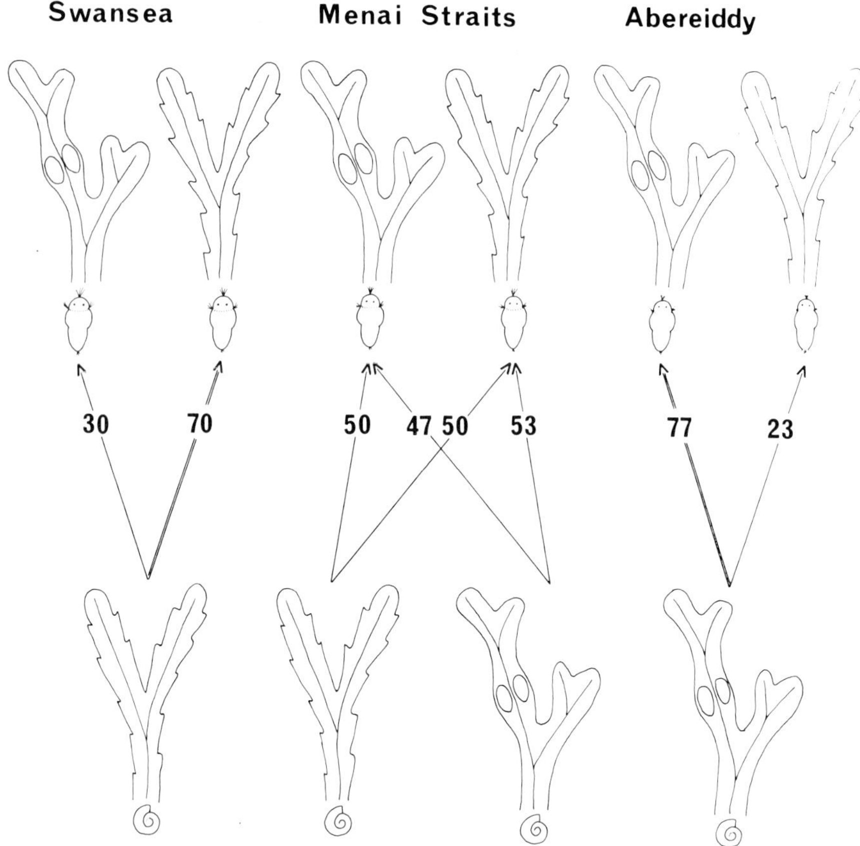

Fig. 1. Larval settlement of *Spirorbis spirorbis* from three different populations: percentage of larvae from each sample settling on *Fucus serratus* and *F. vesiculosus*. (Data from Knight-Jones *et al.*, 1971).

localities along the Nova Scotia coast. The proportion of *Ascophyllum* at a particular tidal level, compared to the *Fucus* spp., declined with increasing exposure from 100% to 45%. The distribution of *Spirorbis* also changed with increasing exposure, from 100% on *Ascophyllum* to a mere 6%; however, at a particular point, predicted by the model, where the abundance of *Ascophyllum* dropped from 59% to 45%, the occurrence of *Spirorbis* on *Ascophyllum* dropped sharply from 43% to 13%. It was suggested that this point marked a change of phenotype and, as final confirmation, larvae from

Ascophyllum-dominant areas selected that alga for settlement at twice the rate of larvae from a population on the other side of the critical point.

This aspect of epiphyte biology deserves further investigation and will doubtless assist materially in explaining how epiphytic species cope with often disjunct, or variably zoned populations of algae, and in distinguishing between truly epiphytic species and those which are simply eurytopic. The advent of *Sargassum muticum* (Yendo) Fensholt in British waters perhaps provides an interesting natural experiment. Withers *et al.* (1975) studied the epibiota of *S. muticum* at four localities on the south coast and recorded 141 species of epiphytic plants and animals; with the exception of two immigrant species of tubeworm (P. Knight-Jones *et al.*, 1975), all appeared to be eurytopic native species. In view of the possibility that this alga may competitively displace certain British fucoids, it was considered reassuring that the Japanese weed proved able to support a large epiphytic community and was thus unlikely to effect a significant change in the faunal balance. It is intriguing to speculate whether native British species will ultimately adapt to this new substratum to the extent of developing the phenotypic variation in larval behaviour patterns observed in some spirorbids.

The nature of the influence exerted by algal substrata on settling larvae is still little understood. That it has a chemical basis is quite evident, but the actual mechanism is not known. In a number of papers, Crisp (1965) and Crisp and Meadows (1962, 1963) have successively demonstrated that barnacle cyprids settle in response to a chemical attraction exerted by individuals of their own species. The attractant substance was found to be a cuticular protein present in the integument of adult barnacles; settlement of the cyprids was dependent on their recognizing the molecular configuration of the protein when adsorbed to a surface, rather than on responding to a gradient of concentration in the water above the settlement surface. Williams (1964), working with *Spirorbis spirorbis* larvae, also demonstrated that the chemical attractant was to be located in the surface of the alga (*Fucus serratus*) and that, again, a gradient of concentration in solution had no effect on settlement. Conversely, Nishihira (1968b) reported that the addition of algal extracts to a dish containing *Coryne uchidai* larvae resulted in immediate settlement.

For many sessile species, the position the animal occupies on a particular alga may be of critical importance to its eventual survival. Settlement on areas of a plant liable to imminent defoliation, for example, would lead to a high post-settlement mortality. Similarly, the observed rugophilic response common to the larvae of many marine invertebrates might result in a concentration of settlement in necrotic pits in the surface of the frond, and invididuals would tend to be lost as the fabric of the plant breaks. That the larvae of some species of epiphyte appear to settle on particular regions of the frond is consequently of interest. Ryland (1959) noted that larvae of *Alcyonidium polyoum* (Hassall) settled preferentially on particular areas of the frond of *Fucus serratus*; when offered pieces of frond cut from four different levels of the plant, they settled preferentially on those taken from immediately below the apices of vegetatively growing branches. The branch tips themselves, and the basal areas of the plant, received significantly less settlement. Stebbing (1972) studied settlement of the bryozoan *Scrupocellaria reptans* (L.) and two species of Spirorbidae on the fronds of *Laminaria digitata* (Huds.) Lamour. In a series of experiments settling larvae were offered a number of discs, each 7.5 cm in diameter, cut from a blade of *L. digitata* at successively greater distances from the intercalary meristem. The results (Fig. 2) suggested that the larvae responded to an age-dependent gradient of attraction in the surface of the alga; in all three species settlement was highest on the discs cut from the youngest part of the plant, close to the meristem, and declined markedly towards the distal end of the frond. An analysis of the distribution of settled larvae of two species of the epiphytic bryozoan *Alcyonidium* on *Fucus serratus* showed a similar result (Hayward and Harvey, 1974a). Nine fronds of *Fucus serratus* bearing laboratory-settled larvae of *A. polyoum*, seven with naturally settled *A. hirsutum* (Fleming) and one with laboratory-settled *A. hirsutum* were analysed. Each frond was divided into a number of areas, defined by dichotomies of the thallus, and the density of larvae in each area could be compared statistically with that on the rest of the plant. A classification test allowed the areas to be divided into groups, within each of which settlement density could be considered comparable. The results are shown diagrammatically in Fig. 3. Three levels of settlement density were recognized; generally, it was highest on the middle regions of the frond, declined towards

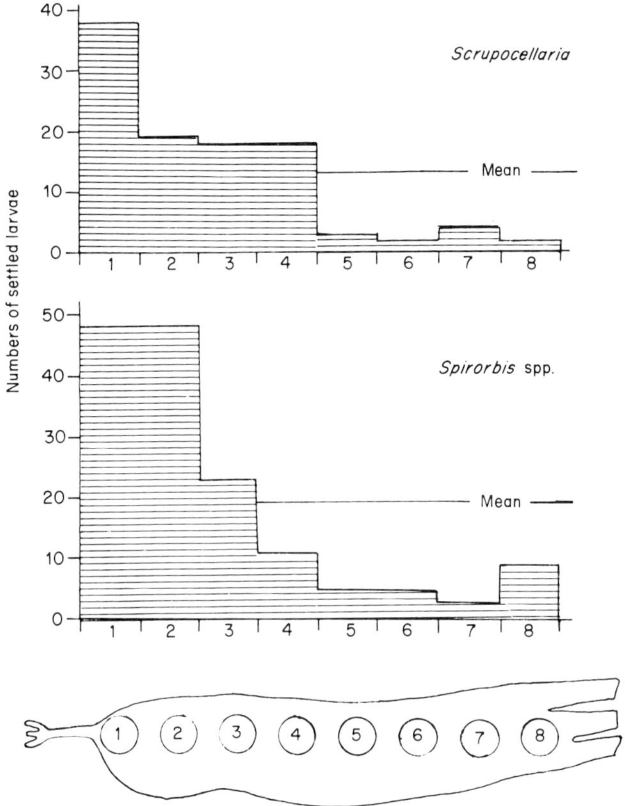

Fig. 2. Settlement of *Scrupocellaria* and *Spirorbis* spp. larvae on discs cut from fronds of *Laminaria digitata*. The histogram columns correspond to the numbered circles in the frond. (From Stebbing, 1972.)

the tips, and was lowest on the basal areas. Some departure from this pattern might be explained by differences in the age gradient along each plant; in Fig. 3, for example, number 11 might be comparable to the upper half of number 2. Plants with extensive growing tips or well-developed receptacles may show more marked differences in density between those areas and the rest of the plant than are found in plants in which both growth and reproduction are at a lower ebb. In both of the above examples, the adaptive strategy of the epiphyte appears to be the same and results in a concentration of the population

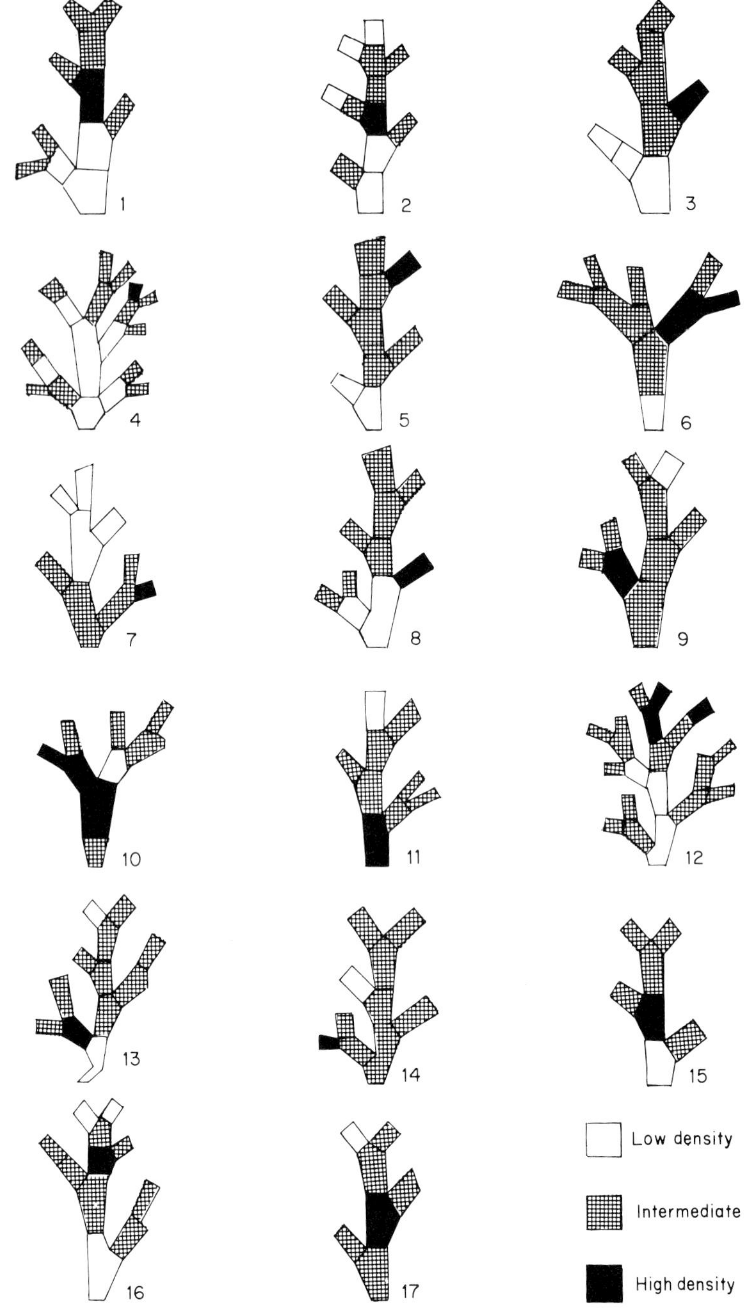
1
2
3
4
5
6
7
8
9
10
11
12
13
14
15
16
17
Low density
Intermediate
High density

on that part of the alga which has the greatest expectation of survival. In *Fucus serratus* the thallus loses foliage basally, and also apically by shedding branches with reproducing tips. In *Laminaria*, the frond disintegrates apically and is renewed annually by growth from the intercalary meristem.

ADAPTATIONS TO AN EPIPHYTIC EXISTENCE

The ability of the larva to select the appropriate substratum and to increase its chances of survival by settling on those parts of the alga most favourable to it are without doubt important adaptations for an epiphyte. Similarly, the ability to adjust patterns of growth and reproduction according to the constraints imposed by the substratum would seem to be a valuable adaptation.

Membranipora membranacea (L.) is perhaps the most specialized bryozoan epiphyte in the North Atlantic region. The colony of *M. membranacea* is lightly calcified and the lateral walls of each zooid incorporate, on each side, a vertical crack which allows a colony a degree of flexibility. The larva of *Membranipora* is a long-lived planktotroph, referred to as a cyphonautes, and must be assumed to have highly developed behavioural patterns to enable it to select its usual substratum after several weeks in coastal waters; it is notable that *M. membranacea* rarely occurs on substrata other than species of *Laminaria*. Ryland and Stebbing (1971) studied the orientation and growth of *M. membranacea* on *L. hyperborea* (Gunn.) Fosl. from the Gower coast and in two isolated populations where it occurred atypically on *Fucus serratus*. On the laminarian frond the cyphonautes did not appear to orientate itself at settlement, but at an early stage of growth the young colonies grew strongly towards the basal part of the frond. The stimulus was not clear, but directional growth could have resulted from a rheopositive response, the colony growing into the current streaming along the frond, or from a response to an age gradient in the surface of the frond. The advantage to the bryozoan was two-fold: colonies tended to grow on to new

---

Fig. 3. Density of settlement of *Alcyonidium* larvae on *Fucus serratus*. Three levels of density indicated by maximum limits of non-significance (5%) revealed by a classification test. (From Hayward and Harvey, 1974a.)

areas of frond, where competition for space would be less intense, and where they would enhance their chances of survival as the distal parts of the frond disintegrated. Growth of *Electra pilosa* (L.) on *F. serratus* was also orientated towards the youngest part of the frond, i.e. the apical regions, but resulted from the orientation of the larvae at settlement. Curiously, the primary zooids of *M. membranacea* on *F. serratus* tended to be orientated towards the basal regions of the plant, but the colonies remained circular and showed no directional growth.

The most unusual adaptation of *Membranipora membranacea* is suggested by the work of De Burgh and Fankboner (1979) on a population of the bryozoan on the bull kelp (*Nereocystis luetkeana* (Mert.) Post. et Rupr.) in Juan de Fuca Strait, Washington. Living kelp plants were provided with a labelled ^{14}C source for photosynthesis and exudates containing dissolved organic ^{14}C were collected. After treatment to remove particulate organic carbon and dissolved inorganic carbon, sea water containing the exudates was added to dishes containing live, feeding colonies of *Membranipora*. Dead control colonies were used to measure the uptake of ^{14}C by adsorption onto skeletal structures and tissues. The uptake of dissolved ^{14}C by the feeding colonies was measured by sampling at hourly intervals and the results, corrected by reference to the controls, suggested that the kelp exudate may constitute a significant source of food for the bryozoan. Clearly, this piece of research has considerable implications for the further study of algal epifaunas and it would be of the greatest interest to discover whether this relationship between the alga and its epiphyte pertains in other populations of *M. membranacea*, and among other sessile epiphytes.

Biological interactions between the alga and its epiphytic burden are little understood, although some algal characteristics have been studied from this point of view. Sieburth and Conover (1965) showed that tannins produced by the gulfweeds *Sargassum natans* (L.) Meyen and *S. fluitans* Børg. possessed a marked antibacterial activity and were also toxic to a number of invertebrate animals. The tannins appeared to be concentrated in the apical regions of the thallus and varied seasonally in activity; as a consequence epiphytes on actively growing plants were restricted to the older parts of the thallus. In a later account (Conover and Sieburth, 1966), it was shown that exudates of two intertidal brown algae, *Ralfsia verrucosa* (Aresch.) J. Ag. and

Fucus vesiculosus also contained tannins which suppressed growth of *Mytilus edulis* L. and *Balanus balanoides* (L.) in tide pools, and were toxic to a number of planktonic organisms. Hornsey and Hide (1976) studied the distribution of antimicrobial activity along the thallus of six British species of algae, including *Laminaria saccharina* and *L. digitata*, and measured the degree of inhibition of *Staphylococcus* cultures by pieces cut from different regions of the frond. For three species, maximum activity was exhibited by the growing tips of the thallus, and for one species it was uniformly distributed over the whole thallus; the *Laminaria* species showed a gradient of increasing activity from the meristem to the tip, although in *L. digitata* this pattern was complicated by an area of minimum activity immediately distal to the meristem. Al-Ogily and Knight-Jones (1977) considered variations in antimicrobial activity in two algal species in relation to the distribution of characteristic epiphytes. *Spirorbis inornatus* L'Hardy and Quiévreux, when settled on *L. digitata* holdfasts, seemed always to be restricted to the inner surfaces of its branches, and on *Himanthalia elongata* (L.) S. F. Gray it occurred only on the undersurface of the basal button. Experiments showed that prospecting larvae consistently settled these areas in preference to the reverse surfaces. By testing pieces of algal tissue against cultures of *Staphylococcus* it was found that antimicrobial activity was significantly higher on the avoided surfaces than on those settled by the larvae.

In these examples, the advantage to the alga does not seem to be equally clear. In *Sargassum*, *Fucus* and *Ralfsia* it is assumed that the effect of high apical concentrations of tannins is to prevent the fouling of delicate growing tips by settling larvae and perhaps to suppress growth of epiphytes on regions of the thallus adjacent to the tips. In *Laminaria*, there is no evidence that settlement or growth is actually inhibited in apical regions; indeed, the older parts of a frond may be thickly covered with epiphytes, but larvae certainly choose to settle in areas of minimum antibacterial activity. However, it seems paradoxical that these areas should correspond with the most vulnerable part of the algae, namely the meristem.

Al-Ogily and Knight-Jones (1977) concluded that *S. inornatus* benefitted from settlement in protected areas within the laminarian holdfast and beneath the *Himanthalia* button. Sieburth and Conover (1965) stated that hydroids were actually damaged by *Sargassum* tannin, and reported mortality of plankters exposed to *Ralfsia* exudates, but there is as yet no other evidence of direct effects of antifouling or antibacterial exudates on epiphytes. The possibility must be considered that the effects are primarily indirect and, for example, that it is the effect of antimicrobial exudates on the nature of the surface film which renders a particular part of an alga unattractive to the prospecting larvae.

A final aspect of algal epifaunas remains to be considered, that of ecological relationships. Dayton (1971) poses the question lucidly in relation to rocky shore epifaunas:

> The concept of community organization suggests more than a description of the assemblage of populations . . . the most convincing demonstration of community structure would be proof that the growth and regulation of the component populations are affected in a predictable manner by natural physical disturbances and by changes in abundances of other species in the community.

Investigations are well advanced in the field of rocky shore ecology and in as much as the communities studied are largely composed of sessile, or non-sessile sedentary, species the problems are very similar to those posed by the study of algal epifanuas. Very little attention has yet been directed towards this topic, although a few accounts may be mentioned briefly. Nishihira (1968c) collected data on seasonal recruitment and growth rates of the hydroid *Sertularella miurensis* Stechow on *Sargassum tortile*, correlated with data on the growth rate of the alga. Hayward and Harvey (1974b) examined growth and mortality of *Alcyonidium hirsutum* on *Fucus serratus* and discussed factors influencing the rates of each. Competitive interactions between a number of epiphytic hydroids on four *Sargassum* species were studied by Nishihira (1971), who showed that the distribution of each epiphyte may be modified by such interaction. Stebbing (1973) also considered the problem in a study on spatial competition between seven sessile epiphytes of *Fucus serratus*. Data on the degree of overgrowth of each species by its competitors showed no clear evidence of a hierarchy of dominance, although one colonial species, *Electra pilosa*, and one non-colonial species, *Spirorbis spirorbis*, were both consistently outcompeted by the other species. It was concluded that much of the pressure for space was relieved by larval behaviour patterns tending to result in settlement on least crowded areas. The *F. serratus* community was the subject of a more comprehensive study by Boaden *et al.* (1975). Of 91 plants and animals recorded from a population of the alga in Strangford Lough, the occurrence and distribution of the 11 most common sessile species were analysed in greater detail. Analysis of competitive interactions produced results which in some cases were related to the zoned distribution of the different epiphytes on the plant (e.g. two sponge species and a colonial tunicate always occurred on the basal areas of the plant) but in some cases may have been attributed to positive interaction; *Alcyonidium* seemed to overgrow all other species, and *S. spirorbis* was again outcompeted in all instances.

The final component in the study of algal epifaunas as ecological communities is that provided by predators. This would include numerous unspecialized predators feeding on the alga or on its epiphytes; an indication of the range of species and their numbers is found in Hagerman's (1966) account of the *F. serratus* community in the Øresund. However, the most important predators are those which are specialized for one particular food source. Thompson (1958) showed that the sea slug *Adalaria proxima* (Alder and Hancock) will choose to feed on *Electra pilosa* in preference to other bryozoans, and that its larvae will only metamorphose successfully after coming into contact with a live colony of *E. pilosa.* In a later paper (Thompson, 1964), the preferred diets of more than 60 British nudibranchs are given. The foods include many epiphytic species and it is probable that in some cases the slugs are as dependent upon their particular food organism as *Adalaria* is upon *E. pilosa.* Seed (1976) studied the distribution of *Membranipora membranacea* and its predator, the nudibranch *Doridella steinbergae* (Lance), on *Laminaria saccharina* fronds in Friday Harbor, Washington. Distribution of the slug paralleled that of the bryozoan, and densities were highest towards the distal areas of the frond where the bryozoan colonies had the lowest proportion of dead zooids. Estimates of the growth rate of the bryozoan and of the consumption of zooids by the slugs provided preliminary data on the dynamic relationships of predator and prey. Further research of this kind will constitute the most useful contribution to our understanding of the ecological structure of algal epifaunas.

REFERENCES

Al-Ogily, S. M. and Knight-Jones, E. W. (1977). Anti-fouling role of antibiotics produced by marine algae and bryozoans, *Nature, Lond.* **265**, 728–729.

Barnes, J. R. and Gonor, J. J. (1973). The larval settling response of the lined chiton *Tonicella lineata. Mar. Biol., Berl.* **20**, 259–264.

Boaden, P. J. S., O'Connor, R. J. and Seed, R. (1975). The composition and zonation of a *Fucus serratus* community in Strangford Lough, Co. Down. *J. exp. mar. Biol. Ecol.* **17**, 111–136.

Colman, J. (1940). On the faunas inhabiting intertidal seaweeds. *J. mar. biol. Ass. U.K.* **24**, 129–183.

Conover, J. T. and Sieburth, J. McN. (1966). Effect of tannins excreted from Phaeophyta on planktonic animal survival in tide pools. *Proc. int. Seaweed Symp.* **5**, 99–100.

Crisp, D. J. (1965). Surface chemistry, a factor in the settlement of marine invertebrate larvae. *Proc. Fifth Mar. Biol. Symp., Botanica gothoburgensia* **3**, 51–65.

Crisp, D. J. and Meadows, P. S. (1962). The chemical basis of gregariousness in cirripedes. *Proc. R. Soc.* B **156**, 500–520.

Crisp, D. J. and Meadows, P. S. (1963). Adsorbed layers: the stimulus to settlement in barnacles. *Proc. R. Soc.* B **158**, 364–387.

Crisp, D. J. and Ryland, J. S. (1960). Influence of filming and of surface texture on the settlement of marine organisms. *Nature, Lond.* **185**, 119.

Crisp, D. J. and Williams, G. B. (1960). Effect of extracts from fucoids in promoting settlement of epiphytic polyzoa. *Nature, Lond.* **188**, 1206–1207.

Dayton, P. K. (1971). Competition, disturbance, and community organization: the provision and subsequent utilization of space in a rocky intertidal community, *Ecol. Monogr.* **41**, 351–389.

De Burgh, M. E. and Fankboner, P. V. (1979). A nutritional association between the bull kelp *Nereocystis lutkeana* and its epizoic bryozoan *Membranipora membranacea. Oikos* **31**, 69–72.

De Silva, P. H. D. H. (1962). Experiments on the choice of substrata by *Spirorbis* larvae. *J. exp. Biol.* **39**, 483–490.

Doyle, R. W. (1975). Settlement of planktonic larvae: a theory of habitat selection in varying environments. *Am. Nat.* **109**, 113–126.

Gross, J. and Knight-Jones, E. W. (1957). The settlement of *Spirorbis borealis* on algae. *Challenger Soc. Ann. Rep.* No. 3, ix, p. 18.

Hagerman, L. (1966). The macro- and microfauna associated with *Fucus serratus* L., with some ecological remarks. *Ophelia* **3**, 1–43.

Hayward, P. J. and Harvey, P. H. (1974a). The distribution of settled larvae of the bryozoans *Alcyonidium hirsutum* (Fleming) and *Alcyonidium polyoum* (Hassall) on *Fucus serratus* L. *J. mar. biol. Ass. U.K.* **54**, 665–676.

Hayward, P. J. and Harvey, P. H. (1974b). Growth and mortality of the bryozoan *Alcyonidium hirsutum* (Fleming) on *Fucus serratus* L. *J. mar. biol. Ass. U.K.* **54**, 677–684.

Hornsey, I. S. and Hide, D. (1976). The production of antimicrobial compounds by British marine algae. III. Distribution of antimicrobial activity within the algal thallus. *Br. phycol. J.* **11**, 175–181.

Jones, D. J. (1973). Variation in the trophic structure and species composition of some invertebrate communities in polluted kelp forests in the North Sea. *Mar. Biol., Berl.* **20**, 351–365.

Kiseleva, G. A. (1967). The effect of the substrate on settling and metamorphosis of larvae of benthic animals. *In* "Bottom Biocenoses and Biology of Benthic Organisms of the Black Sea" (V. A. Vodyanitakii, ed.), pp. 71–84. Akademiy Nauk Ukrainskoi SSSR, Kiev.

Knight-Jones, E. W. (1951). Gregariousness and some other aspects of the setting behaviour of *Spirorbis. J. mar. biol. Ass. U.K.* **30**, 201–222.

Knight-Jones, E. W. (1953). Decreased discrimination during setting [sic!] after prolonged planktonic life in larvae of *Spirorbis borealis* (Serpulidae). *J. mar. biol. Ass. U.K.* **32**, 337–345.

Knight-Jones, E. W., Bailey, J. H. and Isaac, M. J. (1971). Choice of algae by larvae of *Spirorbis*, particularly of *Spirorbis spirorbis. In* "Fourth European Marine Biology Symposium" (D. J. Crisp, ed.), pp. 89–104. Cambridge University Press, Cambridge.

Knight-Jones, E. W., Knight-Jones, P. and Al-Ogily, S. M. (1975). Ecological isolation in the Spirorbidae. *In* "Proc. 9th European Marine Biology Symposium" (Harold Barnes, ed.), pp. 539–561. Aberdeen University Press, Aberdeen.

Knight-Jones, P., Knight-Jones, E. W., Thorp, C. W. and Gray, P. W. G. (1975). Immigrant spirorbids (Polychaeta Sedentaria) on the Japanese *Sargassum* at Portsmouth, England. *Zoologica Scr.* **4**, 145–149.

Linnaeus, C. (1767). "Systema Naturae" (12th edn), Vol. 1, pp. 1–1327. Holmiae, Laurentii Salvii.

Meadows, P. S. and Campbell, J. I. (1972). Habitat selection by aquatic invertebrates. *Adv. mar. Biol.* **10**, 271–382.

Meadows, P. S. and Williams, G. B. (1963). Settlement of *Spirorbis borealis* (Daudin) larvae on surfaces bearing films of micro-organisms. *Nature, Lond.* **198**, 610–611.

Miller, M. C. (1961). Distribution and food of the nudibranchiate Mollusca of the south of the Isle of Man. *J. Anim. Ecol.* **30**, 95–116.

Moore, P. G. (1978). Turbidity and kelp holdfast Amphipoda. I. Wales and S.W. England. *J. exp. mar. Biol. Ecol.* **32**, 53–96.

Nishihira, M. (1966). Ecological distribution of epiphytic Hydrozoa on the Tsuchiya coast near the marine biological station of Asamushi. *Bull. biol. Stn Asamushi* **12**, 179–205.

Nishihira, M. (1967). Observations on the selection of algal substrata by hydrozoan larvae, *Sertularella miurensis*, in nature. *Bull. biol. Stn Asamushi* **13**, 35–48.

Nishihira, M. (1968a). Experiments on the algal selection by the larvae of *Coryne uchidai* Stechow (Hydrozoa). *Bull. biol. Stn Asamushi* **13**, 83–89.

Nishihira, M. (1968b). Brief experiments on the effect of algal extracts in promoting the settlement of the larvae of *Coryne uchidai* Stechow (Hydrozoa). *Bull. biol. Stn Asamushi* **13**, 91–101.

Nishihira, M. (1968c). Dynamics of natural populations of epiphytic Hydrozoa with special reference to *Sertularella miurensis* Stechow. *Bull. biol. Stn Asamushi* **13**, 103–124.

Nishihira, M. (1971). Colonization pattern of hydrozoa on several species of *Sargassum*. *Bull. biol. Stn Asamushi* **14**, 99–108.

Norton, T. A. (1971). An ecological study of the fauna inhabiting the sublittoral marine alga *Saccorhiza polyschides* (Lightf.) Batt. *Hydrobiologia* **37**, 215–231.

Rogick, M. D. and Croasdale, H. (1949). Studies on marine Bryozoa III. Woods Hole region Bryozoa associated with algae. *Biol. Bull. mar. biol. Lab., Woods Hole* **120**, 92–109.

Ryland, J. S. (1959). Experiments on the selection of algal substrates by polyzoan larvae. *J. exp. Biol.* **36**, 613–631.

Ryland, J. S. (1962). The association between Polyzoa and algal substrata. *J. Anim. Ecol.* **31**, 331–338.

Ryland, J. S. and Nelson-Smith, A. (1975). Littoral and benthic investigations on the west coast of Ireland. IV. Some shores in counties Clare and Galway. *Proc. R. Ir. Acad.* B **75**, 245–266.

Ryland, J. S. and Stebbing, A. R. D. (1971). Settlement and orientated growth in epiphytic and epizoic bryozoans. *In* "Fourth European Marine Biology Symposium" (D. J. Crisp, ed.), pp. 105–123. Cambridge University Press, Cambridge.

Scheltema, R. S. (1974). Biological interactions determining larval settlement of marine invertebrates. *Thalassia jugosl.* **10**, 263–296.

Seed, R. (1976). Observations on the ecology of *Membranipora* (Bryozoa) and a major predator *Doridella steinbergae* (Nudibranchiata) along the fronds of *Laminaria saccharina* at Friday Harbor, Washington. *J. exp. mar. Biol. Ecol.* **24**, 1–17.

Sieburth, J. McN. and Conover, J. T. (1965). *Sargassum* tannin, an antibiotic which retards fouling. *Nature, Lond.* **208**, 52–53.

Sloane, J. F., Bassindale, R., Davenport, E., Ebling, F. J. and Kitching, J. A. (1961). The ecology of Lough Ine IX. The flora and fauna associated with undergrowth forming algae in the rapids area. *J. Ecol.* **49**, 353–368.

Sloane, J. F., Ebling, F. J., Kitching, J. A. and Lilley, S. J. (1957). The ecology of the Lough Ine rapids with special reference to water currents V. The sedentary fauna of the laminarian algae in the Lough Ine area. *J. Anim. Ecol.* **26**, 197–211.

Stebbing, A. R. D. (1971). Preferential settlement of a bryozoan and serpulid larvae on the younger parts of *Laminaria* fronds. *J. mar. biol. Ass. U.K.* **52**, 765–772.

Stebbing, A. R. D. (1973). Competition for space between the epiphytes of *Fucus serratus* L. *J. mar. biol. Ass. U.K.* **53**, 247–261.

Thompson, T. E. (1958). The natural history, embryology, larval biology and post-larval development of *Adalaria proxima* (Alder and Hancock). *Phil. Trans. R. Soc.*, B **242**, 1–58.

Thompson, T. E. (1964). Grazing and the life cycles of British nudibranchs. *In* "Grazing in Terrestrial and Marine Environments" (D. J. Crisp, ed.), pp. 275–297. Blackwell Scientific Publications, Oxford.

Wieser, W. (1952). Investigations on the microfauna inhabiting seaweeds on rocky coasts. IV. Studies on the vertical distribution of the fauna inhabiting seaweeds below the Plymouth Laboratory. *J. mar. biol. Ass. U.K.* **31**, 145–174.

Williams, G. B. (1964). The effect of extracts of *Fucus serratus* in promoting the settlement of larvae of *Spirorbis borealis* (Polychaeta). *J. mar. biol. Ass. U.K.* **44**, 397–414.

Withers, R. G., Farnham, W. F., Lewey, S., Jephson, N. A., Haythorn, J. M. and Gray, P. W. (1975). The epibionts of *Sargassum muticum* in British waters. *Mar. Biol., Berl.* **31**, 79–86.

12 Marine and Maritime Lichens of Rocky Shores: their Ecology, Physiology and Biological Interactions

A. FLETCHER

Documentation and Retrieval Section, Leicestershire Museums Service, Leicester, England

Abstract: Almost 450 species of lichen inhabit, and can dominate, the mid-littoral and supralittoral rocks of seashores around Britain. This amounts to about one third of the British lichen flora, rendering rocky shores one of the most important habitats for these plants. Despite this fact, we have relatively little published information on the distribution, biological interactions, physiological properties and economic importance of these maritime/marine organisms. This chapter presents a selective review of the more important publications, supplemented by unpublished observations.

British seashores appear throughout to have a generally similar zonal distribution of lichens, but the presence and abundance of particular species depends on combinations of many environmental variables, including rock chemistry, rock texture, rock topography, climate, tide levels, wind and wave action, light intensity, aspect, salinity, nutritional factors, grazing, competition, and activities such as air and seawater pollution and destruction of habitats by man.

The peculiar properties of lichens, particularly their longevity, slow growth rates, marked accumulation of cations, and preference for specialized habitats, affect their potential for interaction with other plants and animals. They may be directly exploited by other organisms for food and nutrients, shelter and protection, or for their ability to modify the water, light and nutrient content of the environment, as suggested from physiological results. On the other hand, lichens influence other organisms in competing for and eroding away the

---

Systematics Association Special Volume No. 17(b), "The Shore Environment, Vol. 2: Ecosystems", edited by J. H. Price, D. E. G. Irvine and W. F. Farnham, 1980, pp. 789–842, Academic Press, London and New York.

substratum, in using animal waste products (ornithocoprophily), in producing antibiotics, and in accumulating potentially toxic minerals.

It is suggested that the taxonomy, distribution, and ecological and physiological methodology are sufficiently well-known to allow the general marine biologist to study seashore lichens as part of wider ecological programmes involving other organisms.

INTRODUCTION

Lichens are found on rocky seashores in practically all parts of the world. They are most abundant in the "marine-type" climates (Critchfield, 1960) predominating in cool temperate regions where onshore winds, misty days, ample precipitation, and absence of temperature extremes are found, for example in north-west Europe, north-west and north-east America, extreme South America, south-east and south-west Australia, New Zealand and Japan. More limited development of seashore lichen communities occurs in warm-temperate climates of the "Mediterranean-type" countries bordering the Mediterranean Sea, California, South Africa, and parts of Chile, as well as in "warm-humid" climate types of North America and the Baltic Sea. Even tropical climates support lichens on rocky seashores, wherever rocks are shaded from the sun, and polar seashores can be dominated by lichens.

Despite the seemingly widespread distribution of lichens on the rocky shores of the world, the few significant publications deal only with those in north Europe. There are even fewer review articles, and only small sections of works by Smith (1921), des Abbayes (1951) and Kappen (1974) refer to seashore lichens. Consequently, this chapter attempts to fill a gap by placing these organisms in an ecological and physiological perspective. It is concerned both with the factors affecting seashore lichens and, in turn, with the effects which they might have on other organisms.

The chapter is organized into two parts. The first summarizes the distribution patterns of rocky shore lichens in Britain, providing a framework for the data introduced later. The second part comprises three subsections describing (1) the environmental factors which appear, from field evidence, to cause the observed distribution patterns; (2) biological factors which both affect and result from, the presence of lichens on the seashore; (3) physiological and experimental evidence which suggests how these lichens might be adapted to their current environments.

It is hoped that this approach will stimulate future workers to examine seashore lichens from an experimental and conceptual point of view, instead of from the traditional taxonomic and distributional standpoint.

LICHENS OF SILICEOUS ROCKY SHORES

The following account is based on a few published reports, particularly those which used quantitative methods in obtaining field results. Other parts of the account, unsupported by reference citations, utilize the author's unpublished observations.

The organization of this section follows the classification scheme for rocky shore lichen distribution developed by Fletcher (1973a,b), which integrates with that of Lewis (1964). This scheme ranges from the littoral zone, which is the most marine-influenced, through the supralittoral with its three subzones, to the terrestrial zone, which has two recognizable subzones. This "zonation" is, it should be noted, a conceptual one, and does not necessarily relate, except in idealized circumstances, to a "vertical" distribution.

1. Littoral Zone

This is perhaps the most widespread zone of seashore lichens in Britain, being present on shores of all rock-types which experience a variety of environmental conditions. It is only markedly absent from east and south England, where the substrata are easily eroded, but may be seen even there on hard, artificial substrata such as sea walls.

On Anglesey (Fletcher, 1973a), the lower part of this zone (the eulittoral) is rarely dominated by lichens, although *Arthopyrenia halodytes** and *Lichina pygmaea* may just straddle it by penetrating from the drier littoral fringe. *Arthopyrenia sublittoralis* may be locally frequent, in small patches a few cm in diameter, on chalk

---

*Nomenclature and authorities for lichens follow Fletcher (1975a, b) and Hawksworth *et al.* (1980); those for algae follow Parke and Dixon (1976).

or limestone shores where it penetrates down to the level of the uppermost *Laminaria* spp.

The littoral fringe is by contrast a zone of extensive lichen cover. It is dominated by *Verrucaria mucosa* and *V. halizoa* in the lower part, above which is *V. striatula*, followed by *V. amphibia* and finally *V. maura* which marks the top of the littoral zone. *Lichina pygmaea* appears amongst *V. mucosa* and the uppermost barnacles on sunny shores, provided that wave action is neither too great nor too small. *V. mucosa* similarly becomes rare on wave-exposed shores. *Lichina confinis* is common amongst uppermost patches of *V. maura* on sunny, sheltered shores. The three British marine *Arthopyrenia* spp. intermingle with marine *Verrucaria* spp., *A. halodytes* being the most frequent, while *A. "elegans"* (as yet undescribed) is rather rare but widespread. In the upper littoral fringe, *A. sublittoralis* is only common on barnacle and limpet shells.

This zonation pattern of littoral lichens appears to be common throughout Britain, for example in all parts of Ireland (Cotton, 1912; Knowles, 1913; Rees, 1935; Sheard, 1968); in east Scotland (Sheard and Ferry, 1967); in south Wales (Ferry and Sheard, 1969). However, variants have been reported; for example, *Hildenbrandia* spp. may replace *Verrucaria* spp. in the lower littoral fringe (Cotton, 1912; Lewis, 1953; Rees, 1935). Further, a belt of Cyanophyceae was seen overgrowing *Verrucaria maura* in Caithness (Lewis, 1954), although possibly this observation may have reflected only a seasonal variation in pattern (see p. 821).

It is difficult to carry comparisons of littoral lichen distribution farther than this because of the taxonomic confusion manifest in the literature. Many workers have obviously confused *Verrucaria striatula* with the rarer *V. halizoa*, while common species such as *V. ditmarsica* and *V. amphibia* have been overlooked. *Lichina pygmaea* has sometimes been confused with the alga *Catenella caespitosa* and has even been reported to be a summer annual. Since it is unlikely, however, that *Hildenbrandia* could be confused with any marine lichen, reports of its replacing lichens under some circumstances probably reflect differing patterns of distribution around the country. This alga certainly becomes abundant in the littoral on sheltered, north-facing shores, especially beneath the cover of macro-algae.

In some accounts (cf. Knowles, 1913) a bare zone has been

reported to be between *V. maura* and the uppermost barnacles, but such reports have probably overlooked patchy, black ridges of *V. striatula* and thin, brown thalli of *Arthopyrenia halodytes* which only become identifiable through a × 10 hand-lens after wetting the rock surface.

Reports of *Lichina pygmaea* occurring in sheltered sea lochs in west Scotland (Lewis and Powell, 1960) refer to an as yet undescribed species of the *L. confinis* group; this species is restricted to such shores, dominated by *Ascophyllum nodosum* in north-west Britain (Fletcher, 1975a).

The littoral in extreme north Scotland includes the circum-arctic *Verrucaria degelii* (Gilbert *et al.*, 1973), but the precise ecology of the latter has yet to be established.

The littoral lichens are generally restricted to the littoral zone; only *Verrucaria maura* can penetrate into the supralittoral or terrestrial zones, taking advantage of crevices which retain sea water. The constituent species of the littoral zone are morphologically similar to each other, being homoiomerous in organization, subgelatinous in texture (cf. Swinscow, 1968), and reproducing by globose ascocarps (apothecia, perithecia or pseudothecia) which open by a pore. As in non-lichenized marine ascomycetes, ascospore liberation results from passive deliquescence of the ascus; however, unlike those of marine fungi, the ascospores lack appendages. It can be concluded that the marine lichens have their closest affinities with the terrestrial, or freshwater-aquatic, lichens. Marine *Verrucaria* spp. are allied to the "Hydro-Verrucaria" of Servit (1953), while marine *Lichina* spp. accord with the non-marine representatives of the genus (cf. Henssen, 1969). However, marine *Arthopyrenia* spp. have a unique thallus construction, more similar to aquatic lichens than to their terrestrial relatives (Swinscow, 1965).

2. Mesic-supralittoral Zone

This is identical with the "Orange Belt" of Knowles (1913). Its most frequent constituents are orange *Caloplaca marina* and the white-to-grey *Lecanora helicopis, L. actophila* and *Catillaria chalybeia. Arthonia phaeobaea, Lecania erysibe* and *Caloplaca thallincola* are also frequent under suitable conditions (Fletcher, 1973b). Although most authors (e.g. Ferry and Sheard, 1969; Knowles, 1913; Sheard, 1968; Sheard and Ferry, 1967) agree on the distinctiveness of this zone, the separation of subzones within it is inconsistent. Often, *Caloplaca marina* is reported to form a lower zone, with *Lecanora actophila* above, but much local intermingling can occur. In addition, although the mesic-supralittoral zone is easy to recognize, its constituents can vary. For example, on shaded shores, *Caloplaca marina* is replaced by a sparser cover of orange *Caloplaca thallincola*, while on those same shores *Arthonia phaeobaea, Lecania erysibe, Catillaria chalybeia* and *Lecanora helicopis* become more frequent. Consequently, the mesic-supralittoral zone is seldom orange on shaded shores, and becomes leaden-grey, with at best occasional patches of orange *Caloplaca* spp. On the other hand, sunny shores are dominated by creamy-white *Lecanora actophila* and bright orange *Caloplaca marina*, with a reduced cover of grey species. It can be concluded that the "Orange Zone" of Knowles really refers to a sunny-shore lichen zone, while reports of its absence or the inclusion of its constituent species within other zones (Sheard, 1968) are really references to the absence of *Caloplaca* spp. on shaded shores.

The mesic-supralittoral zone has a rich crevice flora containing unique species such as *Solenopsora vulturiensis, Caloplaca microthallina*, and *Bacidia scopulicola*, with *Caloplaca citrina, C. verruculifera* and *Lecanora dispersa* on soft rocks. It follows that this is a particularly variable zone, the nature and extent of which deserve further investigation.

About 20 species are known to inhabit the mesic-supralittoral; just half of these are restricted to it and are exclusively maritime in distribution. Species of this zone have characteristically crustose, often rimose- or cracked-areolate thalli, or are placodoid-lobate. They invariably reproduce by discoid apothecia which have open discs. Their thallus construction is heteromerous, with medullary air spaces and a well-developed cortex, upon which most representatives secrete crystalline secondary metabolites. Few species, however, produce these metabolites within the medulla. The affinities of lichens within this zone are with the terrestrial species; their taxonomy and morphology have little in common with species of the littoral zone.

3. Submesic-supralittoral Zone

This zone was designated by Fletcher (1973b), to account for the regular occurrence of *Xanthoria parietina.* Associated with this species was a selection of lichens from the mesic- and xeric-supralittoral zones. While it is often confused with Knowles "Orange Zone", most authors have felt it necessary to allocate a separate zone to *Xanthoria parietina*, as it appears to be recognizable throughout Britian. However, few authors have indicated that this zone is not always present. For example, *Xanthoria parietina* is rare or absent from shaded shores, while the zone itself becomes diffuse or indistinct on sunny shores exposed to wave or wind action. Here, *Xanthoria parietina* is restricted to crevices and shallow fissures. This species is also a distinct ornithocoprophile and dominates the entire supralittoral and terrestrial zones under conditions of heavy bird-manuring, as suggested by data for the Isle of May (Sheard and Ferry, 1967).

The submesic-supralittoral zone is the lowest part of the shore to be occupied by foliose species, which are less firmly attached to the substratum than crustose species. It seems probable, therefore, that this zone develops only with diminished intensity of wave action. Though few lichens are unique to the zone, over half are exclusively maritime in distribution.

4. Xeric-supralittoral Zone

This zone accomodates the "*Ramalina siliquosa*" belt (Knowles, 1913), with parts of the supralittoral and terrestrial zones as described by Ferry and Sheard (1969) and Sheard (1968). Its most constant members on Anglesey were *Ramalina siliquosa, Rhizocarpon constrictum, Parmelia pulla* and *Anaptychia fusca,* while many other species, such as *Lecanora atra, L. fugiens, Lecidea sulphurea, Lecidella subincongrua* and *Ochrolechia parella,* were also present, intergrading with the submesic-supralittoral and terrestrial zones.

The zone predominates on shores that are neither too sheltered from wind action nor too exposed to it. Consequently, where its species are lacking or where the zone apparently intergrades with submesic-supralittoral or terrestrial zones, the possible effects of wind exposure must be examined. Heavy bird-manuring can also oust the xeric-supralittoral species, which then become replaced by *Xanthoria parietina, X. candelaria* and *Caloplaca verruculifera.* Finally, north-facing situations have a considerably reduced xeric-supralittoral flora.

At Howth Head, Knowles (1913) found that pure stands of *Ramalina siliquosa* occurred (these were still visible to the present author in 1975), without any associated undergrowth of crustose or foliose species. Knowles also noted a "White Belt" which was restricted to sheltered, south-facing shores on which *Ramalina siliquosa* was replaced by crustose *Lecanora atra* and *Ochrolechia parella.*

Obvious representatives of the xeric-supralittoral zone segregated into three sub-zones at Dale, Pembrokeshire (Ferry and Sheard, 1969). The lowermost of these three sub-zones included *Xanthoria parietina* and was partially equivalent to the submesic-supralittoral zone described above. The remaining two sub-zones were apparently unique to that survey. By contrast, the three-zone structure to the supralittoral which occurred at Inishowen, Northern Ireland, bore little resemblance to that found at Dale (Sheard, 1968).

It becomes apparent that while the species of the xeric-supralittoral form a distinct zone they cannot consistently be subdivided. The reasons for this may be as follows. It is in the xeric-supralittoral zone that an orderly sequence of regularly overlapping belts of species seen in the littoral, submesic- and mesic-supralittoral zones, is lost. Instead, the vertical zonation becomes obscured by horizontal zonation. Species are then associated as a result of local variations in topography which affect the patterns of seawater spray deposition, of freshwater run-off, and of tendency to drought. This is primarily due to the lessening influence of tide and wave action, and to the increasing influence of wind-borne spray and factors of terrestrial origin.

The xeric-supralittoral zone is perhaps the least consistent in geographical occurrence. It remains, however, perhaps the most interesting because over half of its constituent species are exclusively maritime in distribution and are restricted to this zone on the shore.

Virtually all lichens that occur in the zone are heteromerous in structure, with discoid apothecia. Crustose representatives are either rimose- or cracked-areolate, while foliose species are typically closely-appressed and narrow-lobed; fruticose species tend to be narrow-lobed or terete. Most xeric-supralittoral species have secondary metabolites that encrust the upper cortex and occur within air spaces in the medulla. These specalized morphologies are thought to be adaptations to a drought-prone environment (Fletcher, 1972b, 1976).

5. *Terrestrial-halophilic Zone*

Few workers have seriously discussed the distinction between maritime and terrestrial lichen floras. However, the terrestrial zone has been defined as one containing those lichens which have a predominantly inland distribution (Fletcher, 1973b). Those species which show a degree of seawater tolerance were designated terrestrial-halophilic and they can be found merging with the soil vegetation on shores which are exposed to moderate wind-action. Typical species include *Caloplaca ferruginea, Fuscidea cyathoides, Parmelia glabratula* subsp. *fuliginosa, P. saxatilis, P. sulcata, Ramalina subfarinacea*, and *Rhizocarpon obscuratum.*

It was postulated that species of this zone receive most of their water and nutrients from terrestrial sources in the form of rainfall, dew, or percolation from soil. They are also able to tolerate occasional inundation by sea water. It is noticeable that *Parmelia saxatilis, P. sulcata,* and *Ramalina subfarinacea*, which contain medullary constituents (salazinic or norstictic acids), become reddened after exposure to extended periods of seawater spray, but resume their normal grey or green-yellow colours after a few days' respite.

Physical abrasion by wind action may discourage colonization by large foliose and fruticose species in this zone.

6. *Terrestrial-halophobic Zone*

All lichens of predominantly inland distribution, but occurring on the seashore in places conspicuously sheltered from seawater spray, belong to this zone. It is of course a highly artificial category and merely allows reference to species of more-or-less accidental occurrence. Such species are often restricted to crevices, hollows or the lee-sides of seashore rocks.

Species commonly encountered in the zone are *Parmelia caperata*, *P. omphalodes*, *Huelia macrocarpa*, *Lecanora badia* and *Sphaerophorus globosus*. Sometimes, in very sheltered sea lochs in west Scotland, lichens more typical of woodland may be found within a few feet of the highest tides. Examples include *Lobaria* spp., *Pannaria* spp. and *Sticta* spp.

Terrestrial-halophobic species are of limited interest to the seashore ecologist, but can be useful in indicating regions of the shore where terrestrial factors predominate, probably permanently, over maritime ones.

GEOGRAPHICAL COMPARISONS

Some 450 species of lichens inhabit British seashores and their ecology and geographical distribution have been indicated by Fletcher (1975a,b). Generally, the seashores in western Britain are richer in species than those in the east, even where the latter are of hard rocky substrata. For example, a shore in Wales might have 150 species, while only 40–60 may be expected on a comparable shore in Northumberland. Lichens conspicuously lacking from eastern seashores are foliose – terrestrial species, sun-species, and those which for various other reasons are known to be restricted to western Britain. It appears likely that this pattern is repeated in Ireland. The west-coast floras there are very species-rich, being similar to those of south-west England. However, the eastern shores of Ireland are less rich. For example, Knowles (1913) recorded only 181 lichens from the Howth Head; this number included a high proportion of species from terrestrial substrata never found on the seashore.

It might be expected that shores in eastern Britain would be more acidic, less sunny and drier than comparable sites in the west, because of the reduced influence of a "maritime" climate. The reduction in the seashore lichen flora of eastern England may however, be due to atmospheric pollution which affects all habitats in this area (Hawksworth and Rose, 1970).

Species restricted to southern and western seashores are *Teloschistes flavicans*, *Lecanora fugiens*, *Roccella* spp. and many others (Ranwell, 1966). Many of these species reach their optimum abundance in Mediterranean or subtropical regions where, incidentally, they are not always restricted to seashores.

Some lichens are restricted to northern coasts in Britain; examples are *Candelariella arctica, Lecanora straminea* (Hawksworth, 1966) and *Verrucaria degelii* (Gilbert *et al.*, 1973). These are essentially circumboreal-arctic species which just penetrate British shores in northern Scotland.

Changes in geographical location also appear to affect the ecology of some species, so that seashore zones need not contain all the same species found elsewhere. This is exemplified by *Parmelia caperata, Pertusaria lactea* and *Parmelia perlata*, which are xeric-supralittoral in Devon but terrestrial-halophobic in Wales. *P. caperata*, in addition, is totally absent from seashores in Scotland.

The degree of development of lichen zones also varies with geographical location in Britain. The xeric-supralittoral zone is much better represented in south-western England and Ireland than in western Scotland, where even wind-exposed shores can bear terrestrial-halophobic genera (e.g. *Pannaria, Sticta, Stereocaulon*). It seems probable that the higher rainfall and lower temperatures prevailing in western Scotland may lead to increased leaching and neutralization, which mitigates the influence of salinity and basic ions arising from seawater spray (see p. 810). In fact, sunny seashores in western Scotland closely resemble shaded shores in Wales. Following this observation, it appears that the lack of terrestrial-zone lichens on shores in south-western Britain may be due to an excess of seawater spray which remains un-neutralized owing to lower rainfall and higher temperatures.

Further variations in the ecology of individual species and their geographical distribution are described in literature dealing with non-British shores. *Lichina confinis*, which is a photophile in Britain and the Baltic (Degelius, 1939; Grummann, 1937) is not found in western France, possibly because of excessive light (Crisp and Fischer-Piette, 1959). Davy de Virville (1938) provided similar observations on the distributional variations in species which are photophilic in Britain. The behaviour of *Verrucaria maura* with respect to latitude is particularly interesting. Throughout Britain it is well-developed on both sunny and shaded shores, but from north Africa to France it is reported to be a shade plant (Davy de Virville, 1932, 1938, 1940; Masse, 1967; Fischer-Piette, 1936). Surprisingly, it is also reported to be a shade plant at higher latitudes, in Scandinavia (Almborn, 1955; Du Rietz, 1925a,b, 1932; Klement, 1953; Lewis,

1965). Why *V. maura* should be apparently sun-tolerant only in Britain remains unexplained.

FACTORS AFFECTING THE DISTRIBUTION

The following paragraphs detail the evidence, available from field observations, which suggests the factors affecting seashore lichen distribution and which, in many cases, may account for the zonation. Each factor is separately dealt with as far as possible, but it is accepted that lichen distribution must depend upon combinations of these factors.

1. Rock Type

The influence of rock types on the distribution of seashore lichens is very great and has always been recognized. The influence can be attributed to the twin properties of chemical composition and texture, but these are not always separable.

(a) Rock chemistry. Practically all existing accounts of rocky shore lichens deal with those of siliceous substrata and it seems generally assumed that the chemical nature of the substratum has little effect on distribution. However, it is possible to recognize different floras on granites and mica-schists, relative to quartzites, sandstones and base-rich basaltic rocks.

The lichen floras of the littoral zone are hardly affected by variations in rock chemistry, but in the supralittoral the differences are profound. Many early observations that littoral lichens are especially well-developed on white quartz may be based on the conspicuousness of these species on such substrata.

Supralittoral quartzites, which are practically pure silica and are nutrient deficient, bear depauperate lichen floras, dominated by *Ramalina siliquosa* with few associated species (Knowles, 1913), or by *Fuscidea cyathoides* and *Rhizocarpon constrictum*, without *Ramalina* (Fletcher, 1973b).

Sandstones often bear species characteristic of soft siliceous rocks, but those with a slightly basic matrix can support characteristic species such as *Opegrapha confluens*. Highly base-rich sandstones are dominated by lichens more usually typical of limestones.

Basic dolerites and basalts, often forming dykes, have different lichen species from surrounding siliceous rocks. *Arthonia phaeobaea* is especially abundant in Anglesey on such dykes in the mesic-supralittoral zone, and crustose species such as *Caloplaca* spp., *Lecanora dispersa* and *Lecania erysibe* assume dense cover in the xeric-supralittoral, where the cover of *Ramalina siliquosa* and *Parmelia* spp. becomes reduced. The factors accounting for these variations in supralittoral floras on siliceous rocks are presumably nutritional, but no more exact data are yet available.

Calcareous seashores have seldom been studied in Britain (Hartley and Wheldon, 1927; Knowles, 1913), especially by quantitative methods (Fletcher, 1972b); some reports exist for elsewhere (Du Rietz, 1925a, 1932; Masse, 1967). About 92 species have been recorded on limestone seashores but only three were observed to be restricted to such substrata (Fletcher, 1976).

The littoral, submesic- and mesic-supralittoral zones contain the only exclusively maritime species, but the patterns of distribution are simplified when compared with siliceous shores. *Arthopyrenia halodytes* dominates the littoral fringe, while endolithic thalli of *A. sublittoralis* extend to the *Laminaria* zone on barnacle-free ridges, which are presumably also ungrazed by limpets. Microsporic representatives of marine *Verrucaria* are restricted to crevices and hard ridges, especially of dolomite (Fletcher, 1972b). The littoral zone becomes more easily recognizable on limestones with the appearance of *Verrucaria maura* in the littoral fringe. The *Lichina* vegetation is normally present and is subject to the influences of aspect and wave action, as on siliceous shores. The calcareous supralittoral lichen flora differs greatly from that on siliceous rocks. While mesic-supralittoral lichens such as *Caloplaca marina, C. thallincola, Lecanora helicopis* and *L. actophila* are common, and a submesic-supralittoral zone of *Xanthoria parietina* is often present, the upper parts of the supralittoral merge imperceptibly with the terrestrial zone and are dominated by *Xanthoria parietina, Catillaria lenticularis, Buellia alboatra, Rinodina gennarii, Lecanora dispersa, Caloplaca citrina* and (on Anglesey) *C. heppiana. Ramalina* spp., *Parmelia* spp. and *Anaptychia fusca* are completely absent. The terrestrial zone only becomes identifiable from the association of its lichens with soil or freshwater drainage. Typical representatives include *Squamarina crassa, Solenopsora candicans, Acrocordia conoidea*, *Collema* spp. and *Leptogium* spp. Aspect and wave action do not seem to affect the presence of lichen species as much on calcareous as on siliceous shores, but local variations of a geographical nature probably occur. For example, *Placynthium nigrum* dominates the supralittoral in northern France, but is confined to crevices and is terrestrial-halophobic in Britain.

The underlying reasons accounting for the differing floras of calcareous and siliceous shores were discussed by Fletcher (1976). It was concluded that the presence of abundant seawater ions low on the shore overcomes the ions emanating from the substratum, so that littoral and submesic-supralittoral floras are identical on shores differing in substratum chemistry. On the upper shore, however, insufficient sea water arises from wind-borne spray, so that rock chemistry exerts a greater influence on the lichen flora. It remains curious that calcareous shores have so few exclusively maritime species. This has been interpreted by supposing that most of the supralittoral lichens on calcareous shores are affected principally by seawater salinity, since their nutritional requirements have been satisfied from the calcareous substratum. On siliceous shores, by contrast, the lichens become segregated according to both their salinity and nutritional tolerances, so that a greater range of species with differing ecological preferences can become established.

Calcium has been specifically implicated as the nutritional factor accounting for these floristic differences between different substrata (Fletcher, 1976). The widespread availability of calcium may account for the homogeneous nature of calcareous supralittoral lichen floras, which are relatively insensitive to environmental variables affecting the deposition or concentration of seawater.

(b) Rock texture. This term involves many attribute gradients, from hard to soft, porous to impervious, smooth to rough, or tendency to flake contrasted with tendency to split into blocks. These texture gradients contribute to gradients in moisture retention capacity, nutrient retention capacity (by absorption), nutrient release (by dissolution), and ease by which lichens can gain or maintain purchase. Temperature may be higher on rocks with less water-absorption capacity, and the abundance of shaded microhabitats is increased on rocks developing fissures or overhangs.

Many authors have attributed the variations in calcareous floras to rock texture rather than chemistry. Southward and Orton (1954) thought that the smoothness of limestone rendered it unsuitable for colonization by *Lichina pygmaea*, while Fischer-Piette (1936) felt that its softness was unsuitable for growth of lichens in general. *Lichina pygmaea* may be more tolerant toward erosion of calcareous substrata than other lichens (Crisp and Fischer-Piette, 1959; Fischer-Piette, 1932). Similarly, *Arthopyrenia sublittoralis* is the only littoral lichen on the very soft chalk rocks of Kent; its endolithic habit may allow it to keep pace with erosion of the substratum. This feature may also account for the predominance of *A. halodytes* on soft littoral rocks elsewhere (Fletcher, 1973a).

Soft rocks may bear a specialized lichen flora in places which are sheltered from erosion. Sandstones and schists are often dominated by *Arthopyrenia halodytes, Lichina confinis* and *Verrucaria prominula* in the littoral zone, *Scoliciosporum umbrinum, Catillaria chalybeia* and *Lecanora dispersa* in the mesic-supralittoral, and *Lecania erysibe, Caloplaca ferruginea, C. citrina, C. verruculifera* and *Opegrapha* spp. in the xeric-supralittoral. Foliose and fruticose species with the exception of *Physcia* spp., are rare on soft supralittoral rocks.

Probably turnover of thalli is more rapid on soft rocks, where the high rate of substratum erosion permits only rapidly growing species to survive. Certainly it is common to see crustose thalli such as *Ochrolechia parella* and *Lecanora atra* peeling away in sheets. This exfoliation results in additional rock-destruction because a layer of substratum is normally pulled away by the departing thallus (Fry, 1927).

It is noticeable that many of the species which are dominant on soft rocks are also frequent in nutrient-rich sites (Fletcher, 1975a). This supports the hypothesis that nutrients are more readily available, either from direct dissolution of the substratum or by absorption of nutrient containing water in the porous substratum.

The hardest rocks usually support a depauperate lichen flora with no especially characteristic species. Hard quartzites were mentioned on p. 800. Wheldon and Travis (1913) noted that floras of soft sandstones differ from those of harder igneous rocks. But on the hard, metamorphosed sandstone formed at their junction, the lichen flora resembled that of the igneous rock and not of the parent sandstone. This effect was attributed to texture, but slower dissolution or fewer absorbed nutrients in the metamorphosed sandstone may also account for the difference.

Rough rocks often have a richer flora than smooth ones (Fletcher, 1973b; Knowles, 1913) and *Lichina pygmaea* in particular has been thought to prefer rough rocks (Evans, 1947; Naylor, 1930; Cotton, 1912). Fissures, especially when producing large cracks and overhangs, can support very specialized floras. Fifty taxa characteristic of such habitats were described by James (1970). Some of these species are extreme xerophytes or sciaphiles and a number appear to be adapted to utilize water vapour for metabolism since liquid water remains unabsorbed by the thalli. Although most of these crevice-inhabiting species are best considered terrestrial-halophobic, some are exclusively maritime in Britain. Examples include *Bacidia scopulicola, Caloplaca littorea, Chiodecton* spp., *Lecanactis monstrosa, Lecania rupicola, Lecanora tenera, Opegrapha cesareensis* and *Solenopsora vulturiensis.* Although these species have been included under the zonation terminology described above (cf. Fletcher, 1975a), it remains doubtful whether this terminology is entirely suitable for organisms with such extreme requirements.

2. The Climate of Rocky Shores

Factors affecting the climate of the littoral zone are well known (Lewis, 1964) but those affecting that of the supralittoral have seldom been discussed (Fletcher, 1973b, 1976; Goldsmith, 1967; Waisel, 1972). Some guidance, however, may be obtained from comparison with the climates of freshwater shores (Geiger, 1965). The following account is based largely on the above sources.

The supralittoral is little influenced by tidal action and sea water and salts are received from wave-splash or wind-borne spray. Wave-splash can deposit heavy quantities of sea water only near the lower part of this zone, but wind-borne spray affects the whole shore. This spray is composed of large water droplets, which fall mainly in the lower supralittoral, and smaller droplets, which fall throughout the supralittoral. The mechanism of droplet formation has been discussed by Knellman *et al.* (1954), and by Edwards and Claxton (1964). Small droplets of sea water are carried to great distances inland, especially after evaporation has reduced them to particles of salts (Fujiwara and Umejira, 1962). These wind-dispersed particulates are so widespread that they are thought to contribute appreciably to natural soil fertility (Eriksson, 1959).

Salt-spray is preferentially deposited on twigs and branches on the seacoast (Edwards and Claxton, 1964), and it is probable that outstanding rock pinnacles and ridges also act as focal points for seawater-spray deposition. The maritime lichen floras of inland monuments on wind-exposed plains, such as at Stonehenge (Laundon, 1968) may be due to deposition of salts carried from seashores many miles away (Fletcher, 1973b). It may be generalized that the splash-affected lower supralittoral would receive the largest amounts of sea water, while outstanding ridges receive more spray than flat surfaces.

At the uppermost part of the shore, soil water of low salinity and containing acidic, humic compounds, percolate downwards (Fletcher, 1973b; Goldsmith, 1967; Kärenlampi, 1966). In consequence, there is a nutritional gradient on the seashore, from base-rich and highly saline water in the lower supralittoral to base-deficient water of reduced salinity and increased organic content in the upper supralittoral and terrestrial zones. Associated with this is a pure-water gradient in that the upper and lower parts of the supralittoral are the wettest, while the middle part is the dryest, receiving less water from the reservoirs in the sea and soil. This middle part, the xeric-supralittoral zone, is in consequence the most drought-prone.

Paralleling these aqueous and nutritional gradients is a temperature gradient. This is potentially highest in the drier xeric-supralittoral zone and lowest in the wetter parts of the shore. In the xeric-supralittoral, relative humidity must be lower and evapotranspiration potential must be higher than elsewhere on shore.

So far, this picture of the supralittoral climate is mainly conjectural and few measurements of the gradients have been made. Salt deposition, pH and water availability have been measured only in the soil at the top of the shore and never on bare rock. In addition, the results of Fujiwara and Umejira (1962) and Edwards and Claxton (1964) were obtained from coastal regions extending far inland and not on rocky shores. Data on the behaviour of water in the supralittoral are based on field observations by the author and quantitative measurements of the rates of water deposition, drying-out, and evaporation potential remain to be undertaken. It follows that much fundamental work needs to be carried out in order to correlate environmental variables with the observed lichen distribution.

A word should be added here about the concept of "exposure" as it has been applied to lichens. This concept is widely recognized (Ballantyne, 1961; Lewis, 1964; Stephenson and Stephenson, 1972) but remains abstract and is not capable of direct measurement. Marine biologists distinguish shores of varying degrees of "exposure" from the biotic situations. Thus a shore bearing a particular community of animal and plant species, in particular combinations of abundance, receives an "exposure" rating. The factors contributing to the exposure rating of a shore include wind action, wave action, tidal regime, tidal action, salinity, silt load, temperature, light, rock type, substratum slope, grazing, competition and many others. Most authors, in dealing with "exposure" and littoral communities, stress the influence of wave action. However, when dealing with lichen ecology, especially in the supralittoral, wind action is probably of even greater importance. It should also be added that the "exposure" rating of a shore need not be consistent throughout the biotic zones. For example, the littoral may have an "exposed shore" community, say on steeply sloping rock, but the supralittoral may bear "sheltered shore" lichen communities if the slope is shallow.

In view of the discussion above, it seems best to qualify references to exposure by using the determining factor, as for example in the terms wind-exposed and wave-exposed, when applying the concept to lichens.

3. Tide Levels

Only the littoral lichens are regularly submerged by the tides, but mesic- and submesic-supralittoral thalli on sheltered shores may be inundated by spring-tides on a few days each year. In tideless areas such as the Baltic and Mediterranean Seas, wind action and changes in atmospheric pressure create alternately submersed and emersed conditions which support a littoral lichen community (Colman and Stephenson, 1966; Du Rietz, 1925a, 1932).

In Britain, some littoral lichens may penetrate to below mean sea level, but all can extend above it. Some thalli of *Lichina pygmaea* always remain at least partially intertidal, even on those shores more exposed to wave action on which it still appears. Thus it is the most truly marine lichen in Britain.

A comparison of the maximum periods of time spent submerged each year by marine lichens in Britain showed values ranging from 44% for *Verrucaria striatula* to 1% for *Lichina confinis* (Fletcher, 1973a). It appears that only one marine lichen is capable of being permanently submerged, namely *Verrucaria serpuloides*, which was dredged from depths of 30 m in Antarctic waters (Lamb, 1973).

Fluctuations in tidal ranges render littoral lichens subject to emersion periods of several weeks at a time during periods of neap tides. These are the driest, hottest times of the year in Britain in summer, and are the coldest and most frost-prone during the winter. Freshwater from rain is also more prevalent in the littoral during neap tide periods, especially in the winter. In spring and autumn, however, daily submergence by the higher spring tides may last for up to six hours. Long-term fluctuations in submersion and emersion by both fresh and sea water have not previously been included in discussions of seashore lichen ecology. This factor does suggest, however, that the ranges of tolerance by lichen species could be much wider than has previously been assumed.

4. *Wind and Wave Action*

The general pattern of response by seashore lichens to increasing violence of wind and wave action appear to be (a) the heights of the zones are raised, (b) the numbers of species are reduced, (c) the total cover of lichens is reduced, (d) certain species become dominant whilst others disappear.

(a) The raising of the heights of lichen zones has often been observed (Jones and Demetropoulos, 1968; Fletcher, 1973a,b; Lewis, 1953; Ferry and Sheard, 1969, Sheard, 1968; Sheard and Ferry, 1967). The reasons for this phenomenon are attributable to the carriage further upshore of sea water by wind and wave action. This allows lichens of all zones to make effective growth at higher levels than on a shore of reduced wind and wave action. On shores where such effects are minimal, lichens of all zones may be inundated by the tides on a daily or otherwise regular basis, but on wind-exposed shores, direct inundation is rare and sea water is carried mostly as splash and spray; in the latter case, presumably, the quantities received are equivalent to those deposited by exceptionally high tides on shores sheltered from wind and wave action. The curious feature is that lichens on sheltered shores thrive on sea water received perhaps on only a few days each year, under exceptional spring tides, whilst the same species on spray-affected shores receive sea water more or less continually throughout the year, but in smaller quantities at a time. This suggests a high degree of adaptibility within different thalli of the same species by perhaps many of the seashore lichens.

Not all lichen zones are equally affected by wind and wave action. For example, on sheltered shores, the mesic-supralittoral zone is poorly represented. This may result from the lack of wind-borne spray so that the submersion-tolerant species quickly give way to terrestrial lichens. Where spray is present, however, the terrestrial species are pushed upshore and the intervening gap becomes occupied by xeric-supralittoral lichens. Where exceptionally high spray deposition occurs, the littoral or mesic-supralittoral zones can develop on rocks intermingled with soil and with angiosperm vegetation. At first sight, it appears curious that supralittoral lichens are apparently less tolerant of spray than are angiosperms; however, it seems that the angiosperms encountered differ according to the degree of exposure to sea winds. Shores sheltered from spray deposition, for example, have broad-leaved grasses and *Calluna vulgaris* (L.) Hull on acidic soils; those receiving spray have *Festuca* spp., on soils of higher pH; whilst on shores subject to heavy spray, *Armeria maritima* (Mill.) Willd. is dominant, on soils approximating in pH and salinity to sea water itself (Fletcher, 1973b; Goldsmith, 1967). In view of this, it might be more accurate to regard the terrestrial zone of angiosperms as penetrating downshore under wind-exposed conditions, so that *Armeria maritima* and its soil accretion cover rocks which would otherwise be covered by xeric-supralittoral lichens.

(b) The reduction in numbers of lichen species on wind-exposed shores results mainly from the absence of foliose genera such as *Parmelia* and *Anaptychia.* Xeric-supralittoral and terrestrial lichens are also absent (see above) and total lichen cover is reduced (see below).

Shores sheltered from spray are not necessarily richer in species, although those present attain greater coverage than on spray-affected shores. Sheltered shores have less available rocky substratum because of the downward penetration of terrestrial vegetation, so that the lichen flora consists only of those species which successfully compete with other lichens, algae and angiosperms.

(c) Total coverage of rock by lichens is greatest on shores sheltered from spray and is reduced by increasing exposure. The reasons are not clear, but physical abrasion may in some way be responsible since wind- or wave-exposed shores have a polished or scoured appearance. Drought caused by wind evaporation, especially in the xeric-supralittoral may also restrict lichens to damper crevices.

(d) Presence or absence of some species, especially *Lichina pygmaea*, have been used in assessments of "exposure" (Ballantyne, 1961; Lewis, 1964), but relatively few other lichens directly indicate the degree of wind or wave action. *Verrucaria mucosa* and *Lichina confinis* are absent from shores receiving appreciable wave action, but *Arthopyrenia halodytes* becomes common. Consequently, the black and greenish colour of the littoral zone below *Verrucaria maura* takes on a brown colour on exposed shores (Fletcher, 1973a).

In the mesic-supralittoral zone, the creamy-white thalli of *Lecanora actophila* show a similar pattern, replacing dark grey *L. helicopis* on wind-exposed shores. Few xeric-supralittoral or terrestrial species are characteristic of wind-exposed shores, but some specialized morphotypes can develop, especially on sunny shores (see p. 816).

5. Light and Aspect

Lichens are normally regarded as photophiles, requiring more light than other plants because such a large proportion of the thallus is fungal and non-photosynthetic (Smith, 1962). Nevertheless, many species are able to exist in shaded conditions, and even seem to prefer them. In only one case does it appear that light has been measured and lichen distribution correlated with it in the field. Here, *Arthopyrenia halodytes* in a marine cave replaced the coralline alga *Lithophyllum incrustans* at a light intensity only 3.3% that of daylight (Grubb and Martin, 1937).

Although the overall patterns of the lichen zonation on north- and south-facing shores are similar, they differ in some respects (Fletcher, 1973b). On shaded shores compared with sunny shores, with other variables constant: (a) the heights of lichen zones are reduced; (b) soil salinity is reduced; (c) total coverage of the substratum is increased; (d) species diversity is increased; (e) photophiles are absent while sciaphiles are common.

The supralittoral zones that penetrate farther downshore on shaded shores are also narrower in vertical extent than on sunny shores. An exception is the terrestrial zone, which widens through its replacement of the xeric-supralittoral zone. Shaded shores usually lack *Armeria maritima* in the terrestrial zone, so that even in wind-exposed places grasses and *Calluna vulgaris* predominate. Thus, the xeric-supralittoral zone does not extend on into the angiosperm zone on shaded exposed shores as it commonly does on sunny exposed shores.

The greater areas covered by lichens and the increased lichen species diversity of shaded shores may be related to increased terrestrial influence. This is supported by evidence that the water percolating downwards from north-facing shores is more acidic and less saline than on south-facing shores (Fletcher, 1973b; Goldsmith, 1967). These observations may in turn be accounted for by the higher humidities and slower rates of drying-out on shaded shores because of reduced temperatures. Greater leaching of the soil above shaded shores results in lowered pH, and in dilution and neutralization of sea water. These factors encourage greater development of terrestrial floras at the expense of supralittoral floras. The generally damper conditions prevailing on shaded shores also permit greater colonization of rock by species which are restricted to crevices on dryer shores, especially when the latter are wind-exposed.

Species with photophilic tendencies become rare or absent on north-facing rocks; they include *Lichina* spp. from the littoral zone, *Caloplaca marina, C. littorea, Lecanora actophila* from the mesic-supralittoral zone, *Xanthoria parietina* from the submesic-supralittoral zone, and brown *Parmelia* spp., *Lecanora fugiens, Buellia subdisciformis*, with many others, from the xeric-supralittoral zone. With the disappearance of photophiles, sciaphiles become abundant; examples are *Verrucaria prominula* in the upper littoral zone, *Catillaria chalybeia, Lecania erysibe* and *Caloplaca thallincola* in the mesic- and submesic-supralittoral zones, and *Buellia punctata, Rhizocarpon obscuratum* and *R. hochstetteri* in the xeric-supralittoral zone.

Species which increase in abundance on shaded shores include *Verrucaria mucosa* and green forms of *V. striatula* in the littoral zone, even on wave-exposed shores; *Lecanora helicopis* and *Caloplaca thallincola* in the mesic-supralittoral; *Lecanora atra, Rhizocarpon hochstetteri, Anaptychia fusca* and *Lecanora polytropa* in the xeric-supralittoral; *Parmelia saxatilis, P. sulcata, Ochrolechia parella* and *O. androgyna* in the terrestrial halophilic zones. It is noticeable that shaded shores have a dirtier, greyer appearance than sunny shores, which are dominated by more white and orange species.

It can be concluded that most of the distributional variation encountered on shaded shores is less attributable to light intensity than to changes in temperature which directly affect the water relations. Few reports directly implicate heat and cold as a factor affecting seashore lichens. However, some authors have concluded that dark rocks may have different lichen floras because they warm up faster (Wheldon and Travis, 1913), while Knowles (1913) thought that limestone rocks would be warmer than siliceous rocks which could account for the different floras.

In the tropics the high temperatures attained by supralittoral rock, which can become too hot to touch, must directly influence the restriction of lichens to more shaded conditions.

6. *Salinity*

Several authors have indicated correlation of lichen distribution with seawater salinity. Santesson (1939) noted that littoral species disappeared with decreasing salinity as the Baltic Sea was entered; the most fully marine species disappeared first. Crisp and Fischer-Piette, (1959) and Davy de Virville and Fischer-Piette (1931) reported survival of upper littoral species into estuaries, while Nelson-Smith (1965) and Fischer-Piette (1932) correlated lichen distribution in estuaries with measured values of salinity. Generally, it appears that the more marine lichens inhabiting the lower littoral fringe die out in waters of less than 20‰, while upper littoral fringe species can be found in waters of 4–20‰ salinity.

It should be remembered however that, in estuarine conditions, salinity is not the only varying factor. The relative proportions of seawater and freshwater ions, including pH, vary, so that direct nutritional factors may play a part in determining which species survive. Estuarine conditions, involving less wave and wind action, often with a reduced tidal range, are furthermore subject to more silt-deposition than on rocky shores; this factor can eliminate littoral lichens.

There appear to be no available accounts of the distribution of supralittoral lichens in estuaries; how far the xeric-supralittoral associations are able to penetrate into regions of reduced salinity, and how the terrestrial associations become established there, are entirely unknown.

Finally, while salinity undoubtedly plays a part in governing the distribution of seashore lichens, that part must be carefully defined. Some authorities regard the vertical zonation of lichens on rocky shores as a response to variations in salinity, and suggest that littoral lichens are in a more highly saline environment than those of the supralittoral; this view is naïve, since *salinity* is a concentration concept which refers to the amount of salts dissolved in a given volume of water. We must separate the effects of quantity of water a part of the shore receives, in a given time, from variations in the concentrations of salts carried by this water. Obviously, littoral lichens receive larger amounts of sea water of normal salinity than those of the supralittoral. However, the concentration of sea salts reaching the various parts of the shore varies, from supersaturated or even solid salt particles under evaporating conditions to dilute or even fresh water when rain, dewfall or run-off are present. Without measurements of the frequencies of salinity variations, it is difficult to postulate what are the relative effects of diluted or concentrated sea water on the lichens of different zones. However, it might be expected that the periods of time exposed to salinity extremes will be least in the littoral zone, where tidal inundation and wave-splash will more regularly lessen their effect, and will be greatest in the supralittoral.

7. *Nutritional Factors*

Field correlations suggest that the concentration and availability of nutrients in the environment play an important part in governing lichen distribution. Seashore lichen zonation correlates well with pH in ground water, which in turn varies with the amount of sea water being deposited (see p. 810; also Acock, 1940; Gillham, 1956; Robertson and Gimingham, 1951; Vevers, 1936). The pH of individual thalli has been measured and found to correlate similarly with environmental position (Du Rietz, 1932). Thalli low on the shore had pH values of 7–8, while upper-shore thalli were more acidic. Thalli on calcareous shores had pH values of 7–8 regardless of position on the shore, thus confirming the discussion (p. 802) of the possible effects of calcareous ions on lichen ecology. Caution must be expressed, however, since the pH of lichen thalli must vary according to the amount of CO_2 being produced as a result of photosynthesis and respiration; the rates vary throughout the day.

Frequent reports implicate bird-manuring (ornithocoprophily) as an ecological factor (Fletcher, 1973b, 1976; Du Rietz, 1932; Grønlie, 1948; Hayren, 1914; Massé, 1967) and at least one lichen species, *Aspicilia leprosescens*, is exclusively associated with seashore-bird perches on siliceous rocks (Sheard, 1965). The neutralizing influence of base-rich bird manure on acidic freshwater run-off can also facilitate growth of lichens which are otherwise not directly dependent on bird manure (Kärenlampi, 1966).

The constituents of bird excreta that primarily affect lichens could be nitrogen or hydrogen ions (Massé, 1967); Fletcher (1976) also implicated calcium in pointing out the similarity of lichen floras of calcareous and bird-manured siliceous rocks. It is also possible that phosphate or organic matter could be responsible. The bird-perch lichen flora possibly also consists merely of opportunistic colonizers that occupy situations vacated by less tolerant species.

Lichens are well-known indicators of the presence of certain metallic cations, especially iron, which colours *Rhizocarpon oederi* and *Huelia macrocarpa* rusty-red (James, 1973; Fletcher, 1975a). Lichens on the seashore more often reflect environmental levels of cation concentration, or can selectively accumulate them, often to very high levels (Fletcher, 1976; Spear, 1974). The presence of radionucleides in seashore lichens has been attributed to fall-out from atmospheric testing of nuclear weapons (Larsson, 1970). Such radioactive ions could accumulate in other organisms via foodchains (James, 1973), as could potential toxins such as copper and cadmium which accumulate to appreciable levels in seashore lichens (Spear, 1974). These possibilities have yet to be explored.

8. Man's Activities

Man can provide artificial substrata, in the form of jetties and break-waters, which allow seashore lichens to exist in estuaries or regions lacking natural rocky substrata. Some normally siliceous species can grow on intertidal wooden posts (Alvin, 1961). However, few other effects beneficial to the lichen flora can be attributed to man. Instead, the destruction and disturbance of natural rocky substrata, oil pollution, production of toxins and air pollution are the most frequent ways in which man affects seashore lichens.

(a) Destruction and disturbance of substrata occur through mechanical damage such as the passage of boats or vehicles, trampling, or modifications or physical removal by building work, mining or quarrying. Damage is noticeable by reduction in species diversity or replacement of the "natural" flora by one which is disturbance-tolerant and presumably more rapidly-growing. The littoral zone may become dominated by *Arthopyrenia halodytes* in disturbed areas, while the supralittoral is dominated by *Lecanora dispersa, Candelariella vitellina* and *Rinodina gennarii.*

(b) Many of the species mentioned above are also common in natural but nutrient-rich situations, but the nutrients responsible are unknown. These floras also arise in places subject to airborne dust or silt arising from industrial processes, and chemical constituents probably account for these supposedly "nitrophilous" communities, although there is as yet no experimental evidence implicating nitrogen. Large amounts of chemicals from agricultural sprays or fertilizers when present in freshwater run-off, modify the supralittoral floras. This effect is manifested by unicellular algae covering the thalli. These can be free-living algae or phycobionts which have broken away from the symbiotic state. Large populations of *Candelariella vitellina* on the seashore are especially indicative of nutrient-enrichment, and this species indicates similar conditions in terrestrial habitats (James, 1973).

Chemical pollution in the marine environment has rarely been related to lichen ecology. However, in one instance, high levels of copper, zinc and cadmium, in concentrations proportional to the distance from the pollution source, were found in littoral thalli near to the estuary of a river draining a disused mining area (Spear, 1974).

(c) Marine oil pollution and subsequent decontamination measures were studied by Ranwell (1968), who listed 19 lichens which were destroyed. Lichens can also show symptoms of possibly sublethal levels of oil pollution (Cullinane *et al.*, 1975). The initial effects of oil inundation were brown discoloration, especially of apothecial discs, and oil adhesion, especially to subgelatinous thalli such as *Verrucaria mucosa*. The oil itself is not thought to be toxic to lichens (Crapp, 1971; Smith, 1968) but studies in laboratory and field conditions revealed that the oil-cleansing agents were particularly toxic (Brown, 1972, 1974). Oil dispersants affect attachment of *Xanthoria parietina*, causing the browned-thalli to peel away from the substratum (Cullinane *et al.*, 1975).

(d) Supralittoral lichens appear to be more affected by air pollution than do littoral thalli; the former disappear in areas such as the Clyde Estuary and north-eastern England, while littoral species survive to a greater extent (Fletcher, unpublished). Presumably sea water has a cleansing influence in the littoral, perhaps neutralizing SO_2 to produce a less toxic ion (cf. Ferry *et al.*, 1973).

BIOLOGICAL FACTORS INFLUENCING SEASHORE LICHENS

Within this section, the growth of seashore lichens, their colonization and succession will be reviewed, followed by an assessment of their interactions with other organisms. General reviews of subjects discussed here are given in Brodo (1974); Hale (1974); and Topham (1977).

1. Growth

Few published accounts exist of the growth of seashore lichens, but their growth rates appear to be low, in common with those of lichens from other habitats.

Lichina pygmaea has been the most intensively studied species. Areas of this plant were cleared and rephotographed after an interval of seven years (Boney, 1961). While the total cover remained the same after this period, it resulted from the partial disappearance of some patches and extension of others. It was suggested that, although small patches were stable, the larger patches were not, being subject to sudden advance or retreat. Boney found that increase in *L. pygmaea* patches was assisted by shaded conditions, but desiccation stabilized them. The radial increase of this plant has been measured at 3–6 cm per annum at a single site, but averaged only 0.5 cm at others (Fletcher and Jones, 1975). The total biomass of *Lichina pygmaea* can be as great as 2 kg/m^2 on a fresh-weight basis

(Colman, 1940) but an overall biomass of less than 0.01 tonnes/km of seacoast has been estimated in northern France (Chassé *et al.*, 1967). These biomass estimates are similar in magnitude to those reached for macrolichens of other habitats (Lindsay, 1978). Estimates of biomass attained by crustose lichens range from 0.1 to 0.5 kg dry weight/m^2, and by foliose seashore lichens from 0.5 to 1.0 kg dry weight/m^2 (Fletcher, 1972a).

Data on rates of growth of seashore lichens have rarely been published. Some preliminary results suggest that crustose species show radial increases of less than 0.1 mm per month, whilst foliose species grow faster, increasing in radius by 0.4–0.7 mm per month (Jones and Fletcher, 1976; Jones *et al.*, 1979). These results showed that growth rates varied widely between different locations and between different species, and even between different thalli of the same species at the same site. Recently, results evaluated using statistical methods of data-treatment have revealed seasonal and climatic correlations, in that the winter climate or cloudy days throughout the year are the most conducive to growth (Fletcher, unpublished).

It is apparent that the great variability in rates of growth necessitates very careful choice of the thalli to be observed if results suitable for comparison between sites and species are desired. Only photographic techniques appear to be precise enough to measure growth rates of as little as 0.1 mm per month, and to obtain statistically significant results a large investment in time and labour is needed (see also Jones *et al.*, 1980, these volumes).

2. Morphological Variation

Marine and maritime lichens appear to be particularly variable in morphology; this is a factor which causes much confusion in their identification. Modern keys to seashore species take this factor into account (Fletcher, 1975a,b).

The eight littoral *Arthopyrenia* species recognized in the older literature were reduced to synonomic status with *A. halodytes* by Swinscow (1965), who felt that their differences in size and prominence of perithecia were environmentally determined. *Verrucaria maura* and other marine *Verrucaria* species are also very variable, depending on the amount of sun and shade in the environment. Thalli from sunny places are black, rimose-cracked and often areolate, while shaded thalli are smooth, continuous and often paler in colour, ranging from brown to green, *Verrucaria striatula* lacks black ridges in shaded places and becomes extremely thin and bright green, but this green tissue disappears in well-lit situations. *Verrucaria mucosa* varies in colour with season, being olive-green in winter and black in summer. The reason for these changes in colour is unknown, since the pigment appears to be structural and is not a normal secondary metabolite which should be extractable with organic solvents.

Supralittoral thalli frequently vary in colour, becoming greener in the winter and in shaded conditions. This effect was explored in *Xanthoria parietina*, where thalli from shaded habitats were found to have thinner cortices and more phycobiont cells than thalli from sunny places (Hill and Woolhouse, 1966). More direct evidence for the influence of habitat on thallus morphology was obtained by transplantation of this species by Richardson (1967). The narrow-lobed, deeper-orange form (var. *ectanea*) common on sunny, wind-exposed seashores grew to resemble the broader lobed, paler-yellow morphotype when transplanted to more sheltered conditions.

The most intensively studied species appear to be those of the *Ramalina siliquosa* group. Knowles (1913) gave extensive notes on the morphology of these plants, finding that thalli from low on the shore were darker in colour and had more forcipate apices when compared with upper shore thalli. Those from open rocks were glaucous, much branched and pustular, while those from south-west and west-facing rocks were short and lacerate. Thalli on east-facing sheltered rocks were soft, dichotomous and forcipate. Accompanying these morphological variations were chemical differences. For example, thalli from high on the shore turned red with potassium hydroxide, but thalli from low on the shore turned yellow or were unaffected. This work was followed up in the quantitative investigations of C. F. Culberson (1965), W. L. Culberson (1967, 1969), Culberson and Culberson (1967) and Culberson *et al.* (1977), who found that the morphotypes and chemotypes select-out according to geographical location, height on the shore and aspect.

The taxonomic status of these morphological and chemical variants has received much attention in the literature since the Culbersons maintained that they constitute genetic differences, deserving specific rank, and that different species occupy different habitats. Opponents of this theory maintain that the variants are responses by no more than two genotypes to differing habitat conditions and do not deserve taxonomic status (Sheard, 1978a,b; Sheard and James, 1976). Intermediate points of view have been expressed by Motyka (1960); Wade (1961); Fletcher (1975a) and Søchting (1976).

It is difficult to comment upon the validity of the opposing viewpoints, except that in general terms lichens are obviously dependent on habitat parameters and are well-known to vary morphologically. The taxonomic status of chemotypes is currently under review (Hawksworth, 1976; Brodo, 1978), but it is still not known whether or not habitat affects the nature of the chemical substances produced by a single species. It is apparent, however, that the mechanisms underlying the effects of habitat on morphology and chemistry of lichens deserve experimental study.

3. Colonization

The process of colonization by lichens on seashore rocks and the dynamics of their populations remain unstudied. Presumably, mycobiont ascospores arrive on a suitable substratum, germinate to form a plaque as described by Ahmadjian (1967), and entrap phycobiont cells of the required species and physiological strain to initiate a symbiosis. It is highly likely that each thallus includes the products from germination of more than one ascospore and phycobiont cell. Consequently, a lichen thallus could be heterocaryotic and could be regarded as equivalent to a population in its own right. Free-living mycobionts have not been reported from seashore habitats, but the phycobionts may well be ubiquitous. The green coloration of upper littoral rocks frequently arises from free-living *Dilabifilium arthopyreniae* (= *Pseudopleurococcus*), which appears to be the phycobiont of marine *Verrucaria* spp. (Fletcher, 1972b; Tschermak-Woess, 1976). *Hyella caespitosa* and *Calothrix scopulorum*, the respective phycobionts of marine *Arthopyrenia* and *Lichina*, are also common and free-living in the littoral zone. Free-living phycobionts have yet to be described from the supralittoral, but since most phycobionts (including *Trebouxia*; Tschermak-Woess, 1978) are now known to be free-living elsewhere, it may be assumed that they are readily available in the supralittoral.

The prothalli of lichen symbioses are often seen on the seashore and are usually recognizable as blackish, dendritic patches on bare rock. The initiation of a new thallus is generally thought to take several years after the substratum becomes newly exposed and it appears that the surface needs to become modified by weathering before lichens can establish (Brodo, 1974; Kristinsson, 1972). The precise period of time for establishment has yet to be determined on the seashore, but careful observations of newly exposed surfaces could provide this information.

The dynamics of seashore lichen populations have never been examined quantitatively and rates of turnover are unknown. However, some qualitative data are available from McLean (1915), who noted three phases of growth in lichens on shingle beaches, namely (a) primary growth, when thalli increased in radius; (b) fusion, when adjacent thalli met and coalesced; (c) decay, when thalli crumbled or eroded at the centre to expose new substrata. It should be added that thalli can undergo all three stages of growth simultaneously, and commonly a single colony is undergoing primary growth or fusion at the circumference, but is decaying in the centre. This process often converts a discoid thallus into a ring or semicircle. It can also allow a thallus to move away from unsuitable habitats. For instance, if increased volumes of water start to be drained by a crevice, the parts of the lichen near to it can die, but the parts farthest away may continue to grow. Thalli of *Xanthoria parietina* can appear to "crawl away" from such crevices at rates of 7 mm per annum (Fletcher, unpublished). It also appears that fragments of lobes remaining when the rest of the thallus has eroded away grow much faster than the parent thallus. Possibly, large thalli in general grow more slowly than small ones, so that mean relative growth rates (MRGR) decline as the thallus ages (Armstrong, 1976).

The process of lichen growth is of further interest in that the centre of the thallus should increase in thickness if growth rates of the central parts equal those at the circumference. But the thickness of the centre of the thallus is invariably little different from that at the circumference. Whether control of growth in different parts of the thallus is internally controlled, or whether it is affected by external factors such as erosion, grazing, or the availability of nutrients, requires further exploration.

4. *Succession*

Natural succession by lichens on bare rock has been conventionally described as being from crustose to foliose than fruticose (McLean, 1915; Vevers, 1936), but many observations contradict this. *Ramalina siliquosa*, for example, can exist in pure stands without an understory of crustose or foliose species (Knowles, 1913), while foliose species such as *Xanthoria parietina, Anaptychia fusca* and *Parmelia* spp. often colonize tufts of *Ramalina siliquosa* and spread from there on to bare rock. In the littoral zone, fruticose *Lichina pygmaea* thalli are rarely associated with crustose lichens directly, perhaps preferring to colonize and spread from crevices. On the other hand, *Caloplaca microthallina* is always epiphytic on *Verrucaria maura*, but cannot be considered to be a stage in a succession.

Succession of lichens may often result from changed conditions within a habitat. Patches of bare substratum arising from the disappearance of the centres of lichen thalli are often colonized by species which need not be normally associated with that of the decaying thallus. For example, the vacated centre of supralittoral *Xanthoria parietina* can be colonized by mesic-supralittoral crevice-species such as *Buellia punctata* or *Catillaria chalybeia*, or by xeric-supralittoral *Ramalina siliquosa*. Sometimes, the old thallus remains to restrict the extension of the newer colonizer.

McLean's phenomenon of "supersession", whereby one lichen overgrows another and replaces it, does not appear to be a regular phenomenon on rocky shores. It is most frequently observed in the terrestrial zone, where crustose *Ochrolechia androgyna* can be so vigorous as to overgrow foliose lichens. The question of whether succession is a natural sequence in lichen colonization remains to be answered, but may be solved by long-term monitoring of newly exposed substrata. For the moment, it appears that crustose, foliose or fruticose species colonize either as a matter of chance or perhaps depend on habitat conditions which favour a particular species irrespective of its morphology.

Only one authority has noted succession after lichens by other organisms (Boney, 1961). After *Lichina pygmaea* was cleared the bared rock became covered by green algae, followed by barnacles. It is possible that *Lichina* eventually spreads from adjacent patches and can overgrow these barnacles, the shells of which form part of the substratum after the death of their occupants. Alternatively, it is possible that the order of succession could vary according to time of year; it is well known that green algae and barnacle-spat predominate in the spring and early summer, so that colonization by *Lichina pygmaea* might best be effected during the autumn and winter.

5. *Competition, Grazing, Shelter*

Littoral lichens actively and successfully compete for substratum with other seashore organisms. Barnacle spat may totally cover *Verrucaria mucosa* and *V. striatula* in the spring, yet few survive to the adult stage on lichen surfaces. Most littoral lichens can overcome reductions in available substratum by growing upon the shells of barnacles and other living marine invertebrates. *Arthopyrenia sublittoralis*, for example, is known from 61 species of animal "host" (Santesson, 1939). The thallus of this species is endolithic and exists within the shell matrix of the host, being visible only as a result of its black pseudothecia. This endolithic habit almost certainly damages the host by eroding away the shell surface. Consequently, lichens could be considered to be competing organisms, but the extent and importance of this activity remains to be assessed.

Competition for substratum between algae and lichens is also frequent (Lewis, 1953). Boney (1961) noted that rock surfaces around patches of *Pelvetia canaliculata* were wholly occupied by littoral lichens which were presumed to be competing for substratum. Algal sporelings are rarely seen directly upon the surface of littoral lichens and it seems that, as with barnacle spat, marine organisms are unable to settle permanently on, or to penetrate into, lichen thalli to obtain purchase on the rocky substratum below. Instead algae are more often associated with crevices, from which they spread and oust lichens, perhaps by shading them from light. Very occasionally, *Pelvetia canaliculata* and *Fucus* spp. grow amongst *Lichina pygmaea* lobes on any bare patches of substratum – often on vacated barnacle shells.

Whilst permanent colonization of lichen-covered rock surfaces by algae is unusual, seasonal colonization is very regular. Starting in late autumn, the upper littoral *Verrucaria* spp. and *Arthopyrenia* spp. become obscured by *Bangia atropurpurea, Porphyra linearis,*

Enteromorpha spp., Cyanophceae and filamentous Chlorophyceae. This is especially noticeable on north-facing and sheltered shores, but all types of shores can be affected. *Lichina pygmaea* is also obscured by *Enteromorpha* spp., *Chaetomorpha* spp., *Porphyra umbilicalis* and *Ulva lactuca*, which entangle with the fruticose lobes. Even supralittoral lichens can bear a crust of Chlorophyceae during the winter months. On rocks used as bird-perches, the lichens become obscured during the winter by littoral algae such as *Prasiola stipitata*.

The phenomenon of seasonal algal colonization allows the lichens to become uncovered during the late spring and remain so until the autumn. However, seasonal coverage must still impose a great strain on the lichen symbiosis since light availability must be severely reduced at a time of year when light intensity is already reduced through climatic fluctuation. In addition, water retained by the algal cover must increase the general wetness of the lichen environment, again at a time when climatic factors reduce the rate of drying-out. The potential effect of nutrients or toxins produced by epiphytic algae must also be mentioned. Despite these seasonal factors, however, or perhaps because of them, it appears that littoral lichens are making their fastest growth during the winter period (see p. 816).

Competition by lichens with other organisms is probably less severe in the supralittoral zone than in the littoral. Lichens are generally only affected where they compete against plants, such as *Armeria maritima*, that accrete soil, and then only near crevices. In these situations, soil and angiosperm cover reduces the amount of rock available for lichen colonization, and may also change the chemical content of the water run-off, making it more acidic and less saline. Such factors will favour a more terrestrial type of lichen community. Shading by angiosperms exerts its greatest effect on sheltered shores, where larger plants such as *Rubus* spp., *Cotoneaster* spp. and *Calluna vulgaris*, or even trees, can overhang the supralittoral rocks. If shading is by summer annuals, however, the lichens are presumably little-affected since their best growth is during the winter period.

It is apparent, then, that since shading takes place at different times of the year in the littoral zone, as compared to the supralittoral zone, the tolerance of lichens to this factor must be evaluated in terms of (a) when shading occurs; (b) the types of plants causing the shading; (c) the metabolic activity of the lichens at that time of the year.

Littoral lichens show evidence of being grazed by limpets from the patterns of radula marks left on the thalli. Limpet-grazing is especially noticeable on *Verrucaria mucosa*, but all crustose species may be affected. If limpet-grazing is severe, then the lichens are to be found only on such parts of the shore as the uppermost littoral fringe, especially in crevices and ridges into which limpets cannot reach.

Grazing by littorinids is also frequent in the littoral but is less obvious, being only visible by scratch marks or trails left upon the thalli, especially if the latter are silt-covered. *Littorina neritoides* (L.) has been noted as cropping lichens with its radula, presumably a reference to fruticose *Lichina pygmaea* (Colman, 1940). It is possible that those littorinids that inhabit crevices in the uppermost littoral fringe on *Verrucaria maura*-dominated rocks are almost wholly dependent upon this lichen for food, since free-living algae are rarely found here except during the winter. Other littoral animals probably graze lichens, but only the isopod *Campecopea hirsuta* (Montagu) has been mentioned as eating away the phycobiont layer of *Lichina pygmaea* (Wieser, 1963).

Invertebrate grazing is also frequent in the supralittoral zone. Gastropods graze the phycobiont-containing upper surfaces of lichens and are also attracted to the soft apothecial discs. Barklice and mites (Søchting, 1976) are also important grazing animals in this zone. An extensive review by Gerson and Seaward (1977) lists lichen-grazing animals from most of the invertebrate orders, and it is highly likely that many of these exploit lichens in the supralittoral zone.

Vertebrates also graze lichens. For example, Gillham (1954) noted that larger fruticose supralittoral species were eaten by rabbits and goats.

In addition to the direct use of lichens for food, many invertebrates depend upon them for shelter. Colman (1940), in a survey of the faunas associated with intertidal plants, found that tufts of *Lichina pygmaea* had the highest numbers of epiphytic animals; for example, up to 16 050 individuals of the bivalve mollusc *Lasaea rubra* (Montagu) were found in 100 g wet weight of lichen. These populations inhabiting a lichen even exceeded those found in *Laminaria* holdfasts. *Campecopea hirsuta* and Diptera larvae were also very numerous. The absolute numbers of epiphytic animals depended on the height at which the lichen occurred; the higher upshore, the lower the numbers. Species diversity of epiphytes was always low, however, compared with other intertidal plants. Only larvae of the fly *Limonia (Geranomyia) unicolor* (Haliday) were restricted to *Lichina pygmaea.* Morton (1954) concluded that *Lichina* tufts provide a habitat analogous to that of rock crevices, providing shelter, protection and shade, and accumulating organic matter upon which the epiphytes could feed. This lichen, it was also concluded, provided the only alternative littoral-zone habitats suitable for expansion of crevice-fauna populations.

Many invertebrates have been found sheltering beneath the thalli of foliose supralittoral lichens (Gerson and Seaward, 1977; Hughes and Tilbrook, 1966; Lagerspetz, 1953; Lindsay, 1978; Madsen, 1940; Tilbrook, 1967). These animals can be sources of food for higher animals. For example, the rock pipit (*Anthus spinoletta spinoletta*) (L.) has been observed pecking-out animals from supralittoral lichen swards (Fletcher, 1973b). Moths may sometimes be encountered with cryptic mimicry of supralittoral lichens, for protection, such as also occurs in terrestrial habitats (cf. Richardson, 1975).

The activities of animals can sometimes damage lichens, even if they are not grazed. Trampling by birds, for example, can lead to impoverished lichen floras in heavily populated localities (Fletcher, 1973b). Large lichen thalli, especially of *Ramalina siliquosa* which can exceed 30 cm length, are only found on vertical rocks inaccessible to animals, including man. Trampling damage appears to be greatest when the lichens are wet, when the entire thallus peels away as a sheet. By contrast, when dry, the brittle thalli fragment, so that at least some portions remain to propagate the plant. It is possible, however, that a degree of trampling and fragmentation is beneficial, since the fragments can serve to disperse the species. It is well known that dispersal of regularly-produced asexual diaspores (isidia and soredia) is effected by invertebrates (Bailey, 1976); this must be important to those diaspore-producing supralittoral lichens. It is worth adding here that some authorities have considered diaspores to be produced in response to damage, so that the whole question of propagation as a result of the activities of animals could form the subject of an interesting investigation.

The only other examples of seashore lichens directly benefitting from the activities of animals appear to be those unique floras resulting from bird-manuring (see p. 813).

In conclusion of this survey of biological influences on seashore-lichen ecology, it is obvious that more quantitative assessments of the effects of animals and lichens are needed. Perhaps the most important aspect is that of lichens as cover, since these life-forms probably have low food value, being of low biomass, and because relatively few animals are capable of digesting fungal chitin (Nielson, 1963). The secondary metabolites produced by many lichens are thought to discourage grazing (Hale, 1972), but there is little evidence that those lichens lacking such substances are more intensively grazed. Hale (1972) provided detailed evidence that grazing of lichens was an extraordinary event, often caused by drought. Gerson and Seaward (1977) suggested that grazing animals could be deterred by high levels of accumulated metal ions, some of which may be toxic.

Atmospheric nitrogen is fixed by marine *Lichina* spp. (Hitch and Stewart, 1973) and may supplement the other sources of this element for grazing animals.

Finally, it has been argued that lichen-grazing could never be a regular phenomenon because no animal population could be supported by organisms of such low biomass and slow rates of growth. Consequently, evolution of such dependence by animals is unlikely (Farrar, 1976a).

PHYSIOLOGY OF SEASHORE LICHENS

Although the body of work available on the physiological ecology of lichens is growing rapidly (Ahmadjian and Hale, 1974; Seaward, 1977; Brown *et al.*, 1976), very little has been published on seashore species. The following account is based on the few publications which exist, and also draws heavily on unpublished work by the author. First the physiology of the isolated bionts will be described, followed by that of the intact thallus with respect to water relations, photosynthesis and respiration, resistance to environmental extremes, light and temperature, and, finally, nutrients.

1. Physiology of Isolated Bionts

The mycobionts and phycobionts of lichens are readily isolated by modern techniques and can easily be cultured (Ahmadjian, 1967), but these methods have not been extensively applied to seashore species. Only the phycobionts of marine *Verrucaria* spp. have been isolated and their culture characteristics described (Fletcher, 1972b; Tschermak-Woess, 1976). *Dilabifilium* Tschermak-Woess (= *Pseudopleurococcus* Snow) from littoral *Verrucaria maura, V. mucosa* and *V. striatula*, showed optimum growth at 720 lumens/ft^2 at 12°C (Fletcher, 1972b). This is a high figure compared with the 400 lumens recorded for *Trebouxia* (Ahmadjian, 1967), which is probably also a seashore lichen phycobiont. Fletcher (1972b) found that the phycobiont growth-rates for *Verrucaria maura* and *V. striatula* were the same in both seawater and freshwater media, but were faster in sea water for the more marine *V. mucosa.*

Isolated mycobionts have only once been investigated. Ramkaer (1978) concluded that the frequency of ascospore germination and rates of hyphal growth for five lichen species depended on the salinity of the medium. Very broadly, the most marine lichens showed greatest tolerance towards salinities exceeding 35‰. However, the figures are not easy to interpret because frequency of germination was time-dependent for some species, whilst in others the ascospores germinated immediately. This effect was independent of salinity. It suggests that perhaps salinity is not the only important variable in these experiments, but submersion frequency, temperature, and the influence of individual ions might also be involved.

2. Physiology of the Composite Thallus

Smith (1962) pointed out that experiments involving isolated symbionts cannot indicate the physiological characteristics of the lichen thallus. This is because the symbiotic state, where both symbionts live together, is maintained by environmental factors (Scott, 1960). These factors, although optimal for maintenance of the symbiotic state, are suboptimal for growth by the free-living bionts. However, if the balance between these factors changes to favour growth by one biont, then the symbiosis may well break down and the bionts separate. It follows that only physiological experiments on the symbionts existing together as a lichen thallus will give results which can be related to field conditions.

(a) Water relations. Experimental work involving the water relations of lichens must consider (i) how much water is taken up; (ii) how quickly it is taken up; (iii) how slowly it is lost. Experimentalists must also consider in what form the water reaches the plant. This can be as liquid, from direct submersion, or in fine-droplet form from spray, or as vapour. These points were investigated in an extensive series of experiments designed to discover whether morphological construction of seashore lichens could have a bearing on their water relations (Fletcher, 1972b). It was discovered that uptake of spray as fine water-droplets was slowest in crustose littoral lichens, but very much faster in non-crustose species. Thick thalli, however, absorbed spray-droplets more slowly than thin thalli of the same species. Littoral zone species also lost water, by evaporation to the atmosphere, at a faster rate than those from the supralittoral, but uptake of water vapour (hygroscopicity) was not significantly different. Generally, littoral lichens lost water faster than they took it up, over periods extending to 200 h, but the reverse was true for supralittoral species.

By comparison with crustose species, foliose lichens absorbed greater amounts of water. Also, the rate of uptake of spray-droplets was particularly fast in individual thalli with narrow lobes. Uptake of water vapour, however, was slower than its loss, though both uptake and loss were much more rapid than for crustose species. Finally, the rate of water loss was less in those foliose thalli which were closely appressed to the substratum.

It was generally concluded that thallus construction, for the 11 species studied, had a great effect on water relations. Adaptations leading to water conservation were (i) close-appression to the substratum; (ii) presence of secondary metabolite crystals in the cortex; (iii) crustose habit; (iv) terete habit; (v) heteromerous construction. Adaptations increasing the rate of spray absorption included (i) cracks in the cortex, or narrow lobes, and (ii) heteromerous construction. Crystals of secondary metabolites within the medulla prevented the thallus from becoming water-saturated.

It became apparent from these experiments that correlations between water relations of lichens and their ecological preferences could only be established in lichens of similar thallus construction. Thus, of homoiomerous thalli, crustose *Verrucaria mucosa* proved to be less efficient at conserving water and absorbing it than did *V. maura*. However, both species of *Lichina*, which have a similar ecology and are also homoiomerous, were even less efficient at conserving water than *V. mucosa*, because they are fruticose. Consequently, it was generalized that whilst a species from a drier habitat need not conserve or absorb water any more efficiently than one from a wetter habitat, the type of morphological adaptations it possessed might allow it to do so.

(b) Photosynthesis and respiration. The amount of water which seashore lichens can absorb hygroscopically can be sufficient to support respiration and photosynthesis. Respiration occurred in *Caloplaca marina* thalli in equilibrium with atmospheres of 15% r.h. at 20°C, and in *Ramalina siliquosa* at 70% r.h. Little ecological correlation with respiration as a function of water derived from water vapour was noted but, when respiration as a function of thallus water-content was compared, it was found that all species from the littoral zone needed to be 30–50% water-saturated while supralittoral species could respire at 5–20% of water-saturation. Optimum respiration rates were at 100% water-saturation for all thalli.

Photosynthesis followed a similar pattern. All species could assimilate when in equilibrium with atmospheres of 50–80% r.h., and little correlation with ecology was noted. However, supralittoral thalli could still photosynthesize at 10–30% water-saturation, while littoral thalli required to be over 40% water-saturated. The biggest influence of water-saturation, however, was on the extent of photosynthesis. All littoral thalli achieved maximum photosynthesis at 100% water-saturation, i.e. when totally submerged, but supralittoral thalli achieved optimum photosynthesis when under-saturated with water, at levels of 90% or less. This meant that conditions of continuous submergence depressed photosynthesis in supralittoral lichens. This result is similar to that of Reid (1960a,b,c), who studied freshwater lichens.

It may be added that the acquisition of a heteromerous morphology, in which the medullary air spaces contain non-wettable medullary crystals, may be a method by which supralittoral thalli can resist becoming water-saturated and can continue to photosynthesize under conditions of heavy spray or rainfall. The littoral species, on the other hand, are better adapted to photosynthesize in submerged conditions, but are less able to do so when partially dried-out.

(c) Resistance to environmental extremes. The relative effects of constant submersion on seashore lichens were discussed by Fletcher (1976). Littoral species were able to maintain photosynthesis after submersion periods lasting 35 days, but in submesic-supralittoral thalli the symbiosis broke down with liberation of the phycobiont, while xeric-supralittoral thalli died. Supralittoral thalli were affected by sea water submersion sooner than littoral species, but the latter were more quickly affected by fresh water. It was concluded that over short periods of 1–2 months, the salinity of the medium over the range 0–35‰ had less overall effect than the continuously wet conditions.

The effects of varying salinity on *Lichina pygmaea* were observed by Feige (1972). Increasing salinity raised the amounts of soluble carbohydrates (principally mannisido-mannitol), while decrease in salinity caused a reduction in the levels of these compounds. Mannitol, the principal respiratory substrate of the mycobiont, was also decreased when soluble carbohydrates were increased. It was concluded that conversion of polysaccharide into mannisido-mannitol instead of into mannitol increases the resistance of the phycobiont to the osmotic stress imposed by seawater. The rates of appearance and disappearance of these compounds depend on seawater concentration (Feige, 1973, 1975).

These results are strikingly similar to those of Farrar (1976b), who suggested that an equilibrium between polysaccharides and monosaccharides exists in lichens, the monosaccharides increasing in periods of environmental stress, such as in drought. It is now thought that 70–80% of the carbohydrates in lichens are used for countering environmental stress, rather than for growth, and this has been invoked as a reason for the slow growth rates of lichens (Farrar, 1976b).

The effects of drought are controversial. Fletcher (1976) found no difference between photosynthetic and respiratory recovery in *Verrucaria maura* and *V. mucosa* after two days subjection to drought at 0% r.h. However, Reid (1969) found that *V. mucosa* took six days to recover from a drought of only one day, and that longer droughts caused permanent impairment of photosynthesis. This factor obviously needs further investigation. Reid (1960a,b,c) found that drought-resistance in itself was not sufficient to account for the zonation of lichens in freshwater habitats. Instead, the relative frequencies and lengths of alternating drought and submersion periods were the more influential.

To test this hypothesis, seashore lichens were subjected to cycles of 21 h drought followed by 3 h submersion over periods of 14 days (Fletcher, 1976). It was found that littoral species died quickly, but supralittoral species experienced breakdown of the symbiosis with liberation of the phycobiont. Again, as with constant submersion, the salinity of the water had less influence than the feature of alternating conditions in itself. It was concluded that maintenance of the symbiosis would be achieved if the dry and wet periods were suitably balanced for each species.

It appears that the time taken by a thallus to recover from a dry or a wet period may account for these results. If the wet conditions arise before the phycobiont has fully recovered from the effects of the previous wet period, then an overall decline in photosynthetic ability will result over a period of time. What is achieved during the recovery period, and how the phycobiont's photosynthetic ability is affected by drought or submersion, are not known.

A decline in photosynthesis is not the only effect of alternating dry and wet conditions (Fletcher, 1972b). In experiments involving whole thalli, the photosynthetic rate increased in some species, as a result of the phycobiont cells multiplying. This was interpreted as another sign of breakdown of the symbiosis. Consequently, in measuring the effects of environmental extremes, it should be remembered that the treatment can cause (i) death of both symbionts; (ii) death of only one symbiont; or (iii) breakdown of the symbiosis to liberate one or both symbionts. It appears highly likely that, in nature, a constant rebalance is being achieved between separate growth rates of the phycobiont and mycobiont in response to environmental factors which alternately favour each symbiont.

(d) Light and temperature. Preliminary results on the effect of temperature on photosynthesis and respiration suggest a normal Q_{10} relationship (Fletcher, 1972b).

The zonation of littoral plants, including lichens, has been related to their temperature resistance (Reid, 1969), but while *Verrucaria mucosa* had similar temperature resistance to the algae (with which it is ecologically associated), *V. maura* was apparently even less resistant. The effects of temperature on seashore lichen ecology are thus inconclusive.

Little is known about the effects of light on the physiology of seashore lichens. The compensation point is strongly dependent on the history of the plant, and in freshly collected *Lichina pygmaea* a value of 300 lumens/ft^2 declined to 200 lumens/ft^2 after a period of 24 h preconditioning (Fletcher, 1972b). Optimum photosynthesis was at light intensities of 800–1000 lumens/ft^2, irrespective of the species (Fletcher, unpublished) and this result is consistent with the growth requirements of the free-living phycobionts (see p. 826).

(e) Nutrients. This subject has been partially covered on p. 812, and has also been extensively reviewed elsewhere (Fletcher, 1976). Careful distinction must be made between osmotic and chemical properties when assessing the effect of sea water. Osmotic properties were implied in the discussion of salinity (page 829), so that the present section will detail the physiological experiments involving the effects of individual ions.

The magnitude of ion uptake by seashore lichens can be very great, as in terrestrial lichens (James, 1973). Concentrations of iron reached 2.5×10^6 over that in sea water in littoral *Verrucaria maura*, while zinc was concentrated by a factor of 8×10^3 (Spear, 1974). Levels of lead can reach 100 p.p.m. of thallus dry weight, and those of iron 55×10^3 p.p.m. (Fletcher, 1976). Even cadmium is detectable in some species at levels up to 2 p.p.m. (Spear, 1974). Sea water is the principal source of these cations, but atmospheric sources such as rainfall and dust may account for most of the lead and iron (Fletcher, 1976; Spear, 1974). A distinction between nutrients derived from seawater or the atmosphere and those from the rocky substratum could not be made, owing to difficulties in comparing rock samples of different surface porosities (Spear, 1974).

No work is available concerning the mechanisms of cation and nutrient accumulation in seashore lichens, but Niebohr *et al.* (1978) have summarized results in this field for lichens in general.

It is uncertain whether cation uptake in seashore lichens is an active, metabolically linked process. However, uptake of phosphate anions appears to be active and to depend on light and temperature in certain species (Fletcher, 1976). The selective absorption of cations was also affected by light availability, but may be linked with ion exchange or pH changes resulting from respiratory or photosynthetic CO_2. This light-influenced selective ion-absorption showed correlations with ecology in two species. The terrestrial-halophilic *Parmelia saxatilis* lost potassium to base-rich media containing calcium and inorganic ions, whilst the submesic-supralittoral *Xanthoria parietina* was unaffected – but only in the light. Further analysis showed that potassium loss was rapid when *Xanthoria parietina* was placed in freshwater, but *Parmelia saxatilis* was unaffected. It was generally concluded that environments such as sea water, and others which are rich in calcium ions, are necessary for *Xanthoria parietina* to avoid losses of potassium. The mechanism for this loss is unknown at present, and whether potassium is lost from within the cell membranes, or is purely from the cell walls and intercellular free-space, requires investigation.

CONCLUSIONS

Quantitative or otherwise well-founded descriptions of lichen distribution on siliceous rocky shores in Britain show reasonable agreement, although the number of publications available is very limited. These descriptions, summarized on the basis of a recently-developed ecological distribution classification system, may have general applicability on rocky shores. However, standardization of methodology is required. It is especially important in this respect that (a) sampling units, whether pin-frames or quadrats, should be sufficiently large to overcome errors due to the large size of individual thalli; (b) transects, if used, should sample the whole shore so that shallow and steep slopes are sampled evenly; (c) if the interface between terrestrial and maritime floras is to be studied, the transect or sampling area should extend to rocks well within the angiosperm vegetation.

Only by critically evaluated and finely discriminatory methods, supported by objectively-based numerical methods of analysis, will it be possible to detect differences and similarities in floras and to provide repeatable descriptions of the distribution of lichens within the six shore zones already known to exist. Such methods could be applied to a range of problems, the most outstanding being (i) the study of estuarine lichens and the description of lichen floras on different rock types, particularly on man-made substrata and (ii) the particularly difficult calcareous flora. Useful studies could also compare maritime rocky shore floras with those of terrestrial conditions to discover the ecological limits of inland-distributed species.

Critically applied descriptive studies may allow us to describe more fully the ecology of seashore lichens in terms of the environmental factors affecting them. A particular aim would be to group together all those species with similar ecological distributions, or to establish their positions along environmental gradients. A final evaluation would allow us to say which species were truly maritime in their ecological requirements and which species merely tolerated maritime conditions as a response to alterations in some other environmental parameter. It is obvious, however, that in order to achieve this evaluation, more work is needed to attempt correlation of lichen distribution with those environmental parameters that have so far rarely been measured.

There are very few existing studies on the growth, dynamics and biological factors affecting lichens on seashores. However, animal and plant interactions, especially the effects of grazing, competition and shelter, offer a promising field of research; integrating with other fields or littoral ecology, these studies could be undertaken by any biologist working in the littoral environment. Biological interactions in the supralittoral offer an almost virgin field, untouched alike by terrestrial and marine biologists.

The well-publicized properties of lichens as environmental indicators could be utilized by marine biologists. Their longevity and slow growth rates make them potential indicators of long-term environmental changes, such as those produced by climate or by chronic pollution, which shorter-lived organisms do not perceptibly register. Such effects could be manifested by changes in lichen growth rates, in population structure, or in modification/simplification of communities. Lichens have an advantage over algae and other seashore organisms as indicators of environmental levels of cations, in that only small amounts of plant material are needed for analysis because of the very high ion-levels attained. Real quantitative relationships between seashore-lichen cation levels and environmental levels still remain to be established.

As yet, we have no picture of the physiology of any seashore-lichen species complete enough to allow us to say why it grows where it does, but there are many indications which could become more definitive with increased data. Research in this field is obviously at a very preliminary stage; of importance so far is the suggestion that no single environmental factor has an overall controlling influence on lichen zonation, individual species possibly existing side by side on the shore for different reasons. For example, some species (e.g. *Xanthoria parietina*) appear to be very wide in their ecological amplitude while others (e.g. *Aspicilia leprosescens*) are very narrow. This introduces problems regarding the selection of which species to work on. For example, a typical sunny shore differs floristically from a shaded shore, even though the lichen zonation of both is apparently determined by tolerance to sea water. It thus becomes necessary to select, for experimentation, species which have similar distributions on both sunny and shaded shores; these species will clearly be insensitive to aspect. When all other determining factors such as temperature, water, nutrients, and morphological structure are considered, it becomes obvious that choice of experimental material can only be made on the basis of secure field-derived distributional evidence.

These general conclusions suggest some of the approaches through which research might profitably be undertaken. There remain few material barriers, other than financial, to the extension of research in this field because seashore lichens (a) are taxonomically better documented and understood than most other seashore organisms; (b) possess well-laid grounds for their ecological description and comparison; (c) have readily available quantitative and numerical methods for their ecological description, especially if works on terrestrial botany are consulted; (d) are covered by extant and well-established physiological techniques for whole-plant experiments.

The final prejudice, that seashore lichens are neither economically nor ecologically important enough to merit attention, can only be overcome by research. It seems inconceivable to the author that lichens, which have presumably existed since the algae and fungi became differentiated and which occupy such extensive tracts of seashores, should not be exerting some significant ecological effects. These effects have so far remained undetected or, more likely, have not yet been sought.

REFERENCES

des Abbayes, H. (1951). "Traité de Lichenologie". (*Encycl. Biol.* **41**, i–x, 1–217.) Lechevalier, Paris.

Acock, A. M. (1940). Vegetation of a calcareous inner fjord region in Spitzbergen. *J. Ecol.* **28**, 81–106.

Ahmadjian, V. (1967). A guide to the algae occurring as lichen symbionts: isolation, culture, cultural physiology, and identification. *Phycologia* **6**, 127–160.

Ahmadjian, V. and Hale, M. E. (1974) (eds) "The Lichens". Academic Press, London and New York.

Almborn, O. (1955). Lavvegetation och lave flora på Hallands Väderö. *K. svenska vetenskAkad. Avh. Naturskydd.* **11**, 1–92.

Alvin, K. L. (1961). Lichens of Skippers Island. *Essex Nat.* **30**, 330–335.

Armstrong, R. A. (1976). Studies on the growth rates of lichens. *In* "Lichenology: Progress and Problems" (D. H. Brown, D. L. Hawksworth and R. H. Bailey, eds), pp. 309–322. Academic Press, London and New York.

Bailey, R. H. (1976). Ecological aspects of dispersal and establishment in lichens. *In* "Lichenology: Progress and Problems" (D. H. Brown, D. L. Hawksworth, and R. H. Bailey, eds), pp. 215–248. Academic Press, London and New York.

Ballantyne, W. J. (1961). A biologically-defined exposure scale for the comparative description of rocky shores. *Fld Stud.* **1**, 1–19.

Boney, A. D. (1961). A note on the intertidal lichen *Lichina pygmaea* Ag. *J. mar. biol. Ass. U.K.* **41**, 123–126.

Brodo, I. M. (1974). Substrate ecology. *In* "The Lichens" (V. Ahmadjian and M. E. Hale, eds), pp. 401–441. Academic Press, London and New York.

Brodo, I. M. (1978). Changing concepts regarding chemical diversity in lichens. *Lichenologist* **10**, 1–12.

Brown, D. H. (1972). The effect of Kuwait crude oil and a solvent emulsifier on the metabolism of the marine lichen *Lichina pygmaea, Mar. Biol., Berl.* **12**, 309–315.

Brown, D. H. (1974). Field and laboratory studies on detergent damage to lichens at The Lizard, Cornwall. *Cornish Stud.* **2**, 33–40.

Brown, D. H., Hawksworth, D. L. and Bailey, R. H. (1976) (eds) "Lichenology: Progress and Problems". Academic Press, London and New York.

Chassé, C., L'Hardy-Halos, M. -Th. and Perrot, Y. (1967). Esquisse d'un bilan des partes biologiques proroquées par le mazout du "Torrey Canyon" sur le littoral du Treger. *Penn ar Bed* **6**, 107–112.

Colman, J. S. (1940). On the faunas inhabiting intertidal seaweeds. *J. mar. biol. Ass. U.K.* **24**, 129–184.

Colman, J. S. and Stephenson, A. (1966). Aspects of the ecology of a "tideless" shore. *In* "Some Contemporary Studies in Marine Sciences" (H. Barnes, ed.), pp. 163–170. Allen and Unwin, London.

Cotton, A. D. (1912). Clare Island survey, part 15. Marine Algae. *Proc. R. Ir. Acad.* **31**, 1–178.

Crapp, C. (1971). The biological consequence of emulsifier cleansing. *In* "The

Ecological Effects of Oil Pollution on Littoral Communities" (E. B. Cowell, ed.), pp. 150–168. Institute of Petroleum, London.

Crisp, D. J. and Fischer-Piette, E. (1959). Répartition des principales espèces intercotidales de la Côte Atlantiques Français en 1954–55. *Ann. Inst. océanogr. Monaco* **36**, 275–388.

Critchfield, H. J. (1960). "General Climatology". Prentice-Hall, New Jersey.

Culberson, C. F. (1965). Some constituents of the lichen *Ramalina siliquosa. Phytochem.* **4**, 951–961.

Culberson, W. L. (1967). Analysis of chemical and morphological variation in the *Ramalina siliquosa* species complex. *Brittonia* **19**, 333–352.

Culberson, W. L. (1969). The behaviour of the species of the *Ramalina siliquosa* group in Portugal. *Öst. bot. Z.* **116**, 85–94.

Culberson, W. L. and Culberson, C. F. (1967). Habitat selection by chemically differentiated races of lichens. *Science, N.Y.* **158**, 1195–1197.

Culberson, W. L., Culberson, C. F. and Johnson, A. (1977). Correlations between secondary product chemistry and ecogeography in the *Ramalina siliquosa* group (lichens). *Pl. Syst. Evol.* **127**, 191–200.

Cullinane, J. P., McCarthy, P. M. and Fletcher, A. (1975). The effect of oil pollution in Bantry Bay. *Mar. Poll. Bull.* **6**, 173–176.

Davy de Virville, A. (1932). Les zones de lichens sur le littoral Atlantique. *Bull. Mayenne Sci.* **1932**, 35–66.

Davy de Virville, A. (1938). Les zones de lichens sur les côtes du Portugal. *Bolm. Soc. Broteriana* **13**, 123–160.

Davy de Virville, A. (1940). Les zones de végétation sur le littoral Atlantique. *Mém. Soc. Biogéogr.* **7**, 205–251.

Davy de Virville, A. and Fischer-Piette, E. (1931). La zone du *Caloplaca marina. Rev. gén. Bot.* **43**, 337–360.

Degelius, G. (1939). Die Flechten von Norra Skaftön. *Uppsala Univ. Arsskr.* **11**, 1–206.

Du Rietz, G. E. (1925a). Die Hauptzuga der vegetation der Insel Jungfrun. *Svensk bot. Tidskr.* **19**, 323–346.

Du Rietz, G. E. (1925b). "Svenska vaxtsociologiska Sallskapets Hedligerll Gotlandische Vegetationsstudien". Uppsala.

Du Rietz, G. E. (1932). Zur Vegetationsokologie der ostschwedische Kustenfelsen. *Beih. bot. Zbl.* **49**, 61–112.

Edwards, R. S. and Claxton, S. M. (1964). The distribution of air-borne salt of marine origin in the Aberystwyth area. *J. appl. Ecol.* **1**, 253–263.

Eriksson, E. (1959). The yearly circulation of chloride and sulphur in nature; meteorological, geochemical and pedological implications. Pt I. *Tellus* **11**, 375–403.

Evans, R. G. (1947). The intertidal ecology of Cardigan Bay. *J. Ecol.* **34**, 273–309.

Farrar, J. F. (1976a). The lichen as an ecosystem; observations and experiment. *In* "Lichenology: Progress and Problems" (D. H. Brown, D. L. Hawksworth and R. H. Bailey, eds), pp. 385–406. Academic Press, London and New York.

Farrar, J. F. (1976b). Ecological physiology of the lichen *Hypogymnia physodes*

II. Effects of wetting and drying cycles and the concept of "physiological buffering". *New Phytol.*·**75**, 115–113.

Feige, G. B. (1972). Ecophysiological aspects of carbohydrate metabolism in the marine blue-green algae lichen *Lichina pygmaea* AG. *Z. Pflanzenphysiol.* **68**, 121–126.

Feige, G. B. (1973). Untersuchungen zur Okolögie und Physiologie der marinen blaualgenflechten *Lichina pygmaea* Ag. II. Die reversibilitat der osmoregulation. *Z. Pflanzenphysiol.* **68**, 415–421.

Feige, G. B. (1975). Investigations on the ecology and physiology of the marine blue-green algae lichen *Lichina pygmaea* Ag.: III. Some aspects of photosynthesis C-fixation under osmoregulatoric conditions. *Z. Pflanzenphysiol.* **77**, 1–15.

Ferry, B. W., Baddeley, M. S. and Hawksworth, D. L. (eds) (1973). "Air Pollution and Lichens". Athlone Press, London.

Ferry, B. W. and Sheard, J. W. (1969). Zonation of supralittoral lichens on rocky shores around the Dale peninsula, Pembrokeshire. *Fld Stud.* **3**, 41–67.

Fischer-Piette, E. (1932). Sur la pénétration des diverses espèces marines sessiles dans les estuaries et sa limitation par l'eau douce. *Ann. Inst. océanogr. Monaco* **10**, 217–243.

Fischer-Piette, E. (1936). Études sur la biogéographie intercotidale des deux rives de la Manche. *J. Linn. Soc.* Zool. **40**, 181–272.

Fletcher, A. (1972a). A method for estimating the dry weights of crustaceous saxicolous lichens. *Lichenologist* **5**, 314–316.

Fletcher, A. (1972b). "The ecology of marine and maritime lichens of Anglesey". Ph.D. Thesis, University of Wales.

Fletcher, A. (1973a). The ecology of marine (littoral) lichens on some rocky shores of Anglesey. *Lichenologist* **5**, 368–400.

Fletcher, A. (1973b). The ecology of maritime (supralittoral) lichens on some rocky shores of Anglesey. *Lichenologist* **5**, 401–422.

Fletcher, A. (1975a). Key for the identification of British marine and maritime lichens. I. Siliceous rocky shore species. *Lichenologist* **7**, 1–52.

Fletcher, A. (1975b). Key for the identification of British marine and maritime lichens. II. Calcareous and terricolous species. *Lichenologist* **7**, 73–115.

Fletcher, A. (1976). Nutritional aspects of marine and maritime lichen ecology. *In* "Lichenology: Progress and Problems", (D. H. Brown, D. L. Hawksworth and R. H. Bailey, eds), pp. 359–384. Academic Press, London and New York.

Fletcher, A. and Jones, W. E. (eds), (1975). "The Second Report of the Coastal Surveillance Unit". Bangor. University College of North Wales.

Fry, E. J. (1927). The mechanical action of crustaceous lichens on substrata of shale, schist, gneiss, limestone and obsidian. *Ann. Bot.* **41**, 437–460.

Fujiwara, K. and Umejira, S. (1962). On the distribution of wind-borne salt on the coastal terrace. *Res. Bull. Coll. exp. Forests Hakkaido Univ.* **21**, 453–464.

Geiger, R. (1965). "The Climate near the Ground". University Press, Harvard.

Gerson, U. and Seaward, M. R. D. (1977). Lichen invertebrate associations. *In* "Lichen Ecology" (M. R. D. Seaward, ed.), pp. 69–119. Academic Press, London and New York.

Gilbert, O. L., Holligan, P. M. and Holligan, M. S. (1973). The flora of North Rona 1972. *Trans. Proc. bot. Soc. Edinb.* **42**, 43–68.
Gillham, M. E. (1954). An annotated list of the bryophytes and lichens of Skokholm island, Pembrokeshire. *N West. Nat.* **25**, 37–48.
Gillham, M. E. (1956). Ecology of the south Pembrokeshire Islands V. Manuring by the colonial seabirds and mammals, with a note on seed distribution by gulls. *J. Ecol.* **44**, 429–454.
Goldsmith, F. B. (1967). "Some aspects of the vegetation of sea cliffs". Ph.D. Thesis, University of Wales.
Grønlie, A. M. (1948). The ornithocoprophilous vegetation of the bird cliffs of Røst. in the Lofoten Islands, Northern Norway. *Nyt Mag. Naturvid.* **86**, 117–242.
Grubb, V. M. and Martin, M. T. (1937). The algal vegetation of a cave. *J. Bot., Lond.* **75**, 89–93.
Grummann, V. J. (1937). Vegetationsökologische Flechtenstudien an *Lichina confinis* und *Verrucaria maura* im Deutschen Kustengebeit von Hiddensee. *Beih. Bot. Zbl.* **61**, 353–408.
Hale, M. E. (1972). Natural History of Plummes Island, Maryland. XXI. Infestation of the lichen *Parmelia baltimorensis* Gyel. & For. by *Hypogastrura packardii* Folsom (Collembola). *Proc. biol. Soc. Wash.* **85**, 287–296.
Halem M. E. (1974). Growth. *In* "The Lichens" (V. Ahmadjian and M. E. Hale, eds), pp. 473–492. Academic Press, London and New York.
Hartley J. W. and Wheldon, J. A. (1927). Lichens of the Isle of Man. *N West. Nat,* **2**, *Suppl.*, 1–38.
Hawksworth, D. L. (1966). The lichen flora of Foula (Shetland). *Lichenologist* **3**, 218–223.
Hawksworth, D. L. (1976). Lichen chemotaxonomy. *In* "Lichenology: Progress and Problems" (D. H. Brown., D. L. Hawksworth and R. H. Bailey, eds), pp. 139–184. Academic Press, London and New York.
Hawksworth, D. L. and Rose, F. (1970). Qualitative scale for estimating sulphur dioxide air pollution in England and Wales using epiphytic lichens. *Nature, Lond.* **227**, 145–148.
Hawksworth, D. L., James, P. W. and Coppins, B. J. (1980). Checklist of British lichen-forming lichenicolous and allied Fungi. *Lichenologist* **12**, 1–115.
Hayren, E. (1914). Uber die landvegetation und flora der meeresfelsen von Tüarmine – Ein Beitrag zur Ehrforschung der Bedeutung des meeres fur die landpflanzen. *Acta Soc. Fauna Flora Fenn.* **39**, 1–193.
Henssen, A. (1969). Three non-marine species of the genus *Lichina. Lichenologist* **4**, 88–98.
Hill, D. J. and Woolhouse, H. W. (1966). Aspects of the autecology of *Xanthoria parietina* agg. *Lichenologist* **3**, 207–214.
Hitch, C. J. B. and Stewart, W. D. P. (1973). Nitrogen fixation by lichens in Scotland. *New Phytol.* **72**, 509–524.
Hughes, A. M. and Tilbrook, P. J. (1966). A new species of *Calvolia* (Acaridae, Acarina) from the S. Sandwich Islands. *Bull. Br. Antarct. Surv.* **10**, 45–53.
James, P. W. (1970). The lichen flora of shaded acid rock crevices and overhangs

in Britain. *Lichenologist* 4, 309–322.

James, P. W. (1973). The effects of air pollutants other than hydrogen fluoride and sulphur dioxide on lichens. *In* "Air Pollution and Lichens" (B. W. Ferry, M. S. Baddeley, and D. L. Hawksworth, eds), pp. 143–175. Athlone Press, London.

Jones, W. E. and Demetropoulos, A. (1968). Exposure to wave action: Measurement of an important ecological parameter on rocky shores on Anglesey. *J. exp. mar. Biol. Ecol.* 2, 46–63.

Jones, W. E. and Fletcher, A. (eds) (1976). "The Third Report of the Coastal Surveillance Unit". Bangor. University College of North Wales.

Jones, W. E., Fletcher, A., Bennell, S. J., McConnell, B. J., Richards, A. V. L. and Mack-Smith, S. (1979). Intertidal surveillance. *In* "Monitoring the Marine Environment" (D. Nichols, ed.), pp. 1–23. Institute of Biology, Symposium No. 24, London.

Kappen, L. (1974). Response to extreme environments. *In* "The Lichens" (V. Ahmadjian and M. E. Hale, eds), pp. 311–380. Academic Press, London and New York.

Kärenlampi, L. (1966). The succession of lichen vegetation in the rocky shore geolittoral and adjacent parts of the epilittoral in the south western archipelago of Finland. *Annls bot. Fenn.* 3, 79–85.

Klement, O. (1953). Die Flechtenflora der Insel Wangerooge. *Veröffentlich des Inst. fur Meeresforsch. in Bremerhaven* 2, 146–213.

Knellman, F., Dombrowski, N. and Newitt, D. M. (1954). Mechanism of the bursting of bubbles. *Nature, Lond.* **173**, 261.

Knowles, M. C. (1913). The maritime and marine lichens of Howth. *Scient. Proc. R. Dubl. Soc.* **14**, 79–143.

Kristinsson, H. (1972). Studies on lichen colonization in Surtsey 1970. *Surtsey Res. Prog. Rep.* 6, 77.

Lagerspetz, K. (1953). Biocoenological notes on the *Parmelia saxatilis – Dactylochelifer latreillei* community of seashore rocks. *Arch. Soc. Zool. Bot. Fenn. Vanamo.* 7, 131–142.

Lamb, I. M. (1973). Further observations on *Verrucaria serpuloides* M. Lamb. the only known permanently submerged marine lichen. *Occ. Pap. Farlow Herb. Crypt. Bot.* 6, 1–5.

Larsson, J. E. (1970). Cs^{137} in lichen communities on the Baltic coast. *Svensk. Bot. Tidskr.* **64**, 173–178.

Laundon, J. R. (1966). Hudson's *Lichen siliquosus* from Wiltshire. *Lichenologist* 3, 236–241.

Lewis, J. R. (1953). The ecology of rocky shores around Anglesey. *Proc. Zool. Soc. Lond.* **123**, 481–549.

Lewis, J. R. (1954). The ecology of exposed rocky shores of Caithness. *Trans. R. Soc. Edinb.* **62**, 695–723.

Lewis, J. R. (1964). "The Ecology of Rocky Shores". English University Press, London.

Lewis, J. R. (1965). The littoral fringe on rocky coasts of S. Norway and W. Sweden. *Bot. Goth.* 3, 129–143.

Lewis, J. R. and Powell, H. T. (1960). Aspects of the intertidal ecology of rocky shores in Argyll, Scotland I & II. *Trans. R. Soc. Edinb.* **64**, 45–100.

Lindsay, D. C. (1978). The role of lichens in Antarctic ecosystems. *Bryologist*, **81**, 268–276.

McLean, R. C. (1915). The ecology of the maritime lichens at Blakeney Point, Norfolk. *J. Ecol.* **3**, 128–148.

Madsen, H. (1940). A study of the littoral fauna of northwest Greenland. *Meddr. Grønland.* **124**, 1–24.

Massé, L. J. C. (1967). Flore et végétation licheniques des Iles Glénan (Finistère). *Rev. Bryol. Lichenol.* **34**, 854–927.

Morton, J. C. (1954). The crevice faunas of the upper intertidal zone at Wembury. *J. mar. biol. Ass. U.K.* **33**, 187–224.

Motyka, J. (1960). De speciebus quibusdam generis *Ramalinae* Ach. europaeis novis et minus cognitis. *Fragm. flor. geobot.* **6**, 637–644.

Naylor, G. L. (1930). Notes on the distribution of *Lichina confinis* and *L. pygmaea* in the Plymouth district. *J. mar. biol. Ass. U.K.* **16**, 909–918.

Nelson-Smith, A. (1965). Marine biology of Milford Haven: the physical environment. *Fld Stud.* **2**, 155–188.

Niebohr, E., Richardson, D. H. S. and Tomassini, F. D. (1978). Mineral uptake and release by lichens: an overview. *Bryologist* **81**, 226–246.

Nielson, C. O. (1963). Laminarases in soil and litter invertebrates. *Nature, Lond.* **199**, 1001.

Ramkaer, K. (1978). The influence of salinity on the establishing phase of rocky shore lichens. *Bot. Tidsskr.* **72**, 119–123.

Ranwell, D. S. (1966). The lichen flora of Bryher, Isles of Scilly, and its geographical components. *Lichenologist* **3**, 224–232.

Ranwell, D. S. (1968). Lichen mortality due to "Torrey Canyon" oil and decontamination measures. *Lichenologist* **4**, 55–56.

Rees, T. K. (1935). Marine algae of Lough Ine. *J. Ecol.* **23**, 69–133.

Reid, A. (1960a). Stoffwechsel und Verbreitungsgrenzen von Flechten II. Wasser-und assimilationshaushalt, Entquellungs-und Submersionsresistenz von Krustenflechten benachbarter Standorte. *Flora, Jena* **149**, 345–385.

Reid, A. (1960b). Thallusbau und Assimilationshaushalt von Laub und Krustenflechten. *Biol. Zbl.* **79**, 129–151.

Reid, A. (1960c). Nachwirkungen Entquellung auf den Gaswechsel von Krustenflechten. *Biol. Zbl.* **79**, 657–678.

Reid, A. (1969). Physiologische Aspekte der Vertikalzonierung von Algen der marinen Litorals. *Ber. dt. bot. Ges.* **82**, 127–141.

Richardson, D. H. S. (1967). The transplantation of lichen thalli to solve some taxonomic problems in *Xanthoria parietina*. *Lichenlogist* **3**, 386–391.

Richardson, D. H. S. (1975). "The Vanishing Lichens". David and Charles, Newton Abbot, London and Vancouver.

Robertson, E. T. and Gimingham, C. H. (1951). Contributions to the maritime ecology of St. Cyrus, Kincardineshire. Part I. The cliffs. *Trans. Proc. bot. Soc. Edinb.* **35**, 370–414.

Santesson, R. (1939). Amphibious pyrenolichens. *Ark. Bot.* **29A**, 1–67.

Scott, D. D. (1960). Studies on the lichen symbiosis I. Relationship between nutrition and moisture content in the maintenance of the symbiotic state. *New Phytol.* **59**, 374–381.

Seaward, M. R. D. (ed.) (1977). "Lichen Ecology". Academic Press, London and New York.

Servit, M. (1953). "Species novae Verrucariarum et generum affinium". *Rozpr. Čsl. Akad. Věd.* **63** (7), 1–11.

Sheard, J. W. (1965). *Lecanora* (sect. *Aspicilia*) *leprosescens* Sandst. new to the British Isles. *Lichenologist* **3**, 93–94.

Sheard, J. W. (1968). The zonation of lichens on three rocky shores of Inishowen, Co. Donegal. *Proc. R. Ir. Acad.* B. **66**, 101–112.

Sheard, J. W. (1978a). The taxonomy of the *Ramalina siliquosa* species aggregate (lichenised Ascomycetes). *Can. J. Bot.* **56**, 916–938.

Sheard, J. W. (1978b). The comparative ecology and distribution and within-species variation of the lichenised Ascomycetes *Ramalina cuspidata* and *R. siliquosa* in the British Isles. *Can. J. Bot.* **56**, 939–952.

Sheard, J. W. and Ferry, B. W. (1967). The lichen flora of the Isle of May. *Trans. Proc. bot. Soc. Edinb.* **40**, 268–282.

Sheard, J. W. and James, P. W. (1976). Typification of the taxa belonging to the *Ramalina siliquosa* species aggregate. *Lichenologist* **8**, 35–46.

Smith, A. L. (1921). "Lichens". Cambridge University Press, London and New York.

Smith, D. C. (1962). The biology of lichen thalli. *Biol. Rev.* **37**, 537–570.

Smith, J. E. (1968). ""Torrey Canyon", Pollution and Marine Life". Cambridge University Press, Cambridge.

Søchting, U. (1976). The *Ramalina siliquosa* aggregate on the Danish Island of Bornholm. *Bot. Tidsskr.* **71**, 87–94.

Southward, A. J. and Orton, J. H. (1954). The effects of wave-action on the distribution and numbers of the commoner plants and animals living on the Plymouth breakwater. *J. mar. biol. Ass. U.K.* **33**, 1–19.

Spear, M. A. (1974). "Inorganic cations in marine and maritime lichens". M.Sc. Thesis, University of Wales.

Stephenson, T. A. and Stephenson, A. (1972). "Life Between Tidemarks on Rocky Shores". W. H. Freeman, Reading.

Swinscow, T. D. V. (1965). Pyrenocarpous lichens: 8. The marine species of *Arthopyrenia* in the British Isles. *Lichenologist* **3**, 55–64.

Swinscow, T. D. V. (1968). Pyrenocarpous lichens: 13. Freshwater species of *Verrucaria* in the British Isles. *Lichenologist* **4**, 34–54.

Tilbrook, P. J. (1967). The terrestrial invertebrate fauna of the maritime Antarctic. *Phil. Trans. R. Soc.* B. **252**, 261–278.

Topham, P. B. (1977). Colonisation, growth, succession and competition. *In* "Lichen Ecology" (M. R. D. Seaward, ed.), pp. 31–68. Academic Press, London and New York.

Tschermak-Woess, E. (1976). Algal taxonomy and the taxonomy of lichens: the phycobiont of *Verrucaria adriatica. In* "Lichenology: Progress and Problems" (D. H. Brown, D. L. Hawksworth and R. H. Bailey, eds), pp. 79–

88. Academic Press, London and New York.

Tschermak-Woess, E. (1978). *Myrmecia reticulata* as a phycobiont and free-living *Trebouxia* – the problem of *Stenocybe septata*. *Lichenologist* **10**, 69–79.

Vevers, H. G. (1936). The land vegetation of Ailsa Craig. *J. Ecol.* **24**, 424–445.

Wade, A. E. (1961). The genus *Ramalina* in the British Isles. *Lichenologist* **1**, 226–241.

Waisel, Y. (1972). "The Biology of Halophytes". Academic Press, London and New York.

Wheldon, J. A. and Travis, W. G. (1913). Lichens of Arran (VC: 100). *J. Bot., Lond.* **51**, 248–253.

Wieser, W. (1963). Adaptations of two intertidal isopods II. Comparison between *Campecopea hirsuta* and *Naesa bidentata* (Sphaeromatidae). *J. mar. biol. Ass. U.K.* **43**, 97–112.

13 The Algal Communities on Floating Structures in Portsmouth and Langstone Harbours (South Coast of England)

R. L. FLETCHER

Department of Biological Sciences, Portsmouth Polytechnic Marine Laboratory, Hayling Island, England

Abstract: Some observations are presented on the structure of marine algal communities attached to the sides of floating structures (pontoons/rafts) situated in Langstone and Portsmouth Harbours, south coast of England, during the period February/March 1979. Two fairly distinct communities are present, a lower, permanently-immersed community and an upper, wave-washed community. The flora of the permanently-immersed regions of the floats is essentially subtidal in composition and is dominated by the large brown algae *Laminaria digitata*, *L. saccharina* and, to a lesser extent *Sargassum muticum*, with a sub-vegetation of brown algae such as *Desmarestia viridis*, green algae such as *Bryopsis plumosa, Cladophora* sp., *Codium fragile* ssp. *tomentosoides, Derbesia* sp. and *Ulva lactuca* and various red algae, in particular *Ceramium rubrum*, *Chondrus crispus*, *Gracilaria verrucosa*, *Griffithsia* spp., *Nitophyllum punctatum* and *Polysiphonia* spp. The flora of the upper wave-washed regions, on the other hand, is more intertidal and supralittoral in composition; it is dominated by green algae, both bladed genera such as *Blidingia* and *Enteromorpha* and filamentous genera such as *Chaetomorpha*, *Cladophora*, *Percursaria*, *Rhizoclonium*, *Ulothrix* and *Urospora*. Only a few brown algae, such as *Petalonia* and *Scytosiphon*, and red algae, such as *Bangia* and *Porphyra*, are present. The wave-washed community is also usually vertically distributed within a number of

Systematics Association Special Volume No. 17(b), "The Shore Environment, Vol. 2: Ecosystems", edited by J. H. Price, D. E. G. Irvine and W. F. Farnham, 1980, pp. 843–874, Academic Press, London and New York.

distinct belts, these approximately corresponding to an upper region dominated by small coccoid and filamentous green algae such as *Ulothrix* and *Urospora*, a mid-region dominated by the green bladed genera *Blidingia* and *Enteromorpha* (with various amounts of the brown algae *Ectocarpus, Petalonia* and *Scytosiphon*), and a lower mixed community of brown algae (particularly *Ectocarpus*, *Giffordia granulosa* and *Petalonia*), green algae (particularly *Cladophora*, *Derbesia* and *Ulva*) and red algae (particularly *Callithamnion*, *Ceramium* and *Chondrus*). Both the composition and vertical extent of the algal communities above the water line are greatly determined by the degree of exposure to wave action/water movement. In the permanently-immersed regions, with increased exposure *L. digitata* replaces *L. saccharina* and a sparse underflora of red algae (*Ceramium rubrum*, *Chondrus crispus* and *Polysiphonia*) replaces the more luxuriant mixed community of green algae (*Bryopsis*, *Chaetomorpha*, *Cladophora* and *Derbesia*) and red algae (*Antithamnion plumula*, *Griffithsia corallinoides* and *Nitophyllum punctatum*) present under the sheltered conditions. In the wave-washed regions, green algae such as *Cladophora*, *Derbesia*, *Percursaria*, *Rhizoclonium* and *Ulothrix* supplement the *Blidingia* and *Enteromorpha* spp. (principally *E. intestinalis* and *E. prolifera*) present under sheltered conditions, while in the localities more directly exposed to wave-beat the latter species are associated with *Ulothrix flacca*, *Ulva lactuca* and *Urospora penicilliformis*, and quite abundant amounts of *Enteromorpha linza*. Increased exposure not only raises various brown algae (such as *Ectocarpus siliculosus*, *Giffordia granulosa*, *Petalonia fascia*, *Pilayella littoralis* and *Scytosiphon lomentaria*) and red algae (such as *Ceramium rubrum*, *Chondrus crispus* and *Polysiphonia brodiaei*) above the water line but appears essential for colonization by *Bangia atropurpurea*, *Petalonia zosterifolia* and *Porphyra umbilicalis*. These observations on artificial floating structures are discussed in relation to a natural shore environment.

INTRODUCTION

Very few studies have been conducted around the British Isles on the marine algal fouling communities attached to the sides of floating structures. The marine algae of buoys was recorded by Grieve and Robertson (1864), Orton (1930), Fraser (1938), Milne (1940) and Lodge (1949), while Orton (1930) and Tittley and Price (1977, 1978) referred to algae collected on pontoons. Investigations of algae colonizing ships' hulls have been even more infrequent (see Orton, 1930; Harris, 1943, 1946; Christie, 1973), although their often dominant occurrence on some vessels, such as supertankers and container ships, causes quite severe economic problems due to the increased drag effect which is exerted. Probably more information on the biology of algal fouling communities on floating structures has been derived from programmes of test panel immersion; the use of non-toxic control panels suspended from rafts to monitor settlement periods of organisms is now common procedure during the field-testing of antifouling paints (see Fletcher and Chamberlain, 1975). Identification of algae on test panels immersed near the waterline has been made by Orton (1930), Harris (1946), Hendey (1951), Stubbings and Houghton (1964), Anon. (1966), Fletcher (1974) and Fry (1975).

The present chapter is concerned with a preliminary survey of the composition and stratification of algal fouling communities attached to the vertical sides of various pontoons and rafts situated in the two adjacent, fully marine harbours of Portsmouth and Langstone (south coast of England). Particular emphasis has been placed on determining the influence of exposure to wave and current action on the algal populations. Floating structures can sometimes extend the distributional limits of algae where suitable natural substrata are unavailable (Milne, 1940; Tittley and Price, 1977); they were used in the present study as a convenient experimental system to examine the algal community on hard substrata in the two harbours and to provide base-line data for monitoring possible pollution effects, especially oil spillage. Such a study also provides valuable information on the locally dominant fouling organisms in these commercially important waters.

PHYSICAL ENVIRONMENT

Langstone and Portsmouth Harbours are two of three fully marine interconnecting natural harbour systems situated in the north-east Solent region (Fig. 1a). Both harbours are shallow, the water depths not exceeding 10 m, and each is almost land-locked, with a narrow channel connecting its southern part with the Solent waters. The intertidal zones are composed predominantly of mudflats and sands, which support a considerable diatom flora (see Hendey, 1951 for Chichester Harbour studies) together with seasonal growths of the thalloid green algae *Enteromorpha* and *Ulva*. The only hard substrata available for algal colonization are the extensive dockyard installations (for example, harbour walls, embankments, pilings) found in Portsmouth Harbour and to a much lesser extent in Langstone Harbour; these occasionally also give way at the base to areas of small stones and pebbles. The vertical sides of these installations

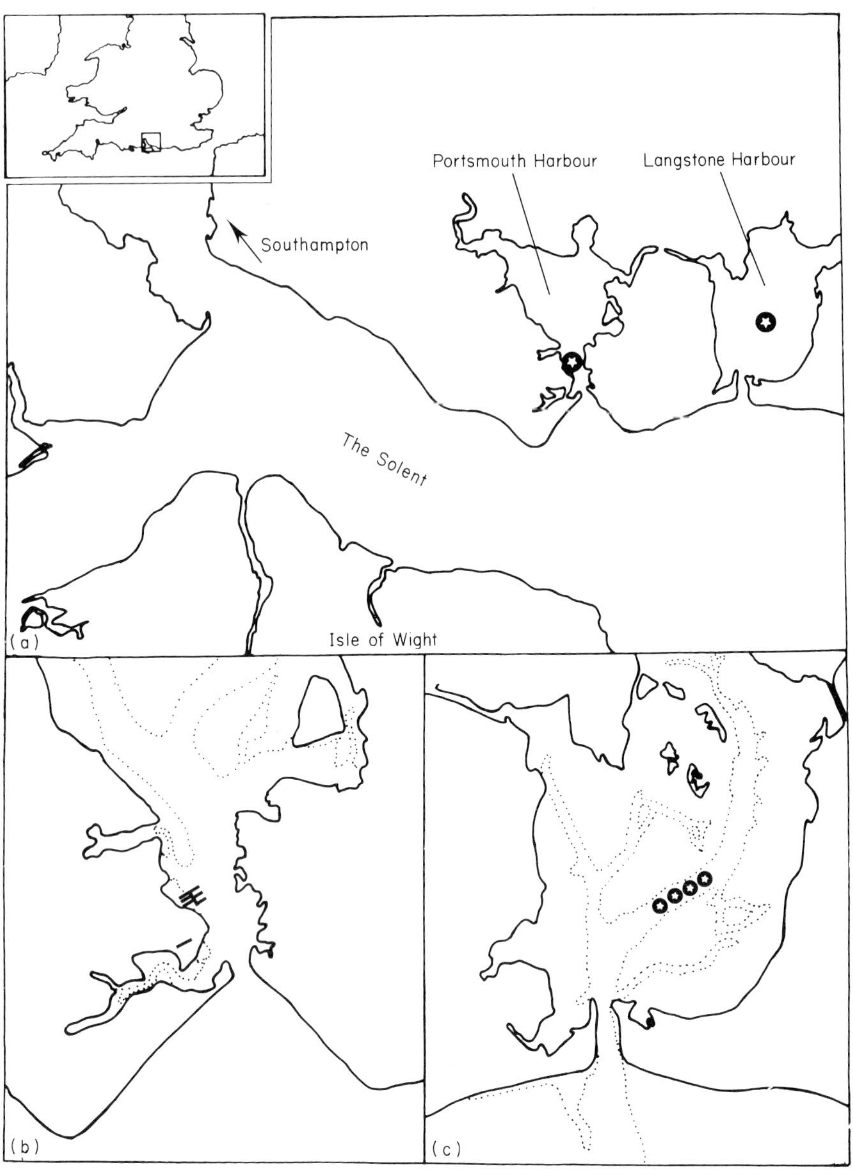

Fig. 1a–c. Maps showing the location and topography of the study sites: (a) Solent Region; (b) Gosport Marina in Portsmouth Harbour; (c) rafts in Langstone Harbour.

support a distinctly-zoned algal community. The upper littoral is mainly dominated by green algae such as *Blidingia*, *Enteromorpha* and *Ulothrix*, with occasionally the red alga *Porphyra*. The mid and lower littoral are dominated by fucoids such as *Fucus serratus*,* *F. spiralis* and *F. vesiculosus*, with an underflora of algae such as *Chaetomorpha linum*, *Ectocarpus siliculosus*, *Enteromorpha linza*, *Pilayella littoralis*, *Polysiphonia spiralis*, *P. urceolata* and *Ulva lactuca*. The dominant sublittoral algae are *Laminaria digitata* and *L. saccharina*, with some *Sargassum muticum* and a largely mixed association of red algae such as *Gracilaria*, *Griffithsia* spp. and *Nitophyllum*. The small stones in the lower intertidal regions are usually quite rich in crustose brown algae such as *Petroderma*, *Pseudolithoderma* and *Ralfsia*; the brown thalloid genera *Petalonia* and *Scytosiphon* are often additionally associated with stones in shallow pools.

The floating structures investigated in Portsmouth Harbour consisted of an interconnecting system of pontoons forming the Gosport Marina (Fig. 1b, Fig. 2a). Some of these extended directly north-eastward from a concrete wall in the relatively narrow south-west region of the harbour, just inside the entrance. The pontoons were supported at intervals by buoyant "floats", consisting of concrete-covered blocks of polystyrene partly immersed in the water (Fig. 2b). The floats supporting the outer pontoons were subjected to much more wave-wash from tidal currents and water movement from passing ships than those situated in the inner regions of the marina. Studies were carried out on the marine algal flora that had developed after 3 to 4 years' immersion on the north-east facing sides of unshaded "end" floats situated in both the exposed and sheltered regions of the marina.

The floating structures in Langstone Harbour consisted of the Ministry of Defence paint-testing rafts, immersed for $3\frac{1}{2}$ years in one of the main central drainage channels to a minimum depth of approximately 4 m of running water (Fig. 1c). The rafts were 19 m long by 7 m wide, constructed of metal tanks with two main central basins into which the test panel frames are immersed (Fig. 2c, d). As the metal rafts had a single mooring, they were not permanently set on any fixed bearing but turned with the tide continually to face the

---

*Nomenclature and authorities follow those employed in Parke and Dixon (1976).

Fig. 2. (a–b) Gosport marina pontoons with support floats.
(c–d) Outer and inner regions of Admiralty Paint Trial Raft.

current. This provided a suitable range of variously exposed vertical sides available for algal colonization, including the inner very sheltered walls, the outer sheltered stern, the more exposed outer mid region and the very exposed outer bow region.

Hydrologically the two harbours show very similar characteristics. They are approximately equal in size (Langstone 19.4 km^2). Both are shallow, with tidal ranges varying between 1.5 m (neaps) and 4.5 m (springs), and have quite rapid tidal streams; Houghton (1959), for example, recorded current speeds, reversing with the tide, ranging from 2.59 km/h (neaps) to 4.64 km/h (springs) in Langstone Harbour. The salinity of the waters, usually 32–34 $^0/_{00}$, is normal for the south coast of England and there is negligible freshwater influx; occasional readings of 29–30 $^0/_{00}$ have, however, been recorded after heavy rain. Sea-surface water temperatures show considerable seasonal variation; readings from Langstone Harbour since 1974 reveal mean monthly values (Table I) ranging from 2°C (February 1979) to 20.2°C (August 1975). Industrial pollution is very light in both harbours although the water transparency is rather poor, not exceeding 1–3 m. Langstone Harbour receives a daily discharge of approximately 40 000 m^3 of sewage effluent.

METHODS

General collections of fouling algae were made from the vertical sides of the floating structures, including both the wave-washed

Table I. Surface seawater temperatures, Langstone Harbour – monthly averages

	1974	1975	1976	1977	1978	1979	Averages April 1974–1979
January		7.0	6.2	4.5	5.3	2.6	5.1
February		5.8	4.3	6.0	3.5	2.0	4.3
March		5.6	5.4	7.5	6.0	4.2	5.7
April	9.7	7.8	8.3	8.5	7.7		8.4
May	12.0	11.0	12.2	12.0	11.8		11.8
June	15.3	15.9	17.3	14.5	15.6		15.7
July	16.5	18.4	20.1	18.0	16.4		17.9
August	17.5	20.2	20.0	18.3	17.7		18.7
September	13.9	16.2	16.6	15.9	16.5		15.8
October	10.2	12.1	14.0	14.0	13.3		12.7
November	8.2	8.5	9.5	9.8	11.0		9.4
December	7.6	5.8	6.0	7.0	6.3		6.5

region above the waterline and the permanently submerged region, during the period late February/early March 1979. Samples were taken on extremely calm days, to enable accurate determination of the true waterline, and from a range of variously exposed sites. Some identification of the samples was carried out in the field, although most of the material was subsequently determined in fresh state in the laboratory. Continuous belt transect techniques were used at some sites to assess vertical stratification of the algae in the wave-washed regions; samples of size 1 cm^2 were removed, commencing from the upper visible limits of the fouling community and extending down to the waterline. Five vertical transects spaced 1 cm apart were usually taken at each site; a collective assessment, based on the scale abundant, common, present, rare, was then made of the abundances of all the species recorded for each 1 cm level above the waterline.

Repli dishes, 10 x 10 cm square and holding 25 compartments, proved particularly useful for collection and storage of the 1 cm square samples prior to determination. At least one, but more usually two, sample sites were investigated for each category of "exposure" studied.

RESULTS

1. *Gosport Marina*

A total of 16 species of Chlorophyta, 9 species of Phaeophyta and 19 species of Rhodophyta was recorded for the Gosport marina (Table II). Some differences observed in the vegetation of the sheltered and exposed regions of the marina are treated separately.

(a) The flora of the outer exposed floats. The fouling community on the upper wave-washed sides of the outer exposed floats was characterized by a prominent zone of green algae which extended from 7–10(–22) cm above the waterline; this was stratified into a number of horizontal belts (Figs 3 and 4). Macroscopic algae dominated the lower 7–8(–15) cm belt, whereas higher up the sides were coated with a green coloured scum comprising various small microscopic green algae of dubious taxonomic identity. These included variously sized *Protococcus*-like algae, some small branched filamentous algae and considerable quantities of attached reproductive spore cells, similar

Table II. Species recorded for Gosport Marina and Langstone Rafts

Chlorophyta	G.M.	L.R.	Phaeophyta	G.M.	L.R.	Rhodophyta	G.M.	L.R.
Blidingia spp.	+	+	*Desmarestia viridis*	+	+	*Antithamnion plumula*	+	
Bryopsis plumosa	+	+	*Ectocarpus siliculosus*	+	+	*Bangia atropurpurea*	+	+
Chaetomorpha linum	+	+	*Fucus* sp.		+	*Callithamnion hookeri*	+	
Cladophora sp.	+	+	*Giffordia granulosa*	+	+	*Callithamnion roseum*	+	
Codium fragile subsp.	+	+	*Laminaria digitata*	+		*Callithamnion tetragonum*	+	+
tomentosoides			*Laminaria saccharina*	+	+	*Callophyllis laciniata*	+	+
Derbesia sp.	+		*Petalonia fascia*	+	+	*Ceramium rubrum*	+	+
Enteromorpha flexuosa	+		*Petalonia zosterifolia*		+	*Chondrus crispus*	+	+
Enteromorpha intestinalis	+	+	*Pilayella littoralis*	+	+	*Cystoclonium purpureum*	+	+
Enteromorpha linza	+	+	*Sargassum muticum*	+	+	*Gracilaria verrucosa*	+	
Enteromorpha prolifera	+	+	*Scytosiphon lomentaria*	+	+	*Grateloupia doryphora*	+	+
Percursaria percursa	+		*Sphacelaria* sp.		+	*Griffithsia corallinoides*	+	+
Rhizoclonium riparium	+	+				*Griffithsia flosculosa*	+	+
Ulothrix flacca	+	+	No. recorded	9	11	*Nitophyllum punctatum*	+	+
Ulothrix pseudoflacca	+	+				*Polysiphonia brodiaei*		+
Ulva lactuca	+	+				*Polysiphonia elongata*	+	
Urospora pencilliformis	+	+				*Polysiphonia nigrescens*	+	+
No. recorded	16	13				*Polysiphonia urceolata*	+	+
						Polysiphonia sp.	+	+
						Porphyra umbilicalis		+
						Porphyra sp.	+	
						Porphyridium purpureum		+
Total no. of species recorded:			Gosport Marina	44				
			Langstone Rafts	40		No. recorded	19	16

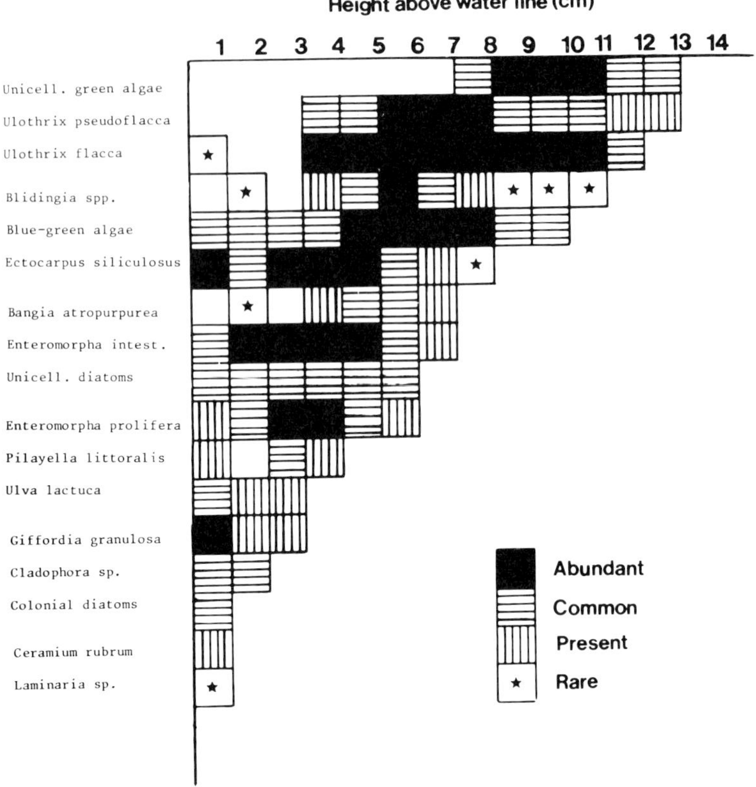

Fig. 3. Gosport Marina. Vertical distribution of marine algae. Outer region, Transect 1. See text for further explanation.

to those of the green genera *Urospora* and *Ulothrix*. *Ulothrix* usually formed the silky community lying immediately below this green scum. The vertical range of this belt varied considerably but reached up to 6–8 cm on occasions, depending upon the degree of exposure; however, the two main constituents, *U. flacca* and *U. pseudoflacca*, were certainly not confined to this upper level but sometimes occurred, often in quite great abundance, almost down to the waterline.

Immediately below the *Ulothrix* community, or sometimes directly below the green scum, was a light green belt of *Blidingia* spp., predominantly *B. minima* with some material resembling *B. marginata* in the upper levels (but see Parke and Dixon, 1976, p. 569, note 40).

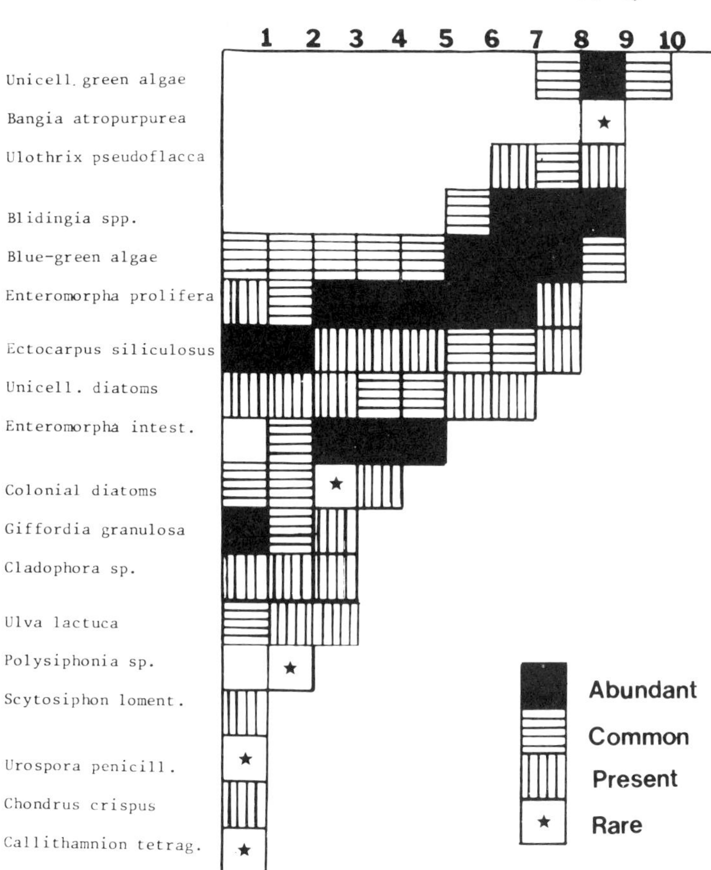

Fig. 4. Gosport Marina. Vertical distribution of marine algae. Outer region, Transect 2. See text for further explanation.

Blidingia was also not restricted to these upper regions but could extend right down to the waterline. Occasional filaments of the red algal genus *Bangia* were found interspersed amongst both the *Blidingia* and *Ulothrix* filaments.

Below the *Blidingia* belt, species of the genus *Enteromorpha* became particularly prevalent, usually producing dark green cover over the surface right down to the waterline. The principal species present was *E. prolifera*, with variable amounts of *E. intestinalis* and

E. flexuosa, although *E. linza* could sometimes be found at the waterline. Sometimes intermixed with *Enteromorpha*, occasionally becoming dominant at a slightly lower level, were filaments of the brown alga *Ectocarpus siliculosus*, although immediately above the waterline *Giffordia granulosa* became particularly abundant. Additional species, occasionally found at this level just above the waterline, included the brown algae *Giffordia sandriana*, *Petalonia fascia*, *Pilayella littoralis*, *Scytosiphon lomentaria* and young *Laminaria* plants, the green algae *Cladophora* sp. and *Ulva lactuca*, and the red algae *Callithamnion tetragonum*, *Ceramium rubrum*, *Chondrus crispus* and *Polysiphonia* sp. In the smaller size-range, both blue-green algae and diatoms contributed quite significantly to the under-flora on the wave-washed regions of the floats. Blue-green algae usually occupied the greatest vertical amplitude, extending from the waterline into the green scum and *Ulothrix* belts; unicellular diatoms were less extensive in their distribution, occurring from the waterline up to approximately the *Blidingia* belt; colonial diatoms were usually restricted to, or just above, the waterline level only.

Below the waterline, in the permanently-submerged zone, the float sides were dominated by *Laminaria* spp. On the outer wave-buffeted floats, large typical *L. digitata* plants were present; however, these were replaced by *L. saccharina* plants with increased shelter or on newly immersed floats (i.e. after approximately one year). Beneath the *Laminaria* canopy, the float sides were largely colonized by fouling animals, in particular encrusting bryozoans and compound ascidians, with only a sporadic occurrence of large red algae such as *Griffithsia flosculosa, Polysiphonia elongata, P. nigrescens* and, in slightly more sheltered regions, the brown alga *Desmarestia viridis*. A prominent zone of algae did, however, occur in the region just below the waterline, in particular red algae such as *Callithamnion tetragonum*, *Ceramium rubrum*, *Chondrus crispus* and to a lesser extent *Gracilaria verrucosa* and *Grateloupia doryphora*, with some of the green alga *Ulva lactuca*.

(b) The flora of the inner sheltered floats. On the sides of the inner sheltered floats, the wave-washed algal community, although present, was much reduced in area, usually extending only 2–5 cm above the waterline with no pronounced zonation of species evident (Figs 5 and 6). Unicellular green algae were usually detectable as a

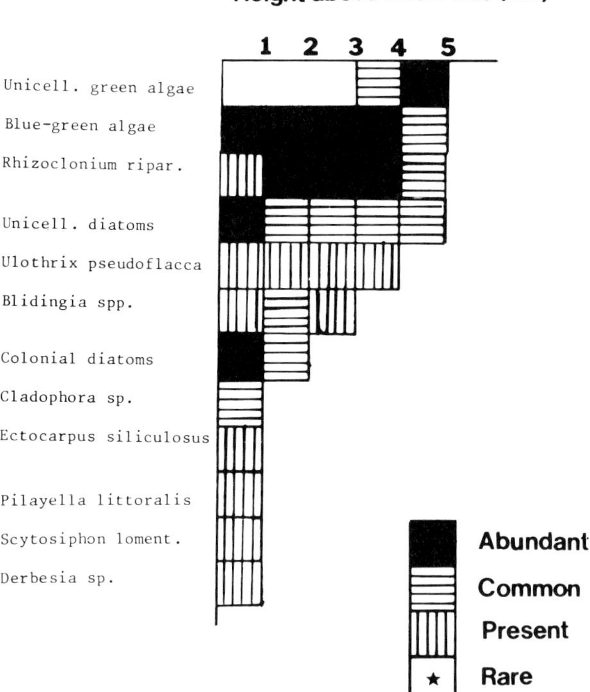

Fig. 5. Gosport Marina. Vertical distribution of marine algae. Inner region, Transect 1. See text for further explanation.

small uppermost belt, below which in the mid and upper levels of the fouling community either *Ulothrix* spp. (*U. flacca*, *U. pseudoflacca*, *U. subflaccida*) or, in particular, *Rhizoclonium riparium* and *Blidingia minima* were dominant. These three genera also commonly extended down to the waterline, although at this level and just above, much greater numbers of algae were present. These commonly included *Enteromorpha prolifera*, which could be quite abundant, *Ectocarpus siliculosus*, *Cladophora* sp. and variable amounts of *Chaetomorpha linum*, *Derbesia* sp., *Percursaria percursa* and *Pilayella littoralis*. Beneath the canopy of all the above species, unicellular diatoms and blue-green algae were quite common, although colonial diatoms tended to be restricted to the waterline level.

Below the waterline, the float sides supported a fairly low-lying association of algae which were secondary foulers on an encrusting

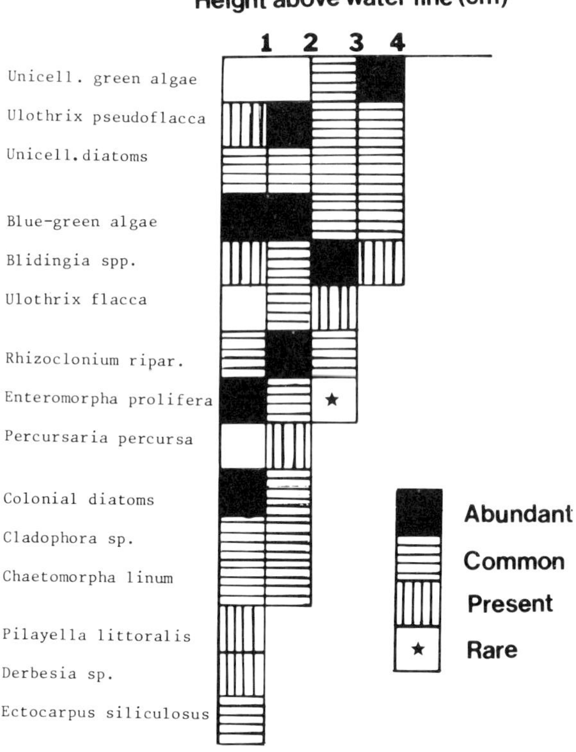

Fig. 6. Gosport Marina. Vertical distribution of marine algae. Inner region, Transect 2. See text for further explanation.

animal community of barnacles, tubeworms and numerous large slipper limpets, *Crepidula fornicata* (L.); only occasional large plants of heavily-epiphytized *Laminaria saccharina* were present with (more rarely) oval-shaped non-digitate blades of *L. digitata*. The dominant algae on the float sides, especially in the lower levels, were colonial diatoms, whilst at the waterline level many more species were to be found. Green algae were particularly common, especially *Cladophora* and *Derbesia* spp., although others frequently identified included *Bryopsis plumosa*, *Chaetomorpha linum*, *Codium fragile* var. *tomentosoides*, *Enteromorpha prolifera* and *Rhizoclonium riparium*. Not uncommon were red algae such as *Antithamnion plumula*, *Ceramium rubrum*, *Griffithsia corallinoides*, *Polysiphonia*

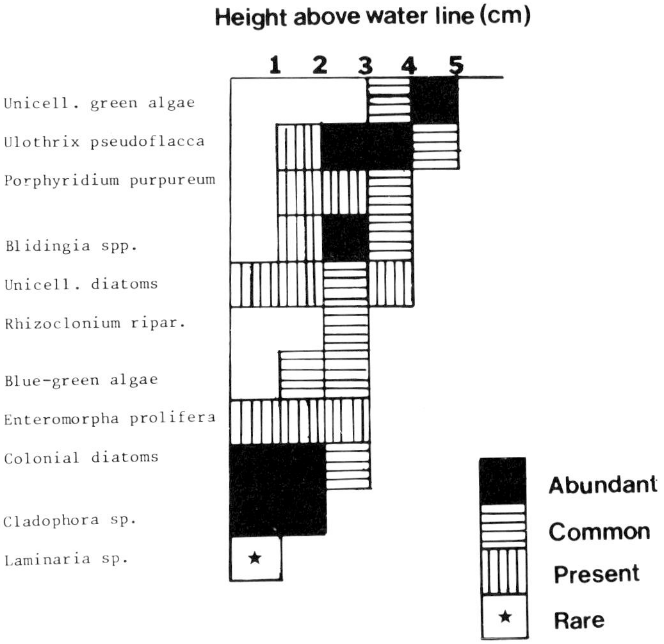

Fig. 7. Langstone rafts. Vertical distribution of marine algae. Inner region, Transect 1. See text for further explanation.

nigrescens and *P. urceolata*, with rare occurrences of *Cystoclonium purpureum*, *Gracilaria verrucosa* and *Nitophyllum punctatum*. Amongst the smaller brown algae, however, only *Giffordia granulosa* was quite commonly detected.

2. Langstone Rafts

A total of 13 species of Chlorophyta, 11 species of Phaeophyta and 16 species of Rhodophyta was recorded for the Langstone Rafts (Table I). Descriptions of the fouling algal communities on the variously exposed walls of the rafts are presented separately.

(a) The flora of the inner sheltered raft walls. The algal fouling community on the wave-washed regions of the inner raft walls was very similar in both vertical amplitude and floristic composition to that recorded on the inner sheltered floats of the Gosport Marina (Figs 7

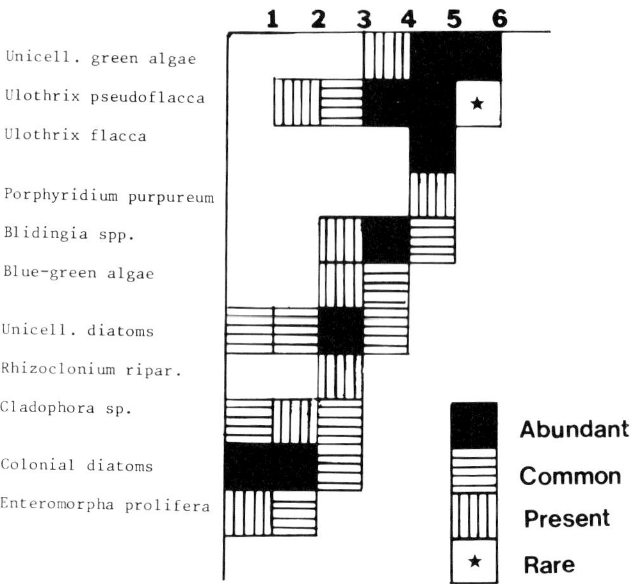

Fig. 8. Langstone rafts. Vertical distribution of marine algae. Inner region, Transect 2. See text for further explanation.

and 8). Growths of algae only extended 5–6 cm above the waterline and were predominantly comprised of species of Chlorophyta. A dark green scum-like growth of unicellular green algae occupied the upper 1–3 cm belt, below which occurred a 2–3 cm light green belt dominated by *Ulothrix* spp. (principally *U. pseudoflacca* with some *U. flacca*), with quite abundant *Blidingia minima* in its lower levels. Commonly associated with the *Ulothrix* spp. was the unicellular red alga *Porphyridium purpureum*. Both *Ulothrix* and *Blidingia* extended down to the waterline, although in the lower 2–3 cm other green algae such as *Cladophora* sp., *Enteromorpha prolifera* and to a lesser extent *Rhizoclonium riparium* were present, usually with quite considerable muddy deposits. At the waterline level, additional algae, including young *Laminaria saccharina* plants, *Polysiphonia* sp., *Sphacelaria* sp. and *Ulva lactuca*, with particularly abundant growths of colonial diatoms, were recorded. As for the previous site, both unicellular diatoms and blue-green algae were common constituents of the underflora in the upper wave-washed regions.

Below the waterline, the fouling community was largely dominated by animals, particularly solitary and compound ascidians, hydroids and tube-building amphipods, although colonial diatom growths were also very abundant. The most conspicuous macroalga present was *Laminaria saccharina*, usually as either large scattered plants or as localized dense stands of young plants; *Sargassum muticum* was not uncommon. Other algae occasionally recorded, particularly near the waterline, were *Bryopsis plumosa*, *Callophyllis laciniata*, *Ceramium rubrum*, *Codium fragile* ssp. *tomentosoides*, *Griffithsia flosculosa*, *Nitophyllum punctatum*, *Polysiphonia brodiaei* and *Ulva lactuca*.

(b) The flora of the outer sheltered raft walls. At the stern of the rafts, algal growths extended approximately 7–8 cm above the waterline (Figs 9 and 10). This increased to approximately 10 cm in small localized areas where paint loss had occurred, leaving a more roughened surface. Unicellular green algae again occupied the highest levels of the wave-washed community, immediately above a quite extensive and dense association of green filamentous algae, principally *Urospora penicilliformis*, with some *Ulothrix flacca* and *U. pseudoflacca*. This *Urospora*-dominated association remained particularly abundant throughout the upper and mid-levels, and not uncommonly extended right down to the waterline. In the mid-levels, however, it usually became subordinate to a well-developed *Blidingia minima* community, whilst slightly further down *Enteromorpha prolifera* thalli predominated. Just above the waterline, the *Enteromorpha prolifera* community was less evident and was largely replaced by a mixed association of *Enteromorpha linza*, *Ectocarpus siliculosus* and colonial diatoms, mingled with variable amounts of *Ceramium rubrum*, *Cladophora* sp., *Petalonia fascia* and *Ulva lactuca*. Below the waterline, scattered *Laminaria saccharina* and *Sargassum muticum* plants occurred down the side with the underflora of red algae such as *Ceramium rubrum*, *Chondrus crispus* and *Cystoclonium purpureum* largely occupying the upper more illuminated levels.

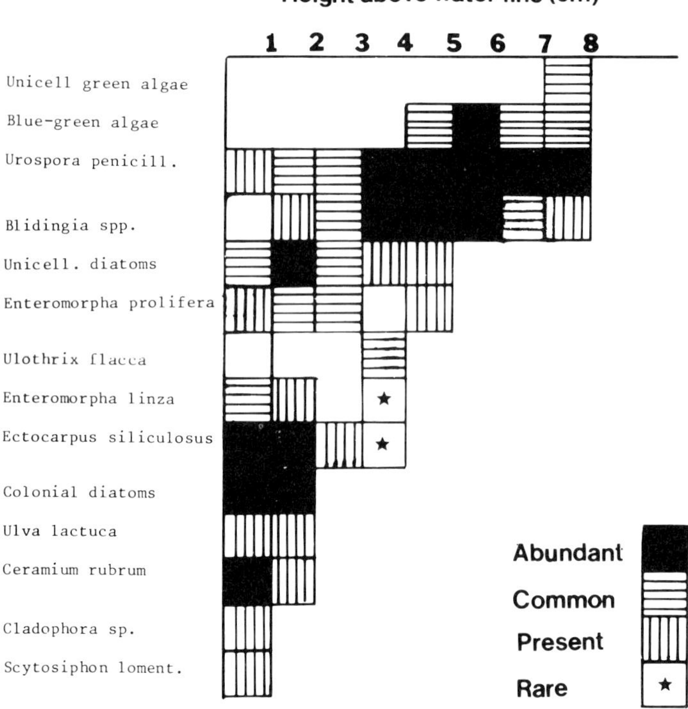

Fig. 9. Langstone rafts. Vertical distribution of marine algae. Outer sheltered region. See text for further explanation.

(c) The flora of the outer mid-region raft walls. The slightly more exposed mid-region of the rafts supported a wave-washed algal community which extended approximately 16–20 cm in height above the waterline, although the floristic composition and basic zonation pattern remained essentially similar to that of the sheltered end (Figs 11 and 12). From the top downwards there was an upper unicellular green algal belt which was successively replaced by a silky, dark green, community of filamentous green algae; this consisted principally of *Urospora penicilliformis* but with localized, sometimes abundant, patches of *Ulothrix flacca*, *U. pseudoflacca* and the red alga *Bangia atropurpurea*. This association extended right down to the mid-level, where it gradually became subordinate

Fig. 10. Langstone rafts. Outer sheltered region. Note large *S. muticum* plant.

to a light green belt formed by a *Blidingia minima* community mixed with quantities of *Enteromorpha prolifera*. Occasional plants of *Fucus ?spiralis* and *Petalonia zosterifolia* were also present at this level. Below the *Blidingia*-dominated belt, the dark green, thalloid blades of *Enteromorpha linza* draped down the sides to the waterline, where they floated out forming a peripheral "skirt" of vegetation. Commonly associated with *E. linza* in the lower 4–7 cm belt were light brown tufts of the brown ectocarpoid alga *Ectocarpus siliculosus*, with scattered occurrences of *Cladophora* sp., *Petalonia fascia*, *P. zosterifolia* and *Scytosiphon lomentaria*. Common waterline species included *Callithamnion hookeri*, *C. tetragonum*, *Chaetomorpha linum*, *Giffordia granulosa*, *Grateloupia doryphora*, *Pilayella littoralis*, *Polysiphonia brodiaei*, *P. urceolata* and *Ulva lactuca*.

(d) The flora of the outer exposed raft walls. The extremely exposed conditions present at the bows of the rafts caused the algal community to extend up to 40–42 cm above the waterline (Figs 13

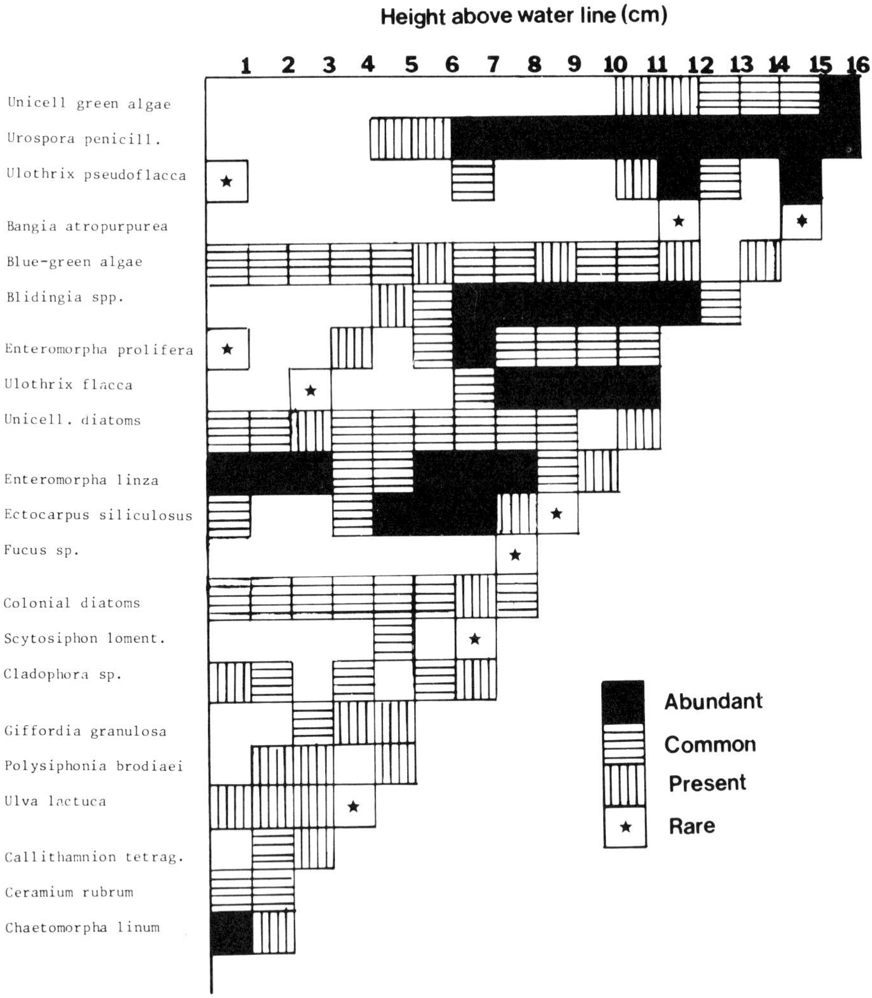

Fig. 11. Langstone rafts. Vertical distribution of marine algae. Outer mid-region. See text for further explanation.

and 14). At the highest levels, the dominant alga was *Urospora penicilliformis*, with usually a subvegetation composed predominantly of unicellular green algae. This association usually extended to approximately half way down the sides of the rafts, a vertical distance of approximately 20 cm, often with few other algae present.

Fig. 12. Langstone rafts. Outer mid-region.

Not uncommonly found in the lower mid-levels, however, were quite dense patches of *Bangia atropurpurea*, with the occasional thallus of *Porphyra umbilicalis*. Although *Urospora penicilliformis* quite commonly extended throughout the lower half of the wave-washed community, a much more diverse flora could be found there, many of the species being zoned. Just below the co-dominant *Urospora*/*Bangia* association in the mid-levels an extensive *Blidingia*-dominated zone appeared and remained conspicuous down to approximately 6–8 cm above the waterline. The subvegetation was quite well-developed and included thalli of *Ectocarpus siliculosus*, *Enteromorpha linza*, *E. prolifera*, *Petalonia zosterifolia*, *Porphyra umbilicalis*, *Ulothrix flacca* and *U. pseudoflacca*. Just above the waterline, some of these species, in particular *E. linza*, *E. siliculosus* and to a lesser extent *P. zosterifolia*, assumed a much more dominant role and the *Blidingia* spp. were present only as a subvegetation along with some *E. prolifera*, *Scytosiphon lomentaria* and *Ulothrix* spp. Although some of these, especially *E. linza* and *E. siliculosus*,

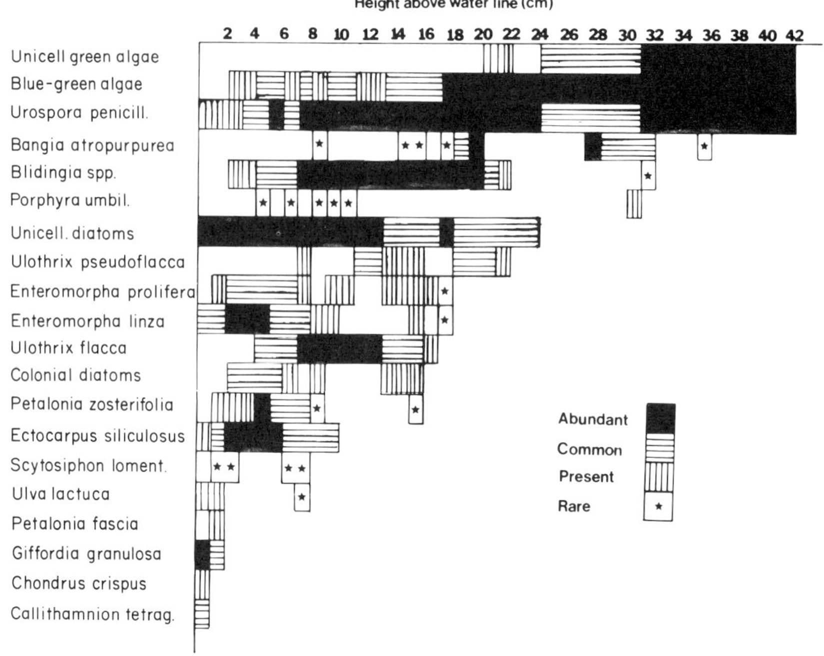

Fig. 13. Langstone rafts. Vertical distribution of marine algae. Outer exposed region. See text for further explanation.

extended right down to the waterline, this level usually supported a number of additional species; these included in particular *Giffordia granulosa*, with *Callithamnion tetragonum*, *Chondrus crispus*, *Petalonia fascia*, *Scytosiphon lomentaria* and *Ulva lactuca*.

The distribution of the diatoms and blue-green algae over the wave-washed levels of both the mid- and exposed raft sides was similar to that of the sheltered side; blue-green algae commonly extended over the whole vertical range, unicellular diatoms were present over two-thirds of the surface and colonial diatoms were largely confined to the level of the lower third. The macroalgal community below the waterline was also similar to that of the sheltered region, with scattered *Laminaria saccharina* plants and varous red algae, in particular species of the genus *Polysiphonia*.

Fig. 14. Langstone rafts. Outer exposed region.

DISCUSSION

The environment provided by floating structures for marine colonizing organisms is unique and certainly differs quite markedly from that of a North Atlantic shore. Probably the most significant environmental aspect of floating structures is that they are not influenced by tidal rhythms; attached organisms therefore are not subjected to the numerous stresses associated with an intertidal shore existence. Organisms are not, for instance, exposed to severe wave action, as waves do not "break" on the surface, whilst continuous immersion prevents problems of desiccation, and temperature and salinity fluctuations. There are no changes in either the quantity or quality of illumination, as normally associated with the rise and fall of a tide, whilst sand-scouring and grazer-activity is usually minimal. (Some grazing activity has been noted by the common limpet *Patella vulgata* L. and the thick-lipped grey mullet *Crenimugil labrosus* (Risso).) Essentially, the environment provided by the sides of floating structures has much more in common with that of the subtidal than with the intertidal. Only the continuous high level of illumination on the sides of the floating structures distinguishes them from subtidal habitats in the North Atlantic.

The strong correlation between these two environments is reflected in the similar floristic composition that they bear. On the permanently-immersed levels of the floating structures, the dominant large algae present were *Laminaria digitata*, *L. saccharina* and *Sargassum muticum*, with a subvegetation of brown algae such as *Desmarestia viridis*, scattered amounts of green algae such as *Bryopsis plumosa, Cladophora* sp., *Codium fragile* ssp. *tomentosoides, Derbesia* sp. and *Ulva lactuca*, and large numbers of red algae; the latter included especially *Ceramium rubrum*, *Polysiphonia elongata* and *P. nigrescens*, with scattered amounts of species such as *Antithamnion plumula*, *Callithamnion hookeri*, *C. roseum*, *C. tetragonum*, *Chondrus crispus*, *Cystoclonium purpureum*, *Gracilaria verrucosa*, *Griffithsia corallinoides*, *G. flosculosa* and *Nitophyllum punctatum*. With some exceptions (notably the presence of *Sargassum muticum*), this association of algae also strikingly resembles that recorded in detailed studies of other floating structures (see especially the lists of species recorded by Grieve and Robertson (1864), Milne (1940) and Lodge (1949) on buoys). If the flora of these floating structures is then directly compared to that of subtidal regions, close correlation is found. For instance, the dominance of *Laminaria* spp. on the hard substrates in both the infralittoral fringe and sublittoral regions around the British Isles has been quite well documented, both for natural surfaces (Kitching, 1935; Lewis, 1953, 1954; Gillham, 1954; Burrows, 1958; Crisp and Southward, 1958; Tittley and Price, 1978) and artificial ones (Lyle, 1926, 1929; Withers and Thorp, 1977). In addition, these laminarian communities are very often reported with a subvegetation not unlike that recorded on floating structures; this includes usually prevalent red algae such as *Callithamnion* spp., *Ceramium rubrum*, *Chondrus crispus*, *Griffithsia* spp., *Nitophyllum punctatum* and *Polysiphonia* spp. (see Lewis, 1953; Withers and Thorp, 1977; Tittley and Price, 1978). Note also the close correlation between the subvegetation of the natural hard subtidal substrates in Portsmouth and Langstone Harbours (see under Physical Environment, p. 845) and that described for the floating structures in the present investigation.

Of particular interest was the occurrence of the community of fouling algae in the region above the waterline on the vertical sides of both types of floating structure. This was due to wave-buffeting and/or vertical motion of the structures which periodically raised the water level up the sides. The flora of this wave-washed region did differ quite markedly from that of the permanently-immersed zone. Green algae were particularly dominant, both bladed genera, such as *Blidingia* and *Enteromorpha*, and filamentous genera, such as *Chaetomorpha*, *Cladophora*, *Percursaria*, *Rhizoclonium*, *Ulothrix* and *Urospora*. Brown algae were less evident, with some ectocarpalean genera such as *Petalonia* and *Scytosiphon*, and very rarely *Fucus* spp., whilst very few red algae, with the exception of *Bangia* and *Porphyra*, extended any great distance above the waterline. A similar waterline community of predominantly green algae has been widely documented on floating structures around the world (Visscher, 1928; Fraser, 1938; Milne, 1940; Harris, 1946; Anon., 1952; Skerman, 1960; Tittley and Price, 1977). The floristic composition of this waterline community is very reminiscent of the intertidal, as noted by Tittley and Price (1977), and has particular affinity with the supralittoral and upper littoral regions, with the occurrence of genera such as *Bangia*, *Blidingia*, *Enteromorpha*, *Porphyra*, *Ulothrix* and *Urospora* (see Rees, 1940; Corlett, 1948; Sundene, 1953; Lewis, 1953; Gillham, 1954; van den Hoek, 1948; Nienhuis, 1969; Klavestad, 1978; Tittley and Price, 1978). Although scattered *Fucus* plants were noted in the wave-washed regions of the Langstone rafts, an extensive fucoid community characteristic of the mid and lower littoral regions of sheltered to fairly exposed shores was usually absent. It may well be that the fucoids are less able than the above genera to survive lengthy periods without immersion in water, but they also, as pointed out by Milne (1940), cannot compete with *Laminaria* in the permanently-immersed zone. Certainly, genera such as *Bangia*, *Porphyra*, *Ulothrix* and *Urospora* are more seasonal in their occurrence (usually being described as winter/spring annuals) and can avoid the more arduous summer period by either dying back (see Rees, 1940; Gillham, 1954; Klavestad, 1978) or moving down the shore (Børgesen, 1905; den Hartog, 1968). Alternatively, it may be that the fucoids are more susceptible to wave action than the above genera; although some degree of wave exposure is necessary to enable these algae to colonize and survive in the wave-washed regions, too much exposure on these vertical surfaces, as some shore studies have shown (Southward, 1953) would be detrimental to their establishment.

The comparative studies on the flora of the variously exposed vertical surfaces did reveal some differences in species composition. In the permanently immersed zone, for instance, although *Laminaria saccharina* was the dominant, most widespread alga in sheltered to semi-exposed localities, under extreme wave-buffeted conditions, such as those on the outer pontoons of the Gosport marina, *L. digitata* often became dominant. This is in agreement with some previous studies, in which it was noted that *L. saccharina* preferred sheltered localities (Evans, 1947; Lewis, 1953) whereas *L. digitata* preferred exposed localities (Kitching, 1935; Crisp and Southward, 1958; Klavestad, 1978). The occasional presence of atypical non-digitate blades of *L. digitata* in sheltered localities (the inner regions of Gosport marina) is also in agreement with observations by Kitching (1935). The subvegetation of these *Laminaria* spp. also differed quite markedly at variously exposed sites, although in general where thick growths of *Laminaria* occurred, e.g. *L. digitata* on the outer Gosport pontoons and *L. saccharina* on one year immersed Gosport pontoons, very few algae were present. In exposed regions, red algae such as *Ceramium rubrum* and *Chondrus crispus* occurred near the waterline whilst further down, with sufficient light, occasional *Polysiphonia* spp. (such as *P. elongata* and *P. nigrescens*) occurred. An increase in *P. elongata* growths with reduced laminarian canopy was also noted by Milne (1940). In more sheltered regions green algal genera became more abundant, including *Bryopsis*, *Chaetomorpha*, *Cladophora* and *Derbesia*, with a variety of more delicate red algae such as *Antithamnion plumula*, *Griffithsia corallinoides* and *Nitophyllum punctatum*.

In the "wave-washed" regions, increased exposure resulted in a marked increase in both the height and diversity of the algal community. Whereas growths of algae only extended 3–4 cm above the waterline in the inner, sheltered regions of the Gosport and Langstone structures, on the outer exposed sites they extended to 10 and 42 cm respectively. A similar upward extension of algal communities with increased exposure has already been well-documented for shores (Børgesen, 1905; Evans, 1947; Southward, 1953; Conway, 1954; Burrows *et al.*, 1954; Lewis, 1957; Klavestad, 1978). On present data, increased exposure resulted in increased algal cover and numbers of species. Although similar findings were made for shore populations by Klavestad (1978), this is not widely supported by most investigators (Stephenson, 1939; Evans, 1947; Southward and Orton, 1954). Certainly, the occurrence of a number of algae in these wave-washed regions was determined by the exposure level. In sheltered localities, green algae such as *Ulothrix pseudoflacca*, *Percursaria percursa*, *Rhizoclonium riparium*, and near the waterline *Derbesia* and *Cladophora* spp., supplemented *Blidingia* and *Enteromorpha* spp. (principally *E. intestinalis* and *E. prolifera*). In more exposed localities, the latter species were associated with *Urospora pencilliformis*, *Ulothrix flacca*, *Ulva lactuca*, and quite abundant *Enteromorpha linza*. Increased exposure not only "raised" various brown algae from the waterline region, in particular *Ectocarpus siliculosus*, with variable amounts of *Giffordia granulosa*, *Petalonia fascia*, *Pilayella littoralis* and *Scytosiphon lomentaria*, but was apparently essential for colonization by *Petalonia zosterifolia*. Red algae were more restricted in their ability to colonize the wave washed zone with relatively few species, such as *Ceramium rubrum*, *Chondrus crispus* and *Polysiphonia brodiaei*, extending marginally above the waterline in exposed conditions; notable exceptions however were *Bangia atropurpurea* and *Porphyra umbilicalis*, which extended up considerable distances on the vertical sides. Many of the above exposure-tolerant algae, such as *Bangia*, *Ulothrix*, *Urospora*, *Enteromorpha* and *Porphyra*, are a common (usually annual) feature of exposed shores (Lewis, 1954, 1957, 1964). *Petalonia zosterifolia*, although rarely recorded, also appears to be locally common in the upper littoral regions of some exposed shores such as Durlston Head, Swanage (unpublished). Its not uncommon occurrence on floating structures in Langstone Harbour, where it has also been observed by the author on buoys, small boats, and the like, has extended its distributional limits into relatively sheltered coastal regions (see also Lodge (1949) for its occurrence on buoys in Port Erin Harbour, I.O.M.); Tittley and Price (1978) have previously commented upon the important influence of floating structures on distributional limits of algae in estuarine situations.

Examination of the structure of the algal community on the wave-washed regions revealed approximately six zones present, from the top downwards:

(1) An uppermost band of microscopic green algae, comprising unicellular forms, coccoid forms, branched filamentous forms and often settled spore stages.

(2) A band of filamentous green algae, principally species of the genus *Ulothrix*, with *Rhizoclonium*, present under sheltered conditions. A wide band of *Urospora pencilliformis* occurs, with occasional plants of *Bangia* and *Porphyra*, under exposed conditions.

(3) A band of *Blidingia* spp., usually with *Ulothrix* as sub-vegetation, with occasional *Bangia* and *Porphyra* in exposed localities.

(4) A band of *Enteromorpha* spp., predominantly *E. prolifera*, with *E. linza* being abundant down to the waterline in exposed localities; occasional *Petalonia zosterifolia*, *Scytosiphon*, *Ectocarpus*, *Porphyra* and *Fucus* occur.

(5) A band of ectocarpoid brown algae just above the waterline, principally *Giffordia granulosa*, with some *Ectocarpus*, *Pilayella*, *Ulva*, *Petalonia fascia* and *P. zosterifolia*.

(6) A mixed assemblage of waterline algae, principally the red genera *Callithamnion*, *Ceramium* and *Chondrus*, with some green algae such as *Ulva* and *Cladophora*; *Derbesia* is present under sheltered conditions.

Similar studies on the vertical stratification of algal fouling communities on floating structures have only been carried out previously by Milne (1940) and his results show some similarity with those of the present study. Three zones were described: an upper zone of filamentous greens, a middle zone of *Ulva* and *Enteromorpha*, and a lower zone of red algae. As commented by Milne (1940), these algal bands represent a compressed zonation comparable to that found on a normal littoral shore. Certainly, a comparable zonation pattern, with an upper community of small green and red algae such as *Urospora*, *Ulothrix*, *Bangia* merging into *Blidingia*, *Enteromorpha*, and with a lowermost fucoid/red algal association, is not uncommonly reported for a variety of shores (van den Hoek, 1958; Nienhuis, 1969; Tittley and Price, 1977, 1978; Klavestad, 1978; den Hartog, 1959).

Overall, the composition and stratification of the algal communities on floating structures, and their modification by environmental factors such as exposure and season of year, show striking correlation with a shore environment. Indeed, direct comparisons can be made between the "wave-washed" regions and the littoral, the permanently-immersed regions and the infralittoral, and to a lesser extent the waterline region and tide-pool habitats. The only littoral features absent from the "wave-washed" regions are the lower placed fucoid cover and barnacle settlement, the latter probably a direct result of the requirement for constant immersion for filter feeding processes. Although the biological features are essentially similar, environmental features of both the "wave-washed" regions and the littoral zone do fundamentally differ in that the former are more rapidly and often less regularly immersed in water. Protracted immersion in sea water resulting from tidal rhythms is not therefore a necessary prerequisite for littoral occupation, nor does it necessarily appear to control zonation; the evidence supports Lewis's (1964) suggestions that these features are more likely to be the results of a complex interplay of many environmental conditions.

ACKNOWLEDGEMENTS

I would like to acknowledge technical assistance by Mrs A. Davis and photographic assistance by Mr K. Purdy and Mr A. Hawton during the preparation of the figures. Thanks are also extended to Mr J. Hepburn and Mr J. Sturgess for acting as boatmen. I also gratefully acknowledge financial assistance for marine algal fouling studies from the Ministry of Defence Procurement Executive, and in particular help and encouragement from Mr D. Houghton, Central Dockyard Laboratory, Portsmouth. Special thanks are extended to Dr E. B. Gareth Jones for his help and interest in the project.

REFERENCES

Anon. (1952). Species recorded from fouling. *In* "Marine Fouling and its Prevention", p. 165 (Woods Hole Oceanographic Institute). United States Naval Institute, Annapolis.

Anon. (1966). "Marine fouling. Hydrological and Biological Co-operative Research". Report of the O.E.C.D. group of experts on the preservation of materials in the marine environment. O.E.C.D. Publications, Paris.

Børgesen, F. (1905). The algal vegetation of the Faeröese coasts with remarks on the phytogeography. *Bot. Faeroes* **3**, 683–834.

Burrows, E. M. (1958). Sublittoral algal population in Port Erin Bay, Isle of Man. *J. mar. biol. Ass. U.K.* **37**, 687–703.

Burrows, E. M., Conway, E., Lodge, S. M. and Powell, H. T. (1954). The raising of intertidal algal zones in Fair Isle. *J. Ecol.* **42**, 283–288.

Christie, A. O. (1973). Spore settlement in relation to fouling by *Enteromorpha*. *In* "Proc. III Int. Congr. Mar. Corrosion and Fouling" (R. F. Acker, B. Floyd Brown, J. R. DePalma and W. P. Iverson, eds), pp. 674–681. Northwestern University Press, Evanston, Illinois.

Conway, E. (1954). The modification and raising of intertidal algal zones on exposed rocky coasts of the British Isles, with special reference to the zonation of Fucaceae. *Rapp. Commun. VIII Int. bot. Congr.* **17**, 133–134.

Corlett, J. (1948). Rates of settlement and growth of pile fauna of the Mersey Inlet. *Proc. Trans. Lpool biol. Soc.* **36**, 3–28.

Crisp, D. J. and Southward, A. J. (1958). The distribution of intertidal organisms along the coasts of the English Channel. *J. mar. biol. Ass. U.K.* **37**, 157–208.

Evans, R. G. (1947). The intertidal ecology of selected localities in the Plymouth neighbourhood. *J. mar. biol. Ass. U.K.* **27**, 173–218.

Fletcher, R. L. (1974). Results of an international cooperative research programme on the fouling of non-toxic panels by marine algae. Bulletin de liaison du Comite international permanent pour la recherche sur las preservation des materiaux en milieu marin. *Trav. Cen. Rech. Etud. océanogr.* **14**, 7–31.

Fletcher, R. L. and Chamberlain, A. H. L. (1975). Marine fouling algae. *In* "Microbial Aspects of the Deterioration of Materials". Society for Applied Bacteriology Techn., Series 9 (D. W. Lovelock and R. J. Gilbert eds), pp. 59–81. Academic Press, London and New York.

Fraser, J. H. (1938). The fauna of fixed and floating structures in the Mersey estuary and Liverpool Bay. *Proc. Trans. Lpool biol. Soc.* **51**, 1–21.

Fry, W. G. (1975). Raft fouling in the Menai strait, 1963–1971. *Hydrobiologia* **47**, 527–558.

Gillham, M. E. (1954). The marine algae of Skokholm and Grassholm Islands, Pembrokeshire. *NWest Nat.* N.S. **2**, 204–225.

Grieve, J. and Robertson, D. (1864). On the distribution of marine algae on the C.L.T. buoys in the Clyde. *Proc. R. phil. Soc. Glasg.* 5, 121–126.

Harris, J. E. (1943). First report of the marine corrosion subcommittee. *J. Iron and Steel Inst.* **147**, 405–420.

Harris, J. E. (1946). Report on anti-fouling research, 1942–44. *J. Iron and Steel Inst.* **154**, 297–333.

Hartog, C. den (1959). The epilithic algal communities occurring on the coasts of the Netherlands. *Wentia* **1**, 1–241.

Hartog, C. den (1968). The littoral environment of rocky shores as a border between the sea and the land and between the sea and the fresh water. *Blumea* **16**, 375–393.

Hendey, N. I. (1951). Littoral diatoms of Chichester Harbour with special reference to fouling. *J. Roy. microsc. Soc.* **71**, 1–86.

Hoek, C. van den, (1958). Observations on the algal vegetation of the northern pier at Hoek Van Holland, made from October, 1953 till August, 1954. *Blumea* **9**, 187–205.

Houghton, D. R. (1959). Tidal measurements in Langstone Harbour, Hampshire. *Dock. Harb. Auth.* **40**, 172–9.

Kitching, J. A. (1935). An introduction to the ecology of intertidal rock surfaces on the coast of Argyll. *Trans. R. Soc. Edinb.* **58**, 351–374.

Klavestad, N. (1978). The marine algae of the polluted inner part of the Oslofjord. A survey carried out 1962–1966. *Botanica mar.* **21**, 71–97.

Lewis, J. R. (1953). The ecology of rocky shores around Anglesey. *Proc. zool. Soc. Lond.* **123**, 481–549.

Lewis, J. R. (1954). The ecology of exposed rocky shores of Caithness. *Trans. R. Soc. Edinb.* **62**, 695–723.

Lewis, J. R. (1957). An introduction to the intertidal ecology of the rocky shores of a Hebridean Island. *Oikos* **8**, 130–150.

Lewis, J. R. (1964). "The Ecology of Rocky Shores". English University Press, London.

Lodge, S. M. (1949). Notes on the flora of Port Erin buoys. *Rep. mar. biol. Stn Port Erin* **61**, 32–33.

Lyle, L. (1926). Marine algae found on a salvaged ship. *J. Bot., Lond.* **64**, 184–186.

Lyle, L. (1929). Marine algae of some German warships in Scapa Flow and of the neighbouring shores. *J. Linn. Soc.* (Bot.) **48**, 231–257.

Milne, A. (1940). The ecology of the Tamar Estuary IV. The distribution of the fauna and flora on buoys. *J. mar. biol. Ass. U.K.* **24**, 69–87.

Neinhuis, P. N. (1969). The significance of the substratum for intertidal algal growth on the artificial rocky shore of the Netherlands. *Int. Revue ges. Hydrobiol.* **54**, 207–215.

Orton, J. H. (1930). Experiments in the sea on the growth-inhibitive and preservative value of poisonous paints and other substances. *J. mar. biol. Ass. U.K.* **16**, 373–452.

Parke, M. and Dixon, P. S. (1976). Check-list of British marine algae – third revision. *J. mar. biol. Ass. U.K.* **56**, 527–594.

Rees, T. K. (1940). Algal colonization at Mumbles Head. *J. Ecol.* **28**, 403–437.

Skerman, T. M. (1960). Ship-fouling in New Zealand waters: A survey of marine fouling organisms from vessels of the coastal and overseas trades. *N. Zeal. Jl Sci.* **3**, 620–648.

Southward, A. J. (1953). The ecology of some rocky shores in the south of the Isle of Man. *Proc. Lpool biol. Soc.* **59**, 1–50.

Southward, A. J. and Orton, J. H. (1954). The effects of wave action on the distribution and numbers of the commoner plants and animals living on the Plymouth breakwater. *J. mar. biol. Ass. U.K.* **33**, 1–19.

Stephenson, T. A. (1939). A constitution of the intertidal fauna and flora of South Africas pt. I. *J. Linn. Soc.* (Zool.) **40**, 487–536.

Stubbings, H. G. and Houghton, D. R. (1964). The ecology of Chichester Harbour, S. England, with special reference to some fouling species. *Int. Rev. ges. Hydrobiol.* **49**, 233–279.

Sundene, O. (1953). The algal vegetation of Oslofjord. *Skr. norske Vidensk. Akad.(1) Mat. Nat. Kl.* 1953 (2): 1–245.

Tittley, I. and Price, J. H. (1977). The marine algae of the tidal Thames. *Lond. Nat.*, **56**, 10–17.

Tittley, I. and Price, J. H. (1978). The benthic marine algae of the eastern English Channel: a preliminary floristic and ecological account. *Botanica mar.* **21**, 499–512.

Visscher, P. P. (1928). Nature and extent of fouling of ships' bottoms. *Bull. Bur. Fish., Wash.* **43**, 193–252.

Withers, R. G. and Thorp, C. H. (1977). Studies on the shallow sublittoral epibenthos of Langstone Harbour, Hampshire, using settlement panels. *In* "Biology of Benthic Organisms" (B. F. Keegan, P. Ó'Céidigh and P. J. S. Boaden, eds), pp. 595–604. (Proc. Europ. mar. Biol. Symp. 11). Pergamon Press, Oxford.

14 | Studies on Aliens in the Marine Flora of Southern England

W. F. FARNHAM

Department of Biological Sciences, Portsmouth Polytechnic Marine Laboratory, Hayling Island, England

Abstract: Many introduced species are known in the British marine flora. Some of the earlier introductions are by now so widespread and well-established that their exotic origins are overlooked, e.g. *Colpomenia peregrina* and *Codium fragile.* Other adventitious species have apparently arrived within recent years. The south coast of England, and in particular the Solent region, seems to provide suitable sites and habitats for the establishment and further spread of many immigrant species. Marine algae of alien origin which have been recorded within recent years include *Grateloupia filicina* var. *luxurians*, *G. doryphora, Solieria chordalis, S. tenera, Neoagardhiella gaudichaudii* and *Sargassum muticum.* The initial problem has usually been in recognizing an "unusual" seaweed as a species introduced from some other part of the world. Ecological observations have been made upon the above species to monitor any further changes in their distribution. Various vectors have been suggested as responsible for long-distance changes in distribution of marine organisms, as natural mechanisms for such dispersal are unlikely. Such transportation agents include shipping, with species carried as fouling organisms or in ballast tanks, and shellfish. It is concluded that early detection of alien species is important, so that any resultant changes in natural ecosystems can be discerned.

Systematics Association Special Volume No. 17(b), "The Shore Environment, Vol. 2: Ecosystems", edited by J. H. Price, D. E. G. Irvine and W. F. Farnham, 1980, pp. 875–914, Academic Press, London and New York.

INTRODUCTION

1. *A Survey of Previous Marine Algal Introductions into the British Isles*

This chapter is concerned with the recent introduction of certain alien marine algae into British waters. Before these events are discussed, previous marine introductions will be reviewed. Taylor (1979) has recently described some of the characteristics shown by exotic species. In this chapter, an alien is broadly defined as any non-indigenous species, which has been fortuitously or deliberately introduced, not necessarily as a result of human activity, and which seems to have become an established member of the British flora or fauna.

The marine benthic algal flora of the British Isles has been well studied for the past two centuries. The culmination of the work of early British phycologists was "Phycologia Britannica" (W. H. Harvey, 1846–1851). A comparison of this compilation with more recent compendia of the British flora, such as "A Handbook of the British Seaweeds" (Newton, 1931) and the later "Check-list of British Marine Algae – third revision" (Parke and Dixon, 1976), shows that additional species of seaweeds have been recorded over the past century or so. This may be explained in various ways. First, some of these more recently recorded species reflect current taxonomic concepts, e.g. the recognition of *Ulva rigida** as a species separate from *U. lactuca*. Secondly, other additions are simply sightings of species which had hitherto been overlooked by collectors. This applies not only to smaller algae or to taxonomically difficult groups but also to larger algae from formerly inaccessible sites or habitats, especially in the sublittoral region. Thirdly, there have been some marine algae detected around the British Isles that actually do represent newcomers. Other aspects of change in the British marine flora were discussed by W. E. Jones (1974). Price *et al.* (1979) have recently described long-term distributional changes – both in time and space – of *Padina pavonica* (L.) Lamour. (= *P. pavonia*), which provides a rare example of a native alga for which the necessary data exist.

---

*Nomenclature of British algae cited follows that given by Parke and Dixon (1976).

Table I lists those marine algae which are considered to have been introduced but which by now are so well-established and extensively distributed that their alien origin is obscured. One of the surprising features of these introductions is that most of them appear to have originated from the Pacific Ocean, and have thus notably extended their geographical range. Fewer examples are known where the introduced species originated from a much nearer source. An example of the latter case is *Laminaria ochroleuca*, which was first reported for the British mainland by Parke (1948).

Many newly arrived species remain unnoticed for some time, this perhaps reflecting the paucity of collections (especially from the sublittoral), but resulting also from misidentifications. This can easily be so where differences from related, indigenous species are but minor. *L. ochroleuca* is illustrative on both accounts. It occurs in the shallow sublittoral which until recently was a poorly-collected area. Furthermore, plants could conceivably have been mistaken for *Laminaria digitata*. Nevertheless, it does seem to represent a relatively recent cross-Channel migrant, perhaps the result of a slight but significant increase in the temperature of the Channel over the past 50 years (Southward, 1960). However, most other algae introduced into this country, even if by way of the European mainland, represent overall incursions to the Atlantic from the Pacific. Often, recognition of these events has been hindered by taxonomic problems, as will be indicated below.

The brown alga, *Colpomenia peregrina*, attracted attention at the beginning of this century by causing considerable losses within the northern French oyster-beds. The problem was that the globose thalli became air-filled and accordingly buoyant, thus floating away with attached oysters. It was not initially appreciated that this alga differed from the previously known European species, *C. sinuosa* (Roth.) Derb. et Sol., until the studies of Sauvageau (1927). Blackler (1963) showed that *Colpomenia* in the Pacific, previously referred to as *C. sinuosa* Saunders, agreed anatomically with *C. peregrina*. It is thus likely that the *Colpomenia* associated with the Breton oyster-beds, viz. *C. peregrina*, came from the Pacific. *C. peregrina* has since spread further in European waters. It was soon noticed along the south-west coast of Britain (Cotton, 1908, although accidentally omitted from Newton, 1931) and later spread further round the British Isles.

Table I. Established introductions of marine algae into the British Isles

Species	Estimated place and date of introduction	Suggested origin	Reference
Codium fragile			
subsp. *atlanticum*	South-west Ireland; 1808	Pacific	Silva (1955)
subsp. *tomentosoides*	R. Yealm, Devon; 1939	Pacific	Silva (1955)
Bonnemaisonia hamifera	Falmouth, Cornwall; 1893	Japan	Holmes (1897)
Trailliella-phase	Dorset; 1890	Pacific	Westbrook (1930)
Colpomenia peregrina	Cornwall, Dorset; 1907	Pacific	Cotton (1908)
Antithamnion spirographidis			
(including *A. sarniensis*)	Plymouth, Devon; 1920s	S. Hemisphere?	Westbrook (1930)
Asparagopsis armata	Co. Galway, Ireland; 1941	Australia	De Valéra (1942)
Falkenbergia-phase	Co. Galway, Ireland; 1939	Australia	C. Harvey and Drew (1949)
Laminaria ochroleuca	Plymouth, Devon; 1940s	Channel Islands; N. France	Parke (1948)

The recognition of an earlier introduction into British (and European) waters was also obscured by taxonomic difficulties. *Codium fragile* was long confused with native, dichotomous species of *Codium*, namely *C. tomentosum* and *C. vermilara*, until Silva (1955) defined this assemblage. The two subspecies of *C. fragile* described by Silva (1955), subspp. *tomentosoides* and *atlanticum*, were probably introduced separately from the Pacific. The latter subspecies was considered by Silva (1955) to have been "introduced from the Pacific within historic times". The former subspecies is of more recent occurrence within the Atlantic. According to Silva (1955), it was first collected in Holland in 1900 and the first British record was from the River Yealm (south Devon) in 1939. Both of these subspecies have spread independently. In some areas, especially along the south coasts of England and Ireland (Parkes, 1975), the indigenous *C. tomentosum* has been outcompeted by *C. fragile*, which has also spread further by colonizing coastline free from *C. tomentosum*. *C. fragile* subsp. *tomentosoides* appeared on the Atlantic seaboard of North America in 1957 (Wood, 1962) and is still undergoing vigorous expansion of its distribution down that coastline (Malinowski and Ramus, 1973). It has now been recorded for the first time in New Zealand waters (Dromgoole, 1975).

Other well-documented instances of introductions of Pacific algae relate to certain red algae. *Asparagopsis armata* was first described by W. H. Harvey (1855) from Australia and has since apparently spread from there into European waters. It was first recorded for the British Isles by De Valéra (1942) for County Galway and the first report of its occurrence in England was by Drew (1950). However, as Dixon (1965) indicated, reports relating to the subsequent spread of *Asparagopsis* in Europe have obscured more fundamental issues. *A. armata* is only known in the gametangial condition. Feldmann and Feldmann (1942) contended that its tetrasporangial generation was represented by a phase so morphologically dissimilar that it had been treated as the separate species *Falkenbergia rufolanosa* (Harvey) Schmitz. This had also been initially described from Australia by W. H. Harvey (1855) and was later reported to be spreading in the Atlantic and Mediterranean (Feldmann and Feldmann, 1942). It was first recorded for Britain by C. Harvey and Drew (1949) on Lundy, where it was later refound by D. Irvine *et al.* (1972). The *Falkenbergia*-phase is more widespread in the British Isles than the *Asparagopsis*-phase. *Falkenbergia* has now been found as far east along the Channel as Lymington, Hampshire (Farnham, unpublished) and as far north as the Orkney and Shetland Isles (Irvine *et al.*, 1975), while the *Asparagopsis*-phase appears to be restricted to the south-west coasts of the British Isles. It would appear that both phases in this life history are spreading independently by vegetative means in the British Isles. *A. armata*, as its specific epithet indicates, produces spinous lateral branches which readily attach to other algae, while *Falkenbergia* grows as a mass of tangled filaments forming "balls" which float and can readily reattach themselves to suitable substrata. Dixon (1964) even questioned whether *A. armata*/*F. rufolanosa* is an Australian introduction. Another species of *Asparagopsis*, *A. taxiformis* (Delile) Trev., is also widely distributed in tropical waters and has been recorded for the Canary Islands (Boergesen, 1929) and the Mediterranean (Feldmann and Feldmann, 1942). It is distinguished from *A. armata* by the absence of spiny laterals but Dixon (1964) commented that British material of *Asparagopsis* is occasionally indistinguishable from *A. taxiformis* on this basis. This reinforces Schiffner's opinion (1931) that *A. armata* and *A. taxiformis* are conspecific. Furthermore, *Falkenbergia hillebrandii* (Born.) Falkenb., said to be the tetrasporangial phase of *A. taxiformis* (Chihara, 1960), is not apparently morphologically distinguishable from *F. rufolanosa* (Dixon, 1964). If these taxonomic opinions are confirmed, then the origins of the European *Asparagopsis* and *Falkenbergia* populations require further reconsideration.

The related alga *Bonnemaisonia hamifera* has also been regarded as an adventive from the Pacific, having first been described from Japanese material in 1891. The first British specimen was collected from Falmouth (south Cornwall) by Buffham in 1893, followed by a collection from Shanklin (Isle of Wight) by Holmes (1897). Westbrook (1930) commented that she had been unable to find *B. hamifera* at Shanklin or elsewhere on the Isle of Wight and this is also the current situation, although it is still to be found at Falmouth (Farnham, unpublished). Cotton (1912) had questioned whether *B. hamifera* was really alien as by then it was known to be more widely distributed in Europe, from Clare Island (west Ireland) to Cherbourg (north France). However, as he admitted (Cotton, 1912), it had been unknown in Europe before Buffham's discovery and accordingly seemed to be a recent arrival.

As with *Asparagopsis*, there is the complication of a pleomorphic life history to consider. Harder and Koch (1949) showed that *Trailliella intricata* Batt. was not an autonomous species but represented the tetrasporangial phase of *B. hamifera*. "*Trailliella*" was recorded in this country slightly earlier than its gametangial phase and has generally spread faster and also further northwards. It was first collected by Holmes at Studland (Dorset) in 1890 (as *Spermothamnion turneri* Aresch f. *intricata* Holmes et Batt.). Westbrook (1930) discussed its further spread around Britain and Europe. McLachlan *et al.* (1969) reported on the current distribution of the phases, both of which are now present on the north-eastern and south-western coastlines of North America. A further complication is that *Bonnemaisonia nootkana* (Esper) Silva in the Pacific has a tetrasporangial phase morphologically indistuiguishable from *T. intricata.*

Although both phases of *B. hamifera* have greatly extended their geographical distributions during this century, there is no conclusive evidence pinpointing Japan as the country of origin. This general assumption (Westbrook, 1930; W. E. Jones, 1974) had been questioned by Cotton (1912), as mentioned previously, and more recently challenged by McLachlan *et al.* (1969). It does not necessarily follow that the country from which a species happened to be described first represents its place of origin. This is probably true for the tubeworm *Mercierella enigmatica* Fauvel (= *Ficoponatus enigmaticus* (Fauvel)), which was first described in France but is native to Australasia (Carlton, 1975). In view of the spread of *B. hamifera* and its *Trailliella*-phase on both sides of the Atlantic, it is surprising that it is not more widespread in the Pacific. The main indication that *B. hamifera* is indigenous to Japan comes from the occurrence of the full range of reproductive phases, i.e. spermatangial, carpogonial, carposporangial and tetrasporangial thalli, which is suggestive of the likely completion of its theoretical life history there.

Antithamnion spirographidis is "of somewhat problematic origin" (W. E. Jones, 1974). Jones cites its origin as from the southern hemisphere, although it was first described from the Adriatic in 1916. Westbrook (1930) discussed its occurrence and spread along both sides of the Channel (as *Antithamnionella sarniensis* Lyle). Sundene (1964) indicated that *Antithamnion sarniensis* (Lyle) G. Feldm. is conspecific with *A. spirographidis*, the former having been described by Lyle in 1922 from the Channel Islands. Westbrook (1930) commented that *A. sarniensis* had not been found around Cherbourg last century by Thuret, but was found there for the first time in 1910 and later was quite abundant. Similarly, it had not been recorded in the Plymouth region by such assiduous collectors as Brebner and Holmes (last century) but Westbrook found it there in the 1920s. It has now been recorded for Lundy (D. Irvine *et al.*, 1972) and west Scotland (McAllister *et al.*, 1967; Price and Tittley, 1978), and so must be considered a well-established member of the British marine flora.

The introductions discussed above are not characterized by the same focal site of introduction into the British Isles, although in so far as can be determined they have usually made their first appearance somewhere along the southern or western coasts of the British Isles. As has been indicated, they have often been well established prior to being discovered and so the early events in their naturalization have been missed.

2. A Survey of Previous Marine Introductions into the Solent

One feature common to many marine species recently introduced into British waters is that they have first been discovered within the Solent region. (In this chapter, the "Solent region" refers to the shores around the Isle of Wight and the adjacent coastline of Hampshire.) Animal introductions are discussed here because similar general considerations apply to them as well as to algae in terms of their arrival, establishment and further spread. Marine introductions originating in the Solent are listed in Table II. Some of these are discussed further.

The Australasian barnacle, *Eliminius modestus* Darwin, has been a strikingly successful colonizer along considerable stretches of the British and European coastlines. *E. modestus* was first found by Bishop (1947) on test panels within Chichester Harbour. Later, Stubbings (1950) examined material collected earlier and concluded that it had been present before 1945. Since that time, *Elminius* has greatly increased its European distribution, as outlined by Crisp (1958). It has now spread round most of the English coastline and has more recently appeared in Ireland, Scotland and Shetland (Hiscock *et al.*, 1978). During the late 1940s, *Elminius* appeared on the European mainland and is now widespread from Germany to Spain. Lewis (1964, Fig. 70) depicts the rate of dispersal by *Elminius* in Europe.

Table II. Previous introductions reported for the Solent region

Species	Group	Date of earliest discovery	Suggested origin	Reference
Spartina alterniflora	Angiospermae	1829	east N. America	Marchant (1968)
Mercenaria mercenaria	Mollusca	1925	east N. America	Mitchell (1974)
Elminius modestus	Crustacea	1940s	Australasia	Crisp (1958)
Styela clava	Tunicata	1950s	Pacific	Houghton and Millar (1960)
Limnoria tripunctata	Crustacea	1957	temperate-tropical seas	Eltringham and Hockley (1958)

A later animal arrival, however, was not immediately identified as such. This was an ascidian reported by Carlisle (1954) as a previously undescribed species, *Styela mammiculata*. He recorded it from Plymouth, although it probably occurred more or less simultaneously in the area of Portsmouth Harbour (Houghton and Millar, 1960). Millar (1960) demonstrated that *S. mammiculata* Carlisle was synonymous with a species described earlier from the Pacific, *S. clava* Herdman, and concluded that *S. clava* constituted a new introduction into British waters from the Pacific. *S. clava* has since spread further along the south coast of England (Millar, 1970), across to Brittany (Dr L. Cabioch, personal communication) and more recently has been found in Cork Harbour, southern Ireland (Guiry and Guiry, 1973).

The bivalve *Mercenaria mercenaria* L. is widely distributed along the Atlantic coast of North America. This hard-shelled clam has often been deliberately introduced into European waters for commercial exploitation but usually without success. On the other hand, colonies have appeared in localities where there had been no attempted transplantations. This may be the explanation for the self-reproducing population in the Solent reported by Heppel (1961), although Mitchell (1974) suggested that this was a deliberate introduction. Naylor (1965) reviewed the biological effects of heated effluents on immigrant warm-water species. This is probably the explanation for the continued existence of *Mercenaria* in Southampton Water, and similarly for that of the wood-boring isopod, *Limnoria tripunctata* Menzies, recorded by Eltringham and Hockley (1958).

The cord-grass *Spartina* has perhaps had a greater overall ecological effect than any of the previous introductions discussed so far. Within the past century it has greatly altered the appearance of long stretches of British and European coastline, by virtue of its rapid spread and exceptional mud-binding properties.

The original species of *Spartina* to be found in Europe was *S. maritima* (Curtis) Fernald, which was widely distributed as small colonies. Those colonies at their northern limit of geographical distribution in Britain and Europe seemed to lack vigour and Marchant (1967) suggested that the species was sensitive to climatic fluctuations. Early in the eighteenth century, another species of *Spartina* appeared around Southampton Water and also in France. This was *S. alterniflora* Loisel, originating from the eastern North American seaboard. An unusual, if not unique, event then occurred around Southampton

Water. Rather than the newly arrived species itself becoming firmly established and spreading further, both species of *Spartina*, previously separated by the Atlantic Ocean, co-existed as outbreeding populations to create a natural hybrid. *S.* x *townsendii* H. and J. Groves. Records of this "species" date from 1870 and since then it has become widespread. This F_1 hybrid is sterile and accordingly can only spread vegetatively. Within the period 1870 to 1890, the initial expansion of *Spartina* took place. This has been explained by the production of a fertile amphidiploid, *S. anglica* Hubbard, derived from the sterile primary hybrid (*S.* x *townsendii*) by chromosomal doubling. As it is not always possible to separate these two hybrid forms in previous records and field collections, both types of hybrid can be collectively referred to as *S.* x *townsendii* agg. (Marchant, 1968). Since the turn of the century, *S.* x *townsendii* agg. has become widely distributed as a major colonizer of unstabilized tidal mudflats, around most of the British coastline and elsewhere in Europe.

Other alien species have been found around the Solent, additional to the list in Table II, but these appeared elsewhere in the British Isles before reaching the Solent. Examples include some of the algae given in Table I, i.e. *C. fragile*, subsp. *tomentosoides*, *B. hamifera* – both phases, *C. peregrina*, *A. spirographidis* and the *Falkenbergia*-phase of *A. armata*, and such animals as the slipper-limpet, *Crepidula fornicata* (L.), and the boring mollusc, *Petricola pholadiformis* Lamarck.

The algae recently introduced into the Solent will be discussed later in more detail, together with other apparently recent aliens occurring elsewhere in the British Isles, but especially along the coast of southern England.

3. A Discussion of Factors Responsible for the Introduction and Further Spread of Introduced Species

The geographical distributional patterns of organisms, whether plant or animal, marine or terrestrial, are not static and changes may occur from time to time. The advent of any species into a new region raises the initial query as to how the species was transported to its new locality. Subsequent investigation into the biology of an introduced species will usually concentrate on its "success", as exemplified by its rate of further spread from the initial site of invasion and its effects upon indigenous members of the flora and fauna living in the same habitat.

The existing boundaries in the distribution of any species may respond to various environmental changes, such as climate, hydrography, and so on. Thus, the southward spread of such typically northern marine algae as *Ptilota plumosa* has been correlated with a general climatic improvement in the British Isles over the past century (Dixon, 1965). As previously mentioned, *Laminaria ochroleuca* is a recent cross-Channel migrant, perhaps in response to slightly elevated sea temperatures. These relatively minor expansions of the boundaries of existing populations are brought about by the natural methods of dissemination, which constitute what Crisp (1958) termed "marginal dispersal". Existing marine communities represent the climax of centuries during which processes of "marginal dispersal" have been operative and which are unlikely to result in any tremendous changes in the near future.

The majority of newly introduced species have been transported considerable distances by a variety of agencies or vectors, and this constitutes the process of "remote dispersal" (Crisp, 1958). Effectively, the difference between these two methods of dispersal is whether the species is transported a short distance or a greater distance away from its previous population. The term "vector" has been used in this context, e.g. Crisp (1958), W. E. Jones (1974), as an extension of its previous biological usage which related to the transmission of parasites only. However, the concept of a "vector" is a convenient one to employ in the wider connotation of the agency responsible for the introduction and spread of species. Doubtless many transportations of species occur but it must be exceptional for any such species to survive the journey and to have a large enough "inoculum" of breeding stock for the establishment of a population in a new area where conditions happen to be favourable. Once such a successful invasion has taken place, then further dispersal may be brought about by either, or a combination of, remote and marginal spread.

Various vectors for the long-distance transportation (remote dispersal) of marine organisms can be suggested. For most introductions, the nature of the vector is conjectural and frequently is suggested by circumstantial evidence related to their time of discovery and initial localities concerned.

An obvious marine vector is shipping, which may carry out this role in two ways. First, species may be transported as fouling organisms attached to the hull. This is the likeliest explanation for the introduction of *Elminius* and *Styela*, both of which are known to occur as components of the fouling community. As shown by Crisp (1958), *Elminius* probably arrived in British waters by the early 1940s. It is possible that wartime conditions may have helped in this introduction. A later war in the 1950s (Korean War) is thought to have resulted in the introduction of *Styela*, which may have been transported from the Pacific to England on naval vessels, such as landing craft. Further circumstantial evidence supporting the role of shipping as an important vector is that most introductions are first found in the vicinity of harbours, e.g. Portsmouth, Southampton, Plymouth, Falmouth and Cork. Involvement of shipping in the further spread of *Styela* is indicated by the recent report of its occurrence around Cork Harbour (Guiry and Guiry, 1973). Transportation of algae attached to ships has been suggested, particularly in those cases where the distribution of an introduced species is disjunct. De Valéra (1942) implicated shipping in the early spread of *Asparagopsis*.

Secondly, shipping can act as a vector by the discharge of ballast in foreign harbours. Marchant (1967) suggested this to be the method by which the North American *Spartina alterniflora* was introduced into Southampton. Discharge of ballast water has been implicated in the dispersal of planktonic species such as *Biddulphia sinensis* Grev. (Hardy, 1956). This diatom is of Indo-Pacific origin and first appeared in European waters at the beginning of the century but by now is an abundant member of the phytoplankton. Boalch and Harbour (1977) have recently reported the introduction of two more planktonic diatoms into the Channel.

Although it is an attractive proposition to cite international shipping as a main vector for introduced species, caution needs to be employed unless additional evidence is forthcoming. The application of antifouling paints to ships' hulls results in a reduced and cosmopolitan flora which is resistant to the toxins and also the varying hydrographic conditions (mainly salinity and temperature) encountered during passage. Additional factors militating against shipping as frequent vectors are the environments offered by harbours, often highly polluted and estuarine, and the quick turnabout times of modern commercial vessels. It may well be that the older forms of shipping with less effective antifouling treatment were a much richer source of possible introductions. It used also to be the practice for at least the smaller trading boats, in the days of sail, to be run directly ashore to unload cargo without entering harbours. On the other hand, the faster speed of modern shipping does subject attached organisms to shorter periods at sea during which unfavourable conditions may be encountered, such as passage through tropical waters for temperate species.

In addition to fouled ships, floating objects such as timbers, buoys and fishing-pots also afford the possibility of transporting attached organisms considerable distances according to the prevailing currents. Lucas (1950) recorded a number of algae cast up on the Dutch coast, some attached to such objects as French fishing-floats. This is probably not an effective method leading to the establishment of successful introductions, because the biomass of attached organisms transported must be low. As Crisp (1958) discussed with respect to the spread of *Elminius*, one of the limiting factors for the establishment and further spread of an invading species must be the number of reproductive units produced to constitute a large enough inoculum. In those instances where only small amounts of a species are transported, a series of repetitious introductions is needed, in order to build up the biomass of the introduced species for its eventual successful establishment.

Another important way by which long-distance introductions are brought about involves the deliberate introduction by Man of commercially important species. This is less true for the marine environment, in which the practice of "mariculture" is still in its infancy as compared with the terrestrial flora and fauna, which has been affected all over the world by international exchanges (see Salisbury, 1964). Marine organisms deliberately introduced into European waters are listed in the report prepared for the International Council for the Exploration of the Sea, I.C.E.S. (Anon., 1972), and are included in the world-wide inventory prepared by Walford and Wicklund (1973).

It has been common practice for many centuries to transplant or relay the indigenous European oyster, *Ostrea edulis* L., into new beds or to augment existing populations. In recent years, many oyster-beds in this country and elsewhere in Europe have been greatly depleted by pollution and disease. Re-stocking of these beds has been attempted with other, hardier or faster-growing species. The Portuguese oyster, *Crassostrea angulata* L., has been successfully transplanted around Europe and later consignments of the Pacific oyster, *Crassostrea gigas* (Thunberg), were exported from Japan and British Columbia. Such deliberate introductions will not be dealt with in detail here. However, as a consequence of deliberate transplantations, many accidental introductions have been effected, e.g. imported oysters themselves acting as vectors. As Elton (1958) commented, "the greatest agency of all that spreads marine animals to new quarters of the world must be the business of oyster culture". This is a regrettable consequence of the initial lack of stringent precautions and quarantining, since many of these accidentally introduced species have proved detrimental to the oyster industry, e.g. the slipper-limpet, *Crepidula fornicata* L., and the oyster-drill, *Urosalpinx cinerea* (Say), (Cole, 1942).

The geographical spread of *Codium fragile* has already been discussed. Ramus (1971) suggested that the *Codium* may have been introduced into eastern North America attached to oysters. Perhaps the same explanation holds good for the initial appearance of *Colpomenia peregrina* in Brittany, also associated with oyster beds there. However, the further colonization of the European coastline by *Colpomenia* probably occurred by marginal dispersal. The thalli of *Colpomenia* are hollow, becoming air-filled and buoyant, and spread by floating away. This is exceptional in that the majority of seaweeds are not likely to float for any significant time or distance when detached. However, a few remarkable instances exist where drift specimens have been found considerable distances away from the nearest site of attached plants. Holmes (1900) found *Gelidium versicolor* (S. Gmel.) Lamour. (as *G. cartilagineum* J. Ag.) unattached on the Isle of Wight. According to Dixon and L. Irvine (1977), the Canary Islands are the nearest site for attached plants of this species. It is probably easier for many marine animals to extend their range because of their production of planktonic larval stages which can be dispersed by water movements. This has probably been an important factor in the subsequent colonization of the European coastline by *Elminius*.

Little is known about the methods of marginal dispersal in the benthic marine algae. The buoyant thallus of *Colpomenia* has been mentioned but this is the exception rather than the rule.

Fragmentation of various algae can occur with the possibility of rhizoidal reattachment, as was shown by Chemin (1928) for a range of red algae. Some algae have become specialized towards this method by the development of tendrils or hooked branches, as in *Asparagopsis armata* and *Bonnemaisonia hamifera*, which facilitate the further spread of such algae by attachment onto floating objects. In other algae, there is the possibility of spores or microscopic germling stages being transported either in the plankton or attached to such vectors as shipping. Virtually nothing is known about the viability and longevity of such stages in the life histories of algae. It is generally assumed that the thin-walled spores produced by marine algae sink and germinate quickly, and are thus unlikely to spread far in the plankton. However, the ability of swarmers of *Enteromorpha intestinalis* to be motile for up to 8 days (W. E. Jones and Babb, 1968) suggests that considerable dispersal of this alga, and any other with comparable swarmers, could take place in the plankton. Many summer annuals are thought to overwinter as multicellular sporelings (Dixon, 1960) and it is these phases which may survive transportation by vectors from one country to another. Usually, major changes in the distribution of macroalgae have been attributed to transportation by vectors rather than to passive dispersal of spores, or other reproductive elements, by water currents but little direct evidence is available to confirm either hypothesis.

As can be appreciated from the varied nature of vectors involved, many potential introductions may be made. That is to say, a wide variety of species is probably transported into new regions without any further development because of unsuitable conditions. Factors required for a successful introduction include the following: suitable vector(s); survival during the transit period; arrival in a new region offering the same or similar habitats to those in the country of origin (e.g. suitable water temperatures; salinity; substratum); the establishment of a large enough breeding-stock from either a single massive inoculum or from a repetitious series of invasions; suitable conditions and vectors for the further spread of the introduced species.

4. A Discussion of Effects Caused by Introduced Species

Little is known of the effects produced by the successful invasion and subsequent spread of most introduced species. This is particularly true for the algae already discussed; the consequences of faunal introductions are perhaps better known because of the commercial interests involved, as in the case of introduced oyster-pests which were discussed by Quayle (1964).

Some introductions appear to have had little discernible effect upon the indigenous biota and simply provide additional components to the ecosystem. *Colpomenia* would seem to be in this category. Despire its present wide European distribution and abundance, especially in summer in rock-pools, no obvious effect has been apparent upon the established flora. In other cases, effects of competition are apparent, and particularly so where related species were established in the host flora. *Codium tomentosum* used to be widely distributed on the south and west coast of the British Isles. Since the introduction of *Codium fragile*, which grows in the same habitats, the former has diminished in abundance whereas the introduced *Codium* has spread further round the British Isles, even into areas where *C. tomentosum* did not grow. This greater competitive ability and "aggressiveness" seems to be a general feature of many introduced species and is not easy to explain. Salisbury (1964), in discussing terrestrial invasions, cites instances where species are easily manageable in their native or original environments but then become rampant in alien environments. This may be explained, easily if not precisely, on the grounds that controlling factors in the country of origin, such as predators or competitors for space, will not have been introduced along with the invading species. In the absence of such constraint, more vigorous biological activities, e.g. growth rate, reproductive strategy and output, may be manifest by the successful alien species.

Certainly the advent of *Elminius* has affected the British native barnacles (Crisp, 1958) and in particular *Balanus balanoides* L., with which it is in direct competition for space and food. There may be further, less obvious, effects resulting from indirect competition. *Elminius* produces a much larger number of larval stages in the summer than does *B. balanoides* and these may then reduce or displace other components of the zooplankton, leading to a smaller adult settlement of other species. In this manner, *Elminius* may affect a wide range of other marine animals through loss of their planktonic larvae.

It is appropriate to mention here the introduced freshwater aquatic plant *Elodea canadensis* Michx. Canadian Pondweed was first noted in England around the middle of the last century and may have been brought in by Canadian timber. *Elodea* quickly became widely dispersed along many rivers and canals throughout the British Isles in such abundance that it hindered the passage of canal barges and choked many land-drainage systems. The spread of *Elodea* was by purely vegetative means, since it is a dioecious species with only female plants having been introduced. However, in recent years there has been a marked decline in *Elodea* populations. The causes of this decline are unknown; grazing is not likely to be a significant factor. Reduced genetic vigour as a result of the vegetative methods of propagation, or limitation by trace elements have been suggested (Salisbury, 1964). This population decrease may well be a general phenomenon for many introduced species. The initial colonizing phase consists of vigorous expansion, either in conditions where resources are available or at the expense of some established members of the native flora and fauna. This pioneer phase may be followed by a decline leading perhaps to a more stable system and better balance within the ecosystem. The relative amounts of ecological disturbance and the time-scale leading to the stabilized phase will vary for each particular case. It is factors such as these which must be taken into consideration when attempting to evaluate the biological effects of introduced species, as and when they are first reported, in case any early remedial action is warranted.

RECENT ALGAL INTRODUCTIONS INTO THE SOLENT

Marine algae which are considered to have been introduced into the Solent are given in Table III. These will be discussed in turn, mainly to provide some account of their initial discovery and present distribution.

1. *Grateloupia filicina* var. *luxurians*

(a) Occurrence and identification. Since 1947 specimens of a large, distinctive red alga have been found around the Solent which had been variously ascribed to such diverse genera as *Helminthocladia*, *Calliblepharis*, etc. Investigations into their anatomy and reproduction showed that none of these identifications was correct and that these specimens must be referred to the polymorphic genus *Grateloupia*

Table III. Recent introductions of algae into the Solent

Species	Date of earliest discovery	Suggested origin	Reference
Grateloupia filicina var. *luxurians*	1947	Pacific	Farnham and L. Irvine (1968)
Grateloupia doryphora	1969	Pacific	Farnham and L. Irvine (1973)
Sargassum muticum	1971	Pacific	Farnham *et al.* (1973)
Neoagardhiella gaudichaudii	1973	Pacific	Farnham and L. Irvine (1979)

(Florideophyceae, Cryptonemiales). Nearly 40 species of this genus have been described and are widely distributed in tropical and temperate seas (Kylin, 1956). Examination of foreign specimens in the British Museum (Natural History) showed closest resemblance between this Solent *Grateloupia* and specimens of *G. filicina* from such countries as Australia and Japan, in particular. The difficulty in identifying the Solent specimens as *G. filicina* was because this same species had already been included in the British flora in such early accounts as W. H. Harvey (1846–1851). Specimens in the British Isles previously ascribed to this species were regarded as rare, being restricted to the south-west, and were very much smaller than the Solent plants.

As suggested by Farnham and L. Irvine (1968), the occurrence of the large plants of *G. filicina* around the Solent could be given various explanations. Their luxuriant growth could be a genetic or ecological response to certain local conditions, such as thermal or organic pollution, promoting enhanced growth. Berthold (1884), Boergesen (1916) and Gayral (1958) all commented that *Grateloupia* spp., including *G. filicina*, show increased growth in waters near towns or rich in organic matter, but none of these authors indicated that the increase in size is of such proportions as would account for the degree of difference between the specimens from the Solent and elsewhere in Britain. Alternatively, the Solent population could belong to a taxon distinct from the usual British *G. filicina*. This could either have passed unnoticed until recent times (which is improbable in view of the careful records kept in this country along the south coast around the turn of the century by such assiduous

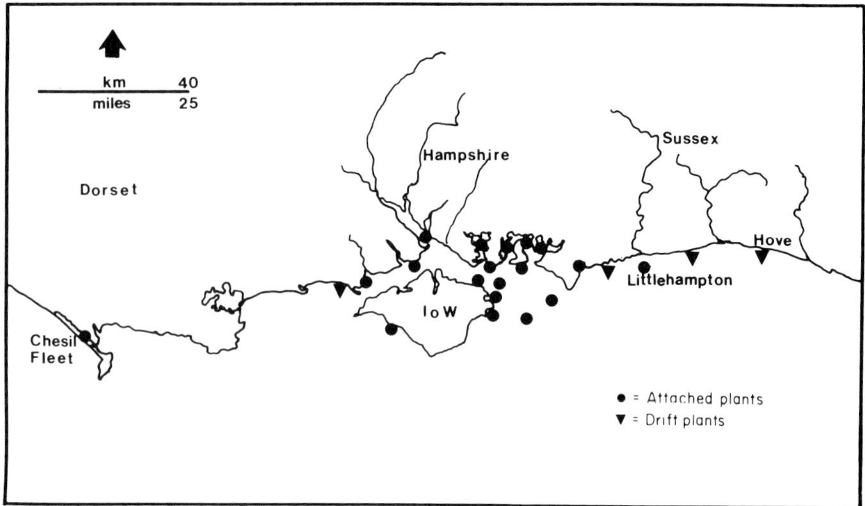

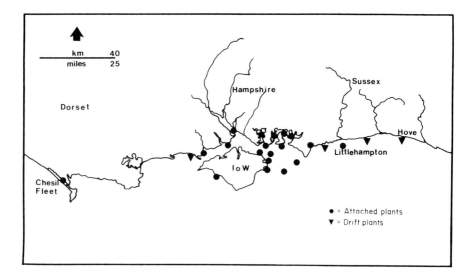

Fig. 1. Distribution of *Grateloupia filicina* var. *luxurians* on the south coast of England. The Solent region is shown in more detail in Fig. 2.

collectors as E. M. Holmes, E. A. L. Batters and their contemporaries), or is a comparatively recent introduction.

Gepp and Gepp (1906) reported on a collection of marine algae from New South Wales, Australia, which included "the finest specimen of *Grateloupia filicina* that we have ever seen". These large plants were described as a new variety *luxurians*. The Solent *Grateloupia* is similar to their type material.

(b) Distribution. G. filicina var. *luxurians* is widely distributed in the Pacific, Indian and warmer parts of the Atlantic Oceans. Figure 1 shows its present English distribution, which is centred around the Solent region. Abundant populations occur on the Isle of Wight at Bembridge and St Helens. On the mainland of Hampshire, var. *luxurians* is to be found within the local harbour complexes. It used to be particularly abundant within Portsmouth Harbour around Horsea Island, until the construction of the M275 motorway and land-reclamation schemes in 1971. Var. *luxurians* is found along Southsea beach and at a similar site between Lepe and Calshot. Within Southampton Water, it has only been found once, growing

on a buoy in the Hamble. Var. *luxurians* extends further west along the Hampshire coast to Lymington (Normandy salterns); drift plants have been found at Milford-on-Sea. The variety has a rather sporadic sublittoral distribution around the Solent.

The only site west of the Solent where var. *luxurians* has been found is in Chesil Fleet, Dorset (Burrows and Farnham, cited by Whittaker, in press). Since this interesting locality had been neglected phycologically for much of this century, it is possible that var. *luxurians* may have appeared in the Fleet before the Solent. Var. *luxurians* has been found further east along the south coast, with drift plants common at Bognor Regis (Sussex) since at least 1966. It was dredged off Littlehampton in 1953 by Drs W. E. Jones and A. Austin. More drift plants have been found between Hove and Brighton.

(c) Ecological observations. The most abundant population occurs at Bembridge. This site consists of an intertidal system of undulating limestone ledges, in between which at low tide are formed extensive shallow lagoons. The flora of these lagoons is rich, with such species as *Cordylecladia erecta*, *Cylindrocarpus microscopicus*, *Derbesia marina* and *Gracilaria bursa-pastoris*. This was one of the reasons for the recent designation of this locality as a Site of Special Scientific Interest (SSSI). Plants are also distributed around the more sheltered local harbours (Portsmouth, Langstone, Chichester and Pagham), where they occur in shallow pools or drainage channels, attached to stones or shells buried in the mud or sand. Associated algae here include *Chondria coerulescens*, *Chondrus crispus*, *Laminaria saccharina* and *Nitophyllum punctatum*.

Seawater temperature and salinity measurements have been made throughout the year at various sites. The lowest temperatures occur in February–March (3–4°C) with summer temperatures in the lagoons and channels exceptionally up to 25°C. Around the Solent, LWST occurs in early morning and late afternoon so that, in summer, the *Grateloupia* plants are not exposed to the full rigours of the midday sun. Lewis (1964) suggested that the time of LWST could be a factor modifying the distribution of certain intertidal organisms. Salinity does not usually vary much but, in parts of Chichester Harbour near freshwater inputs, *Grateloupia* plants may be subjected to salinities of 10–15 ‰ at low water, although for only 1–3 h.

Fertile plants bearing tetrasporangia or carposporangia can be found throughout the year, with greatest fertility in June–July. Tetrasporangial plants generally tend to be more abundant. The seasonal reproductive cycle is not so well-defined as in such other red algae as *Gracilaria verrucosa* (W. E. Jones, 1959).

Numbers of plants within permanent quadrats were counted monthly for one year at Bembridge and Horsea. At both sites, the overall trends were similar, with numbers decreasing from November to midsummer and then a sudden increase of mainly young plants. At this time of year, day length and water temperature are at their maxima.

"Tagged" plants and sporelings grew much faster in summer than in winter; sporelings 50 mm long in May were up to 200 mm in the following month, whereas a sporeling of 58 mm length in November had grown to only 75 mm by the following March. Some "tagged" plants were observed to develop cystocarps, which existed for up to 3 months before discharging spores.

G. filicina var. *filicina* has been only infrequently collected around the Solent, although it has been found at the same sites as var. *luxurians*. Thalli of both varieties have even been found on the same stones, but as quite separate plants. Specimens of var. *filicina* were transplanted from West Looe (Cornwall) into Portsmouth Harbour. They were there found to grow more slowly than var. *luxurians* plants and remained morphologically different. In laboratory culture from spores, sporelings of both varieties, resembling field-material, have been produced. Only in var. *filicina* has the complete *Polysiphonia*-type life history been obtained. These observations indicate that both varieties of *G. filicina* are genetically different and are not ecological variants. We can therefore conclude that var. *luxurians* is a recent introduction into the Solent.

2. *Grateloupia doryphora*

(a) Occurrence and Identification. A blade-like red alga was collected from Southsea beach in May 1969; it had not been found at that site or elsewhere in the Solent previously. Although it was morphologically quite different from *G. filicina* var. *luxurians*, details of its structure and reproduction established it as another *Grateloupia* species. A foliose *Grateloupia* had not hitherto been recorded for the

British Isles, so that this discovery provided yet another example of introduction into the Solent (Farnham and L. Irvine, 1973).

Many foliose species of the genus have been described, often based upon limited material. Ardré and Gayral (1961) made a preliminary taxonomic revision of certain foliose species occurring within the Atlantic and Pacific. They concluded that most species could be reduced to synonymy with *G. lanceola* J. Ag. Later, Dawson *et al.* (1964) agreed with Howe (1914) that *G. doryphora* (Mont.) Howe was representative of the foliose complex in *Grateloupia* and had taxonomic priority. Material of Solent *G. doryphora* agrees well with foreign specimens and in particular with material, illustrated by Abbott and Hollenberg (1976), from the Pacific coast of North America.

(b) Distribution. As indicated in the previous section, *G. doryphora* is widely distributed in the Pacific and Atlantic Oceans. Since the original discovery at Southsea further sites have been noted; these are mainly local harbours although it has not been detected in Portsmouth Harbour (Fig. 2). Its present eastern limit along the English coast is Pagham Harbour (Sussex), where it occurs along with var. *luxurians* (Farnham, 1975), and its western limit in Lepe. *G. doryphora* has not yet been found on the Isle of Wight.

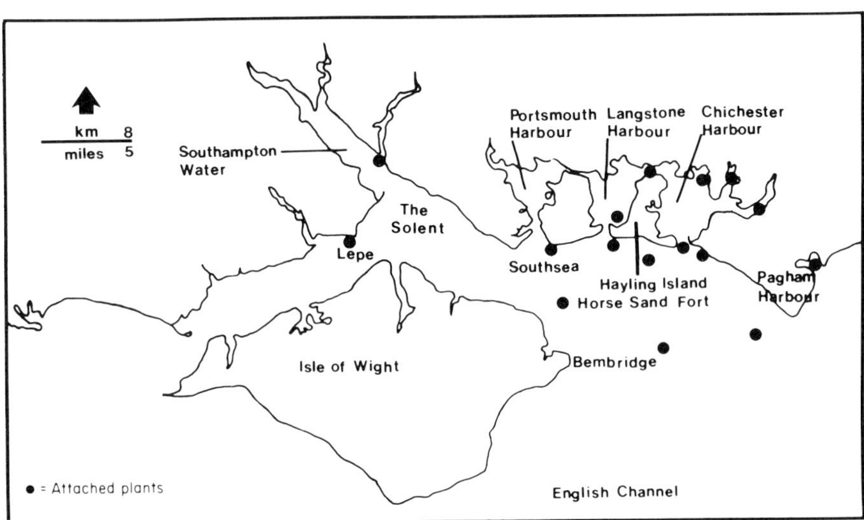

Fig. 2. Distribution of *Grateloupia doryphora* around the Solent region.

(c) Ecological observations. G. doryphora occurs in relatively sheltered sites, as in the Solent harbours, but can also withstand a certain amount of wave action, as indicated by its presence at Southsea. Here, both introduced *Grateloupia* spp. occur in the lower eulittoral-sublittoral fringe. Since 1969, *G. doryphora* has increased in cover at Southsea, while var. *luxurians* has become less abundant.

G. doryphora grows well in the creeks of Langstone and Chichester Harbours. Plants measuring up to 1.0 × 0.2 m have been found, which must make this one of the largest British red algae. Reasons for this enhanced growth probably include the eutrophic conditions in the harbours (Dunn, 1972), little wave action but fast tidal movements, and elevated seawater temperatures (up to 25°C) in summer. *G. doryphora* is more tolerant than var. *luxurians* of reduced salinity; plants have been found in runnels experiencing 5–10 ‰ for 2–4 h before the incoming tide restores the salinity to its full value of 33–34 ‰.

Only a few, small plants (up to 100 mm) have been found in the sublittoral, down to a depth of 5–6 m below C.D. Clearly, *G. dorphora* has not yet colonized the sublittoral zone as effectively as it has the lower eulittoral. This may be due to competition from the indigenous sublittoral algae. In addition, the rather turbid conditions of Solent waters and consequent reduced light penetration in the Solent may inhibit the growth of *G. doryphora* in the sublittoral.

3. *Sargassum muticum*

(a) Occurrence and identification. Sargassum muticum (Phaeophyceae, Fucales) was first reported for the British Isles, and for the Atlantic, when Farnham *et al.* (1973) reported some 30 plants growing in the Bembridge lagoons. However, *S. muticum* must have been present at Bembridge since at least 1971, since a visit shortly after its discovery revealed larger numbers of plants which were subsequently estimated as at least 2 years old. In June 1971, a mature drift *Sargassum* plant had been found at Southsea; this was initially misidentified as one of the pelagic species originating from the Sargasso Sea. It was later correctly identified as *S. muticum*.

Sargassum is a problematical genus, credited with over 200 species. Yendo (1907) described *S. kjellmanianum* f. *muticus* (sic) from Japan, which Fensholt (1955) elevated to specific status. Yoshida

(1978) has recently placed *S. kjellmanianum* Yendo in synonymy with *S. miyabei* Yendo. Tseng and Chang (1954) described a new forma, *longifolia*, of *S. kjellmanianum* from China, which Yoshida (1978) transferred to *S. muticum*. Because Tseng and Chang's paper has not yet been translated from Chinese, it is not known whether f. *longifolia* is present in the Atlantic population of *S. muticum*.

(b) Distribution. S. muticum occurs in the Pacific in Japan (Yendo, 1907), in China (Tseng and Chang, 1954), and along the North American coast, where it was introduced in the early 1940s around southern British Columbia (Scagel, 1956). As Norton (in press) has pointed out, the rate of spread by *S. muticum* down the Pacific American coast has been disjunct and uneven. It had reached Baja California by the early 1970s (Abbott and North, 1972). This represents a spread of over 2000 km in some 30 years. Nicholson *et al.* (in press) consider that this species has not yet reached its southern limit in distribution.

The means of introduction and dispersal of *S. muticum* along the American coastline probably involve both "remote" and "marginal" methods. Circumstantial evidence indicates that the arrival of *S. muticum* into Canada was caused by the importation of Japanese oysters, which were used to restock oyster-beds there (Scagel, 1956). The further spread of *S. muticum* may have been caused not only by the relaying of oysters from British Columbia into new beds, but also by the flotation of unattached *Sargassum* plants, rendered buoyant by their vesicles and subsequently dispersed by currents.

The European distribution has been monitored since 1973, and its rate of spread can be obtained from E. B. G. Jones *et al.* (1974), Lewey (1976), Gray and Jones (1977), Farnham (1978) and Critchley (in press). This alga now occurs along the south coast of England from as far west as Plymouth, south Devon (Boalch and Potts, 1977) to Eastbourne (Sussex) in the east – a distance of over 300 km (see Fig. 3).

The discovery of *Sargassum* on the English coast prompted marine biologists to look for this species on the other side of the Channel. An attached population was found by Gruet (1976) and Cosson *et al.* (1977) at Saint-Vaast-la-Hougue in Normandy. The oyster-parks there have been refurbished with spat of *Crassostrea gigas* imported from Japan, Korea and British Columbia. Gruet *et al.* (1976) pointed

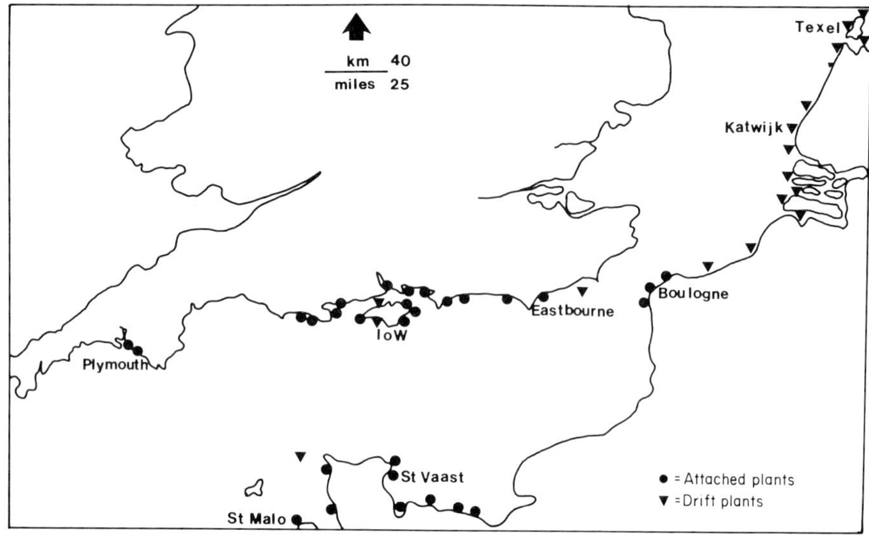

Fig. 3. European distribution of *Sargassum muticum*.

out that various sedentary Pacific animals were also being introduced with the oyster-shells. Since this importation of *C. gigas* into France has been in progress for some years (since at least 1966), it is possible that this population at St Vaast may have been established before the one in the Solent, although the latter happened to have been discovered first. Druehl (1973) expressed the view that international marine transplantations should be controlled more strictly because of the risk of accidental transportation of undesirable species. He predicted "the establishment of *Sargassum muticum* in the eastern Atlantic as a result of this transplant", i.e. importation of Pacific oysters into France. His prophecy has been substantiated! Other sightings of *S. muticum* have been recorded on the Continent. Kopp (1976) found a plant growing in the sublittoral off Barfleur, Compère (1977) collected drift material near Boulogne, and Prud'homme van Reine (1977) recently reported drift plants in the Netherlands.

It is therefore apparent that *S. muticum* is increasing its present distribution in European waters and may even colonize a similar extent of coastline in Europe as that in North America. Hydrographic conditions in terms of salinity and water temperature are generally similar along both these continential coastlines. In the Pacific, *S. muticum* is found in British Columbia with a winter minimum temperature of 1–3°C, whereas in shallow bays in southern California, sea temperatures up to 18°C may be encountered in summer. Kjeldsen and Phinney (1972) demonstrated that estuarine populations of *S. muticum* in Oregon were metabolically tolerant of sea water diluted down to 20‰. Norton (1977) has shown that *S. muticum* sporelings and detached laterals grow in culture over the temperature range 5–25°C. Thus, the potential distribution of *S. muticum* in Europe is considerable – the entire British Isles, and in continental Europe perhaps from Scandinavia down to Spain or Portugal, or even into North Africa. In a shorter space of time, *S. muticum* has spread further from the Solent than either *Grateloupia doryphora* or *G. filicina* var. *luxurians*.

(c) Ecological Observations. Sargassum muticum is found in fairly sheltered sites around the Solent; there, it grows in lower eulittoral lagoons, as at Bembridge and St Helens on the Isle of Wight, in low-water channels within Langstone Harbour, and along the waterline of floating pontoons and landing stages in Portsmouth Harbour. Few plants have been found in the sublittoral and it is considered that, in the rather turbid waters around the Solent, growth of such plants is likely to be poor. It is anticipated that in clearer waters, such as off Dorset and Devon, *Sargassum* may colonize the shallow sublittoral (Jephson and Farnham, 1974). Short accounts of the ecology of *S. muticum* in Britain have been given by E. B. G. Jones *et al.* (1974), Fletcher and Fletcher (1975), Withers *et al.* (1975), Jephson and Gray (1977), Lewey and Farnham (in press), and Critchley (in press).

The rationale for the decision to attempt control of the newly introduced *S. muticum* in English waters is summarized here. An account of this has already been given in E. B. G. Jones and Farnham (1973) and in Farnham and E. B. G. Jones (1974).

The possible effects of the spread of *S. muticum* down the Pacific American coast caused concern to at least some marine biologists there. Druehl (1973), for example, suggested that *S. muticum* might be replacing the eel-grass, *Zostera marina* L. Replacement of native marine plants in English waters by *S. muticum* could disrupt existing ecological relationships and food nets. Furthermore, *Sargassum* plants can also become detached from their holdfasts and float away, forming large free-floating masses. These may become such a nuisance as to affect the recreational usage and amenities of sheltered waters, for example, fouling fishing-lines, tangling round propellers of outboard-powered boats, and rotting on resort beaches. Commercial organizations could be harmed by the blocking of intake pipes or cooling seawater conduits to larger ships and shore installations, such as electricity generating stations. These problems caused by other seaweeds, already occur in England, and the establishment and spread of *S. muticum* would only compound them.

Thus, once marine botanists became aware of the implications of finding *Sargassum* in the Solent, a meeting was held at Portsmouth Polytechnic, on 4–5 May 1973. Eighteen marine biologists from various institutions in the United Kingdom attended to debate what, if any, action might be taken concerning *S. muticum*. This meeting had no official status but was justified by the lack of any Governmental legislation to cover this type of situation in the United Kingdom, although there are controls regulating the importation of land plants. Arguments in favour of eradicating *S. muticum* were proposed principally by Dr D. E. G. Irvine (Polytechnic of North London), supported by Dr G. Boalch (MBA, Plymouth). With regard to the practicality of eradication, most biologists present were not convinced as to the chances of a successful outcome, as the *Sargassum* population in Britain would need to be completely destroyed. However, the decision of this meeting was that the *Sargassum* found in the Solent region represented an undesirable addition to the British marine flora and should therefore be eliminated. Of the methods discussed, the one most acceptable was picking plants by hand. It was estimated that such man-power – made up of volunteers from the general public – would be required over an indefinite period. Gray and E. B. G. Jones (1977) have given a further account of the attempted clearance of *S. muticum* from British shores. It is now clear that hand-picking, even by large parties of enthusiastic volunteers, can only be an interim or palliative measure, rather than a real control, for *Sargassum* populations, because the plants have such a fast growth rate, immense reproductive output, and high regenerative ability. Other approaches which are currently under investigation include the evaluation of suitable herbicides, which would ideally affect only *S. muticum* in the sea (Lewey and

E. B. G. Jones, 1977), and various designs for mechanical clearance, ranging from simple hardware such as tractors fitted with harrows to more sophisticated project-orientated devices.

Despite the above attempts, it is certain that *S. muticum* has established itself along the south coast of England and is likely to colonize further stretches of suitable shoreline around the British Isles.

4. *Neoagardhiella gaudichaudii*

(a) Occurrence and identification. During a recent investigation into the Solent population of *Gracilaria bursa-pastoris*, it became apparent that another red alga, morphologically similar to *G. bursa-pastoris*, had also been collected under the same name. This is generically different from *Gracilaria*, as indicated by its filamentous medulla, zonate tetrasporangia, and ostiolate cystocarps with a central mass of sterile cells. These features are indicative of the genus *Neoagardhiella* (Florideophyceae, Gigartinales), which was defined by Wynne and Taylor (1973). There are two similar species in this genus, *N. baileyi* (Kütz.) Wynne et Taylor, on the North American Atlantic coast, and *N. gaudichaudii* (Mont.) Abbott, on the Pacific coast. The latter was confused with *N. baileyi*, until Abbott's (1978) investigation. The Solent *Neoagardhiella* seemingly fits more closely in habit, anatomical detail, and reproductive detail the description given by Abbott (1978) for *N. gaudichaudii* than that given for *N. baileyi* (Wynne and Taylor, 1973). The earliest collection of *N. gaudichaudii* from the Solent was made in August, 1973. In view of the confusion with *G. bursa-pastoris*, it could well have been present earlier. *N. baileyi* has been re-named *Agardhiella subulata* (C. Ag.) Kraft and Wynne (1979), while *N. gaudichaudii* has been transferred to *Agardhiella* by Ganesan (in press) and to *Sarcodiotheca* by Gabrielson and Hommersand (1980).

(b) Distribution. N. gaudichaudii has a limited distribution in the Solent, having been found only within parts of Langstone and Chichester Harbours and around Hayling Island (see Fig. 4).

(c) Ecological Observations. Only sporadic collections of this alien species have been made in the past 6 years, so that information is

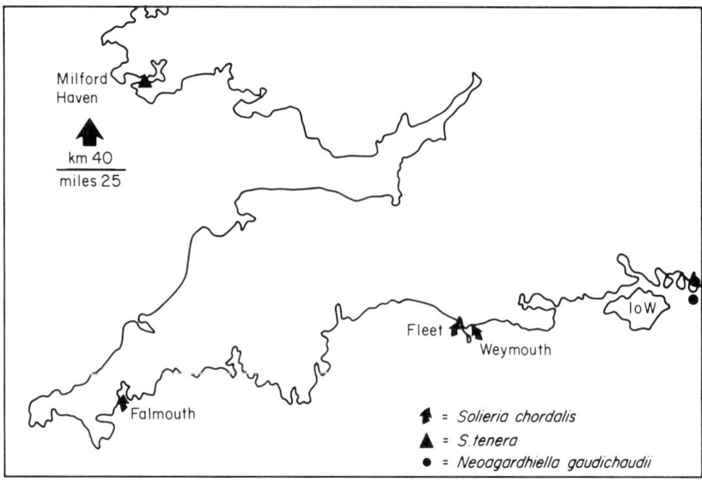

Fig. 4. Distribution of members of the Solieriaceae in Britain.

scanty. Plants have been found mainly in summer, occasionally in great abundance. They are found either unattached, or growing in clumps in the harbour creeks or in the shallow sublittoral (0–5 m). Associated algae include *Brongniartella byssoides, Cryptopleura ramosa, Desmarestia* spp., *Grateloupia* spp., *Laminaria saccharina* and *Ulva lactuca. Neogardhiella* is probably still in the early or pioneer phase of becoming established in the Solent and perhaps cannot even be regarded as a legitimate member of the British marine flora at this stage.

RECENT ALGAL INTRODUCTIONS OUTSIDE THE SOLENT

The Solent is not the only area which has provided new records of marine algae for the British Isles. Table IV lists certain of these, which will be briefly discussed.

It is remarkable that two species of *Solieria* should have been discovered within such a short time of each other, and perhaps even more surprising because *Solieria* occurs in the same family (Solieriaceae) as *Neoagardhiella. S. chordalis* was first found in April 1976, during a sublittoral survey of Falmouth Harbour (Farnham and Jephson, 1977) where the plants were growing on maerl and shell. Later that year, *S. chordalis* was also found in Chesil Fleet and in Weymouth Bay, Dorset (see Fig. 4). Such a disjunct distribution is suggestive of remote dispersal, involving a vector such as shipping. *S. chordalis* is found in northern France

Table IV. Recent additions of marine algae to the British flora

Species	British distribution	Date of discovery	Suggested origin	Reference
Solieria chordalis	Falmouth, S. Cornwall	1976	N. France	Farnham and Jephson (1977)
	Fleet, Dorset	1976		
Solieria tenera	Milford Haven, Pembrokeshire	1978	Atlantic	Farnham and L. Irvine (1979)
Cruoria cruoriaeformis	Falmouth, S. Cornwall	1976	N. France	Blunden *et al.* (in press)
	Galway, W. Ireland	1977		
"Foliose red alga"	Falmouth, S. Cornwall	1977	?	Farnham and Jephson (1977)

and thus seems to be a cross-Channel migrant similar to *L. ochroleuca*. The record by Ardré (1970) for *S. chordalis* in England is erroneous (Mlle F. Ardré, personal communication). The addition of *S. chordalis* to the English flora was anticipated by Holmes and Batters (1891). As with other aliens, it is possible that *Solieria* was always present and has been unnoticed or misidentified. Its life history requires further investigation, since only tetrasporangial plants have been found in this country.

S. tenera (J. Ag.) Wynne et Taylor was first collected by S. Hiscock in July 1978 (as ? *Gracilaria* sp.) at East Pennar Point, Milford Haven, during the Southwest Britain Sublittoral Survey. This material differed from *S. chordalis* in its more robust axes and less proliferous appearance, thus agreeing with specimens of *S. tenera*. This is a warm-water species occurring in the Atlantic (Caribbean, Gulf of Mexico and West Africa). Both carposporangial and tetrasporangial plants have now been collected. In all three of these solieriaceous algae, it has been found that although spores have been discharged in culture from fertile material, none has ever germinated. This could indicate that these species may reproduce more by vegetative propagation than by spore development It has been observed that plants of *S. chordalis*, in particular, easily fragment and undergo rhizoidal reattachment.

An encrusting red alga, *Cruoria cruoriaeformis* (Crouan frat.) Denizot (Florideophyceae, Gigartinales), has been found growing on maerl in Falmouth and Galway. It has not previously been recorded for the British Isles, but Dixon and Irvine (1977) suggested that it was likely to be present. *C. cruoriaeformis* is probably not an introduction from northern France but is much more likely to have been previously undetected. A further foliose red alga has also been found at Falmouth; it is not only unlike any previously known British species but cannot even be given provisional generic identification due to the lack of appropriate reproductive structures. Whether this represents an undescribed indigenous species or an exotic alien therefore cannot yet be stated.

DISCUSSION

Some authors (e.g. Carlton, 1975) stipulate that alien species are only properly so if introduced as the result of human activities, which may be unintentional, as in the case of *Elminius*, or deliberate, as for *C. gigas*. The arrival of other immigrant species may be merely by the process of marginal dispersal, e.g. *L. ochroleuca*. However, the mode of arrival for many adventitious species can only be surmised. Thus, it seems advisable to regard any exotic species which has established itself in a new country as constituting an introduction.

Discoveries of introduced species in the British Isles, especially along the south coast of England, seem to be continuous, particularly within sublittoral harbour areas. This is suggestive of shipping as a vector but may also be a reflection on the "distribution of collectors", especially divers who have recently been surveying these localities. Areas like the Solent may also be conductive to the establishment of alien species, which are usually characterized as pioneer or opportunist, through the occurrence of "open" communities, combined with relative freedom from "closed" communities dominated by fucoids and kelps.

Like many of the established introductions, e.g. *C. fragile*, some of the recent arrivals may also have originated from the Pacific. The main "donor" area for algae introduced into the British Isles could be the Pacific coast of North America, since this is a region common to the geographical distribution of many of our alien species. It is appropriate to note here that the movement of immigrant species is not a one-way process. Successful introductions have occurred from the Atlantic into the Pacific, e.g. the barnacle *Balanus amphitrite* Darwin (Carlton, 1975) and the red alga *Schottera nicaeensis* (Lewis and Kraft, 1979).

As has been indicated, many introduced species are difficult to identify when first found. They may either be confused with native species, e.g. *N. gaudichaudii* and *G. bursa-pastoris*, or may be treated as previously undescribed species. *Cryptonemia hibernica* was described as a new species from Cork Harbour, Ireland, by Guiry and L. Irvine (1974), who considered that this Irish material was taxonomically distinct from a complex of species in the eastern Pacific. Further investigation may indicate that only one polymorphic species of *Cryptonemia* is involved, and that this Irish population represents another Pacific introduction. Inconspicuous species which have recently been recorded for the British Isles, e.g. *C. cruoriaeformis* and *Fosliella limitata* (Chamberlain, 1977), are almost certainly indigenous.

Introduced species may vary in their responses to a new environment. Some may remain locally restricted in their distribution; *G. doryphora*, for example, is still a "Solent species", while others such as *S. muticum* have spread faster and further. Some successful aliens may outcompete indigenous species, as has been suggested for *C. fragile* and *S. muticum*. One alien may even act as vector whereby further adventitious species are introduced; this may be the explanation for the two immigrant spirorbid polychaetes found on *Sargassum* in Portsmouth Harbour by Knight-Jones *et al.* (1975). Ecological consequences of marine transplantations, whether intended or inadvertent, cannot be predicted, as Druehl (1973) pointed out. This should be borne in mind when deliberate introductions are proposed, as in the suggestion to introduce the South Atlantic and Pacific kelp *Macrocystis pyrifera* (L.) C. Ag. into Brittany (Franklin, 1974).

Continuous surveillance of marine communities is required to detect any ecological changes, including the initial arrival of such alien species as discussed here.

ACKNOWLEDGEMENTS

I wish to extend my sincere appreciation to Dr E. B. G. Jones, Mrs L. Irvine and Dr W. E. Jones for their help and encouragement during these investigations. Assistance from the following is also gratefully acknowledged: A. Critchley, Dr P. Gray, S. Hiscock, P. Housden and N. Jephson. I should like to thank the Natural Environment Research Council (Contract GR/3/2261) and the Department of the Environment (Contract DGR/483/36) for financial support.

REFERENCES

Abbott, I. A. (1978). Morphologic and taxonomic observations on *Neoagardhiella* (Gigartinales, Rhodophyta), with emphasis on Pacific populations. *J. Phycol.* **14**, 48–53.

Abbott, I. A. and Hollenberg, G. J. (1976). "Marine Algae of California". Stanford University Press, Stanford.

Abbott, I. A. and North, W. J. (1972). Temperature influences on floral composition in California coastal waters. *Proc. int. Seaweed Symp.* **7**, 72–79.

Anon. (1972). Report of the working group on introduction of non-indigenous marine organisms. *ICES Cooperative Research Report* no. 32: 1–59.

Ardré. F. (1970). Contributions à l'étude des algues marines du Portugal. 1-La flore. *Port. Acta biol., B* **10**, 1–423.

Ardré, F. and Gayral, P. (1961). Quelques *Grateloupia* de l'Atlantique et du Pacifique. *Revue algol.* N.S., **6**, 38–48.

Berthold, G. (1884). Die Cryptonemiaceen des Golfes von Neapel. *Fauna Flora Golf. Neapel* **12**, 1–27.

Bishop, M. W. H. (1947). Establishment of an immigrant barnacle in British waters. *Nature, Lond.* **159**, 501.

Blackler, H. (1963). Some observations on the genus *Colpomenia* (Endlicher) Derbes et Solier 1851. *Proc. int. Seaweed Symp.* 4, 50–54.

Blunden, G., Farnham, W. F., Jephson, N., Barwell, C., Fenn, R. and Plunkett, B. (in press). The composition of maerl beds of economic interest in northern Brittany, Cornwall and Ireland. *Proc. int. Seaweed Symp.* **10**.

Boalch, G. T. and Harbour, D. S. (1977). Unusual diatom off the coast of south-west England and its effect on fishing. *Nature, Lond.* **269**, 687–688.

Boalch, G. T. and Potts, G. W. (1977). The first occurrence of *Sargassum muticum* (Yendo) Fensholt in the Plymouth area. *J. mar. biol. Ass. U.K.* **57**, 29–31.

Boergesen, F. (1916). The marine algae of the Danish West Indies. Part 3. Rhodophyceae. *Dansk bot. Ark.* **3**, 81–144.

Boergesen, F. (1929). Marine algae from the Canary Islands, especially from Tenerife and Gran Canaria. III Rhodophyceae Pt. II. *Biol. Meddr* 8, 1–97.

Carlisle, D. B. (1954). *Styela mammiculata* n. sp., a new species of ascidian from the Plymouth area. *J. mar. biol. Ass. U.K.* **33**, 329–334.

Carlton, J. T. (1975). Introduced intertidal invertebrates. *In* "Light's Manual. Intertidal Invertebrates of the Central California Coast" (R. I. Smith and J. T. Carlton, eds), pp. 17–25. University of California, Berkeley.

Chamberlain, Y. M. (1977). The occurrence of *Fosliella limitata* (Foslie) Ganesan (a new British record) and *F. lejolisii* (Rosanoff) Howe (Rhodophyta, Corallinaceae) on the Isle of Wight. *Br. phycol. J.* **12**, 67–81.

Chemin, E. (1928). Multiplication végétative et dissémination chez quelques algues Floridées. *Trav. Stn biol. Roscoff* 7, 5–62.

Chihara, M. (1960). On the germination of tetraspores of *Falkenbergia hillebrandii* (Bornet) Falkenberg. *J. Jap. Bot.* **35**, 249–253.

Cole, H. A. (1942). The American whelk tingle, *Urosalpinx cinerea* (Say), on British oyster beds. *J. mar. biol. Ass. U.K.* **25**, 477–508.

Compère, P. (1977). *Sargassum muticum* (Yendo) Fensholt (Phaeophyceae) dans le Pas-de-Calais (France). *Dumontiera* **6**, 8–10.

Cosson, J., Duglet, A. and Billard, C. (1977). Sur la végétation algale de l'étage littoral dans la region de Saint-Vaast-la-Hougue et la présence d'une espèce japonaise nouvelle pour les côtes françaises: *Sargassum muticum* (Yendo) Fensholt (Phéophycée, Fucale). *Bull. Soc. linn. Normandie* **105**, 109–116.

Cotton, A. D. (1908). *Colpomenia sinuosa* in Britain. *J. Bot., Lond.* **46**, 82–83.

Cotton, A. D. (1912). Marine algae. *In* "A Biological Survey of Clare Island in the County of Mayo, Ireland and of the Adjoining District" (R. L. Praeger, ed.). *Proc. R. Ir. Acad.* **31**, sect 1 (15): 1–178.

Crisp, D. J. (1958). The spread of *Elminius modestus* Darwin in north-west Europe. *J. mar. biol. Ass. U.K.* **37**, 483–520.

Critchley, A. (in press). Sporeling development of the brown alga *Sargassum muticum*. *Porcupine Newsletter.*

Dawson, E. Y., Acleto, C. and Foldvik, N. (1964). The seaweeds of Peru. *Nova Hedwigia* **13**, 1–111.

De Valéra, M. (1942). A red alga new to Ireland: *Asparagopsis armata* Harv. on the West coast. *Ir. Nat. J.* 8, 30.

Dixon, P. S. (1960). Studies on marine algae of the British Isles: the genus *Ceramium*. *J. mar. biol. Ass. U.K.* **39**, 315–374.

Dixon, P. S. (1964). *Asparagopsis* in Europe. *Nature, Lond.* **201**, 902.

Dixon, P. S. (1965). Changing patterns of distribution in marine algae. *In* "The Biological Significance of Climatic Changes in Britain" (C. G. Johnson and L. P. Smith, eds), Institute of Biology Symposium No. 14, Academic Press, London and New York.

Dixon, P. S. and Irvine, L. M. (1977). "Seaweeds of the British Isles. Volume 1. Rhodophyta. Part 1. Introduction, Nemaliales, Gigartinales". British Museum, London.

Drew, K. M. (1950). Occurrence of *Asparagopsis armata* Harv. on the coast of Cornwall. *Nature, Lond.* **166**, 873–874.

Dromgoole, F. I. (1975). Occurrence of *Codium fragile* subspecies *tomentosoides* in New Zealand waters. *N.Z. J. mar. Freshwat. Res.* **9**, 257–264.

Druehl, L. D. (1973). Marine transplantations. *Science, N.Y.* **179**, 12.

Dunn, J. N. (1972). "A General Study of Langstone Harbour with Particular Reference to the Effects of Sewage". Portsmouth Polytechnic, Portsmouth.

Elton, C. S. (1958). "The Ecology of Invasions by Animals and Plants". Methuen, London.

Eltringham, S. K. and Hockley, A. R. (1958). Co-existence of three species of the wood boring isopod *Limnoria* in Southampton water. *Nature, Lond.* **181**, 1659–1660.

Farnham, W. F. (1975). Seaweeds and their allies (algae). *In* "The Natural History of Pagham Harbour Part II" (R. W. Rayner, ed.), pp. 37–46. Bognor Regis Natural Science Society, Bognor Regis.

Farnham, W. F. (1978). "Introduction of marine algae into the Solent, with special reference to the genus *Grateloupia*". Ph.D. Thesis, Portsmouth Polytechnic.

Farnham , W. F. and Irvine, L. M. (1968). Occurrence of unusually large plants of *Grateloupia* in the vicinity of Portsmouth. *Nature, Lond.* **219**, 744–746.

Farnham, W. F. and Irvine, L. M. (1973). The addition of a foliose species of *Grateloupia* to the British marine flora. *Br. phycol. J.* 8, 208–209.

Farnham, W. F. and Irvine, L. M. (1979). Discovery of members of the red algal family Solieriaceae in the British Isles. *Br. phycol. J.* **14**, 123.

Farnham, W. F. and Jephson, N. A. (1977). A survey of the maerl beds of Falmouth (Cornwall). *Br. phycol. J.* **12**, 119.

Farnham, W. F. and Jones, E. B. G. (1974). The eradication of the seaweed *Sargassum muticum* from Britain. *Biol. Conserv.* **6**, 57–58.

Farnham, W. F., Fletcher, R. L. and Irvine, L. M. (1973). Attached *Sargassum muticum* found in Britain. *Nature, Lond.* **243**, 231–232.

Feldmann, J. and Feldmann, G. (1942). Récherches sur les Bonnemaisoniacées et leur alternance de générations. *Annls Sci. nat. (Bot.)* sér. 11, **3**, 75–175.

Fensholt, D. E. (1955). An emendation of the genus *Cystophyllum* (Fucales). *Am. J. Bot.* **42**, 305–322.

Fletcher, R. L. and Fletcher, S. M. (1975). Studies on the recently introduced brown alga *Sargassum muticum* (Yendo) Fensholt. I. Ecology and reproduc-

tion. *Botanica mar.* **18**, 149–156.
Franklin, A. (1974). Giant kelp for Europe? *New Scientist* **64**, 812–813.
Gabrielson, P. and Hommersand, M. (1980). Taxonomy and phytogeography of the tribe Agardhielleze (Solieriaceae), *J. Phycol.* **16** (Suppl.), 12.
Ganesan, E. (in press). Morphological studies in *Agardhiella* Schusitz (Gigartinales, Rhodophyta) from Venezuela. *Proc. int. Seaweed Symp.* **10**.
Gayral, P. (1958). "Algues de la Côte Atlantique Marocaine". Société des sciences naturelles et physiques du Maroc, Rabat.
Gepp, A. and Gepp, E. S. (1906). Some marine algae from New South Wales. *J. Bot., Lond.* **44**, 249–261.
Gray, P. W. G. and Jones, E. B. G. (1977). The attempted clearance of *Sargassum muticum* from Britain. *Envir. Conserv.* **4**, 303–308.
Gruet, Y. (1976). Presence de l'algue japonaise *Sargassum muticum* (Yendo) Fensholt sur la côte française de Normandie. *Bull. Soc. Sci. nat. Ouest Fr.* **74**, 101–104.
Gruet, Y., Héral, M. and Robert, J. M. (1976). Premières observations sur l'introduction de la fauna associée au naissain d'huitres japonaises *Crassostrea gigas* (Thunberg), importé sur la Côte atlantique française. *Cah. Biol. mar.* **17**, 173–184.
Guiry, G. M. and Guiry, M. D. (1973). Spread of an introduced ascidian to Ireland. *Mar. Poll. Bull.* **4**, 127.
Guiry, M. D. and Irvine, L. M. (1974). A species of *Cryptonemia* new to Europe. *Br. phycol. J.* **9**, 225–237.
Harder, R. and Koch, W. (1949). Life history of *Bonnemaisonia hamifera* (*Trailliella intricata*). *Nature, Lond.* **163**, 100.
Hardy, A. (1956). "The Open Sea – the World of Plankton". Collins, London.
Harvey, C. C. and Drew, K. M. (1949). Occurrence of *Falkenbergia* on the English coast. *Nature, Lond.* **164**, 542.
Harvey, W. H. (1846–1851). "Phycologia Britannica: or a history of British seaweeds containing coloured figures, generic and specific characters, synonyms and descriptions of all the species inhabiting the shores of the British Isles". Reeve, London.
Harvey, W. H. (1855). Some account of the botany of the colony of Western Australia. *Trans. R. Ir. Acad.* **22**, 525–566.
Heppel, D. (1961). The naturalization in Europe of the quahog, *Mercenaria mercenaria* (L.). *J. Conch.* **25**, 21–34.
Hiscock, K., Hiscock, S. and Baker, J. (1978). The occurrence of the barnacle *Elminius modestus* in Shetland. *J. mar. biol. Ass. U.K.* **58**, 627–629.
Holmes, E. M. (1897). Note on *Bonnemaisonia hamifera. J. Bot., Lond.* **35**, 408–409.
Holmes, E. M. (1900). Marine algae. *In* "The Victoria history of the counties of England, Hampshire and the Isle of Wight" (H. A. Doubleday, ed.). Vol. 1, pp. 80–81. Constable, Westminster.
Holmes, E. M. and Batters, E. A. L. (1891). A revised list of the British marine algae. *Ann. Bot.* **5**, 63–107.
Houghton, D. R. and Millar, R. H. (1960). Spread of *Styela mammiculata*

Carlisle. *Nature, Lond.* **185**, 862.

Howe, M. A. (1914). The marine algae of Peru. *Mem. Torrey bot. Club* **15**, 1–185.

Irvine, D. E. G., Guiry, M. D., Tittley, I. and Russell, G. (1975). New and interesting algae from the Shetland Isles. *Br. phycol. J.* **10**, 57–71.

Irvine, D. E. G., Smith, R. M., Tittley, I., Fletcher, R. L. and Farnham, W. F. (1972). A survey of the marine algae of Lundy. *Br. phycol. J.* **7**, 119–135.

Jephson, N. A. and Farnham, W. F. (1974). The Japweed menace. *Triton* **19**, 227–228.

Jephson, N. A. and Gray, P. W. G. (1977). Aspects of the ecology of *Sargassum muticum* (Yendo) Fensholt, in the Solent region of the British Isles. I. The growth cycle and epiphytes. *In* "Biology of Benthic Organisms" (B. F. Keegan, P. Ó'Céidigh and P. J. S. Boaden, eds), pp. 367–375. Eleventh European Symposium on Marine Biology. Pergamon, Oxford.

Jones, E. B. G. and Farnham, W. F. (1973). Japweed: new threat to British coast. *New Scientist* **60**, 394–5.

Jones, E. B. G., Farnham, W. F. and Lewey, S. (1974). "Three Monthly Report on *Sargassum muticum* in the Solent". Portsmouth Polytechnic, Portsmouth.

Jones, W. E. (1959). The growth and fruiting of *Gracilaria verrucosa* (Hudson) Papenfuss. *J. mar. biol. Ass. U.K.* **38**, 47–56.

Jones, W. E. (1974). Changes in the seaweed flora of the British Isles. *In* "The changing Flora and Fauna of Britain" (D. L. Hawksworth, ed.), pp. 97–113. Systematics Association Special Vol. No. 6. Academic Press, London and New York.

Jones, W. E. and Babb, M. S. (1968). The motile period of swarmers of *Enteromorpha intestinalis* (L.) Link. *Br. phycol. Bull.* **3**, 525–528.

Kjeldsen, C. K. and Phinney, H. K. (1972). Effects of variations in salinity and temperature on some estuarine macro-algae. *Proc. int. Seaweed. Symp.* **7**, 301–308.

Knight-Jones, P., Knight-Jones, E. W., Thorp, C. H. and Gray, P. W. G. (1975). Immigrant Spirorbids (Polychaeta, Sedentaria) on the Japanese *Sargassum* at Portsmouth, England. *Zoologica Scripta* **4**, 145–149.

Kopp, J. (1976). Presence d'une phéophycée américaine, *Sargassum muticum*, sur les côtes françaises de la Manche. *ICES Cooperative Research Report*, **1**.

Kraft, G. T. and Wynne, M. J. (1979). An earlier name for the Atlantic North American red alga *Neoagardhiella baileyi* (Solieriaceae, Gigartinales). *Phycologia* **18**, 325–329.

Kylin, H. (1956). "Die Gattungen der Rhodophyceen". CWK Gleerups Forlag, Lund.

Lewey, S. A. (1976). "Studies on the brown alga, *Sargassum muticum* (Yendo) Fensholt, in Britain". M.Phil. Thesis, Portsmouth Polytechnic.

Lewey, S. and Farnham, W. F. (in press). Observations on *Sargassum muticum* in Britain. *Proc. int. Seaweed Symp.* 8,

Lewey, S. A. and Jones, E. B. G. (1977). The effect of aquatic herbicides on selected marine algae. *J. Phycol.* **13**, (Suppl.), 40.

Lewis, J. A. and Kraft, G. T. (1979). Occurrence of a European red alga

(*Schottera nicaeensis*) in southern Australian waters. *J. Phycol.* **15**, 226–230.

Lewis, J. R. (1964). "The Ecology of Rocky Shores". English Universities Press, London.

Lucas, J. A. W. (1950). The algae transported on drifting objects and washed ashore on the Netherlands' coast. *Blumea* **6**, 527–543.

Malinowski, K. C. and Ramus, J. (1973). Growth of the green alga *Codium fragile* in a Connecticut estuary. *J. Phycol.* **9**, 102–110.

Marchant, C. J. (1967). Evolution of *Spartina* (Graminaea). 1: The history and morphology of the genus in Britain. *J. Linn. Soc.* (Bot) **60**, 1–24.

Marchant, C. J. (1968). Evolution in *Spartina* (Gramineae). II. Chromosomes, basic relationships and the problem of *S.* ×*townsendii* agg. *J. Linn. Soc.* (Bot) **60**, 381–409.

McAllister, H. A., Norton, T. A. and Conway, E. (1967). A preliminary list of sublittoral marine algae from the west of Scotland. *Br. phycol. Bull.* **3**, 175–184.

McLachlan, J., Chen, L. C-M. and Edelstein, T. (1969). Distribution and life-history of *Bonnemaisonia hamifera* Hariot. *Proc. int. Seaweed Symp.* **6**, 245–250.

Millar, R. H. (1960). The identity of the ascidians *Styela mammiculata* Carlisle and *S. clava* Herdmann. *J. mar. biol. Ass. U.K.* **39**, 509–511.

Millar, R. H. (1970). British ascidians. *In* "Synopses of the British Fauna (New Series)" (D. M. Kermack, ed.), pp. iv + 92. Academic Press, London and New York.

Mitchell, R. (1974). Aspects of the ecology of the lamellibranch *Mercenaria mercenaria* (L.) in British waters. *Hydrobiol. Bull.* **8**, 124–128.

Naylor, E. (1965). Effects of heated effluents upon marine and estuarine organisms. *Adv. mar. Biol.* **3**, 63–103.

Newton, L. (1931). "A Handbook of the British Seaweeds". British Museum, London.

Nicholson, N. L., Hosmer, H., Bird, K., Hart, L., Sandlin, W., Schoemacher, C. and Sloan, C. (in press). The biology of *Sargassum muticum* (wireweed) at Santa Catalina (California, U.S.A.). *Proc. int. Seaweed Symp.* **8**,

Norton, T. A. (1977). The growth and development of *Sargassum muticum* (Yendo) Fensholt. *J. exp. mar. Biol. Ecol.* **26**, 41–53.

Norton, T. A. (in press). *Sargassum muticum* on the Pacific coast of North America. *Proc. int. Seaweed Symp.* **8**,

Parke, M. (1948). *Laminaria ochroleuca* De la Pylaie growing on the coast of Britain. *Nature, Lond.* **162**, 295.

Parke, M. and Dixon, P. S. (1976). Check-list of British marine algae – third revision. *J. mar. biol. Ass. U.K.* **56**, 527–594.

Parkes, H. M. (1975). Records of *Codium* species in Ireland. *Proc. R. Ir. Acad.* **75**. sect. B, 125–134.

Price, J. H. and Tittley, I. (1978). Marine algae (excluding diatoms). *In* "The Island of Mull A Survey of its Flora and Environment" (A. C. Jermy and J. A. Crabbe, eds). British Museum (Natural History), London.

Price, J. H., Tittley, I. and Richardson, W. D. (1979). The distribution of *Padina pavonica* (L.) Lamour. (Phaeophyta: Dictyotales) on British and adjacent European shores. *Bull. Br. Mus. nat. Hist.* (Bot.) **7**, 1–67.

Prud'homme-van Reine, W. F. (1977). Japans bessenweier aan onze kust. *Zeepaard* **37**, 58–63.

Quayle, D. B. (1964). Distribution of introduced marine molluscs in British Columbia waters. *J. Fish. res. Bd. Can.* **21**, 1155–1181.

Ramus, J. (1971). *Codium*: the invader. *Discovery* **6**, 59–68.

Salisbury, E. (1964). "Weeds and Aliens". Collins, London.

Sauvageau, C. (1927). Sur le *Colpomenia sinuosa* Derb. et Sol. *Bull. Stn Arcachon* **24**, 309–350.

Scagel, R. F. (1956). Introduction of a Japanese alga, *Sargassum muticum* into the northeast Pacific. *Fish Res. Pap. Wash. Dep. Fish.* **1**, 49–59.

Schiffner, V. (1931). Neue und bemerkenswerte meeresalgen. *Hedwigia* **71**, 139–205.

Silva, P. C. (1955). The dichotomous species of *Codium* in Britain. *J. mar. biol. Ass. U.K.* **34**, 565–577.

Southward, A. J. (1960). On changes of sea temperature in the English Channel. *J. mar. biol. Ass. U.K.* **39**, 449–548.

Stubbings, H. G. (1950). Earlier records of *Elminius modestus* Darwin in British waters. *Nature, Lond.* **166**, 277–278.

Sundene, O. (1964). The conspecificity of *Antithamnion sarniense* and *A. spirographidis* in view of culture experiments. *Nytt Mag. Bot.* **12**, 35–42.

Taylor, J. C. (1979). The introduction of exotic plant and animal species into Britain. *Biologist* **26**, 229–236.

Tseng, C. K. and Chang, J. F. (1954). A study of Chinese *Sargassum* III. *Bot. rep.* **3**, 353–366.

Walford, L. and Wicklund, R. (1973). Contribution to the world-wide inventory of exotic marine and anadromous organisms. *FAO Fish. Tech. Pap.* **121**, 1–49.

Westbrook, M. A. (1930). Notes on the distribution of certain marine red algae. *J. Bot., Lond.* **68**, 257–264.

Whittaker, J. E. (in press). The Fleet, Dorset – a seasonal study of the watermass and vegetation. *Proc. Dorset nat. Hist. archeol. Soc.*

Withers, R. G., Farnham, W. F., Lewey, S., Jephson, N. A., Haythorn, J. M. and Gray, P. W. G. (1975). The epibionts of *Sargassum muticum* in British waters. *Mar. Biol., Berl.* **35**, 79–86.

Wood, R. D. (1962). *Codium* is carried to Cape Cod. *Bull. Torrey bot. Club* **89**, 178–180.

Wynne, M. J. and Taylor, W. R. (1973). The status of *Agardhiella tenera* and *Agardhiella baileyi* (Rhodophyta, Gigartinales). *Hydrobiologia* **43**, 93–107.

Yendo, K. (1907). The Fucaceae of Japan. *J. Coll. Sci. imp. Univ. Tokyo* **21**, 1–174.

Yoshida, T. (1978). Lectotypification of *Sargassum kjellmanianum* and *S. miyabei* (Phaeophyta, Sargassaceae). *Jap. J. Phycol.* **26**, 121–124.

15 Control of Algal Life-history by Daylength and Temperature

K. LÜNING

Biologische Anstalt Helgoland, Meeresstation, 2192 Helgoland, West Germany

Abstract: How are the characteristic patterns of seasonal growth and reproduction in benthic marine algae controlled by the environment? From what is known of higher plants, which are much better understood at present than algae, it can be expected that photoperiod and temperature are the main controlling factors. A culture system was developed in which various benthic algae were cultivated at 12 combinations of temperature and photoperiod. A night-break regime was included to test for genuine photoperiodic responses. New photoperiodic reactions were found in the *Trailliella*-phase of the red alga *Bonnemaisonia hamifera* Hariot, which formed tetrasporangia only in short days, at 15°C, as well as in the *Codiolum*-stage of the green alga *Monostroma grevillei* (Thur.) Wittr., which became reproductive again only under short-day conditions, at lower temperatures. In the brown alga *Scytosiphon lomentaria* (Lyngb.) Link, which forms erect thalli under short-day conditions, various photoperiodic ecotypes exist, all with different critical daylengths and obviously adapted to the latitudes at which they are growing. Two species of *Petalonia* also exhibited genuine photoperiodic responses. Various stages of other algae were found to react definitely to temperature, not to photoperiod. Among these are the gametophytes of several representatives of the Desmarestiales and Laminariales, which mature only in a certain range of lower temperatures. The ecological significance of these reactions, which enable the plants to occupy a niche in space and time, is discussed.

Systematics Association Special Volume No. 17(b), "The Shore Environment, Vol. 2: Ecosystems", edited by J. H. Price, D. E. G. Irvine and W. F. Farnham, 1980, pp. 915–945, Academic Press, London and New York.

INTRODUCTION

Since the beginning of this century phycologists have devoted much energy to clarifying the life histories of benthic marine algae, a task which is still not completed but which was fulfilled for many terrestrial plants during the last century. This lagging behind may explain why the question of by what means algal life-histories are regulated by external factors in order to fit the local environment has thus far found few answers for marine algal species. Hundreds of photoperiodic responses have been discovered and analyzed in higher, terrestrial plants, since Garner and Allard (1920) discovered photoperiodism in plants (Vince-Prue, 1975). But until 1967 no photoperiodic response had been convincingly demonstrated to occur in benthic marine algae; it therefore seemed plausible until that time to assume that the seasonal development of algae is regulated exclusively by temperature, which is of course a much more reliable indicator of season under water than on land. The first clear-cut proof of a photoperiodic response in marine algae was demonstrated in the *Conchocelis*-phases of *Porphyra tenera* Kjellm. (Dring, 1967a,b; Rentschler, 1967) and *Bangia atropurpurea** (Richardson and Dixon, 1968; Richardson, 1970), where the formation of fertile cell rows is promoted by short days and where phytochrome is the likely candidate as the photomorphogenetic pigment. A second photoperiodic response, which is however triggered by a blue UV-absorbing pigment and is also light-saturated at extremely low levels as in many phytochrome-mediated responses, was found to be involved in the formation of erect thalli from the prostrate crusts of *Scytosiphon lomentaria* (Dring and Lüning, 1975). From the culture work of various authors, some few more cases are known in which photoperiod may control the algal life-histories, but these still have to be analyzed in detail (see reviews by Dring, 1970, 1974). Recently, Mayhoub (1976) reported that a genuine photoperiodic response controls tetrasporangial formation in the *Hymenoclonium*-stage of the red alga *Calosiphonia vermicularis*. It is to be expected that further detailed investigations of the environmental regulation of algal life-histories will soon reveal more

*As *Bangia fuscopurpurea* in the previous literature cited; all following mentions of all benthic macroalgae that are covered by the British check-list (Parke and Dixon, 1976) employ nomenclature presented in that list.

cases of genuine photoperiodism – indeed, some new examples will be provided in this chapter – but on the other hand such studies will also reveal those cases wherein certain algae in fact detect the ambient season exclusively by temperature. The present investigation is intended to contribute towards this goal, although of the multitude of species and stages which still have to be investigated in this respect, only a very small number can be treated here.

MATERIAL AND METHODS

Throughout this study algal cultures were grown in white fluorescent light (Osram 65 W/19, Daylight 5000 De Luxe), at photon flux densities of 15–20 $\mu E/m^2/s$ (as measured with a Lambda quanta meter; equivalent to an irradiance of about 3–4 W/m^2, or an illuminance of about 750–1000 lux). Unialgal cultures were established by growing spores which had been released from wild material in plastic petri dishes (90 mm diameter, 15 mm high) filled with enriched sea water (PES; Provasoli, 1968). Young stages which had developed from the spores were isolated at an age of 2–3 weeks with forceps under a dissecting microscope. During the first weeks, a medium containing germanium dioxide (2 ml of a saturated solution of GeO_2 in distilled water, added to 1 litre of PES) was used to eliminate diatoms. Afterwards normal PES was used and changed weekly.

Treatments at different daylengths were carried out in a culture system consisting of boxes made of black plastic (8 mm thick PVC; 40 × 25 cm, 12 cm high) equipped with an automatically opening or shutting cover (Fig. 1). An electric time switch triggered a pneumatically operated lever (operating pressure 6–7 bar) which opened or closed the lid instantaneously. In addition, the light-dark status of a box was monitored by a photoelement situated in the interior of the box, which registered continuously on a multi-channel recorder. Two fluorescent lamps (or 3–4 at lower temperatures) were mounted at 40 cm from the top of the boxes, so that the photon flux density given above was obtained.

For basic experiments four systems, each consisting of three boxes (light regimes $8:\overline{16}$, $16:\overline{8}$, and $8:\overline{7.5}:1:\overline{7.5}$), were operated in different constant temperature rooms (± 1°C), at 5, 10, 15, and 20°C. Temperatures were measured continuously by resistance

Fig. 1. Culture system used for photobiological experiments. The unit, consisting of three boxes each equipped with automatically opening or shutting cover, is operated in a constant temperature room.

thermoprobes and registered on a multi-channel recorder. For the determination of critical daylength, a set of 9 (or 12) boxes was used in one constant temperature room. The advantage of this system is to be seen in the fact that the lamps are not included in the light-tight cabinet, which makes it less difficult to maintain a constant temperature within the cabinet.

The following culture scheme was used with representatives of the Scytosiphonales. For establishing unialgal stock cultures the zoospores, released by erect thalli which had been collected at various locations in the field (Table I), were transferred to continuous light, at 15°C. The crusts developing from the germinated spores were isolated as stock cultures. For induction of erect thalli, the crusts were transferred into a short-day regime ($8:\overline{16}$) for 6 weeks (15°C, or 10°C, according to species). Once the formation of the erect thalli had been induced, the latter were allowed to continue growth also in continuous light. At the age of 6 weeks, 20–30 erect thalli (of 5–10 mm length) were transferred into big glass culture vessels (22 cm diameter; 10 cm high; closed with a glass lid; filled with 1.5 l of PES) and cultivated in continuous light for a further 6 weeks (without change of medium). After this time, the erect thalli had reached a length of 5–15 cm and were usually sporogenous. For spore release, the erect thalli were blotted briefly with filter paper, exposed in a dry petri dish for 2–3 h, and then re-immersed in PES. The zoospores, which were released due to this procedure within a few minutes, were seeded into plastic petri dishes (90 or 55 mm diameter; 15 mm high) at such a density that at least 150 (small dish) or 250 plants (large dish) grew in one dish. The bottom of the plastic petri dishes had been scraped with a hot needle prior to filling with PES in order to ensure firm contact of the prostrate system of the plants.

Material for experimentation on the *Trailliella*-phase of *Bonnemaisonia hamifera* was obtained by fragmenting tufts (about 5 mm diameter), which had been pre-cultivated in PES, by means of forceps into units which consisted of 2–3 branches, each with 10–20 cells. For each treatment, 150 units were used in one glass dish (90 mm diameter; 55 mm high) filled with sea water to which less than normal Provasoli enrichment had been added (see below).

Monostroma grevillei was isolated from field samples (containing also *M. arcticum* Wittr.) according to the methods described by Kornmann (1962a) and Kornmann and Sahling (1962, 1977). Negatively phototactic swarmers represent the zoospores of *M. arcticum* and were directly transferred into the treatments at different temperatures and daylengths. Positively phototactic swarmers represent the gametes of *M. grevillei*. The life history of this species was routinely completed in the laboratory within 20 weeks in the following way. The zygotes derived from copulation of the anisogamous gametes were cultivated for 6 weeks in continuous light ($20\,\mu E/m^2/s$), at 15°C. During this time, the diameter of the resultant *Codiolum*-stage increased to a diameter of about 70 μm. For induction of spore formation the *Codiolum*-stages, fixed to glass slides, were transferred to short-day conditions (8 h light per day, photon flux density as before), at 5°C. Zoospores were produced, and blades of 2–5 mm length had grown from these by 12 weeks after the transfer. Subsequently, the blades were grown to fertility for 2 weeks at 15°C, in continuous light.

In all experiments 150 plants (250 in the case of experiments on critical daylength) were counted for the determination of the percentage of plants which had reacted in a specific way. Further details of material and methods are included in the sections below.

RESULTS AND DISCUSSION

In the following, three cases of photoperiodic control will be treated: (1) the formation of erect thalli in the brown algal order Scytosiphonales, with special emphasis on the occurrence of photoperiodic ecotypes in *Scytosiphon lomentaria*; (2) the induction of tetrasporangia in the *Trailliella*-phase of the red alga *Bonnemaisonia hamifera*; (3) the induction of spore formation in the *Codiolum*-stage of the green alga *Monostroma grevillei*. Afterwards several cases will be treated where it has been established that the control of performance of the life history is exerted definitely not by daylength, but by temperature.

1. Photoperiodism in the Scytosiphonales

Scytosiphon lomentaria (Lyngb.) Link grows in all boreal-temperate seas, but does not enter the tropics. In the North Atlantic it has been found from Spitsbergen (78°N; Svendsen, 1959) to the Canaries (28°N; Price *et al.*, 1978), and from Labrador (60°N; Wilce, 1959) to the Bermudas (32°N; Taylor, 1960). On the Pacific side of North America the species occurs from the Bering Sea to Baja California (Abbott and Hollenberg, 1976).

The question of whether the erect thalli are gametophytes or sporophytes has been raised since the beginning of the century (e.g. Kuckuck, 1912; Kylin, 1933) and answered in various ways, depending on whether fusion of the swarmers had been observed or not. Clayton (1979) discussed the problems involved in this differentiation. If no fusion occurs, one may be dealing with only one mating type, and another difficulty for observation of the mating reaction may lie in the "elusive nature of the mating reaction in these algae" (Clayton, 1979). Additonal support for the interpretation of the erect thalli as gametophytes (Kuckuck, 1912; Feldmann, 1949) was supplied by the discovery that a crustose sporophyte bearing unilocular sporangia is involved in the life histories of several Scytosiphonales (see summary of literature in Wynne and Loiseaux, 1976). According to the results of the exhaustive work of Nakamura and Tatewaki (1975), the life history of *Scytosiphon lomentaria* is characterized by a heteromorphic alternation between the erect thalli as gametophytes and the crustose sporophytes. Strains in which the swarmers released by the erect thalli do not fuse are consequently interpreted as following only a parthenogametic type of life history, according to the authors cited. The work of Clayton (1976, 1978, 1979) demonstrates both the complexity of life histories in the Scytosiphonales and the need for further experimental work.

The present study deals only with strains of *Scytosiphon lomentaria* in which no fusion of swarmers was observed. Furthermore, it was not the aim of this study to follow the development of the crusts (or the filamentous prostrate systems, where no firm contact was achieved by the young germling with the bottom of the petri dish) over a period long enough to find the appropriate conditions for obtaining sporangia in the prostrate system.

Several authors (Tatewaki, 1966; Wynne, 1969; Rhodes and Connell, 1973) have reported that from the swarmers released by the erect thalli crusts develop under long-day conditions and crusts bearing erect thalli under short-day conditions as seen in Fig. 2 in the case of the Helgoland strain. Subsequently it was established that, in the case of a strain from Helgoland, genuine photoperiodism is involved in this response (Dring and Lüning, 1975). The critical daylength, as determined at 15°C, was found to lie between 12 and 13 h, and a 1-min light break with a very low irradiance of blue light, given in the middle of a dark period of 16 h, inhibited completely the formation of erect thalli.

Table I (Nos 1–9) shows the results which were obtained with nine photoperiodically active isolates of *Scytosiphon lomentaria* from different localities, the extremes ranging from 32°N (Mexico) to 69°N (Northern Norway). There is a clear relationship between the geographical latitude at which a strain was sampled and the temperature range in which erect thalli were produced under short-day conditions ($8:\overline{16}$). The isolates from 32–48°N (Nos 1–4) produced erect thalli at all temperatures from 5 to 20°C. In the upper interval of this range, it took 3–4 weeks after seeding the zoospores before the erect thalli were visible emerging from the prostrate system; in the lower interval, it required 6–8 weeks. In the isolates from 54–58°N (Helgoland to southern Norway, Nos 5–7), the production of erect thalli was partially prevented at 20°C, but still functioned perfectly at 15°C. The strain from Iceland (66°N, No. 8) was fully blocked in this respect already from 15°C upwards, and the isolate from Tromsö (69°N, No. 9) from 10°C upwards. With increasing

Table I. Development of isolates from different geographical latitudes of *Scytosiphon lomentaria* (S), *Petalonia fascia* (F), and *P. zosterifolia* (Z) at 8 or 16 h light per day, and in a night-break regime (B; $8:\overline{7.5}:1:\overline{7.5}$) at four temperatures. Treatments covered a duration of 4–8 weeks, and percentage of plants which had formed erect thalli from prostrate systems (crustose or filamentous) was determined in 150–250 plants: + = 100–95% with erect thalli; — = 0–5% with erect thalli. Numbers in brackets give percentage of plants with erect thalli, if in the range 5–95%.

Isolate No.	Species	Origin of isolate	Latitude	5°C			10°C			15°C			20°C		
				8	B	16	8	B	16	8	B	16	8	B	16
1	S	Punta Banda (Mexico)	32°N	+	—	—	+	—	—	+	—	—	+	—	—
2	S	Halifax (Nova Scotia)	45°N	+	—	—	+	—	—	+	—	—	+	—	—
3	S	Rovinj (Yugoslavia)	45°N	+	—	—	+	—	—	+	—	—	+	—	—
4	S	Seattle (Washington)	48°N	+	—	—	+	—	—	+	—	—	+	—	—
5	S	Helgoland (Germany)	54°N	+	—	—	+	—	—	+	—	—	(14)	—	—
6	S	Port Erin (Isle of Man)	54°N	+	—	—	+	—	—	+	—	—	(34)	—	—
7	S	Lindesnes (Norway)	58°N	+	—	—	+	—	—	+	—	—	(16)	—	—
8	S	Tjörnes (Iceland)	66°N	+	—	—	+	—	—	—	—	—	—	—	—
9	S	Tromsö (Norway)	69°N	+	—	—	—	—	—	—	—	—	—	—	—
10	S	Flinders, Vict. (Australia)	38°S	+	+	+	+	+	+	+	+	+	+	+	+
11	F	Helgoland (Germany)	54°N	+	(44)	(52)	+	(51)	(34)	+	(48)	(35)	(48)	(16)	(93)
12	Z	Helgoland (Germany)	54°N	+	—	—	(46)	—	—	(38)	—	—	—	—	—

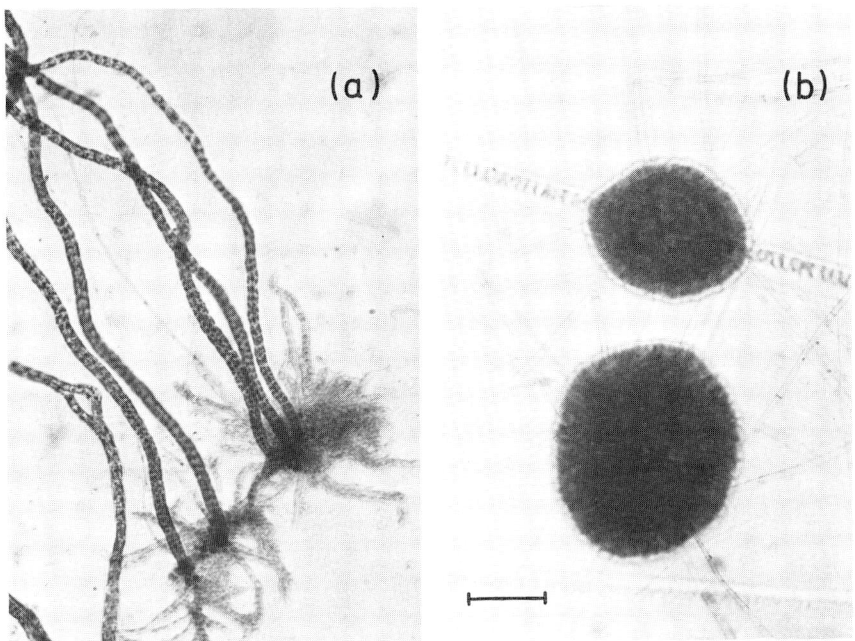

Fig. 2. *Scytosiphon lomentaria* (Helgoland) cultured for 4 weeks at 8 h (a) or 16 h (b) white fluorescent light per day. Scale represents 100 μm.

latitude, there is thus apparently a temperature block preventing the formation of erect thalli at concomitantly lower temperatures. The finding of Rhodes and Connell (1973) that a strain of *S. lomentaria* collected on the Atlantic coast of Virginia (37°N) still formed erect thalli in culture at 21°C at 9 h light per day (but not at 14 h) is in accordance with the reactions of the presently investigated strains originated from 32–48°N (Table I, Nos 1–4).

Another important feature, which is evident from Table I, is the effectiveness of the night-break regime. This fact characterizes all nine strains as showing absolute photoperiodic responses (in the sense of Vince-Prue, 1975), with an induction of almost 100% of the plants by short days, and an inhibition of almost 100% by long days or by an interruption of the long night. In the present study 1 h of white light of comparatively high irradiance (3–4 W/m^2) was used as the night interruption. It seems likely, however, that the energy required for inhibition of erect thalli formation during the night break is much lower, as found earlier in the case of the Helgoland strain (Dring and Lüning, 1975).

There are also non-photoperiodic strains of *Scytosiphon lomentaria*, as reported by Clayton (1978) for cylindrical forms of this species from southern Australia. One of the strains provided by this author has been tested in the present study (Table I, No. 10). The results confirm that erect thalli are produced in this strain under short- and long-day conditions at all temperatures from 5 to 20°C, and that the night-break regime is also not effective.

Two species of the genus *Petalonia*, although only from Helgoland, have also been tested. It can be seen from the data presented in Table I (No. 11) that *P. fascia* (O. F. Müll.) O. Kuntze is not absolutely, but only quantitatively, a photoperiodic plant (in the sense of Vince-Prue, 1975); this means that daylength only induces a certain percentage of the plants to form erect thalli. There is clear quantitative difference in percentage of erect thalli formed between the short-day regime on the one hand and the night-break regime and the long-day regime on the other. However, complete inhibition by short nights is not possible, as was also found to be the case in a strain of this species from the Netherlands (Roeleveld *et al.*, 1974). In contrast to *P. fascia* the second species occurring on Helgoland, *P. zosterifolia* (Reinke) O. Kuntze (Table I, No. 12), shows an absolute photoperiodic response, as in *Scytosiphon lomentaria*. Induction of erect thalli is only partially possible from 10°C onwards and is completely blocked at 20°C.

In order to determine the critical daylength, cultures of the various strains of *Scytosiphon lomentaria* were grown at intervals of 0.5–2.0 h within the range 8–18 h light per day. Figure 3 shows the results for seven strains of this species investigated at 10°C, and for four strains investigated at 15°C. It is obvious that the isolates must be all genetically different as regards the daylength range in which erect thalli can be formed. For example, the Mexican strain produced erect thalli at daylengths up to 11 h, the Helgoland strain up to 12 h, and the Iceland strain up to 14 h light per day (all at 10°C). It is well-known from studies in higher plants (see Hillman, 1962; Cumming, 1969; McMillan, 1974) and also in many insect species (e.g. regarding diapause determination; Beck, 1968) that northern ecotypes have a lower absolute requirement for darkness

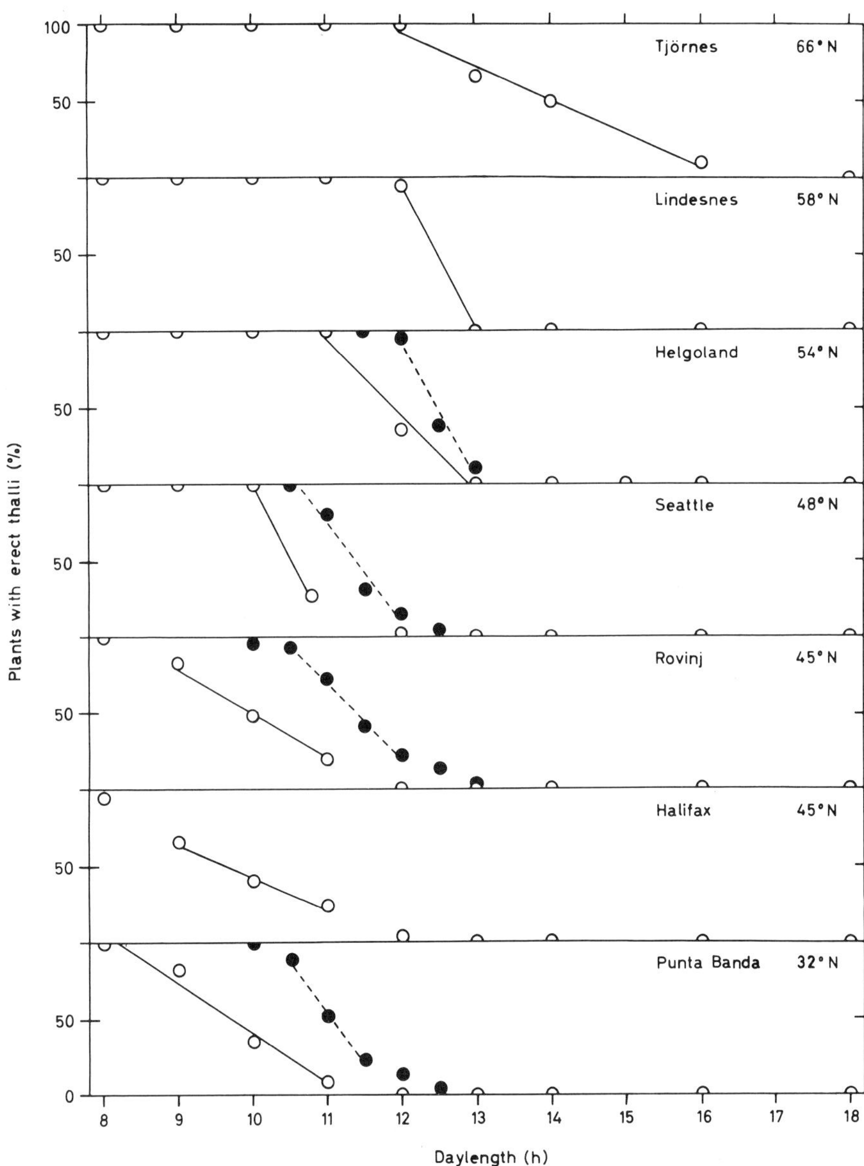

Fig. 3. Effect of daylength on erect thallus formation by different geographical strains of *Scytosiphon lomentaria* at 10°C (open circles) or 15°C (filled circles). Each value is based on a count of 250 plants.

than southern ecotypes of the same species. This accords with the fact that night length from April to August decreases progressively towards north, as pointed out by Cumming (1969). The same phenomenon is encountered again in the case of *Scytosiphon lomentaria*, and one may safely regard the different geographical isolates of this alga, although morphologically similar, as genetically distinct latitudinal or photoperiodic ecotypes. It is furthermore obvious from Fig. 3 that the critical daylength increases with temperature. From 10 to 15°C, the 50% response increased by 1.4 h in the Mexican and Mediterranean strains, by 0.9 h in the strain from Seattle, and by 0.6 h in the Helgoland strain. Such temperature-dependent shifts of the critical daylength are again also known from higher plants (Hillman, 1962).

Since the critical daylength for induction of erect thallus formation decreases from north to south, the period in which only crusts are formed becomes extended along the same gradient, as shown in Table II, where predictions about seasonal development have been based on the results obtained in the laboratory at 10°C and also local temperatures are tabulated. The picture would change slightly if predictions were based on the locally prevailing temperatures, e.g. on an autumn temperature of 5°C in the north (no laboratory data available for this temperature so far), or on autumn temperatures of 15–20° C in the south. Regarding the results available to date on temperature-dependent shifts of critical daylength (Fig. 3) one may predict that the periods of exclusive formation of crusts would be shortened in the south by about a month, but hardly lengthened appreciably in the north, since the change in daylength is so rapid in spring and autumn at high latitudes (Table II).

In all experiments described so far, the swarmers of the erect thalli were transferred immediately into the different regimes of daylength and temperature. Thus the induction of erect thalli formation was possible under short-day conditions right from the beginning. One effect of this kind of treatment was that no symmetrical crusts were formed under short-day conditions, as reported earlier (Dring and Lüning, 1975). Instead, rhizoidal outgrowths appeared early at the margins of the prostrate systems, probably to be interpreted as a means by which the plant fixes the developing erect thalli to the substratum with a widespread attachment system

Table II. Daylength required for induction of 100, 50, and 0% of plants to form erect thalli in isolates of *Scytosiphon lomentaria* from different geographical latitudes. Values were derived from experiments conducted at 10°C. Values enclosed by lines indicate the months in which no induction of erect thallus formation is possible.

Isolate No.	Origin	Latitude	Daylength for induction of erect thalli (h light/day) 100%	50%	0%	Daylength[a] on 21 of month and local water temperatures[b] J	F	M	A	M	J	J	A	S	O	N	D	
1	Punta Banda	32°N	< 8	9.7	> 12	10.4	11.3	12.2	13.1	13.9	14.3	13.9	13.1	12.2	11.3	10.4	10.0	h light/d
2	Halifax	45°N	< 8	9.6	> 12	9.3	10.8	12.2	13.8	15.0	15.6	15.0	13.8	12.2	10.8	99.3	8.8	h light/d
						2	1	1	3	6	10	13	15	14	12	8	5	°C
3	Rovinj	45°N	< 8	10.0	> 12	9.3	10.8	12.2	13.8	15.0	15.6	15.0	13.8	12.2	10.8	9.3	8.8	h light/d
						11	9	10	13	17	23	24	23	23	21	18	12	°C
4	Seattle	48°N	< 9	10.5	> 12	9.0	10.6	12.2	14.0	15.4	16.0	15.4	14.0	12.2	10.6	9.0	8.3	h light/d
						9	8	8	9	10	13	14	14	13	12	11	10	°C
5	Helgoland	54°N	< 11	11.9	> 13	8.2	10.3	12.2	14.4	16.3	17.1	16.3	14.4	12.2	10.3	8.2	7.4	h light/d
						5	4	4	6	9	13	16	17	16	14	10	7	°C
7	Lindesnes	58°N	< 12	12.5	> 13	7.6	9.9	12.3	14.8	17.0	18.2	17.0	14.8	12.3	9.9	7.6	6.5	h light/d
						5	4	4	5	8	11	13	16	14	12	9	7	°C
9	Tjörnes	66°N	< 12	14.0	> 17	5.0	9.0	12.3	16.1	20.3	24.0	20.3	16.1	12.3	9.0	5.0	2.8	h light/d
						3	2	2	2	3	7	9	9	7	6	5	4	°C

[a]Daylength according to Smithsonian Meteorological Tables.
[b]Water temperatures according to the following sources: Chapman (Halifax; personal communication); Zavodnik, 1973 (Rovinj); Weigel, 1978 (Helgoland); Waaland, 1976 (Seattle); Tomczak and Goedecke, 1962 (Lindesnes); Stefánsson, 1969 (Tjörnes). Water temperatures for Punta Banda are not available.

(Fig. 2a). In one experiment with the Helgoland strain, 6-week-old crusts, which had been grown to a diameter of about 1 mm in continuous light, were transferred to short-day conditions ($8:\overline{16}$) at 15°C. Seven weeks later, all crusts had formed erect thalli. From this it is clear that the short-day response takes place in both young germlings and established crusts. In another experiment, swarmers released by the erect thalli of the Helgoland strain were seeded on to scratched Plexiglas slides and transferred to an underwater station at 2 m depth below MLWS in June. The developing crusts survived on the slides when the zoospores, from which they had originated, had settled near or on the scratches. The crusts continued to grow throughout the summer and reached a diameter of about 2 mm by the end of November. In winter, there is little light at this depth near Helgoland due to very turbid water (Lüning and Dring, 1979), and there was practically no further development in the crusts. At the beginning of March, however, numerous erect thalli of up to 5 mm length had developed from the crusts. It thus seems likely that the crusts are perennial stages. It should be noted that the species is mainly to be found in the lower eulittoral region, near Helgoland. However, in the upper sublittoral region, where the field experiment took place, erect thalli of considerable length also occur in late spring and early summer.

The main ecological significance of the photoperiodic response in *Scytosiphon lomentaria* seems to lie in the fact that the swarmers released by the erect fronds are forced to develop first into a solid crust on the rocky substratum; they are prevented from producing a new generation of erect thalli right away, which is possible in the laboratory 2–4 weeks after seeding of the swarmers, under short-day conditions. If one assumed that 2–3 months are required from germination of a swarmer until the formation of a fertile erect thallus under short-day conditions in the field, then it is evident from Table II that by the time new swarmers are produced, daylength has already reached the range which allows only formation of crusts. As a result of the photoperiodic response, a new generation of erect thalli can be produced only from autumn onwards, either by direct vegetative formation from the crusts or by their zoospores, where these exist at this time. At low latitudes, the fact that the induction of erect thallus formation is still possible at high water temperatures in southern strains (Table I) becomes important in autumn, when water temperatures above 20°C occur in the south (Table II). At high latitudes, the "short-day interval" in late autumn and winter can hardly be used by the plants for the formation of erect thalli due to lack of light; the "short-day interval" in spring has to be used instead, since this is followed by a period of increasing light availability. It should be stressed that the induction of erect thallus formation may require a very low irradiance, but for the subsequent formation of the erect thalli sufficient light to support photosynthesis is needed. However, even in March when the induction of erect thallus formation is already prevented by daylength in the south (Table II), total solar radiation at 75° is only 18% of the corresponding value which can be measured at 30°N; only by June are equal amounts of light received at both latitudes (Perl, 1935). For strains which live at high latitudes, it is therefore essential that the induction of erect thalli is not prevented at such short daylengths as in strains living at medium or low latitudes. Another reason for the phenomenon of increasing critical daylength in northern strains may be seen in the fact that the medium daylengths occupy a comparatively short period in spring in the high north, so that there is no need for a sharp critical daylength in the medium range of daylengths.

Obviously, the probably perennial crust represents the growth form best-adapted to survive both severe winter conditions, especially at northern latitudes, and high summer temperatures in the south. The erect thalli of *Scytosiphon lomentaria* disappear in the field during May in the Adriatic Sea (Munda, 1973); by July in the North Sea, at Helgoland; but can still be found in August in Iceland (Munda, 1972). These geographical differences, which are evident again in the phenological pattern of *Petalonia fascia* (Roeleveld *et al.*, 1974), may simply reflect the fact that the erect thalli appear later in the year from south to north and disappear after a certain time interval due to complete disintegration after sporulation. However, it remains to be established whether or not there is also a differential resistance in the crust and the erect thallus towards high temperatures. If it could be demonstrated that the erect thalli do not withstand temperatures as high as do the crusts, it might be understood why the induction of erect thalli is restricted to a comparatively short period in winter in strains living near the southern limit of the species. For instance, based on the present determinations of critical daylength (at 10 and 15°C, Fig. 2), a substantial percentage (more than 50%) of the Mexican plants is induced to form erect thalli only in December and January (Table II).

2. *Photoperiodism in* Bonnemaisonia hamifera

The heteromorphic life-history of *Bonnemaisonia hamifera*, which as the gametophyte alternates with the tetrasporangial phase sometime known as *Trailliella intricata*, was discovered by Koch (1950) in the following way: "At the end of November 1946 tetrasporangia developed in the cultures, which had been standing on the north-east window of the laboratory since summer". From released tetraspores, the gametophytes developed; this life history therefore emerged as previously predicted by Feldmann and Feldmann (1941), who had already clarified the life history of *Asparagopsis armata* and its tetrasporophyte, *Falkenbergia rufolanosa*. Afterwards, Koch was not able to induce tetrasporangia when he continued the culture of the *Trailliella*-phase in a constant temperature room (personal communication). This same difficulty was experienced later on by Shevlin and Polanshek (1978), who cultured the tetrasporangial phase of the Pacific *Bonnemaisonia geniculata*, but could only obtain vegetative growth.

In the course of the present study three isolates of the *Trailliella*-phase, which had been isolated from Helgoland material in 1944 (W. Koch), 1959 (D. Müller), and 1961 (P. Kornmann) and thereafter propagated vegetatively in different laboratories, were cultured at four temperatures and three different daylength regimes. Tetrasporangia were formed in all three isolates in only one set of the 12 possible sets of conditions, that of 8 h light per day and at a temperature of 15°C (Table III, expts 1–3; Fig. 4). Since sporangia were formed neither at 16 h light per day nor in the night-break regime, this response is genuinely photoperiodic, occurring over a narrow temperature range. However, up to 10% only of the tufts had formed sporangia in the short-day regime (15°C), and this only after a long treatment under inductive conditions. Obviously, secondary factors inhibited the expression of the response. When the photon flux density was raised to 20 $\mu E/m^2/s$ and – more importantly – the

Table III. Formation of tetrasporangia in different isolates of the *Trailliella*-phase of *Bonnemaisonia hamifera* at 8 or 16 h light per day, and in a night-break regime (B; 8:$\overline{7.5}$:1:$\overline{7.5}$), at four temperatures (expts 1–3) as well as at different nutrient concentrations (expt 4, modified PES). T: Tetrasporangia were formed (percentage in brackets); v: plants remained vegetative.

Expt No.	Strain	Medium	Duration of expt (weeks)	Photon flux density ($\mu E/m^2/s$)	5°C			10°C			15°C			20°C		
					8	B	16	8	B	16	8	B	16	8	B	16
1	2080[a]	PES	18	12	v	v	v	v	v	v	T (<10)	v	v	v	v	v
2	2089[b]	PES	18	12	v	v	v	v	v	v	T (<10)	v	v	v	v	v
3	2123[c]	PES	12	12	v	v	v	v	v	v	T (<10)	v	v	v	v	v

Expt No.	Strain	Medium	Duration of expt (weeks)	Photon flux density ($\mu E/m^2/s$)	ml of Provasoli enrichment[d] added to 1 litre of sea water[e]						
					0	0.02	0.1	0.2	1	2	20
4	2080[a]	mod. PES	4	20	T(80)	T(96)	T(75)	T(51)	T(52)	T(50)	T(29)

[a]isolated by P. Kornmann in 1961. [b]isolated by D. Müller in 1959. [c]isolated by W. Koch in 1944. [d]1 ml contained 28 μm NO_3–N. [e]1 litre contained 16 μm NO_3–N.

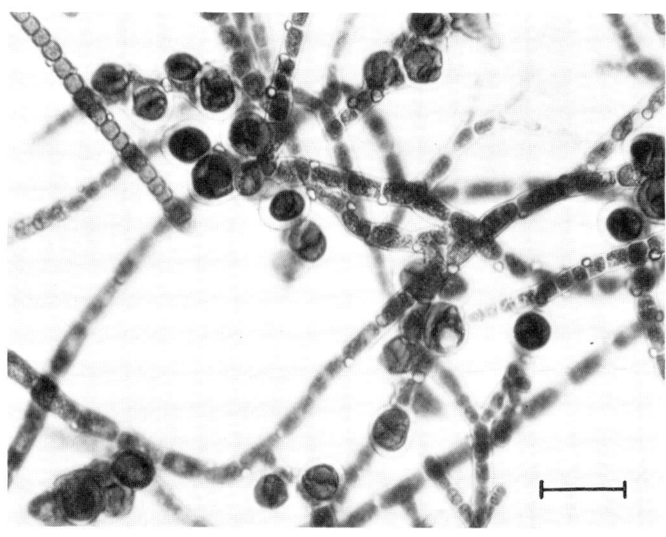

Fig. 4. *Trailliella*-phase of *Bonnemaisonia hamifera* with tetrasporangia, cultured at 8 h light per day and 15°C. Scale represents 100 μm.

plants were cultured during the treatments in sea water, to which had been added either none at all or only 0.02–0.1 ml per litre of Provasoli enrichment, instead of the 20 ml of the original formula (Provasoli, 1968), more than 75% of the tufts formed sporangia at $8:\overline{16}$ and 15°C; the controls in the night-break regime remained solely vegetative (Table III, expt 4). If it is nitrate which at too high a concentration inhibits the onset of reproduction, as is known in the case of several unicellular algae (see Dring, 1974) and also in the *Falkenbergia*-phase of *Asparagopsis armata* (Oza, 1976), significant inhibition of tetrasporangium formation would occur in the *Trailliella*-phase from about 20 μm NO_3–N onwards, corresponding to an addition of 0.2 ml Provasoli enrichment to 1 litre of sea water (containing already 16 μm NO_3–N, Table III). Although the media were changed twice a week in this experiment, in plain sea water there was a tendency for the plants to bleach out. In further experiments, a medium was used which contained 0.1 ml Provasoli enrichment added to 1 litre of sea water, so that in spite of the nutrients added a high percentage reaction could still be obtained (Table III).

From the tetraspores, some of which had already been released 4 weeks after the beginning of the inductive treatment, male and female gametophytes developed; these became fertile after 3–4 months when cultured in continuous white fluorescent light ($20\,\mu E/m^2/s$), at 15°C.

In another experiment, the critical daylength for formation of tetrasporangia was determined at 15°C. After 4 weeks at 8–16 h light per day (hourly intervals) the following percentages of plants bearing tetrasporangia were obtained: more than 92% at 8 and 9 h; 48% at 10 h; 6% at 11 h; 0% from 12 h onwards. Since daylength at Helgoland is still 12.2 h on 21 September (Table II), one may infer that the *Trailliella*-phase must remain vegetative until about this time. In fact, tetrasporangia are found in this plant at Helgoland only from October to December (Kornmann and Sahling, 1977). However, the species invaded the Atlantic only at the end of the last century, originating probably from Japan (see Koch, 1951); one is perhaps more justified in comparing its photoperiodic behaviour with the environmental conditions prevailing at the original locations. In Japan (Fukuoka-Prefecture, Kyushu; 34°N), the *Trailliella*-phase of *Bonnemaisonia hamifera* forms tetrasporangia in the field also from October onwards (daylength < 12 h; see Table II), tetraspores being released in November and December, according to Chihara (1961). The same author reported that the gametophytes in the field in November (17°C), grow throughout the winter (temperature minimum in February, 13°C), attain their maximum size and fertility in late spring (May: 15°C), and disappear soon after release of the carpospores, by mid-summer. At this time the temperature at the Japanese locality begins to rise from 20 to 25°C, so that the species seems to persist through the summer in the form of the *Trailliella*-phase, a similar phenomenon to that seen in *Porphyra tenera*, which passes the summer as the *Conchocelis*-phase (Kurogi, 1959). Chihara (1961) already suspected that daylength might control the onset of sporulation in the *Trailliella*-phase and the present results, which show the effectiveness of the night-break, confirm this hypothesis.

Clearly, the *Trailliella*-phase is able to distinguish between autumn and spring, since formation of tetrasporangia does not occur under short-day conditions when water temperature is 5 or 10°C (Table III). It will be necessary to determine the exact temperature interval which permits induction by a short photoperiod to take place. As to the temperature regime at the original locations, one may predict that the temperature optimum for photoperiodic induction will more probably occur between 15 and 20°C than between 10 and 15°C. Furthermore, the fact that gametophytes are present on the coasts of France and of the British Isles, but that only tetrasporophytes have been found on Scandinavian coasts (Feldman, 1956), may here find explanation. At northern latitudes, temperature may be too low in those autumn months in which daylength has become short enough for photoperiodic induction of sporangium formation (Table II). At Helgoland, where the gametophytes have only been found sporadically in the field (Kornmann and Sahling, 1977), an additional difficulty for their survival may exist in the extremely low light available because of turbid water during the winter months. Nevertheless, gametophytes were very common in the field on Helgoland in 1968 and 1969 (Kornmann and Sahling, 1977), and it is interesting to note that in 1966 and 1967 water temperatures in September were higher by 0.7–0.8°C than the 10-year mean for this month (1965–1975; Weigel, 1978). By contrast, in 1965 and from 1970 onwards, when no gametophytes of *Bonnemaisonia hamifera* were observed in the field, September temperatures have been below the 10-year mean (Treutner, personal communication).

The combination of a short-day regime and high temperatures required for tetrasporangia formation in this alga is unusual in normal culture conditions, where at most "spring" (short days and low temperatures) is imitated, not "autumn", as required here. This explains why other workers (e.g. Koch, Kornmann, Müller; personal communication) failed to obtain tetrasporangia in the *Trailliella* isolates which they cultured for many years in growth chambers with artificial illumination.

3. *Photoperiodism in* Monostroma grevillei

Monostroma grevillei has a heteromorphic life-history, the blades representing the dioecious gametophytes and the *Codiolum*-stage, which develops after copulation of the anisogamous biflagellate gametes, the sporophyte; this latter reproduces the blades again by means of quadriflagellate zoospores (Kornmann, 1962a; Kornmann

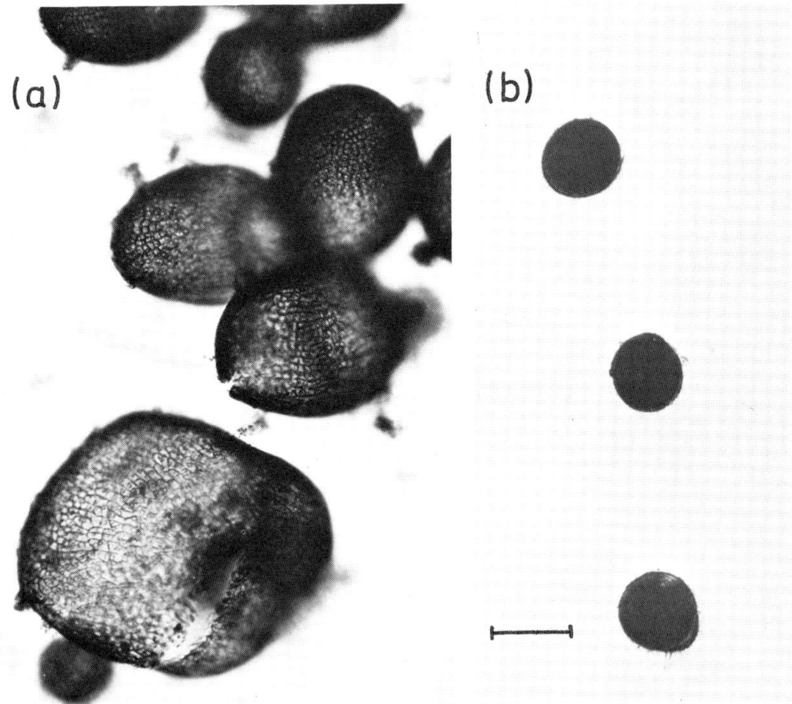

Fig. 5. *Monostroma grevillei* cultured for 20 weeks from zygotes at 5°C and 8 h (a) or 16 h (b) light per day. (a) Saccate thalli have been formed from prostrate systems developed from zoospores which were released by *Codiolum*-stage. (b) *Codiolum*-stage has remained vegetative since start of experiment. Scale represents 100 μm.

and Sahling, 1962, 1977). As can be seen from Table IV (expt 1), the *Codiolum*-stage became sporogenous only in short days (8:$\overline{16}$) and at temperatures from 5–15°C (with a low percentage at the uppermost temperature). From the zoospores prostrate discs developed, and from these the saccate fronds arose (Fig. 5a). Under long-day conditions, however, the *Codiolum*-stage remained vegetative for at least 20 weeks (Fig. 5b). Since the same reaction occurred also in the night-break regime at all temperatures (Table IV), the induction of zoospore formation is obviously due to a genuine photoperiodic response in this alga. In three *Monostroma* spp. occurring in Japan, Tatewaki (1972) also found that the *Codiolum*-

Table IV. Development of *Codiolum*-stages and gametophytes of *Monostroma grevillei* at 8 or 16 h light per day, and in a night-break regime (B; $8:\overline{7.5}:1:\overline{7.5}$) at four temperatures. *Codiolum*-stages were grown from zygotes, gametophytes from germlings derived from zoospores of *Codiolum*-stages. S: $>60\%$ of *Codiclum*-stages sporogenous; (S): $<10\%$ of *Codiolum*-stages sporogenous; v: all *Codiolum*-stages vegetative; D: prostrate disc of gametophyte only; E: erect, saccate fronds formed from all prostrate discs.

Expt No.	Stage	Duration of expt (weeks)	5°C			10°C			15°C			20°C		
			8	B	16	8	B	16	8	B	16	8	B	16
1	*Codiolum*	10	S	v	v	S	v	v	(S)	v	v	v	v	v
2	Gametophyte	7	E	E	E	E	E	E	D	D	D	D	D	D

stages ("cysts") involved in the life histories require short days (10 : $\overline{14}$) and lower temperatures for spore formation.

Once the zoospores have been released and have germinated into small discs, the erect, saccate fronds (later splitting into blades) are formed irrespective of daylength, but only at lower temperatures (Table IV, expt 2). This again has already been stressed in the case of several species by Tatewaki (1972) and in the case of *Monostroma grevillei* by Kornmann (1962).

On Helgoland, the species occurs in form of the blades only from March to May (Kornmann and Sahling, 1977). Although the critical daylength for spore formation still has to be determined, one may postulate that the seasonal cycle of *Monostroma grevillei* is regulated in the following way by daylength and temperature. The zygotes derived from gametes released by the blades in spring remain vegetative and survive the summer as the *Codiolum*-stage, since daylength is too long. In autumn, daylength becomes suitable for induction of spore formation, but temperature is too high in many locations. Only in late winter and early spring does the temperature become low enough to allow photoperiodic induction of spore formation, as long as the days are short enough.

4. *Regulation by Temperature*

Although it is clear from the foregoing that in true photoperiodic responses induction is possible only in a definite although often rather broad temperature range, the actual triggering factor in such reactions is daylength, or better, nightlength. On the other hand, there are clear-cut cases in which daylength is not involved at all in triggering the formation of a certain stage in the life history of a certain alga; temperature or other environmental phenomena, such as light quality (e.g. induction of fertility by blue light and UV in laminarian gametophytes; Lüning and Dring, 1975), are their primary factors.

Table V summarizes the results found on the development of specific stages of various algae not influenced by daylength.

In the life history of *Monostroma arcticum* no sexual stages are involved; the blades reproduce themselves by biflagellate zoospores giving rise to a prostrate disc, from which the blades develop as saccate thalli at low temperature (Kornmann and Sahling, 1962).

Table V. Development of specific stages of various algae at 8 or 16 h light per day, and in a night-break regime (B; $8:\overline{7.5}:1:\overline{7.5}$) at four temperatures. P: prostrate system; E: erect thalli arise from prostrate system (> 50%); F: fertile (> 50%); v: all plants vegetative; C: conchosporangia formed; R: released; N: not released. Symbols in brackets: < 10% of plants formed stage indicated by symbol; –: no survival.

Species	Duration of expt (weeks)	5°C			10°C			15°C			20°C		
		8	B	16	8	B	16	8	B	16	8	B	16
Monostroma arcticum[a,b]	18	E	E	E	E	E	E	P	P	P	P	P	P
Acrosiphonia arcta[a,c]	5	E	E	E	E	E	E	E	E	E	P	P	P
Desmarestia viridis[a,d]	5	F	F	F	(F)	(F)	(F)	v	v	v	v	v	v
Desmarestia aculeata[a,b]	5	F	F	F	F	F	F	v	v	v	v	v	v
Chorda filum[d,e,f]	5	F	F	F	F	F	F	v	v	v	v	v	v
Laminaria digitata[a,d,e]	5	F	F	F	F	F	F	F	F	F	v	v	v
Laminaria hyperborea[a,d,e]	5	F	F	F	F	F	F	F	F	F	v	v	v
Laminaria saccharina[a,d,e]	5	F	F	F	F	F	F	F	F	F	v	v	v
Laminaria japonica Areschoug[d,e,g]	5	F	F	F	F	F	F	F	F	F	v	v	v
Macrocystis pyrifera (L.) C.Ag.[d,e,h]	5	F	F	F	F	F	F	F	F	F	v	v	v
Porphyra miniata[i]	10	C	C	C	C	C	C	C	C	C	–	–	–
Porphyra miniata[i]	20	R	R	R	N	N	N	N	N	N	N	N	N
Lomentaria orcadensis[j]	8	–	–	–	E	E	E	E	E	E	E	E	E

[a]Origin: Helgoland, Germany.
[b]Grown from zoospores of field material.
[c]Grown from gametes of field material.
[d]Started from unialgal culture of filamentous gametophytes.
[e]Male and female gametophytes mixed together. F applies to both sexes.
[f]Origin: Tromsö, Norway.
[g]Origin: Yoishi, Japan; isolated by Y. Sanbonsuga.
[h]Origin: Santa Barbara, California.
[i]Origin: Halifax, Nova Scotia; isolated by L. C. -M. Chen.
[j]Grown from tetraspores of plant from unialgal culture.

As can be seen from Table V, the formation of saccate thalli takes place at 5–10°C, and no photoperiodism is involved, as in the development of the corresponding stage in *M. grevillei* (see above). Saccate thalli transferred to higher temperatures matured at all temperatures from 5–15°C, as already reported by Kornmann and Sahling (1962), irrespective of daylength. *M. arcticum* obviously survives the summer as a disc, and the formation of blades is exclusively induced by appropriately low temperatures in early spring.

The life history of *Acrosiphonia arcta* (Dillw.) J.Ag., in which according to Kornmann (1962b) the filamentous, erect gametophytes reproduce themselves directly from the zygote (or parthenogenetically from gametes), also seems to be regulated exclusively by temperature. From the swarmers of the erect plants, rhizoidal prostrate systems were formed at all temperatures investigated, and erect, filamentous thalli were formed in the range 5–15°C, irrespective of daylength (Table V). In late summer, the formation of erect thalli is thus blocked by high temperatures and the prostrate, rhizoidal system is formed instead; this latter represents the perennial part of the plant and is induced in winter by low temperatures to form the erect thalli again (Kornmann, 1962b).

In the Phaeophyta, the gametophytes of two species of *Desmarestia* and of six species of the Laminariales were investigated (Table V). The general result was that the gametophytes became fertile, irrespective of daylength, at temperatures from 5 to 10°C (*Desmarestia* spp., *Chorda filum*) or from 5 to 15°C (Laminariales). Hence, no photoperiodism seems to be involved in the maturation of the gametophytes, as reported earlier in the case of *Laminaria saccharina* (Lüning and Dring, 1975). Blue light is required for induction of fertility (Lüning and Dring, 1975), and the quantum dose required for induction increases with temperature (Lüning, 1980). High temperatures (e.g. 15–20°C in the case of the *Desmarestia* spp. and *Chorda filum*; 20°C in the case of the Laminariales) block reproduction completely. The fact that no photoperiodism is involved in the maturation of the gametophytes does not rule out, but makes even more likely, the possibility that the sporophytes may become sporogenous at appropriate daylengths only. However, nothing is known about this matter at present.

In the *Conchocelis*-phase of the red alga *Porphyra miniata*, higher temperatures prevent the discharge of conchosporangia which, according to Chen *et al.* (1970), are formed in a broad temperature range. In the present study, it was found that daylength is not involved in the formation of conchosporangia in this species (Table V). In accordance with the results of the authors cited, conchosporangia were formed at all temperatures and daylengths (although 20°C was not survived), but conchospore release occurred only at 5°C, again irrespective of daylength (Table V). This reaction represents a special type of regulation of seasonal development, in that the conchosporangia are formed and are present under a wide range of environmental conditions, but are released only as a result of induction by low temperatures.

The red alga *Lomentaria orcadensis* which reproduces only by tetraspores, is found in the sublittoral zone on Helgoland from May until December (Kornmann and Sahling, 1977). The spores germinate to form crusts, and from these erect plants were formed at all daylength regimes in the temperature range 10–20°C (Table V). Obviously, the erect thalli can arise from the possibly perennial crusts as soon as water temperature is high enough in summer.

CONCLUSIONS

The foregoing examples may have demonstrated that it is possible by a relatively small number of critical treatments to elucidate the developmental responses triggered either by photoperiod or by temperature. It appears crucial that the algae are cultured in different daylength regimes, over the whole temperature range which they are able to survive. Otherwise one might miss a possible photoperiodic response, where this occurs only over a narrow temperature interval, as in the *Trailliella*-phase of *Bonnemaisonia hamifera*. One also has to note the possibility that a species has segregated into various ecotypes, all with different critical daylength and all differing slightly in the temperature range in which photoperiod induction can occur, as seen in the case of *Scytosiphon lomentaria*.

The photoperiodic responses reported above are short-day reactions which occur only when daylength has fallen below a critical value. They are all inhibited by long days (short nights) or – as in many higher short-day plants (Vince-Prue, 1975) – by a night-break regime (two short nights per 24 h) which is photosynthetically almost identical with the short-day regime. However, in the crustose tetrasporophyte of the red alga *Acrosymphyton purpuriferum* (J.Ag.) Sjöst. which forms tetrasporangia only in short days, night-breaks of up to 1 h duration were not effective (Cortel-Breeman and Ten Hoopen, 1978).

In view of the great number of algal species which have still to be investigated as to the regulation of their life histories by photoperiod or temperature, it is premature to try to answer the question of whether regulation by one or the other factor is characteristic for certain ecological groups of species. For instance, the cases known in the Bangiophycidae (Dring, 1967; Rentschler, 1967; Richardson and Dixon, 1968), in the Scytosiphonales and in *Monostroma grevillei* seems to support as plausible the idea that photoperiodism will mainly be found in eulittoral species, for which water temperature is too variable an environmental signal for the detection of season. On the other hand, there are also non-photoperiodic species in the eulittoral region (Table V), and the photoperiodically active red algae *Bonnemaisonia hamifera*, *Calosiphonia vermicularis* (Mayhoub, 1976) and *Constantinea subulifera* Setchell (Powell, 1964) are all sublittoral species. There is no reason why photoperiod should not trigger the seasonal development of algae even at the lower limit of the phytal region, at 150–200 m depth in clear waters, provided that a pigment other than phytochrome transmits the photomorphogenetic stimulus. As Dring (1971) pointed out, the red/far red system (phytochrome) could theoretically still operate through much of the phytal region in coastal "green" waters, where the vertical extension of the phytal region does not reach such great depth as in clear "blue" waters. According to the same author, red and even far red light, although penetrating poorly into water, could still saturate the phytochrome system of sublittoral algae where present in these plants at moderate water depths; there, the plants would exhibit the low saturation levels which are characteristic of phytochrome. However, the finding that exclusively blue light (and probably UV) is effective as night-break in the photo-periodic response of *Scytosiphon lomentaria* suggests the possibility that several different photomorphogenetically-active pigments, independent of red or far red light, may have developed during the evolution of these algae. From both a photobiological and an ecological point of view, it will be interesting to see which pigments mediate the photoperiodic responses in the green alga *Monostroma grevillei* and in the three sublittoral red algal species mentioned above.

ACKNOWLEDGEMENTS

Thanks are due to the following colleagues who provided the author with sporogenous field material or unialgal cultures: Dr L. C. M. Chen, Dr M. N. Clayton, Dr J. M. Jones, Dr W. Koch, Dr P. Kornmann, Dr D. G. Müller, Dr I. M. Munda, Dr Y. Sanbonsuga and Professor J. A. West. Dr A. R. O. Chapman kindly sent temperature data. Furthermore, the author wishes to thank Dr M. J. Dring for many discussions which were fruitful for the present work, and Dr J. W. Markham for correction of the English manuscript. Thanks are also due to Mr J. Meyer, who built the box system and to Ms L. Reiners for skilful assistance with the culture work.

REFERENCES

Abbott, I. A. and Hollenberg, G. J. (1976). "Marine Algae of California". University Press, Stanford, California.

Beck, S. D. (1968). "Insect Photoperiodism". Academic Press, London and New York.

Chen, L. C. -M., Edelstein, T., Ogata, E. and McLachlan, J. (1970). The life history of *Porphyra miniata*. *Can. J. Bot.* **48**, 385–389.

Chihara, M. (1961). Life cycle of the Bonnemaisoniaceous algae in Japan (1). *Sc. Rep. Tokyo Kyoiku Daigaku*, section B, **10**, 121–153.

Clayton, M. N. (1976). Complanate *Scytosiphon lomentaria* from southern Australia: the effect of season, temperature, and daylength on the life history. *J. exp. mar. Biol. Ecol.* **25**, 187–198.

Clayton, M. N. (1978). Morphological variation and life history in cylindrical forms of *Scytosiphon lomentaria* (Scytosiphonaceae: Phaeophyta) from southern Australia. *Mar. Biol., Berl.* **47**, 349–357.

Clayton, M. N. (1979). The life history and sexual reproduction of *Colpomenia peregrina* (Scytosiphonaceae, Phaeophyta) in Australia. *Br. phycol. J.* **14**, 1–10.

Cortel-Breeman, A. N. and Ten Hoopen, A. (1978). The short day response in *Acrosymphyton purpuriferum* (J.Ag.) Sjöst. (Rhodophyceae, Cryptonemiales). *Phycologia* **17**, 125–132.

Cumming, B. G. (1969). Circadian rhythms of flower induction and their significance in photoperiodic response. *Can. J. Bot.* **47**, 309–324.

Dring, M. J. (1967a). Effects of daylength on growth and reproduction of the *Conchocelis*-phase of *Porphyra tenera*. *J. mar. biol. Ass. U.K.* **47**, 501–510.

Dring, M. J. (1967b). Phytochrome in red alga, *Porphyra tenera*. *Nature, Lond.* **215**, 1411–1412.

Dring, M. J. (1970). Photoperiodic effects in microorganisms. *In* "Photobiology of Microorganisms" (P. Halldal, ed.), pp. 345–368. Wiley and Sons, London.

Dring, M. J. (1971). Light quality and the photomorphogenesis of algae in marine environments. *In* "Fourth European Marine Biology Symposium" (D. J. Crisp, ed.), pp. 375–392. Cambridge University Press, Cambridge.

Dring, M. J. (1974). Reproduction. *In* "Algal Physiology and Biochemistry" (W. D. P. Stewart, ed.), pp. 814–837. Blackwell, Oxford.

Dring, M. J. and Lüning, K. (1975). A photoperiodic response mediated by blue light in the brown alga *Scytosiphon lomentaria*. *Planta (Berl.)* **125**, 25–32.

Feldmann, J. (1949). L'ordre des Scytosiphonales. *Trav. bot. déd. à R. Maire, Alger* **2**, 103–115.

Feldmann, J. (1956). La reproduction des algues marines dans ses rapports avec leur situation géographique. *Année biologique* **33**, 49–56.

Feldmann, J. and Feldmann, G. (1941). Un nouveau type d'alternance de générations chez les Rhodophycées: les Bonnemaisoniacées. *Chronica Botanica* **6**, 313–314.

Garner, W. W. and Allard, H. A. (1920). Effect of the relative length of day and night and other factors of the environment on growth and reproduction in plants. *J. agric. Res.* **18**, 553–606.

Hillman, W. S. (1962). "The Physiology of Flowering". Holt, Rinehart and Winston, New York.

Koch, W. (1950). Entwicklungsgeschichtliche und physiologische Untersuchungen an Laboratoriumskulturen der Rotalge *Trailliella intricata* Batters (Bonnemaisoniaceae). *Arch. Mikrobiol.* **14**, 635–660.

Koch, W. (1951). Historisches zum Vorkommen der Rotalge *Trailliella intricata* (Batters) bei Helgoland. *Arch. Mikrobiol.* **16**, 78–79.

Kornmann, P. (1962a). Die Entwicklung von *Monostroma grevillei*. *Helgol. wiss. Meeresunters.* **8**, 195–202.

Kornmann, P. (1962b). Eine Revision der Gattung *Acrosiphonia*. *Helgol. wiss. Meeresunters.* **8**, 219–292.

Kornmann, P. and Sahling, P. -H. (1962). Zur Taxonomie und Entwicklung der *Monostroma*-Arten von Helgoland. *Helgol. wiss. Meeresunters.* **8**, 302–320.

Kornmann, P. and Sahling, P. -H. (1977). Meeresalgen von Helgoland. Benthische Grün-, Braun- und Rotalgen. *Helgol. wiss. Meeresunters.* **29**, 1–289.

Kuckuck, P. (1912). Beiträge zur Kenntnis der Meeresalgen. 11. Die Fortpflanzung der Phaeosporeen. *Helgol. wiss. Meeresunters.* (N.F.) **17**, (Abt. Helgoland), 155–184.

Kurogi, M. (1959). Influences of light on the growth and maturation of *Conchocelis*-thallus of *Porphyra*. I. Effect of photoperiod on the formation of monosporangia and liberation of monospores (1). *Bull. Tohoku reg. Fish. Res. Lab.* **15**, 33–42.

Kylin, H. (1933). Über die Entwicklungsgeschichte der Phaeophyceen. *Lunds Univ. Arsskr.*, N.F., Avd. 2, **29**(7), 1–102.

Lüning, K. (1980). Critical levels of light and temperature regulating the gametogenesis of three *Laminaria* spp. *J. Phycol.* **16**, 1–15.

Lüning, K. and Dring, M. J. (1975). Reproduction, growth and photosynthesis of gametophytes of *Laminaria saccharina* grown in blue and red light. *Mar. Biol., Berl.* **29**, 195–200.

Lüning, K. and Dring, M. J. (1979). Continuous underwater light measurement near Helgoland (North Sea) and its significance for characteristic light limits in the sublittoral region. *Helgol. wiss. Meeresunters.* **32**, 403–424.

Mayhoub, H. (1976). Cycle de développement du *Calosiphonia vermicularis* (J.Ag.) Sch. (Rhodophycées, Gigartinales). Mise en évidence d'une réponse photopériodique. *Bull. Soc. phycol. Fr.* **21**, 48.

McMillan, C. (1974). Photoperiodic responses of *Xanthium strumarium* L. (Compositae) introduced and indigenous in Eastern Asia. *Am. J. Bot.* **57**, 881–888.

Munda, I. (1972). On the chemical composition, distribution and ecology of some common benthic marine algae from Iceland. *Botanica mar.* **15**, 1–45.

Munda, I. (1973). The production of biomass in the settlements of benthic marine algae in the northern Adriatic. *Botanica mar.* **15**, 218–244.

Nakamura, Y. and Tatewaki, M. (1975). The life history of some species of the Scytosiphonales. *Sci. Papers Inst. algol. Res., Hokkaido Univ.* **6**, 57–93.

Oza, R. M. (1976). Culture studies on induction and tetraspores and their subsequent development in the red alga *Falkenbergia rufolanosa* Schmitz. *Botanica mar.* **20**, 29–32.

Perl, G. (1935). Zur Kenntnis der wahren Sonnenstrahlung in verschiedenen geographischen Breiten. *Meteorol. Z.* **52**, 85–89.

Powell, J. H. (1964). "The life history of a red alga, *Constantinea*". Ph.D. thesis, Univ. Microfilms Inc. Ann Arbor, Michigan.

Price, J. H., John, D. M. and Lawson, G. W. (1978). Seaweeds of the western coast of tropical Africa and adjacent islands: a critical assessment. II. Phaeophyta. *Bull. Br. Mus. nat. Hist.* (Bot.) **6**, 87–182.

Provasoli, L. (1968). Media and prospects for the cultivation of marine algae. *In* "Cultures and Collections of Algae" (A. Watanabe and A. Hattori, eds), pp. 63–75. Proceedings of the U.S.–Japan conference, Hakone, September 1966. Japanese Society of Plant Physiology.

Rentschler, H. G. (1967). Photoperiodische Induktion der Monosporenbildung bei *Porphyra tenera* Kjellm. (Rhodophyta-Bangiophyceae). *Planta (Berl.)* **76**, 65–74.

Rhodes, R. G. and Connell, M. U. (1973). The biology of brown algae on the Atlantic coast of Virginia. II. *Petalonia fascia* and *Scytosiphon lomentaria. Chesapeake Sci.* **14**, 211–215.

Richardson, N. (1970). Studies on the photobiology of *Bangia fuscopurpurea. J. Phycol.* **6**, 215–219.

Richardson, N. and Dixon, P. S. (1968). Life history of *Bangia fuscopurpurea* (Dillw.) Lyngb. in culture. *Nature, Lond.* **218**, 496–497.

Roeleveld, J. G., Duisterhof, M. and Vroman, M. (1974). On the year cycle of *Petalonia fascia* in the Netherlands. *Neth. J. Sea Res.* 8, 410–426.

Shevlin, D. E. and Polanshek, A. K. (1978). Life history of *Bonnemaisonia geniculata* (Rhodophyta): a laboratory and field study. *J. Phycol.* **14**, 282–289.

Smithsonian Meteorological Tables (1951). Duration of Daylight. *Smiths. misc. coll.* **114**, 507–512.

Stefánsson, U. (1969). Sjávarhiti á siglingaleid umhverfis Ísland. Hafísinn (Reykjavik) **1969**, 131–149.

Svendsen, P. (1959). The algal vegetation of Spitsbergen. *Skr. Norsk Polarinst.* **116**, 1–47.

Tatewaki, M. (1966). Formation of a crustaceous sporophyte with unilocular sporangia in *Scytosiphon lomentaria. Phycologia* **6**, 62–66.

Tatewaki, M. (1972). Life history and systematics in *Monostroma. In* "Contributions to the Systematics of Benthic Marine Algae of the North Pacific" (I. A. Abbott and M. Kurogi, eds), pp. 1–15. Japanese Society of Phycology, Kobe, Japan.

Taylor, W. R. (1960). "Marine Algae of the Eastern Tropical and Subtropical Coasts of America". University of Michigan Press, Ann Arbor.

Tomczak, G. und Goedecke, E. (1962). Monatskarten der Temperatur der Nordsee, dargestellt für verschiedene Tiefenhorizonte. *Dt. hydrogr. Z., Reihe* B, No. 7 (Ergänzungsheft), pag. var.

Vince-Prue, D. (1975). "Photoperiodism in Plants". McGraw Hill, London.

Waaland, J. R. (1976). Growth of the red alga *Iridaea cordata* (Turner) Bory in semi-closed culture. *J. exp. mar. Biol. Ecol.* **23**, 45–53.

Weigel, H. -P. (1978). Temperature and salinity observations from Helgoland Reede in 1976. *Annls Biol., Copenh.* **33**, 35.

Wilce, R. T. (1959). The marine algae of the Labrador Peninsula and N.W. Newfoundland. *Natl Mus. Canada Bull.* 158, *Biol. Ser.* **56**, 1–103.

Wynne, M. J. (1969). Life history and systematic studies of some Pacific North American Phaeophyceae (brown algae). *Univ. Calif. Pubs Bot.* **50**, 1–88.

Wynne, M. J. and Loiseaux, S. (1976). Recent advances in life history studies of the Phaeophyta. *Phycologia* **15**, 435–452.

Zavodnik, N. (1973). Seasonal variations in rate of photosynthetic activity and chemical composition of the littoral seaweeds common to North Adriatic. *Botanica mar.* **16**, 155–165.

Taxonomic Index

Abarenicola, 749
Acanthaster planci, 711
Acanthina
punctulata, 708
spirata, 712
Acanthuridae, 686
Acarina, 763
Acmaea, 664, 708
conus, 584
digitalis, 584, 724
limatula, 584
paradigitalis, 724
pelta, 584, 724
scabra, 584, 587
scutum, 724
strigatella, 584
tessulata, 655, 673
virginea, 352, 655, 673
Acrochaetiales, 382
Acrochaetium, 465, *see also Audouinella*
Acrocordia conoidea, 801–802
Acrosiphonia, 664
arcta, 938, 939
Acrosymphyton purpuriferum, 940–941
Acrothrix novae-angliae, 402, 406, 408, 414–415, 416, 418, 419, 420
Actinothoe sphyrodeta, 335, 346, 358
Adalaria proxima, 783
Adamsia palliata, 326, 352
Agardhiella
[*gaudichaudii*], 903
subulata, 903
Agarum cribrosum, 402, 406–408, 414–415, 417, 419–420, 519
Aglaophenia, 342, 343, 348, 355, 358
pluma, 768
tubulifera, 335
Agonidae, 695
Agonus cataphractus, 695
Ahnfeltia plicata, 493, 406, 408, 412–413, 418–419
Alaria, 337, 518, 519
esculenta, 334, 346, 360, 402, 406 408, 412–413, 414–415, 418–419
Alcyonidium, 765, 767, 776, 778–789, 783
gelatinosum, 335, 343, 346, 355
hirsutum, 769, 776, 782
polyoum, 769, 776
Alcyonium digitatum, 335, 342, 343, 346, 348, 353, 353, 354, 355, 358, 364
Alvania punctura, 348
Ammodytes, 684
tobianus, 682
Amphilectus fucorum, 334, 342, 348, 358
Amphimonhystera, 739
Amphipholis squamata, 349
Amphipoda, 763
Amphisbetia operculata, 346, 348, 768
Amphiura filiformis, 353
Anaptychia, 808
fusca, 795, 801, 811, 820
Anemonia sulcata, 348, 718
Anguilla anguilla, 682
Annelida, 583, 748
Anomia ephippium, 352
Anoplostoma, 739
viviparum, 733

Antedon bifida, 335, 349, 352, 353, 355
Anthopleura elegantissima, 584, 585, 587
Anthozoa, 583
Anthus spinoletta spinoletta, 824
Antithamnion, 469, 470
cruciatum, 403, 406, 408, 637
floccosum, 403, 406, 408, 414–415, 418–419, 630, 637
plumula, 435, 844, 851, 856, 866, 868
var. *bebbii,* 381
pylaisaei, 403, 406–408, 414–415, 417, 418–419
sarniensis, 878, 881, 882
spirographidis, 386, 878, 881, 885
Antithamnionella sarniensis, 881
Aphanocladia stichidiosa, 386
Apletodon microcephalus, 682, 695
Aplysia brasiliana, 521
Araeolaimus, 738
Arctica islandica, 352
Arenicola, 626, 673
Armeria maritima, 808, 810, 822
Arthonia phaeobaea, 793, 794, 801
Arthopyrenia, 792, 793, 816, 818, 821
"elegans", 792
halodytes, 791, 792, 793, 801, 803, 809, 814, 816
sublittoralis, 791, 792, 801, 803, 821
Arthropoda, 583
Ascidia, 764
mentula, 353
Ascidiacea, 583, 604
Ascidiella, 764
aspersa, 349
Ascolaimus, 739
Ascophyllum nodosum, 402, 406, 408, 412–413, 419–420, 434, 444, 465, 525, 624, 626, 634, 644, 647, 668, 719, 721, 723, 763, 766, 768, 769, 773, 774–775, 793
Asparagopsis
armata, 878, 879, 880, 885, 887, 890, 930, 932
taxiformis, 880
Asperococcus fistulosus, 402, 406, 408, 412–413, 416, 418, 419–420
Aspicilia leprosescens, 813, 834
Asterias rubens, 335, 342, 343, 346, 349, 352, 353, 354, 355, 363, 365, 708, 716, 717, 723
Asterocytis ornata, 496
Asteroidea, 583
Atherina presbyter, 682, 683, 684, 693
Atherinidae, 693
Audouinella, 469, *see also Acrochaetium,*
alariae, 403, 406, 408, 412–413, 416, 418
caespitosa, 637
floridula, 640, 641
membranacea, 403, 406–408, 412–413, 414–415, 417
purpurea, 403, 406, 408, 412–413, 418–419, 433, 437, 461, 629, 630, 653, 657, 660, 666
secundata, 630, 637, 649, 650, 660
Audouinia tentaculata, 352
Aulorhynchus flavidus, 694
Aurelia aurita, 348

B

Bacidia scopulicola, 794, 804
Bacillariophyceae, 377, 384
Bacillariophyta, 583
Balanus, 350, 634, 635, 664
amphitrite, 907
balanoides, 511, 660, 711, 724, 781, 891
balanus, 348, 352, 353
cariosus, 724
crenatus, 334, 342, 343, 346
glandula, 708, 709, 712, 722, 724
Balistidae, 686
Bangia
atropurpurea, 403, 406, 408, 412–413, 416, 418, 419–420, 436, 446, 448, 450, 462, 629, 630,

642, 653, 821, 843, 844, 851, 852, 852, 860, 862, 863, 864, 867, 896, 870, 916
fuscopurpurea, 462, 916
Bangiophyceae, 382, 623
Bangiophycidae, 941
Biddulphia sinensis, 887
Bifurcaria bifurcata, 692
Bittium reticulatum, 348
Bivalvia, 583, 748
Blenniidae, 686
Blidingia, 437, 438, 467, 626, 632, 634, 635, 637, 643, 645, 653, 654, 843, 844, 847, 851, 852, 853, 854, 855, 856, 857, 858, 860, 862, 863, 864, 867, 869, 870
marginata, 433, 629, 630, 657, 660, 672, 852
minima, 402, 406, 408, 412–413, 433, 437, 443, 450, 454, 461, 629, 630, 633, 645, 657, 852, 855, 858, 859, 861
Bonnemaisonia, 382
hamifera, 403, 406–408, 414–415, 878, 881, 885, 890, 915, 920, 921, 930–934, 940, 941, 942
nootkana, 881
Boops boops, 688
Bossiella orbigniana ssp. *dichotoma*, 584
Bostrychia, 469
binderi, 454
radicans, 450, 454
Botryllus schlosseri, 342
Bowerbankia, 342
Brachidontes adamsianus, 603
Brachyistius frenatus, 693
Brongniartella byssoides, 334, 357, 903
Bryopsidophyceae, 381
Bryopsis, 768
hypnoides, 402, 406, 408, 414–415
plumosa, 342, 629, 630, 636, 640, 843, 844, 851, 856, 859, 866, 868
Bryozoa, 346, 347, 349, 583, 763, 767, 769
Buccinum undatum, 352, 354, 355
Buellia
alboatra, 801
punctata, 810, 820
subdisciformis, 810
Bugula
flabellata, 334
plumosa, 335, 342, 343, 346, 358
turbinata, 342, 343

C

Calcarea, 583
Calliblepharis, 892
ciliata, 342, 346, 768
Callionymus lyra, 682, 684
Calliostoma zizyphinum, 348, 352, 355
Callithamnion, 343, 461, 844, 866, 870
corymbosum, 403, 406, 408, 409, 414–415, 416, 418, 419–420
hookeri, 630, 637, 650, 660, 672, 851, 861, 866
roseum, 650, 815, 866
tetragonum, 401, 851, 853, 854, 861, 862, 864, 866
Callophyllis
cristata, 403, 406–408, 414–415, 419–420
lacinata, 357, 851, 859
Calluna vulgaris, 808, 810, 822
Caloglossa leprieurii, 450, 454, 469
Caloplaca, 794, 801
citrina, 794, 801, 803
ferruginea, 797, 803
heppiana, 801
littorea, 804, 810
marina, 793, 794, 801, 810, 828
microthallina, 794, 820
thallincola, 793, 794, 801, 810
verruculifera, 794, 796, 803
Calosiphonia vermicularis, 916, 941, 942
Calothrix, 465

scopulorum, 818
Camacolaimus, 740
Campecopea hirsuta, 823, 824
Cancer pagurus, 352, 718
Candelariella
arctica, 799
vitellina, 814
Caprellidae, 342, 343
Capsosiphon fulvescens, 402, 406, 408, 412–413, 414–415, 416, 418, 419–420, 435, 465, 468, 629, 630, 672
Capulus ungaricus, 352
Carcinus maenas, 353, 690, 708, 709, 718, 721
Carpopeltis rugosum, 584
Caryophyllia smithii, 335, 346, 348
Cassis tuberosa, 714, 715
Castagnea cylindrica, 382
Castalia punctata, 348
Catenella caespitosa, 792
Catillaria
chalybeia, 793, 794, 803, 810, 820
lenticularis, 801
Caulerpa filiformis, 686
Cellaria sinuosa, 335, 346
Cellepora pumicosa, 347, 364
Cephalopoda, 583
Ceramiaceae, 385
Ceramium, 525, 844, 870
byssoideum, 381
cingulatum, 382, 385
diaphanum, 382, 650
eatonianum, 584
fastigiatum
var. *flaccidum,* 385
rubrum, 403, 406–408, 412–413, 414–415, 629, 630, 637, 640, 843, 844, 851, 852, 854, 856, 859, 860, 862, 866, 868, 869
shuttleworthianum, 630, 664
taylori, 385
tenuicorne, 434
Cerastoderma, 348, 349
edule, 352, 708
Ceratocolax hartzii, 403, 406–408, 417
Cerianthus lloydi, 347, 355
Chaetomorpha, 342, 822, 843, 844, 867, 868
capillaris, 636, 649, 660
linum, 402, 406, 408, 412–413, 458, 629, 847, 851, 855, 856, 861, 862
melagonium, 402, 406, 408, 412–413, 649
Chaetophorales, 382
Chara, 466
Chelon labrosus, 682, 683, 687–688, 698
Chiodecton, 804
Chirolophis ascanii, 682
Chlamys
distorta, 352
opercularis, 352
tigerina, 352
varia, 348, 349, 352
Chlorophyceae, 381, 384, 385, 438, 623, 822
Chlorophyta, 397, 402, 431, 583, 621, 622, 629, 630, 850, 857, 858
Chondria
coerulescens, 895
mairei, 382, 386
Chondrus crispus, 403, 406, 408, 412–413, 414–415, 464, 640, 722, 767, 769, 843, 844, 851, 853, 854, 859, 864, 866, 868, 869, 870, 895
Chorda
filum, 402, 406, 408, 414–415, 416, 418, 419–420, 450, 465, 469, 938, 939
tomentosa, 402, 406, 408, 414–415, 416, 418, 419–420
Chordaria flagelliformis, 402, 406, 408, 412–413, 414–415, 416, 418, 419–420
Chordata, 583
Choreocolax polysiphoniae, 403, 406, 408, 412–413
Choristocarpus tenellus, 386
Chromadora macrolaimoides, 747

Chromaspirina, 740
Chromis punctipinnis, 668
Chroodactylon, 382
  ornatum, 469
Chthamalus, 635
  dalli, 584, 585, 587, 724
  fissus, 584, 585, 587
Ciliata
  mustela, 681, 682, 683–684
  septentrionalis, 682
Cingula semicostata, 348
Ciocalypta penicillus, 343
Ciona intestinalis, 353
Cirripedia, 763
Cladophora, 342, 434, 438, 460, 768, 769, 843, 844, 851, 852, 853–862, 866, 870
  albida, 445, 630, 640, 650, 660
  coelothrix, 457
  fracta, 450
  glomerata, 441, 461, 466, 467
  okamurai, 433
  pygmaea, 402, 406–408, 417
  repens, 457
  rupestris, 402, 406, 408, 412–413, 448, 650
  sericea, 402, 406, 408, 412–413, 416, 418, 419–420, 636, 649, 660
Cladophoropsis modonensis, 386
Clathrina coriacea, 356, 358, 359
Clathromorphum,
  circumscriptum, 403, 406–408, 412–413, 414–415
  compactum, 404, 406, 408, 414–415, 418–419
Clava multicornis, 768
Clavelina lepadiformis, 335, 342, 353
Clinidae, 695
Clinitrachus argentatus, 695
Cliona, 342, 343
  celata, 335, 348, 355
Cnidaria, 583
Codiolum, 915, 920, 921, 934–937
  gregarium, 629, 633
  petrocelidis, 649
  pusillum, 402, 406, 408, 412–413
Codium, 463
  fragile, 875, 879, 889, 891, 907, 908
    ssp. *atlanticum,* 878, 879
    ssp. *tomentosoides,* 447–448, 451, 843, 851, 856, 866, 878, 879, 885
  tomentosum, 768, 879, 891
  vermilara, 879
Coelenterata, 763, 768
Collema, 802
Collisella, see Acmaea
Colpomenia
  peregrina, 386, 875, 877, 878, 885, 889, 891
  sinuosa, 601, 877
"*Conchocelis*", 333, 615, 616, 630, 640, 654, 660, 673, 916, 933, 939–940
Conger conger, 682
Conidae, 704
Constantinea subulifera, 941, 942
Copepoda, 673, 746, 763
Corallina, 334, 342, 346, 692. 736
  granifera, 381
  officinalis, 404, 406, 408, 412–413, 414–415, 768
    var. *chilensis,* 584, 585, 587, 601, 602
  vancouveriensis, 584, 585
Cordylecladia erecta, 895
Corella parallelogramma, 353
Corophium, 712, 714
  bonelli, 348
  volutator, 708, 710, 711, 714, 715, 717
Corynactis viridis, 348, 356, 358
Coryne uchidai, 772, 775
Corynospora pedicellata, 382
    var. *tenuis,* 382
Coryphoblennius galerita, 682
Costaria, 519
Cotoneaster, 822
Cottidae, 694
Crangon crangon, 721

Crania anomala, 349
Crassostrea
  angulata, 889
  gigas, 889, 899–900, 907
Crenilabrus, 694
  melops, 682, 684, 687
Crenimugil labrosus, 865
Crepidula fornicata, 856, 885, 889
Crisia, 769
  denticulata, 342, 349, 352
  eburnea, 346
Crisidia cornuta, 349
Crisiidae, 335, 358
Crossaster papposus, 353, 354, 355
Crouania attenuata, 381
    f. *bispora,* 381
Cruoria cruoriaeformis, 905, 906, 907
Crustacea, 583, 604, 748, 769
Cryptonemia, 907
  hibernica, 907
Cryptonemiales, 893
Cryptopleura ramosa, 334, 342, 343, 346, 356, 357, 903–904
Ctenolabrus rupestris, 682
Cucumaria
  lactea, 353
  normanni, 349
  saxicola, 353
Cultellus pellucidus, 352
Cyanobacteria, 533
Cyanophyceae, 377, 384, 792, 822
Cyanophyta, 583, 637, 660
Cyanoplax hartwegii, 584
Cyatholaimus, 743
Cyclopterus lumpus, 682
Cylindrocarpus microscopicus, 895
Cyprina islandica, 717
Cystoclonium purpureum, 404, 406, 408, 414–415, 419–420, 851, 857, 859, 866
Cystoseira, 387
  crinita, 387, 388
  mediterranea, 381
  stricta, 387

D

Dasya rigidula, 381
Dasychone bombyx, 342
Decapoda, 763
Delamarea attenuata, 402, 406, 408, 412–413, 416, 418, 419–420
Delesseria sanguinea, 334, 346, 357, 450, 451, 454, 455, 456, 469, 768
Delesseriaceae, 461
Desmospongiae, 583
Dendrodoa grossularia, 353, 356, 358, 359
Derbesia, 843, 844, 851, 855, 856, 866, 869, 870
  marina, 402, 406, 408, 414–415, 416, 418, 419–420, 895
Desmarestia, 904
  aculeata, 357, 402, 406–408, 414–415, 417, 694, 938–939
  ligulata, 334
  viridis, 357, 360, 402, 406–408, 414–415, 843, 851, 854, 866, 938, 939
Desmarestiales, 915
Desmodora, 740
Desmoscolex, 733
Diastylis rathkei, 752
Dicentrarchus labrax, 681
Dichromadora, 740
Dictyopteris
  divaricata, 772
  membranacea, 346, 454, 455, 456
Dictyosiphon, 440, 465
  foeniculaceus, 402, 406, 408, 412–413, 414–415, 416, 418, 419–420
Dictyota
  dichotoma, 334, 342, 346, 357
  linearis, 381
Digenea, 463
Dilabifilium, 826
  arthopyreniae, 818
Dilophus mediterraneus, 385
Dilsea
  carnosa, 435, 674
  edulis, 435

Diodora apertura, 352
Diplecogaster bimaculata, 682
Diplopeltis, 739
Diplosoma listerianum, 349
Diptera, 674, 824
Discosporangium mesarthrocarpum 381, 386
Distaplia rosea, 342, 343, 349
Distomus variolosus, 364
Ditlevsenella, 741
Dodecaceria fewkesi, 585, 587, 603
Donax faba, 711
Doridella steinbergae, 783
Dosinia exoleta, 352
Dracograllus eira, 733
Dumontia incrassata, 404, 406, 408, 412–413, 416, 418, 624, 642, 643, 670
Dynamena pumila, 768
Dysidea fragilis, 342, 348

E

Echiichthys vipera, 682, 684
Echinocyamus pusillus, 353
Echinodermata, 583, 674
Echinoidea, 583
Echinometra lucunter, 714, 715
Echinus esculentus, 335, 349, 350, 352, 355, 365, 674
Ectocarpaceae, 600
Ectocarpus, 462, 469, 629, 638, 844, 870
  fasciculatus, 402, 406, 408, 412–413, 414–415, 636, 657
  siliculosus, 402, 406, 408, 412–413, 414–415, 416, 418, 419–420, 450, 452, 630, 844, 847, 851, 852, 854, 855, 856, 859, 860–864, 869
Ectoprocta, 583
Egregia menziesii, 583, 584, 585, 587, 591, 593, 598, 601–603
Eisenia arborea, 587, 591, 593, 601
Elachista
  fucicola, 630
  intermedia, 382
Electra pilosa, 334, 780, 782, 783
Elminius modestus, 882, 883, 887, 888, 889, 891, 906
Elodea canadensis, 891, 892
Elysia viridis, 768
Embiotoca jacksoni, 693
Engraulis encrasicolus, 681
Enhydra lutris, 722
Enoploides, 741
Enoplolaimus, 741
Enoplus, 741
Ensis, 624
  arcuatus, 352
Enteromorpha, 402, 406, 408, 428, 437–439, 453, 461–462, 466–467, 469, 600–601, 624, 626, 628, 632, 634–635, 644–645, 662, 664, 674, 694, 723, 768, 822, 843–845, 847, 853, 867, 869–870
  clathrata, 626, 628, 661–662
  compressa, 630, 633, 642, 650
  flexuosa, 450–451, 851, 854
  intestinalis, 412, 434, 437, 450, 453, 455, 457, 469, 628–629, 632–633, 636, 638, 640, 650, 657, 660, 662, 672, 722, 844, 851–853, 869, 890
  linza, 629, 633, 844, 847, 851, 854, 859–864, 896–870
  prolifera, 437, 628–629, 650, 661, 844, 851–853, 855–864, 869–870
  salina, 462
  torta, 657
Entocladia, 382
Erythrocladia, 382
Erythrotrichia, 382, 465
  carnea, 450, 452, 630, 637, 650, 660
Escharoides coccineus, 346
Eucheuma, 454
Euchromadora, 743
Eudendrium ramosum, 348
Eudesme, 670
  virescens, 402, 406, 408, 414–415, 416, 418, 419–420, 670

Euglena, 473
Eugomontia sacculata, 450, 469
Eulalia viridis, 348
Eumorpholaimus, 739
Eupagurus, see Pagurus
Eurystomina, 741

F

Falkenbergia
hillebrandii, 880
rufolanosa, 381, 878, 879–880, 885, 930, 932
Festuca, 808
Ficoponatus enigmaticus, 881
Filograna implexa, 358
Florideophyceae, 623, 893, 903, 906
Flustra, 764
foliacea, 335, 346
Flustrella, 664
Flustrellidra, 765
hispida, 767, 769
Fontinalis, 437
Foraminifera, 749
Fosliella, 382, 673
farinosa
var. *chalicodictya,* 385
var. *farinosa,* 386
var. *solmsiana,* 386
limitata, 907
Fucus, 438, 456, 457–458, 462–463, 511, 651, 692, 694, 768–769, 773–774, 781, 821, 851, 862, 867, 870
F. hybrids, 629, 640, 641, 644, 645, 651
ceranoides, 428, 433, 439, 448–449, 450, 459, 461, 463, 464, 661
distichus, 402, 406, 408, 412–413, 465–466, 723
edentatus, 402, 406, 408, 412–413, 419–420
evanescens, 403, 406, 408, 412–413
serratus, 434, 449–450, 454–455, 465, 525, 634, 644, 651, 719, 762–763, 765, 767–769, 771, 773–776, 778–779, 780, 782, 783, 847
serratus hybrid, 630, 651
spiralis, 403, 406, 408, 412–413, 436, 439, 442, 448, 454, 465, 629, 634, 643–645, 719, 763, 767, 847, 861
spiralis hybrid, 630, 651
vesiculosus, 403, 406, 408, 419–420, 433, 441, 448, 450–452, 454–455, 461, 465–466, 525, 629, 690, 719, 723, 763, 768, 773–774, 781, 847
vesiculosus hybrid, 630, 651
Fuscidea cyathoides, 797, 800

G

Gaidropsarus mediterraneus, 682, 683–684
Galathea
dispersa, 353
intermedia, 352
Gammanema, 741
Gasterosteus aculeatus, 682, 684, 694
Gasterostiformes, 694
Gastropoda, 583, 673–674, 763
Gelidium, 626, 628
amansii, 454
cartilagineum, 889
coulteri, 584, 600
purpurascens, 601
pusillum, 584, 585, 600, 650
versicolor, 889
Geranomyia, see Limonia
Gibbonsia
elegans, 692
metzi, 693
Gibbula, 673
cineraria, 352
tumida, 352
Giffordia, 629, 636, 638
granulosa, 403, 406, 408, 414–415, 416, 418, 419–420, 636, 844, 851–854, 857, 861, 862, 864, 869–870
sandriana, 636, 854

secunda, 636
Gigartina
canaliculata, 584, 585, 587, 602
spinosa, 584, 585
stellata, 404, 406, 408, 624, 626, 630, 634, 640, 642–645, 650–651, 654, 660–661, 664–666, 668, 674, 763, 767, 769
Gigartinales, 903, 906
Giraudya sphacelarioides, 381
Girella nigricans, 688
Gitana, 348
Gobiidae, 686
Gobiesociformes,695
Gobius
cobitis, 682, 687, 690
niger, 682
paganellus, 682, 684
Gobiusculus flavescens, 683
Golfingia vulgaris, 353
Goneplax rhomboides, 352
Goniotrichum, 382
Gracilaria, 465, 469, 847, 906
bursa-pastoris, 895, 903, 907
foliifera, 463
verrucosa, 843, 851, 854, 857, 866, 896
Grantia compressa, 342
Grateloupia, 892–893, 895–898
doryphora, 851, 854, 861, 875, 893, 896–898, 901, 908
filicina, 893, 894
var. *filicina*, 896
var. *luxurians*, 875, 892–896, 897, 898, 901
lanceola, 897
Griffithsia, 843, 847
barbata, 381
corallinoides, 844, 851, 856, 866, 868
flosculosa, 767–768, 851, 854, 866
tenuis, 385
Gymutoclinus rotundifrons, 686

H

Haematopus
bachmani, 708
ostralegus, 708
Halecium halecinum, 342–343, 347–348, 352, 355
Halichoanolaimus, 741
Halichoeres semicinctus, 688
Halichondria panicea, 335, 342, 346, 358
Haliciona, 348
oculata, 342, 343, 355
Halidrys
dioica, 587, 591, 593, 603
siliquosa, 346, 694, 766, 768
Halopteris
filicina, 381, 384, 388
scoparia, 403, 406, 408, 414–415, *see also Stypocaulon*
Halosaccion ramentaceum, 404, 406, 408, 412–413, 418–419
Halosydna gelatinosa, 353
Haplospora globosa, 403, 406, 408, 414–415
Harmothoe, 348
spinifera, 353
Hedophyllum sessile, 706, 721
Helminthocladia, 892
Hemimycale columella, 335, 342
Henricia, 349
sanguinolenta, 353
Hermaea
bifida, 767, 768
dendritica, 768
Hermosilla azurea, 688
Hesperophycus harveyanus, 603
Heteranomia squamula, 348, 349
Heterosiphonia plumosa, 334, 342, 346, 768
Heterostichus rostratus, 690, 692
Hiatella arctica, 342, 348, 349, 352
Hildenbrandia, 792
crouanii, 649
prototypus, 433
rubra, 404, 406–408, 412–413, 414–415, 417, 433, 633, 642

649, 665
Himanthalia, 664
elongata, 768, 781
Hippolyte, 348
Histrio histrio, 691
Holothuroidea, 583, 748
Homarus americanus, 722
Huelia macrocarpa, 798, 813
Hyas araneus, 352
Hydrallmania falcata, 343, 355
Hydrobia, 674
Hydroides norvegicus, 348, 353
Hydrolithon decipiens, 600
Hydrozoa, 346, 347, 349, 583
Hyella caespitosa, 818
Hymeniacidon perleve, 342
Hymenoclonium, 916
Hypoglossum woodwardii, 334, 342, 343, 346
Hypsypops rubicunda, 688

I

Idotea, 690
granulosa, 690, 769
neglecta, 690
pelagica, 769
Inachus, 352
dorsettensis, 352
Insecta, 763
Iridaea cordata, 706
Isopoda, 763
Isthmoplea sphaerophora, 403, 406, 408, 412–413, 650

J

Jania
corniculata, 381
rubens, 381, 387
Janira maculosa, 348, 352
Jasiidae, 343
Jasminiera elegans, 342
Jassa, 636, 673
Jophon hyndmani, 348

K

Kallymenia reniformis, 346
Katherina tunicata, 706
Kellia suborbicularis, 348, 349
Kinorhyncha, 746
Kirchenpaueria pinnata, 348, 352
Kuckuckia spinosa, 382
Kyphosidae, 686, 688
Kyphosus sectatrix, 691

L

Labridae, 687, 694
Labrus, 694
bergylta, 682, 687, 690, 691
Lacuna
pallidula, 768
vincta, 674, 768
Lamellibranchia, 673
Laminaria, 337, 414, 519, 635, 690–692, 695, 721, 764, 768–769, 779, 781, 792, 801, 824, 852, 854, 857, 866–867
complanata, 518
digitata, 334, 346, 403, 406, 408, 414–415, 629–630, 634, 763, 768, 776–777, 781, 843–844, 847, 851, 854, 856, 866, 868, 877, 938–939
groenlandica, 518
hyperborea, 332, 334, 337, 342, 346, 354, 356, 360, 661, 779, 938–939
japonica, 938–939
longicruris, 403, 406–408, 414–415, 417
ochroleuca, 877, 878, 886, 906, 907
saccharina, 346, 454–455, 518, 629, 637, 769, 781, 783, 843, 844, 847, 851, 854, 856, 858–859, 864, 966, 868, 895, 904, 938–939
solidungula, 403, 406–408, 409, 414, 417, 418–419
Laminariales, 338, 915, 939
Lanice conchilega, 352
Lasaea rubra, 823
Latrunculia magnifica, 718

Laurencia, 463, 768
obtusa, 381
Lecanactis monstrosa, 804
Lecania
erysibe, 793, 794, 801, 803, 810
rupicola, 804
Lecanora, 438
actophila, 793, 794, 801, 809, 810
atra, 795, 796, 803, 810
badia, 798
dispersa, 794, 801, 803, 814
fugiens, 795, 798, 810
helicopis, 793, 794, 801, 809, 810
polytropa, 811
straminea, 799
tenera, 804
Lecidea sulphurea, 795
Lecidella subincongrua, 795
Lejolisia mediterranea, 381
Lemanea, 461, 462
fucina, 442–443
Lembos websteri, 348
Lepadogaster lepadogaster, 682
Lepidochitona, 673
Lepidonotus squamatus, 353
Lepidopleurus, 673
Leptasterias hexactis, 708
Leptogium, 802
Leptonemella, 738
Leptophytum laeve, 404, 406–408, 417, 418–419
Leucosolenia coriacea, 356
Lichina, 793, 801, 810, 818, 825
confinis, 792, 793, 799, 803, 807, 809, 828
pygmaea, 763, 791, 792, 793, 803–804, 806, 809, 815, 820–824, 828–829, 831
Ligia
oceanica, 690
pallasii, 707
Limanda limanda, 683
Limapontia capitata, 766, 768
Limnoria tripunctata, 883–884
Limonia unicolor, 824
Lineus longissimus, 352
Linhomoeus, 740
Liparis
liparis, 682
montagui, 682
Lipophrys pholis, 681–682, 684, 687, 691
Lithophyllum, 772
incrustans, 649, 809
proboscideum, 584, 601
Lithothamnia, 334, 342
Lithothamnion, 772
sonderi, 333
Lithothamnium
glaciale, 404, 406–408, 414–415, 417, 654
lemoineae, 404, 406–408, 414–415, 418–419
sonderi, 654
tophiforme, 404, 406–408, 409, 414, 417
Littorina, 662, 663, 691, 708
littoralis, 674
littorea, 657, 674, 722, 723
neritoides, 674, 823
obtusata, 721, 768
planaxis, 584, 587, 602
saxatilis, 674
Lobaria, 798
Lobophora variegata, 386
Lomentaria
articulata, 357, 768
chylocladiella, 386
clavellosa, 629, 630
orcadensis, 938, 940
pennata, 385
verticillata, 386
Lophosiphonia
cristata, 386
scopulorum, 385
Lucernaria quadricornis, 353
Luidea ciliaris, 354, 355
Lysianassa ceratina, 348
Lysidice ninetta, 348

M

Macoma balthica, 708

Macrocystis, 685, 688–689, 692–694
integrifolia, 446
pyrifera, 908, 938–939
Macropipus
depurator, 352
puber, 342, 353
Macropodia rostrata, 352
Majidae, 690
Malacostraca, 673
Margarites groenlandicus, 352
Marthasterias glacialis, 349, 353
Medialuna californiensis, 688
Melanosiphon intestinalis, 403, 406, 408, 412 413
Melosira, 471, 657
nummuloides, 431, 434, 450–452, 458–459, 466, 470
Membranipora membranacea, 346, 345, 769, 779, 780, 783
Membranoptera alata, 334, 342–343, 346, 356–357, 404, 406–408, 414–415, 417–419, 630, 640, 664
Mercenaria, 618
mercenaria, 883–884
Mercierella enigmatica, 881
Metalinhomoeus filiformis, 733
Metridium senile, 353, 355
Microcoleus vaginatus, 438
Microlaimus, 740
Modiolus
modiolus, 326, 345, 350–352, 355, 765
phaseolinus, 349
Molgula, 353
manhattensis, 335, 346, 347, 363
Mollusca, 583, 604, 768
Monhystera, 739
Monia patelliformis, 352
Monoposthia, 740
Monostroma, 462, 518, 627, 633, 674, 935
arcticum, 920, 937, 938, 939
balticum, 434
fuscum, 629, 636
grevillei, 402, 406, 408, 412–415, 416, 418–420, 915, 920–921, 934–937, 939, 941–942
oxyspermum, 433–434, 437
undulatum, 402, 406, 408, 412–413, 414–415, 416, 418–420,
wittrockii, 629–630, 633, 639, 640, 653, 657, 660
Mugilidae, 687
Mullus, 674
Muricidae, 704
Musculus marmoratus, 349, 352
Myoxocephalus scorpius, 684
Myriactula stellulata, 381
Myriocladia lovenii, 403, 406, 408, 412–413, 416, 418–420
Myriogramme
bonnemaisonii, 334, 346
distromatica, 386
unistromatica, 385
Myrionema liechtensternii, 385
Mytilus
californianus, 583, 584–585, 587–588, 603, 708, 712, 721–722, 724
edulis, 343, 349, 352, 363, 365, 511, 603, 636–637, 639, 657–659, 662–663, 673, 708–709, 711, 724, 765, 781
Myxicola infundibulum, 347
Myxilla rosacea, 358

N

Nassarius incrassatus, 348, 352
Naticidae, 704
Nematoda, 673, 746, 729–759, 763
Nemertesia, 764
antennina, 335, 342–343, 346, 348, 355
ramosa, 342, 346
Nemertinea, 763
Neoagardhiella, 903
baileyi, 903
gaudichaudii, 875, 893, 903–904, 907
Neodilsea integra, 404, 406–408, 409, 414, 417–419
Neomysis integer, 708

Nephrops norvegicus, 353
Nephthys, 749
  hombergi, 352, 710
Neptunea antiqua, 352
Nereis diversicolor, 353, 710
Nereocystis, 518–519
  luetkeana, 706–707, 780
Nerophis lumbriciformis, 682, 692
Nitophyllum, 847
  punctatum, 381, 637, 843–844, 851, 857, 859, 866, 868, 895
Nitzschia closterium, 747
Nostoc, 431
Novaculichthys taeniourus, 691
Nucula, 352
  tenuis, 352

O

Obelia
  dichotoma, 354, 363
  geniculata, 346, 768
Ocenebra
  erinacea, 352
  poulsoni, 717
Ochrolechia
  androgyna, 811, 820
  parella, 795, 796, 803, 811
Ocypode ceratophthalmus, 711
Odonthalia dentata, 404, 406–408, 409, 414, 417–419
Oligochaeta, 746, 763
Onchidella celtica, 349
Oncholaimus, 741, 743
Onyx, 741
Opegrapha, 803
  cesareensis, 804
  confluens, 800
Ophiocomina nigra, 347, 351–353, 355
Ophiopholis, 353
  aculeata, 350, 352
Ophiothrix fragilis, 345, 349–352, 354–355, 363–365
Ophiura, 347
Ophlitaspongia seriata, 342
Opuntiella, 519
  californica, 706
Oscillatoria, 657
Ostracoda, 746, 763
Ostrea edulis, 888
Oxyjulis californica, 688
Oxylebius pictus, 688–689

P

Pachygrapsus crassipes, 584
Pachymatisma johnstonia, 335, 346, 356, 358
Padina pavonica, 376, 876
Pagurus, 343
  bernhardus, 347, 352, 355
  pubescens, 352
  prideuxi (*Eupagurus*), 326
Palmaria palmata, 342, 346, 356–357, 404, 406, 408, 412–415, 629, 644
Pannaria, 798–799, 808
Pantoneura baerii, 404, 406–408, 414–415, 417–419
Papenfussiella callitricha, 403, 406, 408
Parablennius gattorugine, 682, 687
Paracanthonchus, 740
Paralabrax clathratus, 693
Paralichthys californicus, 689
Paralinhomoeus, 739
Parapholas californica, 717
Parerythropodium hibernicum, 348
Parmelia, 801, 810, 820
  caperata, 798–799
  glabratula ssp. *fuliginosa,* 797
  omphalodes, 798
  perlata, 799
  pulla, 795
  saxatilis, 797, 811, 832
  sulcata, 797, 811
Patella, 346, 645–655, 664, 673, 691
  vulgata, 334, 865
Patina pellucida, 354, 673, 691, 765, 768
Pavoclinus, 685
Peachia hastata, 347, 353
Pecten maximus, 352
Pelecypoda, 763

Pelvetia
canaliculata, 437, 643, 645, 649, 719, 763, 821
fastigiata, 587, 603
Penitella penita, 717
Pentapora, 764
foliacea, 335, 346
Percursaria percursa, 402, 406, 408, 412–413, 843–844, 851, 855–856, 867, 869
Pertusaria lactea, 799
Petalonia, 843–844, 847, 867, 915, 924
fascia, 403, 406, 408, 412–413, 416, 418–419, 435–436, 629, 637, 641, 674, 844, 851, 854, 859, 861, 864, 869–870, 919, 924, 929
zosterifolia, 403, 406, 408, 412–413, 416, 418–420, 844, 851, 861, 863, 864, 869–870, 919, 924
Petricola pholadiformis, 855
Petrocelis, 664
cruenta, 649
middendorfii, 404, 406, 408
Petroderma, 847
Peyssonnelia, 385
rosenvingii, 404, 406–408, 414–415, 417
Phaeophila, 382
Phaeophyceae, 381, 384–385, 623
Phaeophyta, 397, 402, 440–441, 583, 621–622, 629, 630, 650, 857
Pherusa plumosa, 350
Pholis gunnellus, 682
Phormidium, 437–438, 450, 462
corium, 435, 468
Phoronis hippocrepia, 343
Phragmatopoma californica, 585, 587, 603
Phycodrys rubens, 334, 343, 346, 356–357, 404, 406–408, 414–415, 417, 419–420, 629, 674
Phyllodoce lamelligera, 348
Phyllophora, 334
pseudoceranoides, 342, 404, 406, 408, 414–415
sicula, 342, 346, 357
truncata, 404, 406–408, 414–415, 417
Phyllospadix, 585, 587–588, 598
scouleri, 587, 591
torreyi, 587, 591
Phymatolithon, 768
laevigatum, 404, 406, 408, 412–413, 419–420
lenormandii, 404, 406, 408, 412–413, 414–415, 419–420, 660, 665
polymorphum, 643, 649
rugulosum, 404, 406, 408, 418–420
Physcia, 803
Pilayella littoralis, 403, 406, 408, 412–413, 461, 463, 469, 629, 630, 632, 638, 640, 649–650, 653, 657, 660, 664, 666, 844, 847, 851–852, 854–855, 856, 861, 869, 870
Pileolaria militaris, 768
Pinnotheres pissum, 352
Pisaster ochraceus, 721, 822, 724
Pisces, 674
Placynthium nigrum, 802
Platichthys flesus, 683
Pleurobranchus membranaceus, 352
Pleurococcus, 438
Pleuronectes platessa, 683, 712
Pleuronectiformes, 684
Plocamium cartilagineum, 334, 342, 346, 357, 381, 661
var. *uncinatum,* 381
Plumaria elegans, 404, 406, 408, 409, 412–413, 414–415, 419–420, 768
Plumularia setacea, 343, 352
Podoceropsis excavata, 352
Pollachius virens, 682–683, 692–693
Polycarpa, 349
pomaria, 342, 343
Polychaeta, 380, 583, 673, 756, 748, 763, 768

Polyclinum aurantium, 335, 342, 346
Polyides rotundus, 404, 406, 408, 414–415
Polymastia
boletiformis, 335, 348
mammilaris, 335, 343
Polymnia nebulosa, 352, 353
Polyneura gmelinii, 334, 342–343
Polyplacophora, 583, 673
Polysiphonia, 356–357, 382, 843–844, 851, 853–854, 858, 864, 866, 868, 896
arctica, 404, 406–409, 414, 417
banyulensis, 385
brodiaei, 629, 844, 851, 859, 861–862, 869
elongata, 629, 637, 851, 854, 866, 868
flexicaulis, 404, 406, 408, 412–413, 414–415
lanosa, 404, 406, 408, 412–413, 450, 525, 763, 769
nigrescens, 404, 406, 408, 412–413, 418–420, 640, 851, 854, 856–857, 866, 868
spiralis, 847
subtilissima, 454
urceolata, 404, 406, 408, 412–415, 629, 630, 637, 640, 847, 851, 857, 861
violacea, 637
Pomacentridae, 686
Pomatoceros triqueter, 342, 365–348, 352–353
Pomatoschistus
microps, 683, 721
minutus, 683
pictus, 683
Pomponema, 741
Pontoporeia, 749
Porcellana longicornis, 352
Porifera, 583, 604, 763
Porphyra, 627, 643, 645, 654, 674, 843, 847, 851, 867, 869–870
leucosticta, 445, 629, 637, 640, 660
linearis, 404, 406, 408, 412–413, 416, 418–419, 629, 821
miniata, 404, 406, 408, 414–415, 416, 418–420, 938–940
perforata, 457–458
tenera, 454, 916, 933
umbilicalis, 404, 406, 408, 412–413, 435, 454, 457, 461, 629, 630, 645, 653, 822, 844, 851, 863, 864, 869
Porphyridium purpureum, 851, 857–858
Porphyrosiphon, 657
Porterinema fluviatile, 434
Posidonia oceanica, 387
Potamilla reniformis, 348
Prasiola, 627, 637, 641, 645, 653
crispa, 629–630, 653, 657
stipitata, 402, 406, 408, 412–413, 439, 463, 467, 629–630, 633, 645, 822
Praunus flexuosus, 708–709
Pringsheimiella, 382
Prionitis lanceolata, 603
Protococcus, 850
Protohydra, 748
Psammechinus, 674
miliaris, 351, 353
Pseudendoclonium submarinum, 629, 631, 642, 649, 660
Pseudochama exogyra, 587, 603
Pseudolithoderma, 847
Pseudomonas, 747
Pseudopleurococcus, see Dilabifilium
Pterocladia capillacea, 584, 585
Pterosiphonia dendroidea, 584
Ptilota
plumosa, 357, 661, 886
serrata, 404, 406–408, 414–415, 417
Pugettia producta, 584
Punctaria
latifolia, 403, 406, 408, 414–415
plantaginea, 403, 406, 408, 414–415
Puntazzo puntazzo, 688

Pycnogonida, 763
Pyrogoma anglicum, 348
Pyura tesselata, 349

R

Radicilingua thysanorhizans, 342
Ralfsia, 633, 649, 847
clavata, 630
verrucosa, 649, 780–782
Ralfsiaceae, 587
Ramalina, 801
siliquosa, 795, 796, 800, 801, 817, 820, 824, 828
subfarinacea, 797
Rhabditis, 752
marina, 747
Rhizocarpon
constrictum, 795, 800
hochstetteri, 810–811
obscuratum, 797, 810
oederi, 813
Rhizoclonium, 436–439, 462, 627, 653, 843–844, 867, 870
hieroglyphicum, 462
riparium, 402, 406, 408, 412–413, 433, 437, 445, 448, 450, 462, 629, 650, 657, 660, 851, 855, 856–859
Rhodochorton, 469
purpureum, 433, 461
Rhodomela, 346
confervoides, 342, 404, 406–408, 412–413, 414–415, 637
larix, 722
Rhodophyceae, 381, 384, 385, 603
Rhodophyllis
dichotoma, 404, 406–408, 409, 414, 417
divaricata, 381
Rhodophysema elegans, 404, 406 408, 414–415, 418–419
Rhodophyta, 397, 402, 403, 440, 441, 583, 621–622, 629–630, 850, 857
Rhodymenia, 768
delicatula, 342
pseudopalmata, 334, 346
var. *ellisiae,* 342, 343
var. *pseudopalmata,* 342, 343
Richtersia inaequalis, 733
Rimicola muscarum, 693
Rinodina gennarii, 801, 814
Rissoa, 767
parva, 348, 768
Rivularia, 431
Roccella, 798
Rosenvingiella polyrhiza, 439, 463, 660
Rubus, 822

S

Sabatieria, 739
breviseta, 752
Sabella
pavonina, 353
penicillus, 347
Sabellaria spinulosa, 342, 343
Saccorhiza
dermatodea, 403, 406, 408, 414–415, 416, 418–420
polyschides, 337, 346, 360, 450, 469, 765, 768
Sacheria fucina, 442–443
Sagartia elegans, 334, 343, 346
var. *miniata,* 354, 355
Sarcodiotheca [*gaudichaudii*], 903
Sargassum, 691, 771, 781, 782, 898
confusum, 772
fluitans, 780
hemiphyllum, 772
kjellmanianum, 899
f. *muticus,* 898
f. *longifolia,* 899
miyabei, 899
muticum, 775, 843, 847, 851, 859, 861, 866, 875, 893, 898–903, 908
natans, 780
thunbergii, 772
tortile, 771, 772, 782
Sarpa salpa, 688
Scaridae, 686
Schizoporella unicornis, 765

Schizothrix rubella, 435
Schottera nicaeensis, 342, 907
Scoliciosporum umbrinum, 803
Scophthalmus,
  maximus, 683
  rhombus, 683
Scrobicularia, 749
Scrupocellaria, 335, 358, 769, 777
  reptans, 349, 776
  scrupea, 348, 349
  scruposa, 342, 348, 349
Scypha
  ciliata, 765
  compressa, 765
Scytosiphon, 847, 867, 870
  dotyi, 601
  lomentaria, 403, 406, 408, 412–413, 633, 636–638, 640, 843–844, 851, 853–855, 860–864, 869, 915–916, 919, 921–930, 940–941
Scytosiphonales, 921, 922, 941
Searlesia dira, 724
Septifer bifurcatus, 603
Serpula vermicularis, 353
Sertuarella
  miurensis, 771, 772, 782
  polyzonias, 348, 352
Sertularia
  argentea, 346
  cupressina, 343
Shaskyus festivus, 717
Sidnyum turbinatum, 342, 343
Siganidae, 686
Sigmophora, 741
Siphonocladus pusillus, 386
Siphonolaimus, 741
Sipunculoidea, 748, 763
Solaster endeca, 353
Solea solea, 683
Solenopsora
  candicans, 801
  vulturiensis, 794, 804
Solieria, 904
  chordalis, 875, 904, 905, 906
  tenera, 875, 904, 905, 906
Solieriaceae, 904
Sparidae, 686, 688
Spartina, 884, 885
  alterniflora, 883, 884, 887
  anglica, 885
  maritima, 884
  x townsendii, 885
Spermatophyta, 583
Spermothamnion turneri f. *intricata*, 881
Sphacelaria, 851, 858
  arctica, 469
  cirrosa, 403, 406, 808, 412–413
  fusca, 386
  papilioniformis, 385
  plumosa, 403, 406–408, 414–415, 417–419, 448
  radicans, 629, 640, 641, 660
Sphaerolaimus, 741
Sphaerophorus globosus, 798
Sphaerotrichia divaricata, 403, 406, 408, 412–413, 416, 418–420, 450
Spilophorella, 740
Spinachia spinachia, 682, 684, 694, 708, 709
Spirorbidae, 776
Spirorbis, 777
  corallinae, 768
  inornatus, 768, 781
  rupestris, 768
  spirillum, 353
  spirorbis, 768, 771, 773–775, 782–783
Spongomorpha
  aeruginosa, 402, 406, 408, 412–413, 416, 418–420
  arcta, 402, 406, 408, 412–415, 629, 631, 635–636, 640, 650, 660
Sprattus sprattus, 681
Spyridia filamentosa, 381
Squamarina crassa, 801
Staphylococcus, 781
Steletta grubii, 356, 358, 359
Stelligera stuposa, 348
Stenogramme interrupta, 346

Stenothoe minuta, 348
Stephanolaimus, 738
Stereocaulon, 799
Stichococcus bacillaris, 453, 458, 464
Sticta, 798, 799
Stictyosiphon, 447, 458
  soriferus, 403, 406–408, 414–416, 418–420
Stilophora rhizodes, 381, 435, 461, 469
Stolonica socialis, 335
Streblonema, 401, 649, 660
Strongylocentrotus, 518, 706
  droebachiensis, 353, 705, 721
  franciscanus, 705, 716
  polyacanthus, 722
  purpuratus, 600, 721
Styela
  clava, 883, 884, 887
  mammiculata, 884
Stylarioides plumosa, 353
Stypocaulon scoparium, 381, 384, 388, *see also Halopteris*
Suberites
  carnosus, 347, 348
  domuncula, 343
Syllidae, 352
Syllis
  prolifera, 348
  variegata, 348
Symplocostoma, 743–744
Syngnathus
  californiensis, 693
  rostellatus, 682
  typhle, 682

T

Tanaidacea, 763
Taonia atomaria, 342
Taurulus
  bubalis, 682, 684, 692, 694
  lilljeborgi, 684
Tealia felina, 335, 342–343, 348, 352–355
Tegula
  eiseni, 717
  ligulata, 717
Tellina
  fabula, 353
  tenuis, 712
Teloschistes flavicans, 798
Terebellidae, 352
Terschellingia, 738
Tethya aurantia, 342, 348
Tetraclita squamosa rubescens, 584, 585
Thais [*see also Nucella*], 511, 664
  canaliculata, 724
  emarginata, 708, 709, 722, 724
  lamellosa, 724
  lapillus, 708, 709, 711, 716, 717, 718, 724, 725
Thalassoalaimus, 738
Theristus, 739, 743
Thorogobius ephippiatus, 682
Tilopteris mertensii, 403, 406, 408, 414–415
Tonicella
  lineata, 772
  rubra, 352
Tracheophyta, 585
"Trailliella intricata", 448, 628, 878, 881, 915, 920–921, 930, 931–934, 940
Trebouxia, 818, 826
Tribonema vulgare, 450
Trichotheristus mirabilis, 733
Tricolia pullus, 348
Tringa totanus, 708, 715
Tripyloides, 739
Trissonchulus, 741
Trivia, 674
  monacha, 352
Trophonia plumosa, 350
Tubulanus annulatus, 352
Tubularia, 764
  indivisa, 335, 342, 343, 346, 358
Tunicata, 763
Turbellaria, 748, 763
Turnerella pennyi, 404, 406–408, 417–419

U

Ulothrix, 439, 843–844, 847, 852–855, 863, 867, 869–870
flacca, 402, 406, 408, 412–413, 433, 450, 452, 844, 851–852, 855–856, 959–860, 862–864, 869
oscillarina, 433
pseudoflacca, 433, 851–853, 855–860, 862–864, 869
speciosa, 631
subflaccida, 433, 855
tenerrima, 433, 438
variabilis, 433
zonata, 436
Ulotrichales, 464
Ulva, 342, 467, 518, 627, 629, 633, 640, 644, 674, 707, 844–845, 870
californica, 600
lactuca, 357, 402, 406, 408, 412–413, 414–415, 454, 629, 631, 633, 636, 640–641, 822, 843–844, 847, 851–854, 858, 859–862, 864, 866, 869, 876, 904
pertusa, 454, 772
rigida, 633, 640, 879
Ulvaria obscura, 402, 406, 408, 412–413
Ulvella, 382
Umbonula littoralis, 334, 346, 353, 765
Urosalpinx cinerea, 711, 716, 889
Urospora, 624, 629, 632–633, 635, 637, 639, 645, 653, 660, 664, 843, 844, 852, 867, 869, 870
bangioides, 626, 631, 633, 645, 657, 660
penicilliformis, 402, 406, 408, 412–413, 433, 633, 844, 851, 853, 859–860, 862–864, 869–870
wormskioldii, 402, 406, 408, 412–413, 414–415, 416, 418–420

V

Vaucheria, 428, 431, 434, 437, 438, 657, 661
compacta, 461, 469
geminata, 450
Venerupis
rhomboides, 352
saxatilis, 353
Venus fasciata, 352
Verruca stroemia, 348
Verrucaria, 792, 793, 801, 816, 818, 821, 826
amphibia, 792
degelii, 793
ditmarsica, 792
halizoa, 792
maura, 792–793, 799, 801, 809, 816, 820, 823, 826, 828–829, 831
mucosa, 792, 809–810, 815, 817, 821, 823, 826, 828–829, 830–831
prominula, 803, 810
serpuloides, 807
striatula, 792, 793, 807, 810, 817, 821, 826
Virgularia mirabilis, 353
Volvocales, 621

W

Waerniella lucifuga, 629, 653, 666
Wrangelia penicillata, 381
Wrangelieae, 385

X

Xantho incisus, 690
Xanthoria
candelaria, 796
parietina, 795, 796, 801, 810, 815, 817, 819–820, 832, 834
var. *ectanea,* 817
Xennella, 738
Xyala, 739

Z

Zeugopterus punctatus, 683
Zoarces viviparus, 682
Zostera
marina, 901
noltii, 617
Zygnema, 462

Subject Index

A

Abereiddy, 773, 774
Abiotic factors (*see also all environmental entries*),
  consider with biotic in estuarine distributions, 458–459
  in community ambience, 496
  in distribution/abundance, S. California, 565–603
Absorption efficiencies (*see also* Feeding preferences, Optimal diets),
  in sea urchin diet optimization, 520
Abundance,
  aspects in S. California, causal factors, 565–603
  changes in species with time, 361
  ecological importance assumed proportional to, 581
  effects of algae on fish abundance, 679–686
  estimates by quasi-quantitative methods, 575
  importance in characterizing estuarine flora, 431
  in community recovery studies, 582
  metal-grids in estimates of, 575
  of algae as substrate, increasing epiphyte settlement area, 764
  of intertidal biota/populations in S. California, 585
  of nematodes, 731–734
  of potential prey, in feeding preference models, 518
  of species, indicated by most workers, 347, 350
  seasonal patterns, macrophytes/invertebrates in S. California, 574
Abundance scale,
  for subtidal, making comparable different units, 341
Abundant/frequent biota,
  in N.E. Atlantic subtidal descriptive framework, 330–331
Accessory pigments,
  masking reduced chlorophyll in unhealthy thalli, 566
Acorn barnacles,
  on artificial substrata, 681
Actual hypervolume, *see* Hypervolume
Adaptations,
  to epiphytic existence, 779–783
Add (river), 429
Adriatic Sea (*see also specific locations*), 385, 881, 929
Adventives,
  causes of range changes, 886
  factors responsible for introduction/spread, 885–890
  in the British macrobenthic flora, 875–908
  transportation factors, 886–890
Africa (*see also subdivisions, specific locations*),
  Atlantic north, 329
  West, 906
Age-dependence,
  in attraction gradients, epiphyte growth on "host", 779–780
  in attraction gradients, epiphyte

position on "host", 769, 776–779
Agencies (*see also* Vectors),
in spread/transportation of species, 886–890
Aggregative numerical response, 716–717
Air pollution,
affecting supralittoral lichens, 815
Algae (*for algae in general, see all chapters; for more generalized heads, see entry; for specifics, see below and other subheads*),
advantages to epiphytes, 764
age-dependence of surface-attraction to epiphytes, 769
as direct or indirect food for epiphytes, 764
as direct food for tropical fish, 686
as food resource for temperate fish, 686–689
as habitat for food organisms of temperate fish, 689–691
as nursery areas for young fish, 693–695
as protection for fishes, 691–693
as sediment traps, 764
as shelter for breeding fish, 693–695
as substrata for epiphytic invertebrates, 761–783
characteristics of epiphyte-attracting algae, 766
defoliation consequences for epiphytes, 796
effects of exudates on microbes/plankton/invertebrates, 780–782
effects on distribution/abundance of fish, 679–686
enhancement or depression of attraction to epiphytes, 770–771
epiphyte- unattractive algae, 766, 769
epiphytes characteristic of particular algae, 766
inexact distributional coincidence with epiphyte, 773
in estuaries, 425–475
in the Mediterranean, 371–388
in Newfoundland, 395–421
in stressed environments, characteristics of 425–475, 566–567
in the subtidal, 323–365, 371–388, 395–421
interpretation of algal phenomena in monitoring, 609–674
laminarian holdfast attraction to epiphytes, 769
nature of surface influence on larvae, 775
niche concept in, 487–536
positional importance of epiphyte settlement on 776–779
range utilized by invertebrates, 766
resources provided for epiphytes, 764
surface attractiveness to epiphytes: causes, 766, 769
survival strategy in epiphyte settlement on, 777–779
Algal-dominated facies,
mature state, 609–674
processes of build-up from inoculum sources, 609–674
Algal populations,
detritus from, in amphipod diet, 520
individuals often indistinguisable, 427
in stressed environments, characteristics of, 566–567
Algal surfaces,
age-dependent attraction to epiphytes, 769
enhancement or depression of attraction by other factors, 770–771
nature of influence on larvae, 775
Alginic acid,
decrease in plants into estuaries, 463–464
Algoa Bay (South Africa), 732, 734
Alien animal adventives,

into the Solent, 882–884, 888–889, 891
Aliens,
alien defined, 876
critical biomass for spread/establishment, 888
effects on situation of more careful or wider collecting, 876
in the marine flora of S. England, 875–908
mostly from Pacific USA, 877
origins obscured by extent of establishment/distribution, 877
previously overlooking, 876–877
real newcomers, 876–908
Alien chemicals,
use in dietary co-evolution, 521
Allelochemicals,
as niche dimension characteristic, 517
effects on food preference 520–521
general and definition, 514–515
Almond (estuary), 438
Ambient season,
plant-detected by photoperiod, 916–917, 921–930, 930–937, 940–942
plant-detected by temperature, 916, 921, 924, 937–940
Ambushers,
definition, 700
examples, 704
Amino-acid levels,
effects of salinity on, 464
Ammonium levels,
enrichment effects in Baltic Sea, 466
Amphidiploids,
fertile, of *Spartina*, 885
Amphipods (*see also* Invertebrates),
dominating cool-temperate sedimentary shores, 702
Gammaridean diet, 520
organisms eating them, 702
tube-building as fouling organisms, S. England floating structures, 859
Anacapa Island (California), 568–603
human disturbance of shores, 574
Anglesey, 336, 344, 345, 355, 362, 791, 795, 801
Annuals,
palatability cf. perennials, in algae as diet, 519–520
Anthropogenic disturbance *see* Human disturbance
Anthozoans,
a predominant predator group, 703
Antibacterial activity,
of algal exudates (tannins), 780–782
Antifouling,
effects of algal exudates, 780–782
Antifouling paints,
field-testing of, 844–845
fouling algae reduced to toxin/condition resistant flora, 887–888
use of non-toxic control settlement panels in testing, 845
Antimicrobial activity,
determining distribution of settlement, 781
of tannins, 780–782
Apothecia,
in littoral lichen reproduction, 793
in mesic-supralittoral lichens, 794
in xeric-supralittoral lichens, 796
Appalachee (river), 429
Arctic,
fish in, 680
marine flora of province, 329, 396
Arctic province,
geographical extent, 329, 396
Arctic-Boreal province,
around British Isles, 328–332
geographical extent, 329
Ardmore Bay (Clyde), 467
Ardrossan (Ayr), 617
Area (geographic), *see* Range
Argyll, 344
Arrested succession, *see* Held intermediates,

Arrival phase,
  fragments better than spores, 623
  in settlement sequence partitioning, 621, 623–624
Artificial settlement space,
  in settlement sequence, 628–638
Artificial substrata,
  acorn barnacles and green algae on, attracting fish, 680–681
  affecting shore lichen distribution, 813–815
  as settlement space, 628–638
  augmentation of harbour floras, Newfoundland, 414
  dockyard installations as, 845
  floating structures in S. England harbours, 844–871
  groynes in sandy shore providing rocky shore ambience, 680–681
  importance, 339
  in field culture for microspecies, 427, 471
  possible inclusion in subtidal descriptive framework, 328
  zoned community on dockyard installation verticals, 847
Ascidians,
  alien adventives, 884
  as fouling organisms on floating structures, S. England, 854, 859
  population variability through year, 363
Ascocarps,
  in littoral lichen reproduction, 793
Ascomycetes,
  in marine littoral, 793
Ash content,
  decrease in plants into estuaries, 463–464
Ash-free dry weight,
  for organisms with hard parts, 580
  in disturbed sample analysis, 580
  temporal/spatial variations in, in S. California biota, 565–603
Aspect,
  effect on *Lichina*, 801
  effect on shore lichens in general, 809–811
Assemblages,
  as associations, 325
  described subtidally for various areas, 344–345
  difficulty of comparing workers results, 347, 350
  inappropriate use of "population" for, 326
  of benthic diatoms, 452
  of epibenthic plants/animals, 324
  on seabed, 326
  sedimentary benthic, classification of, 327
  "sublittoral" applied to animals in/on sediments, 336
Assessment of seral stage,
  in monitoring, 609–674
Associations,
  botanical definition, 325
  climax, of *Posidonia*, W. Mediterranean, 387
  commensal definition, 325–326
  excessive recognition of, 387
  in W. Mediterranean infralittoral, 387
  marine invertebrate (epiphyte) – algae (substrata), 761–783
  open Atlantic association, 395–396
  primary association dominated by *Jania*, W. Mediterranean, 387
  recurrent, on sedimentary shores, 327
  terrestrial ecosystem classification, 324
Asteroids,
  a predominant predatory group, 703
  organisms eaten by, 702
Atlantic, north east (*basis for, and mentioned in, most papers*),
  circalittoral/infralittoral subzone boundary in, 332–333
  depth zone terminology, 336–338
  Spartina situation, 884–885

subtidal descriptive framework for, 330–331
Atmospheric pollution,
effects on seashore lichens, 798
Attachment phase,
oil preventing, 639
pollutants acting at, 639
in settlement sequence partitioning, 621, 639
Australia,
alien algae from, 878, 879, 880, 893, 894
south-east, 790
south-west, 790
Australasia, 881, 882, 883
Autecological image,
for W. Mediterranean photophilic infralittoral algal species, 386
Available stock,
in settlement sequence partitioning, 621–623
Average ecological distance,
definition and mathematical sources, 536
Average genotype,
determining ecological characteristics, 494
in ecopotential, 494, 495
in species niche, 494
unrealisable save as theoretical concept, 495
Avon estuary (Forth tributary), 438
Avon (river), 471
Axes (niche), *see* Dimensions (niche)
Ayr, 627

B

Bacteria,
activity of tannins against, 780–782
importance in marine communities, 509–510
Bait-digging,
wash-outs caused by, 659
Baja California, 569, 899, 921
Ballast,
affecting spread of benthic and planktonic species, 887
as method of alien organism spread, 887
discharge of, from ships in foreign harbours, 887
Baltic, 363, 434, 439, 440–441, 445, 452, 461, 465, 466, 469, 790, 799, 806, 811
Banyuls (France), 372, 374, 375, 377, 378, 379, 380, 381, 382, 383, 385, 386
Bare substratum,
as necessary condition in settlement sequence for many algae, 621, 628–638
time of occurrence of prime importance, 631
Bare zone,
erroneous reports for lichens in littoral, 792–793
Barfleur (France), 900
Barklice,
grazing shore lichens, 823
Barnacles,
as fouling organisms on floating structures, S. England, 856, 871
Australasian alien, 882–883
comparative competitive ability, aliens/natives, 891
cyprid larval settlement, 775
deciding isoenzyme strategy, 515–516
dominance on shallow wave-exposed rock, 336
dominating warm temperate and tropical cliff-like shores, 702
eaten by a range of organisms, 702
effect on shore lichen distribution, 801
littoral fringe lichens on, 792
surge-tolerance of, 336
Bathyal zone,
difficulty of field-identification, 333
Bathylittoral,
defined on absence of algae in

Mediterranean depths, 333
difficulty of field identification, 333
equivalence to Mediterranean offshore rocky biocoenosis, 333
need for more G.B. data to separate from sublittoral, 333
Bathythermograph profiles (*see also* Stratification, Thermocline),
in Newfoundland, 409
Beach management, (*see also* Environmental management, Resource management),
in the general light of greater knowledge, 618
legal side complex, 618
pressures growing for, 618
successional interpretation/advice in, 618
Before and after studies,
in Clyde monitoring, 617
in general pollution, 464–465
in S. California intertidals, 602–603
in the species context, 876–908
Behaviour,
in fish, heightening resemblance to marine plants, 679
Behavioural patterns,
in distribution of marine invertebrates, 770–779
Belgium, 752
Bembridge (Isle of Wight), 894, 895, 896, 898, 901
Benthos,
as ecosystem, 509
Bering Sea, 921
Bermuda, 921
Between- site comparisons,
for community structure, by species diversity indices, 581
Bicarbonate levels,
effects in estuaries on growth and photosynthesis, 454–456
Bi-directional water movements, *see* Two directional . . .
Bimodal distributions,
clean/polluted waters, in estuaries, 435, 468
Biochemical defence mechanisms,
in prey/predator relations, 718
Biocoenosis/-ses,
definition of, 325
differences biocoenosis ↔ community, 325
excessive subdivision of W. Mediterranean photophilic infralittoral, 387–388
in terrestrial ecosystem classification, 324
"offshore rocky bottom biocoenosis", 333
of the photophilic algae, 387
opinions on number in W. Mediterranean photophilic infralittoral vegetation, 386–388
similarity of Möbius concept to Petersen community, 325
W. Mediterranean division into Braun-Blanquet named subdivisions, 387
Biogeocoenosis,
relation to ecotope, 505–506
Biogeographic patterns (*see also* Distributions, Distribution factors),
data enhancement in S. California, 567
effects of cluster analysis, S. California, 588–590
mediated by water temperature, S. California Bight intertidals, 566
S. California islands versus mainland comparisons, 590–599
S. California lower shore, islands versus mainland, 590–593
S. California total intertidal comparison, 593–595
Biogeographic provinces,
along English Channel, 328
importance in community comparisons, 332
importance in conservation area selection, 332

S. California Continental Border
/and at overlap of two major, 566
those affecting British Isles, 328–332
Biological factors affecting seashore lichens (*see also* Lichens),
colonization, 818–819
competition, grazing, shelter, 821–825
growth, 815–816
morphological variation, 816–818
succession, 820–821
Biological interactions (*virtually throughout text; see specific entries*),
importance to substrate selection, invertebrate larvae, 770–779
Biomass,
critical level for alien spread in low biomass vector carriage, 888
Biomass measurements,
for disturbed samples, S. California, 580, 581
inapplicability with macroalgal mats/swards of estuaries, 427
low, in lichens, 789–834
macroinvertebrates in S. California, 587
quantification of species by, 427
Bionomic (biological) niche dimensions, 517
Bionts,
in general, lichens, 818–819, 825–828
isolated, of shore lichen constituents; physiology, 826
Biota,
constituent of ecosystem, 327
interpretation of algal-dominated, 609–674
recording data for conservation site selection, 324
richness in S. California, due upwelling, 570
status at times recorded in S. California photosamples, 566
Biotic factors (*see also specific entries*),
in community ambience, 496
in S. California intertidals, abundance/distribution, 565–603
need to consider with abiotic in estuarine distributions, 458–459, 466
Biotic habitats,
importance, 339
in N.E. Atlantic subtidal descriptive framework, 330–331
Biotic relationships,
altered in estuaries, due to reduced species diversity, 442, 458–459
Biotope,
biotope or community habitat, 504
confusion by some authors with habitat, 496
environmental conditions the basis, 327
in classification of terrestrial ecosystems, 324
partial basis for community descriptions, 327
relation to ecotope, 505–506
W. Mediterranean marine infralittoral, 372–388
Bird-manuring,
effect on lichens, 795, 796, 813
Birds,
a predominant predator group, 703
as disturbance agents, 510
predating barnacles, mussels, grazing gastropods, 702
Biscay, 688
Bivalves (*see also* Invertebrates),
adventive alien species to GB, 884
ash-free dry weights of, 580
dominating cool-temperate sedimentary shores, 702
eaten by gastropods, 702
modifying environment, 764
organisms eaten by, 702
sedantary forms as epifauna, 765
Blackwater (river), 429
Blennies (*see also* Fish),
algae important in diet of, 687

general 681–682, 684, 687, 691–692
predate barnacles/mussels, 702
Blue-green algae,
distribution of epilithic forms along estuaries, 430
gelatinous masses in mid-/ upper estuaries, 431
in estuarine mats, 427
on floating structures in S. England harbours, 852–865
predominant cover organisms in most S. California rocky intertidals, 565–566, 585
replacing brown algae in severe pollution, 465
sampled by undisturbed method with infra-red film, 565–566
Blue UV-absorbing pigment,
in formation of erect *Scytosiphon* thalli from prostrate crusts, 916, 941
as photomorphogenetic pigment, 916, 941
Blythe Estuary (England), 735
Body-form (*see also* Growth Forms),
heightened resemblance, due to behaviour, of fish to plants, 679
modifications in fish to resemble marine plants, 679
Body size,
effects on grazing patterns, 707–708
Bognor Regis, 895
Boreal province,
geographical extent, 329
Boreal-Arctic province,
geographical extent, 329
Boston Haven (Lincs.), 429
Bottle-brush forms,
caused by temperature-shock or salinity-shock, 462
Boulders,
as habitat, 339
definitions, 338–339
important to fish in Arctic and (probably) temperate waters, 680
in N.E. Atlantic subtidal descriptive framework, 330–331
limiting factor, 573
loose fields of, S. California, 573
should not be ignored in monitoring, 614
Boulogne, 900
Brackish environments (*see also* Estuaries, Fjords, Lagoons),
estuaries described, 425–475
estuaries compared, 425–475
estuaries cf. other brackish situations, 440–441
fjords, 400, 409, 425, 440–441
lagoons, 425, 440–441
pollution-testing in, by transplantation, 444
validity of inter-estuary comparison, 440
Brackish-water species,
along mid- reaches of estuaries, 428, 431, 432
definition of, 433–434
euryhalinity of, 433
few real examples, 434
general estuarine distribution, 432
Brackish-water submergence,
in fiords, 440
in tube-dwelling diatoms, 439, 471
types in estuarine algae, 439, 471
Brasilenyne,
allelochemical affecting food preference, 520–521
related to rhodophytin, 521
sequestered by animal from algal diet, 521
Braun-Blanquet methods,
applied or not in subtidal algal W. Mediterranean phytosociology, 373, 377, 379, 384
Bravet-Pearson correlation analysis,
in calculating qualitative minimum area, 379
Bray and Curtis percentage distance statistic,

applied to macrophyte/macro-invertebrate cover data, 581–582, 589, 590
Breaking-in phase,
climax mature stages present difficulties for, 639
in settlement sequence partitioning, 621, 638–639
many algae not able to achieve, 628
Bricks,
effect as substrate in Thames Estuary, 439, 459
Brighton, 895
Bristle-brush impingers,
testing availability of algal fragments as inocula by entanglement, 626, 627
Bristol Channel,
animal assemblages, 345, 350, 732
effect on species distributions, 329
Modiolus modiolus community, 350
Britain, East, 798
Britain, North-west,
lichens, 793
Britain, South-west, 877
Britain, West, 798
British Columbia,
oysters imported from, 888–889, 899
British Isles,
biogeographical provinces, 328–332, 934
fish in north, 683, 684
shallow subtidal, 323–365
Brittany,
ascidian spread, 884
depth-zone terminologies, 337
estuaries in, 429
oyster beds, 877
proposed algal introduction to, 908
Broad-fronded red algae,
preferred by some epiphytes, 767
Brown algae,
Clyde/Fairlie Channel/UK species numbers compared, 621
consistently favourable to epiphytes, 767
crustose and thalloid browns on stones below dockyard installations, 847
frequency in Clyde flora, 622
penetration into fiords, 440
reasons for epiphyte attraction, 767
replacement by greens/blue-greens in pollution, 465
selective attenuation into estuaries, 428
zonation patterns on floating structures, 870
zoned on Gosport Marina/Langstone Rafts, 850–871
zoned on verticals of dockyard installations, 847
Browsers,
including euryphagic and specialized species, 764
non-selective, as secondary epiphytes, 766
on algae, 764
some tropical fish specialized as browsers, 678
specialized algal, as primary epiphytes, 766
Bryophytes,
upstream bands in estuaries, 437, 438
Bryozoans,
as epifauna, 765
as epiphytes in general, 770
as fouling organisms on floating structures, S. England, 854
as primary epiphytes, 766
inimical shore-levels overriding acceptance of fucoid substrata, 767
kelp exudates as food sources for, 780
larvae unattracted to fucoid fruiting conceptacles, 767
larval indifference to or avoidance of surface films, 771

larval preferences for algal substrata, 771
larval settlement on inorganic substrata, 771
modifying environment, 764
population variability throughout year, 363
preyed on by sea-slugs (nudibranchs), 783
specialization/adaptations as epiphytes, 779–783
Bunowen (river), 429
Buoys,
as alien-spread vectors, 888
importance, 339, 844
in N.E. Atlantic subtidal descriptive framework, 330–331
marine algae on, 844, 866, 869
means of avoiding complicating tidal emersion along estuaries, 427
permanently submerged flora on, 427
species-poor nature, 626
Bureau of Land Management, South California, 574

C

Cadmium,
in shore lichens, 813, 814
Caithness,
littoral lichens, 792
Calcium levels,
effects in estuaries on algal growth, photosynthesis and distribution, 454–458
increase in plants into estuaries, 463–464
in lichen flora differences, calcareous/siliceous shores, 802
interaction with salinity tolerance in estuarine algae, 450–457
California, 685, 688, 689, 790
California, southern, 565–603
California Current,
general, 568–603
cold, 568
complex eddies/gyres, 569
eastern component of clockwise N. Pacific gyre, 568–569
effect of coast at Point Conception on, 569
main water circulation in S. California Bight, 568–569
moderate flow in two directions, 569
Calorific studies,
of dominant producers/consumers, 575
Calshot (Hants.), 894
Calvi (Corsica), 383, 385
Canada, 396, 397, 398, 899
Canary Islands, 880, 889, 921
Canonical correlation,
in estuarine factor/distribution correlations, 443
Cap Corse, 373
Capacity of individual,
definition, 496
genetically determined, 496
Carbohydrates,
countering environmental stress in lichens, 829–830
Caribbean Sea, 385, 906
Carnivores,
more variety in tropics/warm temperate, 702–703
ocypodid crabs as carnivores/detrital feeders in tropical sediments, 703
Carnivory,
a form of predation, 700
differences from herbivory, 700
β-carotene,
decrease in plants into estuaries, 463–464
Carrigathorna (Lough Ine), 348–349
Carron estuary (Forth, Scotland), 438
Cartesian coordinate system,
in niche space construction, 499
Catastrophic events,
effects of natural, S. California shores, 574–575

Caves,
in N.E. Atlantic subtidal descriptive framework, 330–331
Cell division,
effects of salinity in estuarine algae, 452–453
Ceska similarity test,
in W. Mediterranean homogeneity assessments, 382–383
Chalk,
littoral lichens on, 791–792
Channel Islands (California), 569
biogeographic comparison with mainland, 590–595
effects of human shore-disturbance, 574
lower shore comparison, 590–593
total intertidal comparison, 593–595
Channel Islands (UK), 681, 878, 881
Characteristic species (*see also* Dominant biota),
different understandings of, 345, 347
in community descriptions, 327, 345, 347
patchiness of, 363–364
possibility of inter-area comparisons, 347, 350
Chemical attractants,
in larval settlement, 775
Chemical composition,
alteration of, in estuaries, by pollution, 457
a major factor in estuarine algal distribution, 442, 457–458
of freshwater inflow into estuaries, 442
tolerance experiments in estuarine algae, 443–444
variation in that of species along estuaries, 463–464
Chemical interrelations,
importance at community level, 514–515
Chemical pollution,
affecting shore lichens, 814
Chemotaxonomy,
in shore lichens, 816–818
of estuarine algae, 464
Chemotypes,
in lichens, 789–834, especially 817–818
Cherbourg (N. France), 880, 882
Chesapeake (river), 429
Chesil Fleet (Dorset), 895, 904, 905
Chichester Harbour, 845, 882, 895, 898, 903
Chile, 790
China, 899
Chitin,
in lichens, not digested by many animals, 825
Chitons (*see also* Invertebrates),
choice by larvae of algal substrata, 772–773
grazers on fucoid sporelings/unicells, 702
Chloride levels,
decrease in plants, into estuaries, 463–464
effects in estuaries on algal growths, photosynthesis and distribution, 454–458
Chloride loss,
effects of salinity in estuarine algae, 452–453
Chlorophyll,
in estuarine pollution, 466–467
in niche, 531, 533
reduction, in unhealthy thalli, 566, 578
Circalittoral sub-zone,
algal characterization of Mediterranean circalittoral, 333
animal communites at Lough Ine, 348–349
characterization in British waters, 332, 338
characterization in French waters, 332
communities at Ramsey Island,

Wales, 346–347
definition for N.E. Atlantic, 338
definition of upper/lower circa-littoral, 338
in N.E. Atlantic subtidal descriptive framework, 330–331
misapplication of term to greater depths, 333
need for further study of lower limits of, 333
non-applicability to sedimentary animal assemblages, 336
organisms in, west coast of Ramsey Is., Wales, 334–335
separation by thermocline into "étages", 336–337
variable understanding of term, 336–337
Circumboreal-Arctic lichens,
in northern Scotland, 799
Clams,
heated effluent effects on warm-water immigrants, 884
Mercenaria introduced to GB, 618, 884
Clare Island (Co. Mayo), 880
Classification,
of subtidal marine ecosystems, 323–365
subtidal difficulties on rocky shores, 327–328
subtidal difficulties on sedimentary shores, 327
Clearance experiments,
in Clyde shore intertidal by accident (local amenity reasons), 623
in Clyde shore intertidal purposefully, 632–641
in disturbed sample analysis in S. California intertidals, 579–580, 602–603
in subtidal community development study, 360–361
recovery slower in deeper than in shallow water, 360–361
Cleared surfaces, *see* Clearance experiments
Climate,
broad changes as a cause of biogeographic distribution changes, 886
Climate on rocky shores (*see also* Physical environmental conditions, etc.),
general, 804–806
concept of exposure, 806
littoral well-known, 804
need for much more data, 805–806
soil water, 805
supralittoral ill-known, 804
wave-splash and spray, 804–805
Climatic extremes,
causing ecological reassessment, 567
Climax-association,
in W. Mediterranean infralittoral climax-cycle, 387
Climax community,
as sum of all preceding stages, 659
derived or displaced climax, 659
of sandy/shelly beach at Southannan, 618
Climax-cycle,
in W. Mediterranean infralittoral zone, 387
Climax, ecologically stable,
failure to attain in some marine conditions, 360–361
in marine communities, 359, 361, 659–668
Climax facies,
definition difficult in marine intertidals, 659
of marine algae, 617–618, 659–668
Clinid fish,
experiments proving importance of algal cover to fish, 680
in intertidal rock pools in South Africa, 680, 685–686
Clone selection,
as mechanism responsible for habitat amplitude, 493

"Closed" communities,
effects against aliens establishing, 907
Cluster analysis,
hierarchical cluster analysis, 581
of Newfoundland data, 405–420
of phenological data, 405–406
of S. California biogeography, 588–590
temporal/spatial variations in S. California intertidal biota in terms of, 565–603
Clyde estuary, 429–430, 452, 458, 459, 466, 467, 609–674
Coal Oil Point (California), 568–603
Coal terminal,
in Clyde industrialization, 609–674, especially 610
Coarse-grained species,
competitive aspects of the niche; defined, 502
formulae/mathematical models, 536
"Coastal" circalittoral étage,
definition, 336
probable equivalence to "fronto-littoral" zone, 336–337
relationship to upper circalittoral, 336–338
variable depth range, 336–337
Cockles (*see also* Invertebrates),
grubbing for as beach damage, 618
Coevolution (*implicated aspects throughout many other chapters*),
effects on community structure/stability, 702
effects on diet widths, 713
further intertidal research required, 718
in browser–browse balance, 521
in competitive relationships, 517–521
in predator–prey systems, 701–702, 707, 717–718
use of alien chemicals in, 521
Cold-boreal province,
geographical extent, 329
Colonization,
by shore lichens, 818–819
following major reclamation work, 609–674
introduction of aliens, 875–908
on floating structures, 843–871
Coloration,
algal pigment deepening due to pollution, 466–467
Colour adaptation (*see also* Cryptic coloration),
in fish to merge with dominant colour of local algae, 678
in fish to merge with sand/mud, 684–685
Colour changes,
in exposure to seawater spray of halophilic lichens, 797
Commensal relationships,
"association" used to describe, 325–326
Commercial introductions,
clams (*Mercenaria*), 884
detrimental introductions, 889
listed in reports/inventories, 888
mariculture, 888
oyster restocking/resiting, 888–889
Commercial vessels,
ballast discharge as alien-spreading agency, 887
quick turnround restricting vector function in alien-spreading, 887
Community,
as sets of energy-flow patterns in a continuum, 511–514, 575
changes with depth zones, 332–338
circalittoral animals, Lough Ine, 348–349
community climax, 359–361
community habitat or biotope, 504
concept of, 491, 510
constituent species types in, 361–364
definitions of, 325–328
description by divers, 341

descriptive survey of recurrent subtidal communities, 344–359
development of, 359–361, 582
differences Molander (1928) definition and ecological common usage, 326
dominant biota identifying, 325–327
dynamics of, 567
energetic data in analysis of function, 575
example of description by species listing, 342–343
excessive recognition of, 387
factors important in S. California intertidal community structure, 566
cf. guilds, 509
history of term usage, 325–328
holdfasts as self-contained communities, 769
importance of biogeographical province in comparisons, 332
in framework for subtidal description in N.E. Atlantic, 330–331
in inshore phytobenthos, 487–536
in terrestrial ecosystem description, 324–325
in W. Mediterranean infralittoral, 387
Laminaria hyperborea – associated communities, 354, 356, 357
marine organisation of, S. California, temporal/spatial analysis, 574–603
Modiolos modiolus community, 345, 350–353
naming of subtidal communities, 349–350
need for additional subtidal data, 365
of algae in stressed environments, characteristics, 566–567
Ophiothrix fragilis community, 345, 351, 354–355
organization of, 511–514
organization and structure distinguished apart, 511
position in succession, 659
recovery and development studies, 582
recurrence of, 323–324, 326–327, 345
recurrence of (sedimentary shores), 327
relationship (in concept) to niche for inshore phytobenthos, 506–521
resources used within (niche breadth), 493
sequencing in monitoring, 620–668
species listing in description, 341, 344
stability of, 361–364, 511–514
stenothermal/stenohaline offshore in open sea étage, 336–337
structure of, 323–365, 511–514, 565–603; especially 566, 719–725
subtidal, around Ramsey Is., Wales, 346–347
types in subtidal (GB), 323–365
variability of, S. California, 565–603
wave-exposed overhang communities, 356, 358–359
Community dynamics (*see also* Community),
basic community research towards understanding, 567, 575
Community ecology (*see also* Community),
distinctions from population biology, 513
Community function (*see also* Community),
energetic data in analysis of, 575
Community recovery (*see also* Community),
study method, 582
Community sequencing (*see also* Community),

in monitoring, 620–668
Compact morphology,
a characteristic of algal communities in stressed environments, 566–567
Comparisons,
between-site for community structure, 581
difficulty of, with different workers' epibenthic assemblage data, 347, 350
of characterising species usually possible, 347
percentage cover for S. California sites, animals/plants, 586
Competition (*see also* Spatial competition, Predation/refuges/competition),
a modifying influence (dimension) in niche concept, 500, 516–517
as a concept, 491
as a site-specific intertidal organisation factor within physical environment, 566
between hydroids on algae, 782
in/by shore lichens, 821–823
in structuring communities, 516–517 (contrasting views of importance, 517)
interaction of interspecific with salinity tolerance in estuarine algae, 450–457
interspecific, in estuaries, 436
reduced in estuaries due to lowered diversity, 458–459
reduced in inner fiords, 458–459
Competitive ability,
greater in introduced species, 891
reasons for introduced vigour, 891
Competitive displacement,
of British fucoids by *Sargassum muticum*, 775
Competitive dominants,
development through uninterrupted competition in community, 700–701
Competitive exclusions,
in community structure, 720
inferior and superior competitors, 720
Competitive hierarchies,
effect of predation on, 701, 721
nature and frequency of, 701
Complexity,
of S. California intertidals and other systems, 566
Composite lichen thalli (*see also* Lichens),
shore physiology of, 826–832
Composition,
by groups, of species in S. California intertidals, 582–585
Computers (data storage, retrieval, analysis),
need to produce results treatable by, 324
use in multivariate sorting/grouping techniques, 398
use with large volumes of data, 398
Concavity,
of algal surfaces, affecting epiphyte choice, 766
Concrete blocks,
effects as substrata in Thames, 439, 459
used in Portsmouth Harbour pontoons, 847
use in colonizer/community development studies, 360–361
Configuration (*see also general data in all shore papers*),
of shores, S. California, 571
Conservation,
importance of biogeographical provinces, 332
in the subtidal of the British Isles, 323–365
management of conservation areas, 359
site selection for 324, 359
Conspecificity,

in marine/freshwater forms of some genera, 462
Constant species/area curves,
in qualitative minimum area calculations, 379, 380
Consumers,
calorific studies of dominants, 575
Consumption,
by free-living nematodes, 746–747
Continuum,
a major view of community structure, 513
Coonamessatt (river), 429
Coordinates (niche), *see* Dimensions (niche),
Copper,
in sewage, eliminating estuarine algae, 467
in shore lichens, 813, 814
Coral reefs,
community stability in, 362
fish fauna of, 680, 686–687
Coralline algae (*also occasional mentions in descriptive papers*),
ash-free dry weights of, 580
Cord-grass (*Spartina*),
introduction and spread in UK, 884–885
mud-binding, 884, 885
Cork Harbour (Ireland), 884, 887
Cornwall, 357, 878
Corona del Mar (California), 568–603
Corsica, 385
Cortez submarine bank (California), 567
Cover,
an aspect of structural heterogeneity, 585
by photogrammetry in undisturbed samples, 576–579
general monitoring considerations, 609–674
importance in fish-algal interactions, 679–686
in disturbed samples, 581
in community recovery, 582
percentage cover compared for all sites, S. California animals/plants, 585
predominantly by bluegreens in most S. California rocky intertidals, 565–566
temporal/spatial variations in S. California intertidal biota in terms of, 565–603
parallax as a problem in estimates, 575–576
variations caused by temporal partitioning, 632
Crabs,
as disturbance agents, 510
ash-free dry weights for, 580
commensality, 326
eating algae and being eaten by fish, 690
grapsids grazing algae in tropics/warm temperate, 702
hermit, 326
in tropics, 703
ocypodid crabs in tropics, 703
predating barnacles, mussels, grazing gastropods, 702
Crevice flora,
general to lichens in crevices, 801, 804
littoral lichens, 793
mesic-supralittoral lichens, 794
submesic-supralittoral lichens, 795
terrestrial-halophobic lichens, 797
Crevices,
in N.E. Atlantic subtidal descriptive framework, 330–331
Criteria in description,
objective application of, 324
Critical daylength/nightlength,
the actual trigger in true photoperiodic responses, 937
variation with increasing temperature and latitude in *Scytosiphon*, 926–927
Crustaceans (*see also* Decapod crustaceans, Invertebrates),

those with algal portion of diet, taken by fish, 690

Crusts,
as perennial stages in *Scytosiphon*, 928
lichens, 791–798, 815–818
Mediterranean sampling, 383
on stones in lower littoral, S. England Harbours, 847
overlying, 652, 654

"Crusts-alone" formation,
variations with latitude and temperature in *Scytosiphon*, 926–927

Cryptic coloration (*see also* Colour adaptation),
in fish, to conform with algae, 678, 691–693
in fish, to conform with sand/mud, 684–685

Ctenostomatous Bryozoa, *see* Bryozoa

Cuba, 397

Culturing,
estuarine mud, for microspecies, 427

Current,
effect of, on algal pontoon/raft-fouling communities, 845–871
effects on epiphytic growth, 779–780
influence on substrate choice by invertebrate larvae, 770–779

Current reversal,
in characterising estuarine zones, 432

Current systems,
along/off S. California, 568–571
oceanic, mediating biogeographic pattern, S. California intertidals, 566

Cuticular proteins,
action patterns involved, 775
as larval attractants, 775

Cyphonautes larvae,
of bryozoans, 779–783
settlement on laminarians, 779

Cyprid larvae,
attraction by own cuticular proteins, 775
settlement pattern, 775

Cystoseiretum crinitae,
W. Mediterranean infralittoral subdivision, 387

Cystoseiretum strictae,
W. Mediterranean infralittoral subdivision, 387

Cytological phenomena,
in experiments with salinity on estuarine algae, 452–453

Czekanowski (coverage) similarity test,
in W. Mediterranean homogeneity assessments, 383

D

Dale (Pembrokeshire), 796

Damage (*see also* Disturbance),
by pollution, 573
lack of data-base to assess oil effects, 573

Dana (California), 570–603

Database,
lack of, to assess deterioration of shores, 573

Data storage, retrieval, analysis, *see* Computers *and specific process entries*

Davidson Current (California),
general data, 569–603, especially 569

Daylength,
in algal life-history control, 915–942

Decapod crustaceans (*see also* Crustaceans, Invertebrates),
a predominant predator group, 703
organisms eaten by, 703

Decomposition (*see also* Detritus),
by nematodes, 752

Dee estuary (Hilbre Islands) (Cheshire),
distribution patterns at, 437
point sampling method, 427
two-zone shore, 459

Dee (river, Scotland), 429, 439
Deeper water flora,
 in mixed water with less stable thermocline, Newfoundland, 414
 in Newfoundland, general, 414, 416, 417
Definition,
 ecological theory a prime example of failures in, 491
Defoliation,
 consequences for epiphyte persistence/distribution, 776
Delayed-succession communities,
 in disturbance, 655, 657
Deme terminology,
 applied to algae, 533
Dendrograms,
 in cluster analysis representation, Newfoundland, 406–420
 in cluster analysis representation, S. California, 588–595
Density,
 by photogrammetry in undisturbed samples, 576–579
 in community recovery studies, 582
 in disturbed samples, 581
 intertidal biota in terms of, 565–603
 temporal/spatial variations in S. California intertidal biota, 565–603
De-oxygenation,
 importance to subtidal organisms, 340
Depauperate shore lichen flora (*see also* Lichens),
 on hard rocks in general, 803–804
 on quartzites, 800, 803
Depth limits,
 of algae in Firth of Clyde, 615
 of photosynthetic plants, 337
Depth ranges,
 arbitrary, used in Newfoundland studies, 401, 405
 cluster analysis for Newfoundland ranges, 406–414
 in W. Mediterranean infralittoral, 373–376
 of algae in Firth of Clyde, 615
Depth zones,
 community change with 332–338
 horizon (French) versus zone (English) in term, 337
 in subtidal analysis, description and characterization, 332–338
 in W. Mediterranean infralittoral, 373–376
 terminological difficulties, 336–338
Derived climax,
 overgrazed aspect of beaches as, 659
Desiccation,
 avoidance of effects by growth habit, 456–457
 caused by S. California "Santa Ana" winds, 570
 interaction with salinity tolerance in estuarine algae, 450–457
 problems eliminated by floating structures, 865
 sensitivity to, in estuarine algae, 459–460, 470–475
 stress by, as site-specific intertidal organization factor, S. California, 566
 tolerance experiments on estuarine algae, 443–444
Deterioration,
 in S. California environment due stress by humans/natural phenomena, 573
 lack of base data to assess degree, 573
Detrital feeders,
 amphipods, 520
 invertebrates in general, 764
Detrital food chains,
 in later succession stages, 520
Detritus,
 becoming detritus and being consumed not mutually exclusive, 520
 in amphipod diet, 520

Development pattern,
after widespread disruption, 609–674
colonization/competition/dominance/climax, 359
enrichment period after climax, 359
failure to attain stable climax, 360–361
in recovery from natural/human disturbance, S. California, 600–603
of marine community/ecosystem, 359–361
Devon, 355, 357, 362, 799
Dew,
effect on upper shore lichens, 797
De Wit replacement series technique,
experiments on combined factor effects on competition in estuarine algae, 444, 452
Diatoms,
benthic, in model ecosystem, 452, 473
benthic, in estuaries, 426, 470–475
extreme pollution-induced *Melosira* dominance, 466
field culture on PVC plates, 427
field experiments on effects of grazing, 452
importance of centric in mid/upper estuaries, 430
inhibition of estuarine photosynthesis by, in benthic diatoms, 456
Langstone and Portsmouth Harbour intertidals, 845
multivariate techniques in estuarine distribution, 443
on floating structures in S. England Harbours, 852–865
planktonic aliens spread by ship ballast discharge, 887
simultaneous tolerance experiments to estuarine factors, 443–444, 473
tube-dwelling, in estuaries, 437–439
wide heterotrophic potential of benthic, 459
Diet widths,
effects of predator–prey coevolution, 701–702
in grazers, 705–707
limits of diet width, 713
wider in herbivore grazers; narrower in carnivore grazers, 707
Dietary values,
of algae, 706
cis-Dihydrorhodophytin,
allelochemical affecting food preferences, 520–521
related to rhodophytin, 521
sequestered by animal from algal diet, 521
Dimensions (niche),
bionomic (biological) dimensions, 517
dimensions other than foed resources for plants, 500
fine or coarse realization, 517
generalized axes of importance to benthic marine algae, 531–533
in delimitation of the niche for organisms, 489, 490, 499–500, 515–521
intensive nature of, 502–503
large potential numbers, 499–500
need for few critical axes only, 500
scenopoetic (physically based) dimensions, 517
Direct associations,
fish-algae in temperate waters, 677
Direct counting,
quantification of multicellular algae by, 427
inapplicability with macroalgal mats/swards of estuaries, 427
Disjunct distributions,
shipping as a vector for, in introductions, 887
Displaced climax,
overgrazed aspect of beaches as, 659

Distributions,
algal categories in mid/upper estuaries, 430–431
aspects in S. California related to causal factors, 565–603
effects of algae on fish distribution, temperate waters, 679–686
geographical patterns not static, 885
horizontal, along estuaries, 427, 428–436
inexact coincidence of algae and epiphytes, 773
major factors in estuarine algal distribution, 442
of algae extended by floating structures in absence natural hard substrata, 845
of free-living nematodes, 742–744
of marine invertebrates, 770
of sublittoral species with depth, Ramsey Is., Wales, 334–335
patterns of *Vaucheria* in estuaries, 428
seasonal patterns, macrophytes/invertebrates in S. California, 574–603
seasonal (rainfall/temperature) changes in estuaries, 435–436
sparse literature on estuarine algal distribution factors, 442
Distribution factors – introduced species,
adverse species introduced, 889
agencies or vectors of transportation, 886–889
causes of change, 886
climatic change in, 886
commercial species introduced by Man as vectors, 888–889
floating objects as vector, 888
marginal dispersal in, 886–889
remote dispersal in, 886–889
shipping as vector, 887–888
transportation modes, 886–890
Distribution factors – lichens,
climate of rocky shores, 804–806
human activities, 813–815
light and aspect, 809–811
nutritional factors, 812–813
rock chemistry, 800–802
rock texture, 802–804
rock type, 800–804
salinity, 811–812
tide levels, 806–807
wind and wave action, 807–809
Disruptive effect,
of *Sargassum muticum* possible on existing flora, 901–903
Disturbance,
as site-specific intertidal organization factor, human and natural, S. California, 566, 595
avoidance in sampling, 576–577
care needed with attribution, 510
constructions affecting algal-dominated resettlement sequences, 609–674
delayed succession communities in, 655, 657
deleterious ecosystem changes due to, 359
human and other, documentation through permanent photo-samples, 566
in soft-bottom communities, 510
in S. California mainland versus island biogeographic comparison, 590–595
of existing flora by *Sargassum muticum*, 901–903
promoting coexistence of inferior competitors, 720
response of intertidal communities to natural disturbance, 600–602
slower recoverers heavily impacted by disturbance, 603
to rocky shore through loose boulders, S. California, 573
Disturbed samples,
harvest method in, 579–581
quadrats selected for biological

similarity to undisturbed ones, 579
S. California methods and approach, 579–580
Diurnal rhythms,
in diatoms/euglenoids in estuaries, 471–472
Diversity,
between-habitat (β) diversity, 493
diversity measures, 581
entire landscape diversity (ecotope), 493
of free-living nematodes, 734–742
of intertidal systems of S. California, 566
within-habitat (α) diversity, 493
Dockyard installations,
as artificial substrata, 845
Dominant biota,
algae on rock in shelter, 336
application limitations, in absence of functional interrelationships, 510
barnacles/sponges on shallow wave-exposed rock, 336
brittle stars a good example, 351, 354, 355
calorific studies of, 575
difficulties of applying, in sedimentary seabed communities, 327
habitat zone terminology based on, at depths, 337–338
in community development studies, 360–361
in estuaries, 428
in global stability community, 361
in identifying communities, 325, 327
in N.E. Atlantic subtidal descriptive framework, 330–331
on floating structures in S. England harbours, 844–871
patchiness in, 363–364
primary productivity of, 575
spatial and temporal variations, S. California, 574
successional variations, 364
suspension feeders in strong tidal stream areas, 336
Dorset, 345, 878
Drag effect,
due fouling communities on ships, 844
economic problems created for shipping, 844
Dredging,
disadvantages, 341
Drift,
as agent in marginal dispersal, 889, 899, 902
littorinids cast up due algal overgrowth, 657
off S. California shores, 601
primarily of local origin, 624
transport of substrata by, 624, 657
Drought,
adaptations of lichens to, 797
effect on lichens, 796
Dry weight,
decrease in plants into estuaries, 463–464
in disturbed sample analysis, 580
in non-calcareous species, 580
temporal/spatial variations of in S. California intertidals, 565–603
Duration,
of extreme values in algal estuarine distribution factors, 442–443
Dutch Delta Area and estuaries, 429, 432–434, 438–439, 445–446, 448, 456
Dynamics of predation,
general, 713–717
(attack rate) functional response, 713–714
intensity of predation, 713–714
(attack rate) numerical response, 713–714

E

Early successional plants,
earlier stages dominated by grazing

food chains, 520
more palatable than later ones, 520
Eastbourne, 899
Ecological amplitude,
species of narrower, in outer estuaries, 431
species of wider, in inner estuaries, 431
Ecological importance,
assumption of proportionality to abundance, 581
Ecological processes (*see also specific entries*),
experiments on, 567
Ecological theory,
confusion in application of terms/concepts, 491
confusion in actual concepts, 491
failures to define terms in, 491
Ecopotential,
"average genotype" in, 494
comments on, 496
definition, 494; accepted definition of, 498
difficulties presented, 495
limits unperceived except by species, 495
near equivalence to fundamental niche, 493–494
theoretically satisfying but no practical use, 495, 498
Ecosystem,
definition, 327
primary niches in ecosystem structure, 494
Ecosystem attributes,
confusion in niche concept with species attributes, 493
non-dependence on genotype, 494
Ecotope,
comments on, 496
definition for phytobenthos, 505–506
γ-diversity (entire landscape differentiation), 493
full definition, 505–506
general definition of, 498
practical importance of, 499
relation to habitat/biotope/microlandscape/biocoenosis etc., 505–506
Ecotypic differentiation,
a mechanism responsible for habitat amplitude, 493
Ectocarpoids, 357
Effluents (*see also* Heated effluents),
from direct reduction plant of iron ore terminal, 610
warming by, importance to subtidal organisms, 340
Egypt, 381
Elasmobranch fish,
scyliorhinid eggs laid in subtidal algae, 695
Electronic flash,
in photogrammetry, 577–578
Electrophoresis,
amino-acid analysis of estuarine algae, 464
Emigration,
of species from Atlantic into Pacific, 907
Enclosed sea areas,
effect on Oceanic/Mediterranean-Atlantic species, 329
localized biogeographical change in, 329
Encrusting coralline algae (*see also* Crusts),
as food for chitons, 772–773
Energetic data,
in community function analysis, 575
through primary productivity and calorific studies of dominant biota, 575
Energy flow,
consumption by free-living nematodes, 746–747
metabolism of free-living nematodes, 744–745

production of free-living nematodes, 745–746
through free-living nematode populations, 744–747
Energy maximization premise,
considered, 703, 705
defined, 703
where nutrients limiting, 705
Energy values,
of potential prey, in feeding preference models, 518
England, East, 791
England, South, 791, 879, 884
England, South-west, 798 (*more general statements in texts*)
English channel,
biogeographical provinces along, 328, 329
aliens across, 877
effect on species distribution, 329
Enrichment period,
following community climax, 359
Entanglement phase,
a critical phase, physical or biological, 624
in settlement sequence partitioning, 621, 624–626
Environment (*see more specific aspects*),
changes as a cause of distribution pattern change, 886
deterioration due to excessive-use stress, S. California, 573
Environmental extremes,
carbohydrates in lichens countering environmental stress, 829
resistance to, in shore lichen composite thalli, 829–830
Environmental heterogeneity,
importance in promoting community species richness, 719
Environmental impact,
of shore industrial construction and associated activities, validity of questions/answers, 609–674
on larval behaviour in invertebrates, 770–779
Environmental management (*see also* Beach management, Resource management),
beach data required for, 618
prediction for, 567
Environmental patches,
in optimal patch use, 712–713
Environmental regulation,
of algal life-histories, 915–942
Environmental variability,
broad range in S. California, 566
due to location in overlap of two major biogeographic regions, 566
obscured by local or site specific conditions, 566
Epibenthos,
as ecosystem, 509
Epibios,
as ecosystem, 509
Epifauna,
age of alga important to development, 765
environmental factors modifying, 764–765
many species in common with animal epifauna, 764
of *Sargassum muticum*, 775
on algae, 761–783
Epiflora,
of laminarian stipes, 769
of *Sargassum muticum*, 775
supporting other epiphytes, 769
Epigrowth feeders,
among nematodes, 736–742
Epilithic forms (macroalgae *throughout text*),
microalgae, in estuaries, 470–475
Epipelic forms,
microalgae in estuaries, 470–475
Epiphytes,
adaptations to epiphytic existence, 779–783
age-dependence in attraction to host, 769, 776–779

algal preferences of sessile animals, 767
algal preferences of other groups, 767
attracted to laminarian holdfasts, 769
definition of, 764, 765
distinctions between true epiphytes and eurytopic species, 775
distribution of settlement due to antimicrobial activity, 781
epiphyte (invertebrates) – algae (substrate) associations, often of high specificity, 761–783
examples of primary, 765–766, 768–769
examples of secondary, 766
examples of substrata chosen by primary, 768–769
highly-epiphytized algal state a characteristic of stressed communities, 566–567
? important characteristics of microenvironment for, 517
increasing species diversity, subtidal, 381–382
in settlement sequence partitioning, 648–652
laminarian stipe as substrata, 769
large numbers in W. Mediterranean subtidal, 381–382
microalgae in estuaries, 470–475
microenvironments of, 517
need for definition for study of ecological validity, 765
parts of algal fronds avoided, 767, 769
previous studies of epiphyte–alga association, 762
primary or obligate, defined, 765
range of invertebrate epiphytes in Colman (1940), 763
reactions to disjunct/zoned algal substrata, 775
resources offered epiphyte by algal substrata, 764–765
secondary, defined, 765
survival strategy in settlement on "host", 777–779
use of microepiphytes to characterise pollution, 465
Epiphytism,
in niche concept, 516, 532
Epiphytized algae,
compact communities of, a characteristic of stressed environments, 566–567
Epipsammic forms,
microalgae in estuaries, 470–475
Epizoism,
in niche concept, 516
Equilibrium concepts, 503–504
Equitability,
confounding with richness component of species diversity, 581
as component of species diversity indices, 581
Erect algae,
as subtidal indicators of infralittoral subzones, 337
Erratic weather,
affecting ecological conclusions, 567
Erskine ferry, 657
Establishment phase,
as component of settlement sequence partitioning, 621, 639
exegetic use of earlier phases, 639
Estuaries,
attentuation of red and brown algae along, 428
benthic algae in, 428–441
bimodal clean/polluted distributions, 435, 468
brackish species in mid-reaches, 428
brackish water submergence in, 439
bryophyte bands in, 437
chemical composition of water in, 457–458
chemotaxonomy of estuarine algae, 464
classification into marine/freshwater/brackish algae, 431

classification of types of algae based on estuarine patterns, 426, 434–435
classification of types of estuary based on algae, 426
classification of zones within, 426
comparison with other brackish habitats, 440–441
competition and species diversity lowered, 458–459
competition in, 436
continuous variation cf. distinct morphological types, 469
culturing mud from, for micro-species, 427
definition, 425
differences/similarities between, 426–475
distribution of *Vaucheria* in estuarine conditions, 428
duration of extreme factor values, 442
effect of pollution on *Melosira*, 431
effects of combined factors on inter-species competition, 444
effects of environment on algae, 425–475, especially 460–464 and 468–470
effects of pollution on algae in 430–431, 435–436, 438, 448, 457–458, 464–468
environment, 441–460
estuaries compared, 425–475
estuarine studies listed, 429
experiments on temperature effects, 449–450
factors other than salinity in biota distribution, 432–433
few species usual in benthic floras, 431
fiords, 425, 435, 440–441, 468
freshwater algal species at estuary heads, 428
freshwater zones in, 432
fucoid bands in, 437, 438
general dominance by Chlorophyta, 431
highest nematode abundance in muddy estuaries, 731
hydrographic patterns, 442
importance of abundance in, 431
importance of bluegreens/ *Vaucheria*, 431
increasing importance of green algae, 428, 431
interaction of limiting factors in distribution, 450–457
intraspecific variation in estuarine algae, 468–470
lacking data on bluegreens, 430
lagoons, 425, 440–441, 444, 446
lesser amplitude species of outer, 431
long- and short-life algae along, 430
major factors in distribution of algae, 441–460
marine algal species the main colonisers, 428
measurements of factors/observed distribution correlations, 443
microalgae in (summary of situation), 470–475
Newfoundland, 400–401, 411, 413, 414
pattern of algal categories, mid/ upper, 430–431
reduction of species number along, 428
salinity effects on cytological phenomena, 452–453
salinity effects on photosynthesis/ respiration, 454–456
salinity races, 444–445
sampling in, 427
seasonal horizontal distribution changes, 435–436
shore and supralittoral lichens penetrating, 811–812
species of oligohalinicum, 433
substrata nature in, 459–460

suppression of sexual reproduction in, 470
temperature changes, 447–448
tolerance experiments in algae, 443–444, 469–470
transitional nature, 426
transplantation in tolerance experiments, 444
use of point frames for algal mats, 427
validity of use of estuary as control, 440
variations in plant chemical composition along, 463–464
Venice salinity-zone system applicability, 430
vertical distribution in, 436–439
wide amplitude species of inner, 431
zone characterisation in, 432

Estuarine algae,
brackish-water submergence in, 439
classifications of types based on estuarine patterns, 426, 434–435
lack of a current universally-applicable classification, 435
macroalgae, 425–470
microalgae, 470–475

Estuarine conditions,
effect on *Vaucheria* distribution, 428
general effects on flora, 426
greater physical/chemical complexity than on open coasts, 474
harsher in inner reaches than in outer, 431
often involved in harbours, 887
pronounced effects on Newfoundland flora, 414
salinity as a factor, 430
salinity and tidal emersion effects, 427
transitional nature, 426

Estuarine freshwater zone,
floristic elements, 432
lack of salt penetration, 432

"Étages",
temperature division of circalittoral into, 336–337

Euclidean space, *see* Hyperspace

Euglenoids,
around sewage outfalls in brackish water, 465
in estuaries, 470–475
possible index of water quality, 465

Euhalinicum,
estuarine, 432
marine, 432

Europe, *basis for most papers*

Euryhaline species,
brackish-water submergence in, 439
in estuaries, 432, 446
penetration into fiords, 440
phytoplankton, 457
vertical distribution in estuaries, 436, 437

Euryphagic species,
among browsers and grazers, 764

Eurytopic (physiologically tolerant) species,
among sedentary invertebrates on algae, 764
distinctions between true epiphytes and, 775
low diversity in stressful environments, 359
on *Saccorhiza*, 765
on *Sargassum muticum*, 775
opportunists as secondary epiphytes, 765
spirorbid larvae, 773

Evenness,
in species diversity indices, 581
measured by Pielou's index J′, 581
temporal/spatial variations in S. California intertidal biota in terms of, 565–603

Evolution (*see also* Incipient), 533
speciation

Exe (river), 429, 448, 471, 736

Exegetes,
associated with succession, 670

characterising low littorinid intensity, 657
definition of, 610, 613
location and interpretation of, 659
processes of exegetic significance, 661, 670
use of in monitoring, 609–674
Exmouth, 736
Exonerative monitoring (*see also* Whitewashing),
general comments, 618–619
Exotic species,
characteristics, 876
Exploitation,
deleterious ecosystem changes due to, 359
Exploitation competition,
in affecting niche width, 517
in structuring communities, 516–517
Exposure,
pronounced effects on flora in Newfoundland, 414
Exposure scales,
biologically-defined Ballantine scale, 327
Exterior mucilage (*see also* Surface films),
chemistry of, in algae, 517
discouragement of epiphytes by, 766–767, 769
importance of, to parasite or epiphyte, 517

F

Facies,
definition of, 327
recognised in W. Mediterranean infralittoral, 387
relationship to community, 327
Faeroes, 329
Fairlie Channel, 612, 621, 632, 668
Fairlie Pier, 631
Falmouth, 878, 880, 887, 904, 905, 906
Fecal-Seston,
as ecosystem, 509
Feeding patterns, 517–521
of temperate marine fish, 677, 686–691
of invertebrates and predators, 699–725
on and by nematodes, 736–742, 748–751
Feeding preferences, 517–521
in grazers, 705–707
of temperate marine fish, 677, 686–691
on and by nematodes, 736–742, 748–751
Feeding rates,
in sea urchin diet optimization, 520
Filamentous red algae,
as sediment traps, 767
Fine-grained species,
comparative aspects of the niche; defined, 502
formulae/mathematical models, 536
Finland,
freshwater in Baltic, 441
Fiords,
as brackish environments, 425
compared with estuaries/lagoons, 440–441
distributions in sewage-polluted, 435, 468
in Newfoundland, 400, 409, 425
Firemore Bay (Scotland), 732, 734, 735
Firth of Forth, 617
Firth (Sanda) (Clyde), 616
Fish (*see also specific types*),
a predominant predator group, 703
as disturbance agents, 510
behavioural adaptation to algae, 679
body-form adaptation to algae, 679
cryptic colour adaptation to algae, 678, 691–693
cryptic colour adaptation to sand, 684–685

feeding of temperate marine fish, 677
fish–algal relationships, temperate waters, 677–696
fish feeding on other algal-eating organisms, 690–691
food of algal-associated fish, 689–691
little dependence on algae as direct food, 678
lying flat on or burrowing into sand, 684–685
migrating in with tide to graze algae in tropics, 702
predating grazing gastropods, 702
Fish–algal relations,
algae as breeding shelter, 693–695
algae as food for tropical fish, 686
algae as food resource, 686–689
algae as nursery areas, 693–695
algae as nursery grounds for otherwise offshore fish, 678
algae as protection for fish, 680–683, 691–693
algae shelter food of fish (other fish; invertebrates), 678
background to studies, 678–679
distribution/abundance affected by algae, 679–686
fish of rocky shores attracted to sandy beaches by artificial substrata carrying green algae, 680–681
food organisms of fish, amongst algae, 689–691
indirect studies only available previously, 678
little feeding of fish on temperate algae, 678
predation reduced by algal cover, 678
Fishery science,
importance of fundamental role of plants to, 678
Fishing floats,
as vectors in alien spread, 888
Fishing pots,
as alien-spread vectors, 888
Fitness,
maximised by grazing in *r*-selected species, 519
of individual in niche concept, 490
Fleet (river) (Scotland), 429
Flexibility,
a requirement in concepts in a developing field, 491
need for more crystallized applications currently in ecology, 491
Flinders (Australia), 919, 924
Floating objects,
as vectors in alien spread, 888
restricted success as vector due low biomass, 888
Floating structures,
extending algal distributional limits in absence natural substrate, 845, 869
general zonation patterns on, 870
green algae as waterline community on, 867
habitat more like subtidal than intertidal, 865–866
in provision of baseline data for monitoring possible oil and other pollution, 845
in study of locally-dominant fouling algae/animals, 845
unusual nature of environment provided, 865–866
Flood,
as site-specific unpredictable disturbance factors, S. California intertidals, 566, 574–575
Flowing water,
in narrow channels; epiphyte/algal reaction to, 764–765
Foliose algae,
failure to survive extreme wave-action, 336
Food chains, 517–521
detrital, 520
grazing, 520

Food-partitioning,
based on gross morphology of buccal cavity, in nematodes, 736–742
Food sources (*general to many papers*),
algae as, direct or indirect, for epiphytes, 764
kelp exudates as, for bryozoans, 780
secondary epiphytes using primary as, 766
Foraging methods,
as study in understanding community function, 701
limits of diet width, 713
optimal diets, 703–712
optimal foraging, 703
optimal patch use, 712–713
studied through optimal diets or optimal foraging, 703–713
Formulae,
for niche aspects, 534–536
Fouling communities,
algal variety reduced by modern conditions, 887–888
antifouling paints used against, 845, 887
composition and stratification of algal fouling on vertical sides of pontoons/rafts, 845–847
harbour environments discourage many, 887
in Portsmouth and Langstone Harbours, 845–871
of marine algae on floating structures (pontoons/rafts), 844–871
quick turn round times of ships affecting, 887
Fragmentation,
possible importance where usual reproduction suppressed, 463, 470
possible mechanism of marginal dispersal, 890
Framework for description,
discipline needed to use framework underwater, 344
example of use of subtidal framework, 342–343
of community for monitoring purposes, 619
of subtidal communities in N.E. Atlantic, 330–331
of subtidal habitats in N.E. Atlantic, 330–331
France, 332, 333, 336, 345, 371–388, 679, 687, 799, 877–878, 881, 884, 900, 904–905, 934
Free-living nematodes (*see also* Nematodes),
significance to ecosystem, 729–755
French marine flora,
species new to, 385–386
Frequency,
by photogrammetry in undisturbed samples, 576–579
in community recovery studies, 582
in disturbed samples, 581
percentage, as algal mat sampling method in estuaries, 427
temporal/spatial variations in S. California intertidal biota, 565–603
Frequency/area curves,
in qualitative minimum area calculations, 379
Freshwater algae,
at estuary heads, 428, 432
in estuaries as a whole, 425–475
size reduction down estuaries, 461
Freshwater influence,
in characterising estuarine zones, 432
in sea lochs, 506–507
Freshwater layering,
in sea lochs, 506–507
Freshwater river conditions,
as zone in estuarine characterization, 432
Freshwater run-off,
effect on lichens, 796
Freshwater West (Pembrokeshire), 358

Freshwater zones,
in estuaries, 432
Frontolittoral zone,
probable equivalence to "coastal" circalittoral étage, 336–337
Fucoids,
apical areas generally avoided by epiphytes, 769
chemical composition affected by estuarine pollution, 467
competitive displacement in, 775
detritus in estuaries, 474
effect of levels on shore on otherwise accepting bryozoan larvae, 767
effect of partitioning on settlement, 634
epifauna of, 765
epiphytes on, 651
freedom from epiphytes, 654
hydroid epiphytes on, competition between, 782–783
in settlement patterns, 637, 638
on floating structures, 844–865, especially 867, 871
organisms grazing on, 702, 723
possible biochemical defence mechanisms in, 718
size reduction in estuaries, 461, 469
some fruiting conceptacles unattractive to bryozoan larvae, 767, 769
Fucoid bands,
epiphytes on, 651
competition in, 511
in estuaries, 437–438
on rocky shores, 511
Fucoid sporelings,
organisms by which grazed, 702
Fukuoka–Prefecture, Kyushu, Japan, 933
Functional response (predation intensity),
considered, 714–716
defined, 713–714
stabilizing or destabilizing, 714–716
Fundamental ecological processes (*see also specific entries*),
experiments on, 567
Fundamental niche,
an attribute of species only, or species plus environment?, 494
as physical ambience, 516
comments on, 496
near equivalence to ecopotential, 493–494
principally reflecting species' capabilities but affected by internal/external environment, 495

G

Galapagos Islands,
compared to S. California, 568
Galway, 878, 879, 905, 906
Galway Bay,
animal assemblages, 345
stenohaline/stenothermal offshore communities, 336
Gammarids (*see also* Invertebrates),
diet, 520
Gastropods,
algal preferences, as epiphyte, 767
a predominating predator group, 703
as primary epiphytes, 766
colonial vermetids on warm temperate and tropical cliff-like shores, 702
dominating cool temperate sedimentary shores, 702
eating bivalves, 702
grazing shore lichens, 823
organisms eating them, 702
General susceptibility,
as a benthic macroalgal niche characteristic, 532
Genetic differences, *see* Intraspecific variation
Geographical boundaries,
common to different species' tolerances, 329

Geographical comparisons,
in shore lichens, 798–800
Geographical latitude,
effects on taxonomy of predator and prey, 702
Geographical location,
changes of lichen ecology due to, 799, 800
effect on species characteristic of communities in GB subtidals, 328–332
Geographical range (area),
definition as concept cf. niche/habitat, 505
definition for phytobenthos, 505
Germany, 882
Germling stages,
as stages spread by vectors, 890
as stages spread by water currents, 890
knowledge of longevity/viability of, 890
part of partitioning of settlement sequence, 620–668
Ghana, 451
Glaciation,
in Newfoundland physiography, 400
Global stability,
of community, 361, 362
Glutamic acid levels,
effects of salinity on, 464
Goats,
grazing shore lichens, 823
Gonimoblasts,
in *Antithamnion spirographidis*, 386
Gosport Marina, 846, 848, 850–857
flora of outer exposed floats, 850–854
flora of inner sheltered floats, 854–857
Göteborg, estuaries near (Sweden), 429
Government Point (California), 568–603
Gower (South Wales),
Asterias variability on, 363
descriptive survey of Graves End on, 342–343
kelp epiphytes on, 357, 779
mussel variability on, 363
Gradients of attractiveness,
dependent on "host" age, 769, 776–779
holdfast attractiveness, 769
of algae to epiphytes, 767–769
of parts of algal surface to epiphytes, 769
Grapsid crabs,
grazing algae in tropics/warm temperate zones, 702
grazing algae elsewhere, 690
Gravel,
in subtidal descriptive framework, N.E. Atlantic, 330–331
shore inundation at upper intertidals of mainland S. California; effects, 593
Gravity,
influence on invertebrate larvae substrate choice, 770–779
Grazers,
activity minimal on floating structures, 865
algal grazers more diverse in tropics/warm temperate, 702
as primary epiphytes, 766
definition of, 700
diet widths, 705–707
examples of carnivorous grazers, 704
examples of herbivorous grazers, 704
experimental exclusion of, 362, 452
general relationships in communities, 510, 705–707
grazer recognition of plant value, 706
including specialized and euryphagic forms, 764
in estuaries, 452, 474

inhibited by suspended solid loadings, 655
in subtidal epibenthic animal communities, 362
prey preferences, 705–707
on microbial films, 764
some fish specialized as (on algae) in tropics, 678
types of predatory forms (including grazers), 700
Grazing,
as biotic factor in distribution in estuaries, 458–459
by various organisms on shore lichens, 823–825
effect not always adverse on algae, 520
effects on shore lichen distribution, 801
field-experiments on effects on diatoms, 452
increasing microalgal production in estuaries, 474
in rocky shore "zones" lower limits, 511
mutual, in littorinids, 657
overgrazing, 659
patterns on cool-temperate rocky shores, 702
Grazing boundaries,
increase in algal entities across, 632–641, 660
Grazing food chains,
dominating early succession, 520
Grazing patterns,
on cool-temperate rocky shores, 702
Great Bay (river system, USA), 429, 431, 463
Great Cumbrae, 611, 612, 616
Green algae,
attractive only to motile (specialized herbivore) epiphytes, 767
Clyde/Fairlie Channel/UK species numbers compared, 621
floating structure waterline community predominantly of, 867
frequency in Clyde flora, 622
increasing importance into estuaries, 428
in estuarine mats, 427
lacking rigidity, 766
on artificial groynes in otherwise sandy shore, 681
possessing few sessile epiphytes, 766, 767
replacing brown algae in pollution, 465
seasonal growths on mudflats/sandy intertidals, 845
sewage stimulation of, 466–467
zonation patterns on floating structures, 870
zoned on Gosport Marina/ Langstone Rafts, 850–871
zoned on vertical sides of dockyard installations, 847
Gregarious response,
in invertebrate larval settlement, 771
"Grey area" literature,
effects of pollutants on process probably buried in, 613
Group average sorting,
clustering by, 405
Growth and life-history strategies,
as a benthic macroalgal niche dimension, 515, 532
of shore lichens, 815–816, 818–819
within stressful environments, 566–567
Growth forms (*see also* Body form),
of algae in stressful environments, 566–567
of shore lichens, 816–818
Growth habits,
in algal avoidance of salinity exposure, 456–457
in algal avoidance of desiccation, 456–457

of algae in stressful environments, 566–567
Growth rates,
following transplantation, 575
high, in algal populations in stressed environments, 566–567
of hydroids cf. algae, 782
of shore lichens, 815–816
Guilds,
difference from communities, 509
grazing guild affected by storm, S. California, 601–602
Gulf of Mexico, 906

H

Habitat,
amplitude (expressed in habitat range), 493
between-habitat (β-)diversity, 493
community habitat, 504
confusion by some with biotope, 496
definitions of, cf. niche, 496
general (accepted) definitions of, 498, 504–505
habitat hyperspace, 504
habitat hypervolume, 504
habitat–niche relationship, 504–505
lack of sharp distinctions range/habitat/niche common factors, 505
overlap in application with or equivalence to niche, 492
practical importance of, 498
relation to ecotope, 505–506
within-habitat (intra-community) diversity (α-diversity), 493
Habitats,
definition for, phytobenthos, 504–505
environmental conditions the basis, 327, 328–344
framework for subtidal description, N.E. Atlantic, 330–331
heterogeneity in rocky/sedimentary subtidals, 327–328
in classification of terrestrial ecosystems, 324
partial basis for community descriptions, 327, 328–344
physical, constituent of ecosystem, 327
safeguarding of, as conservation measure, 323–324
selection by invertebrate epiphytes, 770–779
zone terminology for, based on dominant biota, 337–338
Halifax (Nova Scotia), 919, 925, 927, 938
Halogenated cyclic ethers (*see also* Allelochemicals),
affecting food preferences (allelochemicals), 520–521
Hamble (Southampton Water), 895
Hampshire, 882, 894
Hampton-Seabrook (river), 429
Handling time,
defined, 703
constant or not? 711–712
in predation, 700
Harbours (*see also individual entries*),
environments' effect on aliens spread by shipping as vector, 887
Chichester Harbour, 845, 882, 895, 898, 903
Gosport Marina, 846, 848, 850–857
in S. England, 844–871, 875–908
Langstone Rafts, 846–848, 851, 857–865
Hardangerfjord, 440
Harvesting,
as human disturbance of populations, 575
in community recovery and development studies, 582
method for disturbed samples, 579–580
Hayling Island, 903
Headlands,
as common boundaries to species' environmental tolerances, 329

Health,
of plants, assessed by IR film, 566, 578
Heat stress,
through Santa Ana winds in S. California intertidals, 570
Heated effluents (*see also* Effluents),
effects in Clyde, 626
effects on immigrant warm-water species, 884, 893
warming by, importance to subtidal organisms, 340
Heavy metal pollution,
in estuaries, 467
nematodes unaffected by, 753–754
Held intermediates (succession),
by environmental instability, 566–567
by stress, 566–567
Helgoland, 452, 919, 922, 924–930, 933–934, 937–938, 940
Helicopters,
in intertidal surveying, 575
Herbivores and herbivore–plant relations,
among or feeding on invertebrate epiphytes, 764–783
fish–algae in temperate waters, 686–689
fish–algae in tropical waters, 686
important relationships in Clyde, 673–674
in predation patterns, 700–725
in predator–prey research and theory, 515–524, 532
Herbivory,
a form of predation, 700
difference from carnivory, 700
Heteromerous lichens,
in mesic-supralittoral, 794
in xeric-supralittoral, 796
in water-relations, 827–828
Heterotrophic potential,
benthic diatoms with wide, 459
in relation to loading with organic matter/reduced light in estuaries, 442, 459
of algae in estuaries, 442, 459
Hierarchical agglomerative clustering techniques (*see also* Group average sorting),
used on Newfoundland marine algal species, 395, 405
Hierarchical cluster analysis (flexible sorting),
by Bray and Curtis percentage distance statistic, 581
in cover-data analysis, S. California, 581
Hilbre Islands, *see* Dee estuary
Historical floristics,
of Clyde, 617, 621–622
problems in assessment of, 617
regarding introductions, 876–890
History,
of Clyde, in floristic terms, 617, 621–622
of Mediterranean subtidal phytosociological studies, 372–373
of phytobenthic ecology/phenology in Newfoundland, 396–398
of subtidal community study, 325–328
Holdfasts,
as convenient sampling unit, 769
as self-contained communities, 769
attractiveness to epiphytes, 769, 781
fish eggs laid in/on, 679
Holland, 879, 888, 900, 924
Homogeneity,
of W. Mediterranean subtidal algae, for relevés, 377, 382–383
reality versus impression, 382
similarity coefficients higher in photophilic than in sciaphilic vegetation, 383
Homoiomerous lichens,
in littoral zones, 793
in water relations, 827–828

Horizon,
  depth-zone or depth-horizon?, 337
Horizontal distribution,
  along estuaries, 428–436, 470–475
Horizontal gradients,
  of conditions/flora in estuaries, 426
  relation to water quality, e.g. salinity, 427
  removal of tidal emersion complication, 427
Horse mussel,
  beds and community of, 345, 350–351, 352–353
Horsea Island (Hants), 894, 896
Hot water effluent,
  effects in Clyde, 626
Hove, 895
Howth Head (Ireland), 796, 798
Human disturbance,
  affecting shore lichens, 813–815
  assessment by diversity, 581
  as site-specific intertidal organization factor, 566
  avoidance, in sampling, 576–577
  by harvesting, 575
  circumstantial evidence of, S. California, 574
  in S. California island versus mainland biogeographic comparison, 590–595
  of partitioning process in development of algal-dominated facies, 609–674
  of S. California shores in general, 573
  on relatively inaccessible S. California islands, 574
Humic compounds,
  effect on shore lichens, 805
  in percolating soil water over upper shore, 805
Hunterston iron-ore and coal terminal,
  analysis of biota around, 609–674
  construction of, 609–674
  maps, 612, 616
  near power station, 619
Hybrids, natural,
  of *Spartina*, 884–885
Hydrodynamic zones,
  in W. Mediterranean, 336, 374, 376
Hydrogen sulphide,
  effects on epiphytes in polluted brackish waters, 465
Hydrographic patterns,
  changes in, as a cause of biogeographic distribution changes,886
  complexity of, S. California coast, 570–571
  importance as factor in estuarine distributions, 442
  restricting successful alien spread by shipping as hull-carrying vector, 887
Hydroids (*see also* Invertebrates),
  as epifauna, 765
  as fouling organisms, S. England floating structures, 859
  associations with specific algal substrata, 771–772
  competitive interactions between epiphytic, 782
  damaged by algal tannins, 781–782
  effects of algal zonation on substrata choice, 772
  modifying environment, 764
  seasonal recruitment and growth rates, 782
  settlement as opportunists, 363
  spatial competition between epiphytes, on fucoids, 782–783
Hyperspace,
  ecotope hyperspace, 505
  habitat hyperspace, 504
  in niche concept, 490, 500
  measures along niche dimensions delimiting, 501–504
  n-dimensionality, 490, 499–500
  relationship to actual space, 500
  species packing in, 501
Hypervolume,
  actual hypervolume, 500
  ecotope hypervolume, 505

fundamental hypervolume, 500
habitat hypervolume, 504
postinteractive hypervolume, 500
potential hypervolume, 500
preinteractive hypervolume, 500
realized hypervolume, 500
species niche hypervolume defined, 500

I

Ice cover,
as protection from ice scour, 401
on sea of Bonne Bay, Newfoundland, 401
Ice foot,
protection from scour, Bonne Bay, Newfoundland, 401
Iceland, 329, 397, 429, 440, 445, 452, 929
Ice scour,
as unusual stress, 506–507
damage (intertidal and shallow subtidal), western N. Atlantic north of Cape Cod, 395–396
by drifting pack, east Newfoundland, 398–399
by sea ice, west Newfoundland, 401
Iddefjord (Norway), 440, 448
Identification (*see also* Taxonomy),
difficulties due to plastic morphology, 427–428
difficulties of, in algae *in situ*, W. Mediterranean, 376–377
of scientific data for conservation site selection, 324
of species in estuaries, 427–428
of species in relevés (samples), 384–385
taxonomic/determinatory problems, 384–385
Îles de Glénan (N. France),
circalittoral étage depths at, 336
Immigrant species (*see also* Introductions),
effects of heated effluents on warm-water species, 884, 893
greater competitive ability as alien than indigenous species, 891
marginal dispersal in, 207
tubeworms on *Sargassum muticum*, 775
Incipient speciation (evolution),
as a benthic macroalgal niche dimension, 532, 533
Inclination (slope),
mosaic of, in rocks throughout S. California Bight, 566
of beach, as site-specific intertidal organization factor, 566
of rock in determining species present, 338–339
of rock surfaces, 330–331
Indeterminate growth,
as niche dimension characteristic, 517
Indian Ocean, 894
Indicator aspects,
of rocky intertidal systems for future monitoring, 567
Indicator species,
defined, 613
characterising community stage or climax, 613
in Clyde monitoring, 609–674
free-living nematodes as possible, 753–755
Individualistic,
a major view of community structure, 513
Individuals,
indistinguishable in algal mats (estuaries), 427
Industrialization,
of the central part of the Clyde, 609–674
Infauna,
inclusion of visible in epifauna, 338
of sediments, 362
Infralittoral fringe,
organisms on west coast Ramsey Is., Wales, 334–335

Infralittoral sub-zone (*see also* Photophilic infralittoral zone),
characterization in British waters, 332
characterization in French waters, 332
communities at Ramsey Is., Wales, 334–335, 346
definition for N.E. Atlantic, 337
definition of upper/lower infralittoral, 338
domination by photophilous algae, 337
non-applicability to sedimentary animal assemblages, 336
Infralittoral zone,
based on temperature for sedimentary benthos, 336
maximum depth for photosynthetic plants, 337
non-applicability for rocky epibiota, 336
Infrared film (*see also* Photo-samples),
in photogrammetry, 577–579
in quantification of blue-green algae, 565–566, 578
outlines unhealthy thalli with reduced chlorophyll content, 566
used with undisturbed sampling method, 565–566
Ingestion,
rapid, as factor in diet selection, 520
Inishowen (N. Ireland), 796
Initial association,
in W. Mediterranean infralittoral climax-cycle, 387
Inocula sources,
of reproductive elements for algal-dominated facies, 609–674, especially 621, 623
Inoculum type,
fragments, 621, 624
fragments as good as, or better than, spores, 623
in settlement sequence partitioning, 621, 623
spores, 621
Input quantity (arrival, immigration),
low biomass restricting vector success, 888
need *not* be high, 621–624
Insolation,
effects on lichens, 790, 794, 798–799, 800
excessive, as unusual stress, 506–507
variations with latitude, 928–930
Instability, *see* Variability
Intensity of predation, 713–717, 720–722
Interference competition, 516, 609–674
Intermediate niches,
defined, 494
more ecosystem-specific components of primary niches, 494
Intermediate seral communities,
algal populations with stressed characteristics in identifying held subclimax, 566–567
in algal-dominated colonisation in Clyde, 609–674
Inter-population differences,
in ecological theory, 493
mechanisms may differ from habitat amplitude, 493
Interpretations (pre-monitoring),
excessive time needed to solve side-issues since predictive or descriptive data lacking, 617
Interspecific competition,
intertidal zone lower limits affected by, 511
in iron-ore terminal area of Clyde, 609–674
in grazing patterns, 707–708
mid-intertidals structured by, 511, 516–517
Interspecific plant reactions (competition),

in settlement sequence partitioning, 621, 642–652, 653
Interspecific reactions animal/plant (*see* Predation, Grazing),
in settlement sequence partitioning, 621, 652, 653, 654–659
Intertidal,
a stressful environment, 506
easier to study than subtidal, 506–507
penetration into it of "subtidal" species, 506–507
Intertidal ecosystems,
assessment of changes in Scotland, after reclamation work, 609–674
in Newfoundland, 395–421
in Southern California, 565–603
multivariate elucidation of, 398
should not be studied without reference to subtidal, 668
Intraspecific competition,
upper limits and community structure determined by, intertidally, 511
in settlement sequence partitioning, 621, 642–652
Intraspecific variation,
genetic differences in distinct variation, 470
importance of further study, 470, 774–775
importance of reproductive mode in, 470
in estuarine algae, 468–470
in reactions of epiphytes to disjunct/zoned algae, 775
in Spirorbids on *Ascophyllum*, 773–775
in distinction between true epiphytes and eurytopic species, 775
phenotypic variation continuous, 470
Introductions (*see also* Immigrant species),
adverse introductions by accident, 889
agencies and vectors, 886–889
all exotic species as, 907
causes of changes in range, 886
cord-grass (*Spartina*) into UK, 884–885
effects caused by introduced species, 890–892
effects of cord-grass on coastline, 884
factors responsible for introduction and further spread, 885–890
general and conclusions, 906–908
location of known initial introductions, 887
marginal dispersal in, 889–890
need for repetitions, where vector carries low alien biomass, 888
Man and commercial introductions as vector, 888–889
previous, marine algae into British Isles, 876–882
previous, marine algae into Solent, 882–885
recent, marine algae elsewhere in British Isles, 904–906
recent, marine algae into Solent, 892–904
remote dispersal in, 886–889
shipping as vector for, 887–888
transportation methods, 886–890
Invertebrates (marine),
activity of tannins against, 780–782
distribution due to larval and general behavioural patterns, 770–779
feeding on algae and being taken by fish, 690–691
substratum selection by larvae of non-sessile species, 772–773
Ion imbalance,
effects on physiology of estuarine algae, 458
Ireland, 792, 798, 878, 879
Ireland, South-west, 345, 355, 357, 878
Ireland, West, 336, 764

Irish Sea,
effect on species distributions, 329
spider crabs eating algae, 690
Iron,
shore lichens as indicators of, 813
Iron ore,
effects of terminal in Clyde estuary, 609–674
Island Cliff, Lough Ine, 348–349
Isle of Man, 344, 345, 355
Isle of May, 795
Isle of Wight, 880, 882, 889, 894, 897
Isles of Scilly, 736, 743
Isobaths,
significance in division of circalittoral into étages, 336–337
Isopods (*see also* Invertebrates),
dominating cool-temperate sedimentary shores, 702
grazing shore lichens, 823
organisms eating them, 702
wood-borer (*Limnoria*) in Southampton Water, 884

J

Jaccard coefficient,
generating similarity matrix, 405
Jaccard and Sneath similarity test,
homogeneity in W. Mediterranean, 382–383
Japan,
alien algae/animals from, 878, 881, 889, 893, 898, 899, 933, 935
hydroid epiphytes, 770
lichens, 790
Juan de Fuca Strait, Washington, 780

K

K-selection, 519, 520, 532
K-selected species defined, 519
Kelp,
death of, ecological consequence, 364
dominant in infralittoral sub-zone, 337
exudates as food sources for *Membranipora*, 780
failure to survive in extreme wave-action, 336
grazed by few specialized gastropods and sea urchins, 702
holdfasts, stipes, fronds in N.E. Atlantic subtidal descriptive framework, 330–331
in division of infralittoral to upper/lower, 338
Laminaria hyperborea – associated communities, 354, 356, 357
nematodes in holdfasts, 731, 754
possible biochemical defense mechanisms in, 718
upper limit of, as sublittoral boundary, 337
Keny, 803
Keppel Slipway, 634, 642, 646–647, 652, 654
Key (interpretive),
succession, for beach processes, 619, 670
Key aspects,
of rocky intertidal systems for future monitoring, 567
for interpretation of beach processes, 619
Key species,
role of, in community recovery, 575
Korea, 899
Kulczynski similarity test,
for coverage, in W. Mediterranean homogeneity assessments, 382–383

L

Labrador, 397, 921
Labrador current,
effect of arctic waters on east Newfoundland, 398–399
Lagoons,
as brackish environments, 425
compared with estuaries/fiords, 440–441, 444, 446

Laminaria hyperborea-associated communities,
  in subtidal, 354, 356, 357
Laminarians,
  as substratum for *Membranipora*, 779–783
  epifauna of, 764, 765
Langstone Harbour, 845–871, 895, 898, 901, 903
Langstone Rafts, 846–848
  flora on, 851, 857–865
  inner sheltered walls, 857–859
  outer sheltered walls, 859
  outer midregion walls, 860–861
  outer exposed walls, 861–865
Largs Channel, 616
Larval behaviour,
  environmental influence on, in invertebrates, 770–779
Larval choice/discrimination,
  as adaptation to epiphytic existence, 779–783
  of substrate for settlement in invertebrates, 770–779
  nature of algal influence on, 775
  rugophilic response in, 776
  settlement in necrotic pits on algae, 776
Larval responses,
  invertebrates, to algal substrata, 761, 765–766, 770–779
Leith Dock (Scotland), 627, 630–631, 655
Lepe (Hants.), 894, 897
Lichens (shore) (*see also* Biological factors affecting shore lichens),
  affected by percolating soil water, 805
  affected by spray, 804–805
  air pollution in, 815
  as photophiles, 809–811
  as shelter for various organisms, 823–825
  biological factors affecting, 815–825
  bird-manuring in, 813
  chemotaxonomy in, 816–818
  circumboreal-arctic forms, 799
  cleansing agents affecting, 814–815
  colonization by, 818–819
  competition in/by shore lichens, 821–823
  complexities of origin/nature of, 818–819
  concept of "exposure" as applied to, 806
  copper and cadmium in, 813, 814
  distribution factors, 800–815
  effects of wind/wave on, 807–809
  emersion effects, 807
  geographical comparisons in, 798–800
  grazing on, 823
  growth in, 815–816
  growth processes of, 819
  human activities affecting, 813–815
  indicators of metallic ions, 813
  lichen chitin not digested by animals, 825
  light in, 830–831
  littoral zone species, 791–793
  marine and maritime, of rocky shores, 789–834
  marine, closest affinity to terrestrial/freshwater aquatic forms, 793
  mesic-supralittoral species, 793–795
  morphological variation in, 816–818
  nutritional factors/nutrients in, 812–813, 831–832
  oil pollution affecting, 814–815
  pH, 812–813
  photosynthesis in, 828–829
  physiology of composite thallus, 826–832
  physiology of isolated bionts, 826
  predominantly in cool temperate, 790
  prothalli of, 819
  radionucleides in, 813
  resistance to environmental extremes, 829–830
  respiration in, 828–829

salinity effects in, 811–812
sciaphiles in, 804, 809–811
species diversity in shade, 809
submergence times, 807
succession in, 820–821
temperature in, 830–831
terrestrial-halophilic species, 797
terrestrial-halophobic species, 797–798
thalli covered by unicellular algae in pollution, 814
tides in, 806–807
useful organisms for further research, 832–834
water relations in, 827–828
xeric-supralittoral species, 795–797
xerophytes, 804
zinc from disused mines in, 814

Lichen thalli,
forms in shore lichens, 789–834

Life-forms (*see also* Growth habits, Morphology, Morphotypes),
of algae in stressful environments, 566–567

Life histories (*see also* Growth and life history strategies),
changes in estuarine algae, 463
environmental effects of daylength and water temperature on algal, 915–942
life-spans of algae along estuaries, 430
of complex pleomorphic algae, 623–624, 879–881, 921–937
other environmental phenomena as stage determinants, 937–939
short/simple, in algae in stressful environments, 566–567
temperature as stage determinant, 937–939

Life strategies, *see* Growth and life history strategies

Light,
a limiting resource in the intertidal, 585
as a benthic macroalgal niche dimension, 531
influence on invertebrate larvae substrate choice, 770–779
physiology of shore lichens and general life-style, effects on, 809–811, 830–831
variations eliminated on sides of floating structures, 865

Light intensity,
interaction with salinity tolerance in estuarine algae, 450–457

Light penetration (*see also* Turbidity, Water transparency),
a major factor in estuarine algal distribution, 442
low, in estuaries, 442, 459

Light regime,
at Banyuls, 374, 375
difficulty of description in subtidal, 336
predominance of effect on algae, 336
reduction of penetration into estuaries, 442

Light requirements,
estuarine advantage of algae with low, 459
inadequate knowledge of, for estuarine forms, 459
in estuarine microbenthic algae, 472

Limestone,
littoral lichens on, 791–792

Limitations,
on drift, as marginal dispersal agent, 889–890
in methods applied in Newfoundland study, 420–421
in quasi-quantitative sampling/analysis, 575–576
in salinity tolerance of species, 444–445
in SCUBA diving, 373
in subtidal study cf. intertidal, 506–507

Limpets (*see also* Invertebrates),
as grazers on floating structures, 865

coexistence with other invertebrates when dominant cropped, 721
effect on shore lichen distribution, 801
grazing shore lichens, 823
herbivorous grazers on fucoid sporelings, 702, 704
littoral fringe lichens growing on, 792
slipper limpets as fouling organisms on S. England floating structures, 856
small-scale pattern maintained by, lower shore, 655
taken by oystercatchers, 708, 710
widespread and locally dense in S. California, 584, 587

Lindesnes (Norway), 919, 922, 925, 927

Linney Head (S. Pembs.), 358

Littlehampton, 895

Littoral fringe,
extensive lichen cover, 792

Littorinids,
absence of grazing forms from estuaries, 458–459
anchored by *Mytilus* byssus threads, 657, 663
grazing on fucoid sporelings and unicells, 702
grazing on shore lichens, 823
transported by algal buoyancy, 657

Loch Etive (Scotland), 754

Lock (habitat) and key (niche) relationship, 504–505

Long-day regimes,
in *Petalonia fascia*, 924
Scytosiphon crusts from erect thalli swarmers in, 922

Longevity (individual/corporate),
life-spans of algae along estuaries, 430
long-lived species as community constituents, 361, 362
of algal spores/germling stages in dispersal, 890
of many sublittoral epibenthic species, 361
of *Ophiothrix* populations, 351, 354
state of knowledge of, 890

Long-lived species, *see* Longevity

Loose-lying populations,
of plants in brackish conditions, 461

Los Angeles (California),
swell near, 571

Lough Ine (Ireland), 345
circalittoral animal communities, 348–349
laminarian epifauna in rapids at, 764
Saccorhiza epifauna at, 765

Lower circalittoral,
communities at Ramsey Is., Wales, 346
definition for N.E. Atlantic, 338
relationship to "open sea" étage, 336–338

Lower infralittoral,
definition for N.E. Atlantic, 338
communities at Ramsey Is., Wales, 346

Lugworms,
digging for, as beach damage, 618

Lundy Island, 345, 355, 357, 362, 879, 882

Lymington (Hants.), 880, 895

Lynher Estuary (Cornwall), 732, 734, 735, 736, 744, 745, 746, 747

M

Macroinvertebrate species (*see also* Invertebrates; *individual organisms by name*),
biomass measurements, S. California, 587–588
dominant species on cover basis, 585
frequencies compared, S. California, 587
overshadowed by macrophytes in

organic dryweight terms, 587–588
percentage cover compared, all S. California sites, 586
seasonal comparisons of cover, 586
species with highest mean densities, 587
temporal and spatial variations in S. California rocky intertidals, 565–603

Macrophyte species (*see also individual organisms by name*),
frequencies compared, S. California, 587
major S. California macrophyte cover at studied stations, 585
overshadowing invertebrates in organic dryweight terms, 587–588
percentage cover compared, all S. California sites, 586
seasonal comparisons of cover, 586
temporal and spatial variations in S. California rocky intertidals, 565–603

Maerl,
in N.E. Atlantic subtidal descriptive framework, 330–331
in Falmouth Harbour, 904

Magnesium,
increase in plants into estuaries, 463–464

Mangroves,
in Caribbean Sea, 385

Mannitol,
decrease in plants into estuaries, 463–464

Margalef's Index (D′),
for richness (by counts of taxa) in species diversity, 581

Marginal dispersal,
affecting biogeographic distributions, 886
by algal drift, 889–890
causes and definition, 886
differences from remote dispersal, 886
in benthic marine algae, 889–890

Marginal freshwater zone,
current changes in, 432
its climate as basis for the marine lichen situation, 804
in estuaries, 432
instability of, and few species in, the zone, 432
tidal excursion, 432

Mariculture,
early stages of study as yet, 888
eventual effects on alien spread (Man as vector), 888–889

Maritime lichen flora,
distinctions from terrestrial flora, 797

Marseille, 383, 385, 386

Marshall Islands (Pacific), 686

Matching coefficients,
used in Newfoundland analyses, 405

Mathematical models (species niche), 534–536

Mathematics,
in treatment of niche concept, 490, 534–536

Mature stands (*see also* Climax),
in settlement sequence partitioning, 621, 659–668

Measurement,
of estuarine environmental factors, 443
of niche aspects, 534–536
of solar energy at Banyuls, 374
of the physical and chemical environment required, 474–475

Mechanical tolerance and response,
as a benthic macroalgal niche dimension, 531

Mediterranean, 329, 333, 371–388, 687, 688, 790, 798, 806, 880

Mediterranean–Atlantic province,
around British Isles, 328–332
geographical extent and species distribution in, 329

Mediterranean–Boreal province,
geographical extent, 329
Medway (river), 429
Meiobenthos,
nematodes a major component, based on biomass, 731–732, 734
Menai Strait (Anglesey/Wales) (*see also* Swellies), 336, 355, 362–363, 773, 774
Merrimac (river, USA), 429
Mersey (river), 471
Mesohalinicum,
in brackish estuaries, 432
in fiords, 444–445
species of, 432
Metabolism,
of free-living nematodes, 744–745
Metal grids,
in quasi-quantitative abundance estimates, 575
Metamorphosis (larval),
dependent on accurate food organism detection, by some secondary epiphytes, 766, 772–773
dependent on accurate substrate selection in primary epiphytes, 766, 772–773
Meuse (river) (Holland), 429
Mexico (Punta Banda), 919, 922, 924, 925–927, 930
Microalgae (*see also* Diatoms),
benthic forms, in estuaries, 425–475, especially 470–475
"Codiolum"-stages, 633, 649, 934–937
dominating warm-temperate and tropical cliff-like shores, 702
epiphytic/epilithic/epipelic/epipsammic forms, 470–475
in temporal partitioning, 636
on floating structures, S. England, 850–865
overgrowing lichens in pollution, 814
quantitative sampling in estuaries, 427
sediments and substratum for, more important than nutrients in estuaries, 472
Microbial films,
antimicrobial activity of tannins, 780–782
grazers on, 764
Microbiotope,
for habitat characteristics in W. Mediterranean, 388
Microepibiota,
exclusion from most studies because of quantification difficulties, 579
Microepiphyte community,
use of species-composition to characterize pollution in estuaries, 465
Microlandscape,
relation to ecotope, 505–506
Microorganisms,
difficulties of quantification, 579
forming surface films, 770–771
required inclusion in marine benthic community studies, 509–510
Milford Haven, 429, 905, 906
Milford-on-Sea (Hants.), 895
Millport (Cumbrae), 646, 648, 656, 661, 666–667
Miniaturization,
algal vegetation pattern of development in W. Mediterranean subtidal, 377
effects of, on qualitative minimum area for sampling, 377–381
Minimum area, *see* Qualitative minimum area
Miquelon (E. Canada), 369, 397
Misuse of data,
in monitoring generally, 609–674
in site-specific cases, 617–618
Mites,
as secondary epiphytes feeding on primary epiphytes, 766
grazing on shore lichens, 823
Mobility (passive) of spreading phases,

in settlement sequence partitioning, 621, 628
Models,
for aspects of species niche, 534–536
Model ecosystem,
assemblages of benthic diatoms in, 452, 473
Modification of environment,
as by various organisms, 764
analogous to extra surface provision by algae for epiphytes, 764
Modiolus modiolus community,
in subtidal, 345, 350–351, 352–353
Molluscs (*mentioned at intervals in most papers; see also specific organism entries*),
as predators and prey, 702
gastropods a predominant predator group, 703
general to prey–predator situation, 699–725
molluscan fauna of algal feeders taken by fish, 690–691
more variety in tropics, 703
Monitoring,
are *intertidal* algae too robust for it?, 614
chemical or biological the most effective?, 613
cost effectiveness in, 613
data submerged in "grey area" literature, 613
exonerative monitoring, 618–619
expectation of particular results, 618–619
floating structures providing base-line data for, 845
is it purely academic?, 614, 617
monitoring as formalized intuition, 613
rationale for, 609–674
S. California rocky intertidal systems database, 565–603
terminology: difficulties and needs, 671
value of intertidal algae and events in general for, 609–674
value of nematodes as possible indicators for, 753–755
Monitoring programmes,
key/indicator aspects of rocky intertidals, 567
rationale for, 609–674
settlement-period monitoring of organisms on suspended test panels with anti-fouling paints, 845
value of intertidal algae for, 609–674
Monthoux (coverage) similarity test,
in W. Mediterranean homogeneity assessments, 383
Morphology,
conflict in evidence on estuarine effects, 461
effects of estuarine environment on, 460–462
need for more research on estuarine effects, 475
taxonomic implications of variation in, 462
variation in form of shore lichens, 816–818
Morphotypes,
in lichens, 789–834; *especially*, 816–818
Mosaicing,
a normal mature-stand process, 659
by marine algae, of space, 628–638
complex reasons for, 628–638
community mosaicing, 654
in development, 619
Motility of spreading phases,
in settlement sequence partitioning, 621, 628
Mucilage, *see* Exterior mucilage
Mucus, *see* Exterior mucilage
Mucus-trap hypothesis,
in nematode burrowings-lining, 752
in nematode feeding, 742

Mud,
culturing estuarine, for micro-species, 427
epipelic and epipsammic microalgae in estuaries, 470–475
fish burrowing into or lying flat on mud, 684–685
-flats, as intertidals, Portsmouth and Langstone Harbours, 845, 895
in estuaries, 437
in N.E. Atlantic subtidal descriptive framework, 330–331
in Newfoundland, 411
mud-stabilizing by nematodes, 752–753
mud-stabilizing by *Spartina*, 884–885
Mull (Scotland), 344–345, 357
Mullet,
grey mullet feeding on green algae/diatoms, etc., 682–683, 687, 693
thick-lipped grey mullet as grazer on floating structures, 865
Multi-directional water movement,
infralittoral/subtidal zone definition by, 336, 374, 376
Multiple plot procedure,
in qualitative minimum area calculation, 377
Multiple stable points,
several communities in the same habitat, 361, 362
Multivariate sorting/grouping techniques,
in field distribution/environmental factor correlations in estuaries, 443
in numerical description of benthic marine algal distribution, 398
use at phytogeographic level, 398
use in more restricted local areas (as intertidal), 398
use in phytogeography/broad ecology in Newfoundland, 398
Mundesley (Norfolk), 680
Muricid gastropods (*see also* Gastropods),
predators on barnacles/mussels, 702
Mussels,
eaten by a range of organisms, 702
in S. California, the biomass dominant and a cover dominant among macroinvertebrates, 583, 585, 587–588
oil monitoring with, 639
population variability with time, 363
predation on, 365
use as trace-metal indicators, 467
Mutual grazing,
in littorinids, 657

N

Naples, 372, 385, 386
Natural settlement-space,
in settlement sequence, 628–638
Nature reserves,
in shallow seas of GB, 324
Necrotic pits,
consequences of larval settlement in, 776
effect on larval settlement on algae, 776
Neighbourhood stability,
of multiple stable point communities, 361
Nematodes (free-living),
abundance, 731–734
affected by salinity and sediment loads, 754
algal preferences as epiphytes, 767
among bryozoans, 731
among hydroids, 731
as food for secondary consumers, 748–751
as possible indicator group for monitoring, 753–755
decomposition by, 752
distribution of, 742–744

diversity of, 734–742
energy flow through populations (as primary consumers) 744–747
food-partitioning crucial in, 736–742
general use in pollution work, 753–754
highest densities in muddy estuaries/salt marshes, 731
in holdfasts, 731
morphologically very varied, 731, 733
most abundant metazoans of particulate shores, 731
most ubiquitous/abundant/diverse marine metazoans, 744
on larger seaweeds, 731
on particulate shores, 729
penetration depths into sediment shores, 731
resource partitioning in, 742–744
sediment stabilizing/disturbance by, 752–753
sexual partitioning of the food supply, 744
shore habitats incompletely described without, 755
significance to ecosystem, 729–755
spatial and temporal partitioning, 742–744
unaffected by titanium waste or heavy metal pollution, 753–754
Nematophagus organisms,
general, 748–751
macrobenthic carnivores, 750
macrobenthic deposit feeders, 749
macrobenthic suspension feeders, 750
macrobenthos overall, 749–751
other meiofauna, 748–749
vertebrates, 750–751
Nene (river), 429
Nesting sites,
algae as, for fish, 679
Nests (fish),
algal fragments in construction of, 679
Neuston,
as ecosystem, 509
New England, 396
Newfoundland, 395–421
history and background to studies, 396–398
New Hampshire,
Great Bay system, 429, 431
Newport (river, Eire), 429
New South Wales, 894
New taxa (*see also* Rare species),
in W. Mediterranean photophilic infralittoral studies, 385–386
in W. Scotland sea loch lichens, 793
New Zealand, 790, 879
Niche,
accepted definitions, 496–497, 499–504
accepted definition of fundamental niche: a useful construct only, 498
accepted definition of realized niche, 498
as equivalent to habitat plus niche, 493
a theoretical but valid construct, 488–489
Cartesian coordinates in niche space construction, 499
coarse-/fine-grained speces, 502
concept in inshore phytobenthos, 506–521
confusion in previous applications, 489, 489–498, especially, 492–493
ecosystem attributes in, 493
ecotope (γ diversity), 493
equivalence of regeneration/habitat/life-form/phenological niches to niche axes, 497
functional concept of, 492
fundamental niche, 493–495, 498, 503

future predictions/research needs, 522–530
habitat differentiation (β diversity), 493
habitat niche, 497
heuristic and analytical use of niche, 496
history of concept, 489–491
intermediate niches, 494; dismissal of, 498
lack of sharp distinctions niche/habitat/area: common factors, 505
life-form niche, 497
mathematical models for aspects of, 534–536
measures along niche dimensions delimiting hyperspace, 501–504
modifying dimensions in hypervolume, 500
niche breadth, differentiation of resources used within community, 493, 501
niche differentiation (α diversity), 493
niche-habitat relationship, 504–505
overlap in application with or equivalence to habitat, 492
partial niche, 503
phenological niche, 497
place niche (= habitat), 493
practical/theoretical importance of realized niche, 498
previous use in three contrasting senses, 492–493
primary niches, 494; dismissal of, 498
realized niche, 494–495, 498, 503
regeneration niche, 496–497
research stimulus its primary justification, 529–530
species attributes in, 493
species niche, 494, 495, 499–504
species niche hypervolume, 500
zoological origin and early application, 490, 500–501

Niche breadth,
confusion in application, 502
defined, 501
formulae/mathematical models, 535

Niche overlap,
confusion in application, 502
defined, 501
formulae/mathematical models, 535–536

Night-break regimes,
in *Petalonia fascia*, 924

Nitrogen (total),
increase in plants into estuaries, 463–464

Niveaux (= levels),
suitable, in settlement sequence partitioning, 621, 639–641

Non-photoperiodic strains,
in *Scytosiphon*, 924
in other algae, 937–940

Non-selective deposit feeders,
among nematodes, 736–742

Non-sessile sedentary species,
distribution of invertebrate epiphytes due to larval choice, 770–779

Norfolk, 680, 684

"Normal",
characterization of, for monitoring, 609–674
framework for description of, 619, 671
mosaicing in normality, 659

Norstictic acid,
in halophilic lichens, 797

North Africa,
Atlantic, 329, 799
Mediterranean, 329, 385–386, 799

North America,
Atlantic, 879
east, 882, 884
north-east and south-west, 881
north-west, 569
north-west and north-east, 790

Pacific coast, 385, 565–603, 685, 689, 897, 900, 907
North east England, 617
North Sea, 329, 441, 735
Northumberland, 798
North West Europe, 790
Northern species,
absence from some Newfoundland sites, 414
at southern limits in Newfoundland, 396, 409, 420, 421
Norway, 329, 434, 440
Nuclear power stations,
in Clyde industrialization, 610
Nudibranchs (*see also* Mollusca, Invertebrates),
general predation in, 702–703
predation by a few of barnacles/mussels, 702
preferred diets, 783
seasonal and annual changes in populations, 363
Numerical approaches,
in floristic synthesis with large data base, 398
in vegetation descriptions, 398
Numerical response (predation intensity),
aggregative numerical response, 716–717
considered in detail, 716–717
defined, 713–714
reproductive numerical response, 717
stabilizing or destabilizing, 714
Nursery grounds/areas,
algae as, for young of otherwise offshore fish, 678
Nutrient concentrations,
mosaic of, throughout S. California Bight, 566
Nutrient status,
alteration of levels in estuaries by pollution, 457
effects on estuarine microalgae, 472
Nutrition,
effect of factors on lichens, 812–813
effect of factors on shore lichen physiology, 831–832
optimization of diet in, 520

O

Obligate epiphytes,
defined, 765
examples, 765–766
Obligate relations,
absence of, fish–algae in temperate waters, 677
as a benthic macroalgal niche dimension, 532
epiphytes on algae, 765–766
Obtusenyne,
allelochemical affecting food preference, 520–521
related to rhodophytin, 521
sequestered by animal from algal diet, 521
Ocean Beach (California), 568–603
Ocean swell,
island protection from, for S. California coast, 570–571
Oceanic species,
distribution of, 329
Ochiai and Barkman similarity test,
in W. Mediterranean homogeneity assessments, 382–383
Ocypodid crabs,
as carnivores/detritus feeders in tropical sediments, 703
"Offshore rocky bottom biocoenosis",
equivalence in Mediterranean to bathylittoral, 333
possible similarity to levels in GB circalittoral, 333
Oil (*see also* Petroleum resource development),
attempts to provide pre-spill data, S. California, 574
baseline data from floating structure analysis against possible pollution by, 845

bilge oil from iron ore terminal in Clyde, 610
cleansing agents affecting lichens, 814–815
general lack of database against which to assess damage, 573
likely results of spill, in S. California, 602
pollution by, affecting shore lichens, 814–815
preventing proper settlement in Clyde, 639, 650, 655
Santa Barbara spills of 1969, 573
Oligohalinicum,
characteristic species, 433
in upper estuaries, 432
of Dutch Delta area, 433
Omnivores and predators,
among nematodes, 736–742
"Open" communities,
more conducive to establishment of aliens, 907
"Open sea" circalittoral étage,
definition, 336
probable equivalence to "pre-littoral" zone, 336–337
relationship to lower circalittoral, 336–338
variable depth range, 336–337
Ophiothrix fragilis community,
in subtidal, 345, 351, 354, 355
Opisthobranchs (*see also* Mollusca, Invertebrates),
as secondary epiphytes (specialized feeders) feeding on primaries, 766
effect of prolonged exposure and dessication on, 767
metamorphosis (larval) only on favoured food organism, 766
occurrence of some on red algae limited by vertical range of latter, 767
Opportunistic species,
as community constituents, 361
secondary epiphytes as, 765–766
Optimal diets,
defined, 703
further considered, 705, 707
Optimal foraging,
defined, 703
Optimal patch use theory,
defined, 712
concentration on richest environmental patches, 712
foraging outside for comparison, 712
relevant, but requires more testing in intertidals, 712
Optimization,
of food in sea urchins, 520
Ordination methods,
in estuarine factor/distribution correlations, 443
towards identifying sociological units, 384
use in niche concept, 502
Oregon, 772, 901
Oresund, 783
Organic dry weight,
definition, 580, 587
important ecological parameter, 587
in disturbed sample analysis, 579–580
macrophytes overshadowed macroinvertebrates in dry organic biomass, 587–588
results, in different species, 587
Organic material loading,
effect on heterotrophic algal distribution, 442
in estuaries, 442
Organization/structure,
of communites, distinguished apart, 511
Orkney, 880
Orne (river) (France), 429
Ornithocoprophilous species,
of lichens on shore, 795, 796, 813
Oslofjord, 440, 465

Osmoregulatory ability,
possible chemotaxonomic importance in Ulotrichales, 464
Osmotic state,
in estuarine algae, 457–458
Ouse (estuary) (Sussex), 471
Outer Continental Shelf (OCS) (*see also* South California Outer Continental Shelf),
in Pacific USA, 567
Outer Hebrides, 345
Overgrazing,
aspect as a climax or derived/displaced climax, 659
Over-hang communities,
in subtidal wave-exposure, 356, 358–359
Oyster drill,
adverse accidental introduction with oysters, 889
Oyster River (USA), 429, 430
Oysters,
adverse introductions with, 889
as vectors in alien spread, 889, 899
effects of pollution on, 888
losses from French beds due to *Colpomenia*, 877
Portuguese/Pacific oysters, 888
restocking introductions, 888–889

P

Pacific Ocean,
aliens from, 877, 878, 879, 880, 881, 882, 884, 887, 893, 894, 896, 900, 903, 930
main 'donor' area for aliens into European waters, 907
Pacific oyster,
restocking introduction, 889
Pagham Harbour, 895, 897
Parallax,
as a problem in visually-based quasi-quantitative sampling, 575–576
Parasites,
?important characteristics of microenvironments for, 517
microenvironments of, 517
Parasitism,
a modifying influence (dimension) in niche concept, 500, 516, 532
Partial niche,
definition, 503
Particulate (suspended) matter,
in epibenthic organism diets, 326
Particulate shores,
nematodes most abundant metazoans of, 731–732
Partitioning of settlement sequence,
for monitoring, 620–668
on basis of the natural history of a species, 621
Patchiness,
of biota in estuarine systems, 436
of dominant biota, 363–364
Patterns,
development and persistence in rocky marine intertidal, 488
in distribution, abundance and diversity, 488
of biological response of individual, 496
of ecology-reassessment due to climatic extremes, 567
of salinity around a "host" plant, 517
Patuxent (river, USA), 429
Pebbles,
definitions, 338–339
in N.E. Atlantic subtidal descriptive framework, 330–331
in S. England harbours, 845
Pembrokeshire, south, 355, 357, 358, 363
Penetration,
of freshwater/marine species into Baltic, 441
Percentage frequency,
use in point samples of estuarine algal mats, 427
useful for denoting breadth of distribution of taxa, 587

Percolation,
  effects on upper shore lichens, 797
Perennials,
  palatibility cf. annuals in algae as diet, 519–520
Perithecia,
  in littoral lichen reproduction, 793
Permanent data sets, *see* Photosamples
Permanent records, *see* Photosamples
Permanent sampling locations,
  basis of before and after studies, 617
  for photogrammetry of undisturbed samples, 576–579
  marking of, 576
  monitoring locations often very atypical, 614
Perturbations (*see also* Disturbance),
  of environment affecting communities, 361
Petroleum resource development (*see also* Oil),
  base data for monitoring pollution, by, S. California, 567
  implication of natural disturbances in rocky S. California, 573
"Peuplements",
  non-equivalence to "populations", 326
  polyspecific, 326
pH,
  effects on shore lichens, 812–813
Phenological image,
  for W. Mediterranean photophilic infralittoral algal species, 386
Phenology,
  analyzed by cluster analysis, vegetative and reproductive, 405–406
  of phytobenthos around Newfoundland, 395, 405, 414–420
Phenotypic differences, *see* Intraspecific variation
Photic zone,
  lower limits defined, 614–616, 654
Photogrammetric techniques of undisturbed sampling,
  in intertidals of S. California, 576–579
  in lichen growth rate analyses, 815–816
Photography,
  in community recovery/development, 582
Photomorphogenetic pigments,
  blue UV-absorbing pigment, 916, 941
  evolution in algae of several different active pigments dependent on other wave lengths, 341–342
  phytochrome, 916
  pigment other than phytochrome needed for photoperiod trigger in subtidal at more than moderate depths, 941
  triggering photoperiodic responses, 916
Photoperiodic (latitudinal) ecotypes,
  genetically different as regards daylength for *Scytosiphon* erect thallus formation, 924–926
  northern cf. southern ecotypes in general – darkness requirement, 924–926
  of *Scytosiphon lomentaria*, adapted to latitudes at which growing, 915, 921, 922–930
Photoperiodism,
  ecological significance of, in *Bonnemaisonia hamifera*, 933–934
  ecological significance of, in *Monostroma grevillei*, 937
  ecological significance of, in *Scytosiphon*, 928–930
  in algal life-history control, 916–917
  in formation of Scytosiphonales erect thalli, 921–930
  in growth/reproduction in some benthic algae in Newfoundland, 396, 420

in occurrence of ecotypes of *Scytosiphon*, 921–930
in *Petalonia zosterifolia*, 924
in spore formation induction (*Monostroma* "Codiolum"), 921, 934–937
in subtidal, 941
in tetrasporangial induction (Trailliella), 921, 930–934
?mainly in eulittoral species, 941
no absolute correlation of photoperiodism with growth in eulittoral, 941
quantitatively (not absolutely) in *Petalonia fascia*, 924
secondary factors inhibiting expression in Trailliella, 930

Photophiles,
lichens mainly as, 809–811

Photophilic infralittoral biotope,
additional winter study required, 388
physical characteristics in W. Mediterranean, 373–376

Photophilic infralittoral zone (see also Infralittoral Subzone)
additional winter study required, 388
boundary with sciaphilic, W. Mediterranean, 373–376
definition and characterization, 373–376
maximum extent in photophilous algae, 332, 337
W. Mediterranean, on rocky substrata, 371–388

Photophilous (photophilic) algae (*see also* Photosynthetic plants),
dominance depths of, as infralittoral subzone, 337
lower limit of, W. Mediterranean, 384, 388

Photosamples,
as permanent historic data sets, 566
demonstration of seasonality, 566
documentation of quadrat changes, 566
forming quality control, 566
from infrared film, 565–566
use as basis for future, 566

Photosynthesis,
aspects of, in algal niche dimension, 531
effects of salinity on, estuarine algae, 454–456
of shore lichen composite thalli, 828–829
races for performance in, 469

Photosynthetic control,
in growth/reproduction of Newfoundland algae, 420

Photosynthetic plants (*see also* Photophilous algae),
maximum depth, as lower limit of sublittoral, 337, 373

Physical environmental conditions,
as ecosystem constituent, 327
as partial basis for describing communities, 327, 328–344
in estuaries, 425–475
in scenopoetic niche dimensions, 517
intertidal upper limits and community structure determined by, 511
modifying epifauna, 764–765
perturbations of, affecting communities, 361
primary factors affecting Newfoundland flora, 414
primary factors in community determination, S. California, 566, 595–596
species tolerances to, 329
substrate disturbance, island and mainland sites, S. California, 595
variability in subtidals of sedimentary cf. rocky shores, 327–328
"ultimate primacy of", 511
wave shock in, S. California, 596

Physical habitat, *see* Habitat, Physical environmental conditions

Physical tolerance and response,
  as a benthic macroalgal niche dimension, 531
Physiology in seashore lichens,
  light and temperature, 830–831
  nutrients, 831–832
  photosynthesis and respiration, 828–829
  physiology of isolated bionts, 826
  physiology of the composite thallus, 826–832
  resistance to environmental extremes, 829–830
  useful organisms for further research, 832–834
  water relations, 827–828
Phytochrome (red/far red system),
  probable photomorphogenetic pigment in many cases, 916, 941
Phytocoenses,
  in W. Mediterranean infralittoral, 387
Phytogeographical categories,
  in Newfoundland benthic marine algae, 395
Phytogeography,
  relationships of Newfoundland benthic marine flora, 396–397
  use of computerised multivariate techniques in whole flora comparisons, 398
Phytoplankton,
  alien organism spread by ship ballast discharge, 887
  microbenthos production rate higher than, in estuaries, 474
Phytosociology,
  interpretation currently premature, 386
  W. Mediterranean sublittoral benthic photophilic algae, 371–388
  seasonal data missing, 386
Pielou's Index (J′),
  index for evenness in species diversity, 581
Pier piles,
  importance of, 339
  in N.E. Atlantic subtidal descriptive framework, 330–331
  species-poor nature, 626
Plankton,
  animal larvae in, 889
  as ecosystem, 509
  barnacle larvae in, 891
  constituents of, 364
  in epibenthic organism diets, 326
  tannins toxic to, 781
Planktotroph larvae,
  of bryozoans, 779–783
Plasticity (*see also* Growth habits, Morphology, Morphotypes, Life-forms),
  identification problems caused by, 427–428
  in morphology under estuarine conditions, 427–428
Pleomorphic life histories, 623–624, 879–881, 921–937
Plexiglass,
  as field culture surface for estuarine microalgae, 471
Plymouth, 735, 750, 878, 882, 884, 887, 899
Point Conception (California), 567–603
Point Dume, 570–603
Point sampling method,
  for algal mats in estuaries, 427
Poisson statistic,
  in sampling optimization analysis, 576
Pollution,
  alteration of water chemistry by, 457
  aquatic form worst in estuaries, 468
  atmospheric, effects on lichens, 798
  base data for monitoring, 567, 573
  bimodal distributions in clean/polluted fiords, 435
  brackish-water experiments by transplantation, 444

by heavy-metals in estuaries, 467
colour deepening caused by, 466–467
deleterious ecosystem changes due to, 359
effects on algae in estuaries, 430–431, 435–436, 438, 448, 457–458, 464–468
effects on blue-green algae in estuaries, 430
effects of organic on estuarine *Melosira*, 431
effects on oyster beds, 888
from paper-mill affecting algae in fiords, 440
importance to subtidal organisms, 340
in harbours generally, 887
inhibition of photosynthesis by, 456
in restriction of estuarine animals/grazing, 458–459
in S. England harbours, 849, 893
lack of database to assess for shores, 573
possible use of nematodes as indicator species/groups, 753–755
seasonal modification by, 467
thermal or organic, 893
various forms from iron ore terminal on Clyde, 609–674
Polychaetes,
aliens as immigrant species, 775, 881, 908
as secondary epiphytes feeding on primary epiphytes, 766
deposit/filter-feeding, dominating cool-temperate sedimentary shores, 702
eating other polychaetes, 702
organisms eaten by, 702
serpulids on warm-temperate and tropical cliff-like shores, 702
Polyhalinicum,
in brackish estuaries, 432, 445–446
species of, 432, 445–446
Polypropylene-coated paper,
in field note-making, 578
Polystyrene,
concrete-covered, used in Portsmouth Harbour pontoons, 847
Pontoons,
degree of wave-exposure on, 847
importance, 339
in N.E. Atlantic subtidal descriptive framework, 330–331
in Portsmouth Harbour, 844–871; construction, 847
marine flora and fauna on, 844, 850–857
Population,
definition, 326
inappropriateness of term for sea-bed assemblages, 326
non-equivalence to "peuplement", 326
recognized in W. Mediterranean infralittoral, 387
"single-species" population, 326
Population biology,
distinctions from community ecology, 513
Population dynamics,
of shore lichens, 818–819
Population size,
effect on genetic properties and competitive abilities, 495
effect on reproductive element reservoir, 495
Porosity of surface,
affecting settlement patterns/extent, 629–631
in lichen distribution, 802–804
physical nature of substrate important, 439, 459
Port-Cros (Mediterranean France), 377–379, 380–383, 385–386
Port Erin (Isle of Man), 919
Porto Novo (India), 732
Portsmouth Harbour, 845–871, 884, 887, 894–896, 901, 908

Portuguese oyster,
restocking introduction, 889
Postinteractive hypervolume, *see* Hypervolume
Potassium levels,
effects in estuaries on algal distribution, 457–458
Potential hypervolume, *see* Hypervolume
Predation,
and community structure, 699–725
as site-specific intertidal organization factor within physical environment, 566
dynamics of, 713–717
in circalittoral epibenthic animal communities, 362, 365
in communities in general, 510, 516
in marine communities, 511, 517–521
intensity, 713–717
lesser importance to species richness in harsh conditions, 723
modifying influence (dimension) in niche concept, 500, 516
on fish, reduced by algal cover, 678
on *Ophiothrix*, 354
promotion of community species-richness by, 700–701
Predation/refuges/competition,
as a balanced benthic macroalgal niche dimension, 532
Predation tactics,
coevolution with prey defence mechanisms, 701
Predator–prey arms race,
effects on diet widths, 717–718
effects on kinds of predators present, 717–718
effects of phenotype, spatial distribution, productivity of prey, 718
on evolutionary time-scale, 701
Predator–prey systems,
general, 699–725, 517–521
dynamics not well known, 700
multiple systems bewildering, 700
simple single relations actually complex, 700
Predators,
ambushers, 700
categories of predators really extremes in continuum, 700
definition of, 700
exclusion experiments, 725
general relationships in community, 510, 517–521
in reef-lagoon systems, 702
on algal epifaunas, 783
on cool-temperate rocky shores, 702
on cool-temperate sedimentary shores, 702
on tropical, cliff-like shores, 702
on warm-temperate shores, 702
predominantly predator groups, 703, 704
pursuers, 700
searchers, 700
types of predators, 700, 704
Predators on discrete food items,
considered, 702–712
on constituents of algal epifaunas, 783
prey preferences, 708–712
Predictable environments (stable),
effect on species composition of communities, 359–360
Prediction,
general considerations, 617
for environmental managers, 567
of community recurrence after pollution changes, 359
still an art-form, 617
embracing more than just marine algae, 617
Preinteractive hypervolume, *see* Hypervolume
Prelittoral zone,
probable equivalence to "open sea" circalittoral étage, 336–337
Presence of reproductive phase,
in settlement sequence partitioning, 621, 626–627

spore production suppressed leads to enlargement of individual, 627
Prey,
in reef-lagoon systems, 702
on cool-temperate rocky shores, 702
on cool-temperate sedimentary shores, 702
on tropical cliff-like shores, 702
on warm-temperate shores, 702
Prey defence mechanisms,
coevolution with predation tactics, 701
selection for, due to predation pressure, 717–718
sequestering of algal substances, repellent to predators, by herbivores, 520–521
form and colour adaptations of fish to algae, 680, 691–695
Prey evaluation,
by grazers, 706
mechanisms of, in carnivores, 708–710
Prey-recognition time,
effect on diet, 706
length in some cases, 709–710
Primary epiphytes,
defined, 765
as food source for secondary epiphytes, 766
examples, 765–766
listed, with substrate organisms, 768–769
restriction to one or few algal species each, 766
sessile species with discriminatory larvae, 765–766
Primary niches,
defined, 494
Primary productivity,
measurements in dominant intertidal macrophytes, 575
Principal components analysis,
in estuarine factor/distribution correlations, 443
Process-indicating phenomena (*see also* Exegetes),
definition involving, 610, 613
Process-indicating species (*see also* Exegetes),
definition involving, 610, 613
Process-indicating value (*see also* Exegetes, Exegetic value),
in monitoring, 610, 613
Producers,
calorific studies of dominants, 575
Production,
higher production in microbenthos than in phytoplankton of estuaries, 474
in estuarine microalgae, 473–474
in free-living nematodes, 745–746
Proliferation phase,
in settlement sequence partitioning, 621, 628
reattachment during, 628
Proline levels,
effects of salinity on, 464
Propagules,
in *Fosliella farinosa*, 386
in partitioning of settlement sequence, 623, 635
Propagule input,
in relation to plant/plant and plant/animal interactions, 609–674
into established communities, 609–674
to colonization space along the Clyde, 609–674
Prosobranch gastropods (*see also* Mollusca, Invertebrates),
eaten by crabs/fish/birds, 702
few grazing kelp, 702
larval settlement on preferred food algae, 773
less specialized grazers on sporelings, 702
specialized grazers on fucoids, 702
Prospecting larvae,
effect on invertebrate distribution, 770–779

nature of algal influence on, 775
Protection,
of temperate fish by algae, 691–693
Prothalli,
of lichen symbioses on shore, 819
Protozoa,
importance in marine communities, 509–510
Pseudothecia,
in littoral lichen reproduction, 793
Pursuers,
definition, 700
examples, 704
PVC plates,
as settlement panels for diatoms, field culture, 427, 471
Pycnogonids,
algal preferences as epiphytes, 767
as secondary epiphytes feeding on primary epiphytes, 766

Q

Quadrats,
in algal mat point-sampling in estuaries, 427
in computing qualitative minimum area for sampling, 377–381
in documentation of seasonality, 566
in photogrammetry, 576–577
in photosampling to document change in S. California intertidals, 566
in species diversity studies in succession, 646–647
location of, 577
marking permanently of, 576–577
sizes of, 379, 576–577, 579–580, 640–641, 646–647
size of, for disturbed samples, 579–580
small quadrats along transects in successional studies, 640–641
Qualitative minimum area,
approximate definition, 377
for sampling in community, 377–381
for W. Mediterranean infralittoral photophilic biotope, 377
for W. Mediterranean sciaphilic algae, 377
methods of calculation, 377–381
rigorous definition, 377
value dependent on method, 381
Quality control,
in S. California studies, 565–566
of quantification, 565–566
through infrared photosamples reviewed by whole research team, 565–566
Quantitative data (*presented in most papers; see specific entries*)
difficulties of acquiring in subtidal, 341
difficulties with microepibiota, 579
Quasi-quantitative methods,
in benthic organism studies, 575
limitations of, 575–576

R

r-selection, 519, 520, 532
r-selected species defined, 519
Rabbits,
grazing shore lichens, 823
Races,
for general physiological criteria, 469
for salinity-tolerance in species, 445
Radionucleides,
in shore lichens, 813
Radular morphology,
effect on grazing patterns, 707–708
Rafts,
Admiralty Paint Trial Raft, 848
degrees of wave exposure on, 849
flora/fauna on, 851, 857–865
for paint-testing in Langstone Harbour, 847–849

Rainfall,
effect on salinity of S. England harbours, 849
effect on upper-shore lichens, 797, 799
heavy, causing pattern/conclusion reassessment, 567
seasonal effects in estuaries, 435–436
Ramsey Island, West Wales,
barnacle/sponge dominance in shallow wave-exposure, 336
communities in subtidal at, 346–347
zones and distribution of sublittoral species with depth, 334–335
Random processes,
in distribution of marine invertebrates, 770
Range (geographic),
lack of sharp distinctions niche-habitat-area (range): common factors, 505
range phenomena in reproduction, 531
species geographic range as aspect of environmental relations, 505
Ranking of prey, 703, 705
Rare species (*see also* New taxa, Aliens),
in Newfoundland, 401
in southern France and W. Mediterranean, 385–386
Realized niche,
comments on, 496
equivalence/near equivalence to species niche, 494
re-definition, 494–495
total of relations population/environment, 494
Reattachment,
facilitation of marginal dispersal by, 890
of algae to a substrate, 880, 890
Reclamation work,
in intertidal ecosystems, 609–674
Record cards,
for subtidal description of site habitat features, 328
Recording,
of primary data for conservation site selection, 324
Recovery rates and patterns,
of intertidal communities after harvesting, 575, 582
of disturbed quadrats, S. California, 602–603
slow (mostly macroinvertebrate) – and fast (mostly macrophytes) – recovery organisms, 602–603
Recreational use,
effects on S. California shores, 573
Recruitment,
in epibenthic species often slow, 361
low-level in long-lived species, 361
of algae by reattachment, 628
opportunism in, 364
seasonal, 362, 364, 782
Recurrence,
descriptive survey of recurrent subtidal communities, 344–359
of subtidal communities, 323, 324, 326, 349
Red algae,
as sediment-traps, 767
as stipe epiflora, 769
attractiveness as substrate for epiphytes, 767
broad-fronded preferred by some epiphytes, 767
Clyde/Fairlie Channel/UK species numbers compared, 621
filamentous preferred by some epiphytes, 767
frequency in Clyde flora, 622
opisthobranchs on some at restricted shore levels, 767
penetration into fiords, 440
selective attenuation into estuaries, 428
zonation patterns on floating structures, 847, 850–871

Reduction,
in species number into estuaries, 428
Refuges (*see also* Predation/refuges/competition),
algae, as permanent habitats for less mobile invertebrates, 764
algae, for vagile invertebrates at low tides, 764
from predation, 510, 532
in algal size, from grazing, 520
Relative gain (η),
in diet at successional stages, 520
Relevés,
definitions, 371, 373
in homogeneity/similarity assessments, 382–383
in qualitative minimum area calculations, 377–381
in W. Mediterranean phytosociological subtidal study, 383–384, 388
size adopted, 381
Remote dispersal,
by agencies or vectors at biogeographic level, 886–890
differences from marginal dispersal, 886
Remote sampling methods,
disadvantages, 341
Repetitious introductions,
needed to reach critical-level biomass for alien spread, 888
Repli dishes,
used for harbour collections, 850
Replicates,
of quadrats in photogrammetric undisturbed sample analysis, 576
Reproduction,
benthic macroalgal niche dimension, 531
effectiveness of strategies (in niche), 516
effects of salinity, on estuarine algae, 453
general effects of estuaries on algal, 462–463
non-sexual, as niche dimension characteristic, 517
travel by fragments as good as or better than as spores, 623–624
Reproductive capacities,
large in algae in stressed environments, 566–567
Reproductive elements,
as stages spread by vectors, 890
as stages spread by water currents, 890
knowledge extant of longevity/viability of, 890
processes and levels in estuaries, 425–475
processes and levels in more open shores, 609–674
travel by fragments as good as or better than as spores, 623–624
Reproductive numerical response, 716–717
Reproductive periodicity,
alignment of reproductive element reservoir optimum with season and its effects on succession, 609–674
temperature the major factor, 420
winter/spring/summer-fall groups in Newfoundland marine phytobenthos, 395, 405–406, 414, 418–420
Reproductive structures,
presence, nature and frequency, Mediterranean, 384
advantageous for alien spread marginally, 890
rarity of, *Vaucheria* in field, 428
records of rarely found ones, Mediterranean, 386
spores as inoculum type, 621, 623
temperature the main Newfoundland determinant in, 396
Resistance to environmental extremes,

in shore lichen composite thalli, 829–830
Resource management (*see also* Beach management Environmental management),
data provision for S. California authorities, 567
of beaches, 618
predictions for, 567
Resource partitioning (*general as an implied or stated process in most papers: specific heads below and separately in index*),
effect of human activity on, during development of algal-dominated facies, 609–674
in aspects of distribution/abundance/diversity in intertidal/subtidal, 488
in theory and practice of ecology/evolution, 488
spatial and temporal partitioning by nematodes, 742–744
Respiration,
effects of salinity on, estuarine algae, 454–456
in shore lichen composite thalli, 828–829
Restricted (intolerant) species, *see* Ecological amplitude
Rheopositive responses,
advantages, 779–780
in epiphyte growth on laminarians, 779–780
Rhine (river, Holland), 429, 443
Richness (*see also* Diversity),
diversity indices including a component for, 581
confounding with equitability component, 581
temporal/spatial variations of, S. California intertidal biota, 565–603
Rigidity,
of algae, affecting epiphyte choice, 766
Ring phenomena,
due to proliferation and reattachment, 628
in green algae, 628
Roaringwater Bay (S.W. Ireland), 345
Rock chemistry,
accounts of lichens mostly on siliceous substrata, 800
basic dolerites and basalts, 801
calcareous shores, 801–802
differences in lichen flora and physical environments, siliceous/calcareous, 802, 803
effect on seashore lichen distribution of the parameter, 800–802
littoral lichens mostly unaffected, 800
nutrient deficiency of quartzite, 800
sandstones, 800
supralittoral lichen variations with rock type, 800
Rock texture,
effects on shore lichen distribution, 802–804
effects of texture differences on other physical parameters, 802
flaking cf. block-splitting, 802
hard to soft, 802, 803
porous to impervious, 802
smooth to rough, 802
Rock types,
importance, 340
effect on seashore lichen distribution, 800–804
in N.E. Atlantic subtidal descriptive framework, 330–331
Rocky shores,
habitat heterogeneity/environmental variability cf. sedimentary shores, 327–328
species diversity cf. sedimentary subtidals, 327–328
subtidal classification of communities, 323–365

Rovinj (Yugoslavia), 735, 919, 925–927
Rugosity,
of algal surfaces, affecting epiphyte choice, 766
surface rugosity important to fish, 680
Ruzicka (coverage) similarity test,
in W. Mediterranean homogeneity assessments, 383

S

St. Helens (Isle of Wight), 894, 901
St. Lawrence (Canada), 429
St. Pierre (east Canada), 396, 397
Saint-Vaast-la-Hougue (France), 899, 900
Salazinic acid,
in halophilic lichens, 797
Salinity,
as major factor in estuaries, 444–457
avoidance of effects by algae, through growth habit, 456–457
changes reduced on sides of floating structures, 865
different salinity tolerances in ecologically different isolates of many estuarine species, 469
effects of, on estuarine *Vaucheria* distribution, 428
effects of temperature/rainfall on, in estuaries, 435
effects of variation in, in estuaries, 425–426, 442
effects on cytological phenomena, 452–453
experiments in effects on algae, 449–450
fluctuations in fiords, 440–441
fluctuations in lagoons, 441
gradients in Baltic, 441
importance, 340, 442
in N.E. Atlantic subtidal descriptive framework, 330–331
in S. England harbours, 849, 895, 898
interaction with other factors, 445, 450–457
limits for particular species, 444–446
mixture of low and high in S. California, 573
nematodes affected by, 754
patterns around a "host" or "substrate", 517
reduced sites, Newfoundland, 411, 413
salinity races in species, 445
seasonal fluctuations, 440–441
stability of, effects on flora, 445–446
variation patterns in estuaries, 433, 445
Venice salinity zones along estuaries, 430, 432
Saltcoats (Ayr), 617, 621–622, 623
Salt marsh,
highest nematode densities in, 731
Sampling,
by percentage frequency/species in point samples in algal mats, 427
in estuaries, quantitative/qualitative, 427
in Newfoundland, 397
in W. Mediterranean subtidal, 376–377, 383–384
of standing stock in S. California intertidal, 575–581
parallax as a problem in cover estimates, 575–576
problems in estuaries with multicellular benthic algae, 427
Sampling optimization analysis,
by Poisson statistic, 576
Sampling time,
effect on diet, 706
San Clemente Island (California), 568–603

enigmatic depauperate animal population, 588
San Diego, 567, 571
San Miguel Island (California), 568–603
San Nicolas Island (California), 568–603
Sand,
artificial groynes in, with algae/acorn barnacles and attracting otherwise rocky shore fish, 680–681
as intertidals, at Langstone and Portsmouth Harbours, 845, 895
burial by, S. California intertidals, 571–573
determining epibenthic biota, 340
effects of removal of surface, 625
fish burrowing into or lying flat on, 684–685
importance of scour by, 340, 571
in estuaries, 437, 471
in N.E. Atlantic subtidal descriptive framework, 330–331
inundation by, site-specific intertidal organization factor, 566, 571–573, 593, 595
reduction of sandy beach by iron ore terminal, Clyde, 610
rejuvenation of climax, sandy beach, Southannan, Clyde, 618
sand-flats should not be ignored in monitoring, 614
scour minimized on floating structures, 865
Santa Barbara, 938
oil spills (1969), 573
Santa Barbara Island (California), 568–603
Santa Catalina Island (California), 568–603
Santa Cruz Island (California), 568–603
Santa Rosa Island (California), 568–603
Saprobic system (Kolkwitz and Marsson),
attempted application to brackish waters, 465, 466
Scandinavia, 799, 934
Scenopoetic (physically based) niche dimensions, 517
Scheldt (river, Holland), 429
Schotterion,
in W. Mediterranean, infralittoral subdivision, 387
Sciaphiles,
in shore lichens, 804, 809–811
Sciaphilic infralittoral zone,
boundary with photophilic, W. Mediterranean, 373–376
Sciaphilic subtidal vegetation,
in W. Mediterranean, 373
Scotland, east,
littoral lichens, 792
Scotland, north,
lichens, 793
Scotland, west, 882
sea loch lichens, 793
Scour (*see also* Ice scour, Sand scour),
in determining species present, 339, 340
in N.E. Atlantic subtidal descriptive framework, 330–331
Scrapers,
in community recovery and development sampling, 582
in disturbed quadrat sampling, 579
in successional studies, Clyde, 638–641
SCUBA diving,
advantages and restrictions, 373
use in Newfoundland studies, 401
Sea anemones,
commensality, 326
solitary/colonial, as carnivores, 702
zoanthids on warm-temperate and tropical cliff-like shores, 702
Sea grasses,
detritus from, in amphipod diet, 520

Searchers,
definition, 700
examples, 704
Search time,
in predation, 700
Sea slugs, *see* Opisthobranchs, Nudibranches, Mollusca
Seasonal aspects (*in most papers*),
in estuaries, 435–436
of Newfoundland benthic marine flora, 396, 414, 416, 418
of reproductive cycles, 892–904, 915–942
of S. California up-welling, 570
of vegetative cycles, 892–904, 915–942
reproduction, in estuaries, 463
Seasonal growths,
environmental control of patterns, through daylength and water temperature, 915–942
of thalloid green algae on sand/mudflat intertidals, 845
Seasonal species,
as community constituents, 361, 365
in estuaries, 435–436
in Newfoundland, 414, 416, 418
Seasonal studies,
in estuaries, 435–436
in W. Mediterranean photophilic infralittoral zone studies, 383–384
Seasonal variation (*see also* Vegetative/reproductive periodicity),
along estuaries, 435–436
in dominant biota, S. California, 574
in Newfoundland phytobenthos, 396, 414, 416, 418
in niche concept, 516
in percentage cover, S. California sites, animals/plants, 586
in recruitment of hydroids on algae, 782
in S. California up-welling, 570, 573
in water temperatures in S. California Bight, 566
of abundance/distribution of macrophytes and invertebrates for subsequent monitoring, 574–603
of microalgae in estuaries, 470–475
state of study in Mediterranean photophilic infralittoral, 384
Seattle (Washington), 919, 925, 926, 927
Sea urchins,
a predominant predator group, 703
coevolution of prey–predator systems, 518–519
effects of grazing by, 365
grazing kelp, 702
optimization of food, 520
organisms that eat, 702
Sea walls,
littoral siliceous lichens on, 791
Sea-water spray deposition,
effect on lichens, 796, 799
Sea-water tolerance,
in terrestrial-halophilic lichens, 797
Secondary epiphytes,
as non-selective algal browsers, 766
defined, 765
effects on algal population often through numbers, 766
effects on community, 766
example, 766
frequently most of epifauna, 766
larval metamosphosis only on favoured food organism, 766
opisthobranchs as, 766
using primary epiphytes as food source, 766
Secondary metabolites (crystalline),
of lichens, 794, 797, 827–829
Sedentary animals,
non-sessile, distribution by larval choice, 770–779
sessile or non-sessile, epiphytes on algae, 761–783
Sediment-binding turfs,

in estuaries, 460
Sediment loading,
as major factor in estuarine algal distribution, 442, 459, 460, 465–466
cause of two-zone shore, 459
effect on blue-green distribution in estuaries, 430
effects on estuarine vertical zonation, 439, 459
high loading causing algal size-reduction, 461
nematodes affected by, 753–754
Sediment stabilizing/disturbance,
bioturbation, 752
by nematodes, 752–753
mucus-lined burrows, 752
Sediment traps,
algae as, increasing attraction for some epiphytes, 764
filamentous red algae as, 767
Sediment types,
as major factor in microalgal distribution in estuaries, 472
determining species presence, 338
in N.E. Atlantic subtidal descriptive framework, 330–331
Sedimentary benthos,
infralittoral temperature zonation for, 336
sublittoral applied to animals in sediments, 336
classification of assemblages, 327
infauna of, 362
nematodes, 729–755
species diversity, 327–328
Sedimentary shores,
classification of benthic assemblages of, 327
habitat heterogeneity/environmental variability, cf. rocky shores, 327–328
infauna of, 362
in S. California, 571, 573
necessity for inclusion in monitoring process, 614
nematodes in, 729–755
species diversity, cf. rocky shores, 327–328
Selective deposit feeders,
among nematodes, 736–742
Selective development, *see* selective settlement
Selective settlement,
of invertebrate larvae on algae, 761, 765–766
of algae on varying substrata (with selective development), 628–638
Sequencing,
of communities in monitoring in Clyde, 609–674
Seral communities,
identification of held intermediates, 566–567
Seral stages (*see also* Held intermediates),
assessment in monitoring, 609–674
data on, as basis for community understanding, 619
Seral succession (*see also* Held intermediates),
as basis for community understanding, 619
Serpulids,
on different shore types, 702
Sessile epiphytes,
algal preferences, 767, 770–779
distribution due to choice by larvae, 770–779
positional importance of settlement on algae, 776–779
Settlement,
distribution affected by antimicrobial activity, 781
gregarious response in, 771
in algal necrotic pits; mechanism and consequences, 776
of invertebrate larvae, 770–779
opportunism in, 364
partitioning of sequence, 620–668
positional importance in sessile epiphytes, 776–779

space for, 628–638
suitability of surfaces for, 439, 459–460, 628–638, 770–779
survival strategy in epiphyte settlement/growth, 777–779, 780
Settlement behaviour,
by prospecting invertebrate larvae, 770–779
in invertebrate distribution, 770–779
responses to physical factors in, 770–779
role of biological interactions in, 770–779
Settlement panels,
as field-culture technique for microspecies, 427
as pollution-monitoring method, 639
suspended from rafts to test antifouling paints, 844–845
use in community-development study, 360–361, 362
Settlement space,
artificial or natural, 439, 459–460, 628–638, 770–779
Settlement surfaces,
algal substrata as most important factor, 771–772
factors determining suitability for invertebrate larvae, 770–779
general suitability for algae and other organisms, 439, 459–460, 628–638, 770–779
Severn Estuary, 437, 439, 459, 471
Sewage (*see also* Pollution),
algal elimination due to copper from, 467
algal species number reduction due to, S. California, 573–574, 593–594, 595
dumping in Clyde, 610
effluent into S. England harbours, 849
elimination of epiphytes by H_2S sewage conditions, 465
green algal stimulation reacting in other trophic levels, 467
influence on estuarine algal chemistry, 467
pollution in brackish water, 465, 466
pollution in Baltic, 448
pollution in fiords, 435
seasonal periodicity modified by, 467
size reduction due to, 466–467
stimulation of *Ulva*, 466, of green algae, 467
Shanklin (Isle of Wight), 880
Shannon and Weaver Index (H′),
as measure of species diversity, 581, 596–597
calculated for cover data using natural logs, 581, or other base, 581
including richness and evenness components, 581, 596–597
Sharks,
food preference, 521
Shell beach,
rejuvenation of climax community, beach at Southannan, Clyde, 618
Shells,
in littorinid mutual grazing, 657
in mud/sand in S. England harbours, 895
overgrown by algae, in littorinids, 657
Shelter,
provided by algae for epiphytic invertebrates, 689–691, 764
provided by algae for fish, 679–680, 691–695
provided by shore lichens for various organisms, 823–825
Sheltered localities,
causing enriched local floras in Newfoundland subtidal, 396
effects in estuaries, 439, 448
harbours/ports as, for adventive aliens, 875–908

rafts/pontoons in S. England harbours, 843–871
Shetland, 344–345, 350, 352–353, 355, 357, 681, 880
Shipping,
as a potential vector for alien spread, 887–888
attached aliens on hulls, 887
antifouling paints reducing effect, 887
intertidal introduction locations support, as vector, 887
disjunct distributions indicate cause, 887
ballast discharge in foreign harbours a mechanism, 887
polluted and estuarine harbour states reducing effect, 887
quick turn-round time of modern vessels limiting, 887
possible past promotion of vector function by grounding to unload, 888
shorter exposure to adverse sea conditions for aliens in modern shipping, 888
Ships' hulls,
animals on, 887–888
economic problem due fouling drag, 844
marine algae on, 844, 887–888
Shore birds,
as disturbance agents, 510
Shore crabs,
grazing algae and being taken by fish, 690
Shore exposure (*see also* Physical environmental conditions, Wave exposure, Wind, etc.),
concept in lichens, 806
examples of regulatory functions, 767
importance in regulating size/age, 767
importance in regulating species present, 767
Short-day regimes,
in formation of Bangiophycean fertile cells rows, 916
in *Petalonia fascia*, 924
response in both young germlings and established crusts of *Petalonia*, 928
Scytosiphon crusts arising from erect thalli swarmers, 922
sporangial formation in Trailliella in, 930
Short-lived species,
in communities, 361–362
Shrimps,
as disturbance agents, 510
Siliceous littoral lichens,
most widespread zone in GB, except in east and south England, 791
few penetrate to supralittoral or terrestrial, 793
homoiomerous, 793
morphologically similar, 793
taxonomic confusions and effects, 792
Siliceous mesic-supralittoral lichens,
affinities with terrestrial species, 794
"orange belt" of authors, 793
subzones inconsistently separated, 794
species restricted to zone, 794
thallus form, 794
variations between sunny and shaded shores, 794
Siliceous submesic-supralittoral lichens,
confusion with "orange belt", 795
conditions for presence/absence, 795
lowest zone for foliose species, 795
penetrations from mesic and xeric supralittoral, 795
Siliceous rocky shores,
lichens of, 791–798
littoral zone, 791–793
mesic-supralittoral zone, 793–795
xeric-supralittoral zone, 795–797

terrestrial-halophilic zone, 797
terrestrial-halophobic zone, 797–798
Siliceous terrestrial-halophilic lichens,
degree of seawater tolerance in, 797
nutrients from terrestrial sources, 797
Siliceous terrestrial-halophobic lichens,
an artificial category, 797
in crevices, hollows or lee-sides, 797
mainly inland, but on shore in shelter from spray, 797
Siliceous xeric-supralittoral lichens,
intergrading with submesic-supralittoral or terrestrial, 795–796
reasons for zone distinguishing difficulty occasionally, 796
Silt,
determining epibenthic biota, 340
effects in calm weather, 364
in estuaries, 471
in N.E. Atlantic subtidal descriptive framework, 330–331
in Newfoundland, 411
Siltation,
in calm weather, 364
increase with depth, 333
effect on zonation, 333–334
Similarity coefficients,
higher in photophilic than in sciaphilic vegetation, 383
in W. Mediterranean homogeneity assessments, 382
Similarity matrices,
in Newfoundland data, 405
Similarity tests,
based on coverage of species, 383
based on presence/absence of species, 382–383
"Single-species" population,
in definition of "population", 326
Single species stand,
? a worthwhile abstraction, 659
Sites,
local site conditions, cf. broad scale intertidal patterns, S. California, 566
selection, of nature conservation importance, 324
Site-specific autonomy,
due site-specific combinations of factors, 566
in S. California intertidals, 566
Site-specific conditions,
controlled by various site-specific combinations of factors, 566
environmental, obscuring broad overall effects, 566
Size,
continuous variation in some estuarine species, 469
estuarine reduction due to sewage, 466–467, or combination, 461
small, of algae in W. Mediterranean subtidal, 376–377
Skokholm, 357, 358
Skomer, 345, 358
Slipper limpets (*see also* Limpets),
adverse accidental introduction with oysters, 889
as fouling organisms on floating structures in S. England, 856
Slope, *see* Inclination
Smaller species,
often characteristic in Mediterranean infralittoral, 387
Smothering species,
in circalittoral epibenthic animal communities, 362, 365
Snails,
algal preferences as epiphytes, 767
Snow,
effect of melting on fiord salinity, 440
Sodium levels,
effects in estuaries on algal distribution, 457–458
Soft rocks,
affecting turnover of lichen thalli, 803
in shore lichen distribution, 794, 803

specialized flora of, in shelter, 803
Sokal and Sneath similarity test,
in W. Mediterranean homogeneity assessments, 382–383
Solent region, 362, 845–871, 882–885, 892–904, 907, 908
Sorbitol levels,
effects of salinity on, 464
Sørensen similarity test,
in W. Mediterranean homogeneity assessments, 382–383
South Africa, 680, 685, 688, 790
South America (southern), 790
Southampton Water, 362, 884–885, 887, 894
Southannan Beach (Clyde), 612, 617, 618, 624, 625, 643, 652, 654, 655, 658
South-west Britian,
use of habitat criteria described, 341, 345
Southern California Bight, 565–603
physical data on, 568
Southern California Borderland, 568
Southern California Continental Borderland,
at overlap of two major biogeographic regions, 566
Southern California Countercurrent, 569
Southern California Islands, 565–603
Southern California Outer Continental Shelf (OCS),
area defined, 567
area described, 567–574
Southern species,
at northern limits in Newfoundland, 396, 409, 420, 421
Southsea Beach (Hants.), 894, 896, 897, 898
Space,
a limiting resource in the intertidal, 516–517, 585
Spain, 882
Spatial change,
in dominant biota, S. California, 574
water temperature in S. California, 566
Spatial competition (*see also* Competition),
as a niche dimension, 516
between hydroids on *Fucus*, 782–783
important characteristics in, 517
space an intertidal limiting resource, 585
Spatial shuttering,
by algae, 635, 637–638, 640–641
Spearman (coverage) similarity test,
in W. Mediterranean homogeneity assessments, 383
Specialized algal browsers,
as primary epiphytes, 766
Specialized feeders,
as secondary epiphytes feeding on primary, 766
larvae often metamorphose only on favoured food organism, 766
Speciation, *see* Incipient speciation
Species abundance (*see also* Biomass, Frequency, Cover, etc., *for interrelated factors*),
changes in, with time, 361
indicated by most workers as important, 347, 350
Species/area curves,
in calculation of qualitative minimum area, 379
in W. Mediterranean, 378
Species attributes,
confusion in niche concept with ecosystem attributes, 493
"Species clouds",
in species packing, niche concept, 501
Species composition,
of communities in S. California intertidals, 582–585
Species diversity,
compared between biotopes, 381–382

concepts in species diversity theory, 493
formulae/mathematical models, 534–535
in harbours, 381–382
in relation to niche breadth, 501
in relation to species packing, 501
in superficial exposed sciaphilic rocky vegetation, 381–382
in superficial sheltered sciaphilic rocky vegetation, 381–382
in photophilic infralittoral zone, 381–382
reasons for, in photophilic infralittoral, 381–382
reduced, in estuaries, as major distribution characteristic, 442, 458–459
temporal/spatial variations in S. California intertidal biota, 565–603

Species listing,
in describing subtidal communities, 341, 344, 347, 350
example of, 342–343

Species-log area plot,
in calculation of qualitative minimum area, 379

Species niche,
definition, 494
"average genotype" in, 494
based on species ecopotential, 494, 495
equivalence/near equivalence to realized niche, 494

Species novae ineditae,
in W. Mediterranean photophilic infralittoral studies, 385–386

Species packing,
defined, 501
in niche hyperspace, 501
formulae/mathematical models, 536

Specificity,
of algal-invertebrate associations, 762, 766

Spider crab,
grazing algae and being taken by fish, 690

Spirorbids, *see* Polychaetes, Tubeworms

Spitzbergen, 921

Sponges,
as epifauna, 765
encrusting forms dominant on shallow wave-exposed rock, 336
in spatial competition on fucoids, 782–783
population variability through year, 363

Spores (algal),
as reproductive inoculum sources, 621
as stages spread by vectors, 890
as stages spread by water currents, etc., 890
knowledge of longevity/viability of, 890
suppression of production enlarges vegetative individuals, 627

Spore release phase,
in settlement sequence partitioning, 621, 628

Spray (sea),
in lichen colour changes, 797
salt from spray affecting lichens on whole shore, 804–805, 807–809
wind carriage far inland, 805

Stability,
evidence available for, in subtidal communities, 362–363
global stability community, 361
multiple stable points, 361
of communities, 361–364
of environments, 361–364

Stability concepts, 503–504

Stability-time hypothesis,
in community development pattern, 359–360, 364

Stackpole Head (Pembrokeshire),
363–364

Standing stocks,

distribution in relation to tide height, 581
sampling and analysis in S. California, 575–581
Starfish,
effects on mussels, 365
variability on Gower, 363
Stenohaline species,
in estuaries, 431–432, 445, 446
in fiords, 445
in lagoons, 445
stenohaline annuals, 432
stenohaline perennials, 432
Stenohaline offshore communities,
indicating depths of open sea circa-littoral étage, 336–337
Stenothermal offshore communities,
indicating depths of open sea circa-littoral étage, 336–337
Stenotopic (physiologically less tolerant) species,
among sedentary invertebrates on algae, 764
high diversity in predictable environments, 359–360
Stipes,
of laminarians as epiphyte substrate, 769
Stochastic theory,
in feeding preference models, 518
Stonehenge,
maritime lichen flora on, 805
Storms,
affecting grazing guild, S. California, 600–602
as site-specific unpredictable disturbance factor, 566, 574–575
Storm waves,
epiphytes/algae encouraged by lack of, in sheltered narrows, 764–765
island protection for S. California coast, 570–571
Strangford Lough (N. Ireland), 345, 350, 352–353, 735, 737
Strata (biological),
relationship to terrestrial work, 327
use in rocky sublittoral biota, 327
Strategic analysis (market demand curves),
in feeding preference models, 518
Strategy (*see also* Growth and life-history strategies),
overtones in the general concept of "strategy", 515–516
semantic error since the opposite of evolutionary process, 516
Stratification (*see also* Bathythermograph, Thermocline),
fresh water/salt in fiordic estuaries, 440
in S. California hydrographic system, summer, 573
of water temperature in Newfoundland, 409
Stress,
as a cause of held subclimax stages (succession), 566–567
assessment by diversity, 581
greater sensitivity to, due to human disturbance, S. California, 573
Stressed characteristics,
of algal populations in identifying held seral stages, 566–571
Stresses,
human, assessment by diversity, 581
levels of human-induced, 566
levels of natural-induced, 566
Stressful (stressed) environments (unstable),
characteristics of algal populations/communities in, 566–567
effect on species composition of communities, 359
Structure,
cover and structural heterogeneity, 585
effects of estuarine environment on, 460–462
of algal communities/populations in stressed environments, 566–567

Studland (Dorset), 881
"Stuw" zone,
current flow to sea, 432
freshwater species only, 432
species-poor, 432
tidal rise/fall persisting, 432
upstream in estuaries, 432
Sub-Arctic province, 329
Subclimax,
identified by algal populations with stressed characteristics, 566–567
succession held by unstable environment or stress, 566–567
Subcommunities,
definition of, 327
relationship to community, 327
Sublittoral epibenthic ecosystems,
GB, 323–365
Mediterranean, 371–388
Newfoundland, 395–421
Sublittoral fringe,
accepted definition for N.E. Atlantic, 337–338
communities at Ramsey Island, Wales, 346
Sublittoral zone,
accepted definition for N.E. Atlantic, 337–338
communities at Ramsey Island, Wales, 346–347
definition of maximum downwards extent, 333
difficulty of field identification at depths, 333
distribution of species in, with depth, Ramsey Island, 334–335
division into infralittoral and circalittoral subzones, 332
intertidal easier to investigate and more stressful, 506–507
penetration of "intertidal" species, 506–507
Submergence times,
permanent submergence of lichen in Antarctica, 807
in UK shore lichens, 807
Subspecific differentiation,
a mechanism responsible for habitat amplitude, 493
Substrata,
algae as, increase surface area for epiphytes, 764
disturbance of, S. California, 595
selection by invertebrate epiphytes, 770–779
transported by drift, 624
Substratum selection,
factors in choice by invertebrate larvae, 770–779
importance of biological interactions, 770–779
in cyphonautes larvae, 779–781
Substratum stability,
determining epibiota present, 339
factor acting at site-specific level, 566
loose boulder fields reducing, S. California, 573
pronounced effects on Newfoundland flora, 414
Substratum types,
as determinant of species presence, 338–339
as major factor in estuarine algal distribution, 440, 448, 459–460
as major factor in estuarine microalgal distribution, 472
as site-specific factor, 566, 571–573
as settlement space, 628–638, 764
at Ramsey Island, Wales, 346–347
effects on taxonomy of predator and prey, 702
in N.E. Atlantic subtidal descriptive framework, 330–331
in estuaries, 432–433
mosaic of, S. California, 566, 571–573
natural and artificial, 628–638
pronounced effects in Newfoundland, 414

physical nature affecting estuarine vertical zonation, 439
Succession,
as a concept, 491, 510
in marine communities, 510
held intermediate stages due to stress or unstable environment, 566–567
in shore lichens, 800–801
subclimax identification through algal population form, 566–567
the key to interpretation of beach processes, 619, 670
variation of dominants in, 364
Suitable niveaux,
in settlement sequence partitioning, 621, 639–641
Sullom voe, 344
Supersession,
in lichen thalli, 820–821
Surf conditions,
effects of catastrophic events on S. California shores, 575
Surface area,
increased for epiphytic invertebrates settlement by substrate algae, 764
Surface films (*see also* Exterior mucilage),
as biological influence on invertebrate larval settlement, 770–779
indifference to or avoidance of by larvae, 771
variation according to causal microorganisms, 771
variation of attraction with organism, 771
Surface textures,
of algae, affecting choice by epiphytes, 766, 769
Surface-to-volume ratios,
large in algal populations in stressed environments, 566–567
Surtsey, 623
Surveying,
of intertidal by helicopter, 575
Survival phase,
initial colonization usually a wider spread than final mature appearance, 641–642
in settlement sequence partitioning, 621, 641–642
Survival strategy,
in epiphyte settlement and growth, 777–779, 780
Susceptibility, *see* General susceptibility
Susceptible species,
as community constituents, 361
Suspended solid loadings,
virtually all grazers inhibited by, Leith, 655
Suspension-feeders,
success in strong tidal stream areas, 336
Swansea, 773, 774
Swartkops estuary (South Africa), 732, 734
Sweden, 363
Swell,
direct westerly, Los Angeles/San Diego, 571
island protection of S. California mainland shores, 570–571
Swellies, Menai Strait,
suspension-feeders success in strong tidal stream, 336
Symbiosis,
in niche concept, 516
Synecological image,
for W. Mediterranean photophilic infralittoral algal species, 386
Synoptic surveying,
of intertidal at low tide by helicopter, 575

T

Tamar (river), 429
Tangent method, Cain and Castro,
in calculating qualitative minimum area, 379

Tanner submarine bank, 567
Tannins,
antibacterial activity, 780
anti-hydroid activity, 781–782
anti-invertebrate activity, 780–782
anti-planktonic activity, 781–782
Tape recorders,
miniature, in field note-making, 578
Tarff (river) (Scotland), 429
Taxonomy,
climate of taxonomic opinion affecting floristics, 876
confusion in shore lichens due to chemotype and mosphological variation, 816–818
difficulties obscuring recognition of incoming aliens, 879, 907
effects of taxonomic confusion in littoral lichens, 792
implication of variation in estuarine conditions, 462
need for more research on estuarine effects on algal taxonomy, 475
problems caused by reproductive modifications, 463
problems with green microscopic forms, 850
taxonomy and systematics in pre-monitoring database studies, S. California, 574–603
taxonomic overtones of the niche concept, 525–526
Tay (river, Scotland), 429
Tees (river), 429, 439, 463
Temperature, *see* Water temperature
Temperature resistance,
ecological significance of possible differentials, crusts/erect thalli in Scytosiphonales, 929–930
Temperatures (air),
effects on shore lichen distribution, 799
effects on shore lichen physiology, 830–831
Temporal effects in flora, *see* Seasonal variation, Vegetative periodicity
Temporal partitioning,
pre-emption of available space affecting settlement sequence, 632–637, 640–641
Temporal shuttering,
by algae, 635, 637–638
Temporal variation,
seasonal and yearly, island/mainland sites, plants and invertebrates, S. California, 597–599
Terminology for monitoring,
difficulties and needs, 671
Terrestrial lichen flora,
distinctions from maritime flora, 797
Test panel immersion,
source of data on algal fouling communities, 844
Texas, 441, 444, 446
Thallus forms,
simple/compact in algae in stressed environments, 566–567
Thames Estuary, 429, 430, 438, 439, 459, 465
Thermocline (*see also* Bathythermograph profiles, Stratification),
deep in S. California summer, 573
deeper waters with unstable thermocline, Newfoundland, 414
effect in depth distribution of subtidal biota, 336
effects of stable summer thermocline in Newfoundland subtidal, 396, 409
presence/absence in Newfoundland, 409
separation of circalittoral into "étages" by, 336–337
summer presence at Banyuls and W. Mediterranean, 374
Thigmotactic series,
of fish; importance of pool configuration, 680
general to fish, 695
Thiobios,
obligate anaerobically-respiring nematodes in, 745

Thylakoids,
rearrangements of, in low salinity, 461–462
Tidal currents,
strong, affecting flora in Bonne Bay, Newfoundland, 401
Tidal emersion,
affecting lichens, 806–807
avoidance of the complicating factor, in estuaries, 427
Tidal influence,
effects eliminated from floating structures, 865
effect on lichens, 796, 804–806
forming a stressful intertidal environment, 506
in estuaries, 425, 427, 432, 438
influence on standing stock, 581
in supralittoral, 804
temporal/spatial variations in S. California intertidal biota caused by, 565–603
tolerance experiments in estuarine algae, 443–444
Tidal rise/fall,
affecting lichens, 806–807
effects eliminated from floating structures, 865
forming a stressful intertidal environment, 506
in characterizing estuarine zones, 432
influence on standing stock, 581
Tidal stream exposure,
competition for space by suspension-feeders in, 336
in N.E. Atlantic subtidal descriptive framework, 330–331
in S. England harbours, 849
streams weaker in deep water, 364
Time, *see* specific factors for references
Titanium dumping,
nematodes unaffected by, 753–754
Tjörnes (Iceland), 919, 924, 925, 927
Tobruk (Libya), 386
Tolerance experiments,
combined factor effects data needed, 443–444
competition experiment, under combinations of factors, 452
effects of factors on interspecies competition, 444
in estuarine algae, 443–444, 469–470
in lichen physiology, 825–832
light intensity linked to salinity tolerance by, 451–452
on effects of light-regimes on marine algae, 915–942
on tolerance of algae to substrata, 628–638 (*for fuller references, see* Substratum types)
transplantation in field, 444
Tolerance (*see also* Tolerance experiments; *for specific aspects of tolerance, see also the factor concerned*),
to salinity in estuarine algae, 444–457
to salinity, influenced by temperature changes, 435
to salinity/other factor interactions, 450–457
Tolerant species, *see* Ecological amplitude
Topographical features,
affecting shelter/exposure characteristics, 398–401
as determinant of species presence, 338–339
effect on lichens, 789–834
in S. California Bight, 567–574
in S. England harbours, 845–849, 875–908
in subtidal descriptive framework for N.E. Atlantic, 330–331
Torbay, 355
Toxicities (*see also* Tannins),
in foods, 520–521
in biochemical defence mechanisms, 718
of substrata to algae, 636–637

Trace metals,
alteration of levels in estuaries by pollution, 457
in lichen thalli near waste-bringing river outfall, 814
use of algae as indicators of, 467
use of mussels as indicators of, 467
Transect method,
applied to floating structures in S. England harbours, 850
belt transects in S. California photogrammetry, 576–579
in cover estimates as quasi-quantitative, 575
in studying W. Mediterranean infralittoral, 387–388
in successional studies in Clyde, 638–641, 660
poor basis for interpretation, 388
Transplantation,
growth-rate studies following, 575
in estuarine field-tolerance experiments, 444
of fucoids in continuous variation experiments, 470
Trieux (river estuary, France), 471
Trochids,
grazers on fucoid sporelings/unicellular algae, 702
Tromso (Norway), 919, 922, 938
Troon harbour (Scotland), 619, 627, 639, 655
Trophic changes,
as basis for community understanding, 619
Trosa (river, Sweden), 429
Trouble-shooting,
in monitoring, 617–618
detailed example, 672
Tsuchiya, Japan,
hydroids as epiphytes, 770
Tube-worms,
as fouling organisms on floating structures, S. England, 856
alien incursions, 775, 881, 908
as primary epiphytes, 766
immigrant species on *Sargassum muticum*, 775, 881, 908
substrate choice in Spirorbid larvae, 773
Tunicates,
as epifauna, 765
in spatial competition on fucoids, 783
modifying environment, 764
Turbidity (*see also* Light penetration, Water transparency),
as major factor in estuarine algal distribution, 442, 466
cause of two-zone shore, 459
high, in estuaries, 437, 438, 439, 440–441, 442, 459
low, in fiords, 440
of water in W. Mediterranean (Banyuls), 374
Turbulence (water),
greater in winter in W. Mediterranean, 374
infralittoral divided into subzones on, 374–376
in S. California Bight, 570–571
"Turfs",
as compact morphological response in algal populations in stressed environments, 566–567
sediment-binding, in estuaries, 460
turf algae dominating warm-temperate and tropical cliff-like shores, 702
Two-directional water movement,
in hydrodynamic zones in W. Mediterranean, 374, 376
subtidal zone definition by, 336
Two-zone shores,
ascribed to turbidity/sedimentation, 459
distribution of algae, 437, 439
Tyne (river, N.E. England), 429, 439, 463

U

Ulla (river, Spain), 429

Umia (river, Spain), 429
Uncertain taxonomy,
contributions from niche concept approach, 525
in estuaries, 427–428, 462, 463, 464, 474–475
Newfoundland species, 401
W. Mediterranean species, 384–386
Underlying vegetation,
general considerations for subtidal, 323–365
increasing species diversity in W. Mediterranean subtidal, 381–382
in structural complexity of intertidal communities, 585
Undisturbed samples,
S. California methods and approach, 577–579
Undisturbed sampling method,
by photogrammetry, 576–579
in quantification of seasonal/yearly differences in S. California permanent sites, 565–603
used with infrared film for records, 565–566
Unicellular algae,
covering lichen thalli, due to chemical pollution on shore, 814
nitrate inhibiting onset of reproduction, 932
organisms grazing, 702, 707
Unidirectional water movements,
in hydrodynamic zones in W. Mediterranean, 374, 376
Unpredictable disturbances (*see also* Disturbance),
as site-specific intertidal organization factor, S. California, 566
Unsuitable substrata,
as factor in successional patterns, Clyde, 628–638
in estuaries, 459–460
in limiting species geographical distribution, 329
unstable and species-poor, Newfoundland, 414
Upper circalittoral,
definition for N.E. Atlantic, 338
communities at Ramsey Is., Wales, 346
relationship to "coastal" étage, 336–338
Upper infralittoral,
definition for N.E. Atlantic, 338
communities at Ramsey Is., Wales, 346
Upward extension,
of algal communities in "wave-wash" or increasing exposure, 868–869
Up-welling conditions,
local enrichment of S. California intertidals by, 566, 569–570
mosaic of, throughout S. California Bight, 566
S. California seasonal effects, 570, 573
wind-driven upwelling in S. California, 569–570
Urr (river, Scotland), 429

V

Vagile species,
invertebrate epiphytes refuges on algae, low waters, 764
Value for monitoring,
of intertidal macroalgae, 614
Value judgements,
framework for, 671
in monitoring, 609–674
Variability (including Instability),
in shore lichen growth forms, 816–818
instability as a factor in held sub-climax (succession), 566–567
instability in thermocline, 414
in sublittoral epibenthic communities, 362–364
of substrate, due to unstable loose boulders, S. California, 573

Vectors,
adverse species introduced, 889
conditions for success, 886
definition, 886
dispersal after invasion, 886
floating objects as, 888
in spread or transportation of species, 886–890
introduction by Man of commercial species that act as, 888–889
shipping as, 887–888
vector identification by circumstantial evidence, 886
Vegetative periodicity (*see also* Seasonal variation),
in Newfoundland marine flora, 414, 416, 418
temperature the major factor, 420
Veliger larvae,
preferential settlement of prosobranchs of food algae, 773
Venice system,
applicability to estuaries, 430
salinity zones for estuarine classification, 430
Vertical distribution,
in Clyde intertidal flora, 609–674
in GB sublittoral epibenthic ecosystems, 323–365
of algae in estuaries, 436–439, 470–475
of algae in Newfoundland, 395–421
on floating structures in southern harbours, 843–871
Vertical gradients,
of conditions/flora in estuaries, 426
Vertical layering,
canopy above understory, increasing both microhabitat diversity and number of species present, 585
Vertical migration,
of diatoms and euglenoids in estuarine sediments, 471–472
Vertical range,
effect on epifauna of that of "host", 767
Vertical zonation (*see also* Zonation),
in Clyde intertidal, 609–674
in estuaries, 436–439
in Newfoundland flora, 395–421
of lichens on rocky shores, 790–834
on floating structures in S. England harbours, 843–871
subtidal patterns in UK, 323–365
success of intertidal systems, 327
Viability (*see also* Longevity),
of algal spores/germling stages in dispersal, 890
state of knowledge of, 890
Virginia (USA), 923

W

Wales,
general, 798
bryozoan epiphytes of North, 770
Gower, descriptive survey of sites, 342–343
Ramsey Island, West Wales, 334–335, 346–347
littoral lichens of South, 792
Warm-boreal province,
geographical extent, 329
Water quality index,
possible use of euglenoids as basis for, 465
Water relations,
in lichens, whole thalli, 827–828
Water temperature,
in algal life-history control, 915–942
interaction with salinity tolerance in estuarine algae, 450–457
large-scale biogeographic patterns mediated by, in S. California, 566
mixture of low and high in S. California, 573
more reliable season-indicator under water than on shore, 916
Water temperature changes,
along estuaries, 447–448

generally increasing to south, S. California, 571–573
in waters above thermocline, 336
mosaic of temporally/spatially changing temperatures, S. California Bight, 566
reduced on sides of floating structures, 865
slight, in waters below thermocline, 336
with depth and month in W. Mediterranean, 374–375
Water temperature regimes,
depth profiles for Newfoundland sites, 401, 409–410
in estuaries, 432–433
in S. California Bight, 566, 571–573
in S. England harbours, 849, 895, 898
main factor controlling growth/reproduction, Newfoundland phytobenthos, 396, 420
seasonal effects in estuaries, 435
subtidal, around Banyuls (Mediterranean), 374–375
subtidal, around British Isles, 328–332, 336
subtidal, around N.E. Atlantic, 336–337
Water transparency (*see also* Light penetration, Turbidity),
in S. England harbours, 849
mosaic of, throughout S. California Bight, 566
Wave action (*see also* Physical environmental conditions, Wave exposure),
attentuation with depth, 333, 336, 364
effect of exposure to, on algal fouling communities on rafts/pontoons, 845–871
effect on *Lichina*, 801
effect on shore lichens, 792, 796, 801, 807–809
effects of severe, on kelp/foliose algae, 336
island protection from, S. California mainland, 570–571
local enrichment of S. California intertidals by, 566, 596
severity reduced by/on floating structures, 865
strength of, affecting depth distributions, 333, 336
Wave-exposed overhang communities, in subtidal, 356, 358–359
Wave exposure (*see also* Physical environmental conditions, Wave action),
assessment in sublittoral, 339
determining epibiota present, 339
effect on predator and prey taxonomy, 702
in N.E. Atlantic subtidal descriptive framework, 330–331
island protection from, S. California mainland, 570–571
littoral lichens in, 792
mosaic of, throughout S. California Bight, 570–571
use in delimiting community conditions, 327
Wave splash,
supralittoral salts from, 804
Wear (river), 429, 439, 458, 463, 466
Weather (*see also more specific factors*),
affecting ecological conclusions, 567
Weser (river, West Germany), 429
West Indies, 686
West Looe (Cornwall), 896
Westport (river, Eire), 429
West Wales,
Ramsey Island, 334–335
Western Isles (Scotland), 765
Wet weight,
in disturbed sample analysis, 579–580
temporal/spatial variations in S. California intertidal biota, 565–603

Weymouth Bay (Dorset), 904
Whirlpool Cliff, Lough Ine, 348–349
Whites Point (California), 568–603
Whitewashing (monitoring),
exonerative work within organizations, 619
particular results expected, 618
site-deterioration ignored, 618–619
Wind (*see also* Physical environmental conditions, *other specific factors*),
affecting S. California upwelling, 569–570
carriage of salt spray far inland, 805
effects on shore lichens, 795–797, 799, 807–809
reversals in S. California fall/winter, 570
Santa Ana winds causing heating/desiccation, 570
Wooden battens,
as artificial substrata for algal colonization, intentionally placed, 632–633, 635
shore lichens on, 813–814
Wooden pilings,
augmentation of natural flora and substrate, 414
characteristic flora on, Newfoundland harbours, 413, 414
Woodland lichens (*see also* Lichens),
near shore in very sheltered west Scottish sealochs, 798
Woods Hole (USA),
bryozoan epiphytes, 770
Wrasses (*see also* Fish),
algal foods of some significance in some members of group, 687
generally feed very little on algae, 687
many build nests of algae in algae, 694
most strongly associated with algal cover or rocks with algae, 687
predate barnacles/mussels, 702
Wrecks,
importance as substrate and shelter, 339
in N.E. Atlantic subtidal descriptive framework, 330–331
Wrightsville Beach (North Carolina), 735
Wylva (Wales), 619

X

Xanthid crabs,
grazing algae and being taken by fish, 690
Xerophytes,
in shore lichens, 804

Y

Yaquina (estuary, Oregon, USA), 471
Yealm river (Devon), 878, 879
Yoishi (Japan), 938
Yorkshire, 723

Z

Zinc,
in shore lichens, from disused mining, 814
Zonation (*see also* Vertical zonation),
in estuaries, 436–439, 471–472
success of vertical intertidal systems, 327
zones as communities, 511
zones as important but not most productive basis for population ecology, 521–522